"Some people think that systematic theology is impractical for ministry and irrelevant to the spiritual life. Yet God shows us through the example of Sinclair Ferguson that, by the grace of Christ, doctrine sanctifies life and energizes joyful service. This book, written by more than two dozen theologians influenced by Dr. Ferguson, shows how every point of theology can make God's servants more helpful, holy, and happy."

—**Joel R. Beeke**, President, Puritan Reformed Theological Seminary

"Some competent and well-ordered theological writing is intellectually nourishing and instructive, but does little to nurture the heart. Other theological writing rushes so quickly to elicit emotional responses that a suspicion arises that the work is not really about God, truth, and grace, nor primarily about the self-disclosure of our triune God, but about us and how we feel about him. One of the marks of Sinclair Ferguson's great contribution is that over his long years of ministry he has eschewed both poles and given us theology that is, on the one hand, profound and precise and, on the other, wonderfully edifying across the gamut of life and service, calling up responses of both mind and heart. So it is entirely appropriate that this book of essays honoring his life and work takes as its task the same mature synthesis. This book is important not only for what it says, but for what it models."

—**D. A. Carson**, Emeritus Professor of New Testament, Trinity
    Evangelical Divinity School

"This collection of essays—learned, theological, pastoral, and doxological—serves as a fitting tribute to a friend and mentor (to me and many others) who has embodied and championed these very qualities. *Theology for Ministry* repays careful reading, not only as a celebration of Sinclair's life and ministry, but as an exploration of the biblical and confessional truths that should inspire and anchor all our lives."

—**Kevin DeYoung**, Senior Pastor, Christ Covenant Church,
    Matthews, NC; Assistant Professor of Systematic Theology,
    Reformed Theological Seminary, Charlotte

"Sinclair Ferguson embodies the very best of confessional Reformed pastoral theology and ministry in his life, teaching, preaching, and writing. I, like so many others, owe him a spiritual debt that I can never repay. He has nurtured my faith for decades through his ministry, and adorned my life as a friend and counselor. How appropriate that a book on *Theology for Ministry* should be produced in his honor. I am delighted to be able both to contribute to and to endorse this volume, not just because of my love and regard for Sinclair (and his beloved wife, Dorothy!), but because of the sound and edifying contents of this Festschrift. The subtitle tells you what the authors are trying to do, chapter by chapter: *How Doctrine Affects Pastoral Life and Practice*. The reader will quickly note that the subjects of the chapters cover the theological ground and order of the Westminster Confession of Faith, and the substance of each chapter expounds and applies the doctrine pastorally, just as Sinclair has done throughout the whole course of his ministry. I have learned something from every contributor in every contribution, and I think you will, too (especially those of you called to minister to others). May you find here welcome encouragement from the truth of God's Word for the faithful practice of God's ministry to God's people."

—**Ligon Duncan**, Chancellor and CEO, John E. Richards Professor of Systematic and Historical Theology, Reformed Theological Seminary

"*Theology for Ministry* is a fitting tribute to a saint whose heart and mind have blessed the church through his teaching and writing over a lifetime. This impressive collection of essays aptly reflects the emphases of Sinclair Ferguson's instruction—a theologically informed pastoral piety and ministry deep-rooted in the teaching of Scripture. Through a survey of key biblical doctrines, the authors as experienced theologians and practitioners seek to offer solid answers to the question of why theology matters. Each chapter is robust in Scripture, tradition, and practical guidance. In a time when pragmatism too often drives the church, I am delighted that this fine resource will be available to encourage theological reflection on what it means to be godly and effective Christian leaders."

—**S. Donald Fortson**, Professor of Church History and Pastoral Theology, Director, DMin Program, Reformed Theological Seminary, Charlotte

"It has always seemed to me that a Festschrift is one of the most appropriate ways to celebrate the ministry of a Christian scholar. And while Festschrifts require a huge commitment from publishers, I love them: the range of articles that are permeated with a certain celebratory spirit, the biographical sketch of the scholar being honored, and the facility of each piece to be read in a small compass of time. But this is no ordinary Festschrift: here we have a pastoral theology in miniature as each essay investigates how a specific Christian doctrine intersects with Christian praxis and pastoral life. Together this collection of essays captures the heart of the one whose ministry they celebrate, for Sinclair Ferguson has ever stressed that the coals of Christian doctrine are vital for the flame of godly living and pastoral ministry. So it is a joy to highly recommend this book, both for the high esteem in which I hold Professor Ferguson and for the superb essays that it contains."

—**Michael A. G. Haykin**, Chair and Professor of Church History,
The Southern Baptist Theological Seminary

"This is an extraordinary Festschrift because—while honoring the remarkable life and ministry of Dr. Sinclair Ferguson—it will energize and elevate the life of the church for years to come. The reasons are, first, the editors' careful selection and ordering of the twenty-five creedal themes that demonstrate the ineluctable connection between a preacher's doctrine and practice and, second, the superb quality of those chapters—all written by pastoral-hearted academics. Preachers like me, laboring amid the often-mundane duties of ministry, will learn to recharge their divine callings from the deep doctrinal wells of their (soon-to-be-treasured!) copies of *Theology for Ministry*. This magnificent volume is a must for every seminary student's and pastor's library."

—**R. Kent Hughes**, Senior Pastor Emeritus of College Church,
Wheaton; former Professor of Pastoral Theology, Westminster
Theological Seminary

"Because *Theology for Ministry* fulfills the promise of its title, it is a fitting tribute to the diverse and Christ-exalting ministries of exegete/theologian/preacher/pastor/author Sinclair Ferguson. Here is robust biblical and systematic theology, drawn deeply from God's

Word written, articulated confidently in light of the Reformed confessions, and driven pastorally toward the salvation and sanctification of Jesus' beloved bride. The editors and contributors have collaborated to offer to ministers, ministerial candidates, and their mentors a *unified* handbook that shows how the 'whole counsel of God,' focused on God's grace in Jesus Christ, must mold the *practice* of ministry in the church. This integration of theology with ministerial practice makes *Theology for Ministry* 'required reading' for all seminarians, and the ideal textbook for interdisciplinary courses—either initial or capstone—in programs of pastoral preparation."

    —Dennis E. Johnson, Professor Emeritus of Practical Theology,
      Westminster Seminary California

"Romans 12:2 warns us not to be 'conformed to this world,' but so much contemporary ministry practice is shaped by modern secular pragmatism rather than by sustained reflection on biblical truth and theology. Ironically, the pragmatic approach—doing whatever 'works'—leads us away from innovation. I'm old enough to have seen wave after wave of ministry fads that most ministers applied woodenly without much thinking or adaptation to their local contexts. There is no greater need than to help ministers think out the implications of historic scriptural doctrines for life and practice in their own time and place. We have enough 'how-to' manuals that tend to stifle the theologically informed, practical creativity that *Theology for Ministry* provides."

    —Tim Keller, Pastor Emeritus, Redeemer Presbyterian Churches
      of New York City

"Sinclair Ferguson has had an illustrious career with a worldwide reach. By sermon, lecture, and book, he has blended theological acuteness with an ability to speak to a wide audience, from scholars and ministers to regular church members and others. All the contributors to this volume are immensely appreciative of his ministry and regard it as a privilege to participate. These essays are a fitting tribute to Sinclair in gratitude for his work and in expectation of more to come."

    —Robert Letham, Professor of Systematic and Historical Theology, Union School of Theology

"This splendid anthology teams professors and pastors—friends and even family—to engage the range of the Reformed theological loci. *Theology for Ministry* combines biblical treasures and trenchant theological thought. This Festschrift is well named and well honors, for Sinclair B. Ferguson is among this era's superlative pastoral theologians whose fruitful ministries will grace the church for generations to come."

—**Peter A. Lillback**, President, Westminster Theological Seminary

"Anyone who is familiar with the writing and teaching of Sinclair Ferguson knows what he has stood for: the faithful, skillful exposition of biblical truth without compromising its depth, and the application of such truth within the church. This superb volume, a collection of essays written by some of the most able-minded scholars and pastors in today's Reformed church, will stand firmly within that same legacy. It is thus not only a fitting tribute to Dr. Ferguson, but an important resource that will be treasured by students and expositors for years to come."

—**Iver Martin**, Principal, Edinburgh Theological Seminary

"From the lectern, from the pulpit, and from his pen, Dr. Sinclair Ferguson has served the church as a theologian—one who teaches about God and who leads others to worship God in reverence and awe. For five decades, he has faithfully executed the office of minister as a true pastor-teacher. Warm, winsome, and encouraging, he is a gift to the church. This book by a stellar cast of his students, colleagues, and brothers-in-arms is also a gift to the church. These essays herald the truth that ministry needs theology, and they offer a generous and vibrant vision that the church today urgently needs."

—**Stephen J. Nichols**, President, Reformation Bible College; Chief Academic Officer, Ligonier Ministries

"This collection of profoundly biblical, helpfully applicable, and surprisingly compact studies of doctrinal topics is an outstanding contribution to the life of any Christian, but especially to a pastor. Its premise: God revealed or 'expressed' biblical truth to help his people 'embody' that same truth in their manner of life and ministry. Those whose lives are shaped by biblical beauty rightly glorify the Lord.

"This is a worthy tribute to Dr. Ferguson, for he not only faithfully ministers so as to express biblical truth in as much of its beauty as he possibly can, but also embodies that peerless beauty in his manner of life. One cannot be with Dr. Ferguson for long without either sensing or actually saying to oneself, 'This man has been with Jesus.'

"This masterful collection of treasured insights may well help the reader to draw much closer to the pattern of our King in ministry and truth. I stand the thankful debtor to every contributing author and to the careful editorial work that compiled this collection. Relish the richness of these outstanding contributions to true pastoral ministry."
—**Joseph V. Novenson**, Pastor to Senior Adults, Lookout Mountain Presbyterian Church

"This book obeys Philippians 2:29–30, which directs those who discharge the work of Christ to 'honor such men.' Sinclair Ferguson is worthy of the honor that this book ascribes to him because what is true for me is true for thousands of other pastors worldwide: Sinclair Ferguson has taught me how the truths of the gospel shape and sustain pastoral ministry. I owe him more than I know and love him more than he would believe."
—**Dane Ortlund**, Senior Pastor, Naperville Presbyterian Church

"This book is a significant contribution to a neglected issue: systematic theology is of great value in pastoral ministry. This value is often not understood or appreciated. Accordingly, the book has chapters that deal one by one with all the major headings of systematic theology, including those whose relation to pastoral ministry is less obvious and therefore all the more important to notice and trace out. The book is especially welcome because it is dedicated to Dr. Sinclair Ferguson, himself a blessing to pastoral ministry, an embodiment of gifts and service in both theology and pastoral ministry."
—**Vern Poythress**, Distinguished Professor of New Testament, Biblical Interpretation, and Systematic Theology, Westminster Theological Seminary

"When requested to consider providing an endorsement for *Theology for Ministry* in honor of the life and ministry of my professor, friend, and colleague Dr. Sinclair Ferguson, I took only seconds to say yes—for two reasons. First, in a day when the church desperately needs models and mentors for the next generation of pastors to lead Christ's church in fulfilling the Great Commission, with God-glorifying, Christ-exalting, Spirit-filled, gospel-saturated ministries, I can think of no one better to set before them in this present age. Then to also have a majestic distillation of his ministry—'how doctrine affects pastoral life and practice'—is glorious. Second, this volume, written with a richness that causes the reader to anticipate the turning of every page, celebrates and propagates the glorious truths of God's Word to be preached and embraced in the life and ministry of a pastor-preacher. Enjoy and give thanks to the Lord for his choice servant Dr. Sinclair Ferguson and the gospel breadth and depth he proclaims and embraces in his life and ministry."

—**Harry L. Reeder III**, Senior Pastor, Briarwood Presbyterian Church, Birmingham, Alabama

"Sinclair Ferguson has been my mentor, teacher, pastor, and friend in some form or another for almost half a century. It is eminently fitting that pastor-theologians should honor him with this superb volume of essays. Individually, each chapter is a treasure in itself, but collectively, they form a coherent and rich source of material, addressing the very nature of what a pastor-theologian is and does. A treasure store of biblical wisdom that honors one of our finest and that is sure to enrich the church of today and tomorrow."

—**Derek W. H. Thomas**, Senior Minister, First Presbyterian Church, Columbia, SC; Chancellor's Professor, Reformed Theological Seminary; Teaching Fellow, Ligonier Ministries

"Reformed theology is sometimes pilloried for an imbalance of theoretical overload and practical lightness. Anyone who knows the work of Sinclair Ferguson will realize that this myth is not worth a ripe tomato. He stands in line with the great 'linkers' of theology and practice in the Reformed tradition, a worthy successor in the spirit of the Heidelberg Catechism, John Owen and the Puritan divines, Wilhelmus à Brakel, Robert Murray M'Cheyne, Rabbi Duncan, and of course John Calvin himself. The value of this volume is found in its reflecting on the implications of the various *loci* of theology in a way that honors Dr. Ferguson's calling and work. And should perchance an alien from another planet wish to know him better, presentations of his qualities as teacher, pastor, preacher, author, and friend round off this essential reading."

—**Paul Wells**, Editor in Chief, *Unio cum Christo*; Emeritus Professor, Faculté Jean Calvin, Aix-en-Provence, France

"Dr. Sinclair Ferguson is the quintessential pastor-theologian, appropriately recognized in this valuable collection of articles that should have long-term usefulness."

—**Luder Whitlock**, President Emeritus, Reformed Theological Seminary

"I will be adding *Theology for Ministry* to my required-reading list for seminary students. Twenty-six pastor-theologians, touching on every major area of ministry, winsomely demonstrate how theology gives shape to a godly pastorate. That this book honors Sinclair Ferguson is especially appropriate—his books, lectures, and sermons mine God's Word and Reformation theology, and set their riches before God's beloved church. I can think of no better model of ministerial work."

—**Charles M. Wingard**, Associate Professor of Pastoral Theology, Dean of Students, Reformed Theological Seminary, Jackson

THEOLOGY
FOR
MINISTRY

THEOLOGY
FOR
MINISTRY

How Doctrine Affects
Pastoral Life and Practice

Edited by

WILLIAM R. EDWARDS
JOHN C. A. FERGUSON
CHAD VAN DIXHOORN

P&R
P U B L I S H I N G
P.O. BOX 817 • PHILLIPSBURG • NEW JERSEY 08865-0817

Printed in the United States of America

ISBN: 978-1-62995-655-8 (cloth)
ISBN: 978-1-62995-656-5 (ePub)

Library of Congress Cataloging-in-Publication Data

Names: Edwards, William R., (William Rob), editor. | Ferguson, John C. A.,
    editor. | Van Dixhoorn, Chad B., editor.
Title: Theology for ministry : how doctrine affects pastoral life and
    practice / edited by William R. Edwards, John C.A. Ferguson, Chad Van Dixhoorn.
Description: Phillipsburg, New Jersey : P&R Publishing Company, [2022] |
    Includes bibliographical references and indexes. | Summary: "Deeply connecting
    theology with practice, this book encourages rich biblical-theological reflection
    for growing and sustaining a vibrant ministry-applying more than twenty key
    Christian doctrines to pastoral work"-- Provided by publisher.
Identifiers: LCCN 2020055219 | ISBN 9781629956558 (hardcover) | ISBN
    9781629956565 (epub) | ISBN 9781629956572 (mobi)
Subjects: LCSH: Pastoral theology. | Church work.
Classification: LCC BV4011.3 .T454 2022 | DDC 253--dc23
LC record available at https://lccn.loc.gov/2020055219

To
Sinclair B. Ferguson

With gratitude for teaching us *theology for ministry.*

CONTENTS

Contents

Contents

FOREWORD

It is a privilege to stand, as it were, at the entryway of a book and to open the door for guests, inviting you to come in and enjoy a rich collection of essays. The chapters that make up *Theology for Ministry* have been written as a present for and tribute to Sinclair B. Ferguson. The volume has been limited to just twenty-six chapters, but the authors represent a much larger group of colleagues, friends, and former students who also wish to honor him—and that is to say nothing of the many of us who have learned from his writings and benefited from his ministry in churches and at conferences around the world.

It is no exaggeration to say that, under God, Sinclair has been the means of introducing many pastors, and in turn their congregations, to a robust and Christ-centered theology. He would no doubt be surprised and a little amused to learn of his role as pastor to the pastors, even in churches that he has never visited. He may be surprised, too, at how regularly he is quoted by people whom he has never met and who have difficulty pronouncing his name.

Dr. Ferguson is a professor of systematic theology who has a unique ability to write books intended for children that are also read by pastors, who in turn teach the material to their people (confession is good for the soul). It is not unusual for able and well-respected authors to seek his theological guidance before going to print. His voluminous works have become for many a kind of theological Internet "googled" by budding theologians. One can imagine two students, talking over coffee; one says: "How are we to understand the unity of the divine presence in three persons?" to which his friend replies: "Why don't we Ferguson it!?" as they search through the professor's chapter titles and volume indexes to find the answer. (Yes, an implausibly advanced picture for Ferguson, who in the age of email, Twitter, and text remains the champion of the handwritten note.)

Given the privilege of this moment as the doorkeeper of this book, I want to mention what these essays do, and then ask why they were written—hazarding a guess of my own.

The scholarly essays in this volume were not written to explain the breadth of Sinclair's influence, although the afterword on friendship comes very close. Rather, they try to offer reflections that honor his own persistent interests in theology and the importance of theology for pastoral life and ministry.

But why have all these busy, well-respected pastor-theologians taken time to contribute these essays? Is it out of a sense of collegiate responsibility? Or in justifiable admiration for Sinclair's academic ability? Is it because of the strength of his personality and his platform presence? Is it his down-to-earth love of murder mysteries and the way that he can introduce Lord Peter Wimsey into important theological conversations? Maybe it is their admiration for his quiet humor that goes unnoticed if we're not paying close attention?

I'm not sure whether the editors will allow my conjecture to stand, but I think these men took the time to write this book because Dr. Sinclair B. Ferguson still wears his lanyard, with the plastic name tag, when he speaks at conferences—conferences at which he is the keynote speaker. Given the fact that the attendees have come to listen to him, and that he is immediately recognizable to all, he does not need to identify himself. He does not need to—and yet he does.

Perhaps this will help to explain what I mean. Visitors to the Ronald Reagan Library in Simi Valley, California, take a tour while wearing headphones and listening to commentary given by the late president himself. In the reproduced "Oval Office" in the Reagan Library, he explains that he never regarded that as being *his* office; it was merely a place that he was privileged to have access to for a time. Reagan explains that he took his task so seriously that when working, he purposely never removed his suit jacket. Commenting on what might seem to some a strange, almost superstitious practice, he concludes, "You see, it is possible to take the office seriously without taking yourself too seriously."

This, I submit, goes a long way to explaining S. B. F.'s worldwide influence. He is the conference speaker who is never too "big" to wear his name tag. He does not take himself too seriously. It probably helps that he was born in Glasgow (he can explain), and there is no doubt that Dorothy, his children, and the best of his friends have played a large part in the formation of his character. Nonetheless, this humility is not merely a natural virtue. It is rather that Sinclair, after fifty years of "active service," is still amazed that God chooses to put his treasure in earthen vessels and in his providence has given this Glaswegian the immense privilege of gospel ministry.

Were it not for that character—and even more, that gospel!—this book of essays would never have been compiled. But here they are: a treasure trove to inform our minds, stir our hearts, and make us more useful in seeking to correctly handle the Word of truth.

> This is the one to whom I will look:
> he who is humble and contrite in spirit
> and trembles at my word. (Isa. 66:2b)

Alistair Begg
Parkside Church
Cleveland, Ohio

ACKNOWLEDGMENTS

On behalf of the editors, I express gratitude to the authors for the time and energy given to contribute to this book dedicated to my father, Sinclair Ferguson. I know what it will mean for him, because I know what you mean to him as colleagues, brothers, and friends in Christ. The time you have shared with him in churches, conferences, seminaries, writing books, and not least the hospitality that you and your families have shown to him has been a blessing in countless ways over the years.

A work of this scale requires a great deal of attention to detail. We are very grateful to G. B., Andrew Becham, Ben Hein, and Blake Franze and his trusted team of helpers for their assistance. They have skillfully applied themselves over many hours to help ready the manuscript for publication and compile the bibliography. We record here our gratitude to Reformed Theological Seminary and Westminster Theological Seminary for making that assistance possible.

Special thanks also to the publishing team at P&R for taking on the project and for their guidance and patience throughout. We wish to especially mention Acquisitions Director Dave Almack, who kindly offered guidance at the start of the project; Director of Academic Development John Hughes for his faithful oversight in producing the book; and copyeditor Karen Magnuson for her careful reading of the text and grace in corresponding with us. Knowing that we have been in their highly capable hands has been greatly assuring along the way.

Each of us was taught by Sinclair Ferguson at Westminster Theological Seminary and remember those times in his classes with thankfulness. As Chad Van Dixhoorn and Rob Edwards, now teaching at Westminster, express in their chapters, we have all benefited from his ministry in our own ministries. I am deeply grateful to them for inviting me to join them as an editor while the project was well underway.

The genesis of the idea for the book and the impetus that has brought it to fruition are theirs and so also the greater credit for it. For me to join in their wish to honor a much-loved seminary professor in this way and to be among them as they have poured themselves into producing this book has been a memorable experience.

For myself, along with my brothers, David and Peter, and my sister, Ruth, we have shared the added blessing of having Sinclair Ferguson as our father. In a book dedicated to him, it seems obvious to us that his wife and our mother, Dorothy, must also feature among the acknowledgments. As a family, we know that without her love, support, constancy, and willingness to share in both the joys and the sufferings of gospel ministry, the wide reach of his ministry, especially in the United States, would not have been possible. She has exemplified to us in the home, as my father wrote of her, "a life lived in practical devotion to Him."[1]

As editors, we owe a special debt to our families and especially to Emily Van Dixhoorn, Angie Edwards, and Louise Ferguson, wives who have so lovingly supported us in our callings in gospel ministry. They have faithfully given of themselves in enabling us to produce this book.

A note of thanks also belongs to those for whom we respectively work in seminary and church contexts. We hope the book will be received and enjoyed as a token of gratitude for the daily support we receive from you.

Our highest debt in presenting *Theology for Ministry* is to our God and Savior, Jesus Christ, upon whom all gospel ministry, and theology of ministry, depends. Our ministry is, after all, his ministry, and we simply serve as fellow workers with the gifts he's provided. Together we give thanks and praise to him for allowing us a share in this privileged vocation. Our prayer is that this volume may prove a blessing for gospel ministers, elders, and students especially, and a means to the furtherance of God's good purposes and glory.

John C. A. Ferguson, for William R. Edwards and Chad Van Dixhoorn

1. Sinclair B. Ferguson, *The Trinitarian Devotion of John Owen*, Long Line of Godly Men Profile (Orlando, FL: Reformation Trust, 2014), xviii.

ABBREVIATIONS

ANF	Alexander Roberts, James Donaldson, and A. Cleveland Coxe, eds., *Ante-Nicene Fathers* (1885; repr., Peabody, MA: Hendrickson, 1994)
BECNT	Baker Exegetical Commentary on the New Testament
ESV	English Standard Version
JETS	*Journal of the Evangelical Theological Society*
JSNT	*Journal for the Study of the New Testament*
KJV	King James Version
NASB	New American Standard Bible
NICNT	New International Commentary on the New Testament
NIGTC	New International Greek Testament Commentary
NIV	New International Version
NovTSup	Novum Testamentum Supplements
NPNF	Philip Schaff, ed., *Nicene and Post-Nicene Fathers, Series I* (1888; repr., Peabody, MA: Hendrickson, 1994)
NRSV	New Revised Standard Version
NSBT	New Studies in Biblical Theology
OPC	Orthodox Presbyterian Church
PG	J.-P. Migne et al., eds., *Patrologia Graeca* (Paris, 1857–66)
PMLA	*Publications of the Modern Language Association of America*
PRJ	*Puritan Reformed Journal*
RTS	Reformed Theological Seminary
SBJT	*Southern Baptist Journal of Theology*
TNIV	Today's New International Version
WCF	Westminster Confession of Faith
WLC	Westminster Larger Catechism
WSC	Westminster Shorter Catechism
WTJ	*Westminster Theological Journal*

INTRODUCTION

WILLIAM R. EDWARDS

Pastors need theology for ministry because the substance of ministry is speaking for God. Pastors serve as ambassadors for Christ. A ministry of reconciliation is entrusted to them. God makes his appeal through them. The substance of their message is "be reconciled to God" (2 Cor. 5:18–20). In fact, we may say that theology is *for* ministry, explicating the fullness of this message and equipping pastors for its faithful proclamation both in public and in private, for both the gathering and the perfecting of the saints. As Christ clearly states to his disciples, this labor will entail many difficulties, and thus pastors need the personal encouragement that comes from "the depths of the riches and wisdom and knowledge of God" (Rom. 11:33), the confidence that comes from "the whole counsel of God" (Acts 20:27), and ever-deeper insight into "the mystery of Christ" made known by revelation (Eph. 3:3–4).

A temptation in practical theology is to focus on technique and skill without relating theological substance to pastoral practice. The literature, at times, is experience-based and pragmatic rather than clearly grounded in coherent biblical and theological reflection. Systematic theological works, on the other hand, may fail to connect the substance with practice, neglecting to explore and express the relevance or implications of doctrines beyond the clear statement of truth.

The purpose of this collaborative effort is to demonstrate the relationship between theology and practice from authors experienced in both. We believe that the church thrives when pastors comprehend how God's whole counsel shapes and impacts their entire ministry, and when practices are not baptized by a few biblical texts but are instead rooted in thoughtful biblical exegesis. Thus, each chapter in this volume builds on the rich biblical-theological reflection that a

vibrant ministry demands. The aim, however, is not merely exposi-
tional and theological but devotional and practical, concrete rather
than abstract. Each contributor is currently or has at one time been a
pastor and draws from his own experience as well as the experience
of other pastors, past and present. At the same time, each contributes
out of the gifts uniquely bestowed on him, shaped and sharpened by
his own experience and practice in various ministry settings.

Each contributor has also been impacted by a particular pastor-theologian who, for us, exemplifies what we seek to bring together
in this volume: biblical and theological reflection in service to the
church, for the encouragement of gospel ministers, as well as the good
of those they serve in ministry. Sinclair B. Ferguson is a model pastor-theologian in our day. Now in his fiftieth year of service to Christ
and his church, Sinclair continues to cultivate a theologically rich
and personally winsome ministry among his colleagues, students, and
readers, which has been demonstrated in his own years of pastoral
ministry. These essays are written in his honor by a few from among
the many who have been greatly influenced by his life and work, as is
evident in various ways through the following chapters.

As we explore theology for ministry through these essays honoring a teacher and a friend, we are reminded that theology is
important in its own right—the queen of the sciences, as it has been
called—because God himself is the one true and glorious King over
all. Theology matters because "from him and through him and to
him are all things" (Rom. 11:36). And for this very reason, theological reflection is absolutely essential for ministry. While much of
this book will focus on how doctrine ought to impact ministry, we
are also concerned to show that doctrine ought to impact ministers,
especially in view of the many personal struggles as well as external
difficulties pastors face.

At the time of writing this introduction, the general consensus is that over the past thirty to fifty years, much has changed in
ministry, with the result that "pastoral leadership does not seem to
offer the promise of a life well lived."[1] This appears evident from

1. L. Gregory Jones and Kevin R. Armstrong, *Resurrecting Excellence* (Grand
Rapids: Eerdmans, 2006), 24. Various studies conclude that social changes over the
past two generations have greatly altered ministry experience. See Dean R. Hoge

the large numbers of those leaving the ministry within the first five years, with some statistics indicating a fourfold increase since the 1970s.[2] The mainstream media has taken note, too, with an article in the *New York Times* concluding: "Members of the clergy now suffer from obesity, hypertension and depression at rates higher than most Americans. In the last decade, their use of antidepressants has risen, while their life expectancy has fallen."[3] Studies indicate that many in ministry are unhappy and would leave for some other line of work if they could.[4]

In response, at the start of the twenty-first century, the Lilly Foundation funded a ten-year project, "Sustaining Pastoral Excellence," distributing grants totaling in the millions of dollars to many different organizations, with the aim of conducting research to better understand the negative conditions of pastoral ministry and develop strategies for positive change.[5] Although operating with diverse theological commitments, these various studies are tied together by the use of the social sciences. The studies explore the habits and practices of pastors in their various traditions with the guiding question of what defines and sustains excellence in ministry, utilizing qualitative research methods in the analysis of data to develop their descriptions and reach their conclusions.[6] These studies prove helpful in many

---

and Jacqueline E. Wenger, *Pastors in Transition* (Grand Rapids: Eerdmans, 2005), 3; Bob Burns, Tasha Chapman, and Donald Guthrie, *Resilient Ministry: What Pastors Told Us about Surviving and Thriving* (Downers Grove, IL: InterVarsity Press, 2013), 12; Bob Wells, "Which Way to Clergy Health?," accessed October 15, 2020, https://faithandleadership.com/programs/spe/resources/dukediv-clergyhealth.html.

2. Jones and Armstrong, *Resurrecting Excellence*, 24; Paul Vitello, "Taking a Break from the Lord's Work," *New York Times*, August 1, 2010, accessed December 14, 2013, http://www.nytimes.com/2010/08/02/nyregion/02burnout.html?page wanted=all&_r=0.

3. Vitello, "Taking a Break from the Lord's Work."

4. Jackson W. Carroll, *God's Potters: Pastoral Leadership and the Shaping of Congregations* (Grand Rapids: Eerdmans, 2006), 160.

5. Holly G. Miller, "Sustaining Pastoral Excellence: A Progress Report on a Lilly Endowment Initiative" (Durham, NC: Leadership Education at Duke Divinity, 2011), 3–7, accessed April 22, 2014, http://pastoralexcellence.com/pdfs/Final_SPE _Report2011.pdf.

6. Miller, "Sustaining Pastoral Excellence," 7–11. For an example describing the methodology used, see Burns, Chapman, and Guthrie, *Resilient Ministry*, 265–69.

ways, noting commonalities in experience that coalesce into themes that frame life in ministry. The hopeful expectation through all of this work is that "a new narrative about ministry is coming into being," one that replaces the discouraging narrative of irrelevance, ineffectiveness, and mediocrity.[7]

The various studies inevitably include some measure of biblical and theological reflection. The primary focus, however, is on the immediate causes that make pastoral ministry uniquely difficult in our current setting. So while biblical notions of excellence in ministry are considered, the data gathered on contemporary experience is at the heart of the analyses. While valuable in bringing to light particular difficulties that our current ministry culture may create, this approach potentially overshadows deeper biblical-theological commitments essential to meeting the challenges that ministers face in every age.[8]

This book aims to encourage a thriving ministry through examining the biblical-theological framework that must inform our ministry in a way that addresses both the pastor and his work. This book presents a theology for ministry—and ministers. The premise in what follows is that the current need is not so much to develop a new narrative for pastoral ministry, but to recover the rich biblical-theological framework for ministry found in Scripture that is grounded in the triune God and his decrees, the person and work of Christ, and the application of all the benefits and blessings that come to us through the Spirit in our union with Christ, together with the various associated doctrines traditionally included in the theological encyclopedia.[9] Thus, the hope is to see beyond immediate difficulties to the larger setting of all ministry throughout these last days, stretching from Christ's resurrection until his return, so that those

7. Craig Dykstra, "On Our Way: The Sustaining Pastoral Excellence Initiative," plenary address, Lilly Endowment Annual Report, Indianapolis, May 11, 2011, accessed April 22, 2014, http://pastoralexcellence.com/pdfs/DykstraPlenaryAddress .pdf.

8. For further reflection on these matters, see William R. Edwards, "Participants in What We Proclaim: Recovering Paul's Narrative of Pastoral Ministry," *Themelios* 39, no. 3 (2014): 455–69.

9. The chapters of this volume generally follow the chapters of the Westminster Confession of Faith.

laboring in ministry will do so with the vital theological framework required for faithful service.

In various places, the apostle Paul presents what appears to be a rather grandiose view of his ministry, such as when he describes his "insight into the mystery of Christ, which was not made known to the sons of men in other generations," a mystery that, he says, was "made known to me by revelation" (Eph. 3:3–5). He boldly envisions his labors in relation to great Old Testament prophets, going so far as to compare himself to Moses, leaving the clear impression that his is the greater and more glorious work (2 Cor. 3:11–13). These portrayals, on first read, may seem to imply an exaggerated sense of self-importance.[10] It is not, however, Paul's self-perception that leads to this exalted view of his ministry. Instead, Paul understands that the greatness of the age ushered in by Christ's death and resurrection exalts his work. It is not his contribution that brings distinction. This grand and decisive epoch of redemption—the fullness of time and the finality of revelation— attributes greatness to Paul's own labors in ministry.[11]

Paul concludes his first letter to the Corinthians with a reminder of what he refers to as the matter "of first importance" in the gospel he preaches: "that Christ died for our sins in accordance with the Scriptures, that he was buried, that he was raised on the third day in accordance with the Scriptures" (1 Cor. 15:3–4). The death and res- urrection of Christ together constitute the focal point of the gospel he proclaims. Yet this climactic moment of redemption is not simply the summary of Paul's message. Jesus' death and resurrection are of first importance as the events that inaugurate a new era of redemp- tion, which then shapes his entire conception of ministry. Through it, Paul proclaims the coming of an age within which his ministry takes place, a redemptive epoch of which his ministry is truly a vibrant

10. John Calvin notes this, describing how Paul "boasts that he 'begat' the Corinthians 'through the gospel' [1 Cor. 9:2]," and that "in many passages he not only makes himself a co-worker of God but also assigns to himself the function of imparting salvation [1 Cor. 3:9 ff.]." John Calvin, *Institutes of the Christian Religion*, ed. John T. McNeill, trans. Ford Lewis Battles, 2 vols., Library of Christian Clas- sics 20–21 (Philadelphia: Westminster, 1960), 4.1.6.

11. Geerhardus Vos describes Paul as "arguing from the glory of the message to the distinction of the bearer." Geerhardus Vos, "The More Excellent Ministry," in *Grace and Glory* (Edinburgh: Banner of Truth, 1994), 85.

part. Paul understood, as Geerhardus Vos observes, that "the servant is, as it were, made part of the wonder-world of salvation itself."[12] Ministers of this gospel do not tell the story of salvation as if standing at a distance, but instead are made participants in the unfolding drama of the last days inaugurated by Christ's death and resurrection. According to Herman Ridderbos, "Paul's preaching itself is taken up into the great eschatological event."[13] His ministry is also a part of God's redemptive provision, inseparable from this age of fulfillment.

The point is that Paul thinks theologically about his ministry. These themes are integral to the framework of ministry, and thus essential to faithful endurance in the work of ministry. Narrowly viewed, eschatology may be approached as an area of study concerned with distant events and consequently largely fruitless for practical ministry. As considered above, however, its concern is not with obscure matters but with the great mystery revealed in Christ's death and resurrection. The great end has now truly begun. Jesus himself is "the beginning, the firstborn from the dead" (Col. 1:18). All gospel ministry must maintain this outlook. To quote Vos again, "The joy of working in the dawn of the world to come quickens the pulse of all New Testament servants of Christ."[14] Or at least it should, and it will only when these "last things" are maintained as the "first thing" in ministry. The end begun with Christ's death and resurrection is always of first importance, and must be as we consider the work of ministry.

Here we are illustrating the general thesis of our book. But the larger point is this: when a rich theological perspective is lost, so is the larger story for our ministry. Bereft of such a vision, we are left simply with the things immediately before us, our work defined primarily by our current activity rather than the age of consummation that has now come. Apart from this vibrant biblical vision, the pastor's attention will be limited to his own labors while missing the

---

12. Vos, "The More Excellent Ministry," 87.

13. Herman Ridderbos, *Paul: An Outline of His Theology*, trans. John Richard de Witt (Grand Rapids: Eerdmans, 1975), 47.

14. Vos, "The More Excellent Ministry," 90. Elsewhere, Vos states, "All eschatological interpretation of history, when united to a strong religious mentality cannot but produce the finest practical theological fruitage." Geerhardus Vos, *The Pauline Eschatology* (Phillipsburg, NJ: Presbyterian and Reformed, 1979), 61.

grand narrative that gives them true significance. When this occurs, the tasks of ministry become wearying in their repetition: sermons to prepare and worship to order with the approach of each Sunday; more counsel to offer, possibly with little hope of change if experience proves true; meetings with elders that focus primarily on pressing needs. David Hansen laments how, in the work of the pastor, "theology's venerable 'already and not yet' has become 'what needs to be done today and what can be left until tomorrow.'"[15] The immediate pressures and demands of pastoral ministry may cause us to lose sight of this final epoch of redemption in which we serve. And without this larger story, the burdens of ministry may quickly become unbearable and the source of great discouragement. Ministry needs theology.

Much more could be said about the manner in which Paul understands ministry—and much will be said in the following chapters. And yet while biblical-theological realities inform each of the essays, the structure of this book follows a fairly traditional systematic arrangement. Carlton Wynne, Robert Letham, and Douglas Kelly treat the foundational topics: Scripture, God, and the divine decrees. Ian Hamilton and Michael McClenahan tackle the outworking of the divine decrees in chapters on creation and providence—including hard providence.

The book then pivots to address realities after the fall through the doctrine of humanity, treated by John McClean, and outlines the rubric through which redemption is proffered, in David McWilliams's chapter, focusing especially on the covenant of grace. What follows, naturally, are Lane Tipton's and David Gibson's chapters on Christ and his work, and Philip Ryken's and Dennis Johnson's chapters on union with Christ and the Holy Spirit. The appropriation and application of that redemption are discussed in the next six chapters, roughly following the pattern found in the Westminster Confession of Faith and other Reformation and post-Reformation confessions: John Ferguson addresses the doctrine of justification, Ligon Duncan adoption, and Rob Edwards sanctification. Cornelis Venema then considers the twin graces of faith and repentance, Paul Wolfe perseverance, and Joel Beeke assurance.

---

15. David Hansen, *The Art of Pastoring: Ministry without All the Answers* (Downers Grove, IL: InterVarsity Press, 1994), 20.

Other subjects, critical for pastoral ministry, include the law and liberty, respectively authored by Philip Ross and David Strain. Bob Godfrey then provides a biblically grounded vision for worship. The doctrine of the church and the communion of the saints are addressed by Mark Garcia and Craig Troxel. And Chad Van Dixhoorn writes pastorally on the sacraments. Daniel Strange provides a theologically rich perspective on missions. Michael Horton closes the theologically constructive section with a chapter on eschatology—understanding that biblical eschatology not only ushers in the day of salvation but also serves as the pattern for ministry with a redemptive purpose.

In the final chapter, Chad Van Dixhoorn talks about the life and ministry of the one whom we seek to honor with these essays, Sinclair B. Ferguson, including his lifelong labors as a teacher and writer, set within the context of a wide pastoral ministry, including service to particular churches but also extending out to the broader church, and as a result pastoring, nurturing, and encouraging many other pastors as well. Concluding the volume is a rich reflection on friendship by Bill Edgar, comparing and contrasting cultural expressions of friendship with its truest revelation in Christ and in the relationships had in him.

Additional features are provided at the end of each chapter. These include key terms for the essay that correspond to glossary entries at the end of the volume. Also provided are discussion questions and recommendations for further reading. We hope these elements will help extend both comprehension and application of each doctrine addressed.

It should also be noted that the authors have produced these essays in the context of many and varied pastoral duties. As Sinclair says of his own writing, it is often "squeezed into, or out of, an occasional hiatus in the sheer busy-ness of ministry."[16] And yet each has embraced Sinclair's encouragement to be "stretched a little beyond their normal pulpit or lectern preparation."[17] We, as editors, express our gratitude for their contributions. Our hope is that this has led to growth in us all and that the Lord will use these labors to enrich others.

16. Sinclair B. Ferguson, *Some Pastors and Teachers: Reflecting a Biblical Vision of What Every Minister Is Called to Be* (Edinburgh: Banner of Truth, 2017), xii.
17. Ferguson, *Some Pastors and Teachers*, xii.

Recent studies into the decline of pastoral ministry may provide accurate descriptions along with immediate reasons for the demise of many who become discouraged in the work. Such conditions should be addressed. Yet to be truly understood, these experiences must be placed into a theological framework in which Christ and his ministry for us remain central.

In his work *The Resurrection of Our Lord*, William Milligan reminds us: "The Living Lord is with us, who once knew every such disappointment as we experience, and every such cause of despondency as weakens us; who once sighed over the stubbornness of men more deeply than we can sigh, and shed more tears for those who refused to listen than we can weep. Yet he triumphed; and he comes to us now that he may communicate to us his joy of victory."[18] Such is the vision of Scripture, and the same must be shared by all whose ministry is built on this foundation once laid, that we might rejoice even as we long for his return. And so we offer to you this *Theology for Ministry*.

---

18. William Milligan, *The Resurrection of Our Lord* (New York: Macmillan, 1917), 222.

1

SCRIPTURE

Foundational for Life and Ministry[1]

R. CARLTON WYNNE

How should a right doctrine of Scripture, rooted in the Bible's self-testimony,[2] shape the life and ministry of a pastor? What is it about Scripture that makes it central, even indispensable, to pastoral ministry? How does the Bible guarantee its sufficiency for preaching, teaching, and defending the faith? How should a right grasp of Scripture buoy a pastor's soul as he drives to the home of grieving parents? How can Scripture fortify him to preach unpopular truths or to begin a difficult conversation with a church member? How does the Bible lead

1. This essay is offered with abiding admiration for Sinclair Ferguson, a trophy in life and ministry of the personal Christ speaking in the Scriptures.

2. In the traditionally Reformed view, Scripture's role as the principle of knowing or cognitive foundation (*principium cognoscendi*) of theology accounts for the priority of Scripture's self-witness when discovering what Scripture is. For systematic treatments of this topic, see Richard A. Muller, *Post-Reformation Reformed Dogmatics*, vol. 2, *Holy Scripture* (Grand Rapids: Baker Academic, 2003), 151–61; Francis Turretin, *Institutes of Elenctic Theology*, ed. James T. Dennison Jr., trans. George Musgrave Giger, 3 vols. (Phillipsburg, NJ: P&R Publishing, 1992–97), 1:89 (2.6.11); Herman Bavinck, *Reformed Dogmatics*, ed. John Bolt, trans. John Vriend, vol. 1, *Prolegomena* (Grand Rapids: Baker Academic, 2003), 210–14; John Murray, "The Attestation of Scripture," in *The Infallible Word: A Symposium by the Members of the Faculty of Westminster Theological Seminary*, ed. Ned B. Stonehouse and Paul Woolley, 2nd ed. (Phillipsburg, NJ: P&R Publishing, 2002), 1–54.

a pastor to finish his race with joy in this fallen world? The answers to these questions reveal the many-sided "wisdom of God" (Eph. 3:10) that radiates from the Bible he has given us. Within the scope of this discussion, three key elements of the doctrine of Scripture deserve attention: (1) the inspiration of Scripture; (2) the accommodated character of Scripture; and (3) the redemptive-historical design of Scripture. Under these three headings we will explore other attributes of Scripture (authority, sufficiency, clarity, necessity, finality, and efficacy) and see how they, too, bear on the pastor's life and ministry.

The Inspiration of Scripture

No aspect of the doctrine of Scripture is more basic for understanding what the Bible is than its inspiration. Though he does not treat the point exhaustively,[3] Paul provides a key entry point in 2 Timothy 3:16 ("All Scripture [πᾶσα γραφή] is breathed out by God [θεόπνευστος] and profitable [ὠφέλιμος] for teaching, for reproof, for correction, and for training in righteousness"). As B. B. Warfield masterfully demonstrates in his discussion of this text, the verbal adjective *theopneustos*, which appears only here in the whole Bible, indicates that Scripture—indeed, "all Scripture" (*pasa graphē*), i.e., not just the Old Testament, but also the New Testament[4]—finds its origin in God and is the product of his creative breath.[5] The whole

---

3. As Ferguson notes, though the doctrine of inspiration is central to the Scripture's testimony to itself, the way in which the Spirit providentially generated the Scriptures "must be discovered exegetically, not dogmatically, in an *a posteriori* manner, by the examination of the whole of Scripture, with special attention to its reflection on the mode of the production of its various parts." Sinclair B. Ferguson, *Some Pastors and Teachers: Reflecting a Biblical Vision of What Every Minister Is Called to Be* (Carlisle, PA: Banner of Truth, 2017), 360.

4. Though the Old Testament was in view at the time of Paul's writing, the scope of his statement is extensive, including all that can be counted as "Scripture." So George W. Knight III, *The Pastoral Epistles: A Commentary on the Greek Text*, NIGTC (Grand Rapids: Eerdmans, 1992), 447–48; Ceslas Spicq, *Saint Paul: Les Épîtres Pastorales* (Paris: Librairie Lecoffre, 1947), 787–88; Edward J. Young, *Thy Word Is Truth: Some Thoughts on the Biblical Doctrine of Inspiration* (1957; repr., Carlisle, PA: Banner of Truth, 2008), 21.

5. Benjamin B. Warfield, *The Inspiration and Authority of the Bible*, ed. Samuel Craig (1894; repr., Philadelphia: Presbyterian and Reformed, 1948), 283. Warfield

of Scripture is "breathed out" by God with the same purity and power as the words he thundered from Mount Sinai.

Inspiration does not entail that the Bible on our desks is divine, but it does mean that its human words are also God's words, a verbal reflection of his divine character (e.g., personal, trustworthy, and true; see Rev. 3:14; 21:5; cf. Isa. 65:16). In fact, the Bible so closely identifies God's Word with God himself that at one point the two appear as coordinate subjects in adjoining texts: "For the word of God is living and active, sharper than any two-edged sword, piercing to the division of soul and of spirit, of joints and of marrow, and discerning the thoughts and intentions of the heart. And no creature is hidden from his sight, but all are naked and exposed to the eyes of him to whom we must give account" (Heb. 4:12–13). As the written Word of God, the Bible lays bare the thoughts and attitudes of its hearers because God, its author, searches all hearts and human plans (1 Chron. 28:9; Jer. 17:10). Similarly, just as God exercises absolute authority (Ex. 3:14; Acts 17:24–26) over all creation, so the Bible does not derive its authority from logical inferences or human proofs, but possesses that authority inherently in the writings themselves from the moment of their origin.[6] That is, Scripture is as "self-authenticating" (*autopistos*) as is God himself, though one will acknowledge this from the heart only when persuaded by the Holy Spirit (cf. 1 Cor. 2:12–16).[7]

shows from patristic literature that *theopneustos* bears "a uniformly passive significance" (275); cf. 245–96, esp. the conclusion that "Scripture is called θεόπνευστος in order to designate it as 'God-breathed,' the product of Divine spiration, the creation of that Spirit who is in all spheres of the Divine activity the executive of the Godhead" (296). For arguments that the conjunction "and" (*kai*) between the adjectives ("inspired *and* useful") supports a predicative ("All Scripture is inspired") rather than an attributive ("All inspired Scripture . . .") interpretation, see Philip H. Towner, *The Letters to Timothy and Titus*, NICNT (Grand Rapids: Eerdmans, 2006), 589; Knight, *Pastoral Epistles*, 447.

6. Ned B. Stonehouse, "The Authority of the New Testament," in *The Infallible Word: A Symposium by the Members of the Faculty of Westminster Theological Seminary*, ed. Ned B. Stonehouse and Paul Woolley, 2nd ed. (Phillipsburg, NJ: P&R Publishing, 2002), 93.

7. John Calvin, *Institutes of the Christian Religion*, ed. John T. McNeill, trans. Ford Lewis Battles, vol. 1, Library of Christian Classics 20–21 (Louisville: Westminster John Knox, 2011), 1.9.2, 1.7.5; cf. 3.1.1–3; 3.2.15, 33–36. Summarizing these thoughts, Calvin writes: "For even if it [i.e., Scripture] wins reverence for itself

To say that the biblical text is "inspired," then, is to affirm that the written text is nothing less than divine speech, the "Word of God inscribed in letters," as Ursinus put it.[8] Confident of this, Jesus appealed repeatedly to the Old Testament as a faithful expression of God's authority, will, and purpose (e.g., Matt. 19:18–19; Mark 10:6–8; 14:49) and as the end of all argument (Matt. 4:1–11; 19:18–19; 22:31–32, 43–44)—even commenting at one point, in a confident aside, that "Scripture cannot be broken" (John 10:35). Moreover, Jesus, the promised Messiah, presented himself as the central redemptive subject matter and consummative goal of Old Testament revelation (Luke 24:44–49; John 5:39).[9] This point, in turn, bears directly on the writings of the New Testament as inspired Scripture. The apostles embraced the Old Testament as a testimony to Christ (see, e.g., Acts 2:14–41; cf. 4:24–25) and were commissioned by him to add to the Old Testament canon their own authoritative witness to his saving work.[10] As a result, the apostles recognized their own preaching and writing, including that which was recorded in the New Testament, as God's

---

by its own majesty, it seriously affects us only when it is sealed upon our hearts through the Spirit. Therefore, illumined by his power, we believe neither by our own nor by anyone else's judgment that Scripture is from God; but above human judgment we affirm with utter certainty (just as if we were gazing upon the majesty of God himself) that it has flowed to us from the very mouth of God by the ministry of men" (1.7.5).

8. Zacharius Ursinus, *Loci Theologici*, col. 434, quoted in Muller, *Post-Reformation Reformed Dogmatics*, 2:193.

9. Lane G. Tipton, "Christocentrism and Christotelism: The Spirit, Redemptive History, and the Gospel," in *Redeeming the Life of the Mind: Essays in Honor of Vern Poythress*, ed. John M. Frame, Wayne Grudem, and John J. Hughes (Wheaton, IL: Crossway, 2017), 129–45.

10. Herman N. Ridderbos, *Redemptive History and the New Testament Scriptures*, 2nd rev. ed. (Phillipsburg, NJ: P&R Publishing, 1988), 17–18; Herman N. Ridderbos, "The Canon of the New Testament," in *Revelation and the Bible: Contemporary Evangelical Thought*, ed. Carl F. H. Henry (Grand Rapids: Baker, 1958), 193–94. For an account of the New Testament as "an organic development of the Messiah's redemptive work, fully consistent with, and in fact authorized by, the OT expectation," see C. E. Hill, "God's Speech in These Last Days: The New Testament Canon as an Eschatological Phenomenon," in *Resurrection and Eschatology: Theology in Service of the Church: Essays in Honor of Richard B. Gaffin, Jr.*, ed. Lane G. Tipton and Jeffrey C. Waddington (Phillipsburg, NJ: P&R Publishing, 2008), 203–54; the quote is from Hill, 207.

authoritative speech.[11] For example, Paul rejoiced that when the Thessalonians received the message he delivered to them, they "accepted it not as the word of men but as what it really is, the word of God, which is at work in you believers" (1 Thess. 2:13). Similarly, Peter enjoined his readers to remember not only "the predictions of the holy prophets," but also, and with equal reverence, "the commandment of the Lord and Savior through your apostles" (2 Peter 3:2). Again and again, the New Testament writers indicate that their written witness to the glorified Christ is the very Word of God (Mark 1:1; 1 Cor. 14:37–38; 2 Cor. 13:3; 2 Thess. 2:15; 2 Peter 3:16; Rev. 1:1–3), "words not taught by human wisdom but taught by the Spirit" (1 Cor. 2:13).

Scripture's Authority and Sufficiency for Ministry

The Bible ought to be believed and obeyed because its authority depends "wholly upon God (who is truth itself) the author thereof: and therefore it is to be received, because it is the Word of God" (WCF 1.4). This believing and obeying begins for a pastor in yielding his whole being to what Scripture says. He must consume the Bible and be consumed by it, so that its words become the joy and delight of his heart (Jer. 15:16; cf. Rev. 10:9) and a fire and hammer in his soul (Jer. 23:29). In a brief article encouraging ministers to use the Greek New Testament, J. Gresham Machen declared that "whatever else the preacher need not know, he must know the Bible; he must know it at first hand, and be able to interpret and defend it."[12] Not only will heeding Machen's words make a pastor's performance of his duties more thrilling, it will increase his trust that, through this Word, Jesus Christ by the Holy Spirit still abides with and cares for his church, including the pastor himself.

In particular, by reflecting on what Scripture is and says, the pastor will grow in confidence that the Word is made for the work to

---

11. On the New Testament authors' view of their own divine authority, see Michael J. Kruger, *The Question of Canon: Challenging the Status Quo in the New Testament Debate* (Downers Grove, IL: InterVarsity Press, 2013), 119–54.

12. J. Gresham Machen, "The Minister and His Greek New Testament," in *Machen: Selected Shorter Writings*, ed. D. G. Hart (Phillipsburg, NJ: P&R Publishing, 2004), 212; originally published in *The Presbyterian* 88 (February 7, 1918): 8–9.

which he is called. Even more, as he enters the pulpit, the pastor will know that insofar as he faithfully expounds the Scriptures, what he speaks carries divine authority. From that perspective, Heinrich Bullinger's maxim is true: "The preaching of the word of God is the word of God" (*Praedicato verbi Dei est verbum Dei*).[13] This is not to suggest that the Bible is anything less than the Word of God or that the preached Word becomes anything more than a by-product of Scripture, properly interpreted and expounded. Nevertheless, the Bible itself commissions the preaching of Scripture as uniquely communicating God's Word to sinners (see Rom. 10:14–17). As John Calvin writes, God "deigns to consecrate to himself the mouths and tongues of men in order that his voice may resound in them."[14] It is no wonder, then, that the reading and preaching of Scripture have been central to church worship for centuries.[15]

Receiving and heralding the Bible as God's Word demand that faithful pastors lovingly press its truth even in those areas so rapidly degenerating in our late-modern age, such as sexual ethics, gender determination, and biblical justice. "Let God be true," writes the apostle, "though every one were a liar" (Rom. 3:4). Nothing engenders a pastor's otherworldly commitment to speak the truth in love (Eph.

13. Though commonly attributed to the Second Helvetic Confession (written by Bullinger in 1561), this statement is actually a marginal heading that, according to Edward Dowey, reflects "an authentic lifelong preoccupation of Bullinger with the *viva vox.*" Edward A. Dowey Jr., "The Word of God as Scripture and Preaching," in *Later Calvinism: International Perspectives*, ed. W. Fred Graham, Sixteenth Century Essays and Studies 22 (Kirksville, MO: Northeast Missouri State University, 1994), 9. Bullinger expands on this statement, writing, "Wherefore when this Word of God [i.e., Scripture] is now preached in the church by preachers lawfully called, we believe that the very Word of God is preached, and received of the faithful; and that neither any other Word of God is to be feigned, nor to be expected from heaven: and that now the Word itself which is preached is to be regarded, not the minister that preaches; who, although he be evil and a sinner, nevertheless the Word of God abides true and good." Philip Schaff, *The Creeds of Christendom, with a History and Critical Notes: The Evangelical Protestant Creeds, with Translations*, vol. 3 (New York: Harper & Brothers, 1882), 832.

14. Calvin, *Institutes*, 4.1.5; cf. Pierre C. Marcel, *The Relevance of Preaching*, ed. William Childs Robinson, trans. Rob Roy McGregor (New York: Westminster, 2000), 21.

15. See Hughes Oliphant Old, *The Reading and Preaching of the Scriptures in the Worship of the Christian Church*, 7 vols. (Grand Rapids: Eerdmans, 1998–2010).

4:15) than a Spirit-wrought conviction that Scripture is God's Word. By contrast, too many pastors shade their commitment to Scripture by qualifying the "is" in the statement, "The Bible is God's Word," as though the Bible were merely a human record of religious experiences designed to facilitate new encounters with God today, or simply an instrument of God's self-revelation, but not his verbal revelation itself. Such conceptions are the bitter fruit of theological modernists such as Adolf von Harnack (1851–1930) and the Swiss theologian Karl Barth (1886–1968).[16] If they are to love well, to hate evil, and to pursue righteousness in their ministries (Amos 5:15; Rom. 12:9), pastors must eschew such verbal and theological maneuvers and hold fast to the Scriptures as God's written revelation.

This approach does not dismiss contemporary intellectual and cultural challenges to what Scripture says. Instead, it recognizes that standing on the Scriptures as God's inspired Word is the very key to preaching, teaching, and counseling with power and persuasion. Paul teaches that God's general revelation through nature, including the law written on the heart that conscience apprehends, indelibly stamps a true knowledge of God upon every human being (Rom. 1:19–21, 32). Yet the apostle adds that without the regenerating work of the Spirit, all unbelievers willfully "suppress the truth" that they know (including the truth of their moral obligation to God), and that this leads them into all manner of intellectual and moral futility (Rom. 1:18, 21; Eph. 4:18). Scripture's inspired authority should therefore lead pastors to use the Scriptures to expose the tragic consequences and contradictions of unbelief en route to extolling the mysteries of biblical revelation and the person of Christ as the only safe refuge for sin-sick souls.[17]

16. In a manner consistent with his broader theological project, Barth decried the orthodox doctrine of inspiration as "deplorable," since it implied that the text of Scripture, in its entirety, abides as the Word of God written. See Karl Barth, *Göttingen Dogmatics: Instruction in the Christian Religion*, ed. Hannelotte Reiffen, trans. Geoffrey W. Bromiley, 2 vols. (Grand Rapids: Eerdmans, 1991), 1:217. Cf. Barth, *Church Dogmatics*, 4 vols. (Edinburgh: T. & T. Clark, 1956–75), I/1, 118.

17. For an excellent example of this apologetic approach, see Cornelius Van Til, *Why I Believe in God* (Philadelphia: Committee on Christian Education, Orthodox Presbyterian Church, 1948); Cornelius Van Til and Eric H. Sigward, "A Letter to Francis Schaeffer," in *Unpublished Manuscripts of Cornelius Van Til*, electronic ed.

The imperative of grounding all preaching and apologetics in the authority of Scripture as the very Word of God closely relates to its sufficiency for all of ministry. God intends that through the Scriptures his people would be made "wise for salvation through faith in Christ Jesus" (2 Tim. 3:15).[18] Beyond this evangelistic purpose, Paul adds that Scripture is useful "for teaching, for reproof, for correction, and for training in righteousness" (v. 16), with the more ultimate purpose (*hina*, v. 17) that "the man of God"—any believer, but especially, in context, any new covenant minister—might be "complete [ἄρτιος], equipped for every good work" (v. 17).[19] Taken together, these texts teach that Scripture is thoroughly sufficient for the central aim of a pastor's ministry, namely, that he "may present everyone mature [τέλειον] in Christ" (Col. 1:28). Though Christians will be perfect or fully grown, in body and soul, only at Christ's return (cf. 1 Thess. 2:19–20; 5:23), the Spirit uses the preaching of Scripture to bring about the firstfruits of this transformation in the hearts of God's people. The minister who expends his energy (cf. "For this I toil" [κοπιῶ], Col. 1:29) in the Spirit in this way brings joy to heaven and health to his church. For the risen Christ imparts his resurrection life to the saints through a pastor's labors (Eph. 1:19–20; James 1:17). Even more, the pastor's Word-ministry to others will become a ministry of inner transformation to his own soul, ever conforming him to the image and glory of Christ (2 Cor. 3:18; 4:10).[20]

Scripture is also sufficient for all the ways in which a believer's fellowship with Christ reverberates from the heart and beyond the pew into every area of life. The Bible does not provide Christians with detailed instructions for things such as paying parking tickets. But it does contain all the divine words we need to live for God in every context (including when paying parking tickets!).[21] Cornelius Van Til

(New York: Labels Army Co., 1997).

18. Ferguson, *Some Pastors and Teachers*, 364.

19. The TNIV's gender-neutral language ("so that all God's people may be thoroughly equipped") obscures Paul's primary intent to equip and encourage Timothy, as well as those who would follow him, for the work of pastoral ministry.

20. Geerhardus Vos, *Grace and Glory: Sermons Preached in the Chapel of Princeton Theological Seminary* (Grand Rapids: Reformed Press, 1922), 128.

21. John M. Frame, *The Doctrine of the Word of God* (Phillipsburg, NJ: P&R Publishing, 2010), 221.

captures the wide scope of Scripture's authority and sufficiency when he writes:

> The Bible is thought of as authoritative on everything of which it speaks. Moreover, it speaks of everything. We do not mean that it speaks of football games, of atoms, etc., directly, but we do mean that it speaks of everything either directly or by implication. It tells us not only of the Christ and his work, but it also tells us who God is and where the universe about us has come from. It tells us about theism as well as about Christianity. It gives us a philosophy of history as well as history. Moreover, the information on these subjects is woven into an inextricable whole.[22]

The wise pastor will strive to disciple his flock into an understanding of the ways in which Scripture speaks, "either directly or by implication," into every area of life.

Because God's Word gives us "all things necessary for His own glory, man's salvation, faith and life" (WCF 1.6), it ought to shape how a pastor plans and leads a worship service. It should frame and pervade every prayer, song, sermon, and sacrament. The Bible should guide the counsel he gives to a depressed teenager, drive the loving rebuke he issues to an unrepentant adulterer in his church, suffuse the comfort he extends to a new widow, and fuel the hope he carries for the lost in his neighborhood. While others shelve the Scriptures to become entertainers of goats rather than feeders of sheep, we must declare with William Still, "Let goats entertain goats, and let them do it out in goatland"![23] A pastor must feed his flock with "the whole counsel of God" (Acts 20:27) as one who knows that the Bible, as is the Christ it reveals, is true food and drink (cf. John 6:55), both for his people and also for himself. Show me a pastor for whom the Bible is the song of his heart and the source of his deepest convictions, and I will show you a pastor who speaks with the power of heaven behind his words, yet who walks in a spirit of humility and in utter dependence on God.

22. Cornelius Van Til, *Christian Apologetics*, ed. William Edgar, 2nd ed. (Phillipsburg, NJ: P&R Publishing, 2003), 19–20.
23. William Still, *The Work of the Pastor*, rev. ed. (Fearn, Scotland: Christian Focus, 2010), 23.

The Accommodation of Scripture

As the inspired Word of God, the Bible is accommodated to our finite and fallen condition. Even apart from sin, our creatureliness demands that we receive God's self-disclosure gradually, according to the various relations that he wills to establish with us out of the exhaustive fullness of his unchangeable existence.[24] Compared to him, all believers, even the most elderly, remain "little children" (1 John 5:21), utterly dependent on him for any true knowledge of his majesty and goodness. Before the final resurrection, neither our minds nor our bodies can bear the glory (or "weight") of God's self-disclosure in heaven (1 Cor. 15:50), from which even the angels shield their eyes (cf. Isa. 6:2). Thankfully, in the Bible, the God whose exhaustive self-knowledge no one can fathom speaks to us in ways that we can understand. As Calvin writes, God is pleased to "accommodate the knowledge of him to our slight capacity."[25] Mysteriously, and without altering his transcendent deity, the triune God communicates to us in a book that uses our bodily capacities of sight and sense to bring his truth and wisdom home to our hearts (cf. Ps. 51:6). God is not at all hampered by our limited channels of creaturely reception, since "the hearing ear and the seeing eye, the Lord has made them both" (Prov. 20:12). As God's created image-bearers inhabiting the world he has made, we are fit receptacles of his special revelation.

24. See Herman Bavinck, *Reformed Dogmatics*, ed. John Bolt, trans. John Vriend, vol. 2, *God and Creation* (Grand Rapids: Baker Academic, 2004), 106: "Just as a child cannot picture the worth of a coin of great value but only gains some sense of it when it is counted out in a number of smaller coins, so we too cannot possibly form a picture of the infinite fullness of God's essence unless it is displayed to us now in one relationship, then in another, and now from one angle, then from another."

25. Calvin, *Institutes*, 1.13.1. It is sometimes missed that, in context, Calvin is refuting the "Anthropomorphites," who mistakenly "imagined a corporeal God" given the way Scripture occasionally attributes human characteristics or behavior to God. Yet the principle of divine "accommodation" through revelation is multifaceted in Calvin's thought and pervades his understanding of God's dealings with the world. See, e.g., Arnold Huijgen, *Divine Accommodation in John Calvin's Theology: Analysis and Assessment* (Göttingen: Vandenhoeck & Ruprecht, 2011). Hanson argues that the exegetical principle of accommodation goes back at least to Origen. See R. P. C. Hanson, *Allegory and Event: A Study of the Sources and Significance of Origen's Interpretation of Scripture* (Louisville: Westminster John Knox, 2002), 225–28.

Sadly, the intrusion of sin has crippled our spiritual ability to acknowledge the truth of what God has plainly revealed, both in creation and in Scripture (Rom. 1:18–23; 1 Cor. 2:14). Without the renewing power of the Spirit, we are all, deep down, "hostile to God" (Rom. 8:7) and lie under his wrath and curse. In this condition, were God to confront us with his flaming majesty as it blazes before the angels, we could not help but condemn ourselves as Isaiah did, crying out: "Woe is me! For I am lost" (Isa. 6:5)—literally, cut off, undone, and doomed to die.[26] Were it not for God's forbearance, even the glory revealed in Scripture would destroy us (cf. Ps. 130:3–4; Jer. 23:29; Rev. 2:16). Yet it is precisely here that the brightest rays of divine grace shine forth in the accommodated Scriptures. For God has met our deepest need by giving us the redemptive revelation of Jesus Christ in permanent, written form.[27] In the Bible, God approaches fallen and forgetful men and women in the fullness of his justice and grace and introduces us to a world of salvation and fellowship with himself through Jesus Christ. The accommodated character of Scripture, therefore, means not only that God speaks in it intelligibly to his creatures, but that the words he has given are just what we as sinners need.

This aspect of the doctrine of Scripture is the antidote to pastors' perennial temptation to avoid reading and preaching on hard passages. I well remember being assigned as a young minister to preach on the defiling of Dinah in Genesis 34 at my home church. Another time I was called on as a first-time guest preacher to read Ezekiel 23 (go ahead, I'll wait as you look it up) to a congregation. Both occasions made me sweat! But they were lessons in divine providence and in the truth that God gave us every chapter of his Word for the building up of his church. While every sermon should take into account the makeup of its hearers, pastors magnify God's wisdom in giving us the Scriptures when they do not shy away from preaching any portion of his Holy Word.

Thankfully, the books of Scripture exhibit a variety of genres and styles, attractive elements of artistic form, concrete expressions,

26. Edward J. Young, *The Book of Isaiah, Chapters 1–18*, vol. 1 (Grand Rapids: Eerdmans, 1965), 247n28.
27. Geerhardus Vos, *Biblical Theology* (Grand Rapids: Eerdmans, 1948; repr., Carlisle, PA: Banner of Truth, 2007), 20–21.

and an unembellished simplicity that appreciates the complexity of human life.[28] All of it together reflects the richness of the triune God, the supreme Artist and Architect of the universe and the source of our salvation (cf. Ps. 104:24; Prov. 8:22–31; Rom. 11:33; 1 Cor. 1:30).[29] But as the revelation of the transcendent God, the Bible also contains some things that are "hard to understand" (2 Peter 3:16)—unfamiliar historical references and literary figures, ancient idioms, elaborate arguments, and layered narratives originally laid down in Hebrew and Greek (and Aramaic). Though we can overcome some of these challenges by careful study and Bible translations, Scripture is filled with profound mysteries that defy full comprehension. In fact, every text in Scripture carries an infinite depth of meaning, since its language (indeed, all language) is rooted in the communicative fellowship of the Trinity, which no creature can plumb.[30]

Nevertheless, the Bible so plainly reveals those things that are necessary for salvation that any reverent, serious inquirer can grasp them sufficiently without interpretations handed down by priest, pope, or prosperity preacher streamed online.[31] In the Bible, the eternal God opens his hand to satisfy the desires of needy sinners (cf. Ps. 145:16). Though many turn away in unbelief, the true believer who opens his Bible or hears it faithfully preached will say with Peter, "Lord, to whom shall we go? You have the words of eternal life" (John 6:68).

Scripture's Clarity and Necessity for Ministry

That Scripture so wonderfully accommodates our creatureliness and fallenness speaks directly to the challenges of pastoral ministry. What pastor has pondered the plight of the lost, the needs of his family and flock, and the gravity of his calling, and not felt his own

28. See Leland Ryken, James C. Wilhoit, and Tremper Longman III, eds., *Dictionary of Biblical Imagery* (Downers Grove, IL: InterVarsity Press, 1998).

29. Bavinck, *Reformed Dogmatics*, 2:206.

30. For more on the infinite depth of divine communication within the Trinity and, consequently, in Scripture, see Vern S. Poythress, *God-Centered Biblical Interpretation* (Phillipsburg, NJ: P&R Publishing, 1999), 19–25; Vern S. Poythress, *In the Beginning Was the Word: Language—A God-Centered Approach* (Wheaton, IL: Crossway, 2009), esp. 17–41, 85–90, 163–69.

31. Cf. WCF 1.6.

finitude crashing upon him like a tidal wave? If he looks for help from pastoral networks on social media, he is deluged with an endless stream of digital articles, blog posts, and videos, many by megastar ministers who seem to hover effortlessly above the challenges of church life. If he shuts off such channels and contemplates his own soul, he may sense a toxic blend of guilt, resentment, anger, and anxiety bubbling up within him as he remembers his own sins or the sins of others against him. If, at last, he suppresses his emotions and musters the grit to carry on, he may well face the emptiness of heart that awaits a man who proclaims God's saving mercy to others while neglecting it himself. Where is he to turn for refuge and relief?

Thankfully, God is pleased to save pastors (1 Cor. 9:25–27) and to make his power perfect in their weakness (2 Cor. 12:9) by giving to them, and working in them, divine words that are sufficiently clear to all. The essential clarity of Scripture reminds pastors that God calls them not to perform supernatural feats of spiritual strength, but simply to live within the limits of their creatureliness in utter dependence on him. God graciously enables them to do this by cultivating in them a love and an appetite for the Bible itself. As they preach and teach the Bible's clear message without hindrance, the church experiences Scripture's power for human living. The Bible is a mirror that exposes the heart (James 1:23–25), a hammer that shatters pride (Jer. 23:29), a lamp that yields knowledge and lights the way (Ps. 119:105), and a seed that imparts new life (1 Peter 1:23). Thomas Watson describes the Bible as "the compass by which the rudder of our will is to be steered; it is the field in which Christ, the Pearl of price, is hid; it is a rock of diamonds."[32] Charles Spurgeon speaks of it as his living companion, declaring:

> No other writing has within it a heavenly life whereby it works miracles, and even imparts life to its reader. . . . Why, the Book has wrestled with me; the Book has smitten me; the Book has comforted me; the Book has smiled on me; the Book has frowned on me; the Book has clasped my hand; the Book has warmed my heart.

32. Thomas Watson, "Sermon VIII: How We May Read the Scriptures with Most Spiritual Profit," in *Puritan Sermons 1659–1689*, ed. James Nichols, 6 vols. (Wheaton, IL: Richard Owen Roberts, 1981), 2:63.

The Book weeps with me, and sings with me; it whispers to me, and it preaches to me; it maps my way, and holds up my goings; it was to me the Young Man's Best Companion, and it is still my Morning and Evening Chaplain.[33]

What one Reformed divine writes about Christians, therefore, goes double for pastors: those who love the Bible will exhibit in return an "earnest and indefatigable effort to procure for ourselves an abundant supply of the divine Word, and to use it and enjoy it, as a thing on which the life and salvation of our soul hinges."[34] What could be more necessary to pastoral ministry than for the Bible to be the pastor's refuge, his refreshment, and his feast?

Our gratitude for the Bible increases when we realize that God was not compelled to give it to us. In that specific sense, Scripture is not absolutely necessary. But Scripture is necessary if any are to be saved, sanctified, and brought home to glory.[35] For Scripture alone reveals the redemptive plan of God, commanding all to lay hold on Christ through faith and, in him, to receive all his saving benefits.[36] While creation resounds that God is the eternal, righteous, and good Creator (cf. Rom. 1:20, 32), Christians can know that Jesus loves them, "for the Bible tells me so." In this way, Scripture is necessary to the pastor who longs to see saving faith and joy flourish among his flock.

Paul draws out the God-ordained link between Christ, faith, and preaching when he writes, "How then will they call on him in whom they have not believed? And how are they to believe in him of whom they have never heard? And how are they to hear without someone preaching? . . . So faith comes from hearing, and hearing through the word of Christ" (Rom. 10:14, 17). Underlying Paul's argument is the fact that because Scripture alone reveals the Christ who must be

---

33. Charles Haddon Spurgeon, "The Word a Sword," in *The Metropolitan Tabernacle Pulpit Sermons*, 63 vols. (London: Passmore & Alabaster, 1888), 34:112.

34. Petrus van Mastricht, *Theoretical-Practical Theology*, vol. 1, *Prolegomena*, ed. Joel R. Beeke, trans. Todd M. Rester (Grand Rapids: Reformation Heritage Books, 2018), 185.

35. As Turretin puts it, "God indeed was not bound to the Scriptures, but he has bound us to them." Turretin, *Elenctic Theology*, 1:57 (1.2.2).

36. See Calvin, *Institutes*, 3.1.1, 3.2.2.

believed, it is Scripture that must be heard, and therefore it is Scripture that must be preached.

God promises that as the Word goes out, the Spirit will grant faith to those to whom he will (John 3:8) and, in turn, that those sealed in the body of Christ will offer worship that is well pleasing to God (cf. Ex. 29:18, 41; 1 Peter 2:5; Rev. 8:4). Here, too, Scripture is necessary to pastoral ministry. For the church exists to worship God, and God accepts only that worship that conforms to the standards and directions laid down for us in his Word (Heb. 12:28; cf. Lev. 10:1–3). By neglecting Scripture, some have displaced worship with all sorts of agendas for human flourishing (e.g., social initiatives, producing art, building community). Others long for something more transcendent but, still hampered by a this-world focus, subtly redefine worship as an experience to be received from God ("How was your worship today?") or from the musicians up front (i.e., "the worship team"). To be sure, God must work the desire to worship into the heart, and in that sense it originates with him; and music is a divine gift meant to move our affections and prompt in us genuine zeal.[37] But true worship entails giving to God the honor due his name according to the instructions he has revealed. In these ways and more, Scripture is necessary to sustain a pastor's soul, to save his flock, and to satisfy God's people with his steadfast love.

The Redemptive-Historical Design of Scripture

A third feature of Scripture—and one that reflects its divine inspiration and human accommodation—is its redemptive-historical design. The Bible has not come to us as a textbook of abstract theological truths. Rather, it records and exhibits God's practical care for his people through a long history of his redemptive words and deeds. Why is this the case? The answer rests on two precious realities: (1) true religion consists of a human being's fellowship with God in covenant and (2) God, who desires to be known in this way,

37. R. B. Kuiper, "The Glory of the Christian Church," *Presbyterian Guardian* 20, no. 12 (1951): 230; Jonathan Edwards, *The Works of Jonathan Edwards with a Memoir by Sereno E. Dwight*, ed. Edward Hickman, 2 vols. (Carlisle, PA: Banner of Truth, 1974), 1:242.

has opened the door to covenant fellowship with himself by acting and speaking in history, preeminently through his incarnate Son (see Heb. 1:1–2). To be precise, then, the ultimate reason why God's verbal revelation in Scripture covers ages and spans epochs is not human finitude or sin, but that (after the fall) his word-revelation marched in step with the great redeeming work by which God was leading generations of his people into the riches of heavenly glory in fellowship with himself. "Revelation is the interpretation of redemption," Geerhardus Vos writes; "it must, therefore, unfold itself in installments as redemption does."[38]

But there is something more. Intriguingly, Vos adds that the redemptive process, as Scripture reveals it, developed over millennia because it advanced according to the natural development of the human race.[39] In other words, after the fall, the God who "made from one man every nation of mankind to live on all the face of the earth" (Acts 17:26) did not leave his people as orphans, but attuned his redemptive work to their specific needs as creatures bound to space and time. God condescended to covenant with real individuals in history—first with Adam and his offspring and then, after the fall, with his people in Jesus Christ—all with a view to revealing the depths of his eternal glory through a new creation of righteousness and peace. At the most basic level, therefore, it is because human beings are historical creatures, and because God desires to redeem his people in the reality of their settings, that he wove his word- and deed-revelation into the course of history, culminating in the formation of the Scriptures.

In light of its development, Scripture's redemptive-historical design reminds us that the whole Bible is a testimony to God's wise and loving care for his covenant people. It explains why the Old

38. Vos, *Biblical Theology*, 6.

39. "As soon as we realize that revelation is at almost every point interwoven with and conditioned by the redeeming activity of God in its wider sense, and together with the latter connected with the natural development of the present world, its historic character becomes perfectly intelligible and ceases to cause surprise." Geerhardus Vos, "The Idea of Biblical Theology as a Science and as a Theological Discipline," in *Redemptive History and Biblical Interpretation: The Shorter Writings of Geerhardus Vos*, ed. Richard B. Gaffin Jr. (Phillipsburg, NJ: P&R Publishing, 2001), 8.

Testament lays the creational foundation for the entire movement of history (Gen. 1–2) before tracing the organic growth of the one gospel of Christ, first adumbrated through promissory types and symbols (see Rom. 1:1–3; 16:26; 1 Cor. 15:1–5) and then in the work of Jesus Christ and in the witness of the apostles (Luke 24:45–47; Acts 1:8; 3:18). The Old Testament types and symbols were special instances of God's love for his "church under age," just as the open disclosure of the gospel in the New Testament increases the blessing (WCF 19.3). As Calvin explains:

> The Lord of old willed that his people direct and elevate their minds to the heavenly heritage; yet, *to nourish them better in this hope*, he displayed it for them to see and, so to speak, taste, under earthly benefits. But now that the gospel has more plainly and clearly revealed the grace of the future life, the Lord leads our minds to meditate upon it directly, laying aside *the lower mode of training* that he used with the Israelites.[40]

Scripture is the product of God's covenantal concern for his people, centered on the person and work of Jesus Christ. It is written evidence of the Father's steadfast love for us as our Creator and Lord (Mal. 2:10; Heb. 12:9), of the grace of the Lord Jesus Christ toward us as our Shepherd and King (John 10:11; cf. Ezek. 34:23; 37:24), and of the fellowship of the Holy Spirit with us as our Helper and Teacher (John 14:26; 1 John 2:27).

Scripture's Finality and Efficacy in Ministry

Scripture's redemptive-historical and Christ-centered design is of great benefit to pastors. One of the primary benefits is the firm and certain knowledge that Scripture is God's final redemptive revelation to the world before the return of Christ. As the Westminster Confession of Faith puts it, now that Christ has come, the "former ways of God's revealing his will unto his people" are "now ceased" (WCF 1.1). Expanding that point, once we recognize that the central subject

---

40. Calvin, *Institutes*, 2.11.1 (emphasis added); cf. 2.11.5.

matter of all postfall special revelation is God's objective redemptive work in history, and that it climaxed initially in the humiliation and exaltation of Christ, it is plain that no further redemptive revelation is necessary, nor will it be forthcoming. God has "in these last days" (Heb. 1:2) spoken to us by his Son and has poured out the power of his Spirit to the church at Pentecost. By that Spirit, Christ gave unique and unrepeatable authority to his apostles, as his plenipotentiaries, to proclaim, and eventually to inscribe, divinely sanctioned testimony for the church age regarding the fact and meaning of his finished work.[41] That is to say, Christ's finished redemptive work correlates to a final revelatory word from God concerning it. Or, as Richard Gaffin aptly states, "Their [i.e., the apostles'] witness is the foundational witness to the foundational work of Christ; to the once-for-all work of Christ is joined a once-for-all witness to that work (Eph. 2:20)."[42]

Because Scripture's focus is Christ and his finished work, together with its many implications, pastors should not treat the Bible as if it were designed to deliver specific directions for dealing with the ad hoc circumstances and contingent choices of twenty-first-century Westerners (e.g., whom to marry, which job to accept, where to live). Certainly, Scripture offers a Christ-centered worldview in terms of how we can and should approach these questions (see above on Scripture's sufficiency for ministry). But the Bible is neither a fortune cookie nor a self-help manual. Rather, from Genesis to Revelation, the Bible unfolds "the gospel of God . . . concerning his Son" (Rom. 1:1, 3) and anticipates the glorious eschatological consummation to come. For this reason, pastors should preach a biblical text with a view to lifting their congregations' eyes of faith to the ascended Christ, who works repentance, renews faith in the promises of God, and orders all of life under the benevolent reign of our Father in heaven. This is done only when the pastor explains

---

41. See Ridderbos, *Redemptive History and the New Testament Scriptures*, 12–24, 36–38.

42. Richard B. Gaffin Jr., "The New Testament as Canon," in *Inerrancy and Hermeneutic: A Tradition, A Challenge, A Debate*, ed. Harvie M. Conn (Grand Rapids: Baker, 1988), 176. Cf. Oscar Cullmann, "Scripture and Tradition," trans. Joseph E. Cunneen, *Cross Currents* 3, no. 3 (1953): 264; Ridderbos, *Redemptive History and the New Testament Scriptures*, 25.

every text of Scripture within the larger horizon of the redemptive accomplishment of Jesus Christ. Such was Jesus' practice when he explained to his disciples that "everything written about me [περὶ ἐμοῦ] in the Law of Moses and the Prophets and the Psalms [ἐν τῷ νόμῳ Μωϋσέως καὶ προφήταις καὶ ψαλμοῖς] must be fulfilled" (Luke 24:44). Luke's ensuing note that Jesus "opened their [i.e., the disciples'] minds to understand *the Scriptures* [τὰς γραφάς]" (v. 45)—i.e., the Scriptures in their entirety—confirms that a redemptive-historical interpretation of the Scriptures is no optional hermeneutical approach for ministers today. It is what the Scriptures, in all their Christ-centered glory, require.

Another benefit of recognizing the redemptive-historical design of Scripture is that it leads to increased confidence that, by the power of the Spirit, the Bible is effectual to accomplish all of God's saving purposes (cf. Isa. 55:10). This is the case because Christ's fulfillment of the Old Testament includes that the Scriptures be proclaimed for the sake of "other sheep" who will believe in him (John 10:16, 27). "Thus it is written," he announced, "that the Christ should suffer and on the third day rise from the dead, *and that repentance for the forgiveness of sins should be proclaimed in his name to all nations*, beginning from Jerusalem" (Luke 24:46–47).[43]

What a privilege belongs to the pastor who holds and heralds the Word of God. He does it with the heavenly promise that in the Lord his labor, while dismissed by a world lost in sin, is not in vain (1 Cor. 15:58). Just as the apostle John wrote his Gospel "so that you may believe [ἵνα πιστεύητε] that Jesus is the Christ, the Son of God, and that by believing [ἵνα πιστεύοντες] you may have life in his name" (John 20:31), so the pastor who handles the Bible in accord with its design as God's historically wrought, Christ-centered revelation can carry on, knowing that by God's grace, his efforts will introduce those with ears to hear into eternal fellowship with their Savior through faith. But even if many turn away, he will restore to preaching and teaching a proper emphasis on God's objective work of redemption in Christ, together with all the entailments of that work for the church's life, and it will please his Father in heaven. And on the last day, his

43. Cf. Hill, "God's Speech in These Last Days," 208.

efforts by the Spirit will be met with the words that will make all his trials pale by comparison: "Well done, good and faithful servant. You have been faithful over a little; I will set you over much. Enter into the joy of your master" (Matt. 25:23).

Conclusion

In Jesus' longest recorded prayer (John 17:1–26), commonly known as his High Priestly Prayer, our Lord said, "Sanctify them in the truth; your word is truth" (v. 17). These words reveal the depth of the Savior's love for his disciples and his desire for their safekeeping in the name of his Father after his departure (cf. v. 11). Just as the Father consecrated his Son and sent him into the world (10:36), so Jesus prays that the Father would set apart, or "sanctify" (ἁγιάζω), his disciples as his holy witnesses in the world (cf. 17:18–19).[44] Significantly, Jesus says that the means and context of this work of sanctification would be nothing less than "the truth," that is, the truth of God's redemptive self-disclosure, which Jesus embodied in climactic form and which is now enshrined in Scripture.[45] From this perspective, it

44. Though the same verb (ἁγιάζω) is used in John 17:17 ("sanctify them"; ἁγίασον αὐτοὺς) and 19 ("I consecrate myself"; ἐγὼ ἁγιάζω ἐμαυτόν) to denote the setting apart for service to God, Morris observes that in the case of the disciples, such service necessarily includes an inward renewal unto holiness. See Leon Morris, *The Gospel according to John: The English Text with Introduction, Exposition and Notes*, NICNT (Grand Rapids: Eerdmans, 1995), 647–48.

45. Some have thought that Jesus was referring to himself, the eternal Word, when he declared that "your word [λόγος] is truth" (John 17:17). E.g., Cyril of Alexandria, *Commentary on the Gospel according to S. John*, vol. 2 (London: Walter Smith, 1885), 529–30; Augustine of Hippo, "Lectures or Tractates on the Gospel according to St. John," in *St. Augustin: Homilies on the Gospel of John, Homilies on the First Epistle of John, Soliloquies*, ed. Philip Schaff, trans. John Gibb and James Innes, Select Library of the Nicene and Post-Nicene Fathers of the Christian Church 7, 1st ser. (New York: Christian Literature Company, 1888), 405. Yet a close look at the prayer and its context suggests that in John 17:17 Jesus was thinking of God's oral or even written revelation, particularly the way in which the Old Testament speaks about itself (see, e.g., 2 Sam. 22:31; Ps. 119:14, 151, 160). E. J. Young adduces three reasons for this interpretation. First, Jesus "identifies the Word of God as something distinct from himself" in John 17:6 ("they have kept your word") and 14 ("I have given them your word"). Second, the fact that Jesus lived on earth "in the very atmosphere of the Old Testament Scriptures" suggests

is fair to say that just before he experienced the most excruciating moments of his earthly ministry, Jesus turned his attention to the character of Scripture ("your word is truth") and to its practical purpose ("Sanctify them in the truth") in the lives of his people.[46]

The Father answers Jesus' prayer wherever a right doctrine of Scripture shapes the ministry and life of a pastor. As we have seen, the inspired, accommodated, and redemptive-historically designed Scripture pours forth countless blessings for the pastor and his work. The Bible is authoritative in its content, sufficient in its scope, clear in its message, necessary for salvation, final in history, and effective for redeeming sinners and building up the saints. When a pastor faithfully studies, preaches, and teaches this Bible to the flock under his care, especially when he is borne by the power of heaven and the prayers of the saints, he participates, as God's chosen spokesman, in the historical unfolding of "the mystery of Christ" (Eph. 3:4; cf. Col. 4:2), the cosmic plan of redemption conceived in God's eternal counsel and centered on the life, death, and resurrection of Jesus Christ, the Lord and heir of all things (Matt. 28:18). And in this way, a proper doctrine of Scripture renders its highest service to the church of Jesus Christ, which he purchased with his own blood (Acts 20:28).

---

that he was "giving expression to the thought of the Old Testament, and most likely was basing the form of His expression upon the longest of the Psalms." Third, a reference to God's verbal revelation fits the historical context of Jesus' imminent departure, after which his disciples would be "constrained to depend upon His Word." Young, *Thy Word Is Truth*, 261–62. Chrysostom, who also sees John 17:17 as referring to God's written Word, notes that Paul teaches that it is by this Word that God sanctifies his church (Eph. 5:26). John Chrysostom, "Homilies of St. John Chrysostom, Archbishop of Constantinople, on the Gospel of St. John," in *Saint Chrysostom: Homilies on the Gospel of St. John and Epistle to the Hebrews*, ed. Philip Schaff, trans. G. T. Stupart, Select Library of the Nicene and Post-Nicene Fathers of the Christian Church 14, 1st ser. (New York: Christian Literature Company, 1889), 303.

46. Strictly speaking, the third-person plural pronoun in John 17:17 (αὐτοὺς) and the demonstrative pronoun in John 17:20 (τούτων) share the same referent—namely, the apostles—though Jesus' petition in verse 20 ("I do not ask for these only, but also for those who will believe in me through their word") widens the scope to include "all the disciples of the Gospel, so long as there shall be any of them to the end of the world." John Calvin, *Commentary on the Gospel according to John*, trans. William Pringle, vol. 2 (Edinburgh: Calvin Translation Society, 1847), 181.

Key Terms

inspiration
redemptive history

Recommendations for Further Reading

Gaffin, Richard B., Jr. "The New Testament as Canon." In *Inerrancy and Hermeneutic: A Tradition, A Challenge, A Debate*, edited by Harvie M. Conn, 165–83. Grand Rapids: Baker, 1988.

Murray, John. "The Attestation of Scripture." In *The Infallible Word: A Symposium by the Members of the Faculty of Westminster Theological Seminary*, edited by Ned B. Stonehouse and Paul Woolley, 1–54. 2nd ed. Phillipsburg, NJ: P&R Publishing, 2002. First published 1946.

Ridderbos, Herman N. *Redemptive History and the New Testament Scriptures*. 2nd rev. ed. Phillipsburg, NJ: P&R Publishing, 1988. First published 1963.

Tipton, Lane G. "Christocentrism and Christotelism: The Spirit, Redemptive History, and the Gospel." In *Redeeming the Life of the Mind: Essays in Honor of Vern Poythress*, edited by John M. Frame, Wayne Grudem, and John J. Hughes, 129–45. Wheaton, IL: Crossway, 2017.

Young, Edward J. *Thy Word Is Truth: Some Thoughts on the Biblical Doctrine of Inspiration*. 1957. Reprint, Carlisle, PA: Banner of Truth, 2008.

Discussion Questions

1. According to the Bible, what does it mean to say that Scripture is inspired? How does inspiration relate to each of Scripture's attributes (authority, sufficiency, clarity, necessity, finality, efficacy)?

2. What are some ways in which Scripture is accommodated to our finite and fallen condition?

3. What is the deepest reason why God gave the text of the Bible over long ages of time?

4. How does the Christ-centered character of Scripture account for the finished canon of Scripture?
5. How does the preaching of Scripture fit within the redemptive-historical purposes of God?
6. How should the efficacy of Scripture inform the pastor's ministry? His expectations? His efforts?

2

THE TRINITY

The Doctrine of God and the Pulpit

*Wherein is A MOST ABSTRUSE TEST CASE, in which the
monstrous tergiversations of sundry adversaries are craftilie
dismantled in a ghostlie and agreeable manner and the faithe of the
most noble fathers gathered at Nicaea and Constantinople in the
yeares of our Lord 325 and 381 vindicated from all false calumnies
and aspersions, together with divers admonitions relating to the
publick declaration of the same. Written by D. Robt. Letham,
Minister of the Gospell, in honour of that most eminent Divine
and Minister of the Gospell, D. Sincl. Ferguson.*[1]

We are all familiar, I'm sure, with the demand for relevance. It has
dominated the church ever since I can remember, which is longer
than I care to recall but not quite as long as the subtitle of this essay
might lead you to believe. The tyranny of the present is ever with
us, never more than when the preacher is expected to be cool and
to appeal to the latest passing fad. There is a sense in which this is a
necessity; the congregation to which we preach must be engaged with

1. Sinclair Ferguson's lucid biblical and doctrinal preaching and writing, with
clear connections to Christian living, are widely valued by us all. This paper, based
on sermonic material, attempts to follow this trajectory.

the message, and the preacher must address the real world. Problems arise when the immediate circumstances dictate the message.

A while ago I preached on a theme that I can only describe as the most searingly relevant that could ever be conceived. It touches every aspect of life—encompassing the entire cosmos and the world around us—and reaches to the heart of the gospel. Before it, all else fades into insignificance. It should be enough to satisfy the most acute demands of the present moment. I preached on the generation of the Son by the Father in eternity.

I have never heard a sermon on this theme. Indeed, in over sixty-five years since I became conscious of sermons, I can count those that I have heard on the Trinity—the Christian doctrine of God—on the fingers of one hand.

On the doctrine of God in general, the tally is not much better. One year, when I sat in the pew of a well-known church in Cambridge, sans minister, a pantheon of preachers filled the pulpit, each of whom preached on themes related to sanctification. I concluded that it represented a Pelagian tendency, with evangelicalism exhibiting all the anthropocentric characteristics of post-Enlightenment individualism.

Yet as I have said, the eternal generation of the Son is about the most relevant topic one can have. Not that too many think so. Some have rejected the doctrine, while others dismiss it as unimportant, speculative, and of little consequence. In this they set themselves against the historic teaching of the Christian church—Catholic, Orthodox, Protestant—and call on themselves the anathemas of the Second Council of Constantinople (553): "If anyone shall not confess that the Word of God has two nativities, the one from all eternity of the Father, without time and without body; the other in these last days, coming down from heaven and being made flesh of the holy and glorious Mary . . . let him be anathema."[2] For the sake of argument, perhaps the fathers were wrong; maybe theologians and exegetes down the centuries have been uniformly misguided—after

2. Capitulum 2, *The Second Council of Constantinople, 553 A.D.*, in Henry R. Percival, *The Seven Ecumenical Councils of the Undivided Church: Their Canons and Dogmatic Decrees*, Select Library of Nicene and Post-Nicene Fathers of the Christian Church 14, 2nd ser. (repr., Edinburgh: T. & T. Clark, 1997), 312.

all, the church is not infallible. But it would require overwhelming evidence to establish the charge.

Again, not many congregations might be able to appreciate the importance of eternal generation and be able to intelligently hear a sermon on it. It so happens that I have ministered to ones who *could* understand what is at stake, insofar as it is possible to do so. Notwithstanding, we recite the Nicene Creed on a regular basis. This great ecumenical creed, confessed through the centuries, contains the line that the Son was "begotten by his Father before all ages, . . . begotten not made."[3] The familiar Christmas hymn "O Come, All Ye Faithful" has the words "very God, . . . begotten, not created." Do we want to encourage singing and confession that is blind to what is sung and confessed? Is ignorant repetition acceptable? Without teaching, these words are meaningless sounds.

At a conference in the USA on the Trinity a few years back, a prominent evangelical—a household name—asked me publicly where in the Bible the eternal generation of the Son was to be found. I suspected that he did not accept that it was biblical. I also gathered that he required explicit proof texts for every element of faith, something at variance with classic Christian interpretation.[4] I shot back, "The whole Bible." Certainly there are individual passages that exhibit the doctrine—Hebrews 1:3 was cited by another scholar, a Roman Catholic—but the whole sense of Scripture and its overall doctrinal fabric require it. Without it, the structure of the doctrine of the Trinity would collapse and all else would be threatened. I have addressed this elsewhere.[5]

3. Translation by R. P. C. Hanson, *The Search for the Christian Doctrine of God: The Arian Controversy 318–381* (Edinburgh: T. & T. Clark, 1988), 816, from the Greek text of the Nicene Creed printed by G. L. Dosetti, *Il Symbolo di Nicea e di Constantinopoli* (Rome: Herder, 1967), 244ff.

4. Gregory Nazianzen, *Oration 31*, 3, 21–24; WCF 1.6, in *The Confession of Faith, the Larger and Shorter Catechisms with the Scripture Proofs at Large, Together with The Sum of Saving Knowledge* (Applecross, Scotland: Publications Committee of the Free Presbyterian Church of Scotland, 1970), 22.

5. Robert Letham, *Systematic Theology* (Wheaton, IL: Crossway, 2019), 114–21; Robert Letham, *The Holy Trinity: In Scripture, History, Theology, and Worship*, rev. and expanded ed. (Phillipsburg, NJ: P&R Publishing, 2019), 193–201. See also Kevin Giles, *The Eternal Generation of the Son: Maintaining Orthodoxy in Trinitarian Theology* (Downers Grove, IL: IVP Academic, 2012).

Here are some factors that demonstrate the significance of the dogma. In listing them, I hope the reader will see how vital it is to preach about God. It appears blindingly obvious—but the obvious is too often overlooked!

The Generation of the Son Is a Mystery beyond Our Knowledge: It Demonstrates God's Greatness and Our Limitations

From the fathers onward, the church has recognized that the internal relations of the Trinitarian hypostases are beyond our grasp. God is incomprehensible; we cannot encompass him by our thoughts. A favorite passage used in the early church was Isaiah 53:8, "who shall declare his generation?"[6] To our oh-so-sophisticated sensibilities, this is not good exegesis of Isaiah. Yet maybe at least part of the problem lies elsewhere. The fathers were living at a different time, while we are often oblivious to the ways that post-Enlightenment practices, requiring each book to be read in isolation, restrict what we can see in the text. The way that the fathers saw it was that the relation of the Son to the Father is a mystery beyond our intellectual capabilities. The idea, still purveyed by some, that the doctrine of the eternal generation of the Son was the product of a speculative frenzy is as far from the mark as can be. It was not a matter of clever logic or brilliant philosophizing, but a mystery to be adored rather than investigated, as Calvin would have said. It shows in clear relief our own limitations. It placards before us that we are not the center of the universe and leads us to recognize that our place is in submission to God. His ways are past finding out. The extent to which we can even begin to plumb them is on the basis of what he has revealed and the degree to which he chooses to illuminate our minds. "Who are you, O man, to answer back to God?" (Rom. 9:20).

Some say that "these are meaningless, empty words, of no use to our faith, since we cannot ever know what is meant by the generation of the Son." How can we believe what we cannot understand? it is claimed. This is wrong; it is to put the cart before the horse. We

6. Irenaeus, *Against Heresies*, 2.28:5–9, *ANF* 1:400–406. On the incomprehensibility of eternal generation, see Origen, *On First Principles*, 1.4, *ANF* 4:247; Basil of Caesarea, *On the Holy Spirit*, 14, *PG* 32:88–89.

do not understand in comprehensive fashion in order to believe; we believe in order to understand (Heb. 11:3). If we were to believe only what was fully within our mental grasp, we would be masters of our fate, the final arbiters of what was true. This cannot be. Even the clearest statements of the Bible have a depth and richness that is never-ending (Rom. 11:33–36). As we grow older, we find that there is more in what we once took for granted than we could ever realize. The surpassing mystery of the Trinity is there to be believed, to instill worship. On that basis, perhaps we may be given further insight in God's own time. While we cannot comprehend what goes on in the inner life of the Trinity, enough is given to us that we can appreciate something of the nature of the mystery that has been revealed.

The Generation of the Son Demonstrates That the Son Is One in Being and of the Identical Nature as the Father

The Trinitarian controversy of the fourth century was a matter of public discussion, the subject of gossip in barbershops, on the street corner, and in private homes. The Arians and Eunomians would ask, "Were you a father before you begat your son?" Given the obvious negative reply, they would eagerly follow up with the clincher: "Neither was God before he begat his Son." These people believed that the Son began to be at some point. He was not one with God from eternity. He was a creature. Their line of argument was from human realities to the divine; as it is with us, so it is with God. The assumptions underlying their argument were wrong. While created realities may, and sometimes do, give indications of what God may be like, the normal line of thought should be in the other direction. After all, God precedes his creation.

The orthodox responded to this tactic with the rejoinder that fathers generate sons who are of the same nature. Consequently, the Son is of the same nature as the Father. He is one with God eternally and indivisibly. His generation by the Father establishes the point. Generation entails identity of nature. It shows that whoever has seen the Son has seen the Father (John 14:9). It proves that Jesus is the ultimate revelation of what God is like. It means that God is just like Jesus. It requires us to pay close attention to what Jesus says, since in doing so we will be brought face to face with God himself. This is at the heart of the gospel.[7]

The Generation of the Son Demonstrates That the Son Is Eternally Distinct from the Father

I have mentioned that eternal generation undergirds the doctrine of the Trinity. Since this is so, it demonstrates that God is personal, an indivisible union of love. The Father is not the Son, and the Son is not the Father. Every bit as much as the fact that the Son is of the same identical being as the Father, and eternally so, eternal generation displays eternal distinctions between the two, and between the Holy Spirit also.

Beyond this, it points to the stunning truth that love is at the heart of the universe that God created. The three are one, yet the three are distinct. Their indivisible union is one of love. The creation in which we are a part is not a harsh, random, impersonal cosmos, ruthless and meaningless, but is brought into existence, formed and shaped by the infinitely loving God. As God's special creatures, we have a right to feel at home in the world God made.[8]

The Generation of the Son Demonstrates Not Only That God Is the Living God, but That He Is Life Itself

"In him was life," we read of the Son (John 1:4). It is not that there is such a thing as life, God's being the perfect exemplification of it; God cannot be the exemplification of something external to himself. He *is* life; he defines what life is. He is brimful of life, vibrant, infinite. The fact that the Father eternally communicates to the Son his hypostatic identity, in the unity of the indivisible being of the Trinity, marks this emphatically.

7. For the fourth-century Trinitarian controversy, see Hanson, *Search for the Christian Doctrine of God*; Lewis Ayres, *Nicaea and Its Legacy: An Approach to Fourth-Century Trinitarian Theology* (Oxford: Oxford University Press, 2004); Letham, *Holy Trinity*, 109–207.

8. Herman Bavinck, *Reformed Dogmatics*, ed. John Bolt, trans. John Vriend, 4 vols. (Grand Rapids: Baker Academic, 2003–8), 1:321; James Eglinton, *Trinity and Organism: Towards a New Reading of Herman Bavinck's Organic Motif* (London: Bloomsbury, 2012), 149.

The Generation of the Son Enables God to Create Freely and Sovereignly

Without the generation of the Son and the spiration of the Spirit, God would not have been able to freely bring other entities into existence and grant them contingent, finite life.[9] If God were a static block of concrete, he could hardly create. Because God is life, he grants us life. Whereas he is life itself, he has granted to his creatures life on a finite, contingent basis. Our life is given by God, dependent entirely on his will. We might never have existed. Once created, we depend on him for continuance every nanosecond. On the other hand, God is life itself and is so necessarily; there is no possibility of its being otherwise. The Tree of Life in Genesis 2 indicates that we can receive life as a gift only from the hands of God.

Humanity Chose to Rebel against God, Preferring Death to Life

When Adam sinned, breaking God's commandment, he made a fateful choice against the indivisible and living God, against the Father who begets the Son and spirates the Spirit, against the Son who is begotten and shares in the Spirit's procession, and against the Spirit who proceeds. Adam's act was thereby a choice for death, a determination to rebel against the giver of life (Rom. 6:23). In this sense, that the wages of sin is death is entirely appropriate; the penalty fits the crime. Death features prominently in the early chapters of Genesis in the aftermath of the fall. It entails that obedience and faithfulness to God is the way of life for us, in harmony with the living God.

The Living God Offers Us Eternal Life in His Son, Promising That We Will Participate in the Life He Has by Nature

"In him was life, and the life was the light of men" (John 1:4). "God loved the world in this way, that he gave his only-begotten Son

9. Bavinck, *Reformed Dogmatics*, 2:240.

that whoever believes in him should not perish but have everlasting life" (John 3:16, my translation). The resurrection proves it. United to Christ, we rise with him to eternal and indestructible life. Need I say more?

The Path from the Doctrine of Eternal Generation Leads Straight to the Heart of the Gospel

From our perspective, the generation of the Son is about the most abstruse teaching imaginable. It is an impenetrable mystery. Notwithstanding, it lies at the heart of who God is and what his purposes are for the human race. It is directly relevant; nothing could be more so than this.

It is relevant for unbelievers. It highlights the point that we face a situation of life or death. Existentially, the gospel presents before us an eternity with one of two starkly contrasting destinies. The one is that we head for everlasting death, away from the presence of the living God, away from life in its fullest sense. This is an utterly withering prospect in so many senses. Alternatively, we embark on the way of life.

It is relevant for the church. It affirms that the purposes of God are dynamic. It directs us to the reality that the gospel is intended to promote human flourishing. It affirms the inherent goodness of creation and mandates our enjoyment of it. Behind all this, as the basis of all things, it suggests the biblical teaching that we are made to be "partakers of the divine nature" (2 Peter 1:4) and thus to share on a creaturely level in the life that the Son possessed in his incarnate state.

It is relevant for the pulpit. It should galvanize us as we preach, for it carries us on to consider the life that we share in Christ, the transformation that the Spirit is energizing (2 Cor. 3:18). The gospel is explained in legal, forensic categories in many places, in terms of atonement, justification, and the like. This is not all, however, for there is this powerful, existential side to it that, if anything, is even more significant, since it is the reality in connection with which the forensic is the scaffolding.

The doctrine of God must be the bull's-eye on the preacher's dartboard, the center of our thinking, living, and preaching. From our side, Christianity has at its heart knowing and loving God. If we know God, we will want to know about him. If a man claims to love his wife but knows little about her, and shows no desire to find out more, it is questionable whether he loves her at all. I have found it striking, however, how many people in congregations who are otherwise keen listeners to preaching either feign boredom or actually go to sleep if the subject turns to God. Books about time management, marital relationships, and ministerial strategy sell widely, books on the doctrine of God less so. It goes without saying that a crucial element of the preacher's task is to reorient the mindset of people in the pew, making sure that first he has done so himself. This reorientation will focus on the Father's revelation in Christ, the Son, and on the transforming work of the Spirit.

Someone once asked me to provide reasons how and why the doctrine of the Trinity should impact our thinking, our preaching, and our time in study and preparation for ministry. If I were to do so, I would be defeating my purpose. To provide reasons less than God for why we should love, honor, and serve him makes as much sense as coming up with logical and extraneous reasons why someone should love wife, husband, or children.[10] *He* is the reason why we are called to preach; *he* is the one to whom we invite people to be reconciled; *he* is the one whom to know is life eternal; it is above all because of *him* that we toil in our studies, spend time on our knees, and are so earnest in our sermons (John 17:3). Because God is the indivisible Trinity, he is love; look at the cross, where for us and our salvation "one of the Trinity died according to the flesh."[11] Because the Father generates the Son and spirates the Spirit, he is life. He is the reason we exist, and

10. Rik Van Nieuwenhove remarks of St. Bernard of Clairvaux, in his work *On Loving God*, 8:23: "Bernard raises the question 'why and how should God be loved.' He answers that God himself is the reason why he is to be loved." Rik Van Nieuwenhove, *An Introduction to Medieval Theology* (Cambridge: Cambridge University Press, 2012), 113.

11. Attributed to Leontius of Jerusalem and the Scythian monks. See John Meyendorff, *Christ in Eastern Christian Thought* (Crestwood, NY: St. Vladimir's Seminary Press, 1975), 77; Aloys Grillmeier, *Christ in Christian Tradition*, vol. 2, *From the Council of Chalcedon (451) to Gregory the Great (590–604)*, part 2, *The Church of Constantinople in the Sixth Century*, trans. Theresia Hainthaler and John Cawte (London: Mowbray, 1995), 317–43.

he is bringing us to our ultimate goal of union with him in Christ. If we are not excited by this, maybe it is best for us to take a break from the ministry for a while, perhaps for a well-planned sabbatical. For one thing is sure: if we are not spurred to thought and action, neither will our congregations be. Moreover, any specific edicts I might make could only divert us from this most vital matter.

In more practical terms, we need to shape the liturgy around communion with the Father, the Son, and the Holy Spirit, ever one and indivisible. Worship begins with God. The initiative is his, not ours. He calls us to worship; we respond. He speaks to us in his Word; we believe. He communes with us in the sacraments; he elicits our response. He dismisses us with his blessing; we go in peace to love and serve the Lord. We worship the Father, in the Spirit and in the truth that is Jesus Christ. In Christ the Son, we have access by the Spirit to the Father.[12] The one name of the Father, the Son, and the Holy Spirit is the new covenant name of God, named over every entrant to the Christian church, however young or old (Matt. 28:19–20). It follows that our preaching and our prayers need to be intentionally Trinitarian. The great liturgies will help; a good seasoning of Cranmer will add spice and flavor to the blandest fare.

Christian worship is communion with the living, loving, vibrant, triune God; Christian living is the same. Both are lived out in a world that is in rebellion, marked by hatred and death, but that this God has redeemed and will transform.

The doctrine of God must be central to our ministries. Even at its most recondite, with the eternal generation of the Son, it is vital and necessary to a healthy church, integral to the gospel of Christ. That, I suggest, is relevant.

Key Terms

anthropocentric
eternal generation

---

12. Yes, you have a liturgy even if you despise liturgies; it is better that you acknowledge it. Even the old-style Plymouth Brethren had an order of sorts, often predictable—as it was sometimes said, "ten thousand thousand are their texts but all their sermons one."

hypostases

Pelagianism

Recommendations for Further Reading

Giles, Kevin. *The Eternal Generation of the Son: Maintaining Ortho-doxy in Trinitarian Theology*. Downers Grove, IL: IVP Academic, 2012.

Letham, Robert. *The Holy Trinity: In Scripture, History, Theology, and Worship*. Rev. and expanded ed. Phillipsburg, NJ: P&R Publishing, 2019. Pp. 193–201.

Sanders, Fred, and Scott R. Swain. *Retrieving Eternal Generation*. Grand Rapids: Zondervan, 2017.

Discussion Questions

1. How can we ensure that our preaching and teaching are centered in God in practice and not merely in theory?

2. Given that we have been baptized into the one name of the Father, the Son, and the Holy Spirit (Matt. 28:19), that true worship is in the Holy Spirit and in the truth incarnate, Jesus Christ (John 4:21–24), and that in Christ the Son we have access to the Father by the Holy Spirit (Eph. 2:18), what might need to change in our preaching, praying, and worship?

3. How far should the robust and vibrant Trinitarianism of the Nicene Creed (dating from the Council of Constantinople in 381), in its distillation of the biblical exegesis of the early church, confessed by the whole church for the last sixteen hundred years, shape and mold our thinking and living?

3

THE DECREES OF GOD

What Every Pastor Must Know[1]

DOUGLAS KELLY

The eternal God of Holy Scripture is, throughout the inspired pages, Creator, Sustainer, Redeemer, and final Judge. In being and doing these majestic things, God controls all that happens to these ends that show forth his glory. In the earliest part of Holy Scripture, God creates all things out of nothing (cf. Gen. 1–2). He never ceases overseeing and controlling all things outside himself, so that every aspect of the created order answers to his will. He organizes what might be called an original sort of "chaos"—i.e., the pervasive watery mass on the first day of creation—into a beautiful "cosmos" throughout the work of the following days, concluding with the Sabbath of rest on the seventh day.

Following Adam's fall, all through the long saga of redemption, God is planning, and always intervening, to carry out his purposes. B. B. Warfield said that to be personal is to act with purpose, and Scripture shows God as doing just that.[2] This chapter considers what

---

1. Sinclair Ferguson's pastor was the Rev. William Still of Aberdeen, whom I knew well when I was studying in Edinburgh at the same time. Mr. Still once said to me (after a meeting of the Christian Union): "I consider Sinclair to be a young giant." The years that followed have proved that observation to be true.

2. Benjamin B. Warfield, *The Plan of Salvation* (Philadelphia: Presbyterian Board of Publication, 1915), 12.

pastors must know and teach about God's purpose, and how faith in a decreeing God informs the Christian pastor's own life and ministry.

An All-Comprehensive Plan

The first point that we must acknowledge about God's plan may be the most difficult: even the fall was included in the all-comprehensive divine plan, for Christ is said to be "the Lamb slain from the foundation of the world" (Rev. 13:8).[3] In Peter's sermon in Acts 4:28, even the murderous anger of the Christ-haters is included in God's plan: "For to do whatsoever thy hand and thy counsel determined before to be done." Similarly, in Acts 2:23, Peter declares that it was in the counsel of God for the wicked to take Christ to death: "Him, being delivered by the determinate counsel and foreknowledge of God, ye have taken, and by wicked hands have crucified and slain." Though difficult, pastors must preach the truth of God's all-comprehensive plan because God's Word teaches this truth.

God Has Included "Secondary Causes" in His Plan

Note carefully that even though an event is in the counsel of God from eternity, it does not relieve the wickedness of those who perpetrate evil. God's determinate counsel is never said anywhere in Scripture to relieve the wicked of their sin against God's law.

And although it is difficult to understand with our limited human minds, God has definitely included natural causes and human motivations and choices in his great plan. This is assumed throughout the Bible and is the basis for final judgment (as in Matthew 25). In traditional terminology, the Primary Cause (God) includes in his overarching decrees secondary causes (as nature and mankind). Hence, choices we make on earth directly affect our eternity. That does not mean that God is unaware of the future in granting us spontaneous choice, for "known unto God are all his works from the beginning of the world," according to Acts 15:18. Because God is of infinite wisdom, he knows exactly how to order ahead of all time

3. Scripture quotations in this chapter are from the KJV.

his decrees for everything that will happen, and yet include in that divine ordering the spontaneity involved in the choices of humankind. We are in no position to comprehend such heights and depths of God; our place is to humbly follow his Word.

As the Scottish theologian John Dick wrote:

> We are not required to reconcile the divine decrees and human liberty. It is enough to know that God has decreed all things which come to pass, and that men are answerable for their actions. . . . If everything in religion were level to the comprehension of reason, there would be no room for faith. It is better to believe humbly, than to reason presumptuously.[4]

The book of Revelation gives us the overarching details of the conclusion of the history of the cosmos, clearly indicating God's overseeing of every aspect of world history from beginning to end. The wedding supper of the Lamb is planned in every part, and will certainly transpire at the conclusion of redemptive history (cf. Rev. 19:9). Although we should not presume to provide a full account of the complexities of God's comprehensive plan as it relates to human actions, we must confidently teach these great truths as they magnify God's glory.

God Orchestrates Human and Natural Causes to Achieve His Plan

It is plain that Paul, in Ephesians 1:11, includes absolutely all things in the counsel of God, from beginning to end: "In whom also we have obtained an inheritance, being predestinated according to the purpose of him who worketh all things after the counsel of his own will." This reality of God's controlling of all things, usually behind the scenes, is assumed by the same Paul in Romans 8:28–30:

> And we know that all things work together for good to them that love God, to them who are the called according to his purpose. For

---

4. John Dick, *Works of John Dick*, vol. 1, *Theology* (Philadelphia: F. W. Greenough, 1830), 358.

whom he did foreknow, he also did predestinate to be conformed to the image of his Son, that he might be the firstborn among many brethren. Moreover whom he did predestinate, them he also called: and whom he called, them he also justified: and whom he justified, them he also glorified.

In short, for all things to work together for good (as here in the case of the redemption of the elect), then God must control all things.

In the Old Testament, we see, for instance, the "chance" flight of an arrow that hits wicked King Ahab at just the right place, in the joints of his armor, thus causing him to bleed to death (1 Kings 22:34). This confirmed the word of the holy prophet Micaiah, who had told Ahab that he would not return alive from this battle (22:15–23). Joseph said to his fearful brothers, after the death of their father, Jacob: "But as for you, ye thought evil against me; but God meant it unto good, to bring to pass, as it is this day, to save much people alive" (Gen. 50:20).

Long before Joseph's time, Pharaoh's daughter "happened" to go down to the river with her maidens to wash, and saw the beautiful baby boy Moses, floating in a basket on the water. She then adopted him as her son and named him "Moses," meaning "drawn out" (Ex. 2:5–10).

And long after Joseph, in the time of Queen Esther, the emperor "happened" to experience insomnia, and asked his servants to read the recent chronicles of his kingdom. That way, he learned about the goodness of Mordecai (a Jew, and uncle of Esther) in taking action to spare his life. From there, things worked out to spare the Jews from a massive pogrom. The emperor's inability to sleep that night was obviously in the plan of God. And by it, God's people were saved. Thus, very small matters are in the divine plan, as well as naval and land battles, rain and hail, storms and wind: "He sendeth forth his commandment upon earth: his word runneth very swiftly. He giveth snow like wool: he scattereth the hoarfrost like ashes" (Ps. 147:15–16). We are often unable to see what the Lord is doing in the world, through our ministries, and within the church. We don't know what he will do with a bold stand; we don't know what effect pointed sermons or difficult conversations might have. But we do know that he is working all things together for good, according to his perfect plan. With this confidence, we are called to be faithful.

Faith

Faith in God plays its part in accomplishing the purposes of the Lord. Hebrews 11:33–34 states that "through faith [God's people] subdued kingdoms, wrought righteousness, obtained promises, stopped the mouths of lions[,] quenched the violence of fire, escaped the edge of the sword, out of weakness were made strong, waxed valiant in fight, turned to flight the armies of the aliens." David prays for God's intervention in Psalm 31:1–2: "In thee, O LORD, do I put my trust; let me never be ashamed: deliver me in thy righteousness. Bow down thine ear to me; deliver me speedily: be thou my strong rock, for an house of defence to save me." He adds in verse 15: "My times are in thy hand: deliver me from the hand of mine enemies, and from them that persecute me."

It is the help of God, rather than human strength, that saves an army and a nation. Psalm 33:16–19 demonstrates this truth: "There is no king saved by the multitude of an host: a mighty man is not delivered by much strength. . . . Behold, the eye of the LORD is upon them that fear him, upon them that hope in his mercy; to deliver their soul from death, and to keep them alive in famine."

Prayer

Prayer to the Lord is an ordained way for his people to attain his specific help. While not being dependent on prayer and faith, or anything else outside himself, God has chosen prayer as a major way of access to him for his assistance. His honoring petitionary prayer is—far from being a weakness in God—a mighty strength that brings about his greater glory, and is a way of knitting his people's hearts to him in greater love and trust. And perseverance in prayer is one of the modes by which we are bound ever closer to him through practical necessities.

Jesus shows us in a parable the frequent necessity of continuing in prayer to God for the answer to be given. In Luke 11:5–8, Jesus speaks of a man who, at midnight, was given an unexpected visit by a friend. Naturally, the host wanted to feed the man, but his cupboard was bare. So he went to a friend's house and asked him to lend him some bread. At first, the friend did not want to do it, since it was so late; it might disturb his sleeping children. But the needy man persisted, and was given what he wanted. What Jesus says in verse 8 is very important for us to understand what God is doing when we have to keep on praying: "I say unto you, Though he will not rise and give him, because he is his friend, yet because of his importunity he will rise and give him as many as he needeth."

In other words, it took more than friendship (though surely that was basic); it also took "importunity" (that is, keeping on and keeping on). Certainly, God is our friend above all, for "he . . . spared not his own Son, but delivered him up for us all" (Rom. 8:32). But the Lord wants us, like the needy man in ancient Judea, to keep on asking, to keep on coming to him in prayer. God needs no help to become our friend, but we need the frequent experience of coming into his gracious presence with our petitions. That is one of the ways that we are experientially reminded of who he is!

The Order of God's Decree

In my view, human minds cannot go very far in attempting to discern the order of the decrees within the mind of God. We cannot go beyond Scripture, and the inspired writings do not take us into the workings of the divine mind, as far as I can tell.

Certainly, there is a kind of order in John 3:16: "For God so loved the world, that he gave his only begotten Son, that whosoever believeth in him should not perish, but have everlasting life." The love of the Father sent the beloved Son into this world to save us. The love of God is behind any sort of order, and "God is love" (1 John 4:8).

Many distinguished theologians (especially in the seventeenth century) sought to discern what order the mind of God took in decreeing the salvation of the elect and the reprobation of the lost. To read their careful and pious work is to admire their efforts. One could say that among the Augustinians and Calvinists, they tended to fall into two theological categories: *supralapsarian* and *infralapsarian*.

These terms (*lapsus* refers to the fall of mankind in Adam) attempt to answer the question whether God decreed the election and reprobation of humans without regard to their fall, or whether he made such decisions beforehand. Herman Bavinck has carefully and fairly discussed the differences between both approaches, as well as their strengths and weaknesses.[5] I need not repeat his research here. But I will refer to his apt assessment of both positions:

> In this sequence election and reprobation precede not only faith and unbelief, renewal and hardening, but also before the fall and creation. At this point, however, one problem immediately asserted itself. It was an established Reformed doctrine that the election of Christ and of the church occurred in connection with each other in one single decree, whose object, therefore, was the "mystic Christ." . . .
>
> The churches, however, always objected to this supralapsarian view. As a result, there is not a single Reformed Confession that offers this representation. . . . They were without exception infralapsarian in character and clothed in mild and moderate terms.[6]

Let us note two significant matters pertaining to this question here: (1) the impossibility of going inside the mind of God, and (2) the plain teaching of Scripture of the unity of the decree, in that all the elect are chosen in Christ.

First, the impossibility of going inside the mind of God. I doubt that those holding to either the supralapsarian or the infralapsarian position actually thought they could do this. But the questions they raise assume a certain ability to do so. The major problem is that we humans necessarily have a certain linear mode in our thought: that is, we have to think and plan one thing before another. But we cannot read this limitation back into God, for he, and he alone, is able, as an infinitely wise mind, to take all matters into consideration at the same time.

How could we know either that he had to consider the creation first, then the fall, and then election, or that he had to go in another

---

5. Herman Bavinck, *Reformed Dogmatics*, ed. John Bolt, trans. John Vriend, vol. 2, *God and Creation* (Grand Rapids: Baker Academic, 2004), 361–66.

6. Bavinck, *Reformed Dogmatics*, 2:366.

direction? Since he is God, it seems that he would have been fully able to think them all together at the same time, without the limitation of any linearity, as is the case with us. The old Southern Presbyterian theologian Robert L. Dabney used to say frequently, "This is a question that ought never to have been raised!" And he may well be right.

Second, the plain teaching of Scripture of the unity of the divine decree includes the elect *in Christ*. Louis Berkhof states it well:

> Reformed Soteriology takes its starting point in the union established in the *pactum salutis* [covenant of salvation] between Christ and those whom the Father had given him, in virtue of which there is an eternal imputation of the righteousness of Christ to those who are his. They begin the *ordo salutis* with regeneration or with calling, and thus emphasize the fact that the application of the redemptive work of Christ is in its incipiency a work of God. This is followed by a discussion of conversion, in which the work of regeneration penetrates to the conscious life of the sinner, and he turns from self, the world, and Satan, to God. Conversion includes repentance and faith, but because of its great importance the latter is generally treated separately. The discussion of faith naturally leads to that of justification, inasmuch as this is mediated to us by faith. And because justification places man in a new relation to God, which carries with it the gift of the Spirit of adoption, and which obliges man to a new obedience and also enables him to do the will of God from the heart, the work of sanctification next comes into consideration. Finally, the order of salvation is concluded with the doctrine of the perseverance of the saints and their final glorification.[7]

Without taking anything away from Berkhof's discussion of what transpires in the sinner who believes, we must note here that it deals (properly) with what transpires within the believer, but it does not imply that God himself is limited to a linear conception of what is happening in that believer. We may not read the general order of salvation within the Christian back onto the mind of God.

---

7. Louis Berkhof, *Systematic Theology* (Carlisle, PA: Banner of Truth, 1959), 418.

The Union of Believers with Christ in the Same Decree

This necessary union with Christ is set before us in Ephesians 1:3–14:

> Blessed be the God and Father of our Lord Jesus Christ, who hath blessed us with all spiritual blessings in heavenly places in Christ: according as he hath chosen us in him before the foundation of the world, that we should be holy and without blame before him in love: having predestinated us unto the adoption of children by Jesus Christ to himself, according to the good pleasure of his will, to the praise of the glory of his grace, wherein he hath made us accepted in the beloved. In whom we have redemption through his blood, the forgiveness of sins, according to the riches of his grace; wherein he hath abounded toward us in all wisdom and prudence; having made known unto us the mystery of his will, according to his good pleasure which he hath purposed in himself: that in the dispensation of the fulness of times he might gather together in one all things in Christ, both which are in heaven, and which are on earth; even in him: in whom also we have obtained an inheritance, being predestinated according to the purpose of him who worketh all things after the counsel of his own will: that we should be to the praise of his glory, who first trusted in Christ. In whom ye also trusted, after that ye heard the word of truth, the gospel of your salvation: in whom also after that ye believed, ye were sealed with that holy Spirit of promise, which is the earnest of our inheritance until the redemption of the purchased possession, unto the praise of his glory.

Let us notice here that "spiritual blessings in heavenly places" primarily refers not to what we will be granted in heaven (although verse 11 probably includes the fuller blessings of heaven), but to what God is now giving us while we are still in this world. These blessings, absolutely needful to the believer while he is on earth, are housed in Christ, who is now seated in heaven beside the Father.

These blessings, now available to us, include holiness (Eph. 1:4), adoption (v. 5), redemption and forgiveness (v. 7), all wisdom and prudence (v. 8), inheritance (v. 11), and sealing of the Spirit of promise (v. 13). Our having been chosen in Christ precedes the bestowal of the blessings (v. 4). It is not that we first had these qualities and on that ground were divinely chosen, but rather that we were chosen to be given these transforming blessings in Christ.

We note also that election is unto holiness (Eph. 1:4), and that predestination is to adoption (v. 5). It is likely that verse 5 is epexegetical of (i.e., clarifies and explains more fully) verse 4. This means that election does not flow from holiness, but establishes it, and that the love of God for us causes predestination. Regarding salvation, therefore, we must remember that God's love stands behind his every decree.

The Importance of the Union of the Believer with Christ as the Operative Factor

This passage demonstrates in detail how it is through this relationship of union with Christ that these spiritual blessings come to us as believers. Believers (like all the rest of fallen humankind) were once in the first Adam (cf. Rom. 5:12–21), but they have been taken out of him and placed into the last Adam. Thus, the blessings flow to us through him because we abide in the Vine (cf. John 15). This relationship with Christ is not caused by our believing and persevering as the determining factors; rather, our believing and persevering spring from our relation to Christ, constituted in the counsel of God before the foundation of the world. That is why we believe.

Let us note the many times that the concept of "in him" or "in Christ" is stated in Ephesians 1: "chosen . . . in him" (v. 4); "before him in love" (v. 4); "adoption . . . to himself" (v. 5); "accepted in the beloved" (v. 6); "in whom we have redemption" (v. 7); "gather together . . . all things in Christ" (v. 10); "in whom . . . we have obtained an inheritance" (v. 11); "in whom . . . ye were sealed with that holy Spirit of promise" (v. 13). Indeed, as Paul says elsewhere, "all the promises of God in him are yea, and in him Amen" (2 Cor. 1:20).

What the opening chapter of Ephesians describes as predestination in Christ is paralleled in Romans 8 by the conformity of the believer to Christ. Romans 8:35–39 describes this hard world with its good and evil that we all must experience. God is using both the good and the evil occurrences in our lives to shape us into the same pattern: conformity to his Son. We were chosen from eternity by the Father to be made like his Son. That is the greatest blessing that could ever be contemplated, and one wishes that the "prosperity preachers" proclaimed this as the ultimate prosperity that God will bring to his people!

So, then, the Father's plan for his adopted children is to increasingly shape them into the likeness of his eternal, only-begotten Son. In the realms of eternity, long before their births, the Lord foresaw them as somehow existing within his Son. As the Father's love was always upon his Son, so his love rested upon all those who would be called into union with his Son through faith and the Holy Spirit. This reality, which far surpasses all our thoughts, is conveyed in the Greek verb *prognosko*.

Prognosko ("whom he did foreknow," Rom. 8:29), while certainly including the reality of prevision or foresight, means far more. It is not a mere foreseeing, for God knows all things anyway. *Ginosko* (in Greek) or *yada* (in Hebrew) generally implies "to know with affection" or "to love." For instance, Abraham was known differently from others: that is, he was specifically loved by God (cf. Gen. 18:19). In Exodus 2:25, God saw the suffering of Israel, and "knew" them, or "set his love upon them." Psalm 1:6 declares that "the LORD knoweth the way of the righteous"; that is, he loves them. Of course, he is well aware of the way of the wicked, but does not "know" them in the same way.

Jesus speaks in Matthew 7:22–23: "Many will say to me in that day, Lord, Lord, have we not prophesied in thy name? and in thy name have cast out devils? and in thy name done many wonderful works? And then will I profess unto them, I never knew you: depart from me, ye that work iniquity." Yes, he knew exactly what they were doing, but their love was not set upon him, and he did not "know" them—i.e., his love was not upon them, as it was upon his elect (see also Matt. 25).

Paul asks in Romans 11:2, "Has God cast away his people whom he foreknew?" The true remnant of Israel, whom God foreknew, upon whom was his eternal love, will never be cast away. This kind of true personal knowledge is the question raised by Paul in Galatians 4:9: "But now, after that ye have known God, or rather are known of God, how turn ye again to the weak and beggarly elements, whereunto ye desire again to be in bondage?"

True knowledge of God (love) and false knowledge of the world (vanity) are the issues in 1 John 3:1: "Behold, what manner of love the Father hath bestowed upon us, that we should be called the sons of God: therefore the world knoweth us not, because it knew him not." This kind of knowledge goes with a spiritual intimacy that is essentially equivalent to saving union with Christ.

The High Priestly Prayer

We could say that the great blessings prayed upon us in Christ's High Priestly Prayer are parallel to the blessings of union with Christ in Ephesians 1, and to the hope of being conformed to Christ in Romans 8. These blessings in the High Priestly Prayer are (1) glory, (2) eternal life, (3) knowledge of God, and (4) sanctification. These blessings come through knowing Christ, through union with him. They cannot be found apart from him. In John 17:6 and 9, the Father gives us as his people to the Son, and then the Son gives us back to the Father for safekeeping (vv. 10–11). Then Christ prays for our oneness with God. This is the continuing and eternal source of all these blessings.

Hebrews 2:8–15 sets forth the union of Christ with human flesh in order to take it down into death, and then bring it up into new life:

> But we see Jesus, who was made a little lower than the angels for the suffering of death, crowned with glory and honour; that he by the grace of God should taste death for every man. . . . For both he that sanctifieth and they who are sanctified are all of one: for which cause he is not ashamed to call them brethren. (Heb. 2:9, 11)

That is why Christ "took not on him the nature of angels; but he took on him the seed of Abraham" (Heb. 2:16).

Sanctification is the great blessing spoken of in this text. It is parallel to the spiritual blessings found in Ephesians 1, Romans 8, and John 17, all of which are coordinated in Christ according to God's decree. We humans must be "*all of one*" with Christ in order to receive his sanctification. We have to be united to him to have it.

Thus, John Calvin writes:

Therefore, to share with us what he has received from the Father he had to become ours, and to dwell within us. For this reason, he is called "our head" (Eph. 4:15), and "the first-born among many brethren" (Rom. 8:29). We also, in turn are said to be "engrafted into him" (Rom. 11:17), and "to put on Christ" (Gal. 3:27): for, as I have said, all that he possesses is nothing to us until we grow into one body with him.[8]

The Continuing Nature of This Corporate Connection

Christ is now (since his victory on earth) the head of the body to the church (cf. Eph. 1:2–23). We are "saved by [or, perhaps, *in*] his life" (Rom. 5:10). Because he lives, we will live also (John 14:19). The risen Christ asked Saul of Tarsus, "Why persecutest thou me?" (Acts 9:4). This is a very moving aspect of the continuing reality of our union with Christ: he identifies with us in our suffering. And as we have already seen, our standing with God for all eternity is because we are "accepted in the beloved" (Eph. 1:6). This will always be the truest fact about us, and it always continues; it constitutes who we really are. We can be certain of this because of God's sure decree.

Key Terms

infralapsarian
supralapsarian

Recommendations for Further Reading

Bavinck, Herman. *Reformed Dogmatics.* Edited by John Bolt. Translated by John Vriend. Vol. 2, *God and Creation.* Grand Rapids: Baker, 2004. Pp. 337–405.

Murray, John. "Calvin on the Sovereignty of God." In *Collected Writings of John Murray.* Vol. 4, *Studies in Theology.* Edinburgh: Banner of Truth, 1982. Pp. 191–204.

8. John Calvin, *Institutes of the Christian Religion*, ed. John T. McNeill, trans. Ford Lewis Battles, vol. 1, Library of Christian Classics 20–21 (Louisville: Westminster John Knox, 2011), 3.1.1.

Warfield, Benjamin B. "The Significance of the Confessional Doctrine of the Decree." In *Benjamin B. Warfield: Selected Shorter Writings*. Vol. 2. Phillipsburg, NJ: P&R Publishing, 2001. Pp. 93–102.

Discussion Questions

1. What is the pastoral significance of the conviction that every sin is included in God's decree? Consider how this might be applied, or misapplied, in ministry.
2. How does the doctrine of God's decree relate to God's glory, and how might this be magnified in our ministry?
3. How does God's eternal sovereign decree coincide with human freedom and spontaneity? How might you address the person who concludes, "If all things happen because of God's decree, then my actions have no ultimate significance"?
4. How does God's decree affect practical matters such as faith and prayer?
5. How should God's decree for us in Christ motivate us to pursue a life of sanctification?

4

CREATION

The Essential Setting for
Proclaiming Christ

IAN HAMILTON

The Shorter Catechism of the Westminster Assembly succinctly summarizes the Christian doctrine of creation as "God's making all things of nothing, by the word of his power, in the space of six days, and all very good" (WSC 9), and regarding humanity that "God created man male and female, after his own image, in knowledge, righteousness, and holiness, with dominion over the creatures" (WSC 10). We live not in a meaningless cosmos but one designed, sustained, and directed by the God of the Bible. We, as human beings, are not a chance amalgam of atomic and subatomic particles but are fashioned for a unique relationship with God and the rest of creation. Everything that a pastor preaches from his pulpit, or ministers in the homes of his congregation, or shares one to one in coffee shops, is predicated on these truths.

My first recollection of studying theology at Edinburgh University was asking my New Testament lecturer to explain his theological presuppositions before he embarked on his course of teaching. Looking a little nonplussed, he said that he wasn't sure he had any, and then asked me what mine were. My response, as I remember, was this: "That God is and that he has revealed himself truly in the pages of the Bible as Creator and Redeemer" (to my and perhaps also to his surprise, we got on well, though he could never quite understand that I believed what I believed).

The great truths revealed in Genesis 1–3—God's uniqueness, sovereignty, and plurality; his *ex nihilo* creation; men and women made in the image of God; creation's initial perfection; the reality and malevolent activity of Satan; Adam and Eve's sin and cosmic fall; and God's promise of a Deliverer from the seed of woman—form the foundation and shape the superstructure of biblical ministry. But biblical truths are not chunks of brute fact merely to be understood and acknowledged. Martin Bucer's well-known words, "True theology is not theoretical, but practical. The end of it is living, that is to live a godly life," remind us that doctrine produces godly gospel instinct. Furthermore, that instinct must inform pastoral ministry, such as is evident in the work of Martin Bucer as well as the writings and pastoral ministry of Sinclair Buchanan Ferguson.[1]

Creation's Ultimate Purpose

If we are rightly to understand God's *purpose* in creating the heavens and the earth, and men and women in his own image and likeness, we need to do so through the lens of what Paul writes in Colossians 1:15–16, that Jesus Christ "is the image of the invisible God, the firstborn of all creation. For by him all things were created, in heaven and on earth, visible and invisible, whether thrones or dominions or rulers or authorities—all things were created through him and for him." Creation was made "for him." God's purpose in creation was not merely to display his power and sovereignty, but to create a cosmos for the praise and glory of his Son.

Creation is not first for our sakes, but for Christ's sake. There is a God-ordained Christocentricity to creation. Not only is Jesus "the

---

1. I have known Sinclair Buchanan Ferguson for almost fifty years, and he has modeled for me what preaching is, the pastoral exploration and application of the unsearchable riches of Christ. Throughout his long years in ministry, Dr. Ferguson has taught the intimate relationship between exegesis and theology, always with an eye on the implications for life. It is a privilege to contribute to this essay in his honor.

firstborn of all creation," he is "the firstborn among many brothers" (Rom. 8:29). Understanding this fundamental truth of creation cannot but shape and style a gospel minister's pastoral ministry. Jesus Christ will never be an appendage. He will never merely be an application. If God the Father created all things for his Son, then Jesus Christ will always be front and center in any exposition of God's Word.

This is no less true in one-to-one pastoral ministry. Many Christians look for some practical wisdom that will help them cope with, and even triumph over, difficulties and trials. This is understandable. Yet what is often overlooked, or perhaps never even considered, is the practical relevance of reflecting on the grace and glory of the Lord Jesus Christ.

Matthew 11:28–30 is one of the high points of new covenant revelation: "Come to me, all who labor and are heavy laden, and I will give you rest. Take my yoke upon you, and learn from me, for I am gentle and lowly in heart, and you will find rest for your souls. For my yoke is easy, and my burden is light." Here we see Jesus preaching himself to the weary and heavy laden. He holds out his grace and tenderness to men and women burdened and bowed down by sin and failure. In essence, he is saying: "Look to me. Come to me." This is not unbridled arrogance speaking. This is the God-man, fully conscious of who he is and what he is able to do, inviting sin-burdened men and women to rest the weight of all they are on the grace and sufficiency of who he is.

If we have been created for Christ, then our greatest need is both to know this and to give ourselves to knowing this Jesus Christ. A minister's pastoral empathy will, above all, be seen in his resolve to lead his congregants, corporately, familially, and individually, to discover the abundant life and the hope that is to be found in Jesus Christ (John 10:10). The goal of creation in Christ keeps us on track pastorally.

Foundational Truths

Having considered the overall Christ-centered dimension of creation, we need to reflect on further foundational truths embedded in the account of creation and subsequent events in the garden, together with their bearing on pastoral ministry.

God Is the One True and Living God

First, we do not live in an impersonal universe: "In the beginning, God created the heavens and the earth" (Gen. 1:1). As God's covenant people are rescued out of their four hundred years of bondage in Egypt, and as they embark into the unknown at God's command, God reveals to them, through his servant Moses, that Yahweh, their covenant Lord, is the sovereign Creator of the heavens and the earth. For four hundred years, the Israelites had resided in a pluralistic culture. Day after day, they would have been confronted with the polytheism and pagan rituals of Egypt. The worship of the sun god Ra, the creator god Amun, and the mother goddess Isis, at the head of a pantheon of other more minor deities, would have been the proliferating atmosphere of Egyptian society. Now, God's people are being reminded with stunning clarity that "God, Israel's God, made the heavens and the earth."

Pastoral ministry in the twenty-first century is no less confronted with pluralism and polytheism. Belief systems abound. The church has often retreated in the face of militant pluralism. Sometimes the retreat is into societal disengagement. Sometimes, more tragically, the retreat is into societal compromise, watering down the absolute uniqueness of what we read in Genesis 1:1. More than ever, Christians need to be regularly reminded of who their God is. That he is the Creator of all things. That he is not one of many, but the unique and only. The rest of Genesis 1 unpacks who Israel's God is:

1. He is the sovereign Creator of all things; therefore, worship him alone.
2. He created the sun, moon, and stars; worship and serve him, not them.
3. He created all the animals; worship him and not them. Do not make images and idols of God's creatures as the Egyptians did.
4. He made you in his image and after his likeness; therefore, live with humility, thankfulness, and dignity. You are not mere animals; you are God's special and unique creation.

Nothing more elevates the mind and heart of a believer than to sit under ministry that exalts God. The opening words of Genesis 1 summon pastors to be God-saturated men and God-saturated preachers.

Humankind Has a Unique Creation and Calling

Second, we are God's unique and special creation: "Then God said, 'Let us make man in our image, after our likeness. And let them have dominion over the fish of the sea and over the birds of the heavens and over the livestock and over all the earth and over every creeping thing that creeps on the earth.' So God created man in his own image, in the image of God he created him; male and female he created them" (Gen. 1:26–27). The creation of man on the sixth day is the climax of God's creating activity.

It is striking that God does not set apart a day uniquely for the pinnacle of his creation. Man shares his creation on the sixth day with the creation of "living creatures according to their kinds—livestock and creeping things and beasts of the earth according to their kinds" (Gen. 1:24). Human beings share a common sixth-day origin with mere animals. It should not surprise us, then, that there is a manifest congruity between men and women and the animal creation. But unlike the mere animal creation, men and women are made in God's image and after his likeness. Adam was created to husband God's creation, to exercise dominion and responsibility, not to ravage the creation for his own interests.

Later we will notice the physicality of God's image in mankind. Here we simply notice that God's image is not located within us; we are, *in toto*, God's image. The New Testament gives us insight into the visible character of God's image. In Ephesians 4, Paul exhorts the believers in Ephesus to "put on the new self [better: *man*], created after the likeness of God in true righteousness and holiness" (Eph. 4:24). For Paul, this does not mean that for a Christian, his new life in Christ is a restoration to the life that he lost when Adam fell into sin. The "true righteousness and holiness" that are to define and describe a Christian are not what Adam lost, but what Jesus Christ has won. Isaac Watts expressed this truth well:

> Where he displays his healing power
> Death and the curse are known no more;
> In him the tribes of Adam boast
> More blessings than their father lost.[2]

2. Isaac Watts, "Psalm 72, part 2" (1719).

Faithful pastoral ministry will seek to exemplify that "true righteousness and holiness," as well as preach it and apply it to the people of God. The "family likeness" is to mark the lives of God's people. What we read in Genesis 1:26–27 finds its fullest realization in the new covenant revelation that we are saved "to be conformed to the image of his Son" (Rom. 8:29). A biblically faithful pastoral ministry will never let God's people forget their high and holy calling.

The biblical doctrine of the *imago Dei* further impresses on us that every individual we encounter, inside and outside the church, has innate dignity and value. Dignity and value are not found in anything this world confers on us, nor on anything we might achieve. The fact that God made us gives uniqueness, value, and dignity to who we are, irrespective of our wealth, possessions, education, achievements, social standing, or whatever else.

Many people in our disordered, broken, dysfunctional world think badly of themselves. It is true, of course, that "all have sinned and fall short of [lack] the glory of God" (Rom. 3:23). The Bible will not allow us to hide from the humbling truth that "none is righteous, no, not one; no one understands; no one seeks for God. All have turned aside; together they have become worthless; no one does good, not even one" (vv. 10–12). That said, the most broken, dysfunctional, and wicked of men and women have been made in the image of God (Gen. 1:27). No one is a brute beast. We remain God's image in our sinfulness and rebellion. That image has been defaced, marred, and all but obliterated. But even so, the Bible tells us, we are yet God's image.

Part of a pastor's calling, then, is to address men and women outside as well as inside the church as God's image-bearers, men and women of innate dignity and worth. Human beings are not merely a higher form of animal life. The unscientific doctrine of evolution demolishes human dignity. That said, a faithful pastor will not seek to give people a better "self-image," as if that were all they needed to make life pleasant. He will tell them that they are "fearfully and wonderfully made" (Ps. 139:14). That their significance depends not on what they do but on who they are. The biblical doctrine of creation gives transcendent identity to men and women no matter their economic status, their color of skin, their social status, their education. "The living God made you. He has made you in his image and likeness. He supports and sustains your every breath. Recognize your significance. Bow down and worship."

This is why chauvinism in all its ugly forms, abuse of any kind, racism, and social and educational snobbery are so abhorrent and are condemned without qualification in the Bible.

The pastoral significance of the biblical doctrine of creation is immense and also a huge challenge to pastors, and to Christians in general. We are called to minister the love and grace of God into a world that "lies in the power of the evil one" (1 John 5:19). In recent times, this challenge has become acute. The so-called sexual/gender revolution has transformed the face of society almost throughout the world. Legislation that the Word of God calls abominable is passed and promoted. Increasingly, Christians are being penalized for refusing to embrace the LGBTQI agenda that has become the new norm. Christians are rightly filled with revulsion as a tidal wave of ungodliness sweeps over the nations. This new state of affairs poses a pressing question to gospel ministers: How are we to preach the gospel of God's grace in Jesus Christ to such a world? What we read in Genesis 1 is profoundly helpful. God made men and women in his image. Everyone born of woman bears in his or her life, however scarred and defaced, the image of God. Sin did not obliterate God's image. It tragically defiled it, but it did not utterly extinguish it. This is the tragedy of men and women in their sin. It is not just that they sin, but that they sin as the image-bearers of the living God. We must never look on men and women, even in the wickedness of their rebellion against God, as less than what they are. Like God, we must hold out our hands all the day long to disobedient sinners, calling them to turn to God in Christ for mercy and salvation (see Rom. 10:21, quoting Isa. 65:2).

Pastoral ministry will therefore welcome sinners, but never affirm their sin (see Luke 15:1). Nor will a faithful pastor hide from sinners the solemn judgment that hangs over the unrepentant, however unpopular it makes him. The Pharisees' charge against Jesus, "This man receives sinners and eats with them" (v. 2), is a charge that the self-righteous should always be directing toward faithful gospel ministers. God takes no pleasure in the death—including the present spiritual, separating death—of the wicked, and neither should we (see Ezek. 33:11).

God's Creation Entails Community

Third, we are created in the image of the God who is three but one, who is one but three. The God in whose image men and women are created is a God who exists in eternal community: "Let *us* make man in our image, after *our* likeness" (Gen. 1:26). The "us" has often been understood as a plural of majesty, and that may well be included in its meaning. In the light of the whole testimony of Scripture, however, it is better to see here a first adumbration of God's essential plurality, a plurality that reaches its fullest exposition in Jesus' words in Matthew 28:19, "Go therefore and make disciples of all nations, baptizing them in the name of the Father and of the Son and of the Holy Spirit." One name, three persons. This is the God in whose image we are made. This truth tells us that just as God exists in community, so individual men and women are to live in community. Just as God is not a solitary monad, so human beings are not created to be solitary monads. We were made for fellowship. The Christian life cannot be lived in isolation. The New Testament uses a number of pictures to emphasize and reinforce this truth. The church is the one body of Christ, all members being vitally united to all other members. The one bride of Christ, united as one spiritual beloved of the Savior. The one temple of the living God, joined together as living stones.

The church of God is not a disparate society of believing men and women, who come together on a Sunday for spiritual refreshment. God's church is his family, the body of his Son, the temple of his Spirit. It is in vital community that we "grow in the grace and knowledge of our Lord and Savior Jesus Christ" (2 Peter 3:18). It is "together with all" the "saints" (1 Cor. 1:2) that we learn how high and wide and deep and broad is the love of Christ (Eph. 3:18). The apostle Paul develops this truth graphically in his letter to the church in Ephesus:

> Speaking the truth in love, we are to grow up in every way into him who is the head, into Christ, from whom the whole body, joined and held together by every joint with which it is equipped, when each part is working properly, makes the body grow so that it builds itself up in love. (Eph. 4:15–16)

Spiritual growth, growth in love, growing up "into him who is the head, into Christ," happens in community, not in isolation.

The Material World Matters, as Do Our Physical Bodies

Fourth, our bodies matter. The biblical doctrine of creation further impresses on us the concrete physicality of the believing life. Our bodies are not mere receptacles for our undying souls. When God made man in his own image, the image was not located "in" man; he and she were in the totality of their humanity the image of God. This, in part, is why the Christian hope is not the immortality of the soul, but the resurrection of the body. It is in "this hope" that we are saved (Rom. 8:24).

Too often in the history of the church, the body that God has made has been depreciated. This is remarkable because our Lord Jesus Christ "became flesh" (John 1:14). He did not put on flesh as a man might put on a shirt or jacket. He "became" flesh. Men and women are not immortal souls encased in flesh. We are made by God as psychosomatic beings. At death, our undying souls are separated from our bodies. But the separation is temporary, awaiting the coming of our Lord Jesus Christ, when he "will transform our lowly body to be like his glorious body, by the power that enables him even to subject all things to himself" (Phil. 3:21).

The pastoral implications are not difficult to grasp. Because we are created as psychosomatic unities, ministers of the new covenant should pastor the whole person. Sometimes what is presented as an exclusively spiritual need is remedied by the commonsense counsel to take exercise or develop more sensible sleeping patterns (sometimes requiring more, sometimes less, sleep!), all in submission to God, recognizing our creaturely limitations. The words of the psalmist may at first sight seem ordinary and prosaic, but they are a recognition that we are psychosomatic men and women who need to understand the material limits of our capacities: "It is in vain that you rise up early and go late to rest, eating the bread of anxious toil; for he gives to his beloved sleep" (Ps. 127:2).

Our bodies are the ordained means through which God ordinarily accomplishes his purposes in this world. We see this in God's first command to Adam and Eve: "And God blessed them. And God said to them, 'Be fruitful and multiply and fill the earth and subdue it, and have dominion over the fish of the sea and over the birds of the heavens and over every living thing that moves on the earth'" (Gen. 1:28). Adam and Eve were to use their newly created bodies to fulfill God's command. The filling and subduing of the earth would not happen automatically. It would happen as the first man and woman used their minds, hands, and feet to accomplish the divine ordinance.

If nothing else, a pastor will surely want to teach the dignity of manual labor. In Western civilization, there has been an increasing demeaning of manual labor during the past half-century. The impression is often given, and at times even promoted, that the more paper qualifications you have, the more significant you are. The Bible witnesses at its outset to the dignity of manual labor.

It should not surprise us that when Paul comes to highlight the one adequate response that a Christian is to make to the "gospel of God . . . concerning his Son" (Rom. 1:1–3), he writes, "I appeal to you therefore, brothers, by the mercies of God, to present your bodies as a living sacrifice, holy and acceptable to God, which is your spiritual worship" (12:1). Sanctification is radically physical. The devotion that God seeks from his children is not theoretical; it is psychosomatic. Our devotion to God is to be expressed in and through what we do with our bodies. It matters what we look at with our eyes, what we do with our hands, where we go with our feet, what we think with our minds. Sanctification is not a theory; it is a lifestyle of concrete, embodied, loving obedience to God.

Paul had earlier in his letter to the Romans highlighted this truth: "Let not sin therefore reign in your mortal body, to make you obey its passions. Do not present your members to sin as instruments for unrighteousness, but present yourselves to God as those who have been brought from death to life, and your members to God as instruments for righteousness" (Rom. 6:12–13).

Far from being a prison house for the soul, the human body is inextricably bound up with an immaterial soul. The Christian hope is not the immortality of the soul; it is the resurrection of the body (Rom. 8:23; 1 Cor. 15:42–49). Our physical bodies are not incidental to our identity as children of God. As we live out our calling to be light and salt in a decaying and putrefying world, we look forward to the day when Jesus Christ "will transform our lowly body to be like his glorious body, by the power that enables him even to subject all things to himself" (Phil. 3:21).

Biblically faithful pastoral ministry will accent this fundamental truth.

The Goodness of the Created Order and the Far Reach of the Fall

Fifth, in the beginning everything God made was "very good." The closing words of Genesis 1, "And God saw everything that he had made, and behold, it was very good" (Gen. 1:31), are a pastoral anchor point for gospel ministers. When God created the heavens and the earth, his creation was pristine; it was without spot or blemish. There was nothing discordant, nothing out of place, nothing that was not "very good." The opening chapter of Genesis is a necessary reminder that what is now is not what once was. Paul tells the church in Rome that "the whole creation has been groaning together in the pains of childbirth until now. And not only the creation, but we ourselves, who have the firstfruits of the Spirit, groan inwardly as we wait eagerly for adoption as sons, the redemption of our bodies" (Rom. 8:22–23). The present "groaning" of creation is the result of Adam's sin, which brought sin and death, misery and futility, into the heart of God's very good creation.

This state of things is the dark, sinister reality into which pastors are called to minister the Word of God. Sin has brought into God's creation a multiplex of miseries. Every individual is marred by a broken relationship with God and a broken relationship with everyone born of woman. More than that, sin has infected every aspect of our beings (Rom. 7:18). The doctrine of total depravity does not mean that we are as bad as we could possibly be. It does mean, however, that sin's infection is total; it has touched every facet of our lives.

This truth cannot but profoundly influence a pastor's ministry from the pulpit and as he ministers more informally to Christ's sheep under his care. Sin is not an occasional blemish that mars our lives. It is a deep-rooted malignancy that needs radical spiritual surgery. This is what the gospel of the grace of God in Jesus Christ has come to accomplish. The remedy for our sin, originating as it did in the representative action of our first head, Adam (Rom. 5:12–19), first humbles us, but then wonderfully gives us hope. The humbling comes with the realization that we are helpless to deal with our sin, which separates us from God and brings us under his just condemnation. The hope comes when we hear that "in Christ God was reconciling the world to himself, not counting their trespasses against them" (2 Cor. 5:19). United to our first head, Adam, we were condemned with all men (Rom. 5:18). But when through faith we become united to God's "better man," Jesus Christ, we become the inheritors of "justification and life" (Rom. 5:18).

The biblical doctrine of creation and the fall of God's first man, Adam, ensures that the pastor does not merely address particular sins in his ministry. Every pastor who takes seriously the truths embedded in Genesis 1–3 will address the "original sin" that is ours because of our union with our first head, Adam. The early chapters of Genesis impress on us that we sin because we are sinners, not that we are sinners because we sin. Our great need is to be taken out of Adam and be savingly united to Jesus Christ.

Pastoral ministry has, therefore, a fundamental twofold focus: First, it seeks to bring men and women, boys and girls, by God's grace, out of their death-union with Adam and into a life-union with Jesus Christ. Second, it seeks to help all those united to Christ to grasp the profound and glorious implications of that life-union. "Know who you are" is one of the recurring themes in Paul's letters, notably in 1 Corinthians. Six times in the sixth chapter, Paul asks his readers, "Do you not know?" (1 Cor. 6:2, 3, 9, 15, 16, 19). He is reminding them what is true about them because they are in Christ (see 1 Cor. 1:9) and indwelled by the Holy Spirit (6:19).

Understanding the doctrine of creation as revealed in Genesis 1–3 compels a pastor to minister the grace and hope found in God's better Adam, our representative head, the serpent-crusher, Jesus Christ.

The Sinister Reality

This pastoral note introduces us to the dark shadow that came insidiously to corrupt God's very good creation by deceiving into sin and rebellion our creational head, Adam. Not only must a biblically faithful pastor be courageous in seeking to lay bare our death-union with Adam and the sin that infects every strand of our being, he must understand that behind Adam and our sin lies, lurks, a sinister darkness. The apostle Paul alerted the church in Ephesus to this truth: "we do not wrestle against flesh and blood, but against the rulers, against the authorities, against the cosmic powers over this present darkness, against the spiritual forces of evil in the heavenly places" (Eph. 6:12).

Alongside the pristine beauty of God's creation so beautifully displayed in Genesis 1, the dark shadow of sin and its master and instigator, the devil, looms over Genesis 3. Pastoral ministry that seeks to be more than superficially therapeutic must reckon with this enemy. The apostle Peter, no doubt still conscious of his own calamitous failure, exhorted his readers to "be watchful. Your adversary the devil prowls around like a roaring lion, seeking someone to devour" (1 Peter 5:8).

Understanding this spiritual warfare will in no way cause a pastor to ignore human responsibility. It will, however, give the pastor the insight to see beyond the individual to the dark menace of Satan, on the prowl, looking for someone, some unsuspecting someone, to devour. The Bible nowhere explains the devil. He is a creature, a fallen, malignant creature. Out of nowhere, he appears in Genesis 3 in the guise of a serpent. As the text unfolds, we see the subtlety and malignancy of this serpent. Slowly but surely, he deceives and seduces God's first man and woman into willful disobedience. Nowhere is Adam seen to be less than culpable. But behind his sin lay the seductive voice of the "deceiver of the whole world" (Rev. 12:9). There is an unseen enemy to reckon with. It will therefore be a pastor's concern to help those to whom he ministers to become cognizant of the wiles, methods, stratagems of this enemy (see 2 Cor. 2:11; Eph. 6:11).

But this enemy is also active in the lives and circumstances of believers whom he has not managed to seduce into sinful rebellion against God. The story of Job is helpful here. Job belonged to a fallen world. He was by nature a sinner, though a sinner saved by God's grace. It is striking, then, that as the book of Job opens, it does so with an affirmation that Job "was blameless and upright, one who feared God and turned away from evil" (Job 1:1). In the following verses, we see God's servant overwhelmed by a series of devastating calamities. All these calamities were orchestrated by Satan. The significance of the opening words becomes clear. The afflictions that engulfed Job's life were not, of themselves, the result of his sin: "An enemy has done this" (Matt. 13:28).

More than Job, the Lord Jesus Christ was assailed by the devil throughout the whole course of his life. As he began his public ministry, he was "tempted by the devil" (4:1). This temptation was not an occasional feature in Jesus' life. Speaking to his disciples as the shadow of the cross began to penetrate his human soul, Jesus said, "You are those who have stayed with me in my trials" (Luke 22:28) (or "temptations," KJV). From Herod's "slaughter of the innocents" (Matt. 2:16–18) to the mocking of the soldiers as he hung on the cross, "If you are the King of the Jews, save yourself!" (Luke 23:37), Jesus was exposed to the wicked schemes of the devil (Eph. 6:11). Conscious as he was of the evil one's sinister activity, Jesus warned his disciples, "Watch and pray that you may not enter into temptation" (Matt. 26:41). To the last, Jesus was ministering to his disciples.

A pastor who does not understand the reality of the devil and the powers of darkness is unfit to care for God's people. A pastor must, more than others, have his spiritual senses "trained by constant practice to distinguish good from evil" (Heb. 5:14).

Ministering the Word of God effectively and sensitively requires this twofold understanding of creation's fallenness and the unseen but present activity of the devil. It is true, wonderfully true, that our Lord Jesus has "disarmed the rulers and authorities and put them to open shame, by triumphing over them in him" (Col. 2:15). Satan is a defeated foe, but he remains troublesome and vindictive, full of schemes. And so we must know our enemy and how to stand against him.

A faithful pastor will want his people to know that the resources they need to enable them to stand "against the schemes of the devil" (Eph. 6:11) will be found alone "in the Lord" (v. 10). Even as redeemed men and women, we need nothing less than the "strength of his might" (v. 10) if we are to keep standing in "the evil day" (v. 13). Paul is highlighting the spirit of utter dependence on the Lord that must characterize our engagement in spiritual warfare. He makes the same point to the believers in Corinth: "For though we walk in the flesh, we are not waging war according to the flesh. For the weapons of our warfare are not of the flesh but have divine power to destroy strongholds" (2 Cor. 10:3–4).

In everything, Jesus is the prototypical man of faith. It is the new covenant ministry of the Holy Spirit to replicate in believers what he first formed and forged in Jesus. The Gospels give us a dramatic example of Jesus' repelling the devil as he lived in his trustful servant-obedience to his Father. As Jesus began his public ministry, he was "led up by the Spirit into the wilderness to be tempted by the devil" (Matt. 4:1). On three occasions, the devil tempted Jesus to step outside the will of his Father and abandon the way of the cross. On each occasion, Jesus replied, "It is written" (vv. 4–10). As he found himself in a barren wilderness, hungry after forty days of fasting, confronted by the devil, Jesus drew on the authority, wisdom, grace, and truth of the Word of God. He had complete trust in the Holy Scriptures. He armed himself against the insidious, pressing temptations of the evil one with God's written Word. This Word was not a lucky charm to ward off evil. It was the living Word of the living God, embedded with God's own infallible wisdom. Jesus was exercising trust and confidence in the goodness, wisdom, and power of his Father.

The reality and activity of the devil punctuate the whole of the Bible, from Genesis to Revelation. Satan is a creature, a fallen creature. He can do nothing beyond what the sovereign Lord gives him permission to do. Evil is a dark mystery. How could this creature rebel against a holy, sovereign, omnipotent God? When did he do so? How was he able to seduce Adam and Eve into sin? Why does God give this evil one permission to do anything at all? These and other questions no doubt rise in our minds. But God's ways are higher than our ways, as Isaiah reminds us (Isa. 55:7–8). His ways are past finding out, as Paul reminds us (Rom. 11:33–36). There will inevitably be a note of unembarrassed humility running through a pastor's ministry. Often, we will be constrained to say with Paul, "O the depths. . . . His ways [are] past finding out" (v. 33 KJV). That said, our great need is not to understand the origin of evil, or to have all our questions answered, but to know that we are "more than conquerors through him who loved us" (8:37).

The Serpent-Crusher

In the midst of the cosmic tragedy of Adam's sin, God announced a sentence of doom on the serpent and a promise of hope for Adam and his posterity: "The LORD God said to the serpent, . . . 'I will put enmity between you and the woman, and between your offspring and her offspring; he shall bruise your head, and you shall bruise his heel'" (Gen. 3:14–15).

From this moment, the biblical narrative, and human history, is the unfolding exposition of God's double announcement.

There is little doubt that God is promising to raise up one from the seed of woman who would fatally crush the serpent, but who would himself be wounded in the battle. Read in the fuller light of the New Testament, Genesis 3:15 is a shining promise of rescue and hope. The last word will lie not with the serpent, Satan, but with God and his Champion. On his cross, the Lord Jesus Christ "disarmed the rulers and authorities and put them to open shame, by triumphing over them in him" (Col. 2:15).

One of the predominant notes in a pastor's ministry, from the pulpit and from house to house (Acts 20:20), will be to herald the triumph of the Crucified and the crushing of that "ancient serpent, who is the devil and Satan" (Rev. 20:2). At the center of Jesus' triumph is his sin-bearing, sin-atoning death on Calvary's cross. The promise made in the solemn wake of Adam's sin has come to its climactic fulfillment in the cross and resurrection of Jesus Christ. Faithful pastoral ministry will be marked by the exposition, "the expository adulation," of the sin-atoning, wrath-exhausting, Satan-vanquishing cross work of Jesus Christ. The triumph of the seed of the woman will be the joyful pulse beat of a faithful pastor's ministry.

Repristinated Cosmos

The biblical doctrine of creation impresses on us that there is a God-ordained *telos* to creation, as we noted earlier: "For by him all things were created, in heaven and on earth, visible and invisible, whether thrones or dominions or rulers or authorities—all things were created through him and *for him*" (Col. 1:16). In creating the heavens and the earth, God was not simply displaying his majestic power, beauty, and wisdom. He had a master plan in mind. That master plan was to find its omega point in the repristination of the cosmos under the headship of the God-man, Jesus Christ. Paul makes the point in Ephesians 1:9–10. He tells us that God has made "known to us the mystery of his will, according to his purpose, which he set forth in Christ as a plan for the fullness of time, to unite all things [again] in him, things in heaven and things on earth."

When Adam sinned, God's good creation was defaced. Sin came into the world (Rom. 5:12). Satan became the god of this world (2 Cor. 4:4). The whole world came under the diabolical rule of the enemy of our souls (1 John 5:19). The whole creation is currently in "bondage to corruption" and waits to "obtain the freedom of the glory of the children of God" (Rom. 8:21). Adam's sin was a cosmic tragedy. But God already had a purpose, and that purpose was to "unite all things in [Christ], things in heaven and things on earth" (Eph. 1:10). Paul makes a similar statement in his letter to the Colossians, where he speaks of God's reconciling all things to himself in Christ, things in heaven and things on earth, "making peace by the blood of his cross" (Col. 1:20). The whole creation that was lost through the fall will be restored to God through Christ.

Paul uses a wonderfully vivid verb in Ephesians 1:10 to capture the glorious cosmic unity that God is in the process of accomplishing in Christ. The ESV translates it "*to unite* all things in him"; the NIV, "*to bring unity* to all things . . . under Christ"; the KJV, to "*gather together in one* all things in Christ"; the NASB, "*the summing up* of all things in Christ." The verb appears in only one other place in the New Testament, Romans 13:9, where Paul says that God's commandments are "*summed up* in this word: 'You shall love your neighbor as yourself.'" It is clear that ἀνακεφαλαιόω contains the idea of "gathering together and bringing into a unity." The context, however, suggests another way to translate this Greek compound. In Ephesians 1:22, Paul tells us that the Father has given Christ as "head over all things." Creation has a "head," who is Jesus Christ. Literally, ἀνακεφαλαιόω is translated "to *head* up *again*." It may, then, be better to hear Paul telling the Ephesians that God's purpose, "which he set forth in Christ," was "*to head up again* all things in him." Before Adam's rebellion, God's Son was the "head" of creation. The triune God's rule over creation was mediated through the Son. God's ultimate purpose, then, is to reestablish the Son as the head of creation. It is imperative that we understand that God's purpose in salvation focuses not ultimately on us but on his Son. Paul makes this explicit in Romans 8:29: "For those whom he foreknew he also predestined to be conformed to the image of his Son, in order that he might be the firstborn among many brothers."

Pastoral ministry is rooted in the opening chapters of Genesis. To attempt to minister into this broken, dysfunctional, wicked, and rebellious world without expounding the elemental truths of Genesis 1–3 would be like trying to explain Act 2 of *Hamlet* without reference to Act 1. The space-time history of the opening chapters of Genesis grounds our experience in this world and provides the foundation on which God establishes his gracious purpose that culminates in the gospel of Jesus Christ. If our calling is to lift up and hold out God's "second man" and "last Adam" (1 Cor. 15:45–47), we need to do so in such a way that our hearers are taught about the first Adam, his creation from the dust of the earth, his tragic fall, and God's promise to send one from the seed of woman to crush the serpent and restore all things to God (vv. 24–28).

Key Terms

Christocentricity
ex nihilo creation
pluralism and polytheism
psychosomatic
theological presuppositions

Recommendations for Further Reading

Alexander, T. Desmond. *From Eden to the New Creation*. Grand Rapids: Kregel, 2009.

Bavinck, Herman. *Reformed Dogmatics*. Edited by John Bolt. Translated by John Vriend. Vol. 2, *God and Creation*. Grand Rapids: Baker Academic, 2004.

Godfrey, W. Robert. *God's Pattern for Creation: A Covenantal Reading of Genesis 1*. Phillipsburg, NJ: P&R Publishing, 2003.

Pipa, Joseph A., and David W. Hall, eds. *Did God Create in 6 Days?* Dallas, GA: Tolle Lege, 2006.

Robertson, O. Palmer. *Christ and the Covenants*. Phillipsburg, NJ: Presbyterian and Reformed, 1987.

Schaeffer, Francis A. *Genesis in Space and Time*. Downers Grove, IL: InterVarsity Press, 1972.

VanDoodewaard, William. *The Quest for the Historical Adam*. Grand Rapids: Reformation Heritage Books, 2015.

Discussion Questions

1. What was the purpose of God's revealing his work of creation in Genesis 1, first to the people of the exodus, and then to the church throughout history?
2. Why is it important to think about presuppositions, our own and others', as we discuss the Bible's teaching on creation?
3. How should the truth of the *imago Dei* influence how we think about and treat other people, whoever they are?
4. How should the Bible's teaching on creation affect how we think about and treat the environment we live in?
5. In what ways does the truth that the living God is our Creator shape and style how we think and behave?
6. How should a church's pastoral ministry be influenced by what the Bible teaches us about God the Creator?

5

PROVIDENCE

Confidence in God's Purpose
to Perfect His People[1]

MICHAEL McCLENAHAN

Christians are not the only people who think about the idea of providence. The order and rhythms of the natural world have long moved human thought toward the idea of a higher controlling power. In his famous work "On Providence," Seneca wrote that "everything moves forward according to a law that is fixed and passed for eternity. Fate is our guide, and the amount of time that remains for each of us was determined at the first hour of our birth."[2] It is hardly surprising that this is the case. God himself testifies to everyone that God is Lord and God is good: "he did not leave himself without witness, for he did good by giving you rains from heaven and fruitful seasons, satisfying your hearts with food and gladness" (Acts 14:17).

This chapter sets out the Christian doctrine of providence. It begins by setting the doctrine of providence in its only proper

---

1. Sinclair Ferguson has been a very good friend to the church on the island of Ireland. His frequent visits, his preaching, and his writing have strengthened many of his brothers and sisters. We thank God for him and for his faithful ministry.

2. Seneca, "On Providence," in *Seneca: Dialogues and Essays*, trans. John Davie (Oxford: Oxford University Press, 2007), 14.

71

context—the unchanging perfection of God's holy life. It is the doctrine of God that sets the context for the Christian doctrine of providence, allowing it to take on its unique shape and life-sustaining power. It is here that all the failings in Seneca's pagan teaching about providence are clearly seen. Providence is not Stoic fate: in Seneca, the gods are subject to the rule of fate—true providence is the outworking of the perfect divine purpose for the creation. Therefore, this chapter sets out the argument that a Christian doctrine of providence has three central aspects. First, it is the doctrine of *God's* providence. Second, it is a doctrine rooted in the *wisdom* and *power* of God *preserving* and *governing* the created order. Finally, it is a doctrine with a *telos* or a purpose. In order to draw out the elements in this argument, the chapter proceeds with an exposition of the following dogmatic thesis: *The Christian doctrine of providence is a teaching of unspeakable consolation, rooted in the life of God as Father, Son, and Holy Spirit. God is the infinitely wise and powerful Lord of heaven and earth, who preserves and governs all his creatures and all their actions to their appointed ends. Such is the wisdom and power of God that his holy and good will for the perfection of his creatures comes to pass, to the praise of his glorious grace.* The chapter concludes with specific applications to ministry from the theological content of the essay.

It is important to note carefully the structure and order of the argument. The doctrine of providence is not developed by the church because there are problems to be solved. It is certainly the case that the biblical doctrine of providence raises many vexing and difficult issues, but as "with all dogmatics, *disputatio* is subordinate to *expositio*. Dogmatics has a twofold task: an analytic-expository task, in which it attempts orderly conceptual representation of the content of the Christian gospel as it is laid out in the scriptural witnesses; and a polemical-apologetical task in which it explores the justification and value of Christian truth-claims."[3]

---

3. John Webster, *God without Measure: Working Papers in Christian Theology*, vol. 1, *God and the Works of God* (London: Bloomsbury T. & T. Clark, 2016), 130. Webster's essays in this volume, "On the Theology of Providence" and "Providence" (cited below), will both repay careful study.

The Christian Doctrine of Providence Is a Teaching of Unspeakable Consolation, Rooted in the Life of God as Father, Son, and Holy Spirit

Many distortions of the doctrine of providence are traceable back to a failure to think rightly about God. Good theology does not seek to separate the doctrine of providence from other Christian teaching, as though all the questions and problems raised by this article of faith could be resolved if it were removed from the interconnected body of Christian thinking and examined isolated and all alone—under a microscope. There are, of course, many apparently sophisticated theological attempts to address the anxieties created by this teaching that follow just this method.[4] Many more popular variations that articulate versions of the doctrine are really nothing more than sentimentalized reworkings of Seneca's encomium to fate. Older readers may remember Doris Day's famous rendition of the now-iconic ballad by Jay Livingston and Ray Evans: "Que Sera Sera"—*whatever will be, will be.* The song itself was later adapted and ingrained in large sections of British cultural life when it became a mainstay sporting anthem.[5] It gave impetus to the phrase "cheerful fatalism."

This is just one popular example of the distortion of the doctrine of providence when God is forgotten or reimagined. The problem with these distortions is not simply that they are disordered, which they are, but that they rob people of the comfort and hope that this teaching should bring to the redeemed children of Adam. John Webster writes that part of the deformation of the doctrine comes when "there is a gradual 'anonymization' of providence. Little significance is accorded to the identity of the agent of providence, which can be

4. The superlative modern example of this ailment might be Jürgen Moltmann, *The Trinity and the Kingdom* (Minneapolis: Fortress Press, 1993), in which Moltmann redefines the doctrine of God almost entirely in order to redefine the relationship between Creator and creatures.

5. At this point, it is probably worth noting that this cultural appropriation of the song moved it a long way from the famous plot function it provided in Alfred Hitchcock's 1958 movie *The Man Who Knew Too Much*. It is certainly the case that Doris Day's little pagan ditty is now the most popular song "on providence" in common usage in the United Kingdom. If you doubt that, Google it.

stripped down to a nameless causal force, the term 'providence' itself often becoming a substitute for 'God.'"[6]

Christian theology must resist this tendency, and it has been doing so for quite some time. In his foundational work *City of God*, Augustine contrasts arguments about pagan trust in the "gods" and Christian confidence in the one God, Lord of heaven and earth. Centuries later, the boldness and courage of Augustine's vigorous apologetic should still press upon the thinking of the church. He writes: "In this matter there is no power at all in those gods whom the Romans considered they had to worship by means of frivolous ceremonies. . . . I have shown that the notion of 'destiny' must be dismissed, so that no one, once convinced that the propagation and preservation of the Roman Empire was not due to the worship of those gods, should attribute it to some 'destiny' or other, and not to the omnipotent will of God most high."[7]

It is notable that this is precisely what the great Reformed confessions achieve. On this matter there is no hesitation, no equivocation. First, the Belgic Confession (1561):

> This doctrine affords us unspeakable consolation, since we are taught thereby that nothing can befall us by chance, but by the direction of our most gracious and heavenly Father; who watches over us with a paternal care, keeping all creatures so under his power, that "not a hair of our head (for they are all numbered), nor a sparrow, can fall to the ground, without the will of our Father", in whom we do entirely trust; being persuaded that He so restrains the devil and all our enemies that without His will and permission, they cannot hurt us. (Belgic Confession, art. 13)

The theological point is clear—the "unspeakable consolation" that the doctrine of providence brings flows from the knowledge that it is God, our gracious heavenly Father, who guides history in every detail and ensures that there is no such thing as chance.

6. John Webster, "Providence," in *Mapping Modern Theology: A Thematic and Historical Introduction*, ed. Kelly M. Kapic and Bruce L. McCormack (Grand Rapids: Baker Academic, 2012), 209.

7. Augustine, *City of God*, trans. Henry Bettenson (London: Penguin, 1984), 196–97.

Second, the Westminster Confession of Faith (1646): "God the great Creator of all things doth uphold, direct, dispose, and govern all creatures, actions, and things, from the greatest even to the least, by His most wise and holy providence, according to His infallible foreknowledge, and the free and immutable counsel of His own will, to the praise of the glory of His wisdom, power, justice, goodness, and mercy" (WCF 5.1).

It is important to note that the Westminster divines spoke of "God the great Creator" in an earlier chapter of the confession using the grammar of Western catholic Trinitarianism. On this matter there was no disruption at the Reformation—God is the three persons, the eternal relations of Father, Son, and Spirit: "The Father is of none, neither begotten, not proceeding: the Son is eternally begotten of the Father: the Holy Ghost eternally proceeding from the Father and the Son" (WCF 2.3).[8] It is this One, the triune God, whose providence is determinative for the "greatest even to the least" in the order of creation. God is thus fully alive, and providence is the "overflow of God's abundant life."[9] None stand outside his will.

It is this point that is clear in Scripture. Paul says that God "works all things according to the counsel of his will" (Eph. 1:11). The difficulties that arise from the Christian doctrine of providence do not arise because Scripture is unclear—it is the very clarity of the Bible

8. As John Bower notes, this restatement of Reformed catholic orthodoxy was accepted by the assembly "wholly unchanged from the original." John R. Bower, *The Confession of Faith* (Grand Rapids: Reformation Heritage Books, 2020), 13. For an excellent summary of Christian teaching on the divine processions and divine life, see Scott R. Swain, "Divine Trinity," in *Christian Dogmatics: Reformed Theology for the Church Catholic*, ed. Michael Allen and Scott R. Swain (Grand Rapids: Baker Academic, 2016), 78–106. Note also the delightful echo of the Trinity in the first ten words of WCF 5.4: "The almighty power, unsearchable wisdom, and infinite goodness of God."

9. Webster, *God without Measure*, 1:135: "The doctrine of providence begins from the doctrine of God of which it is a function. It is important to begin far back in the doctrine of God—not simply with, for example, divine power or intelligence but with God's complete inner life which he is from himself as Father, Son and Holy Spirit, that is, with the eternal plenitude of the divine processions in which consists divine blessedness. Providence is an aspect of the uncaused wonder of the overflow of God's abundant life. God's perfection includes his infinite love; he is himself an inexhaustible fountain of life; he bestows life in limitless generosity."

that brings so many questions to the foreground. It is important to remember that the difficulties that arise for the (post)modern mind are hardly new; they are variations on age-old questions. Consequently, the doctrine has been endlessly examined. Before moving on to the way in which this doctrine has been articulated, it is important to pause for a moment and reflect on its unspeakable consolation. There is only one true and living God. He is God the Father, God the Son, and God the Holy Spirit. He is the God who "comforts us in all our affliction" (2 Cor. 1:4) and who holds each of his children by the hand (Isa. 41:13). It is this living Lord who in Jesus Christ has redeemed his people from their sins. When the church of Christ confesses belief in divine providence, it is this Lord, and no other, who is the God of providence. The question to ask when thinking about providence must be: "Is He not your Father? Has He not loved you with an everlasting love?"[10]

God Is the Infinitely Wise and Powerful Lord of Heaven and Earth, Who Preserves and Governs All His Creatures and All Their Actions to Their Appointed Ends

The Reformed tradition has spoken of providence according to three particular aspects. Each is important in expounding the biblical material and highlighting particular facets of the doctrine. But there is only one divine work of providence considered in these various ways. First, providence is expressed as *preservation*. In Scripture, the ideas of creation and preservation are closely linked. The Creator is also the Preserver:

> For the Lord is a great God,
>   and a great King above all gods.
> In his hand are the depths of the earth;
>   the heights of the mountains are his also.
> The sea is his, for he made it,
>   and his hands formed the dry land. (Ps. 95:3–5)

---

10. Wilhelmus à Brakel, *The Christian's Reasonable Service*, ed. Joel R. Beeke, trans. Bartel Elshout, 4 vols. (Grand Rapids: Reformation Heritage Books, 1992), 1:352.

While it is true that men and women are appointed stewards of the earth, and will be held to account for the manner in which they have treated the generosity of God to them, it is not the case that human beings will ever be the ultimate destroyers of the created order. The annihilation of the world by nuclear weapons, the obliteration of life by biological weapons, and ultimate environmental destruction— these are all well beyond the power and reach of creatures. The Lord will preserve his creation and guide it to his own end: "Say among the nations, 'The LORD reigns! Yes, the world is established; it shall never be moved'" (Ps. 96:10). Robert Letham highlights the role of the Noahic covenant in the preservation aspect of the doctrine of providence: in "this covenant, God promises preservation from universal judgement by flood."[11] This is important in illustrating the historical manifestation of the divine will—the eternal will to preserve is made manifest in this covenant.

Yet providence as preservation is not restricted to the Noahic covenant. The point about preservation is doing much more in Reformed theology than merely outlining the significance of the Noahic covenant. Divine preservation—linked as it is to creation *ex nihilo*—is fundamentally concerned with God's preserving decree toward created being qua created being. God alone is uncreated; he is *a se*, "from himself." Created being is from God. The preservation aspect of the doctrine of providence highlights the benevolent wisdom of the Creator's will. He brought created being into existence, and it is his unalterable will to thus preserve it: "world without end," as the liturgy repeats. Richard Muller offers a helpful pithy definition of *conservatio* ("conservation, preservation"): "specifically, the preserving or protecting of the created order by its Creator."[12]

The divine work of preservation, like the divine work of creation to which it is so closely linked, is a work of God. Like creation, it is a great mystery. Not mystery in the sense that creatures have yet to figure it all out—but mystery in the sense that it is far beyond the ability of creatures to comprehend. It is in this sense, simultaneously

11. Robert Letham, *Systematic Theology* (Wheaton, IL: Crossway, 2019), 294.

12. Richard A. Muller, "Conservatio," in *Dictionary of Latin and Greek Theological Terms: Drawn Principally from Protestant Scholastic Theology*, 2nd ed. (Grand Rapids: Baker Academic, 2017), 77.

both severe and sublime, that "mystery is the lifeblood of dogmatics."[13] Katherine Sonderegger remarks: "Divine Mystery is not a sign of our *failure* in knowledge; but rather our *success*. It is because we *know* truly and properly—because we obey in faith the First Commandment— that God is mystery."[14] Creatures must stand amazed at the eternal wisdom of God in his works of providence: "For who has known the mind of the Lord, or who has been his counselor?" (Rom. 11:34).

Second, providence is expressed as *concurrence*. In this aspect of the discussion of providence, theology considers the relationship between divine action and the creatures who are the objects of his life-giving love. What does it mean to say that God acts? What does it mean to say that creatures act? If God acts, does that not mean that creaturely acts are rendered meaningless? This aspect of the discussion is technically very important and pastorally vital. To take the latter issue first, it is not unusual for those coming to terms with divine sovereignty and providence to lapse into a kind of grotesque "Reformed fatalism," with teaching about divine causation simply overwhelming the sinful soul into a state of lethargy and spiritual torpor, a soul sickness measurable in prayerlessness, in secret sinful patterns, and particularly in a callous disregard for the lost and the global mission of the church. The cure for this malady is careful instruction in the distinction between primary and secondary causes—or, to express it in more scriptural terms, a sustained meditation on the exhortation to "work out your own salvation with fear and trembling, for it is God who works in you, both to will and to work for his good pleasure" (Phil. 2:12–13).

The basic point to grapple with here is that God in his work of creation has endued his creatures with causality: "In creating, God has placed powers in substances."[15] He gives his creatures a particular nature; the nature he gives them has particular qualities. Wilhelmus à Brakel puts it beautifully when he says that all "creatures

13. Herman Bavinck, *Reformed Dogmatics*, ed. John Bolt, trans. John Vriend, 4 vols. (Grand Rapids: Baker Academic, 2003–8), 1:29.

14. Katherine Sonderegger, *Systematic Theology*, vol. 1, *Doctrine of God* (Minneapolis: Fortress, 2015), 24.

15. Geerhardus Vos, *Reformed Dogmatics*, ed. and trans. Richard B. Gaffin Jr., 5 vols. (Bellingham, WA: Lexham Press, 2012), 1:189.

have received an independent and unique existence from God so as to move in a manner unique to themselves."[16] If a man is to jump into the air, he must exert his muscles, and he must cause that motion by a decision of his mind. He is in a proper sense the cause of his jumping—yet not the primary cause because it is only in the omnipotent God that creatures "live and move and have [their] being" (Acts 17:28). The creature will jump only when the creature wills to jump, and he will freely will to jump only when his Creator so enables it. As Herman Bavinck notes, "Christian theology teaches that the secondary causes are strictly subordinated to God as the primary cause and in that subordination nevertheless remain true causes."[17] The strength of these true secondary causes, in which creatures are entirely dependent on the power of God, is entirely natural to them as secondary causes. There is no overwhelming of their nature, no trampling on their liberty. Rather: "God's love of creatures includes his creation of them with a particular nature. . . . They possess causality, [and] this causality is secondary or medial. . . . 'Secondariness' is not a deficiency, a violation of creaturely agency, but a specification of the agency lovingly bestowed on us by God who summons us into his service."[18]

The matter under discussion here is nothing other than the nature of theism itself. At the very heart of biblical theism is the notion of a hierarchy of causes. It is God himself who is the First and Ultimate

---

16. À Brakel, *Reasonable Service*, 1:336.

17. Bavinck, *Reformed Dogmatics*, 2:613. Bavinck's discussion of this matter is clear and instructive, particularly 614–15. Not all agree, for example, G. C. Berkouwer, *The Providence of God* (Leicester, UK: Inter-Varsity Press, 1972), 154–60. Berkouwer offers a less favorable assessment of the schema of primary and secondary causation than that outlined here. The basic weakness of Berkouwer's argument is his assumption that the language of causation inevitably means that first and second causes will be treated as comparable: "The terms, by their arrangement (first-second), nevertheless suggest a causal circle in which God and man are alike involved" (155). Thus, either God is bound to the world or sin is brought into the sphere of divine causality. Suffice to say at this stage that there are better readings of Thomas Aquinas in the history of Reformed theology. For example, Francis Turretin, *Institutes of Elenctic Theology*, ed. James T. Dennison Jr., trans. George Musgrave Giger, 3 vols. (Phillipsburg, NJ: P&R Publishing, 1992–97), 1:489–538, esp. 6.4.5 (502); Paul Helm, *The Providence of God* (Leicester, UK: Inter-Varsity Press, 1993), 86–87.

18. Webster, *God without Measure*, 1:140.

Cause of all things, but in the created order that actually exists (as opposed to the ones that might be imagined), created causes are established and not invalidated by divine causation.[19]

Finally, providence is expressed as *government.* God rules over all. There are two ways in which this wonderful truth may be considered. On the one hand, the Scriptures set before us the universal and sovereign rule of God. Even foolish earthly rulers come to acknowledge this truth:[20]

> At the end of the days I, Nebuchadnezzar, lifted my eyes to heaven, and my reason returned to me, and I blessed the Most High, and praised and honored him who lives forever,
>
> > for his dominion is an everlasting dominion,
> >   and his kingdom endures from generation to generation;
> > all the inhabitants of the earth are accounted as nothing,
> >   and he does according to his will among the host of heaven
> >   and among the inhabitants of the earth;
> > and none can stay his hand
> >   or say to him, "What have you done?" (Dan. 4:34–35)

This is what it means to confess God's providential government over his creation: "none can stay his hand." It is this hand of God that feeds every living thing (Ps. 145:15–16), including the birds of the air (Matt. 6:26). It is the sovereign King of heaven who "gives to all mankind life and breath and everything" (Acts 17:25). God's loving care for the world he created is beautifully set forth in the polemic of the closing chapters of Job (38:1–39:30). On the other hand, there is more to say about God's government of the world: most importantly, that the government of the world has now been placed into the hands of the risen and ascended Christ. That most glorious indication at

---

19. The language of secondary causes' being "established" comes from WCF 3.1. This argument is all just another way of saying that Thomas Aquinas is a much better guide to Philippians 2:12–13 than Søren Kierkegaard, whose famous essay "Fear and Trembling" alludes to the text in the title, but that is all. See Søren Kierkegaard, *Fear and Trembling,* trans. Alastair Hannay (London: Penguin, 1985).

20. So keep praying for them, especially in public worship (1 Tim. 2:1–2).

the onset of the new creation—"he has risen" (Matt. 28:6)—points to the reality of the victorious life of the resurrected Son. It is this risen and ascended Christ who possesses all authority in heaven and earth (v. 18). It is this glorious Christ who sits in the place of highest honor at the right hand of God (Acts 2:34). It is Jesus Christ who is Lord of lords and King of kings.

Biblical teaching about the ascension and heavenly reign of the Lord Jesus is deeply instructive when wrestling with the perennial question of sin that arises in discussions of divine providence. À Brakel, in his treatment of providence, which is so warm and pastorally helpful, raises this perennial issue when he says that "God's government also encompasses sin, for otherwise the entire human race, being sinful in its deeds, would be removed from God's government."[21] Of course, at this point the Christian faith denies emphatically that God is the author of sin.[22] One important approach that theologians take in responding to the issue involves further distinguishing the responsibility of primary and secondary causes. Without doubt, this is an important argument to develop in this context, but the argument will not succeed without careful exegetical and theological treatment of a much broader and fundamental point: Christ the King is holy. The ascended Lord is utterly resplendent, majestic, and luminous in his being and therefore in all his ways: "His eyes were like a flame of fire, . . . and his face was like the sun shining in full strength" (Rev. 1:14, 16). It seems more than a little plausible that this is why most believers do not feel the pressure of the "problem of evil" in a continuous existential way. The reason is that the knowledge of providence—specifically here the knowledge of God's government and sovereign rule—is linked so closely with the knowledge of faith. To be more specific, the gospel brings life and light to lost souls and creates in them a true knowledge of God. This gospel knowledge is created by the Word and Spirit as the eyes of the heart

---

21. À Brakel, *Reasonable Service*, 1:343.

22. See WCF 3.1: "neither is God the author of sin." It is true that nearly all Reformed theologians and confessions deny that God is the author of sin. As ever, Jonathan Edwards presses the use of language in order to clarify the material questions at issue. On this question, as on a number of others, it results in the most arresting language. See, for example, the discussion of the language of "author of sin" in Edwards by Helm, *Providence of God*, 173.

are opened and the soul is reoriented to God as he really is—sovereign, holy, merciful, and good. While it is true that we "simply cannot solve the riddles presented to us by the providence of God in life," it is also true that the pilgrim who knows God by the grace of the gospel knows that the Lord Most High is too pure even to look upon evil, let alone commit sin (Hab. 1:13).[23] And so the church echoes the words of Augustine: "It is clear that God, the one true God, rules and guides these events, according to his pleasure. If God's reasons are inscrutable, does that mean that they are unjust?"[24]

Such Is the Wisdom and Power of God That His Holy and Good Will for the Perfection of His Creatures Comes to Pass, to the Praise of His Glorious Grace

There is always a temptation to conceive of providence in a way that distances God from his preservation and government of all things. But there is no aloofness with God. He is exalted and majestic—he is also our contemporary. He is with us. His presence with his creatures always has a *telos*, a goal. It is in this way that the infinite relates to the finite, the Creator to the creature. In other words, the preservation and government of creation is not static. He is the Lord of history. Not in the sense that he is constituted by and shaped through the history of creation; this cannot be, because he is the fullness of the perfection of his own life. Rather, his presence with his creatures is the momentum by which all things move to their appointed end. As Bavinck notes, "providence serves to take the world from its beginning and to lead it to its final goal."[25] This final goal, this end of his creatures, is the glorification of the elect of God in a reborn creation.

Scripture teaches the church about the divine *telos* in many different ways, but it is particularly in the great stories of the Bible that the doctrine of God's governing providence is displayed. Think of the great narrative accounts of the Old Testament—there is nothing static

23. Herman Bavinck, *The Wonderful Works of God: Instruction in the Christian Religion according to the Reformed Confessions*, trans. Henry Zylstra (Glenside, PA: Westminster Seminary Press, 2019), 163.

24. Augustine, *City of God*, 216.

25. Bavinck, *Reformed Dogmatics*, 2:609.

or restrained about the divine presence. God is ever calling, leading, drawing, sustaining, and delivering his people. They are pilgrims, on a journey to "a better country, that is, a heavenly one" (Heb. 11:16). And on that journey, he bore them "on eagles' wings and brought [them] to [him]self" (Ex. 19:4). One of the most familiar examples of this *telos* is seen in the story of Joseph: betrayed, enslaved, persecuted, imprisoned, forgotten, delivered, restored, empowered, exalted—his life both prophetic, in that he lays down the pattern for the greater Joseph to come, and epic, because his solitary life is the pattern of the great pilgrimage of God's people throughout time.[26] Even Joseph's bodily remains were subject to the divine *telos* (Heb. 11:22).

The great *telos* of God is the glorification of his own name in the perfection of the creatures of his love: "For from him and through him and to him are all things. To him be glory forever. Amen" (Rom. 11:36). The Lord Jesus delivers individual fallen creatures from their sins. They have names, and he knows them—they are Mary, and Philip, and James, and Susannah, and myriads and myriads more. He is also the cosmic Christ: "For in him all the fullness of God was pleased to dwell, and through him to reconcile to himself all things, whether on earth or in heaven, making peace by the blood of his cross" (Col. 1:19–20). Ultimately all things have a *telos*, an appointed end, because the God who made all things is the triune God of mercy and grace who wisely and powerfully moves all things to that end. This is why the doctrine of providence, God's preserving and governing all his creatures and all their actions, is a matter of "unspeakable consolation" to God's children and the subject of their eternal praise: "To him who sits on the throne and to the Lamb be blessing and honor and glory and might forever and ever!" (Rev. 5:13).

Conclusion

How might the doctrine outlined in this chapter be applied to the practice of Christian ministry? There is, of course, the immediate point that the lives and ministries of pastors are in the hands of God.

26. See the beautiful summary of this point in Sinclair B. Ferguson, *Preaching Christ from the Old Testament* (London: Proclamation Trust, 2002), 17.

The appropriation of this teaching into the heart weans the soul from sinful habits such as self-reliance, prayerlessness, anxiety, pride—the applications are manifold. More positively, the main doctrinal building blocks in this argument provide the kind of nourishment that rejuvenates the soul. It is the theology that Paul testifies to when he speaks of "all his energy that he powerfully works within me" (Col. 1:29). This teaching has the important role of reminding ministers that God has sovereignly ordained the means and the end. The means are, in the inexhaustible mercy of God, means *of grace*, and it is the privilege of ordained ministers of Word and sacrament that these means of divine grace come to God's people through pastors who are themselves the recipients of such very great grace. What else might be said?

First, sustained attention to the doctrine of providence recalibrates the heart to the sovereignty and glory of God. The doctrine of providence is a striking and arresting truth; God is in control. Of course, many unbelievers simply scoff—the wicked man thinks that God will never see, that God has forgotten (Ps. 10:11). It is possible for God's own children to grow "brutish and ignorant" and to misinterpret the order of the world almost completely (Ps. 73:22). Yet true heavenly wisdom teaches the heart to sing: "Hallelujah! For the Lord our God the Almighty reigns" (Rev. 19:6). Here the eyes of faith must gaze so that the heart may be strengthened by the rule of God. One of the great legends in the history of the church (imagine that it were true!) is that the great hymn of praise *Te Deum Laudamus* ("God, we praise you") was an improvised antiphonal creation of St. Ambrose and St. Augustine at the latter's baptism. Whatever the origins of the Ambrosian hymn, it certainly captures something of the resplendent glory of the triune God and his Christ: "Heaven and earth are full of the majesty of thy glory." The doctrine of providence is a wonderful teacher when it turns the heart away from self to the God who is the source of all life, wisdom, and joy. Ministers of the Word and sacraments need the eyes of their hearts continually opened to the divine majesty before they turn and open their lips to edify the church.

Second, this doctrine will help pastors "wait for the LORD" (Ps. 27:14). The hope of the leaders of the people of God is in the Lord alone—waiting for him to bring growth (1 Cor. 3:6). Yet godly waiting for the Lord is never passive. Providence is, in the delightful words of Stephen Charnock at the end of his famous treatise, a doctrine that teaches what it means to "wait upon him obedientially." Christian leaders in particular need not think "God's time too long." Rather, serious meditation on providence is a reminder that "God's methods appear in the end both wiser and better than our frames. Infinite goodness aims more at our welfare, than our shallow self love; and infinite wisdom can conduct things to our welfare better than our short-sighted skill. He that knows all the moments of time, knows best how to time his actions."[27]

The knowledge that God is working out his good and loving purpose adds meaning to the apparent banality of much of the life of obedience—particularly in many necessary aspects of the ministry of the gospel. Pastoral administration is no more thrilling than any other sort of administration, and in Christian ministry there is an abundance of work that simply must be done. Meetings must be attended, papers should be read, reports need to be written. Most of this labor is not particularly glamorous or invigorating. In the end, every aspect of a minister's calling is work and so is subject to frustration in a fallen world. Yet the uplifting doctrine of God's providence means that God—who has ordained all the means to the great end of the perfection of the church—hears the cry of his undershepherds: "establish the work of our hands!" (Ps. 90:17).

Not all of life is banal or commonplace. There are times of great moment—times when decisions seem to shape the future in the most extraordinary way. Times when pastors are placed in the spotlight of history and called on to make their confession of Christ and bear the cruel scorn and fierce rejection of this present age. Of course, this does not happen only to pastors. The blood of the martyrs has flowed like a great river for many generations, and the persecutor's zeal often lacks discrimination between leaders and people. Yet down through the centuries, it has often been the way of God in his providence that the leaders of the church have been given the first opportunity to make the great confession—to choose Christ over earthly life. It is

---

27. Stephen Charnock, *A Treatise of Divine Providence*, in *The Works of the Learned Divine Stephen Charnock*, 2 vols. (London, 1684), 2:91.

God's providential gift to his people that their leaders are often set apart to show the way to heaven—to show that faithfulness to Christ the Lord means that there is a cross before there is a crown.

On Broad Street in Oxford, England, there is a small brick memorial set into the street. It is known as the "martyrs' cross." It marks the place where in October 1555 the Protestant bishops Nicholas Ridley and Hugh Latimer were burned at the stake during the great persecution of Queen Mary. They were two of several hundred Protestants who died in those awful years. As they were consumed by flames, it may have seemed that the light of the gospel itself was being extinguished in England. The next year, the former Archbishop of Canterbury, Thomas Cranmer, suffered the same fate. As they died, these men could not see the future—it was not for them to see the great days of spiritual life under Queen Elizabeth, the reformation of the universities, and the recovery of gospel preaching in pulpits throughout the parishes of England. They could not see the great London Synod in the middle years of the seventeenth century that would produce a confession of faith and catechisms that would reshape the world and endure for centuries. They saw none of these things. Yet as he was being burned alive, in some of the most famous words in English history, Latimer exhorted Ridley:

> Be of good comfort, Master Ridley, and play the man: we shall this day light such a candle by God's grace in England, as (I trust) shall never be put out.[28]

So speaks the man of God, who knows the Lord, and trusts in his wise and good providence.

Key Terms

concurrence
providence
telos

28. John Foxe, *Foxe's Book of Martyrs: Select Narratives*, ed. John N. King (Oxford: Oxford University Press, 2009), 154.

Recommendations for Further Reading

Bavinck, Herman. *The Wonderful Works of God: Instruction in the Christian Religion according to the Reformed Confessions*. Translated by Henry Zylstra. Glenside, PA: Westminster Seminary Press, 2019. Pp. 144–65.

Helm, Paul. *The Providence of God*. Leicester, UK: Inter-Varsity Press, 1993.

Letham, Robert. *Systematic Theology*. Wheaton, IL: Crossway, 2019. Pp. 292–311.

Watson, Thomas. *All Things for Good*. Edinburgh: Banner of Truth, 1986. Reprint of *A Divine Cordial*. London, 1663.

Webster, John. "On the Theology of Providence." In *God without Measure: Working Papers in Christian Theology*, vol. 1, *God and the Works of God*. London: Bloomsbury T. & T. Clark, 2016. Pp. 127–42.

Discussion Questions

1. Why is it important to think about who God is before we try to talk about the doctrine of providence?
2. What aspects of God's revealed character might help us as we consider the doctrine of providence?
3. How would you explain primary and secondary causation using your own words?
4. How might meditation on passages of Scripture that speak of the holiness and purity of Jesus Christ (such as Rev 1:14, 16) help you to live in a world full of darkness and evil?
5. As you think about the future, how does the knowledge of the Lord's providence strengthen you on your pilgrimage to the heavenly city?

6

HUMANITY

The Need of Theological Anthropology for Everyday Ministry[1]

JOHN McCLEAN

An Ordinary Pastoral Day

Pastor Steven drove home, his mind awhirl. The day had begun at the bedside of Margaret, a long-term church member, dying of heart failure. Her faith faltered with her heart, and she was lonely and fearful. He spent the rest of the morning with Jack and Alice, coming to terms with the announcement made by their only daughter that she would marry her lesbian partner. In tears they wondered, "What did we do wrong?" Could they reclaim their relationship with her? Should they refuse to permit her and her partner to visit their home?

In the afternoon, Steven skimmed through the most recent of a never-ending stack of emails, replying to the most urgent. With relief, he caught a quiet hour in his favorite café, studying the opening verses of Romans 12 for Sunday's sermon: "Do not conform to the pattern of this world, but be transformed by the renewing of your

---

1. It is a pleasure to contribute to this volume, which honors Sinclair Ferguson and his contribution to Christ-focused theology and ministry. I have benefited immensely from his writings.

89

mind" (Rom. 12:2).[2] What would change the "minds" of his congregation when the world seemed so forceful? His Bible software explained that the Greek word for "mind" (*nous*) is "the thinking, reasoning, and planning aspect of human existence and awareness . . . representing simply the whole of human existence and experience."[3] That made renewed minds an incredible project. What, he wondered, did it mean to offer his body to the Lord "as a living sacrifice" (v. 1)?

As he left the café, he was stopped by Reg, a friend made over coffee. A month ago, in a long conversation, Reg had explained that he lost his faith when his brother, a church elder, abandoned his wife. For Reg, the hypocrisy was devastating. Steven had listened and empathized, pointing out that Jesus condemned hypocrisy, trying to get Reg to think more about Jesus than his brother. He had made no apparent progress. Reg's update was that his brother had been in touch with his wife, and now with Reg, to ask for forgiveness. "There is no way I'm forgiving him," he snarled, "but I think she might be ready to take him back—more fool her!" While Steven tried to formulate a reply, Reg walked out, leaving the café door swinging. He had not been asking for advice!

After a raucous evening meal and hurried family devotions, Steven left Angela to supervise bedtime while he chaired a difficult elders' meeting to consider filling the role of youth coordinator. Some elders championed Gillian, a young woman newly graduated from a local seminary; others wanted a wider search for an experienced male candidate. The parties separated along familiar fracture lines. They respected each other, but tempers frayed, and they left the meeting with the acrid taste of division, but no decision.

Now, driving home, Steven struggled to focus his thoughts or even to turn them into prayer. His body ached, his mind buzzed, and his heart sank. He tried to prepare to listen to Angela and not simply dump on her. Maybe, late this evening, a half-hour of late-night sports on TV would let him wind down enough for bed.

2. Unless otherwise indicated, Scripture quotations in this chapter are from the NIV.

3. A. C. Myers, "Heart," in *The Eerdmans Bible Dictionary* (Grand Rapids: Eerdmans, 1987), 721.

Theological Anthropology

To state the obvious, pastoral ministry concerns people. A pastor deals with people in all their stages of life, with their complex histories and relationships, their joys and celebrations, and their conflicts and fears. He seeks to apply God's Word to them and to help them understand their lives in the light of the gospel. And the pastor is human—finite and foolish.

It follows that anthropology, the study of human life, is a core element of pastoral theology. This chapter offers a theological anthropology—a study of human life in light of the knowledge of God, grounded in the Scriptures. There are, of course, other versions of anthropology—philosophical, cultural, social, and physical. The disciplines of psychology and sociology, the medical sciences, and even linguistics are all aspects of anthropology. A theological anthropology must acknowledge the place of these, and guide Christians on how to interact with them. First of all, however, it must be a theological discipline, considering humanity in light of God's revelation and our relationship to him.

What anthropological issues face Pastor Steven in his "ordinary" day? He aims to support Margaret through the age-old experience of fear in dying, and Jack and Alice through new questions of sexuality and family life. He wants to challenge the influence of the world and see the congregation transformed in thought and deed. He wonders about how to present Christ to Reg. He leads conflicted elders who have to clarify their view of gender and church staff roles. Meanwhile, he is busy with his family and he should attend to his own well-being. This chapter focuses on such immediate pastoral questions, while wider cultural issues come into view in the background.[4]

---

4. The concept of *image of God* has been central to recent discussions of anthropology, and it has often been expected to provide the basic insights, or at least the organizational structure, for discussions. See Cornelis van der Kooi and Gijsbert van den Brink, *Christian Dogmatics: An Introduction* (Grand Rapids: Eerdmans, 2017), 260–66; Michael Horton, "Post-Reformation Reformed Anthropology," in *Personal Identity in Theological Perspective*, ed. Richard Lints, Michael S. Horton, and Mark R. Talbot (Grand Rapids: Eerdmans, 2006), 60–66. For the sake of this essay, I will simply consider humans as created, and then as fallen sinners.

Humans as Creatures

We are creatures: limited and dependent. Sleep is the most obvious reminder of our dependent finitude.[5] It is God's good gift (Pss. 3:5; 127:2) for physical, psychological, and emotional health. It should also be an act of trust in God (4:8) as we resign ourselves to his protection and oversight. As never before, we need to learn to live within creaturely limits, accepting our need for rest (Gen. 2:3; Ex. 20:9–11; Mark 2:27–28) and trusting and thanking God for his provision (Matt. 6:11, 25–34; Phil. 4:6; 1 Peter 5:7). Steven is running on the edge of his capacity; no doubt others around him are as well. Understanding his creatureliness might help him reflect on his own patterns and offer a model of wise living for his congregation.

Looking beyond himself, Steven must view all people as God's creatures and understand them in light of their relationship to God (the exercise of this chapter). One of the other foundational truths of anthropology is that all humans share a common humanity. In Australia, indigenous people were treated wickedly, but evangelical Christians insisted that Aboriginal and Torres Strait Islanders were "one blood" (Acts 17:26 KJV) with Europeans and deserved justice.[6] This same truth challenges racism in all cultures.[7] The New Testament church was multicultural (Rom. 10:12; 1 Cor. 12:13; Col. 3:11), a demonstration that Christ redeems people from "every nation, tribe, people and language" (Rev. 7:9). Our shared humanity also provides a basis for protection of the unborn and to ensure that ministries include people with disabilities.[8]

---

5. See John Baillie's famous address "The Theology of Sleep," in *Christian Devotion: Addresses by John Baillie* (London: Oxford University Press, 1962), chap. 11. See also David P. Murray, "A Theology of Sleep," *PRJ* 6, no. 2 (2014): 318–27; Adrian Reynolds, *And So to Bed . . . A Biblical View of Sleep* (Fearn, Scotland: Christian Focus, 2014).

6. See John Harris, *One Blood: 200 Years of Aboriginal Encounter with Christianity: A Story of Hope*, 2nd ed. (Sutherland, New South Wales, Australia: Albatross Books, 1994); for a summary: Meredith Lake, *The Bible in Australia: A Cultural History* (Kensington, Australia: UNSW Press, 2018), 90–104.

7. John Piper, *Bloodlines: Race, Cross, and the Christian* (Wheaton, IL: Crossway, 2011).

8. See George C. Hammond, *It Has Not Yet Appeared What We Shall Be: A*

Body and Soul

Humans are "body and soul." We are thoroughly physical with wonderful, beautiful bodies (1 Sam. 9:2; Ps. 139:13–14; Song 5:10–16).[9] The importance of bodies is underlined by the incarnation of the Son (John 1:14) and our final redemption in glorified bodies (Rom. 8:11, 23; 1 Cor. 15:35–54; Phil. 3:21). Yet we are more than physical. We have an inner life and can exist in a nonbodily "intermediate state" (Luke 23:42–43; 2 Cor. 5:6–8; Phil. 1:21–23; Rev. 6:10).[10] The body is spiritually relevant—the body is for the Lord, and the Lord for the body (1 Cor. 6:13). Steven is right to consider how to help his congregation avoid the Corinthian view that bodies and physical behavior are relatively unimportant. This can be reinforced by current ideology that views bodies as limitations to be transformed and transcended.[11]

Pastoral care attends to bodies. Rest, diet, and exercise are basic spiritual disciplines. Spiritual depression may have an organic basis and benefit from medical treatment. Architecture and aesthetics make a difference to how people listen to a sermon and experience worship.

We also risk the other extreme of materialism. Many people not only reject the idea of nonmaterial reality but can hardly imagine it. This remains an apologetic challenge. It also provides the frame of reference for much psychological and medical care. It is important in Christian pastoral care to critique assumptions that everything about a person can be explained in terms of the body, including the brain.[12]

Reconsideration of the Imago Dei in Light of Those with Severe Cognitive Disabilities (Phillipsburg, NJ: P&R Publishing, 2017).

9. See Gregg R. Allison, "Toward a Theology of Human Embodiment," *SBJT* 13, no. 2 (Summer 2009): 5–17; Rodney Clapp, *Tortured Wonders: Christian Spirituality for People, Not Angels* (Grand Rapids: Brazos, 2004).

10. Cornelis P. Venema, *The Promise of the Future* (Edinburgh: Banner of Truth, 2000), 35–75. In my view, the fact of the intermediate state settles the question whether it is possible to have a Christian "physicalism" in which the "soul" has no distinct existence from the body but is entirely a function (or an emergent property) of the body. See Terence Nichols, *Death and Afterlife: A Theological Introduction* (Grand Rapids: Brazos, 2010), 118–19.

11. See Brent Waters, "Man Reconstructed: Humanity beyond Biology," *Concordia Theological Quarterly* 77, no. 3 (2013): 271–85; Nancy R. Pearcey, *Love Thy Body: Answering Hard Questions about Life and Sexuality* (Grand Rapids: Baker, 2018).

12. See Michael R. Emlet, "What's in a Name? Understanding Psychiatric Diagnoses," *Journal of Biblical Counseling* 30, no. 1 (2016): 66–93.

Verbal

Humans are made by and for words. God's covenant relationship with us is determined by his words of promise and command. We receive and share wisdom by words (Prov. 1:2; 2:1; 4:4–5, 20). Good words bring blessing and life; evil words are deeply scarring and have great power for evil: "The words of the reckless pierce like swords, but the tongue of the wise brings healing" (Prov. 12:18). In a posttruth world of insulting polemics, Christian communication is to be honest and kind (Eph. 4:25, 29).

Words are the basic tool of pastoral ministry. Steven is called to teach God's Word (Acts 20:27) and is charged with guarding the deposit of apostolic doctrine (2 Tim. 1:14). He aims to listen attentively and seeks to speak wisdom that directs, encourages, and refreshes God's people. Pastoral conversations should be a form of gospel ministry, applying God's Word to the particulars of the life of God's people.

Communal

Our existence, identity, and prosperity are shared. We grow to maturity in a family (Gen. 24:66–67; Prov. 3:35–4:27). The foreigner, the fatherless, and the widow need protection because they lack the usual safety of family (Deut. 10:18; 24:17, 19–21; Pss. 94:6; 146:9). We do not simply rely on others for growth and physical protection—our identity and self-understanding arise from our relationships.

Jesus' kingdom is a new society or a renewed community in which people find a welcome and security. How different this is from the individualism of Western culture, reinforced by consumerism, social media, and the demise of voluntary organizations.[13] The result is that social isolation and loneliness are significant problems in modern society.[14]

---

13. For a theological examination of the various forms of individualism, see Jake Meador, *In Search of the Common Good: Christian Fidelity in a Fractured World* (Downers Grove, IL: InterVarsity Press, 2019), 29–46; David H. Kelsey, *Eccentric Existence: A Theological Anthropology* (Louisville: Westminster John Knox, 2009), 391–402.

14. Adrian Franklin, "A Lonely Society? Loneliness and Liquid Modernity in Australia," *Australian Journal of Social Issues* 47, no. 1 (2012): 11–28; Michelle Lim,

Steven will keep this in mind as he cares for Margaret. Loneliness is a common experience of dying, especially in modern society and medical systems. One of the great contributions of churches is to keep the dying in their fellowship, when "warm human support is their first and foremost need."[15] He will also consider how the church supports Jack and Alice and their stressed family system. Maintaining healthy relationships among the elders is more important than selecting the best youth coordinator, though the former should aid the latter.

Rational

We self-consciously understand our environment and respond appropriately to it.[16] To be rational is to be accountable, to have reasons for what we understand and do, and to be responsible for and able to test those reasons. Reasoning is not strictly separable from other human activities such as trusting and feeling, though it is distinguishable from them.[17] The rational capacity of humans is apparent in the Bible from the place that it gives to wisdom and understanding (Ex. 36:1; 1 Chron. 22:15; Prov. 14:8; Eccl. 12:1), as well as argument and reason (Acts 17:2, 17; 18:4, 19).

Recognition of our rationality is the basis for Christian commitment to education. We promote the development of the human ability to investigate and understand the world. Steven has the task to help people understand God from his Word and to understand their lives in light of that. As he talks with Reg, he is not simply an empathetic listener. He wants to reason with him (Acts 17:2; 18:4, 19; 24:25)—whatever the school of apologetics to which he subscribes.

Australian Loneliness Report (Melbourne: Australian Psychological Society, 2018), accessed August 25, 2019, https://apo.org.au/node/202286.

15. Kathryn A. Holewa and John P. Higgins, "Palliative Care—The Empowering Alternative: A Roman Catholic Perspective," *Trinity Journal* 24, no. 2 (2003): 213–14.

16. See Olli-Pekka Vainio, "*Imago Dei* and Human Rationality," *Zygon* 49, no. 1 (March 2014): 121–34.

17. Alan G. Padgett, "Faith Seeking Understanding: Collegiality and Difference in Theology and Philosophy," in *Faith and Reason: Three Views*, ed. Steve Wilkens (Downers Grove, IL: InterVarsity Press, 2014), 89–91.

Passionate and Affective

We not only *think*, but also *feel*. The Bible reflects the range of our feelings: lament (Ps. 137), exultation (Ps. 47), despair (Ps. 88), longing (Ps. 24), bitterness (Ps. 73), and contentment (Ps. 23). Jesus felt compassion (Matt. 9:36), love (John 13:1), indignation (Matt. 12:6), joy and gladness (Luke 10:21), anguish and fear (Matt. 26:37; Mark 14:33; Luke 12:50).[18] In modern thought, we often refer to feelings as *emotions*—noncognitive, involuntary, and bodily. The older view—which is closer to Scripture—is that we have *passions* and *affections* that are open to direction by our understanding and reflection. The passions are unruly and uncontrolled, closely tied to bodily appetites; affections are "directed towards goodness, truth and, ultimately God."[19] Love, for instance, can be a passion (when we love the wrong thing) and an affection (when we love God).

The passions and affections spring from the "heart" (Hebrew *leb*; Greek *kardia*), which is the center of human existence (e.g., 1 Kings 3:9, 12; 2 Chron. 29:31; Prov. 14:30, 33; Matt. 6:21; Luke 2:19; 10:27; Rom. 1:21; 1 Cor. 14:25). The "heart," much the same as the "mind" about which Steven was reading, is the seat of volition, moral responsibility, passion, affection, and cognition, the full inner reality of a person. The heart, directed by passions and affections, determines so much of how we act. We are to love God with all the heart, soul, and mind (Matt. 22:37). Jesus says that "the mouth speaks what the heart is full of" (Luke 6:45) and that sin comes "from the heart" (Matt. 15:18).

Christian thinkers have often recognized how people are directed by their passions and affections. Famously, Blaise Pascal wrote, "The heart has its reasons of which reason knows nothing."[20] He considered that we perceive God by the heart and not by reason.[21] He (the great

18. David J. Atkinson, "Emotions," in *New Dictionary of Christian Ethics & Pastoral Theology*, ed. David J. Atkinson et al. (Downers Grove, IL: InterVarsity Press, 1995), 341–43. See Phillip Michael Lasater, "'The Emotions' in Biblical Anthropology? A Genealogy and Case Study with יִרְאָה," *Harvard Theological Review* 110, no. 4 (2017): 520–40, who argues that the biblical concepts are far closer to the classical passions/affections.

19. Thomas Dixon, *From Passions to Emotions: The Creation of a Secular Psychological Category* (Cambridge: Cambridge University Press, 2003), 29.

20. Blaise Pascal, *Pensées*, trans. A. J. Krailsheimer (London: Penguin, 1966), no. 423.

21. For Pascal, the heart is the human faculty that knows things immediately

polymath) does not dismiss reason, but his famous quote reminds us that desires, fears, memories, and love have a powerful influence.

Most pastors are aware of this power. They recognize that passionate reactions are a telling guide to our deepest commitments and deserve attention. They know that preaching must engage the mind but also the heart and must aim to direct the affections.[22] In preparing and leading worship, the pastor needs to help pair head and heart. Because passions are powerful, we are open to being misled and manipulated through them. The wise pastor guards against this risk.

Sexed and Gendered

Sex and gender are contested aspects of human life in current society. The Bible's view is that we have sexed bodies, designed for sexual relationships and reproduction, created "male and female" (Gen. 1:27).[23] Our gender, or our sexual identity, is already given to us by God. We don't achieve anything by desperately trying to redefine ourselves.[24]

Jack and Alice face questions about sexual ethics and the implications for their family. No doubt somewhere Steven will also need to help people think about relating to someone who identifies as transgender. More regularly, he will have to help his congregation think about what it means to be a man or a woman in a culture that is utterly confused about sex and gender. All of this needs to be guided by a well-formed biblical anthropology.

In marriage, God has given an order of loving headship and submission within that relationship (Eph. 5:21–25). This pattern in marriage is parallel with appointment of the suitably qualified men as church elders responsible for teaching and ruling (1 Cor. 14:29–35;

---

and intuitively. See Klaas Bom, "Heart and Reason: Using Pascal to Clarify Smith's Ambiguity," *Pneuma* 34, no. 3 (2012): 345–64.

22. Murray Capill, *The Heart Is the Target: Preaching Practical Application from Every Text* (Phillipsburg, NJ: P&R Publishing, 2014).

23. See Christopher Chenault Roberts, *Creation and Covenant: The Significance of Sexual Difference in the Moral Theology of Marriage* (New York: T. & T. Clark, 2007); Jonathan Cahana, "Dismantling Gender: Between Ancient Gnostic Ritual and Modern Queer BDSM," *Theology & Sexuality* 18, no. 1 (2012): 60–75.

24. Andrew T. Walker, *God and the Transgender Debate: What Does the Bible Actually Say about Gender Identity?* (Centralia, WA: Good Book Company, 2017).

1 Tim. 2:11–3:7; Titus 1:6–9).[25] Steven needs to address these aspects of relationships carefully and patiently, since Western culture increasingly finds them repressive and even incredible.

In response to the culture, some evangelicals risk making too much of male-female differences.[26] Men and women are both humans! Adam's first reaction to Eve was that "this is now bone of my bones and flesh of my flesh" (Gen. 2:23). One of the important things that the Bible says about gender is that men and women are meant for partnership. God makes Eve to be for Adam a "helper as his partner" (v. 18 NRSV). Paul, in the midst of instructions on how men and women should conduct themselves differently, reminds us that "in the Lord woman is not independent of man, nor is man independent of woman" (1 Cor. 11:11).

Thus, Steven will help the congregation understand that men and women are different from each other, called to different roles in family and church life, and need to work together well. That will have implications for the selection of the new youth coordinator—though we do not yet know what they will be.

Communion and Conformity in Covenant

This list of human features is nowhere near exhaustive but is at least a reminder of the complex wonder in God's design for humanity. Important as they are, they do not form the core of human existence.

Fundamentally, we are made to know the triune God. The Westminster Shorter Catechism famously inscribes this: "Man's chief end is to glorify God and enjoy him forever" (WSC 1). To speak of a "chief end" is to indicate the purpose and goal of existence. Humans particularly glorify God by "enjoying" him in communion and conformity to him in a covenant relationship (Heb. 1:14; 1 Peter 1:12).[27]

---

25. Claire Smith, *God's Good Design: What the Bible Really Says about Men and Women* (Kingsford, Australia: Matthias, 2012).

26. John McClean, "'Do Not Conform': Thinking about Complementarianism as Contextualisation," in *The Gender Conversation*, ed. Edwina Murphy and David Starling (Macquarie Park, Australia: Morling Press/Eugene, OR: Wipf & Stock, 2016), 173–85.

27. See chapter 7 on covenant theology for further discussion of this important framework for anthropology; see also Horton, "Post-Reformation Reformed Anthropology," 46–60.

We properly understand humanity only in this light. Each of the features of humanity noted above is designed to be engaged in worship, love, and obedience to God, serving him in his world. They function in harmony with each other only in conformity to him.

Sin—A Theological Reality

Though made for communion with God, humans have turned away from him, breaking the covenant. We become idolaters, worshiping other things and ourselves (Rom. 1:21–23). According to Brian Rosner, idolatry "plays a central role in the Bible's overarching narrative." Idolatry can be the explicit worship of false gods, or the attempt to worship God through images, which misrepresent him and claim to control him. Yet it goes beyond explicitly religious activity, because all human activity has a religious dimension. Whenever something takes God's place of "ultimate value," we confuse "creation with the Creator" and are guilty of idolatry.[28] As worshiping creatures, we always have something to which we devote ourselves, be it possessions, sexual pleasure, an ethnic group, or political power.[29]

Sin also consists in refusing to love God and loving other things instead.[30] Jesus told his opponents that they refused to recognize him because they did not love God (John 5:42).[31] Paul frames an analysis of sin in terms of love: humans are "lovers of themselves" (*philautos*) and "lovers of money" (*philarguros*), "not lovers of the good" (*aphilagathos*), "lovers of pleasure" (*philedonos*) rather than "lovers of God" (*philotheos*) (2 Tim. 3:2–4). John warns his readers not to love "the world or anything in the world" (1 John 2:15).[32]

---

28. Brian S. Rosner, *Known by God* (Grand Rapids: Zondervan, 2017), 61.

29. For an analysis of sin as idolatry, see G. K. Beale, *We Become What We Worship: A Biblical Theology of Idolatry* (Downers Grove, IL: IVP Academic, 2008).

30. See James K. A. Smith, *You Are What You Love: The Spiritual Power of Habit* (Grand Rapids: Brazos, 2016).

31. D. A. Carson, *The Gospel according to John*, Pillar New Testament Commentary (Leicester, UK: Inter-Varsity Press/Grand Rapids: Eerdmans, 1991), 264.

32. John's vocabulary of love clearly includes a benevolent sense, since believers are to love brothers and sisters (1 John 2:10; 3:16–18) in practical service. Yet John also speaks of loving God (4:20–21), and this is not a matter of seeking God's well-being and includes an element of desiring God as well as serving him with

Sin is also disobedience. In Romans 5, Adam's sin (*hamartano*) is described as both "trespass" (*paraptoma*, Rom. 5:18) and "disobedience" (*parakoe*, v. 19). From his act, sin entered the world (v. 12), so it was followed by "many trespasses" (v. 16). To sin is to act against God in disobedience to a command. So Scripture often catalogues sin against God's commands (Ps. 10:1-11; Rom. 1:28-31; Gal. 5:19-21).

To understand humans as creatures who fail to worship, love, and obey God is to analyze them theologically. It is not enough to work in existential, psychological, social, or even moral terms. Sin has enormous ramifications in all those aspects of life, but it must be understood in strictly theological terms as the root of human ruin.

Sin, however, is more than our acts. It is also a power that can be personified (Gen. 4:7; Rom. 7:9). It rules us and enslaves us (Ps. 119:133; John 8:34).[33] We may boast in sin, imagining that we demonstrate our freedom in the fantasy that we belong only to ourselves and are able to determine our own rules. That thought is part of the deception of sin. We may *feel* that we choose our own path, but in fact we are enslaved to sin and unable to free ourselves from it. The Westminster Confession of Faith says that humanity has "wholly lost all ability of will to any spiritual good accompanying salvation" and is "altogether averse from that good, and dead in sin" (WCF 9.3). Sin, then, is also a "state." Michael Horton reminds us that the "state" precedes the actions. He affirms: "Sin is, first of all, a *condition* that is simultaneously judicial and moral, legal and relational. . . . We sin because we are sinners rather than vice versa. Standing before God as transgressors in Adam, we exhibit our guilt and corruption in actual thoughts and actions."[34]

Horton's comment highlights why a Christian doctrine of sin must include *original sin*. Apart from the historical fact of Adam's original sin, we are unable to clarify that humanity is created good, radically fallen, and redeemed in Christ. Henri Blocher rightly asks,

---

devotion and fear. See Colin G. Kruse, *The Letters of John* (Leicester, UK: Apollos/ Grand Rapids: Eerdmans, 2000), 94.

33. For fuller analysis of these dimensions of sin, see van der Kooi and van den Brink, *Christian Dogmatics*, 305–9 (emphasis original).

34. Michael Horton, *The Christian Faith: A Systematic Theology for Pilgrims on the Way* (Grand Rapids: Zondervan, 2011), 427.

"If evil is 'invincible' as a dimension of being, . . . should we not conclude that it will never be defeated and 'cast out'?" He insists that "only historical evil, sin, the foe of both God and humankind, and true hope . . . go together. Only if the problem is historical will the solution happen."[35]

As in all other areas of theology, there is a mystery about sin. That may seem surprising, since it is sometimes claimed that the doctrine of sin is the one empirically verifiable Christian doctrine. In fact, the genuine Christian doctrine of sin is not so verifiable. Certainly, we can catalogue human malice, folly, and error, and perhaps even demonstrate that no one is free from these. Yet the full depth of human sin is apparent only against the holiness of God. When humans are assessed against human standards, then "sin" hardly appears to be sinful. The fullest insight we can gain into the depth of sin is from the vantage point of redemption. The magnitude of the work of Christ in the accomplishment of redemption and the depth of the work of the Spirit in its application together bring to light the depth of human sin.

In a culture that rejects a theological perspective, Steven has to keep reminding himself and his people of the reality and tragedy of sin. It is all too easy to settle for nontheological perspectives, and it is socially and even personally discomforting to view people as sinners. Human life is tragic. We have been brought down from the heights by our own flaws. Each of us is both a victim and also a perpetrator, to be treated with compassion and caution!

The simple point about the reality and depth of sin must not obscure the complexity of the human predicament. Since every feature of human existence is distorted by sin, life becomes entangled in deliberate evils, thoughtless malice, and ignorant folly, which ramify in guilt, regret, resentment, conflict, deceit, disillusion, and injustice. Everyone and each community carry layers of sin and its effects, which cannot be simply undone. Reg's family situation illustrates this, and no doubt it is true for Jack, Alice, and their daughter. Steven must remember this reality as he leads the elders. Each of them has a complex, sin-stained history that will impact his contribution to decisions.

---

35. Henri Blocher, *Original Sin: Illuminating the Riddle* (Leicester, UK: Apollos, 1997), 62.

The Consequences of Sin

The most tragic result of sin is lost communion with God. Eden was a garden-temple where Adam and Eve could enjoy God's presence; the tragic loss is marked by expulsion from Eden. The "curses"—disorder of the environment, pain in childbirth, tensions in marriage, difficulty in work, and even death itself—announce the consequences that flow from this deepest and most terrible result of sin (Gen. 3:14–19). Paul describes pagans as being "without hope and without God in the world" and "darkened in their understanding and separated from the life of God" (Eph. 2:12; 4:18). The inevitable consequence of sin is that we are not able to enjoy the One for whom we were made.

A further consequence of sin is that humans are under God's condemnation. The forensic language of Scripture is indispensable: God is Lawgiver and Judge (Gen. 18:25; Ps. 94:2; Heb. 12:24; James 4:12; 1 Peter 4:5). In his holy love, he responds to human sin with condemnation and righteous wrath (1 Sam. 26:21; Ps. 37:38; Prov. 11:21; Isa. 13:11; Amos 3:14; Zeph. 1:12; Rom. 2:12; 1 Thess. 4:6; Heb. 9:27; Rev. 20:10–15). Here, the discussion of anthropology could transfer to that of theology proper to consider wrath as an expression of God's holy love.[36] Keeping the focus on a biblical account of humanity in relation to God, we can say that humans have become God's enemies, guilty, condemned, and facing punishment and death (Ex. 23:7; Rom. 1:32; 5:12; 6:21, 23).

Steven's gospel ministry offers God's answer to the greatest human need. Only in Christ is death overcome. Only in Christ are condemned sinners acquitted and estranged enemies brought home. Bruce Springsteen's insight "Everybody's got a hungry heart" echoes Augustine's aphorism: "you have made us for yourself, and our hearts are restless till we find our rest in you." Augustine, of course, named the cause and not just the symptom. Margaret, Jack and Alice and their daughter, along with Reg, Angela, and the church elders, and Steven himself, need to be brought home to God in Christ—either reassurance that they are home or the news that will bring them there.

36. See Tony Lane, "The Wrath of God as an Aspect of the Love of God," in *Nothing Greater, Nothing Better: Theological Essays on the Love of God*, ed. Kevin J. Vanhoozer (Grand Rapids: Eerdmans, 2001), 138–67; Horton, *Christian Faith*, 270–72.

Sin leaves no part of the human person untouched. This point is emphasized by the claim that sin has to do with our heart (Ps. 51:2–10; Jer. 17:9; Ezek. 11:19; Matt. 12:33–35). The very center of our being is gripped and enslaved. Paul teaches that those in the state of sin— "governed by the flesh"—not only are hostile to God and refuse to submit to God's law, but cannot submit to or please him (Rom. 8:7–8) and are unable to accept the things of the Spirit (1 Cor. 2:14). Reformed theology has described the extent of sin as *total depravity*. John Calvin, with typical flair, describes the human state: "the whole man is overwhelmed—as by a deluge—from head to foot, so that no part is immune from sin and all that proceeds from him is to be imputed to sin."[37] *Total depravity* does not mean that humanity is as evil as it could be, but it does mean that no part of the human is unaffected by sin and that we are unable to extract ourselves from sin or choose to do good.

Sin destroys us internally. As we fail to love, worship, and obey God, we lose our identity—we lose self-knowledge (Jer. 17:9) and, ironically, we lose self-control (Gal. 5:17, 23). Sin also destroys humanity communally, wreaking damage in our relationships. The first evidence of the effects of sin was that Adam and Eve sought to cover themselves from each other (Gen. 3:7). Soon they turned to mutual recrimination (vv. 12–13); in the next generation, Cain murdered Abel (4:8). In our corrupted relationships, "this world" leads us away from God (Eph. 2:2).

The final consequence of sin is eternal death and destruction as God's judgment (Gen. 2:17; Ps. 90:7–10; Rom. 5:12; 6:23; 1 Cor. 15:21). Spiritual death holds unregenerate sinners and brings physical death (Eph. 2:1–2; Rom. 8:6). Eternal death (or the second death, Rev. 20:6; 21:8) is the finalization of the state of spiritual death. This is the full and final expression of God's anger against sin. Believers participate in spiritual life, even though they die physically (John 11:25), and do not face the second death.

Christians continue to struggle with sin and need to fight temptation, so this account of sin is highly relevant to Christian life and ministry. Steven needs to be aware of the ongoing power of sin in his

37. John Calvin, *Institutes of the Christian Religion*, ed. John T. McNeill, trans. Ford Lewis Battles, 2 vols., Library of Christian Classics 20–21 (Philadelphia: Westminster, 1960), 2.1.9.

own life. Has ministry "success" become his idol? Biblical insight into sin will help him recognize how easily he can be deceived about his own motivations and underline the need to guard his heart (Prov. 4:23). Steven will be aware of sin as a source of conflict among the elders. The two sides are likely to be committed to goals that they have not fully acknowledged. Spiritual leadership will involve helping them address these, not simply searching for a political compromise (or a win).

Steven's view of sin reminds him that Reg's objection to his hypo-critical brother, while very understandable, is unlikely to be the whole story behind his loss of faith. Idols of his heart keep him from recon-sidering Christ. Steven will think and pray about how to help Reg see that. No one is able to see his own desperate situation, nor can he will or work himself free from sin. Real insight and freedom require the work of the Holy Spirit through the gospel.

Everyone, believer and unbeliever, lives under the sentence of physical death (Gen. 3:19; Heb. 9:27). Christ has defeated death, and believers may face it with confidence as a defeated enemy, but face it they must. How tragic if Margaret is coming to terms with that only in her last days. In a culture that avoids thinking about death, a key task of pastoral ministry it to prepare people for it.[38]

The Wider Context of Sin

The tragedy of human sin has a shadowy backdrop of sinful evil powers. There is a "dominion of darkness" (Col. 1:13; see also Matt. 12:26) headed by Satan (Eph. 2:2), with lesser powers also in play (1 Cor. 15:24; Jude 6).[39] Though temptation never excuses our actions, Satan plays a part in instigating sin (Gen. 3:1, 4; John 8:44; 2 Cor. 11:3;

38. For a classic treatment, see Jeremy Taylor, *Holy Living and Holy Dying*, vol. 2, *Holy Dying*, ed. P. G. Stanwood (1651; repr., Oxford: Oxford University Press, 1981); recently Bill Davis, *Departing in Peace: Biblical Decision-Making at the End of Life* (Phillipsburg, NJ: P&R Publishing, 2017).

39. For a review of the New Testament material dealing with Satan, see Thomas J. Farrar and Guy J. Williams, "Diabolical Data: A Critical Inventory of New Testament Satanology," *JSNT* 39, no. 1 (2016): 40–71; and their analysis in "Talk of the Devil: Unpacking the Language of New Testament Satanology," *JSNT* 39, no. 1 (2016): 72–96.

1 John 3:8; Rev. 12:9; 20:2, 10). He and his demons have real power to deceive and to hold sinners captive (2 Cor. 4:4; Gal. 4:8). They hold some lives in deep bondage (1 Sam. 18:10–11; Matt. 12:22; Mark 5:4; Acts 19:16). Modern scholarship has tended to "demythologize" the powers and principalities (especially in Paul's letters), and even the church has ignored this theme of human life. Christ has defeated the powers, so Christians should not live in fear of them (Luke 10:18; Rom. 8:38; Col. 2:15). At the same time, we must not be naive about our real spiritual enemies (Eph. 6:12; 1 Peter 5:8).[40]

Finally, it is important to underline that God restrains the full effects of sin (Gen. 3:22–23; 4:15; 20:6). This is often called the *doctrine of common grace*. In this age, God limits his judgment on sin (Gen. 6:3; Rom. 2:4; 2 Peter 3:9) and promotes the good of the world both in the nonhuman world and in human society (Rom. 13:3–4; 1 Tim. 2:1–2; 1 Peter 2:14). John Murray describes common grace with rich insight:

> He . . . causes nature to teem with the gifts of His goodness. . . .
> He . . . endows men with gifts, talents, and aptitudes; He stimulates
> them with interest and purpose to the practice of virtues, the pur-
> suance of worthy tasks, and the cultivation of arts and sciences that
> occupy the time, activity and energy of men and that make for the
> benefit and civilization of the human race. He ordains institutions
> for the protection and promotion of right, the preservation of lib-
> erty, the advance of knowledge and the improvement of physical
> and moral conditions. . . . Occupying the energy, activity and time
> of men they prevent the indulgence of less noble and ignoble pur-
> suits and they exercise an ameliorating, moralizing, stabilizing and
> civilizing influence upon the social organism.[41]

Reflection on the depth and complexity of sin is bleak. This is accentuated when Steven realizes that his church and family are involved in a cosmic contest between God's redemption in Christ and the powers of sin, the world, and the devil. Yet he can rest in two great truths.

40. See Sharon Beekmann and Peter Bolt, *Silencing Satan: Handbook of Biblical Demonology* (Eugene, OR: Wipf & Stock, 2012).
41. John Murray, "Common Grace," *WTJ* 5, no. 1 (1942): 12.

First, God in his sovereign patience restrains sin and delays judgment, allowing the creation to still display his glory and goodness. There is much good in the world, and Steven can rely on God to faithfully sustain that. Second and more importantly, Christ has come as Redeemer of his people and his world. He has conquered sin, death, and Satan. That has not been a major theme of this chapter because it is treated in other chapters, yet a Christian account of humanity is incomplete apart from redemption. There have been points at which we have considered humanity in the state of grace. Later chapters explore in detail the work of grace as well as the final state of glory.

Both common grace and special grace enable believers, such as Steven and the members of his church, to face the full reality of sin with confidence and even joy. The goodness of life as a creature underlines the tragedy of sin; Christ's victory enables us to live with hope in the midst of the tragedy.

Who Am I?

Personal identity is one of the great questions of contemporary life and can summarize much of this chapter and many of the themes of Steven's ministry.[42] Our identity as creatures rests in being made for God and being known by him. Our culture, however, suppresses the real source of the self and has removed many of the traditional sources of secure identity. We are left to define ourselves and inevitably feel lost and insecure. The various means we use to establish an identity—family, occupation, achievement, reputation, race, nationality, gender, sexuality, abilities, possessions, power, personality—become idolatrous searches for self that never satisfy. Like all other idols, they fail to deliver what they promise. Understood as features of human life created by God and provided for our care, they are aspects of our identity; expected to carry the entire load, they collapse under the weight.

In Christ, we are restored to communion with God in conformity to him, loved and chosen by him, made his heirs, and included

---

42. The following paragraphs draw on Rosner, *Known by God*. See John McClean, Review of *Known by God: A Biblical Theology of Personal Identity*, by Brian Rosner, *Themelios* 43, no. 3 (December 2018): 516–20.

in his family. In him, we are able to live confidently and humbly as ourselves. Steven's own spiritual walk and leadership depend on continuing to grow in knowledge of his God, and himself as a son of God. Much of his ministry involves helping believers to grasp that same security in Christ and to live consistently with confidence in him in the face of death, regret, busyness, conflict, and all the other realities of living as redeemed sinners in a still-fallen world. As an evangelist, he offers reconciliation and security with God. Theological anthropology frames his entire ministry and helps him discern practical wisdom for the task. It also reminds him that leading people to grow in communion with God in conformity to Christ is the great act of true humanism.

Key Term

theological anthropology

Recommendations for Further Reading

Bavinck, Herman. *Reformed Dogmatics*. Edited by John Bolt. Translated by John Vriend. Vol. 3, *Sin and Salvation in Christ*. Grand Rapids: Baker Academic, 2006.

Cortez, Marc. *ReSourcing Theological Anthropology: A Constructive Account of Humanity in the Light of Christ*. Grand Rapids: Zondervan, 2017.

Ferguson, Sinclair B. *John Owen on the Christian Life*. Edinburgh: Banner of Truth, 1987.

Gurnall, William. *The Christian in Complete Armour*. Reprint, Edinburgh: Banner of Truth, 1964.

Lloyd-Jones, D. Martyn. *Spiritual Depression: Its Causes and Cures*. London: Pickering & Inglis, 1965.

Discussion Questions

1. How may pastors attend to the ongoing power of sin in their own lives?
2. How might Steven best pastor Reg regarding his loss of faith?

3. In what ways does Scripture affect our understanding of emotion?

4. What lessons have you learned from this chapter on sin?

5. What truths allow Christians to rest despite the depth and complexity of sin?

7

COVENANT

The Structure of Reformed Theology and Environment of Reformed Piety[1]

DAVID B. McWILLIAMS

Reformed theology is covenant theology; hence, Reformed piety is covenantal piety. Consequently, the contours of covenant theology impact at every point the Reformed minister and believer in the pursuit of holiness and growth in grace. Even a cursory reading of the Westminster Confession of Faith demonstrates its pervasive, architectonic framework as an indispensable, biblical, revelatory category determining the most intimate facets of our communion with God. What is covenant theology, and how does it shape the work of pastors? The magnitude of the question calls for a sixfold answer and a fivefold reflection.

Covenant Theology Is Biblical Theology

Covenant is a pervasive theme undergirding the Bible's unity. As the biblical interpreter is engrossed in his historical and linguistic

1. Sinclair Ferguson has been mentor and friend for over four decades. My life has been enriched beyond measure by his kindness, counsel, and prayers. Sinclair, "I thank my God upon every remembrance of you" (Phil. 1:3 KJV).

task, his preoccupation with the method, mode, and epochs of revelation will deepen his appreciation of the unity that pervades the historical unfolding of God's redemptive plan. This unity is that of God's covenant of grace. The diversity of administrations does not disrupt the unified, redemptive theme of the covenant of grace (Rom. 5:12–21; 2 Cor. 3:6–11; Gal. 3:15–22).

A basic understanding of the covenant theme is essential to appreciating the redemptive-historical, Christocentric purpose of Scripture. The point here is not simply to note the frequency with which the Bible uses the term *berith* or *diathēkē* but to recognize the pervasive thoroughness with which the *concept* of the covenant is found, even when the lexical stock may be absent. The covenant of grace is the very transcript of God's relationship with man. The Bible is a covenant book, and God's purpose for his creation is covenantal (Rev. 21:3). Indeed, God is a covenant God.

Covenant Theology Is Trinitarian Theology

By way of covenant, God deigns to enter into a relationship with man. Given God's transcendent character, this is truly remarkable. Astonishingly, God also condescends to have a relationship with repentant sinners: "For thus says the One who is high and lifted up, who inhabits eternity, whose name is Holy: 'I dwell in the high and holy place, and also with him who is of a contrite and lowly spirit, to revive the spirit of the lowly, and to revive the heart of the contrite" (Isa. 57:15). Indeed, because of the Creator-creature distinction, it is a wonder that God relates to man, and all the more after his fall into sin. The Westminster Confession of Faith expresses the relationship of transcendence and covenant in this classic formulation:

> The distance between God and the creature is so great, that although reasonable creatures do owe obedience unto Him as their Creator, yet they could never have any fruition of Him as their blessedness and reward, but by some voluntary condescension on God's part, which He hath been pleased to express by way of a covenant. (WCF 7.1)

God's condescension to fellowship with man is of the essence of covenant. As mentioned, however, this is even more astounding because of man's rebellion in our first parent, Adam.

Man in the first covenant possessed the ability to fulfill its legal terms but also possessed the power to transgress. "Our first parents, being seduced by the subtlety and temptation of Satan, sinned in eating the forbidden fruit" (WCF 6.1). With the tragic loss of original righteousness and communion with God, our first parents became "dead in sin, and wholly defiled in all the parts and faculties of soul and body" (6.2). Therefore, our first parents' "being the root of all mankind, the guilt of this sin is imputed; and the same death in sin, and corrupted nature, conveyed to all their posterity descending from them by ordinary generation" (6.3). Man cannot now initiate communion with God, not only because of the Creator-creature distinction, but also because of the awful sin separating us from the holy God. Because man was now "incapable of life" by terms of the first covenant,

> the Lord was pleased to make a second, commonly called the covenant of grace; wherein, He freely offereth unto sinners life and salvation by Jesus Christ; requiring of them faith in Him, that they may be saved, and promising to give unto all those that are ordained unto eternal life His Holy Spirit, to make them willing, and able to believe. (WCF 7.3)

This carefully worded confessional language speaks of the covenant in terms of redemptive history. Man failed in the covenant of works; God was pleased to make a second covenant, the covenant of grace.

We totally misunderstand the Bible and the confession, however, if we fail to grasp that this redemptive covenant was God's eternal plan formulated for those "ordained unto eternal life" (WCF 7.3). The covenant of grace requires contemplating the historical outworking of God's redemptive plan in light of God's eternal, decretive purpose. The covenant of grace was made with Christ and the elect in him in eternity past. The Shorter Catechism says plainly in answer to question 20, "Did God leave all mankind to perish in the estate of sin and misery?," that

> God, having out of his mere good pleasure, from all eternity, elected some to everlasting life, did enter into a covenant of grace, to deliver them out of the estate of sin and misery, and to bring them into an estate of salvation by a Redeemer.

The Larger Catechism summarizes biblical teaching on this theme by identifying the members of the covenant of grace as Christ and God's elect in union with him: "The covenant of grace was made with Christ as the second Adam, and in him with all the elect as his seed" (WLC 31). Though the covenant unfolds in history, in epochs, God's eternal purpose in Christ antedates the covenant's historical unfolding. Covenant and election are distinguishable, but coordinate and inseparable.

The Scriptures teach that the Son received a commission from the Father to shed his blood to redeem God's elect. In the first chapter of Ephesians, God reveals that his *motive* in election is love, that the *cause* is his own will, that the *purpose* is his own glory, and that the *central feature* of his decree is Christ. Not one part of the Father's glorious purpose has been decreed apart from Christ as the *central feature* of his decree. "The incarnation of Christ, and his mediation thereon," John Owen reminds us, "were not the procuring *cause* of these eternal counsels of God, but the *effects* of them, as the Scriptures constantly declare." "But," Owen continues, "the design of their accomplishment was laid in the person of the Son alone."[2] The end of God's decree is "to unite all things in him, things in heaven and things on earth" (Eph. 1:10). "His person, therefore," observes Owen,

> is the foundation of the church—the great mystery of godliness, or the religion we profess—the entire life and soul of all spiritual truth—in that all the counsels of wisdom, grace and goodness of God, for redemption, vocation, sanctification, and salvation of the church, were all laid in him, and by him were all to be accomplished.[3]

2. John Owen, "Christologia: Or, A Declaration of the Glorious Mystery of the Person of Christ—God and Man," in *The Works of John Owen*, vol. 1, *The Person of Christ* (Edinburgh: Banner of Truth, 1972), 62.
3. Owen, 64. The Reformed, following the Synod of Dort, have not ascribed

Precisely how to speak of the eternal plan of God to redeem sinners, and bring to fruition new creation, has been much debated in the history of Reformed thought. A detailed discussion of this would involve a perceptive and incisive understanding of the covenant of redemption. The great takeaway for us at this point, however, is that the eternal covenant of grace is necessarily Trinitarian and that the eternal covenant of grace is therefore not to be conceived as a bargain or a contract.

The relationship between the members of the Trinity is one of infinite love, companionship, fellowship, and friendship. The one God in three persons is eternally sharing communion, needing nothing and no one outside the triune Being. The covenant of grace made with God's people reflects the mutual companionship between the members of the Trinity. Though personally distinct, the members of the Trinity are one in being and share (perichoresis) one another's life and bliss: "The Father is wholly in the Son, and the Son wholly in the Father, even as he himself declares: 'I am in the Father, and the Father in me.'"[4] The covenant made with elect sinners is determined by God's purpose to establish fellowship with them after the pattern of that eternal fellowship within the Trinity.

Notice, for example, some of the petitions of Jesus' prayer to God before going to the cross, his High Priestly Prayer: "And this is eternal life, that they know you, the only true God, and Jesus Christ whom you have sent" (John 17:3). "Holy Father, keep them in your name, which you have given me, that they may be one, even as we are one" (v. 11). "But now I am coming to you, and these things I speak in the world, that they may have my joy fulfilled in themselves" (v. 13). "The glory that you have given me I have given to them, that they may be one even as we are one, I in them and you in me, that they may become perfectly one, so that the world may know that you sent me

---

to Christ *fundamentum electionis* ("foundation of election") but have ascribed to Christ the expression *fundamentum salutis* ("foundation of salvation"). In other words, the work of Christ did not lead God to elect sinners to be saved, but electing love springs from the Father's heart and those chosen are saved by the Son.

4. John Calvin, *Institutes of the Christian Religion*, ed. John T. McNeill, trans. Ford Lewis Battles, 2 vols., Library of Christian Classics 20–21 (Philadelphia: Westminster, 1960), 1.13.19.

and loved them even as you loved me" (vv. 22–23). "I made known to them your name, and I will continue to make it known, that the love with which you have loved me may be in them, and I in them" (v. 26). Clearly, the relationship that God establishes with his elect for whom Jesus was about to shed his precious blood was founded in and reflective of the communion that the Son had with the Father before the world ever was. Indeed, the Son came to reveal the Father (1:18). The Son reveals the Father to his elect (Matt. 11:27); from Jesus we have the knowledge of God (1 John 5:20), the "eternal life, which was with the Father and was made manifest to us" (1:2). Our fellowship is with the Father and with his Son (v. 3).

This language, easily multiplied, takes us back into the internal relations between the members of the Trinity and grounds our fellowship in eternal perichoresis. This eternal relationship was fellowship, not a bargain, and friendship, not a contract. Therefore, we draw this almost unimaginable and overwhelmingly beautiful conclusion: the covenant that God makes with us has its eternal origin in the infinitely blissful fellowship shared by the members of the Trinity one with another. In the covenant of grace, God sovereignly and infinitely condescends to make with us not a pact, not a contract, not a bargain, but a permanent bond of love and friendship in Christ reflective of eternal, Trinitarian beatitude. This explains those many places in Scripture that describe the covenant as fellowship (Gen. 5:22; 6:9), friendship (James 2:23), marriage (Mal. 2:10–16), and fatherly condescension (2 Cor. 6:16–18). This is why the covenant formula finds its ultimate fulfillment in the new heaven and new earth: "Behold, the dwelling place of God is with man. He will dwell with them, and they will be his people, and God himself will be with them as their God" (Rev. 21:3).

In sum, God's covenant of grace with his people is possible because God is a covenant God; therefore, the covenant of grace that God makes with his people springs from the Father's infinite love for Christ and those chosen in him. The covenant of grace is, be it noted with a sense of deep worship, a covenant of friendship, fellowship, love, and joy made with his people.[5]

5. One of the most felicitous and positive insights of Herman Hoeksema relates to this theme. See, for example, Herman Hoeksema, *Reformed Dogmatics* (Grand Rapids: Reformed Free Publishing, 1966): "God is in Himself a covenant God . . .

Covenant Theology Is Redemptive Theology

The Covenant of Works

It is a mystery to be received on authority of God's Word that Adam was created upright, but lapsable. Adam's breach of the first covenant provided the historical basis for the covenant of grace, though purposed in eternity past. The relationship between God and Adam was certainly "covenantal." Genesis 2 utilizes the covenant name (Gen. 2:4–5, 7–9, 15–16, 18–19, 22). Hosea 6:7 might well refer to this covenant. Arguably, one or both of the specially designated trees in the garden functioned sacramentally, as signs and seals of the covenant. Most importantly, the headship of Adam harmonizes with the notion of covenant solidarity.

The matter of covenant solidarity is crucial. Romans 5:12–21 is foundational for establishing the doctrine that the guilt of Adam's sin is imputed to his posterity and that the corruption of man is the penal consequence of Adam's disobedience. All human beings were in Adam representatively, and so are justly liable for his sin. Just as the head of a corporation who breaks the law brings down the entire corporation he represents, so Adam's sin brought down humanity. As the Shorter Catechism puts it: "The covenant being made with Adam, not only for himself, but for his posterity; all mankind, descending from him by ordinary generation, sinned in him, and fell with him, in his first transgression" (WSC 16).

The truths of federal representation and imputation (crediting, reckoning) together form the plank on which the necessity of the atonement is built. Both truths are necessary for establishing the concept of the penal substitution of Christ for sinners. Since the wages of sin is death, "the death of Christ is then seen to be the real infliction of the originally threatened curse."[6]

The consideration of this covenant is necessary for understanding the covenant of grace. As the Confession of Faith says: "Man, by his fall, having made himself incapable of life by that covenant, the

---

not according to a decree or according to an agreement or pact, but according to His very divine Nature and Essence" (319), and "the covenant is the very essence of religion . . . in which God reflects His own covenant life" (322).

6. Hugh Martin, *The Atonement* (Edinburgh: Banner of Truth, 2013), 5.

Lord was pleased to make a second, commonly called the covenant of grace" (WCF 7.3; cf. WLC 30–31).

Paul's presentation of sin and the gospel stands or falls with the historicity of the first Adam: "Therefore, . . . sin came into the world through one man, and death through sin, and so death spread to all men because all sinned" (Rom. 5:12). Indeed, to deny Adam's historicity not only involves a denial of the biblical view of sin, but also radically alters the biblical concept of redemption. Denial of the historicity of Adam obliterates the comparison and contrast of the first and last Adams: "For as by the one man's disobedience the many were made sinners, so by the one man's obedience the many will be made righteous" (v. 19). That some are willing to question the historicity of Adam indicates the influence of systems alien to biblical Christianity, which disregard this covenant structure and undermine a commitment to biblical authority. Such denial indicates apostasy.

The Covenant of Grace and the Work of the Mediator

The covenant defines and delimits the parameters of Christ's mediation and atoning work in at least six ways.

First, the covenant concept *underscores the eternal origin and decretive foundation* of the Lord's merciful plan of redemption. That a redemptive counsel is contemplated in the divine decree of election is, as already indicated, beyond dispute. The Son redeemed those given to him by the Father (John 6:37–44; 10:14–16, 27–30; 17:2, 6, 19, 22, 24). The covenant of grace was made with Christ and with God's elect in him (WLC 31). The covenant of grace, in time and space, is the actualization of God's eternal redemptive plan.

Second, the covenant concept *provides the rationale for the incarnation of the Son*. That the Son is the eternal God, the second person of the Trinity, is the great presupposition of the whole of Scripture apart from which the Bible would be meaningless. Why did the Son become incarnate? Why did God become man? Why were the two natures—deity and humanity—perfectly united in the one person of Jesus Christ? Why this stupendous miracle "whereby the Eternal was made in time, the Infinite became finite, the Immortal, mortal, yet continuing eternal, infinite, immortal"; why did the Son of God become incarnate "not by ceasing to be what he was, but by becoming what he was not"?[7] The answer is provided in the covenant of grace.

God the Son became man that "he might be thoroughly furnished to execute the office of Mediator and Surety" (WCF 8.3) of the covenant of grace. Atonement is a covenant concept. Only a sinless substitute could redeem from sin. Only God become man could meet that prerequisite and redeem sinners (2 Cor. 5:21; Heb. 4:15; 7:26; 1 Peter 2:22, 24; 1 John 3:5). But man, having fallen in Adam, owed the debt to the broken law of God. Only man could obey the law broken by man (Gal. 4:4–5). Because it was man he came to redeem, the Mediator between God and man must himself be man (1 Tim. 2:5; Heb. 2:10–18). And as Mediator, Christ in Scripture is pointedly called the *Mediator of the covenant* (Heb. 8:6; 9:15; 12:24). Therefore, only a man could become the High Priest of sinners (2:17–18; 4:15–16; 5:1–2).

Third, the covenant of grace, providing as it does the rationale for the incarnation of our Lord, also necessarily *provides the rationale for the offices of Christ*: Prophet, Priest, and King (Deut. 18:15; Ps. 110:4; Acts 3:22; 5:31; 1 Tim. 6:15; Rev. 17:14; cf. WSC 23–28). The incarnation is the foundation of these offices. Christ could be none of these to his people were he not God and man; "had he not been partaker of our nature, we could have received no benefit—not that without which we must eternally perish—by any office that he could have undertaken."[8]

Fourth, the covenant of grace provides the framework for understanding the categories of the atonement of Christ: sacrifice, suffering, suretyship.

The covenant of grace provides the framework for understanding the sacrifice of Christ.

The sacrificial system of the Old Testament was covenantal in nature. The blood of the sacrificial victim was the "blood of the covenant" (Ex. 24:8; Matt. 26:28). Moreover, the Old Testament system provides the categories used in the New Testament to describe the atonement of Christ. The concept of sacrifice is clearly taught in the

7. Owen, "Christologia," 46.
8. Owen, "Christologia," 87.

New Testament (1 Cor. 5:7; Eph. 5:2; Heb. 10:14) and points to the Old Testament as the pattern for understanding the sacrificial death of Jesus (Heb. 9:16–24; 13:10–13).

Patrick Fairbairn notes that the burnt offering represented the whole sacrificial institution (Deut. 33:10). To summarize: Offered morning and evening, it pointed to the perpetual efficacy of the sacrifice of Jesus and is in many respects the quintessential type. Essential to the sacrificial system were actions of victim selection, identification with the sacrifice by the laying of hands on the head of the victim, and sacrifice by bloodletting. In each instance, the sacrificial system underscores the essential aspect of the work of Christ—that of *substitution*! The victim, a perfect one of its kind, represented the indispensable need of a sinless substitute. The laying of hands on the head of the victim represented the transference of guilt from the worshiper to the vicarious sacrifice. Finally, the shedding of the victim's blood pointed to the merciful provision of Christ as the sinner's substitute who would remove the guilt of the sinner and satisfy the divine anger by the shedding of his own precious, covenant blood.[9]

The shedding of blood to redeem sinners is grounded within the nature of the Godhead. It is particularly grounded on the justice of God. In the provisions of the covenant of grace, the demands of God's justice are met (Rom. 3:21–31).

The covenant of grace provides the framework for understanding the sufferings of Christ.

By "the sufferings of Christ," we mean his *active obedience*, Christ's keeping all the commands of God on our behalf, and his *passive obedience*, his taking upon himself the penalty due our sins.

Adam's first sin laid the groundwork for the necessity of the covenant of grace historically considered. It was the voluntary work of the last Adam to obey the demands of the first covenant broken by man through his rebellion. The violated covenant of works necessitated, historically, the work of Christ. Christ's work is one of obedience, a meriting of salvation for lost sinners. All his sufferings were the

---

9. Patrick Fairbairn, *The Typology of Scripture* (Grand Rapids: Guardian Press, 1975), 2:265–77.

sufferings of his obedience to the Father's commission. The obedience of Christ that merited our salvation is one, complete, and perfect obedience, though distinguishable as *active* and *passive*.

First, Christ obeyed the righteous requirements of God's law, which we as sinners have broken. Christ was "born under the law" for the purpose of redeeming sinners under law (Gal. 4:4–5) so that sinners, who have no righteousness of their own through the law, might have a righteousness that comes by faith (Phil. 3:9). Christ obeyed where Adam rebelled:

> Therefore, as one trespass led to condemnation for all men, so one act of righteousness leads to justification and life for all men. For as by the one man's disobedience the many were made sinners, so by the one man's obedience the many will be made righteous. (Rom. 5:18–19)

The obedience of Jesus Christ to the Father was obedience rendered as the last Adam, reversing the curse, restoring sinners, and gaining for them much more than was lost by the first Adam through his rebellion. He rendered that perfect, personal obedience required in the first covenant. Satisfaction meets the penal sanctions of the law, and perfect obedience meets its positive requirements. This was as necessary as punishment in our stead.

Second, Christ obeyed his Father in taking upon himself the penal obligations that we sinners sustained to the law. The wages of sin is death (Rom. 6:23; Phil. 2:6–8). It is those precise wages that Christ took upon himself to pay by his sacrifice in the place of sinners. Christ's work for sinners was forensic and substitutionary (Isa. 53:6; Rom. 4:25; 1 Peter 2:24; 3:18; 1 John 2:2). His entire life as well as his death was one act of obedient substitution for sinners, who have broken God's law and incurred guilt through original sin and the actual transgressions that proceed from it. This leads us to consider the next category.

The covenant of grace provides the framework for understanding the suretyship of Christ.

As representative and substitute for his spiritual seed in the covenant, Christ was made surety. He is termed a "guarantor" (*enguos*) of a better covenant in his priestly work (Heb. 7:22). Christ took upon himself the legal obligations of his covenantal seed. He became a surety for the debt of the elect by substituting himself as "guarantor" in the place of the debtor. All the sins of the elect were laid on him as the scapegoat of God's provision (Lev. 16:21). As substitute for his elect (2 Cor. 5:21), Jesus by his death guarantees their salvation through the covenant of grace.

A fifth consideration is that *the covenant of grace is the unfolding in time of the eternally decreed plan of the triune God.* Though the covenant is rooted in eternity, it is revealed by means of historical and epochal progress. Those very epochs, however, are pervasively covenantal. To understand the organic, progressive, historical, linguistic, and epochal structure of the Bible is to begin to understand the very transcript of God's eternally purposed covenant with men. This is what Geerhardus Vos meant by the "principle of periodicity" or the "principle of successive *Berith*-makings."[10]

Two implications of great importance meet us here. First, the covenant of grace is essentially one through all ages, although its administrations differ with the progress of covenantal epochs. The vital principle of the covenant of grace in every epoch is Christ, the Mediator of the covenant (Gen. 3:15; Gal. 3:15–25).

The second implication is this: because the covenant of grace is rooted in the decree of God and the Father's commission of the Son, and since the end of the covenant of grace is union and communion with God ("I will be your God, and you shall be my people," Jer. 7:23), then in its inner essence the covenant is coterminous with the decree of election.[11] The purpose of Christ's atonement, the shedding of covenant blood, is to redeem those chosen by the Father.

---

10. Geerhardus Vos, *Biblical Theology* (Grand Rapids: Eerdmans, 1948), 25.

11. Herman Bavinck's comments are helpful in *Our Reasonable Faith*, trans. Henry Zylstra (Grand Rapids: Baker, 1977), 278–79: "Inasmuch as the covenant of grace enters into the human race in this historical and organic manner, it cannot here on earth appear in a form which fully answers to its essence. Not only does there remain much in the true believers which is diametrically opposed to a life in harmony with the demand of the covenant: Walk before My face, and be upright; be holy for I am holy. But there can also be persons who are taken up into the covenant of grace as it manifests itself to our eyes and who nevertheless on account

One final implication of the covenant scheme for the work of Christ in the covenant framework is that the grace of God in Christ is *unconditional grace*. Much discussion has revolved around the question whether the covenant is conditional or unconditional. If our starting point for understanding the covenant is the decree of God and the commission of the Father, the answer is clear. The covenant of grace, in its essence, is unconditional. The covenant is a sovereign administration of grace.[12]

Conditional is a slippery and often controversial term. The salvation of God's elect is secured absolutely in the covenant of grace not because there is nothing that needs to occur ("conditions") in order for us to be forgiven and accepted by God, but because the triune God is totally committed to fulfill the necessary conditions for us. The "condition" of our forgiveness is the sacrifice of Christ as sinless substitute; the "condition" for our acceptance is Christ's perfect obedience; the "condition" of our receiving the benefits of Christ is faith and repentance, which is supplied by the Holy Spirit, who grants these gifts of grace. Hence, the covenant of grace in its *essence* is unconditional.

Even those things that might seem to us conditional in relation to the covenant are promissory in Christ. Hellenbroek's catechism asks: "What does God require in the covenant?" The answer is in full accord with unconditional grace: "That which God requires in it, is also a promise of the covenant, namely, faith in Jesus Christ."[13] The insight here is that God gives to his elect what he required of the elect in the covenant. Thomas Boston reminds us that "a surety engageth for the whole of the sum payable" and:

> The sum of the matter lies here: If Christ did in the covenant become Surety in way of caution for his people's performing some deed; the performing of the condition of the covenant, properly

of their unbelieving and unrepentant heart are devoid of all the spiritual benefits of the covenant." He continues to speak of "two sides of the one covenant of grace. One of these is visible to us; the other is perfectly visible to God, and to Him alone."

12. On this point, see John Murray, *The Covenant of Grace* (London: Tyndale Press, 1977), 18.

13. Quoted in Wilhelmus à Brakel, *The Christian's Reasonable Service*, ed. Joel R. Beeke, trans. Bartel Elshout, 4 vols. (Ligonier, PA: Soli Deo Gloria, 1992), 1:434.

so called, is divided betwixt Christ and them; however unequal their shares are: and if the performing of the condition is divided betwixt Christ and them, so far as their part of the performance goes, the reward is of debt to them, which obscures the grace of the covenant.[14]

This matter is of fundamental consequence for the presentation of the gospel of Christ. This is not hairsplitting over an insignificant matter. If the covenant is presented conditionally, the grace of God must also be presented conditionally. If the covenant is presented apart from its root in election, the covenant of grace is transposed into a hopeless covenant of works, which we as sinners could never fulfill.[15] But this is not the case. The work of Christ meets all the conditions, and the covenant of grace is to us one of pure, unadulterated, unconditional grace. This is the gospel view of the covenant. Christ met all the conditions and requirements and provides all that is needed for our entrance into salvation with all its benefits.

Covenant Theology Is Election Theology

Paul brings to the fore the internal and external distinction of the covenant of grace by writing that "they are not all Israel, which are of

14. Thomas Boston, *Works*, vol. 8, *A View of the Covenant of Grace* (Wheaton, IL: Richard Owen Roberts, 1980), 425–26.

15. Bavinck, *Our Reasonable Faith*, 272: "After all, when the covenant of grace is separated from election, it ceases to be a covenant of grace and becomes again a covenant of works. Election implies that God grants man freely and out of grace the salvation which man has forfeited and which he can never again achieve in his own strength. But if his salvation is not the sheer gift of grace but in some way depends upon the conduct of men, then the covenant of grace is converted into the covenant of works. Man then must satisfy some condition in order to inherit eternal life. In this, grace and works stand at opposite poles from each other and are mutually exclusive. If salvation is by grace it is no longer by works, or otherwise grace is no longer grace. And if it is by works, it is not by grace, or otherwise works are not works (Rom. 11:6). . . . So far from election and the covenant of grace forming a contrast of opposites, the election is the basis and guarantee, the heart and core, of the covenant of grace." The application of these stellar words to the error of "the Federal Vision" is apparent. Bavinck's words with what we have written above strike at the very heart of the pernicious error that flows from conditionality.

Israel" (Rom. 9:6).[16] He identifies the covenant of grace with the elect: "the children of the promise are counted for the seed" (v. 8). Of Jacob and Esau, though both circumcised children of Isaac, only Jacob was elect of God (vv. 11–13). Clearly, election defines the inner essence of the covenant.

The essence of the covenant is sovereign promise. Some, like Esau, are of the covenant, "in" the covenant only externally and visibly. Election determines the relation of the promise to the covenant; the promise is absolute. We may not be Calvinistic in our doctrine of electing grace and Arminian in our doctrine of the covenant of grace. The covenant of grace is anchored in the eternal, decretive purpose of God and is worked out in history. Through families,

> God has graciously promised to show mercy unto thousands of them that love Him and keep His commandments; the decree of election runs largely in their loins, and through their faithfulness in rearing a holy seed, the Church is perpetuated, and new recruits are constantly added to the communion of the saints.[17]

There is a clear distinction between those who are of the seed of the flesh and those who are of the seed of the promise: "They which are the children of the flesh, these are not the children of God: but the children of the promise are counted for the seed" (Rom. 9:8). There are children who are associated with the covenant externally who are not heirs to the promise, not "in" the covenant as to its essence: "They are not all Israel, which are of Israel" (v. 6).

We have already observed that the covenant of grace is made with Christ and the elect in him. The line of election runs right through the contours of covenant history, establishing the essence of the covenant as inseparable from election. The covenant promise guarantees the salvation of the children of promise. Consequently, the covenant once again is seen to be in its essence unconditional. There are those who have merely an external relation to the covenant and those who are internally related to the covenant. In the unfolding generations,

16. Scripture quotations in this section are from the KJV.
17. James Henley Thornwell, *Collected Writings*, 4 vols. (Edinburgh: Banner of Truth, 1974), 4:340.

God preserves the remnant according to the election of grace (Rom. 11:5). This truth should stir those of us who minister the Word to do so with the aim of maturing our congregations always with future generations in mind.

Covenant Theology Is Consummation Theology

The goal of the covenant of grace is the glory of the triune God and that his people fellowship with God in his Trinitarian love. The covenant extends to the fulfillment of God's eternal purpose in the new creation, the eternal state. When covenant theologians veer toward Pelagianism, they no longer hold to the biblical theology of the covenant. "For from him and through him and to him are all things. To him be glory for ever" (Rom. 11:36).

God is his own end; what he has planned in fellowshipping with his people accords with his own purpose to glorify himself. And particularly, the world was created in order that the Son might be glorified in re-creation. God's excellencies will be known, loved, and adored by saved sinners (Eph. 1:15–23; Col. 1:15–20). Nothing is so calculated to put to death self-centeredness, and to fill the heart with hope, as the knowledge that the end of all things and of God's covenant with sinners is his own glory. This is truly the eschatology of victory that beckons us (Rev. 21–22). The consummation is described in covenantal terms: "I will be their God, and they shall be my people" (Jer. 31:33; see also Rev. 21:7). The consummation will be the fulfillment in perfection of the covenant of grace.

Covenant Theology Is Pastoral Theology

Reformed theology is covenant theology, and therefore Reformed piety is covenantal piety. Covenant theology overflows with implications for pastoral piety and labor. In what ways will the covenant form pastoral piety? Here are five reflections.

First, covenant theology calls upon pastors, in all that they do, to *commune with the Trinity*. The Belgic Confession, having confessed the numerical oneness of God's being in which are three persons, then in article 9 confesses astoundingly: "All this we know, as well from the testimonies of holy writ, as from their operations, and chiefly by those we feel in ourselves." Feeling arising from the operations of the Trinity is the result of the new heart given by God's Spirit (Ezek. 36:26–27), "for our partaking or communion with God consists in the communion or partaking of the Holy Ghost"; indeed, "the sum of all that Christ purchased for men was the Holy Ghost"[18] (Gal. 3:13–14). It is not mysticism to realize that sweetness of fellowship with God through the operations of the Holy Spirit is felt within the soul. "The friendship of the LORD is for those who fear him, and he makes known to them his covenant" (Ps. 25:14). Should not our attentive listening to the covenant Word of God result in deep feelings of love and gratitude? This covenant fellowship is reflected, for example, in Jonathan Edwards's delight in the Trinity, where we find the essence of covenant theology at its best:

> God has appeared glorious to me, on account of the Trinity. It has made me have exalting thoughts of God, that he subsists in three persons; Father, Son and Holy Ghost. The sweetest joys and delights I have experienced have not been those that have arisen from a hope of my own good estate; but in a direct view of the glorious things of the gospel.[19]

Theology's goal is covenant fellowship. Theology is unto godliness. "Let not the wise man boast in his wisdom, let not the mighty man boast in his might, let not the rich man boast in his riches, but let him who boasts boast in this, that he understands and knows me" (Jer. 9:23–24). Pastor, do you agree that you should radiate experiential piety in your life and preaching? Go to the Lord in secret prayer and humbly commune with the Father in his love, with the Son in his blood, and with the Holy Spirit in his effectual, saving application of the covenant of grace to the soul. Let this conscious, covenantal fellowship grip you, change you. Make this the constant priority of your ministry. Let your soul relish this fellowship and gain a heart that cannot live without the place of secret communion. It is out of

18. Jonathan Edwards, *An Essay on the Trinity* (Cambridge: James Clarke, 1971), 110, 124; see also p. 116.

19. Jonathan Edwards, *Memoirs*, in *The Works of Jonathan Edwards*, 2 vols. (Edinburgh: Banner of Truth, 1974), 1:xlvii.

such union and communion that you will teach your people the way of holiness. To love the Lord is to be in love with sanctification.[20]

Second, covenant theology calls us pastors to *learn to reflect covenant grace in our ministries.* Apply the balm of Gilead to the hurting. Respond to those who are unkind with the kindness that has been shown you. Do not view his flock as a commodity, or with anger, or with indifference. Remember, on Sunday you will lift your hands to pronounce the Trinitarian benediction on God's people in the words of 2 Corinthians 13:14. This is a pronouncement of the covenant bond of God with his people, a bond of fellowship with the members of the Trinity. Have you seen God's face in Christ? Then show the fatherly character of God and the tender mercies of the Lord to his people.

Third, covenant theology calls upon preachers to *stress the reliability of God's promise.* God's tried people need to hear frequently that the God of the covenant always keeps his promises! There is so much in life that *seems* to contradict this reality. Tell God's people that God's oath to Abraham was made on the strength of God's own unchangeable character and provides for God's people a "steadfast anchor of the soul" (Heb. 6:13–20; see also Gen. 15:1–21; Deut. 29:13–14; 1 Chron. 16:15–18). It is a promise that God will save his people, that he redeems his own, that nothing can separate us from his love, a promise, yes—eaten and drunk down at the communion table—that what he has done for us in the past will last for eternity. And it is a promise that God's people may even take to the graves of their covenant children. As the fathers of Dort so ably put it, "in virtue of the covenant of grace, . . . godly parents have no reason to doubt of the election and salvation of their children, whom it pleaseth God to call out of this life in their infancy" (Canons of Dort 1.17).

Fourth, covenant theology means that we *minister God's Word, emphasizing sovereign grace and gratuitous mercy in Christ.* Let covenant mediation be your constant theme. "For when we think of God apart from a mediator, we can only conceive of Him as being angry with us, but when a mediator is interposed between us, we know that

20. Wilhelmus à Brakel, *The Christian's Reasonable Service* (Grand Rapids: Reformation Heritage Books, 1999), 1:441. Bartel Elshout points out that à Brakel "uses the word *verliefd* to describe the disposition of the heart of the godly," literally saying that "the godly are in love with sanctification."

He is pacified towards us." "Thus the duty of ministers is to apply to us the fruit of Christ's death."[21] Tell your congregation that the covenant of grace is just that, *gracious*! Tell them that the gospel is free. Preach the finished work of Christ, call sinners to Christ, the covenant Tree of Life! Do not separate the benefits of Christ from Christ in whom are the benefits. Clothe your preaching with the Christ of the covenant.

Fifth, covenant theology *encourages a pervasive eschatological focus* in our preaching and work with people. Let your ministry overflow with hope. The covenant of grace grounded in the Trinitarian nature of God cannot be a mere means to an end of salvation; rather, the Scriptures represent God's covenant with his elect as the end itself. The covenant formula is repeated at the end of the Bible as a summary of God's intention from the beginning: "Behold, the dwelling place of God is with man. He will dwell with them, and they will be his people, and God himself will be with them as their God"—indeed, "they will see his face" (Rev. 21:3; 22:4). The supralapsarian instinct on this point is certainly right: what is last in execution was first in intention. Constantly help God's dear people to live in the reality of these wonders. Help God's people, who live in union with Christ in his humiliation and exaltation, to lift up their faces hopefully in the midst of this fallen world and sing *Te Deum Laudamus*!

Key Terms

    decrees of God
    election
    penal substitution
    piety

Recommendations for Further Reading

Bavinck, Herman. *Reformed Dogmatics*. Edited by John Bolt. Translated by John Vriend. Vol. 3, *Sin and Salvation in Christ*. Grand Rapids: Baker Academic, 2006. Chap. 5.

21. John Calvin, *The Second Epistle of Paul the Apostle to the Corinthians and the Epistles to Timothy, Titus and Philemon*, ed. David W. Torrance and Thomas F. Torrance, trans. T. A. Smail, Calvin's Commentaries (Edinburgh: Oliver and Boyd, 1964), 78–79.

Boston, Thomas. *A View of the Covenant of Grace.* Vol. 8 of *Works of Thomas Boston.* Wheaton, IL: Richard Owen Roberts, 1980. Pp. 376–604.

Hoeksema, Herman. *Reformed Dogmatics.* Grand Rapids: Reformed Free Publishing, 1966. Pp. 285–336.

Robertson, O. Palmer. *The Christ of the Covenants.* Phillipsburg, NJ: Presbyterian and Reformed, 1980.

Vos, Geerhardus. "Doctrine of the Covenant in Reformed Theology." In *Redemptive History and Biblical Interpretation,* 234–67. Phillipsburg, NJ: P&R Publishing, 1980.

Discussion Questions

1. What is the sixfold answer to the question "What is covenant theology?" And how does this sixfold answer "hold together" and provide unity to the concept of *covenant theology*?
2. Regarding these six categories:
   a. Why is it essential to begin with the Bible and the Trinity?
   b. How does covenant theology provide the rationale for the work of Christ?
   c. How do covenant and election relate?
   d. How does the covenant of grace point us to our blessed hope?
   e. What does it mean that the covenant of grace is pastoral?
3. How does the covenant of grace provide the context for our fellowship with the Trinity? Ponder the quotation from Belgic Confession article 9: "All this we know, as well from the testimonies of holy writ, as from their operations, and chiefly by those we feel in ourselves."
4. How does the covenant of grace help us stress the reliability of God's promises?
5. What is the connection between the covenant of grace and the sovereignty of grace?
6. How does pondering the covenant of grace necessarily lead to an eschatological focus?

8

THE PERSON OF CHRIST

The Deeper Protestant Conception and

the Church's Heavenly-Mindedness

LANE G. TIPTON

Sinclair Ferguson's work as a pastor and theologian has consistently sought to develop and apply in various ways the theology contained in the Scriptures of the Old and New Testaments, as summarized by the ecumenical creeds and Reformed confessions of the church.[1] His published works unite in a common concern to honor the being, persons, and glory of the triune God, while maintaining a robust Christ-centered understanding of the gospel. The God-glorifying and Christ-centered themes in his published works stand in admirable contrast to a century of theological approaches that diminish the immutable and self-contained God of Scripture in order to reconceptualize his relation to the world and, by extension, redefine the gospel of Jesus Christ.

1. Along with J. I. Packer and R. C. Sproul, Sinclair Ferguson shaped my early development as a Christian through his numerous expositions of Reformed theology and practice. I, along with countless others, owe him a debt of gratitude for his service to the Lord these many years.

While the theological influences on Ferguson are numerous, for our purposes it is useful to recognize that he inherited the tradition of classical Reformed theism from John Owen and shares an interest in redemptive history with Geerhardus Vos, and his colleague Richard Gaffin.[2] His advocacy of Owen's theology proper emerges throughout *The Trinitarian Devotion of John Owen*, and the influence of Gaffin's redemptive-historical approach appears frequently in *The Holy Spirit*. Ferguson's work reminds us that a Christ-centered approach to covenant history demands that we affirm that the triune God remains immutably absolute and self-contained in the works of creation and redemption (Mal. 3:6; James 1:17).

This essay will probe the interface of classical Reformed theism and biblical theology pioneered by Geerhardus Vos and seek to develop some implications of what Vos called the "deeper Protestant conception,"[3] particularly as it bears on the heavenly-mindedness of the church. The hope is that the convergence of dogmatic and biblical-theological points of view will have a deep practical value that helps to calibrate the church's life toward the ascended Christ in heaven to the glory and worship of the self-contained triune God.

The Triune Creator in the Deeper Protestant Conception

Geerhardus Vos, the father of Reformed biblical theology, advocated as a dogmatic theologian what he termed "the deeper Protestant conception" regarding the "new relation"[4] willed by the triune God to image-bearing Adam before the fall in the work of creation.

Put tersely, the living and impassible persons of the immutable and self-contained Godhead do not change in the sovereignly willed new relation to creation. The triune God undergoes no essential or personal change in the freely willed new relation to creation. To

---

2. For Ferguson's appreciation of Vos, see Ferguson's essay "What Is Biblical Theology?," in *Some Pastors and Teachers: Reflecting a Biblical Vision of What Every Minister Is Called to Be* (Carlisle, PA: Banner of Truth, 2017), 417–48.

3. Geerhardus Vos, *Reformed Dogmatics*, ed. and trans. Richard B. Gaffin Jr., vol. 2, *Anthropology* (Bellingham, WA: Lexham Press, 2014), 2, 14.

4. Geerhardus Vos, *Reformed Dogmatics*, ed. and trans. Richard B. Gaffin Jr., vol. 1, *Theology Proper* (Bellingham, WA: Lexham Press, 2012), 177–78.

affirm a "real change"[5] in God as triune Creator, whether that change finds its locus in the essence or in the persons of the Godhead, would ascribe to God the qualities found in the creature, thereby denying in the Creator-creature relation what is affirmed about God in the Creator-creature distinction, namely, that in God the triune Creator "no time distinction exists."[6] In the new relation to creation, the relation itself changes, the creature in relation to God changes, but the self-contained triune Creator remains essentially and personally immutable and impassible in the sovereignly willed new relation to creation.

In the sharpest possible contrast to the deeper Protestant conception stands the trend inherent in all forms of correlativism or theological mutualism. Karl Barth, the chief architect of what we might call the deeper *modernist* conception, insists that there is initially an absolute and qualitative difference between God and man in the Creator-creature distinction. Barth's dialectical approach also insists, however, that in the Creator-creature relation God participates with the creature in a "third time" dimension that he termed "God's Time for Us" in the "Christ-Event."[7] It is in the primordial "Event" of mutual participation between God and man in a "third time" that Barth reconceived the identity of God. Contrary to the deeper Protestant conception, for Barth, God's identity is entirely dependent on the creature in a correlative relationship between God and man in the event of Jesus Christ in a third time dimension (*Geschichte*). That third time is a supratemporal event in a dimension (*Geschichte*) that is entirely distinct from our ordinary calendar time (*historie*). This is the mutualistic deeper modernist conception that stands on the polar far side of the deeper Protestant conception.

The Reformed logic of the new relation exposes all forms of theological mutualism, because the logic of the new relation in the deeper Protestant conception demands that we do not deny in

---

5. Vos, *Theology Proper*, 178.

6. Vos, *Theology Proper*, 178.

7. For an outstanding exposition and penetrating critique of this central structural strand in Barth's theology of the Creator-creature relation, see James J. Cassidy, *God's Time for Us: Barth's Reconciliation of Eternity and Time in Jesus Christ* (Bellingham, WA: Lexham Press, 2016).

the Creator-creature relation what we have already affirmed in the Creator-creature distinction, namely, the pure actuality of the self-contained triune Creator entirely apart from the relation to the creature. Barth's deeper modernist conception, and all forms of theological mutualism like it, denies that the triune God remains self-contained and immutable entirely apart from his relation to creation as well as in relation to his creation. The identity of the self-contained God is at no point dependent on the creature, because God does not as Creator participate in some *tertium quid* along with the creature, whether that third thing is time, or being, or historical contingency.

The deeper Protestant conception must, therefore, be set in contrast to the deeper modernist conception of Barth and all other forms of theological mutualism. The difference does not concern one or two isolated points; rather, it relates to the entire conception of the God-man relation. This essay aims to make this distinction clear through Vos's notion of the deeper Protestant conception, which reaches from the new relation to creation, to its perfection in the *historia salutis*, to its application in the *ordo salutis*, to its bearing on the church's call to heavenly-mindedness.

The Deeper Protestant Conception of the Doctrine of Christ: Relation of Origin and the New Relation to Creation

Herman Ridderbos, in his magisterial work *Paul*, examines more specifically the eternal *person* of the preincarnate Son of God's sovereignly willed new relation to creation in light of Colossians 1:15–16. Ridderbos insightfully speaks of "Paul's Christological Interpretation of Creation." Verse 15a denotes the relation of origin of the Son to the Father prior to the new relation to creation, and verses 15b–16 denote the new relation in its comprehensive scope that includes the invisible heaven and visible earth.[8]

---

8. For those interested in some of the exegetical insights that underlie the theological conclusions developed below, see my essay in the Gaffin Festschrift: Lane G. Tipton, "Christology in Colossians 1:15–20 and Hebrews 1:1–4: An Exercise in Biblico-Systematic Theology," in *Resurrection and Eschatology: Theology in Service of the Church: Essays in Honor of Richard B. Gaffin, Jr.*, ed. Lane G. Tipton and Jeffrey Waddington (Phillipsburg, NJ: P&R Publishing, 2008), 177–202.

Colossians 1:15a: The Image of God and the Trinitarian Relation of Origin

Ridderbos, with his characteristic depth of understanding, observes: "By calling Christ the Image of God he thus identifies Christ's glory with that of God himself. . . . And the same thing applies to Colossians 1:15 . . . [so that] there is . . . special mention of Christ's glory as the Pre-existent One in these passages."[9] He says that "it is evident here anew, therefore, to what extent the divine glory of Christ, even already in his preexistence with the Father prior to his redemptive revelation, determines and underlies the Pauline Christology," and this yields the proper conclusion that "we have before us (in Col. 1), therefore, a christological interpretation of Genesis 1."[10] Colossians 1:15–16 therefore supplies a rich resource to further develop from the Scriptures the depth and beauty of the deeper Protestant conception of the God-world relation. Let us attempt such a development.

Two main exegetical considerations underwrite Ridderbos's interpretive conclusion that the "image of the invisible God" in Colossians 1:15a denotes the eternal Trinitarian relation of origin, rather than the human nature of Jesus as the incarnate and created image of God, and that the "firstborn of all creation" in verse 15b denotes his absolute ontological distinction from the created order as the Creator of all things (and thus absolute lordship over it).

First, the poetic structure of the strophic arrangement requires that Colossians 1:15–16 denotes the eternal Son in his eternal relation to the Godhead (v. 15a) and in his new relation to creation (vv. 15b–16), prior to and entirely apart from his incarnation in postfall calendar time (cf. Gal. 4:4; Col. 1:18–20). The passage is arranged in terms of two strophes (Col. 1:15–16, 18b–20), with a transition separating them (vv. 17–18a). In Ridderbos's language, the first strophe denotes the eternal Son's "preexistence" prior to his incarnation, and the second strophe denotes the resurrected Son's "postexistence" inaugurated in his bodily resurrection.[11] The key for interpretation of the

9. Herman N. Ridderbos, *Paul: An Outline of His Theology*, trans. John Richard de Witt (Grand Rapids: Eerdmans, 1975), 70.
10. Ridderbos, *Paul*, 71.
11. Ridderbos, *Paul*, 70–73.

first strophe, then, rests in the fact that the whole denotes the Logos as *asarkos* in his eternal ontic status as the Image-Son (v. 15a) and in his economic function as the Creator-Son (vv. 15b–16).

Second, and related, "image" and "firstborn" are mutually interpretive of the Son's eternal preexistent identity in relation to the Godhead and created order, respectively. This becomes quite clear when the explanation in Colossians 1:16b for the status of "firstborn" rests in the fact that "by him all things were created" (Col. 1:16a). The Son, as firstborn of all creation, is the one "by [whom] all things were created," including things "invisible" and things "visible" (v. 16c). His status as firstborn, then, is the natural consequence of his relation of origin to the Father (cf. Ridderbos above) in verse 15a—the uncreated image of the invisible God. Image supplies the theological rationale for the Son's categorical preeminence as the uncreated "firstborn over all creation" in verse 15b. Only the one who personally subsists distinctly as the entire essence of God, and in that relation "images" the invisible God in a personal relation of origin, can be the one "by whom all things were made," whether things in "heaven" or "on earth" (v. 16b). To put it in summary terms, verse 15a brings into view the eternal relation of origin and subsistence, and verses 15b–16 the new relation to creation (see Vos above).

The logic of the new relation from the divine side is that the person of the Son does not change in the sovereignly willed new relation to creation. Just as the "Father of lights . . . [has] no variation or shadow due to change" in his relation to creation (James 1:17), so the eternal "image" of the immutable Father does not change like shifting shadows in his relation to creation as the "firstborn" (Col. 1:15b). The eternal Son, in his freely willed new relation to creation, does not change. Put in capsule form, "image of the invisible God" denotes the immutable person of the Son in the relations of origin, subsistence, and coinherence, and "firstborn over all creation" denotes the immutable person of the Son in his sovereignly willed new relation to creation. The Son remains immutable and living in each distinct relation. This is the substance of the deeper Protestant conception when applied to the doctrine of the person of Christ.

It is especially in the language regarding the Son as the "image of the invisible God" that Ridderbos proves uniquely insightful. He says, regarding Colossians 1:15a specifically, that "by the designation Image of God he [the eternal Son] is on the one hand distinguished from God, and on the other hand identified with God as Bearer of the divine glory."[12] To render Ridderbos's language in dogmatic terms, being "distinguished from God" brings into view an incommunicable personal property (relation of origin) and a relation of personal coinherence (perichoresis). Being "identified with God" brings into view the Son's distinct personal subsistence as the simple and undivided divine essence. The person of the Son is thus distinct from the person of the Father, yet identified with the essence of the Father. This is, as far as we can render it, Ridderbos's point regarding the features of the Son's eternal glory.

Relating this material to Adam as the created image of God requires that we bring into view the relation of origin between the unoriginate Father and the only-begotten Son of God (John 1:1–3; Col. 1:15a; Heb. 1:3; James 1:17), on the one hand, and the new relation of the triune God and the created image of God (Gen. 1:27; 2:7; Col. 1:15b–16), on the other hand. As the only-begotten Son of the Father, the Son subsists distinctly and entirely as the undivided essence of God. In this subsistent relation, he is distinctly and entirely God. As the only-begotten Son of the Father, he also exhaustively indwells the Father in a relation of exhaustive personal coinherence (perichoresis). In this coinherent relation, he is both personally related to and personally distinguished from the Father. The Son distinctly subsists as the undivided essence of God and exhaustively indwells the Father's person without confusion or conflation of personal properties, and he remains such at every point in the new relation to Adam as the created image of God under the covenant of works (Gen. 1:27; 2:7–17). The divine person of the Son at no point in the work of creation begins to subsist in created properties, as do the human properties that subsist in Adam's created nature as the image of God. Rather, the person of the Son always personally subsists only as the simple and immutable divine essence in the works of creation and redemption.

As Ridderbos notes, Paul denotes the relation of origin between the Father and the Son by using the language of the created "image"

12. Ridderbos, *Paul*, 70–73.

of God (Gen. 1:27; 2:7). Paul uses the language of "image" to denote the eternal relation of the Son to the Father, yet at the same time, in light of it, moves on in Colossians 15b–16 to offer a "Christological interpretation of creation." Paul's logic is that the creation of Adam as the image of God in natural religious fellowship with God replicates at the creaturely level the eternal mystery of immutable and living Trinitarian persons in the beatitude of Trinitarian perichoresis. Adam's natural religious fellowship in covenant with God is a creaturely replica of the subsistent and coinherent relations of the eternal Godhead. The religious fellowship inherent in the image of God is therefore best understood to be a replication on the finite and creaturely level of the Trinitarian perichoresis. The subsistent and coinherent relations of the Godhead anchor conceptually the character of Adam as the created image of God in covenant with God (Gen. 1:27; 2:7–17).

Colossians 1:16b: The New Relation to Creation and the Invisible Heaven

In Colossians 1:16, Paul presents the cosmic architecture of the new relation and speaks of the creation of all things "in heaven and on earth, visible and invisible." Several lines of argument converge to suggest that included in this language is heaven as the royal dwelling place of the uncreated image of God and firstborn over all creation.

Colossians 1:16b presents the sum total of the creation of the upper and lower registers of the created order in a chiastic structure as follows:

A Heaven
  B Earth
    B' Visible
A' Invisible

The new relation to creation includes all things, visible and invisible, heavenly and earthly, which is precisely what the absolute beginning of Genesis 1:1 brings into view. As Meredith Kline argues extensively in *God, Heaven and Har Magedon*, Colossians 1:16b is inspired apostolic commentary on Genesis 1:1 and Nehemiah 9:6. He says:

Genesis 1:1. What this opening verse states is that God, in the beginning, created both the upper and lower spatial spheres. "The heavens and the earth" is not just a merismus, a pair of antonyms which as a set signifies totality. The phrase rather denotes concretely the actual two components that together comprehend all of creation. . . . More precisely, what Gen 1:1 affirms is that God created not just the spatial dimensions immediately accessible to man, but the heavens too, that is, the invisible realm of the divine Glory and angelic beings. This interpretation is reflected in the apostle Paul's Christological exposition of Gen 1:1, declaring that the Son created "all things that are in heaven and that are in earth, visible and invisible, whether they be thrones, or dominions, or principalities, or powers" (Col 1:16; cf. John 1:1–3). Similarly Nehemiah, reflecting on the Genesis creation account, finds a reference there to the invisible heaven of the angels (Neh 9:6), and the only possible referent is "the heavens" of Gen 1:1.[13]

"Heaven" in Colossians 1:16 is thus a distinct created and concrete realm that is currently veiled from sight. It is the archetypal dwelling place of God after which provisional earthly dwelling places are patterned, whether it be protological Eden or the typological tabernacle or the temple(s) (cf. Ex. 25:40; Ezek. 28:13–16; Heb. 8:5; 12:22). Accordingly, heaven is the original "temple" of God populated with an angelic host (Neh. 9:6; Isa. 6:1–7). This is brought into view when Paul speaks in Colossians 1:16c of all things visible and invisible, including "thrones or dominions or rulers or authorities." Heaven, the invisible heaven of verse 16, is thus a created yet veiled dimension of the cosmic order brought into being in the absolute beginning. As such, it is a royal temple dwelling of the glory of the triune God. As Kline states, "the glory of the heavenly Presence is a royal glory, the glory of a king with myriad of servants in attendance about his throne."[14] In fact, "because heaven's King is the Lord God, the thrice-holy One (Isa. 6:3; Rev. 4:8) whose Presence sanctifies a place, the royal house of heaven is at the same time a holy house, a

13. Meredith G. Kline, *God, Heaven and Har Magedon: A Covenantal Tale of Cosmos and Telos* (Eugene, OR: Wipf & Stock, 2006), 228–29.
14. Kline, *God, Heaven and Har Magedon*, 6.

temple."[15] He notes that "the New Testament Apocalypse repeatedly designates the heavenly seat of God's judgment throne as a 'temple' or the holy 'tabernacle' of the covenant (Rev. 11:19; 14:15, 17; 15:5–8; 21:11, 23)."[16] Likewise, the book of Hebrews presents the tabernacle (and temple) as a "copy" and "shadow" of heaven itself (cf. Heb. 8:5; 9:23–24), Mount Sinai as a provisional earthly projection of heavenly Mount Zion (cf. 12:18, 22), and the land of Canaan as a typical topographical sketch of the heavenly city (cf. 11:9–16; 12:22; 13:14).

In the absolute beginning, the image of the invisible God, the firstborn of all creation, created the invisible heaven-temple and filled it not only with angels, but with his glory and Spirit. Colossians 1:16d makes explicit that "all things" are both "through him and for him." All of creation is through him and for him. It is important to realize the relation between the invisible heaven (the upper register) and the visible earth (the lower register) in Paul's Christological interpretation of creation. As we have just surveyed, the upper register, invisible heaven, is the created and substantial archetype and pattern after which the lower register, the visible heaven and earth, is the created and substantial ectype. It is especially with reference to Adam and Eden that we can understand the insight in this text that is expanded on in the rest of the Scriptures (as surveyed so briefly above). Adam, the created image of God (Gen. 1:27; 2:7), replicates the uncreated image of God (Col. 1:15), even as Eden (Gen. 2:8), the visible and provisional dwelling place (Ezek. 28:13–16), replicates heaven (Gen. 2:2; Col. 1:16; 3:1–2; Heb. 4:4; 8:1–2).

The movement of Adam's successful probation under covenant in Eden would bring Adam and his created earthly environment into the glory realm of heaven (the prefall parallel to Colossians 1:20 and the reconciling of all things in heaven and on earth). Such a consummative event would not only bring transformation to the lower register but also effect its perfect conformity to the created glory of the upper register. The temple dwelling of God in heaven would be unveiled to sight as all good and holy things on earth and in heaven would be united in the realization of Sabbath rest (Gen. 2:2; Heb. 4:4,

15. Kline, *God, Heaven and Har Magedon*, 7.
16. Kline, *God, Heaven and Har Magedon*, 7.

9–11). Entering into Sabbath rest for Adam would involve his person and earthly environment being transformed and conformed to the heavenly temple dwelling of God for the perfection of covenantal worship. This would entail removing of the veil that would hide from view the concrete and substantial glory of the heavenly temple dwelling of God as long as Adam remained under probation (2 Peter 3:13; Rev. 21:1–2).

Colossians 1:16, then, surveys the sum total of created reality, visible and invisible, that is "through him and for him" as the image of the invisible God and the firstborn of all creation (Col. 1:15b–16) and sets the frame of reference for what follows in the second strophe. Here we must recall the parallel between Colossians 1:16 and Colossians 3:1–2. Paul's call to "seek the things that are above, where Christ is," and to "set your minds on things that are above" (3:1–2)—in contrast with the things "that are on earth" (v. 2)—is grounded in the distinction Paul makes between the invisible heaven and visible earth in the chiasmus of Colossians 1:16. In fact, the command to pursue heavenly-mindedness in Colossians 3:1–2 is a direct and self-conscious outworking of the distinction between the invisible heaven and visible earth set forth in Colossians 1:16. Thus, there is a clear and direct parallel between the programmatic theological framework of Colossians 1:16 and Paul's command to pursue and set the mind on things above where Christ is and not on the things of the earth.

The Redemptive Perfecting of the New Relation to Creation: The *Historia Salutis* (Col. 1:18b–20)

What was not realized by Adam because of his sin and fall is realized in the humiliation and exaltation of the "second man" and "last Adam" (1 Cor. 15:47, 45), which is the fundamental content of the second strophe that runs from Colossians 1:18b through 20. Colossians 1:18b–20, when understood in terms of the deeper Protestant conception, is the redemptive modification and perfection of the new relation to creation in the humiliation and exaltation of Jesus Christ. Verse 18b specifies that the resurrection of Christ as the "firstborn from the dead" marks the "beginning" of the new creation, the once-for-all eschatological accomplishment of the original purpose contemplated in the first creation with Adam under the covenant of works (Gen. 1:28; 2:7–17; 1 Cor. 15:44–47; Col. 1:15, 18). The bodily resurrection of Christ as "firstfruits" of the one great resurrection harvest (1 Cor. 15:20), constituting him the "last Adam" and "a life-giving spirit" (v. 45), perfects once and for all the religious fellowship that constitutes the Adamic image of God (v. 49). In this he is the "firstborn among many brothers" as he enters into his heavenly inheritance as raised from the dead (Rom. 8:29; see also Rom. 8:17; 1 Peter 1:3–5). The natural religious fellowship of the image of God has been instantly brought to consummate perfection in the historical event of Christ's bodily resurrection from the dead. The resurrection of Christ is itself the de facto once-and-for-all modification of the new relation to creation brought to its consummate perfection. In the event of bodily resurrection, the natural bond of religious fellowship with God, originally given to Adam, has reached its climactic fullness.

But another event beyond bodily resurrection advances Christ as resurrected into the invisible heaven, and that event is his bodily ascension into heaven on the day of Pentecost (Acts 1:9–11). It is in his ascension in the Spirit on the day of Pentecost that Christ undergoes a supernatural bodily translation from the visible earth to the invisible heaven. It is not simply as raised, but more specifically as ascended, that the "last Adam" is the "man . . . from heaven" (1 Cor. 15:45, 47). Jesus' ascension advances what began in the event of bodily resurrection, namely, the consummation of the natural religious fellowship inherent in the created image of God, to its consummation in heaven at the right hand of God (Acts 2:28, 32–33; Rom. 8:29; 1 Cor. 15:49; Col. 3:1; Heb. 1:3).

Colossians 1:18 makes it clear that all of this is true of Christ "firstborn from the dead" and, as such, "preeminent" in all things. As firstborn from among the dead, he is the "firstborn among many brothers" (Rom. 8:29). He is the firstborn in the sense that he himself is the first to be translated bodily into heaven to sit at God's right hand (Col. 1:15; 3:1; Heb. 8:1–2). As firstborn from the dead, he is the first to rise up in his flesh and ascend into heaven to sit in the glorious presence of the Father in the full power of the Holy Spirit (Jer. 17:12; Acts 2:27; Heb. 1:3). As firstborn from the dead and ascended into heaven, Jesus Christ is the first to enter into the heavenly temple prepared in the absolute beginning for Adam to enter (Gen. 1:1; 2:2; Heb. 4:4–11). As the firstborn, he has bodily ascended into the heavenly Jerusalem atop the heavenly Mount Zion (Heb. 12:22–24). As the firstborn from among the dead, Jesus Christ is the "beginning" (Col. 1:18) of the one great resurrection harvest that will ascend into heaven, bearing the image of the heavenly man (1 Cor. 15:47, 49).

The Redemptive Application of the Perfected New Relation in Christ: The *Ordo Salutis* and the Christian Life

The new relation to creation is modified and perfected de facto by Christ in his bodily resurrection from the dead. But this resurrection life extends to all who are united to him by the Spirit and through Spirit-gifted faith (John 5:24; 20:5; 1 Cor. 1:30; Eph. 2:6–8). The ascension of Christ into heaven, his reception of the Spirit as raised and ascended, sets the context of the application of the new relation realized in the bodily translation of Christ into heaven. That application is in a two-age translation of the church into heaven through union with the ascended Christ.

What is true of the firstborn from the dead is true of him in a single event of bodily translation into heaven (cf. John 20:5–6). But the bodily translation into heaven that occurred once and for all in his ascension is applied to his church in a two-age translation of the bodies of believers into heaven, the inner man and then the outer man (2 Cor. 4:16–5:10). It is the fact of bodily translation into heaven that grounds the commandments to seek what is above, where Christ is, seated at the right hand of God (Col. 3:1–2). Believers are commanded to seek that heavenly place. To seek that which is above is to seek Christ himself (vv. 1–2).

What has happened in the once-for-all event of the resurrection of Jesus from the dead as the last Adam is nothing less than the *beginning* of a *bodily translation* from the lower register, the "visible earth" of Colossians 1:16, into the upper register, the "invisible heaven" of Colossians 1:16. In fact, it is precisely the blood of Christ's cross that reconciles all things on earth and in heaven (Col. 1:20; Rev. 21:1–2). Union with Christ brings about the realization of the church's bodily translation into heaven in a two-age movement (Ephesians 2:6 for present resurrection and 1 Corinthians 15:50–58 for future resurrection). Jesus' bodily translation into the invisible heaven is the "beginning" that finds its full realization in his church in union with him at the end of the age (Col. 3:4; 2 Peter 3:13; Rev. 21:1–2).

In the bodily ascension of Christ, as he is by the Spirit seated at the right hand of God in heaven, the path of eternal life and everlasting joy in fellowship with the Father in the Holy Spirit has been perfectly realized (Acts 2:28). That path is most basically a translational path that is defined in terms of bodily resurrection followed forty days later in calendar time by bodily ascension (1:9–11). The translation from the visible earth to the invisible heaven is not merely a temporal but a spatial-dimensional transition. Christ's bodily translation was once for all accomplished two thousand years ago, and that translational event in redemptive history is the foundation for the church's hope in union with him by the Spirit and through Spirit-gifted faith. The fruition of Christ's resurrection as the "firstborn from the dead" (Col. 1:18) involves his bodily entrance into the "invisible heaven" of Colossians 1:16, and the "blood of his cross" entails the same bodily translation into the invisible heaven for the church (v. 20).

In light of the doctrine of Christ developed as such, we can understand the heavenly-minded character of the Christian life in union with the crucified and ascended Christ. Colossians 3:1–2 recapitulates the "invisible heaven" and "visible earth" distinction from the chiasmus in Colossians 1:16. The invisible heaven of Colossians 1:16 *is* the "things that are above, where Christ is, seated at the right hand of God" (Col. 3:1). The fundamental contrast that moves from 3:1 to 3:2 turns on the "things that are above" in direct contrast to the "things that are on earth." Specifically, "things that are above" is parallel to Colossians 1:16 and the invisible heaven. Picking up on that language again in 3:2, Paul commands that we set our minds on those "things that are above" and "not on things that are on earth." This explicates the upper- and lower-register distinction in Colossians 1:16 with specific reference to the Christian life. The church is to "seek" the things above, where Christ is, and "set the mind" on things above.

Paul does not speak in Platonic or Gnostic categories, since he is speaking of the created, concrete, and substantial invisible heaven where Christ has bodily ascended. This is referred to in Jesus' teaching as "my Father's house" (John 14:2). Jesus told his disciples while on earth that he would leave and "prepare a place" for them so that "where I am you may be also" (v. 3). "My Father's house" is an image that helps us understand the nature of the "things that are above" where Christ will "go" in order to "prepare a place" for his covenant people. The invisible heaven is likened to a home where your Father dwells and where your Savior has ascended. It is there that he lives, and it is there that he will bring your soul when you pass into glory at death. It is there that he will bring your body, raised with your soul, on the last day. But the point is that the "things that are above" are a dwelling place of the Father, the Son, and the Holy Spirit, likened to a house—a place where you are to live forever.

The "things that are above" also bring into view Christ "sitting at the right hand of God" (Col. 3:1). The Father's house is a holy and royal dwelling place that has a throne in its midst. In Isaiah 6:1–7, when God revealed himself to Isaiah to inaugurate the prophet's ministry, he appeared as one "sitting upon a throne," and the "train of his robe filled the temple" and the seraphim encircled him in worship. Isaiah did not see the copy of heaven contained in the earthly temple. He saw the living God, surrounded by living seraphim, seated on a throne in heaven, and that heavenly temple realm was filled with the glory of God's presence. That heavenly temple with that heavenly throne is the place where the ascended Christ is, seated at the right hand of God (cf. Heb. 8:1–2, 5; 9:23–24).

Notice the verb in Colossians 3:1: *seek* those things above, where Christ is, seated at God's right hand. Seeking is a self-conscious activity of faith. To seek those things above is an activity that grows directly out of being united to the ascended Christ by Spirit-gifted faith, and it is by faith that you seek those things above, where Christ is. To seek those things above is to cultivate an ongoing desire for Christ, for heaven, for the currently veiled glory associated with Christ, seated at God's right hand. We walk by faith, not by sight (2 Cor. 5:7). It is by faith that we seek the things above, the heavenly things, *where Christ is.*

Paul is simply echoing the teaching of Jesus in Matthew 6:19–21: "Do not lay up for yourselves treasures on earth, where moth and rust destroy and where thieves break in and steal, but lay up for yourselves treasures in heaven, where neither moth nor rust destroys and where thieves do not break in and steal. For where your treasure is, there your heart will be also." Do not set your affection supremely on the things of this earth. Moth and rust can corrupt. Moths can eat away at precious things stored away on earth. They can corrupt the beauty of your most prized possessions in this world. And rust can corrode the most radiant and valuable objects that you might prize as invaluable. Such possessions are temporary—they do not endure forever. Thieves can breach and steal. Your most valued possessions in this age can take up wings and fly away before your eyes. Wealth and earthly possessions are as fleeting as human life. This world, this age, the visible earth in its present form, is filled with transient things that are passing away.

But in direct contrast to this, notice what Jesus says about treasure in heaven. Moth and rust cannot corrode what is in heaven. Peter tells us in 1 Peter 1:4 that your inheritance in heaven is imperishable and undefiled, reserved in heaven for you. This inheritance in heaven is beyond moth and rust—it cannot be corrupted. It is "reserved" (KJV, NASB)—or, perhaps better, *preserved*—in heaven for you by the power of the ascended Christ. No thief can enter in and steal this inheritance. No one is able to enter into heaven, destroy the ascended Christ, and take your inheritance in him. This is the comfort for the church as she has a fellowship in Christ's sufferings.

To sum up, there is a structural, organic theological relationship between the new relation to creation (Col. 1:16) and its perfection and application in the *historia* and *ordo salutis*. The relationship that God sustains to his creation, evident in Paul's description of the Son in Colossians 1:15–17, is maintained and further manifested throughout salvation. Thus, there is an organic relation between what has been perfected by Christ and what is applied to the church. All of this leads directly to the heavenly-mindedness of those united to Christ.

Pastoral Application

The point, put most basically, then, is this: pastors, along with all other Christians, are to seek the things above, where the ascended Christ is seated, *because that glorious realm abides forever as it has been filled with the Spirit of Christ.* Associated with this glory-filled realm is truth. Associated with this glory-filled realm is righteousness. Associated with this glory-filled realm is the cross of the ascended Christ. After the earthly cross came heavenly glory, first for Christ, and now for those of you united to him and seeking those things above, where he is. Let this be your strength in suffering, including suffering in your ministry (2 Cor. 4:16–18; Phil. 3:10–12).

Continue to seek him, raised and ascended into heaven, and do not set your mind on the wicked things of the earthly-minded. The earthly-minded confess and prize as absolute the fading and corrupting things of this present age and this present earth. They worship idols. The heavenly-minded confess as absolute the immutable triune God and possess the permanent and abiding things of the age to come and located in heaven, where Christ is, as ascended. They worship the absolute triune God in union with the ascended Christ. Pastors, worship in such a way as to cultivate this heavenly-mindedness in yourself, and impart it to others.

Ask, knock, and seek. As you seek, you will find. As you knock, it will be opened to you. And as you ask, Christ himself will make himself known to you by his Word and Spirit. Ask him to teach you, and he will show you that you participate in the fellowship of his sufferings on earth, even as you are raised with him to walk in newness of life. As raised with him, you are a present possessor of the glory of heaven itself, the place where Christ is, because your life is hidden with Christ in heaven. The secret of all this—the heart of the revealed mystery—is that by the Spirit and through faith, *Christ is in you* and *you are in Christ* (Rom. 8:9–11; Col. 1:27). Your life is hidden with Christ in God (Col. 3:3), and when Christ is revealed in the glory of heaven, you will appear with him there forever, in the glory of a new heaven and a new earth (Col. 3:4; 2 Peter 3:13; Rev. 21:1–4). Let this be the hope and *telos* of your every service to Christ.

Seek him. Find him. Listen to him. Trust him. Follow him. In the ascended Christ are the paths of life and the pleasures forever at the right hand of God (Acts 2:28). In Spirit-engendered union with him, as you seek him, you will find him in heaven. Finding Christ in heaven is only for the heavenly-minded—which is what you are in Christ Jesus. Geerhardus Vos advanced the deeper Protestant conception in its practical value for the Christian life, observing as follows in his most mature work:

> The life of this earth as a mere passing episode in time is not worth the aeonian toil expended upon it. Precisely because the Christian other-worldliness is inspired by the thought of God and not of self, it involves no danger of monastic withdrawal from or indifference to the present world. The same thirst for the divine glory which is the root of all heavenly-mindedness, also compels the consecration of all earthly existence to the promotion of God's kingdom. Here also the by-product cannot continue, if the main object of pursuit is lost sight of or neglected. But, what is most serious of all, the vanishing of the belief in the transcendent importance of the world to come would most surely spell the death of the Christian religion itself. Whatever may have been possible under Old Testament conditions, in the beginnings of revelation, it is absolutely impossible now with the New Testament behind us to construe a religious relationship between God and man on the basis of and within the limits of the present life alone.[17]

It is this message that the church of Jesus Christ so desperately needs to hear and embrace by Spirit-gifted faith. This is the good news to be proclaimed to a lost and a dying world. It is this message that Dr. Ferguson has heralded throughout a gospel ministry that has directed all who suffer with Christ to the place of comfort where he is, seated at the right hand of God, in heaven (Col. 3:1; Heb. 8:1).

Key Terms

historia salutis
image of God
new relation
ordo salutis
relation of coinherence

---

17. Geerhardus Vos, "Eschatology of the Psalter," in *Pauline Eschatology* (Phillipsburg, NJ: Presbyterian and Reformed, 1991), 364.

relation of origin
relation of subsistence

Recommendations for Further Reading

Kline, Meredith G. *God, Heaven and Har Magedon: A Covenantal Tale of Cosmos and Telos*. Eugene, OR: Wipf & Stock, 2006. Pp. 1–60.

Ridderbos, Herman N. *Paul: An Outline of His Theology*. Translated by John Richard de Witt. Grand Rapids: Eerdmans, 1975. Pp. 44–90.

Van Til, Cornelius. *An Introduction to Systematic Theology*. Nutley, NJ: Presbyterian and Reformed, 1974. Pp. 206–14.

Vos, Geerhardus. *Reformed Dogmatics*. Edited and translated by Richard B. Gaffin Jr. Vol. 1, *Theology Proper*. Bellingham, WA: Lexham Press, 2012. Pp. 3–76, 156–82.

Discussion Questions

1. If "image of the invisible God" refers to a Trinitarian relation of origin, then what does that imply about Adam's creation as the image of God?
2. If "firstborn of all creation" refers to the Son in his "new relation" to creation, how does that amplify Vos's teaching about the nature of that new relation?
3. How does Colossians 1:16 amplify the teaching from Genesis 1:1, Nehemiah 9:6, and Isaiah 6:1–7 regarding the creation of the invisible heaven in the absolute beginning?
4. How does Colossians 3:1–2 relate to Colossians 1:16 and 20?
5. How does the ascension of Christ relate to the commandment for the church to seek those "things that are above" (Col. 3:1–2)?

9

THE WORK OF CHRIST

Remembering the Forgetfulness of
God in Pastoral Ministry

DAVID GIBSON

". . . begotten before all ages of the Father according to the Godhead,
and in these latter days, for us and for our salvation, born of the
Virgin Mary, the Mother of God, according to the Manhood."
(Chalcedonian Creed, A.D. 451)

Introduction

What does God desire from his people?

In pastoral ministry, one encounters many different mental images of God in the minds of parishioners. Sinclair Ferguson has written of the anxious conscience of the worshiper faced by the Rev. John McLeod Campbell in nineteenth-century Scotland, where the preaching of the gospel was being heard as a demand for greater self-righteousness with little assurance of the love of God in Christ.[1] This problem is neither

1. Sinclair B. Ferguson, "'Blessed Assurance, Jesus Is Mine'? Definite Atonement and the Cure of Souls," in *From Heaven He Came and Sought Her: Definite Atonement in Historical, Biblical, Theological, and Pastoral Perspective*, ed. David Gibson and Jonathan Gibson (Wheaton, IL: Crossway, 2013), 612. This essay is typical of the ways in which Sinclair has edified the church with theological writings that

innately Scottish (!) nor the result of federal Calvinism, but rather, Ferguson argues, betrays the bent of the fallen human heart and its natural blindness to grace. Humanity's maxim appears to be *facere quod in se est* ("do what lies within you"), or "heaven helps those who help themselves."[2] Within this default setting, God is perceived either (1) as a headmaster or policeman, rulebook in one hand and baton in the other, so that what he wants is strict adherence to the set standard, or (2) as a genial grandfather, beaming a benign smile, expressing his desire that we simply do our best. Personal temperament dictates which image of God we gravitate toward.

In contrast, wise pastors know that it is the work of Another, not ours, that matches the divine intention and merits God's approval. What *Christ* does reveals what God desires: "Behold, I have come to do your will, O God" (Heb. 10:7).

In this chapter, I will argue that the doctrine of the work of Christ shows that what God wants for his people, what he desires and loves, is *the fellowship of perfection*. His original intention for creation and creatures to be perfect forever in his presence is restored by the work of Christ in his life, death, resurrection, ascension, and session at the right hand of the Father. This doctrine needs both a close-up lens (looking at what Christ does) and a wide-angle lens (taking in where, why, and how Christ does it); it requires us to see the work of Christ as the culmination of a single biblical story about creation gone awry but now given, gloriously, the promise of redemption and perfect restoration. I will do this by sketching a biblical-theological reading of Hebrews 10:1–18 to highlight key applications of the work of Christ to the labor of pastoral ministry. I will seek to show how the argument of these verses takes its narrative shape from the wider biblical narrative of the mediatorial offices of Prophet, Priest, and King, which Christ fulfills so wonderfully. Alert readers will spot the presence of three classical parts to the doctrine: the reason for Christ's work, its covenantal activity, and its ultimate achievement. To be as concrete

---

explore the depths of the gospel and its application to pastoral ministry. In my denomination, the International Presbyterian Church, by treating younger men as brothers, Sinclair has been a friend to many at formative stages of our development and a source of much wisdom and encouragement.

2. Ferguson, "'Blessed Assurance, Jesus Is Mine'?," 630–31.

as possible, I aim to show that the very heart of pastoral ministry is remembering the glorious truth that God forgets our sins because of the work of Christ, and yet his work is all the more stunning because forgiveness of sin is not the best answer we can give to the question of what God desires for his children.

This passage shows us several key aspects of the work of Christ that pastoral ministry needs to remember. I will focus on three of them.

Pastoral Ministry Remembers Our Crushing Problem (Heb. 10:1–4)

The opening verses of Hebrews 10 provide the vital context for the doctrine of Christ's work: he came to save his people from their sins. There is no way to escape our sin apart from the work of the Lord Jesus Christ. Hebrews 10:1–4 shows this to us in a surprising way—surprising because, in showing the inadequacy of the Old Testament sacrificial system, the writer knows full well that the constant shedding of blood in the work of the Levitical priesthood was God's idea. He provided sacrifice as a means of atonement, and yet, verses 1–4 argue, this very system still leaves us with the crushing problem of our sin.

The writer shows this problem in four ways. First, these sacrifices had an *insubstantial character*: "the law has but a shadow of the good things to come instead of the true form of these realities" (Heb. 10:1). We know from everyday life that no one wants to live in the realm of shadows. You can see your shadow and it is real, but you cannot actually touch it or have a conversation with it. Hebrews teaches that the cross of Jesus Christ towers over world history and casts a long shadow all the way back through the pages of the Old Testament and that the shape of the shadow is a lamb, a goat, a bull, an altar—none of those things was the real thing.

Second, note their *repetitive nature*: "continually offered every year" (Heb. 10:1) and "every priest stands daily at his service, offering repeatedly the same sacrifices" (v. 11). A friend of mine once had a faulty boiler, which again and again, week after week, had to be manually topped up. The very fact of repetition points to an inadequacy in the system. He constantly did the same work over and over again, when the right person with the right skills and the right equipment and the right qualifications (and for the right price) was able to fix it once and for all. The nature of the Old Testament sacrificial system was this: a priest's work was never done.

Third, these sacrifices had an *inadequate achievement*: they could not "make perfect those who draw near" (Heb. 10:1) by cleansing their consciences (v. 2). In fact, here we see what God intended in the system: "in these sacrifices there is a reminder of sins every year" (v. 3). Instead of being an annual reminder of sins forgiven, the sacrifices were an annual reminder of sin that needed to be forgiven. Again, we know what this is like in the world we live in. Sticking an IOU for your rent to the fridge door every month does not make you feel any better each time you walk into the kitchen; it simply reminds you of the outstanding debt that must still be paid.

And fourth, these sacrifices had *invalid materials*: "For it is impossible for the blood of bulls and goats to take away sins" (Heb. 10:4). The essence of the sacrificial system was substitution, but the economy of substitution is that it must be like for like. In a prisoner exchange, as opposing forces gather at the truce line, as one man steps forward and walks to safety, the other side does not release a herd of goats. The comparison of worth must be transparent. Our sin cannot be atoned for by an animal.

These verses come as the writer to the Hebrews is urging his readers to see that no one can save from sin apart from the Lord Jesus. Herman Bavinck shows quite powerfully how, among all peoples of the world in every age, there is always the need and hope of redemption from a sense of misery. Culture affords the genius of human progress but with it, too, pride and instability. And with all its wealth and power, civilization "only shows that the human heart, in which God has put eternity, is so huge that all the world is too small to satisfy it."[3] The world over, we know that something is wrong, but we do not know how to fix it. Miroslav Volf suggests that the essence of modernity is its claim that the fissures of the world can be repaired

---

3. Herman Bavinck, *Reformed Dogmatics*, ed. John Bolt, trans. John Vriend, vol. 3, *Sin and Salvation* (Grand Rapids: Baker Academic, 2006), 327–28.

and healed through the twin strategies of social control and rational thought. But, he argues, it is patently absurd to deny the expulsion of paradise from the beginning of history while expecting its creation at the end of history. Rather, "none of the grand recipes that promise to mend all the fissures can be trusted," for none have ever succeeded in eradicating the evil of the human heart.[4] The work of Christ alone addresses the crushing problem of our sinfulness.

When Christian theology and the church forget that the eternal Son became incarnate *for our salvation*, radical harm ensues for the gospel. There has always existed theological speculation about whether the Son would have become incarnate anyway regardless of the fall—G. C. Berkouwer calls the position at best "a border-opinion in the Christian church"—but on this account, as Berkouwer perceives, not only do incarnation and atonement have their intimate relationship loosened, so, too, the incarnation begins to take on a different character altogether.[5] Christ does not come to save but to exemplify, to teach, and at best to suffer empathetically or as victim, not vicariously. When salvation from sin ceases to be causal in the mission of Christ, then it is common to speak freely of the kingdom of God as being at hand while at the same time muting the voice of the King: "*Repent* and believe in the gospel" (Mark 1:15). B. B. Warfield shows with compelling force how a description of the Christian faith that does not portray Christ himself as tracing his work with the jarring outline of a cruel cross will be many things, but not Christian.[6]

This means simply that the gospel minister is constrained to keep in front of him the fact that the work of Christ is the work of a *Savior*,

4. Miroslav Volf, *Exclusion and Embrace: A Theological Exploration of Identity, Otherness, and Reconciliation* (Nashville: Abingdon, 1996), 28.

5. G. C. Berkouwer, *The Work of Christ* (Grand Rapids: Eerdmans, 1965), 21–22. See the treatment in John Calvin, *Institutes of the Christian Religion*, ed. John T. McNeill, trans. Ford Lewis Battles, 2 vols., Library of Christian Classics 20–21 (Philadelphia: Westminster, 1960), 2.12.4: "the only reason given to us in Scripture that the Son of God willed to take our flesh, and accepted this commandment from the Father, is that he would be a sacrifice to appease the Father on our behalf" (468).

6. Benjamin B. Warfield, "The Essence of Christianity and the Cross of Christ," in *The Person and Work of Christ* (Philadelphia: Presbyterian and Reformed, 1970), 479–530.

and therefore, the story of his own work is to be structured by that story if it is to retain its integrity. Theological liberalism is far from being the only danger.

There is a modern pastoral version of "incarnation anyway": the presence of Christ in the life of the minister and his people becomes divorced from the reason for the presence of Christ in the world in the first place. Instead of coming "for us and for our salvation," as the Nicene Creed confesses, Christ came for us and for our happiness, comfort, and success in the world. Any manner of individual contextual alternatives may be inserted here. We pursue the same career goals as everyone else around us, but with the difference that Jesus is there for us as our "coach." When ministry is infected with this virus, the language of sin and forgiveness and grace and the gospel recedes from our regular vocabulary in shepherding and inevitably drifts instead toward either the theologically didactic or the relationally therapeutic, depending on our personal inclination. On the one hand, ministers quickly become messiahs, saving their people from all manner of social, relational, and economic ills. On the other hand, in doing so, we become quick to counsel but slow to explore and expose the persistent presence of sin as the root of all our ills and the gravest of offenses toward God.[7] It is possible to do many things in ministry without living and dying by the main thing: the gospel of a cleansed conscience before God because of Jesus.

Having seen that pastoral ministry remembers our crushing problem of sin, and therefore our need of a Savior, the question now in front of us is *how* Christ saves us from our sins.

Pastoral Ministry Pursues a Vital Contrast (Heb. 10:5–14)

We might easily think that the writer of Hebrews is pressing a contrast between the sacrifice of animals on the one hand and the superior sacrifice of Christ on the other. This is certainly true, of course, not least in the contrast between the constant repetition of the former and the once-for-all nature of the latter (Heb. 10:12). The

7. Eugene H. Peterson recounts a vivid personal example of just such a drift in his own ministry that is worth careful reflection. See *The Pastor: A Memoir* (New York: HarperCollins, 2012), 130–42.

main contrast, however, is not between types of sacrifice per se, but between types of human action that bring pleasure to God.

Note how Hebrews 10:5 actually comes as a surprise in the flow of the passage. After the impossibility of animal sacrifice to deal with sin so decisively outlined in 10:1–4, when in verse 5 we come to the advent of Christ, we might expect a contrast with the effectiveness of Christ's sacrifice. But instead we learn that "sacrifices and offerings you have not desired . . . ; in burnt offerings and sin offerings you have taken no pleasure" (vv. 5–6). Something brings God more pleasure than sacrifice: "a body you have prepared for me. . . . 'Behold, I have come to do your will, O God'" (vv. 5, 7). As Michael Horton puts it, not an animal sacrifice but a *living* sacrifice is required for redemption.[8]

This should give us pause as we flesh out the doctrine of Christ's work, for the obedience of Christ is here taking center stage. Bavinck notes: "In theology this rich idea has frequently not come into its own. Often Christ's suffering has been separated from the act of obedience expressed in it and thus made into an object of pious reflection."[9] In fact, the obedience of Christ is the overarching biblical concept for explaining how Christ saves us, and here we touch the heart of the matter.

Soteriology is the story of two Adams: "For as by the one man's disobedience the many were made sinners, so by the one man's obedience the many will be made righteous" (Rom. 5:19).[10] What the first Adam undid, the second Adam repairs. Human beings, covenant partners who do his will, are what God desires. Delighted devotion, wholehearted love, humble submission, and joyful, intimate relationship—this is what Adam was invited to return to God. What God sought from the very beginning was pristine shalom, covenantal wholeness, consummated relational perfection in the garden and to the ends of the earth, humankind living in God's Sabbath rest; but what God's covenant partner returned instead was pride, suspicion,

8. Michael Horton, *Lord and Servant: A Covenant Christology* (Louisville: Westminster John Knox, 2005), 225.

9. Bavinck, *Sin and Salvation*, 377.

10. An earlier and much more abbreviated form of my argument here appeared in *Tabletalk*, December 2014, and is used here with permission.

unbelief, and rebellion—and all was lost. The sacrificial system was instituted to remedy the problem of human disobedience, but it could not produce human obedience. Yet what about the second Man? Wonderful beyond words is the fact that before he came to die, Jesus came to live.

All of this helps us to note, as we penetrate Hebrews 10 further, that Christ's person and work are inseparable: a body prepared for him and a divine will executed by him. It is *who* Christ is that makes possible *what* Christ achieves. Reformed theology is right to hold that what emerges in these verses is a clear picture of Christ as Mediator, with the Man Christ Jesus able to represent both his people and his Father perfectly. Gloriously, "he does not stand between two parties: he *is* those two parties in his own person."[11] Here, in the "I have come" language, is what John Owen calls the infinite condescension of his mediatorial office: the one who comes to take human nature is the eternal Son, the Lord of glory.[12]

It is necessary that our Savior be a man, truly human like us. Scripture is clear that God is the only Savior, and yet because humans have sinned, God's justice demands that only a human can pay for sin. In the words of the Heidelberg Catechism, because of his righteousness, "God will not punish another creature for what a human is guilty of" (Q14). This is stunning: if only God in himself saved us, it could have destroyed the moral fabric of the universe. We need a Savior who is human. The Chalcedonian Creed makes it clear that when the eternal Son, "begotten before all ages of the Father," joined himself to human nature in the womb of the virgin, then that same Son, our Lord Jesus Christ, was "truly God and truly man, of a reasonable soul and body; . . . in all things like unto us." He was not a divine being who appeared to be human. Jesus was not "God in human skin." He was a man, fully human in every way.

But the creed also adds two crucial words: "in all things like unto us, *without sin*." As the answer to Heidelberg Catechism question 16 puts it, "God's justice demands that human nature, which has sinned, must pay for its sin; but a sinner could never pay for sin." To be a

11. Bavinck, *Sin and Salvation*, 363 (emphasis in translation).
12. John Owen, *The Glory of Christ: His Office and Grace* (1684; repr., Fearn, Scotland: Christian Focus, 2004), 93–106.

fallen human being is to "increase our guilt every day" (Q13). We need a Savior who is like us (human) to be able to pay for our sin, and we need a Savior who is unlike us (sinless) to be able to pay for our sins. It is common in modern theology to argue that in taking human nature, the Son of God took *fallen* human nature. The assertion is that because we have fallen natures, Jesus cannot be truly like us unless he, too, has a fallen human nature. But this short-circuits the magnificent beauty of Christ's obedience. Fallenness is not intrinsic to being human; if it were, Adam would not have truly been a man. The Word became flesh to go right back to the very beginning, so to speak, and to do as a man what Adam failed to do. In the womb of his mother, he is both completely identified with us (he is human) and distinct from us (he is free of all Adamic guilt). The language of the Spirit's "overshadowing" Mary in the miracle of the incarnation (Luke 1:35) hints at both new-creation and new-exodus themes.[13] It is best to say that Christ relives Adam's life not from the point of the fall onward, but from the point of creation onward. He is the last Adam and the new Israel, facing their temptations and fighting their battles, only now triumphing at every point at which they failed.

At the same time, the obedient self-offering of Jesus is not just the offering of a human life. The one who dies is the one who remains "in very nature God." Heidelberg Catechism answer 14 says that "no mere creature can bear the weight of God's eternal anger against sin and release others from it." Sin against an infinite God requires an infinite payment, but a finite human cannot render this to God outside an eternal hell. We need a Savior who is more than a man. Christ's death, because of who he is as the God-man, is of infinite value and fully satisfies the righteous demands of an infinitely holy God.

These considerations about the person of the Mediator mean that we must never separate the work of the Mediator from his person, as though what Christ does and gives could be received in isolation from receiving Christ himself. Although the phrase is inexact, there is a sense in which it is vital to see that Christ has come to *be* someone for us before he *does* something for us. That is to say, the cross is effective

---

13. Cf. Sinclair Ferguson, *The Holy Spirit* (Leicester, UK: Inter-Varsity Press, 1996), 38–39.

because it is *this* Christ who dies on it: "This, to use an Augustinian term, is *totus Christus*, the whole Christ, the person in whom incarnation has been accomplished and in whom atonement, resurrection, ascension and heavenly reign are now realized."[14] In simple terms, this means that the vocabulary of pastoral ministry—preaching the good news of justification, adoption, reconciliation, sanctification, and so on—must never become divorced from the grammar of ministry: preaching Christ himself and showing how what Christ gives is effective because of who Christ is.[15]

The rest of Hebrews 10 makes this clear by showing the office of Mediator in three parts: Christ is Prophet, Priest, and King. From who he is flows what he does. This ancient way of portraying Christ's work, the *munus triplex*, receives classic elaboration in John Calvin, who establishes exactly the kind of connection we have outlined above by showing that there is one office (Mediator) in three parts (Prophet, Priest, King), not three separate offices, because "under the law prophets as well as priests and kings were anointed with holy oil"; and the Savior bears the name *Christ*, "the Anointed One." It is because Christ is the Mediator that he is Prophet, Priest, and King, and by performing and fulfilling the work of each of these typological roles, Christ brings salvation to us.[16]

Christ speaks as Prophet: "I have come to do your will" (Heb. 10:7). The revelation here of the will of the Father is not in itself actually new, for Christ's words are a quotation from Psalm 40, and indeed parallel the incident narrated in the Old Testament where disobedient King Saul learns that the Lord does not have as great delight in burnt offerings and sacrifices as in obedience (1 Sam. 15:22). The concept is covenantal, not novel, but Christ speaks here as Prophet

---

14. Sinclair Ferguson, *The Whole Christ: Legalism, Antinomianism, and Gospel Assurance—Why the Marrow Controversy Still Matters* (Wheaton, IL: Crossway, 2016), 46.

15. See Berkouwer, *Work of Christ*, 20: "In human relationships it is possible—out of ingratitude—to isolate the gift from the giver and still enjoy it, and there are also 'unknown givers' in the background. But Christ is not such an unknown giver. He gives himself, and therefore his gift is never an isolated richness. Every gift would lose its richness and vivifying power when isolated and considered apart from his person."

16. Calvin, *Institutes*, 2.14.2.

par excellence in two ways: he authoritatively interprets the Scripture to be about himself (Heb. 10:7), and in so doing he establishes a new landmark in redemptive history: "He does away with the first in order to establish the second" (v. 9). Christ does not now stand alongside the sacrificial system as a superior alternative; his very words render it obsolete while establishing himself as absolute. Bavinck puts it beautifully: "He is the law and the gospel in his own person. He is not a prophet only by the words he speaks but primarily by what he is."[17]

Alongside this, Christ's priestly work is evident here in two main ways. We know from the book of Leviticus that the sacrificial rites contained thanksgiving offerings and guilt offerings. Thanksgiving offerings relate to the kind of life that God always intended humanity to live in his presence and are what Adam should have offered in the garden; guilt offerings become necessary after the fall and relate to the kind of life that we now experience. In the second Adam, we see the fulfillment of both types of sacrifices. Throughout his whole life, Christ offers himself as a sacrifice of praise to his Father—"I have come to do your will" (Heb. 10:7)—and in his death, he offers himself as a sacrifice of atonement for sin. The life Jesus lived prepared for the death Jesus died, because his obedient life climaxes in his sacrificial death on the cross: "But when Christ had offered for all time a single sacrifice for sins, he sat down at the right hand of God" (v. 12).[18]

Christ's royal work is also present: he "sat down at the right hand of God, waiting from that time until his enemies should be made a footstool for his feet" (Heb. 10:12–13). Here the promise God gives to his King to make the ends of the earth his possession and to see the ultimate destruction of all that is evil (Ps. 2) is applied to Jesus. The King is now waiting and watching, royal rule expressed in divine patience as much as in regal power. At the same time, we observe such a close connection between priestly and kingly work, the royal following on from the sacrificial, that here we see an excellent example of why it is not easy to separate out the three parts of Christ's work

17. Bavinck, *Sin and Salvation*, 337.

18. For a brilliant treatment of this, see Michael Horton, "Obedience Is Better than Sacrifice," in *The Law Is Not of Faith: Essays on Works and Grace in the Mosaic Covenant*, ed. Bryan D. Estelle, J. V. Fesko, and David VanDrunen (Phillipsburg, NJ: P&R Publishing, 2009), 315–36.

and assign them to discrete elements of his obedience.[19] Calvin, for example, in drawing on other parts of the New Testament, describes Christ's offering of himself on the cross in royal language: "There is no tribunal so magnificent, no kingly throne so stately, no show of triumph so distinguished, no chariot so lofty, as is the gibbet on which Christ subdued death and the devil."[20]

Not only are we unable to separate the three parts of Christ's office from one another, even as we distinguish them, but we should also see that Christ's office as Mediator in the *munus triplex* extends through what is known as the *doctrine of the two states*, Christ's humiliation and exaltation (traced in outline in Philippians 2:5–11, for instance). The letter to the Hebrews shows us that not only is Christ Prophet, Priest, and King in his humiliation (his conception, and life lived unto death), but so, too, he is these things in his exaltation, from heaven ruling his world as Prophet by his word and interceding as Priest in the power of an indestructible life, waiting as King to come to defeat his enemies and to judge the living and the dead. Our salvation depends on *both* humiliation and exaltation, so that the resurrection saves with the cross and the cross with the resurrection. Calvin explains: "we divide the substance of our salvation between Christ's death and resurrection as follows: through his death, sin was wiped out and death extinguished; through his resurrection, righteousness was restored and life raised up."[21] It is this conception that leads Calvin to one of his most eloquent descriptions

19. Bavinck and Berkouwer together point out how Reformed dogmatics has always been cautious about trying too hard to delineate exactly what in Christ's life and work belongs to each particular office. Sometimes there are clear distinctions; other times, what has been attached to one turns out to be just as plausibly attached to another. Cf. Bavinck, *Sin and Salvation*, 366; Berkouwer, *Work of Christ*, 20.

20. Calvin, commenting on Colossians 2:15, in *Calvin's New Testament Commentaries: The Epistles of Paul the Apostle to the Galatians, Ephesians, Philippians and Colossians*, ed. David W. Torrance and Thomas F. Torrance (Grand Rapids: Eerdmans, 1965), 336.

21. Calvin, *Institutes*, 2.16.13. Cf. the helpful treatment by Gavin Ortlund, "Resurrected as Messiah: The Risen Christ as Prophet, Priest, and King," *JETS* 54, no. 4 (December 2011): 749–66. "Our salvation consists of both a bloody cross and an empty tomb, both a Friday afternoon's agony and a Sunday morning's vindication— and the latter is not merely proof of the gospel, but part of the gospel" (751).

of the unity of Christ's work in relation to his person in both humiliation and exaltation:

> We see that our whole salvation and all its parts are comprehended in Christ. . . . If we seek strength it lies in his dominion; if purity, in his conception; if gentleness, it appears in his birth. . . . If we seek redemption, it lies in his passion; if acquittal, in his condemnation; if remission of the curse, in his cross; if satisfaction, in his sacrifice; if purification, in his blood; if reconciliation, in his descent into hell; if mortification of the flesh, in his tomb; if newness of life, in his resurrection; if immortality, in the same; if inheritance of the heavenly kingdom, in his entrance into heaven; if protection, if security, if abundant supply of all blessings, in his kingdom; if untroubled expectation of judgment, in the power given to him to judge. In short, since rich store of every kind of good abounds in him, let us drink our fill from this fountain, and from no other.[22]

We may say that the reason that anyone in Christ is a new creation (2 Cor. 5:17) is that Christ himself is a new creation, the firstfruits of the age to come entering the old age in advance, in his own person uniting heaven and earth, and therefore able not merely to herald the new world order but in himself to actually bring it. The gospel we preach is that Christ himself is the gospel.[23]

In all the interpenetrations of the *munus triplex*, and in their operations across both states, we observe again how crucial throughout is Christ's obedience. This is because the *munus triplex* itself is a proto-anthropology: Christ's office does not arrive de novo with his coming, nor even with the presence of Israel on the world stage, but rather, "the three offices with which Christ was commissioned are a reference to the original calling and purpose of man."[24] Typologically, they are a depiction of what Adam was meant to be and do in the garden of Eden. As prophet, he received God's word and was required

---

22. Calvin, *Institutes*, 2.16.19.

23. Cf. Ferguson, *Whole Christ*, 44.

24. Herman Bavinck, *The Wonderful Works of God: Instruction in the Christian Religion according to the Reformed Confessions*, trans. Henry Zylstra (Glenside, PA: Westminster Seminary Press, 2019), 316.

to speak it in turn to Eve and their descendants; as priest, he was to return the sacrifice of praise to God in the garden-temple sanctuary; as king, he was to exercise dominion over the earth as God's image-bearer—and in executing his office in this threefold way thereby cultivating the garden to fill the earth and subdue it.[25] The coming of Christ into the world is the definitive act in this Adamic saga because his offering of himself makes perfect for all time, and it is vital to grasp that this is so because offering himself in death was the climactic act of his offering a perfect life to the Father. As Calvin puts it, "Our Lord came forth as true man and took the name and person of Adam in order to take Adam's place in obeying the Father, to present our flesh as the price of satisfaction to God's righteous judgment, and in the same flesh, to pay the penalty that we had deserved."[26] Horton states what we often fail to observe: "The cross can only be regarded as standing synecdotally for the whole of Christ's life and obedience."[27] Calvin makes a similar point, but from the angle of observing the narrative structure of Christ's death, his very passion unfolding in a way that shines the spotlight on the fact of his voluntary, willing obedience. Christ could not have suffered just any kind of death (such as being murdered by thieves or slain in an insurrection). It was essential that Christ died in this particular way—tried in a kangaroo court, arraigned by false witnesses, sentenced to death unjustly, and executed between two thieves—precisely because in so doing he is seen as a blameless man before the judgment seat as a criminal and taking the role of a guilty man. "Thus we shall behold the person of a sinner and evildoer represented in Christ, yet from his shining innocence it will at the same time be obvious he was burdened with another's sin rather than his own."[28]

What, then, is the effect of Christ's saving work for us, and what might application of this passage look like?

---

25. For more development of this, cf. G. K. Beale, *The Temple and the Church's Mission*, NSBT 17 (Leicester, UK: Inter-Varsity Press, 2004); Jonathan Gibson and Mark Earngey, eds., *Reformation Worship: Liturgies from the Past for the Present* (Greensboro, NC: New Growth Press, 2018), 1–22.

26. Calvin, *Institutes*, 2.12.3.

27. Horton, *Lord and Servant*, 220.

28. Calvin, *Institutes*, 2.16.5.

Pastoral Ministry Rejoices in a Perfect
Relationship (Heb. 10:15–18)

The work of Christ perfects for all time those who are being sanctified (Heb. 10:14). The following verses make clear exactly what this means: it is the arrival among God's people of a covenant in which God has taken his law and put it in our hearts and written it on our minds (v. 16). This is nothing less than the fulfillment of the covenant of grace ("I will be your God, and you shall be my people," Jer. 7:23), a return to the garden, where Adam and Eve knew and loved God's law with wholehearted delight, and it is an anticipation of the end of time when God himself will dwell with us, when heaven and earth will once again be united as they were in the beginning. It is a picture of the closest possible relationship between God and his children. Wonderfully, it is a relationship in which God forgets our sin: "I will remember their sins and their lawless deeds no more" (Heb. 10:17).

Throughout this chapter, I have been trying to tease out various threads that might allow us to say that God desires something more than the forgiveness that comes from sacrifice. *He desires the relationship that comes from obedience.* We have some sense of this in all our relationships. As spouses, parents, friends, we know that after wrongdoing, forgiveness restores communication and breaks down barriers (or at least it should). But something is better than forgiveness, and it is simply the open, free-flowing sheer joy in each other that comes when we are relating to each other as we should in the first place. Forgiveness is great, yes, but better by far than tearful apologies is actually living as we ought in selfless delight, enchanted with God and loving our neighbor as ourselves.

I suggest that in large measure this is the glorious gospel of Hebrews 10. Horton states the case so well: "the goal of redemption is not simply restoration, 'paradise restored,' but the consummation; and for this not only forgiveness but the perfect fulfillment of the law was required. Jesus recapitulated in himself the history of Adam and Israel in order to bring us not only out of ruin into a state of innocence, or guilt into forgiveness, but to bring the whole of creation into the everlasting Sabbath."[29]

29. Horton, *Lord and Servant*, 220.

The point is that "one may be forgiven and yet not be righteous,"[30] and the message of Hebrews is that it is precisely *both* these grace-gifts that Christ has won for us. A second Adam has walked the earth, one who brought God more pleasure than any burnt offering ever could, precisely because his whole life was an offering of praise. He returned to God what every human being in every age and place should return to God, but none do: devoted, delighted obedience. Why is it that God does not remember our sins and lawless acts? Why has he forgotten them? Not, of course, because he has a memory problem. It is because he has chosen to remember something else instead: Christ's life of willing delight in doing his will—*and that obedient life is ours.* The imputation of Christ's obedience to the believer needs to be the very heartbeat of our ministries. The offering of Christ's life was his active obedience and the offering of death his passive obedience, and *both* are necessary to save us. In his death, Christ gave himself up to the judicial punishment for sin, but he was an acceptable offering because he was a guilt-free and wholly obedient man, and so was worthy of taking the place of guilt-laden, disobedient sinners.

Our own societal individualism impacts our reading of Scripture to such an extent that, more than simply viewing ourselves as autonomous individuals, we view Christ as a private individual when, in fact, he comes to us in the Bible clothed in the titles of covenant union. Christ is a second Adam, and neither first nor second Adam acts alone. What one does, he does for those who belong to him. As a husband as head of his wife is fully responsible for her welfare, so Adam and Jesus as heads of their families bear complete responsibility for them. The actions of the one implicate those who are his, either in disobedience or in righteousness. Just as Adam made us sinners, so Christ makes us righteous. He is a King for his people, a Bridegroom for his bride, a Shepherd for his sheep, a Master for his friends, a Savior for sinners, a Head for the body, a Vine for the branches. As Bavinck points out, "his entire life was an act of self-denial, a self-offering *presented by him as head in the place of his own.*"[31]

---

30. Horton, *Lord and Servant*, 224.
31. Bavinck, *Sin and Salvation*, 379 (emphasis added).

Indeed, such union with Christ is part of the very goal of creation itself: "We live *coram Deo*—before God—as the creatures he made according to his image and likeness. Yet the goal of our creation is greater, namely to live *in* God, being united to him as much as is possible for a creature."[32]

This means that the central task of pastoral ministry is to rejoice in Jesus' perfect relationship with God and to read our own relationship with God—and, by implication, the very definition of our ministries—in light of his primary, perfect relationship with God. This looks like immersing ourselves in the glory of union with Christ, understanding it deeply and living and preaching it tirelessly as the astonishingly good news that it is. Scottish theology has given to the church some extremely rich reflections on the application to pastoral ministry of union with Christ in all its facets, what it means for it to be true that "as to him, so to us." I want to give two examples.

The Rev. William Still, the minister of Gilcomston South Church in Aberdeen (1945–97), delivered an address to the Crieff Fellowship in 1979 entitled "The Minister as Feeder of Souls." Speaking after nearly forty years of parish ministry, the Rev. Still's paper is part autobiographical reflection, part exposition, with the single aim of displaying the work of the minister as dying daily in order to feed one's people the death of the Savior. William Still's text was this: "I am the living bread that came down from heaven. If anyone eats of this bread, he will live forever. And the bread that I will give for the life of the world is my flesh" (John 6:51). I suspect that today, were many of us to address the same topic, we would focus, at best, on a theology of preaching or the character of the preacher, or at worst on the techniques of communication. Instead, the Rev. Still offers a profound theology of "feeding." Christ feeds his people by breaking the living bread of his body in death, such that what ministers offer to their people—indeed, all they have to offer—is Christ crucified. This is the content of the Word of God with which ministers feed their flocks; but *because that is its content*, then God does something to his ministers as they do this—he makes them real-life examples of the

---

32. Michael Horton, *Calvin on the Christian Life: Glorifying and Enjoying God Forever* (Wheaton, IL: Crossway, 2014), 83.

death of Jesus: "we must identify with him, absolutely, as if it was *our* flesh that was being broken for the people."[33] This is the profoundly biblical, deeply Pauline conception of ministry whereby God gives his servants thorns in the flesh, places our light in jars of clay, makes us weak to display his strength, and leads us to always carry "in the body the death of Jesus, so that the life of Jesus may also be manifested in our bodies" (2 Cor. 4:10). As Still says, "The true bread is Christ, only, whose bread can only be handled by, and handed to the people by crucified hands—by flesh, willing to become itself, broken bread and poured out wine for the people."[34]

Further applications of union with Christ in his office as Mediator can be made. The Scottish theologian Hugh Martin (1821–85), in "A Letter to My Daughters on the Prophetic Office of Christ," gives a charming exposition of the infinite riches that flow to the minister and his people from being united to Christ in his own relationship with the Father. Martin recognizes that the question in front of the minister, daily in his study and his pastoral work, weekly in each sermon, is the question that towers above all others: "What think ye of Christ?"[35] It is worth pausing to ask how we would answer that today and where we would turn to flesh out our answers.

Martin suggests that what will really fill our minds with understanding and our hearts with love for the Lord Jesus is knowing him "as the supreme office-bearer in the Church." It is the "Son of his bosom" whom God has given to the church as its "official, regular, standing Instructor" *before it is ever the minister.*[36] This makes the relations between the persons of the blessed Trinity the primary relationship for the pastor to delight in as the wellspring of his own spiritual affections. That is to say, because the Father shows the Son all that he does, in then communicating this to his people as Prophet,

---

33. William Still, "The Minister as Feeder of Souls," unpublished address given at the 1979 Crieff Conference, Scotland, with the theme: "The Word of God as Life and Nourishment for Souls."

34. Still, "The Minister as Feeder of Souls." For a similarly rich version of this argument, see William R. Edwards, "Participants in What We Proclaim: Recovering Paul's Narrative of Pastoral Ministry," *Themelios* 39, no. 3 (2014): 455–69.

35. In Hugh Martin, *Christ Victorious: Selected Writings of Hugh Martin*, ed. Matthew J. Hyde and Catherine E. Hyde (Edinburgh: Banner of Truth, 2019), 403–25.

36. Martin, *Christ Victorious*, 405–6.

the Son changes our status from servants to friends precisely because of the intimacy of knowledge of God that he shares with us: "No longer do I call you servants, for the servant does not know what his master is doing; but I have called you friends, *for* all that I have heard from my Father I have made known to you" (John 15:15). Pastors quickly become servants—serving God, serving the church family, serving the denomination—but all such servitude must flow from friendship with Christ because his own office of Prophet defines the nature of our relationship to him. What he does for us means that we can be friends with him. If we lose daily friendship with Christ, pastors next lose a ready ease and deep love of sharing his words and instead come to view ourselves as the repositories of truth and wisdom for our people. But intimate friendship with Christ, as Prophet in his office of Mediator, leads us to say of him, "You are the most handsome of the sons of men; grace is poured upon your lips; therefore God has blessed you forever" (Ps. 45:2). If we love him like this, we will be unable not to speak about him like this to our people.

And grace will flow from our lips.

Conclusion

Sinclair Ferguson has provided a devastating exposé of the theological fault lines in the way that John McLeod Campbell responded to his people's troubled consciences, while nevertheless also recognizing the desideratum of his pastoral impulse in the care of souls. McLeod Campbell longed that his people "might be free to serve God, with a pure disinterested love to Him."[37] This was surely right. The work of the pastor is to know and to show that the ground of this freedom is found not in us but in the work of Christ because he has done away with all the ways in which we are tempted to seek his favor in ourselves.[38] At the root of this is a focus on ourselves even though, counterintuitively, the best way to see ourselves in relation to God is not to look at ourselves but to focus on Jesus' relationship with God. Without a steady gaze on Christ as Prophet, Priest, and King, pastors

37. Ferguson, "'Blessed Assurance, Jesus Is Mine'?," 613.
38. See the helpful study by Jared C. Wilson, *The Pastor's Justification: Applying the Work of Christ in Your Life and Ministry* (Wheaton, IL: Crossway, 2013).

either will try to be these offices for their people or will watch as their flock tries to be them, too, without Jesus.

For instance, ministers soon discover that the rite of sacrifice is alive and well in all our hearts. We offer the sacrifice of time—after sinning, we wait a while before drawing near to God. We bring to God the sacrifice of a daily quiet time. As ministers, we carry before God, and the church, the sacrifice of service—we think that the fruit of gospel work is dependent on our workaholic schedules. And in it all, we remember the wrong thing about ourselves and forget the right thing about God—in Jesus alone, God remembers our sins no more.

So, too, forgiveness is the necessary vocabulary of gospel ministry, but the gospel minister is not long in ministry before he encounters all the multifaceted problems of forgiveness in his own heart and the hearts of the flock. Some cannot forgive others. Many cannot forgive themselves. Others long for forgiveness from someone with every fiber of their being. In it all, we are up against the fact that, left to our own devices, we cannot do what God can do: forget our sins. We remember them. We return to them and linger over them, prodding their memory and nursing their effects on us and others— yet in Jesus, God remembers our sins no more. We may be unable to forget our own sins or the sins of others, but the offering to God of Jesus' perfect life instructs us that when such remembering is used to hold sin against ourselves or against others, it is not because we have measured sin rightly but because we have measured Christ's offering wrongly. His life is sufficient to cover our wrongs. His death is enough to forgive our sins.

Yet as liberating as this is, the doctrine of the work of Christ leads us on to an even more glorious, cosmic reality: Christ can forgive *and* make righteous. He has completed Adam's work, fulfilled his mandate, restored what was lost, paid what was due, borne the curse, and so creation and creatures will again one day enter our perfect Sabbath rest.

Is there any greater news in all the world than this?[39]

---

39. I am grateful to John Ferguson, Jonathan Gibson, and Jonty Rhodes for their comments on an earlier version of this chapter.

Key Terms

exaltation of Christ
federal Calvinism
humiliation of Christ
session

Recommendations for Further Reading

Gibson, David, and Jonathan Gibson, eds. *From Heaven He Came and Sought Her: Definite Atonement in Historical, Biblical, Theological, and Pastoral Perspective.* Wheaton, IL: Crossway, 2013.

Letham, Robert. *The Work of Christ.* Contours of Christian Theology. Leicester, UK: Inter-Varsity Press, 1993.

Murray, John. *Redemption Accomplished and Applied.* Grand Rapids: Eerdmans, 1955.

Still, William. *The Work of the Pastor.* Rev. ed. Fearn, Scotland: Christian Focus, 2010.

Discussion Questions

1. What truths assure a Christian of God's love?
2. How are faith and assurance related?
3. Why must the Savior be both God and man?
4. God desires a relationship that comes from obedience more than forgiveness from sacrifice. How does this observation affect your understanding of God?
5. In what ways should Christ's work be imaged in a pastor's work?
6. How may pastors be helped to forget their own sins and those of others in their congregation?

10

UNION WITH CHRIST

Gospel Ministry as Dying
and Rising with Jesus

PHILIP GRAHAM RYKEN

The most famous and influential doctrine from the Protestant Reformation is justification by faith alone. But as theologians reflected more broadly on the connection between justification and other aspects of salvation, another beautiful doctrine came to increasing prominence as a Reformed distinctive: union with Christ.

Simply put, this doctrine teaches that when we trust in Jesus, the Holy Spirit so closely unites us to Christ's death and resurrection that everything that is his becomes ours. It is not just Christ's righteousness that belongs to us by faith, but all the other blessings of salvation, too.

As we will see, the doctrine of union with Christ has held a central place in the thinking of Reformation theologians across the centuries—from John Calvin to John Owen to John Murray. Indeed, one church historian goes so far as to identify union with Christ as "the normative dogma of Reformed Christianity."[1] The reason for this, of

---

1. Gordon S. Wakefield, *Puritan Devotion: Its Place in the Development of Christian Piety* (London: Epworth Press, 1957), 5.

171

course, is that union with Christ holds an equally central place in the New Testament, especially in the writings of the apostle Paul.

What I hope to show in this chapter is how central this doctrine can also be for the practice of pastoral ministry. My starting and ending point is Paul's holy ambition in Philippians 3:10–11: "that I may know [Christ] and the power of his resurrection, and may share his sufferings, becoming like him in his death, that by any means possible I may attain the resurrection from the dead."

In these verses, Paul expresses a desire that flows directly from the gospel—specifically, from the death of Jesus for our sins and his resurrection from the grave with the free gift of eternal life. From what he says, we can sense how desperately the apostle wanted the cross and the empty tomb to become integral to his Christian experience. Sinclair Ferguson has lovingly described union with Christ as a doctrine that "engages our whole being."[2] This was obviously true for Paul, and it ought to be equally true for every other minister of the gospel. Enlivened and empowered by our crucified and risen Lord, we carry out every aspect of pastoral ministry in union with Christ.[3]

Stated more simply, gospel ministry is dying and rising with Jesus.

Union with Christ in Biblical Theology

Being united to Christ is one of the central concerns of the New Testament. Again and again, the apostle Paul emphasizes the necessity of being found "in Christ" (Phil. 3:9). This is because he knows that it is only in Christ that salvation's blessings are located: "Blessed be the God and Father of our Lord Jesus Christ, who has blessed us *in Christ* with every spiritual blessing in the heavenly places" (Eph. 1:3). This vital relationship summarizes our salvation and describes

---

2. Sinclair B. Ferguson, *Some Pastors and Teachers: Reflecting a Biblical Vision of What Every Minister Is Called to Be* (Edinburgh: Banner of Truth, 2017), 526. Writing this essay has been a labor of my love for Dr. Ferguson, whose wise counsel, generous friendship, profound teaching, heartwarming preaching, and exemplary Christian life have inspired me to pursue the highest ideals in gospel ministry.

3. An earlier version of this chapter was published in *The Practical Calvinist: An Introduction to the Presbyterian and Reformed Heritage*, ed. Peter A. Lillback (Fearn, Scotland: Mentor/Christian Focus, 2002).

the new life that God has given us to live. "If anyone is *in Christ*," Paul says, "he is a new creation" (2 Cor. 5:17).

Given the consistent priority that the Bible places on being "in Christ," the doctrine of union with Christ properly occupies a primary place in systematic theology. It also provides the essential context for our Christian experience. Through our union with Christ, we are joined to him at every point in his saving activity. We were predestined in Christ. On the basis of our union with him, we are not only justified, but also adopted and sanctified. It is also in the image of Christ that one day we will be raised and glorified. Therefore, as John Murray has written, "union with Christ is really the central truth of the whole doctrine of salvation. . . . It embraces the wide span of salvation from its ultimate source in the eternal election of God to its final fruition in the glorification of the elect."[4] Without beginning and without end, every aspect of salvation is entailed in our union with Christ.

It is not surprising, then, that union with Christ became a prominent theme in the theology of the Reformers and their successors. To give the most notable example, union with Christ served as one of the organizing principles for Calvin's *Institutes*. "We must understand," Calvin famously wrote, "that as long as Christ remains outside of us, and we are separated from him, all that he has suffered and done for the salvation of the human race remains useless and of no value for us. . . . All that he possesses is nothing to us until we grow into one body with him."[5] Calvin went on to teach that it is the Holy Spirit who unites us to Christ by faith.[6] Thus there is a double bond. By faith we bind ourselves to Christ; by his Spirit Christ binds us to himself, and thereby "makes us participants not only in all his benefits but also in himself."[7] Earlier in the *Institutes*, Calvin had beautifully celebrated the implications of union with Christ for our spiritual experience:

4. John Murray, *Redemption Accomplished and Applied* (Grand Rapids: Eerdmans, 1955), 161, 165.

5. John Calvin, *Institutes of the Christian Religion*, ed. John T. McNeill, trans. Ford Lewis Battles, 2 vols., Library of Christian Classics 20–21 (Philadelphia: Westminster, 1960), 3.1.3.

6. Calvin, *Institutes*, 3.1–2.

7. Calvin, *Institutes*, 3.2.24.

"We see that our whole salvation and all its parts are comprehended in Christ (Acts 4:12). We should therefore take care not to derive the least portion of it from anywhere else. . . . Since rich store of every kind of good abounds in him, let us drink our fill from this fountain and from no other."[8]

Later Reformed theologians adopted Calvin's emphasis on union and communion with Christ. The doctrine exercised a formative influence on the theology of the English Puritans, who considered union with Christ to be the source of all blessing and the fountainhead of true spiritual joy.[9] According to John Owen, for example, union with Christ "is the cause of all other graces that we are made partakers of; they are all communicated to us by virtue of our union with Christ. Hence is our adoption, our justification, our sanctification, our fruitfulness, our perseverance, our resurrection, our glory." Hence also is our experience of divine affection, for as a result of union with Christ, "there is love in the person of the Father peculiarly held out unto the saints, as wherein he will and does hold communion with them." As the summation of all spiritual blessings and the full expression of God's love, union with Christ is "the principle and measure of all spiritual enjoyments and expectations."[10]

Properly understood, the doctrine of union with Christ pulses with the heartbeat of genuine piety—a heart of faith joined to the Savior of love. As the Old Princeton theologian Archibald Alexander insisted: "If Christ be in us there will be communion. . . . He will sometimes speak to us—He will speak comfortably to us—He will give tokens of his love. He will invite our confidence and will shed abroad his love in our hearts. And if Christ be formed within us we cannot remain altogether ignorant of his presence. Our hearts, while he communes with us, will sometimes burn within us."[11]

8. Calvin, *Institutes*, 2.16.19.

9. To give just two examples, the English Puritan Thomas Case in *The Morning Exercise Methodized* (London, 1660) and the Scottish Presbyterian Thomas Boston in *Human Nature in Its Fourfold State* (Edinburgh, 1720; repr., Edinburgh: Banner of Truth, 1964) both organize their teaching on salvation around the doctrine of union with Christ.

10. John Owen, *The Works of John Owen*, 23 vols. (Edinburgh: Banner of Truth, 1992), 21:149–50, 2:22, 54, 20:146.

11. Archibald Alexander, "Col. 1:27, 'Christ in you the hope of glory,'" quoted

The Suffering and the Glory

When Reformed theologians describe the work of Christ, they often make a distinction between his humiliation and his exaltation.

Humiliation is the work of Christ in suffering and dying for sin. It includes everything that Christ endured in his earthly travails, starting from the first moment that he came into this world. The Son of God left behind the glories of heaven. He became a human being, was born in a stable, and endured all kinds of indignities at the hands of fallen humanity. Then at the end of it all, he died the God-forsaken death of the cross. The Westminster Shorter Catechism summarizes the humiliation of Christ by saying that it "consisted in his being born, and that in a low condition, made under the law, undergoing the miseries of this life, the wrath of God, and the cursed death of the cross; in being buried, and continuing under the power of death for a time" (WSC 27).

Exaltation is the work of Christ in conquering sin and death through his resurrection and ascension. After the cross, there came a crown. God raised Jesus from the dead, lifted him up to heaven, and exalted him to the highest place, where he gave him the name that is above every name. To quote again from the Shorter Catechism, Christ's exaltation consisted "in his rising again from the dead on the third day, in ascending up into heaven, in sitting at the right hand of God the Father, and in coming to judge the world at the last day" (WSC 28).

These two aspects of Christ's work—humiliation and exaltation—are both clearly in view in Philippians 3:10–11, which mentions both the sufferings and the glories of Christ.[12] When Paul expresses that he wants to know Christ "and" the power of his resurrection "and" the fellowship of sharing in his sufferings, he is not saying that he wants to know several different things, but declaring that to know Christ *is* to share in his crucifixion and resurrection. According to Sinclair Ferguson, Paul wanted the kind of "fellowship with Christ, or union

---

in W. Andrew Hoffecker, *Piety and the Princeton Theologians* (Phillipsburg, NJ: Presbyterian and Reformed, 1981), 34.

12. There is a similar movement from death to resurrection in Romans 5–6 and Colossians 2–3.

with him, in which all that Christ had done for him in his life, death, resurrection and ascension was brought into his life through the ministry of the Holy Spirit."[13]

Earlier, in Philippians 2, the apostle traced the trajectory of Christ's work, the grand parabola of redemption that swept from equality with God down to the obedience of crucifixion, and then back up to the highest place in the cosmos. In order to accomplish our salvation, God the Son went from glory to glory by way of the cross. In chapter 3, as Paul contemplated what Christ had done, he said, in effect, "Now, *that's* the Jesus that I want to know: the crucified and glorified Christ—the Christ who suffered, died, and rose again." Philippians 3:10–11 takes Philippians 2:5–11 and makes it personal. Paul took the whole wide sweep of the saving work of Jesus Christ and applied it to his own spiritual experience. To put his desire in the categories of systematic theology, the apostle wanted to be united to Christ in both his humiliation and his exaltation.

In order to attain this knowledge of Christ, it was necessary for Paul first to declare his personal spiritual bankruptcy. In the first part of Philippians 3, he tells us the story of his salvation. All the things he had formerly counted as assets—his ethnic heritage, his educational background, his ecclesiastical pedigree, his ethical standards—had to be written off as liabilities (Phil. 3:4–7). Only then could Paul be justified by faith in Christ, not by works, which could never save anyone. Furthermore, compared to the superlative joy of knowing Christ, Paul calculated that his greatest religious achievements added up to nothing more than a filthy pile of refuse (*skubala*, v. 8). The best thing, the most valuable thing, the surpassingly great thing was to know Christ and to be found in him. Paul gave up everything else to be united to Jesus Christ, and to find salvation in him by faith. His testimony is a reminder that a minister can find true identity only in Jesus—not in religious activity, theological affiliation, or public notoriety, but only in Christ alone.

Now the apostle's burning, passionate desire was to know Christ and his resurrection power, to share in his sufferings, and to become

---

13. Sinclair B. Ferguson, *Let's Study Philippians* (Edinburgh: Banner of Truth, 1997), 81.

"like him in his death" (Phil. 3:10). In one sense, this is a surprising declaration, for if anyone knew Christ already, it had to be the apostle Paul. The man had known Christ for decades, ever since he met him on the road to Damascus (Acts 9). If there was any doubt about Paul's relationship to Christ, this was dispelled in Philippians 3:8, where he testified to "the surpassing worth of knowing Christ Jesus my Lord." But knowing Christ only made Paul want to know him all the more—another challenge to our own Christian experience. As well as we know Jesus, do we still want to know him better than ever?

Paul's highest and most heartfelt ambition was to become ever more closely identified with the crucified and glorified Christ. So he emphatically declared, "I want to know Christ." He was writing these words not simply as a Christian, but also as a pastor. It was in his gospel ministry—more than anywhere else—that he prayed for God to satisfy his desire to be humiliated and exalted with Christ.

Being united to Christ in suffering and glory became Paul's primary paradigm for gospel ministry. His message was also his methodology. Whenever the apostle speaks about the sufferings of his calling, he invariably puts them in the context of God's resurrection glory. And whenever he preaches the Christ of the empty tomb, he also proclaims him as the crucified Savior. Paul really was "*always* carrying in the body the death of Jesus" (2 Cor. 4:10; cf. 1 Cor. 15:31). We see his full ministry paradigm in the simple exhortation he gave to Timothy: "Remember Jesus Christ, risen from the dead, the offspring of David, as preached in my gospel, for which I am suffering" (2 Tim. 2:8–9). Earlier Paul had invited his protégé to "share in suffering for the gospel by the power of God" (1:8). In advocating an approach to pastoral ministry that is as practical as it is theological, Paul was preaching what he practiced. We do not simply proclaim the gospel; we live it.

Becoming like Jesus in His Death

To follow the pattern of Christ's own ministry, in which the cross came before the crown, we must begin with the sufferings of the ministry. Pastoral ministry is not a matter of life and death, but a matter of death, then life: "we suffer with him in order that we may also be glorified with him" (Rom. 8:17; cf. 1 Peter 4:13). And if what Paul says in Philippians 3:10–11 is any indication, we should expect gospel ministry to contain suffering as well as glory—maybe in equal parts. Pastoral ministry is cruciform: "The pastor who is most Christlike is not the one who is most gloriously fulfilled in every moment of his ministry, but the one whose ministry has in it unbelievable elements of crucifixion."[14]

The biblical history of gospel proclamation is primarily a story of suffering, which should help us have proper expectations for the pastorate. Few if any biblical preachers were successful by any worldly standard, and for every success there seem to be dozens of failures. For every man who turned the nation back to God, many others were mocked and persecuted, some so severely that they were tempted to leave the ministry or even to despair of life itself. God said, "I will send them prophets and apostles, some of whom they will kill and persecute" (Luke 11:49). As we read this verse, we look in vain for a third category, but there are only two: the persecuted and the dead.

Even a brief review of the Old Testament prophets—of long-suffering Moses, persecuted Elijah, rejected Isaiah, weeping Jeremiah, and all the rest—reveals that most of them were called mainly to suffer. In this way, they anticipated the sufferings of Christ. It is said of Moses that he suffered "the reproach of Christ" (Heb. 11:26). In other words, he suffered the disgrace that Christ later suffered, which is really another way of saying that he suffered in union with Christ. The same could be said of the other prophets, which explains why Jesus could prove the necessity of his humiliation from what they endured. "Was it not necessary that the Christ should suffer these things and enter into his glory?" he asked his disciples on the road to Emmaus. "And beginning with Moses and all the Prophets, he interpreted to them in all the Scriptures the things concerning himself" (Luke 24:26–27; cf. 1 Peter 1:11).

Jesus suffered many indignities at the hands of the evil men who plotted to have him killed. On various occasions he was accused of insanity, illegitimacy, and blasphemy. He was unlawfully arrested, unfairly accused, unjustly convicted, and unmercifully beaten. But

14. Dave Goetz, "Tour of Duty," *Christianity Today*, April 1, 1996, https://www .christianitytoday.com/pastors/1996/spring/6l2022.html.

he endured his greatest sufferings on the cross, where he died a God-forsaken death. His crucifixion was the apotheosis of the humiliation suffered by his prophets (see Luke 11:47–51). As Stephen said in his challenge to the Sanhedrin: "Which of the prophets did your fathers not persecute? And they killed those who announced beforehand the coming of the Righteous One, whom you have now betrayed and murdered" (Acts 7:52; cf. Luke 6:23).

Remarkably, at the time of his death Jesus had virtually nothing to show for his ministry. Nearly everyone had rejected him. He had had relatively few followers to begin with, but at the end he had only eleven disciples, and even they abandoned him. His public ministry turned out to be no more successful than Isaiah's. People were forever hearing Jesus, but never understanding him; forever seeing his miracles, but not perceiving his message (Matt. 13:13–15; cf. Isa. 6:9–10). And Jesus suffered greatly for this. "O faithless generation," he groaned, "how long am I to be with you? How long am I to bear with you?" (Mark 9:19). We find the lament of this Suffering Servant previously recorded in the book of Isaiah: "[God] said to me, 'You are my servant, Israel, in whom I will be glorified.' But I said, 'I have labored in vain; I have spent my strength for nothing and vanity'" (Isa. 49:3–4). At the time of Jesus Christ's death, his preaching ministry could hardly be judged as anything except a failure. The main thing it seemed to accomplish was getting him killed.

And what of Christ's followers? What happened to them? According to the best historical records, nearly every one of his original disciples died a violent death. The first martyr was Stephen, who, as far as Scripture records, preached only one great sermon before being stoned (Acts 7). These men suffered all these things because they were united to Jesus Christ in his sufferings and death.

The one who endured the most excruciating torment was the apostle Paul. When Paul first came to Christ, God showed him how much he would suffer for the sake of the gospel (Acts 9:16). And suffer he did. Paul faced trouble, hardship, hunger, homelessness, and distress. He was frequently imprisoned and often on the run—in danger by land and by sea. He was whipped, beaten, stoned, and left for dead (1 Cor. 4:11, 13; 2 Cor. 6:4–10; 11:23–27). Then there were all the sufferings that Paul experienced in ministry: his anguish for lost souls (Rom. 9:1–5), his ceaseless spiritual concern for the church (2 Cor. 11:28–29), his tearful entreaties with Christians who were struggling to follow Christ (Acts 20:31).

What this means is that Paul's prayers were answered! He did indeed become like Christ in his death—specifically in the context of his gospel ministry.

Sharing in Christ's Sufferings

What does this litany of misery teach us about pastoral ministry?

Any minister who knows his Bible can hardly expect to escape suffering—specifically suffering for the cause of Christ. Martin Luther wrote: "Those who are in the teaching office should teach with the greatest faithfulness and expect no other remuneration than to be killed by the world, trampled underfoot, and despised by their own. . . . Teach purely and faithfully, and in all you do expect not glory but dishonor and contempt, not wealth but poverty, violence, prison, death, and every danger."[15]

Some critics may be tempted to think that Luther was exaggerating, that his view of gospel ministry was unduly negative. No doubt his perspective was colored by the unique struggles he faced in the Age of Reformation. Yet any authentic pastoral theology must be adequate to the task of ministry under conditions of the most extreme hardship, such as that which many ministers suffer today in many parts of the world. The truth is that being united to Christ in the ministry of his gospel always involves conflict within the church and some measure of opposition from without. Inevitably there will be unfair criticisms, unfortunate misunderstandings, unfounded rumors, and unjust accusations. These hardships cannot be avoided; they are to be expected. It is simply a fact: "we share abundantly in Christ's sufferings" (2 Cor. 1:5). Pastoral ministry could not be in union with Christ unless it entailed difficulty, discouragement, and sometimes death.

Nevertheless, many ministers are surprised by suffering. Unmet expectations are one of the main reasons why some become

---

15. Martin Luther, *Luther's Works*, ed. Jaroslav Pelikan (St. Louis: Concordia, 1955–58), 12:220–21.

discouraged and unproductive or may leave the ministry altogether. Often there has been a failure to grasp the implications of pastoral ministry in union with Christ. The words of Thomas à Kempis are striking for their contemporary relevance:

> Jesus today has many who love his heavenly kingdom, but few who carry his cross; many who yearn for comfort, few who long for distress. Plenty of people he finds to share his banquet, few to share his fast. Everyone desires to take part in his rejoicing, but few are willing to suffer anything for his sake. There are many that follow Jesus as far as the breaking of bread, few as far as drinking the cup of suffering; many that revere his miracles, few that follow him in the indignity of the cross.[16]

How rare it is to find a minister who desires fellowship with Christ if it includes sharing in his sufferings. Yet according to Paul, the trials of pastoral ministry are to be embraced. "I *want* to know Christ," he said, and for him this included wanting to share in his sufferings. The apostle's emphasis was on knowing Christ, but he placed that knowledge specifically in the context of participating in Christ's humiliation. This flies in the face of the career goals of the average pastor, at least in America and the West. A sincere willingness to suffer with Christ cannot come from the human nature, but only from God's Spirit.

The life of the missionary Helen Roseveare bears remarkable witness to the fellowship of sharing in Christ's suffering. When Roseveare first came to faith in Christ as a student at Cambridge University in the 1940s, evangelist Graham Scroggie "wrote Philippians 3:10 in her new Bible, and told her: 'Tonight you've entered into the first part of the verse, "That I may know Him." This is only the beginning, and there's a long journey ahead. My prayer for you is that you will go on through the verse to know "the power of His resurrection" and also, God willing, one day perhaps, "the fellowship of His sufferings, being made conformable unto His death."'"[17]

16. Thomas à Kempis, *The Imitation of Christ*, trans. Ronald Knox and Michael Oakley (New York: Sheed and Ward, 1959), 76–77.

17. This account, including the quotations from Helen Roseveare's writings, comes from Justin Taylor, "A Woman of Whom the World Was Not Worthy: Helen

As her faith deepened, and she sensed a growing calling to ministry, Roseveare continued to reflect on Paul's words. During one missionary gathering, she resolved, "I'll go anywhere God wants me to, whatever the cost." Afterward, she went up into the mountains and prayed, "O.K. God, today I mean it. Go ahead and make me more like Jesus, whatever the cost. But please (knowing myself fairly well), when I feel I can't stand anymore and cry out, 'Stop!' will you ignore my 'stop' and remember that today I said 'Go ahead!'?"

Roseveare's prayers to be united to Christ in his sufferings were answered many years later when soldiers attacked her medical clinic in Congo, destroying the facilities and taking her captive. The missionary was brutally raped. She later recounted, "On that dreadful night, beaten and bruised, terrified and tormented, unutterably alone, I had felt at last God had failed me. Surely He could have stepped in earlier, surely things need not have gone that far. I had reached what seemed to be the ultimate depth of despairing nothingness."

In the darkness, though, Roseveare remembered her long-ago prayer and sensed the Lord saying to her, "You asked Me, when you were first converted, for the privilege of being a missionary. This is it. Don't you want it? . . . These are not your sufferings. They're Mine. All I ask of you is the loan of your body." She also sensed the Lord's comforting presence. "Through the brutal heartbreaking experience of rape," she wrote, "God met with me—with outstretched arms of love. It was an unbelievable experience: He was so utterly there, so totally understanding, his comfort was so complete—and suddenly I knew—I really knew that his love was unutterably sufficient. He did love me! He did understand! . . . He was actually offering me the inestimable privilege of sharing in some little way in the fellowship of His sufferings."

Why Paul Wanted a Crucified Ministry

The apostle Paul would have recognized Helen Roseveare as a kindred spirit and true sister in Christ. In his epistles, as Paul reflected

Roseveare (1925–2016)," *The Gospel Coalition*, December 7, 2016, accessed October 29, 2020, https://www.thegospelcoalition.org/blogs/justin-taylor/a-woman-of -whom-the-world-was-not-worthy-helen-roseveare-1925-2016/.

on the role of suffering in gospel ministry, he expressed manifest joy in suffering for the cause of Christ. "Now I rejoice in my sufferings for your sake," he wrote in Colossians 1:24. Or to the Corinthians: "I am content with weaknesses, insults, hardships, persecutions, and calamities" (2 Cor. 12:10). Paul really did *want* to know Christ by sharing in his sufferings! He was like the apostles in Jerusalem, who left the Sanhedrin, "rejoicing that they were counted worthy to suffer dishonor for the name" (Acts 5:41).

There were at least two reasons for Paul's readiness to share in Christ's sufferings. One was his belief that they were necessary for the evangelization of the lost. The world could not understand the message of the cross unless those who preached it were themselves marked by its suffering and shame. This is the meaning—at least in part—of Paul's enigmatic claim "in my flesh I am filling up what is lacking in Christ's afflictions" (Col. 1:24). This verse has nothing to do with the extent of the atonement, of course, but everything to do with missions and evangelism. What is still lacking is the communication of the gospel by a suffering church. The unsaved people of the world cannot see Jesus hanging on the cross, but they can see a community that shares in his sufferings and thus confirms the truth of his passion. The sufferings of the apostles—and, by implication, of the church and its ministers today—were public exhibitions of Christ and his cross. Paul thus described himself as part of a procession being led out to die in the arena (1 Cor. 4:9) or to die for the honor of a conquering king (2 Cor. 2:14).[18] Sharing in suffering was the very heart of the apostle's strategy for making known the crucified Christ. As we have seen, he was "always being given over to death for Jesus' sake" (4:11). These sufferings were far from pointless; they were for the sake of the lost, "so that as grace extends to more and more people it may increase thanksgiving, to the glory of God" (v. 15).

Another reason for Paul's passion to know Christ in his sufferings is that such fellowship affords a deep, personal knowledge of Christ. This is one of the promised blessings of gospel ministry. As George

18. See Scott J. Hafemann's compelling dissertation, *Suffering and the Spirit: An Exegetical Study of II Cor. 2:14–3:3 within the Context of the Corinthian Correspondence*, Wissenschaftliche Untersuchungen zum Neuen Testament, Reihe 2, 19 (Tübingen: J. C. B. Mohr, 1986).

Whitefield once observed, "Ministers never write or preach so well as when under the cross; the Spirit of Christ and of glory then rests upon them."[19] Anyone in the pastorate inevitably faces one form of suffering or another, and in the fellowship of sharing Christ's sufferings will also enjoy the fruit of union and communion with him. During seasons of hardship and difficulty, a minister experiences the closest possible identification with Christ. At the same time, Christ makes the closest possible identification with his suffering ministers. Paul learned this at the time of his conversion, when the Lord said to him, "I am Jesus of Nazareth, whom you are persecuting" (Acts 22:8; cf. 9:4–5). Christ is so closely united to his suffering people that he considers every incarceration and abuse they endure as an assault on his own person.

All of this helps explain why Paul wanted so very badly for the humiliation of Christ to be worked out in his own life and ministry. What he desired was not the sufferings themselves, but the fellowship of sharing them with Christ. He reasoned that since he was a minister of the gospel, difficulties were bound to come, and that when they came, it would be much better to experience them in union with Christ. Paul knew that hardship is woven into the fabric of any faithful pastoral ministry. This is to be not only expected, but also embraced as part of the minister's communion with Christ. Suffering is one of God's gifts, "for it has been granted to you that for the sake of Christ you should not only believe in him but also suffer for his sake" (Phil. 1:29).

This does not mean that suffering needs to be sought out. It will come on its own, according to the will of God, in the manner and measure that he intends. It will come in all the sorrows that a shepherd shares with his flock and in all the burdens he bears on their behalf. In the meantime, there are other ways for a minister to nurture his communion with the crucified Christ. The kind of spiritual intimacy that Paul sought comes not only from outward suffering, but also inwardly from dying to self. This, too, is part of what it means to be united with Christ in his death, following the way of his cross. The minister must be able to say, with the apostles, that "what we

19. George Whitefield, *Works* (London, 1771), 4:306.

proclaim is not ourselves" (2 Cor. 4:5); "but we preach Christ cru-cified" (1 Cor. 1:23). In order to preach this way, however, he must first be able to say: "I have been crucified with Christ. It is no longer I who live, but Christ who lives in me" (Gal. 2:20). It takes a crucified preacher to preach a crucified Christ.

As one aspect of his union with Christ, the pastor must die to self in all its hideous forms: self-indulgence, self-promotion, self-love, and self-will. He must be dead to pride, dead to financial gain, dead to recognition and approval. All of this must be put to death—if a pastor is to know Christ and the fellowship of sharing in his sufferings.

The notable Scottish minister William Still—who mentored Eric Alexander, Sinclair Ferguson, and many other faithful pastors—gave his spiritual autobiography the noteworthy title *Dying to Live*. There, he wrote about a form of union with Christ that every preacher needs to experience in order to be fully effective and maximally fruitful in ministry. "From the moment that you stand there dead in Christ and dead to everything you are and have and ever shall be and have," Mr. Still wrote, then "every breath you breathe thereafter, every thought you think, every word you say and deed you do, must be done over the top of your own corpse or reaching over it in your preaching to others. Then it can only be Jesus that comes over and no one else."[20]

The Power of Christ's Resurrection

As much as Paul had to say about knowing Christ in his suffer-ings and death, he also understood that union with Christ entails exaltation as well as humiliation. After all, his ministry was a *gospel* ministry—one grounded in both the crucifixion and resurrection of Jesus Christ.

In Philippians 3:10–11—the summary statement for his theol-ogy of pastoral ministry—the apostle began not with suffering, but with glory: "that I may know [Christ] and the power of his resurrec-tion" (Phil. 3:10). If this starting point seems surprising, we should remember how Paul came to know Christ in the first place. He met Jesus not at the foot of the cross, but at the throne of glory—not at

---

20. William Still, *Dying to Live* (Fearn, Scotland: Christian Focus, 1991), 136.

Calvary, but on the Damascus road, where he saw a radiant vision of the risen Christ. Paul also ended his aspiration statement with glory, hoping "by any means possible" to "attain the resurrection from the dead" (v. 11). "By any means possible" does not indicate doubt, as though Paul (of all people!) lacked the certainty of his salvation. Elsewhere he is emphatic in the assurance of his eternal hope, as he is in Romans 6:5: "For if we have been united with him in a death like his, we shall certainly be united with him in a resurrection like his" (see also Rom. 8:38–39; 1 Cor. 15:20; 2 Tim. 1:12). What he expresses in Philippians 3, therefore, is not so much doubt as it is amazement—amazement that God would raise a sinful man such as him from the dead. The apostle's "by any means possible" is "an expression of expectation."[21] What he wanted to know is also what he expected to see: God's resurrection power.

What is the power of Christ's resurrection? Specifically, and explicitly, it is the life-giving power of God the Holy Spirit. The Scripture teaches that "according to the Spirit of holiness," Christ "was declared to be the Son of God in power . . . by his resurrection from the dead" (Rom. 1:4). The Holy Spirit is therefore the effective transforming agent of God's resurrection power both for Christ and for the Christian. As Paul later reasoned, "If the Spirit of him who raised Jesus from the dead dwells in you, he who raised Christ Jesus from the dead will also give life to your mortal bodies through his Spirit who dwells in you" (8:11). To know the power of the resurrection, therefore, is to know the revitalizing power of the Holy Spirit—the greatest power there is.

When Paul asserted his desire to know Christ's resurrection power, he was announcing his intention to live and serve by the power of God's Spirit, who alone gives power for gospel ministry. This was true in the ministry of Jesus. Before the resurrection, his followers remained uncertain of his identity and thus lacked the courage to live for his kingdom. It was only when Jesus rose from the dead that they came to a full understanding of his saving work and began to experience resurrection-empowered success in their ministry.

---

21. Friedrich Blass, Albert Debrunner, and Robert W. Funk, *A Greek Grammar of the New Testament and Other Early Christian Literature*, rev. ed. (Chicago: University of Chicago Press, 1961), para. 375.

As soon as the apostles believed in the risen Christ, they were commissioned to proclaim his saving message. That message was the good news of salvation for sinners through both the cross and the empty tomb. So the resurrection was essential to apostolic preaching. When Peter preached in Jerusalem, and when Paul preached in places such as Pisidian Antioch and Athens, it was not simply the crucifixion, but also the resurrection that animated their presentation of the gospel (see Acts 2:24–32; 13:30–37; 17:31–32). Whenever the apostles preached, they said, "We are witnesses" (e.g., 2:32; 3:15; 5:32; 13:31), meaning eyewitnesses of the resurrection of Jesus. Here is how Hughes Oliphant Old explains the connection between what the apostles witnessed and what they preached:

> It was the risen and exalted Christ who sent those who experienced him as risen and exalted to proclaim his resurrection glory. Not only that, but the proclamation that Jesus is the risen and exalted Christ was constitutive of the Church. It planted it; it brought it into being. It was the essence of the apostolic ministry. The highest and holiest office of the apostle is to proclaim that Christ has risen. The proclamation of the resurrection is the heart and center of all Christian preaching.[22]

The resurrection was significant to the apostles for another reason as well. It was not simply the basis for their message, but also the source of their power. Their proclamation of the risen Christ became a performative act that brought the dead back to spiritual life. The same Spirit who had raised Jesus from the dead was now at work in the apostolic proclamation of the gospel. The Son of God had ascended to glory, and from his place of exaltation he had sent his Spirit. This explains why Jesus had promised his disciples that by faith, remarkably, they would do even greater things than he had done (John 14:12): he was sending them by his Spirit, so that the very power of his resurrection would be at work in their ministry. Michael Horton writes that after Pentecost "the apostles, deputized by the

---

22. Hughes Oliphant Old, *The Reading and Preaching of the Scriptures in the Worship of the Christian Church*, 7 vols. (Grand Rapids: Eerdmans, 1998–2010), 1:202.

Son and empowered by the Spirit, became witnesses whose preaching did exactly what was prophesied by Ezekiel. By preaching—and not just by preaching anything, but by preaching the gospel—the dead were raised."[23]

As we have seen, the ministry of the Old Testament prophets was marked primarily by humiliation. The same can be said of the ministry of Jesus Christ—up until the time of his death. In a sense, his ministry had been humiliating. But everything changed with the resurrection. Then the Spirit was unleashed in all his saving power, and as a result the ministry of the gospel now reveals God's power to save sinners. This ministry is not exercised without suffering; the "already-not yet" dynamic of redemption is as evident in the pastorate as anywhere else. But through the preaching of the risen Christ, the Spirit is inaugurating the glories of the coming age. Therefore, for the minister in union with Christ, there is exaltation as well as humiliation in fulfilling the duties of his calling. Paul's pastoral theology is not merely a theology of the cross, but also a theology of glory.

How Ministry Comes to Life

The life-giving power of the Holy Spirit is the source of all effective gospel ministry. Any success we see is resurrection-empowered. First, the Holy Spirit has the power to regenerate (see John 3:5). Paul experienced this power in his own conversion. When he met the risen Christ on the Damascus road, the light was so dazzling that he was blind for three days. But one of Christ's ministers came and said to him, "The Lord Jesus . . . has sent me so that you may regain your sight and be filled with the Holy Spirit" (Acts 9:17). As the scales fell away from Paul's eyes, he was filled with the regenerating Spirit, and at once he began preaching that Jesus is the Son of God (v. 20). Paul's ministry of the gospel, in turn, led to the conversion of others. The same resurrection power that he experienced in his conversion was also at work in his preaching, as it is in all preaching, to bring spiritual life from spiritual death. Through the preaching of God's Word,

---

23. Michael S. Horton, *Covenant and Eschatology: The Divine Drama* (Louisville: Westminster John Knox, 2002), 267.

sinners receive eternal life by the Holy Spirit; through the proclamation of a risen Savior, they are granted the blessings of resurrection life. Thus the minister prays, as Paul prayed, for God's blessing on the ministry of God's Word, through the powerful work of God's Spirit (see Eph. 1:18–20).

Another way to say all this is that Paul wanted others to know through his gospel ministry what he already knew through his spiritual experience: the resurrection power of Jesus Christ. Everyone needs to know this transforming power. It is what ministers need when they feel like failures. It is what people in their congregations need when they are trying and failing to escape the enslavement of addictive sins, drowning in oceans of grief, seeking healing from a history of abuse, crying out for the reconciliation of broken family relationships, and struggling with all the other agonies of a fallen world. It is what the artist needs in order to avoid despair, the businessperson needs to resist greed, the street person needs to overcome oppression, and the churchgoer needs to be healed from hypocrisy. We all need a fresh and powerful work of God the Holy Spirit, who alone is able to bring the dead back to life.

If it is to be effective, everything a minister does must be done in the resurrection power of the Spirit—not just the evangelism that first brings people to Christ and the preaching that helps them to grow in godliness. When Paul announced that he wanted to know Christ and the power of his resurrection, he was asking for the sovereign work of God's Spirit, who alone enables the various duties of pastoral ministry to fulfill their divinely appointed purpose. It is the Spirit who answers pastoral prayer. It is the Spirit who transforms sinners through private counsel in the practical application of biblical teaching. It is the Spirit who makes baptism an effectual sign of God's saving grace. It is the Spirit who makes Christ present in the bread and the wine of the Lord's Supper.

Perhaps most importantly of all, it is the Spirit who blesses the public ministry of God's Word by doing his saving and sanctifying work, as we have seen. Preaching is a matter of life and death—not only for the hearers, whose souls hang in the eternal balance, but also for the preachers, who are dying and rising with Jesus as they proclaim his gospel in the power of his Spirit. We exercise the ministry of the Word, like the ministry of the sacrament, in union with Christ. The great Baptist preacher Charles Spurgeon is reported to have mounted each of the fifteen steps of London's Metropolitan Tabernacle pulpit, saying, "I believe in the Holy Ghost."[24] If this story is true, then Spurgeon was conducting his ministry in union with the Christ who is present in the church by his living Holy Spirit.

Crucially, the Spirit is at work not only in a minister's evident successes, but also in his apparent failures. In every struggle, a faithful minister can take consolation in the inescapable presence of the risen Christ. As William Milligan wrote more than a century ago: "The Living Lord is with us, who once knew every such disappointment as we experience, and every such cause of despondency as weakens us; who once sighed over the stubbornness of men more deeply than we can sigh, and shed more tears for those who refused to listen than we can weep. Yet he triumphed; and he comes to us now that he may communicate to us his joy of victory."[25]

Perhaps this is the best place to emphasize that dying and rising with Jesus are not two successive stages in gospel ministry; they are constantly present as closely related experiences. As William R. Edwards explains in his excellent essay on suffering in pastoral ministry, for Paul, "the dimensions of death and resurrection in ministry" are "not experienced sequentially but simultaneously." "In other words," Edwards goes on to explain, "Paul does not describe an experience of death that is then followed by an experience of resurrection. They are not separate moments or distinct occasions. Both are present at the same time. . . . It is not first death and then resurrection. The pattern is *always* death and *also* resurrection."[26]

In his epistles, the apostle repeatedly testifies to the gospel paradox that was displayed in his ministry. As he ministered in union with Christ, Paul experienced both humiliation and exaltation. And it was humiliation that compelled him to rely more completely on the

---

24. The story is recounted in John R. W. Stott, *Between Two Worlds: The Art of Preaching in the Twentieth Century* (Grand Rapids: Eerdmans, 1982), 334.

25. William Milligan, *The Resurrection of Our Lord* (New York: Macmillan, 1917), 222.

26. William R. Edwards, "Participants in What We Proclaim: Recovering Paul's Narrative of Pastoral Ministry," *Themelios* 39, no. 3 (2014): 462.

exalting power of God's Spirit (see 1 Cor. 2:3–4; 2 Cor. 1:8–9). "There-fore," he said, "I will boast all the more gladly of my weaknesses, so that the power of Christ may rest upon me. For the sake of Christ, then, I am content with weaknesses, insults, hardships, persecutions, and calamities. For when I am weak, then I am strong" (2 Cor. 12:9–10; cf. 4:7). Paul's sufferings in ministry so strengthened his grasp on God's resurrection power that he was able to say, "We who live are always being given over to death for Jesus' sake, so that the life of Jesus also may be manifested in our mortal flesh" (4:11). Or again: "For he was crucified in weakness, but lives by the power of God. For we also are weak in him, but in dealing with you we will live with him by the power of God" (13:4).

These verses show that it was through his suffering that Paul came to know Christ in the power of his resurrection. Christ has already endured his humiliation and entered his exaltation. We are one step behind, waiting to be glorified. In our present sufferings, it is encouraging to know that our Savior has passed this way before. But it is even more comforting to know that the risen and exalted Christ is with us now, by his Spirit, to sustain and comfort us in our humil-iation. Soon his resurrection will raise us beyond all suffering, but in the meantime, we participate in his grace as our ministries portray the same gospel that we proclaim.

Attaining the Resurrection of the Dead

When the final resurrection comes at last, we will witness the Holy Spirit's power to glorify. Here it must be emphasized that most of the greatest glories of gospel ministry are deferred benefits. This was true in the ministry of Jesus Christ. After apparently laboring in vain and spending his strength for nothing, that Suffering Ser-vant declared his expectation of coming exaltation: "yet surely my right is with the LORD, and my recompense with my God" (Isa. 49:4; cf. 53:10–12). Isaiah's suffering Christ looked forward in faith and believed that he would be fully rewarded for his gospel labors.

The hope of deferred glory is of particular encouragement to pas-tors who are burdened by heavy cares and discouraged by apparent fruitlessness in ministry. Like their Lord, ministers of the gospel labor in barren fields with the hope of a harvest that will not be reaped until eternity. The Puritan Richard Sibbes wisely advised ministers to wait patiently for the rewards of their ministry:

> Let us commit the fame and credit, of what we are or do to God. *He will take care of that*, let us take care to be and to do as we should, and then *for noise and report*, let it be good or ill as God will send it. . . . We should be carried with the Spirit of God, and with a holy desire to serve God and our brethren, and to do all the good we can, and never care for the speeches of the world. . . . We'll have glory enough BY-AND-BY.[27]

The apostle Paul was looking for glory "by-and-by." Thus, his definition of success in ministry was future-oriented. He did not think that he had fully grasped the knowledge of Christ, but still wanted to "press on toward the goal for the prize" (Phil. 3:14). As he went on to write: "But our citizenship is in heaven, and from it we await a Savior, the Lord Jesus Christ, who will transform our lowly body to be like his glorious body, by the power that enables him even to subject all things to himself. Therefore, my brothers, whom I love and long for, my joy and crown, stand firm thus in the Lord, my beloved" (Phil. 3:20–4:1; cf. 1 Peter 5:4).

Paul was trusting in the power of the Holy Spirit, not only for his own glorification, but also for the glorification of the church. This is the ultimate goal and crowning glory of any preaching ministry: to present the elect unto God, ready to receive their eternal inheritance. "For what is our hope or joy or crown of boasting before our Lord Jesus at his coming?" the apostle asked the Thessalonians. "Is it not you? For you are our glory and joy" (1 Thess. 2:19–20; cf. 2 Tim. 4:8). The exaltation of a pastoral ministry, which is rarely glimpsed in this life, will be fully displayed only at the second coming, when God will reveal his Son in the risen church. When—by any means possible—we rise with Jesus, we will know his power to the fullest measure.

---

27. Richard Sibbes, *Works of Richard Sibbes*, ed. Alexander Grant, 7 vols. (1862–64; repr., Edinburgh: Banner of Truth, 1973), 1:xxiii–xxiv.

Key Terms

exaltation of Christ
humiliation of Christ
union with Christ

Recommendations for Further Reading

Billings, J. Todd. *Union with Christ: Reframing Theology and Ministry for the Church*. Grand Rapids: Baker, 2011.
Letham, Robert. *Union with Christ: In Scripture, History, and Theology*. Phillipsburg, NJ: P&R Publishing, 2011.
Murray, John. *Redemption Accomplished and Applied*. Grand Rapids: Eerdmans, 1955.
Wilbourne, Rankin C. *Union with Christ: The Way to Know and Enjoy God*. Colorado Springs: David C. Cook, 2016.

Discussion Questions

1. What is the relationship between union with Christ and the many other blessings of the believer's salvation?
2. What stories, conversations, or teachings from the Gospels illustrate or display the humiliation of Jesus Christ? The exaltation of Jesus Christ?
3. What trials and sufferings have you experienced in ministry, and what have you learned from them about dying with Christ?
4. What successes have you experienced in ministry, and what have you learned from them about being raised with Christ?
5. From your relationships in the church or your knowledge of church history, who are your favorite examples of believers whose lives and ministries embody what it means to live and die with Christ?
6. Paul wanted to share in the fellowship of Christ's sufferings because he believed this was essential for the evangelization of the lost, and also because he wanted to experience deeper intimacy with Jesus. From your study of the Scriptures and

your own life in ministry, what are some additional reasons to pursue union with Christ in his humiliation and exaltation?

7. What are some ways that you have seen the Holy Spirit at work through your ministry of the gospel? When have you been most conscious of the Spirit's resurrection power?

8. What fruit from your life and ministry do you hope and pray will be revealed at the coming of Jesus Christ?

11

THE HOLY SPIRIT

New-Creation Power for
God's Redeemed People

DENNIS E. JOHNSON

Gospel Ministry Is the Ministry of the Spirit

The Bible's revelation of the person and work of the Holy Spirit has implications for pastoral ministry that far exceed the space allotted to this chapter. The pastor-theologian and friend whom we honor with this volume has himself authored an illumining study of the Holy Spirit, rich in biblical-theological, systematic-theological, and pastoral insights.[1] He draws not only on his own study of Scripture but also on the wisdom of Reformed forebears such as John Calvin, John Owen, George Smeaton, and Abraham Kuyper.[2] Compared to

---

1. Sinclair B. Ferguson, *The Holy Spirit*, Contours of Christian Theology (Downers Grove, IL: InterVarsity Press, 1996). This study of the Holy Spirit, along with everything else that I read and hear from Sinclair, moves me to thank God for giving such an insightful and Christ-exalting pastor and theologian to his church.

2. John Calvin, *Institutes of the Christian Religion*, ed. John T. McNeill, trans. Ford Lewis Battles, 4 vols. (Philadelphia: Westminster, 1967); John Owen, *Pneumatologia, or, A Discourse concerning the Holy Spirit*, vol. 3 of *The Works of John Owen*, ed. William H. Goold (1850–53; repr., London: Banner of Truth, 1965); George Smeaton, *The Doctrine of the Holy Spirit*, 2nd ed. (1889; repr., Edinburgh: Banner of Truth, 1974); Abraham Kuyper, *The Work of the Holy Spirit*, trans. Henri de Vries

such a wealth of resources, this essay can offer only a sketch of the Spirit's vital role in pastoral ministry.

Dr. Ferguson's volume and the older classics devote much attention to the Holy Spirit's mission as the divine Applier of the salvific benefits that Jesus Christ achieved for his people.[3] These Spirit-imparted benefits—regeneration, which enables faith and effects our union with Christ for justification, adoption, sanctification, and glorification—have profound ramifications for pastoral ministry.[4] When pastors apprehend the sovereign grace of God's Holy Spirit in bringing Christ, in all his redemptive mercy and power, to broken people, we are both humbled and heartened. Humbled, because our roles as planters and waterers pale in contrast to the almighty God who gives life and causes growth (1 Cor. 3:5–9). Heartened, because the Spirit conveys life even through us, his fragile earthen vessels (2 Cor. 4:7–12). Because these aspects of "redemption applied"[5] are discussed elsewhere in this volume, our focus here will be on the Spirit's work specifically in the persons and practices of pastors, who minister his Word and shepherd his flock.

Our starting point is the apostle Paul's characterization of gospel ministry in the new covenant era as "the ministry of the Spirit" (2 Cor. 3). Paul described the Christians of Corinth as "a letter from Christ delivered by us, written not with ink but with the Spirit of the living God, not on tablets of stone but on tablets of human hearts" (v. 3). The "tablets of stone" allusion contrasts new covenant gospel ministry to Moses' mediation of the old covenant. Apostles such as Paul (and, implicitly, other heralds of the apostolic gospel) inscribe God's Word not on mere stone (Ex. 31:18; 32:15–16), but on human hearts. Moses' ministry, though attended by sensory "glory," was a "ministry of death" and condemnation (2 Cor. 3:7, 9). But now, that

---

(1900; repr., Grand Rapids: Eerdmans, 1956).

3. Benjamin B. Warfield, "The Spirit of God in the Old Testament," in *Biblical and Theological Studies* (Philadelphia: Presbyterian and Reformed, 1952), 131: "In both Testaments the Spirit of God appears distinctly as *the executive of the Godhead*" (emphasis original).

4. Calvin, *Institutes*, 3.1.1: "To sum up, the Holy Spirit is the bond by which Christ effectually unites us to himself."

5. John Murray, *Redemption Accomplished and Applied* (Grand Rapids: Eerdmans, 1955).

old covenant has been eclipsed by the surpassing glory of "the ministry of the Spirit"[6] and of righteousness (vv. 8–9). Though beset by affliction and personal inadequacy (catalogued in 1:8–11; 4:7–18; 6:4–10; 7:5–7; 10:1–12; 11:6; 11:21–12:10; 13:1–4),[7] Paul and his colleagues convey "the aroma of Christ" that imparts life to some, while confirming others in spiritual death (2:14–16). They can conduct a ministry with such momentous consequences because "God . . . has made us sufficient to be ministers of a new covenant, not of the letter but of the Spirit. For the letter kills, but the Spirit gives life" (3:5–6).

Paul's claim is stunningly bold. Frankly facing his own frailty, he nonetheless asserts that when we proclaim Christ, whether to thousands or to dozens or to one, the life-igniting power of the Holy Spirit invests our ministry with a glory that "must far exceed" the splendor of Sinai (2 Cor. 3:9–11). Do we, who minister the new covenant inaugurated by Jesus' sacrifice, approach our daily duties with expectations befitting the Spirit's heart-transforming power? Is it with a reverent awareness of the Spirit's holy presence that we prepare and speak sermons, pray with and for stained and suffering people, offer counsel and care, and nurture others by discipleship and discipline?

The descent of the Holy Spirit on the day of Pentecost marks the redemptive-historical transition from the era of promise to the era of fulfillment, and the quantum leap forward in the ministries of the people of God. That great leap was precipitated by the incarnation and redemptive mission of Jesus Christ. Old Testament prophets announced that the suffering and subsequent glory of the Messiah would bring the long-anticipated unleashing of the Holy Spirit in new-creation power to gather, fill, equip, grow, and glorify God's

---

6. Smeaton, *Doctrine of the Holy Spirit*, 277–78, calls "the ministry of the Spirit" in 2 Corinthians 3:8 "an extraordinary expression," commenting that "the gospel ministry, whether in the hand of the apostles—the chief functionaries—or of ordinary office-bearers, is exercised with the accompanying power of the Holy Spirit sent down from heaven."

7. Smeaton, *Doctrine of the Holy Spirit*, 278: "We find united in the history of the apostles the greatest apparent opposites: weakness and power, emptiness and sufficiency, limitation and the boundless resources of omnipotence, the earthen vessel ready to go to pieces at the slightest pressure, and the excellency of power, an unimposing agency with the mightiest force that stirs humanity; in a word, what Milton calls 'the unresistible might of weakness.'"

redeemed people. Through the Holy Spirit, Christ is now creating a Spirit-ual sanctuary, composed of living stones (1 Peter 2:4–6; 4:14),[8] "a dwelling place for God by the Spirit" (Eph. 2:21–22). Through the Spirit, Christ is creating one new man (Eph. 2:14–18), one body in which each member is enabled by the Spirit to serve the health of the whole (1 Cor. 12:4–13; Eph. 4:1–16). We begin the Bible's story of God's Spirit and ministry, therefore, with expressions of anticipation before Pentecost.

Anticipations of the Holy Spirit's Arrival to Empower Ministry

The Old Testament records various operations of God's Spirit before Pentecost, in creation and providence (Gen. 1:2; Ps. 104:30) as well as in redemption (Ps. 143:10; Isa. 63:7–14).[9] In the Old Testament, the Spirit's soteric work (especially regeneration and sanctification) generally becomes visible through its fruit in individuals' speech and behavior. When we see the actions of Noah, Abraham, Joseph, David, and others, we see the display of their faith (Heb. 11). The sobering reality of total depravity leads us to infer that the Spirit's mysterious power brought their otherwise sin-deadened hearts to life (John 3:8; Eph. 2:1–10). Yet the Old Testament itself rarely identifies the Holy Spirit by name as the Originator of this new life in the experience of Old Testament saints.[10] Typically, Old Testament statements about the Holy Spirit's regenerating and sanctifying operations

8. Dennis E. Johnson, "Fire in God's House: Imagery from Malachi 3 in Peter's Theology of Suffering (1 Peter 4:12–19)," *JETS* 29, no. 3 (September 1986): 285–94.

9. Warfield, "Spirit of God in the Old Testament," 127–56, surveys the "cosmical, theocratic, and individual" relations and operations of God's Spirit, progressively revealed in the chronological development of the biblical canon: "God in the world, God in the theocracy, and God in the soul" (132).

10. Ferguson, *Holy Spirit*, 24–25, understands David's plea to "take not your Holy Spirit from me" (Ps. 51:11) as referring not primarily to the Spirit's gifting for rule, symbolized in his royal anointing (a gifting also received—temporarily—by David's predecessor, Saul, 1 Sam. 10:6–12; 11:6; 16:14), but more profoundly to the Spirit's saving and transforming presence in his heart: "on [David's] lips the prayer has a personal-subjective-soteriological, and not merely an official-objective-theocratic, orientation. It is personal fellowship with God, not merely the security of his monarchy, that concerns him here."

occur in predictions of a future era in which the Lord would come to save and judge in new ways. Through Ezekiel, for example, the Lord promised, and then portrayed in visionary symbolism, a future "resurrection" of the covenant people by the life-generating power of the Spirit: "I will remove the heart of stone from your flesh and give you a heart of flesh. And I will put my Spirit within you, and cause you to walk in my statutes and be careful to obey my rules" (Ezek. 36:26–27; see 37:1–14). Isaiah portrays the future coming of the Spirit on Israel's offspring as water poured out onto parched ground, bringing fruitfulness: coming generations will confess that they belong to the Lord (Isa. 32:15; 44:1–5). The Lord's promise through Jeremiah, without mentioning the Spirit, envisions the same heart transformation: "the days are coming . . . when I will make a new covenant. . . . I will put my law within them, and I will write it on their hearts" (Jer. 31:31, 33). These latter prophets elaborate Moses' prediction that after Israel's treason and exile, their merciful, faithful Lord would "circumcise your heart and the heart of your offspring, so that you will love the LORD your God with all your heart and with all your soul, that you may live" (Deut. 30:1–6).

When the Old Testament describes the Holy Spirit's operation within its own historical epoch, the reference is typically to the Spirit's ministerial empowerment, enabling individuals to serve the covenant people. The Spirit filled craftsmen to build the tabernacle (Ex. 31:3). He descended on elders, enabling them to render wise and just decisions (Num. 11:17–30). He empowered captains, judges, and kings to battle Israel's enemies (Num. 27:18; Judg. 6:34; 1 Sam. 11:6; 16:13). He gave prophets God's words to speak to God's people (2 Sam. 23:2; 1 Kings 18:12; Ezek. 11:5; Zech. 7:12).

Old Testament texts anticipate a future escalation of the Holy Spirit's ministry-empowering activity in two directions: an individual concentration and a corporate expansion. On the one hand, prophets foresaw the appearance of a Spirit-endued royal descendant of David (Isa. 11:1–5) and a Spirit-anointed prophetic Servant of the Lord (42:1–9; 61:1–4). This Servant is distinct from Israel, tasked with restoring Jacob's remnant and also extending salvation to Gentile nations (49:5–6; see 52:11–53:12). Yet although the Servant is an individual distinguished from Israel, he is also identified with Israel (44:1; see 43:10–11). Therefore, the prophets foresaw not only a uniquely Spirit-empowered King-Prophet to come, but also a broader outpouring of the Spirit to enable all of God's people to serve God's holy community. Moses longed that God would pour out his Spirit not merely on seventy elders, but on all of the Lord's people (Num. 11:29). Moses' longing became the Lord's promise through the prophet Joel:

> And it shall come to pass afterward,
>   that I will pour out my Spirit on all flesh;
> your sons and your daughters shall prophesy,
>   your old men shall dream dreams,
>   and your young men shall see visions.
> Even on the male and female servants
>   in those days I will pour out my Spirit. (Joel 2:28–29)

In other words, the prophets' anticipation of the Spirit's future outpouring to *impart spiritual life* is complemented by a promise that the Spirit will *disseminate ministerial capacities* among all the people of God.

The Arrival of the Spirit to Empower Ministry

With the coming of the Messiah, anticipation for the last-days outpouring of the Holy Spirit intensified. John announced that the coming Lord would baptize with the Holy Spirit and with fire (Matt. 3:11; Mark 1:8; Luke 3:16; John 1:32–33). Jesus himself sent signals that his mission would climax in the Spirit's arrival in unprecedented fullness (John 7:37–39). Jesus' sending of the Spirit would usher his friends into a deeper communion with himself and his Father than they had enjoyed while he was physically among them (14:16–18). Moreover, the Spirit's arrival would empower them to serve God's purposes for his expanding kingdom. The Spirit of truth would testify on Jesus' behalf, so the apostles would testify as well (15:26–27). As the divine Advocate, the Spirit would press God's indictment against the unbelieving world through the apostles and their successors (16:7–15).

Jesus taught his followers to pray, assuring them that, as human fathers give their children wholesome, not harmful, gifts, "how much more will the heavenly Father give the Holy Spirit to those who ask him!" (Luke 11:13). After his resurrection, Jesus announced that the Spirit-baptism that he himself would administer was imminent. The Spirit would empower his apostles to be his witnesses to the end of the earth (Luke 24:49; Acts 1:4–8). So his followers spent the days between his ascent to heaven and the Spirit's descent from heaven in prayer, awaiting the Father's gift (Acts 1:14). Moses' yearning and God's promise were about to be fulfilled.

On the day of Pentecost, the Spirit descended on 120 followers of Jesus (Acts 1:15; 2:1). This group included not only apostles, but also women, Jesus' brothers, and others (1:13–14). Peter explained that the outpouring of the Spirit was the act of Jesus, the risen and ascended Lord and Christ (2:33–36). The declaration of God's mighty deeds in diverse dialects, spoken in regions across the Roman Empire and beyond, fulfilled God's promise through Joel to pour out his Spirit on all his people, young and old, male and female (vv. 15–21).

The apostles' distinctive mission as witnesses to Jesus' resurrection was the focus of the Spirit's enabling arrival (Acts 2:32). Jesus had prepared them for this mission by providing "many proofs" of the substantial reality of his risen body (Acts 1:3, summarizing Luke 24:36–43; cf. John 17:20; 20:19–28). Their calling as eyewitnesses appears often in Luke-Acts (Luke 1:1–2; 6:12–16; 24:48–49; Acts 1:2, 15–26; 2:32, 40; 3:15; 5:32; 10:39–42; 13:31; see 22:15; 26:16).

Yet the Spirit also distributed his gifting across the entire community of disciples, giving utterance to all (Acts 2:4). Later, Peter and John would affirm their apostolic role as witnesses, adding that the divine Spirit who likewise testifies is given not to apostles only, but to all "those who obey him" (5:30–32). Subsequently, men "full of the Spirit and of wisdom" ministered to widows' material needs (6:1–7) and spoke the good news about Jesus (Stephen, 6:8–7:53; and Philip, 8:4–40). When persecution dispersed believers from Jerusalem, "those who were scattered went about preaching the word," while the apostles themselves—Christ's handpicked eyewitnesses—remained behind (8:1–4). As in Jerusalem (6:7), so also in Judea, Samaria, and beyond, "the word of God increased and multiplied"

(12:24; 19:20) through the words of ordinary Christians, as well as the eyewitness testimony of apostles. Thus, Acts sketches the Spirit's expanding embrace, conferring on all believers gifts to advance the church's mission and maturity.

New Testament epistles elaborate the implications of the Spirit's distribution of his ministerial empowerment among all who belong to Christ. Paul compares the church to one body in which diverse members need and are needed by one another, since "the same Spirit" imparts various, enabling varieties of service (1 Cor. 12:4–31; see Eph. 4:7–16). The Spirit's expansive ministry-enablement is in view when Peter speaks of God's "varied grace," by which some speak while others serve "by the strength that God supplies" (1 Peter 4:10–11). The Spirit's role in the ministries of all of Christ's members merits fuller discussion and careful attention by pastors and elders, but this theme lies beyond our scope in this chapter.

The Presence, Purity, and Power of the Spirit in the Person of the Pastor

Paul's epistles explore the Holy Spirit's role in the persons and the practices of the apostles and of the pastors who follow them in new covenant ministry. The heartening and humbling truth that our service is "the ministry of the Spirit," carried out in the presence and by the power of Christ's indwelling Spirit, must first mold pastors' persons, our mindset and character, even before we turn to the responsibilities of our calling.

The Spirit's faithful presence and heart-searching omniscience mean that he knows intimately sorrows and longings that we cannot put into words (Rom. 8:26–27). This reality brings comfort amid ministry's miseries. Moreover, he is uniquely qualified to weigh the integrity of our character and our conduct, our hidden motives and our visible actions. Our words must not misrepresent ourselves, our Master, or his message, since God the Spirit is ever-present to witness all that we are and think and say (Rom. 1:9; 9:1; 2 Cor. 1:23; 2:17; 4:2; Phil. 1:8; 1 Thess. 2:5, 10).

Pastors are called not only to speak with integrity but also to live exemplary lives. Although we do not claim to have "arrived" at the

Christlikeness for which we strive (Phil. 3:12–14), we must be able to say with a clear conscience, "Brothers, join in imitating me, and keep your eyes on those who walk according to the example you have in us" (3:17; see 4:9; 1 Cor. 4:16; 11:1; 1 Thess. 1:5–8; 2:3–12). Our sanctification progresses only as we cultivate a constant, lively dependence on God's Spirit of holiness. He is the one who began a good work in us—enabling us both to desire and to do what pleases God (Phil. 2:13)—and he will "bring it to completion at the day of Jesus Christ" (1:6; see 1 Thess. 5:23–24; 2 Thess. 2:13).

Yet pastors, of all people, know that the "work of God's free grace" that we call *sanctification* is not a process in which Christians can be merely passive. It is a lifelong pilgrimage in which we are increasingly "enabled" to die to sin and live to righteousness (WSC 35). The fruit of the Spirit—love, joy, peace, patience, kindness, goodness, faithfulness, gentleness, self-control—is produced in those who intentionally "walk by the Spirit" and "keep in step with the Spirit" (Gal. 5:16, 22–23, 25).

Recognizing the eternal consequences of gospel ministry (2 Cor. 2:14–17), our own vulnerability (4:7–12; 6:4–9; 11:23–31), and the formidable evil forces arrayed against the church (Eph. 6:12), we desperately need the sanctifying, Satan-disarming Spirit of God to wage war for our own souls, as well as for those we serve. The apostle is not embarrassed to ask fellow believers to pray "in the Spirit" that chains and legal, even lethal, threats will not intimidate or silence him. Instead, he wants to proclaim Christ with courage and clarity (Eph. 6:18–20; Col. 4:3–4). He anticipates that through others' "prayers and the help of the Spirit of Jesus Christ," he will experience "deliverance"—that when he stands in the imperial court, he will be delivered from shame, so "that with full courage now as always Christ will be honored in my body, whether by life or by death" (Phil. 1:19–20).[11]

11. Scholars debate whether the "deliverance" that Paul expects (Phil. 1:19) is from Roman custody and/or capital punishment, from present miseries through martyrdom, or from sin and death ("deliverance" as eternal salvation). A case for interpreting "deliverance" (*sōtēria*) in this context as "rescue from intimidating fear and shame," which would dishonor Jesus' name, is offered in Dennis E. Johnson, *Philippians*, Reformed Expository Commentary (Phillipsburg, NJ: P&R Publishing, 2015), 71–75.

Paul's spiritual "son" Timothy had a tender heart that cared for others (Phil. 2:19–22). But Timothy's tender heart was apparently vulnerable to fear (1 Cor. 16:10–11) and to shame over the cost of discipleship. So the apostle challenged Timothy to "fan into flame" the (Spirit-imparted) gift that he had received, since "God gave us a spirit not of fear but of power and love and self-control" (2 Tim. 1:6–8). The divine Spirit banishes cowardice and in its place imparts power, love, and prudent self-discipline. These words to Timothy, in the first postapostolic generation, still speak courage to daunted pastors today.

Scripture presents sad instances in which effective, even Spirit-empowered ministry was divorced from Spirit-wrought holiness in a leader's character. King Saul started well as Israel's royal defender, in the power of the Spirit (1 Sam. 11:1–15); but he ended badly (16:14–23; 18:6–19:24; 28:1–25). Judas, one of the Twelve, exorcised demons in the power of God's kingdom (Matt. 10:1–15); but he betrayed the King, revealing his true nature as "the son of destruction" (John 13:21–30; 17:12). Even when preachers are themselves strangers to the Spirit's heart-transforming power, God can make his message, on their tongues, life-giving to others. Nevertheless, we must heed Puritan Richard Baxter's admonition: "Take heed to yourselves, lest you should be void of that saving grace of God which you offer to others, and be strangers to the effectual workings of that Gospel which you preach."[12] It is perilous to belong to a church in which the Spirit is working, while one personally defies his presence and resists his purifying power (Acts 5:1–11; Heb. 6:4–8; 10:29–31). How much worse to preach to others and yet to disqualify oneself through unbelief (1 Cor. 9:27)! On the other hand, gospel heralds who taste the sweetness of the good news and enjoy "the fellowship of the Holy Spirit" (2 Cor. 13:14; cf. Phil. 2:1) rejoice to watch their living Lord bearing fruit through their service (John 15:4–5).

---

12. Richard Baxter, *Gildas Salvianus: The Reformed Pastor* (London, 1656), in *The Practical Works of the Rev. Richard Baxter* (London: James Duncan, 1830), 14:53, also available in abridged form as *The Reformed Pastor*, ed. William Brown (abr. eds. 1829, 1862; repr., Edinburgh: Banner of Truth, 1974), 51.

The Presence, Purity, and Power of the Spirit
in the Practices of the Pastorate

We will briefly consider four practices at the heart of the new covenant "ministry of the Spirit": preaching, counseling, discipline, and prayer. Pastors must engage in each of these ministry activities with dependence on the Holy Spirit's intimate presence, anticipating that he will exert his life-changing power through our faithful efforts.

The Holy Spirit and Pastoral Preaching

Every aspect of our preaching ministry is dependent on the Holy Spirit. If the preacher is to understand God's Word, which he is called to proclaim, he himself needs the illumining work of the Spirit. Paul reminds the Christians of Corinth that when he first brought them God's good news, his unimpressive speaking style ensured that people came to faith not through human rhetoric but by "demonstration of the Spirit and of power" (1 Cor. 2:1–5). Then he goes deeper than issues of delivery style. He traces his message back to its source in "things God has revealed to us through the Spirit" (v. 10). Now, revelation—that gift of receiving and expressing God's truth in Spirit-given words (v. 13)—belongs distinctively to the apostolic and prophetic offices (Eph. 3:3–5). Yet the wider principle, that *only* through God's Spirit can anyone understand "the things freely given us by God" (1 Cor. 2:11–12), applies to other preachers and all believers. Sermon preparation in all its phases—text selection; exegesis; historical, literary, and canonical analysis; theological integration and meditation; application; structure; illustration—must be pursued with a sense of our need for the risen Lord to open the Scriptures to our understanding (Luke 24:32) and to open our minds to their message (24:45; see Acts 16:14). It is all too easy for pastors to slip inadvertently into a practical deism in studying and teaching the Bible. Practical deists may affirm that the Holy Spirit breathed out the Scriptures in the *past*. But in the press of daily duties, they ignore their need for his *present* illumining presence. In the seventeenth century, John Owen described the danger of divorcing ministry of the Word from dependence on the Spirit:

It was "through the Holy Ghost that [Jesus] gave commandments unto them," Acts 1:2. These commandments concern the whole work in preaching the gospel and founding of the church; and these he gives unto them through the actings of divine wisdom in the human nature by the Holy Ghost. . . . Without his assistance he forbids them to attempt any thing, verses 4, 8. . . . And this is the hinge whereon the whole weight of it doth turn and depend unto this day. Take it away, . . . and there will be an absolute end of the church of Christ in this world;—no dispensation of the Spirit, no church. He that would utterly separate the Spirit from the word had as good burn his Bible. . . . But blessed be God, who hath knit these things together towards his elect, in the bond of an everlasting covenant! Isa. lix, 21.[13]

Owen affirms that God's Spirit opens the meaning of Scripture not by bypassing, but by working through our study and reflection: "the actings of divine wisdom in the human nature by the Holy Ghost." In our exploration of the Bible, the Spirit uses means, so we must be conscientious "craftsmen" in handling the Word (2 Tim. 2:15). But we must not trust in the means. Only God's Spirit can unfold and apply the message that he breathed out through prophets and apostles. In avoiding the mysticism and subjectivism that appear elsewhere in the church, Reformed pastors must not drift into reliance on lexica and commentaries, skills and systematic theologies, forgetting our need for God's Spirit to open his message to our hearts, and our hearts to his message.

Our dependence on the Holy Spirit applies to our communication of the Word as well. At Pentecost, Christ's outpouring of the Spirit gave his followers words to proclaim the mighty works of God (Acts 2:4, 11). That pattern—filling by the Spirit, imparting words of witness about Jesus—reappears later in Acts (4:8; 13:9; see also Luke 1:41–45, 67–79). When authorities forbade speaking the gospel, the church turned to the Lord in prayer, pleading, "Grant to your servants to continue to speak your word with all boldness." His answer came in a fresh impartation of the Spirit, renewing their courage:

13. Owen, *Pneumatologia*, 3:192–93.

"And when they had prayed, the place in which they were gathered together was shaken, and they were all filled with the Holy Spirit and continued to speak the word of God with boldness" (Acts 4:29–31).

Paul relied on the help of God's Spirit not only in threatening situations (Phil. 1:19–20), but also in his evangelistic outreach. He reminded the Thessalonians:

> Our gospel came to you not only in word, but also in power and in the Holy Spirit and with full conviction. You know what kind of men we proved to be among you for your sake. And you became imitators of us and of the Lord, for you received the word in much affliction, with the joy of the Holy Spirit. (1 Thess. 1:5–6)

The Holy Spirit displayed his presence in Paul's presentation and character, but also in his listeners' joyful response. His preaching was effective not because of his intellectual or rhetorical skills, but because of the heart-permeating, life-giving power of God's Spirit (Rom. 2:29; 1 Cor. 2:1–5; 2 Cor. 3:1–6; Phil. 3:3).

The Holy Spirit and Pastoral Counseling

Pastors bring Christ's Word not only corporately through preaching to congregations, but also personally through counseling individuals and families. Jesus' undershepherds must address a vast variety of spiritual challenges confronting the flock of God. God's indictment of Israel's negligent shepherds portrays the diversity of these needs:

> The weak you have not strengthened, the sick you have not healed, the injured you have not bound up, the strayed you have not brought back, the lost you have not sought, and with force and harshness you have ruled them. So they were scattered . . . , with none to search or seek for them. (Ezek. 34:4–6)[14]

Some of us (myself included) find this aspect of our pastoral responsibility more daunting than preaching from a pulpit and leading

14. See Martin Bucer, *Concerning the True Care of Souls*, trans. Peter Beale (1538; repr., Edinburgh: Banner of Truth, 2009), 69–197. Most of Bucer's treatise is structured by the profile of pastoral care in Ezekiel 34.

public worship. We do our duty to reach out to the brother snared in sin, to the couple contemplating divorce, to the grieving widow, or to the estranged and distant member. But we know that we are beyond our depth. Our stores of wisdom are scant, our capacity for compassion is thin, our courage to confront (in love) is feeble. Such personalized shepherding exposes the paucity of our personal resources. Yet as uncomfortable as this exposure is, we need it. Paul experienced this painful paradox of ministry in Jesus' name: "For the sake of Christ, then, I am content with weaknesses, insults, hardships, persecutions, and calamities. For when I am weak, then I am strong" (2 Cor. 12:10). The strength that overrides our weakness and works through our weakness is the heart-purifying power of the Holy Spirit, the invincible divine Agent of sanctification.

In our calling as peacemakers, pastors can and must draw on the reality of the Spirit's commitment to make God's children one. When interpersonal frictions and competing agendas threaten the unity of Christ's people, in congregations or in families, we can appeal to the truth that, by uniting us to Christ, the Spirit has made us one. So Christians are called to "maintain the unity of the Spirit in the bond of peace" by engaging each other in "humility and gentleness, with patience, bearing with one another in love" (Eph. 4:2–3). Jesus' sacrifice for us and the Spirit's presence with us converge to move and enable us to reject bitterness and anger, and instead to express kindness, forgiveness, and love (4:30–5:2).

Whenever pastors (or other believers) discover that brother or sister "caught in any transgression," we must reach out to restore the person in the gentleness of the Holy Spirit (Gal. 6:1–5). Paul's directive flows from the contrast that he just drew between the works of the flesh and the fruit of the Spirit (5:16–26). The "flesh" (sin-stained, sin-disabled human nature) produces not only sins of the body (sexual impurity, drunkenness, etc.) but also conflict-generating sins of the self-absorbed heart (enmity, strife, jealousy, dissensions, etc.) (5:20–21). By contrast, God's Spirit bears fruit that unites and purifies (love, joy, peace, patience, kindness, goodness, faithfulness, gentleness, self-control). As people born of the Spirit (4:28–29) and alive through the Spirit, Christians must walk by the Spirit and keep in step with the Spirit (5:16, 25). So Paul's address to "you who are spiritual" (6:1) does not set apart a distinctive class of mature Christians or church officers. Rather, all who belong to Christ Jesus have the Spirit. English versions typically interpret "spirit of gentleness" (*en pneumati praütētos*) (1 Cor. 4:21) as referring to the believer's attitude; but the preceding context identifies gentleness (*praütēs*) as a fruit of God's Spirit (*karpos tou pneumatos*) (Gal. 5:22–23). So, as one pastor concludes, "a case can be made for an upper-case 'S' translating a *Spirit of gentleness*."[15] Whether or not one perceives in "spirit/Spirit of gentleness" a specific reference to the third person of the Trinity, the preceding context, at least, reinforces our need for the Holy Spirit when we are called to reach out gently to correct fellow Christians snared in sin.

The Holy Spirit and Pastoral Discipline

When repeated gentle efforts to restore meet resistance, love for Christ's reputation and for the unrepentant brother or sister compels shepherds to exercise their delegated authority through formal discipline. In such situations, as pastors and elders confer soberly, seeking wisdom and grace beyond their own, the Lord's promise of his personal presence imparts assurance and accountability:

> If [your brother] refuses to listen to [witnesses], tell it to the church. And if he refuses to listen even to the church, let him be to you as a Gentile and a tax collector. . . . If two of you agree on earth about anything they ask, it will be done for them by my Father in heaven. For where two or three are gathered in my name, there am I among them. (Matt. 18:17–20)

We might wonder how, after his ascension, the Lord Jesus is "among" those gathered in his name when the church must administer disci-

15. David B. McWilliams, *Galatians: A Mentor Commentary* (Fearn, Scotland: Christian Focus, 2009), 211: "A **spirit of gentleness** can refer to the Holy Spirit or to the human spirit. In either case the source of **gentleness** is the Holy Spirit (5:23)" (boldface original). Others, though interpreting *pneuma* as a reference to believers' attitude, note that gentleness is a fruit of God's Spirit (Gal. 5:23). E.g., Herman N. Ridderbos, *The Epistle of Paul to the Churches of Galatia*, NICNT (Grand Rapids: Eerdmans, 1953), 212; F. F. Bruce, *Commentary on Galatians*, NIGTC (Grand Rapids: Eerdmans, 1982), 260; and Timothy George, *Galatians*, New American Commentary 30 (Nashville: Broadman & Holman, 1994), 412.

pline to its members. He is present by his Holy Spirit, who indwells the church. Jesus fulfills his promise to come to us through the arrival of the Spirit of truth to reside within and among Jesus' followers (John 14:16–18, 23).

In 1 Corinthians 5, therefore, Paul appeals to the presence of Christ's Spirit in the assembled church when a member must be disciplined. The apostle is geographically distant (hence he is writing); but when the church gathers, he himself is present to pronounce judgment, for his spirit/Spirit "is present, with the power of our Lord Jesus" (1 Cor. 5:3–5). Gordon Fee explains:

> [Paul] is not allowing that because he is not physically present he is not truly present and therefore he must act *as though* he were. Rather, he is emphasizing the fact that he is indeed present in the Spirit, and that is *why* he can act as he does. . . . When the Corinthians are assembled, the Spirit is understood to be present among them (see on 3:16); and for Paul that means that he, too, is among them by that same Spirit.[16]

Paul does not call these Christians to pretend that he is present, but to recognize that, through Christ's Spirit, Christ's apostle is, in fact, in their midst. Likewise, Acts 5:1–11 records a terrifying incident when sudden supernatural judgment befell professing believers who had cynically dismissed the presence of God's heart-searching Spirit in the church: "Ananias, why has Satan filled your heart to lie to the Holy Spirit[?] . . . You have not lied to man but to God" (vv. 3–4; see v. 9). God's Spirit ordinarily protects God's people through the authority, wisdom, and diligence that his presence imparts to pastors and elders. When the family of God must discipline a wayward member in love, we thank God that we are not confined to our own finite perspectives and powers of persuasion. Rather, we humbly, hopefully rely on the Spirit's boundless wisdom and his heart-piercing power to work repentance, rescue, and restoration.

Related to the Spirit's involvement in discipline is his guidance

---

16. Gordon D. Fee, *The First Epistle to the Corinthians*, NICNT (Grand Rapids: Eerdmans, 1987), 204–5 (emphasis original).

of shepherds as they consider the application of God's Word to the church's life together. A classic example is the early dispute over the standing of uncircumcised Gentile believers and its resolution by a council of apostles and elders (Acts 15). After "much debate," Peter testified that he had watched God pour out his Spirit on Gentiles, without requiring circumcision (15:7–11; see 10:44–48). God "made no distinction between us and them, having cleansed their hearts by faith" (15:8–9). To Peter's testimony, Barnabas and Paul added their own report of God's welcome to Gentiles in Cyprus and Asia Minor (v. 12). James interpreted these events as fulfilling the words of the prophets, citing Amos 9:11–12 (Acts 15:16–18). Finally, the council expressed its consensus in a letter (vv. 19–29).

Notably, the process that produced consensus—interpreting events in the light of Scripture—is the same process by which pastors and elders today strive to discern what serves the well-being of Christ's church. Admittedly, Peter, Barnabas, and Paul reported extraordinary displays of God's power that had previously occurred (see Acts 10:46; 13:11–12; 14:8–10). But during the council itself, no apostle or prophet received and spoke a new revelation from God to resolve the question (contrast 11:27–30; 21:10–14). Instead, these leaders reached consensus through the ordinary means of deliberation and debate, interpreting their experiences of God's work in the light of God's Word. They were confident that God's Spirit was guiding in their discussion and decision, so they introduced their conclusion in these striking words: "For it has seemed good *to the Holy Spirit* and to us" (15:28). No new revelation, but rather careful reflection on how God's Word addressed the situation. And their conclusion "seemed good to the Holy Spirit."

Christ leads his church through men marred by weakness, lacking in wisdom, courage, integrity, compassion, and other attributes that set Jesus himself apart as the Good Shepherd. Yet we draw encouragement from the assurance that Jesus is "in the midst of the lampstands," his churches on earth, through his Holy Spirit (Rev. 1:12–13, 20; 2:1–2). Remembering this reality in our staff meetings, in sessions and councils, in presbyteries and classes, in synods and assemblies will instill in us awe, dependence, and expectation that the Spirit of truth will lead us into his truth (John 16:13) and knit us together in love (Eph. 4:1–6, 15–16). Our speaking and our listening take place *coram Deo*, before the face of God. The Spirit's holiness and patience set a guard over our mouths, a watch over our lips (Ps. 141:3), making us pause to consider what we say and how we say it. He opens our ears and humbles our hearts, making us quick to hear and slow to speak, ready to listen to what the Spirit says to the churches from his Word, through one another (James 1:19; Rev. 2:7).

The Holy Spirit and Pastoral Prayer

The apostles linked "prayer and . . . the ministry of the word" as the central priorities to which they must devote themselves (Acts 6:4). Pastors and evangelists "plant" and "water," but God alone makes his Word germinate and grow in human hearts (1 Cor. 3:5–9). That fact transforms our prayers for God's people.

Paul's Prison Epistles show his pastoral priorities in intercession for fellow Christians. He asked the Lord to make their love abound in knowledge and discernment, filling them with the fruit of righteousness (Phil. 1:9), and to fill them with the knowledge of God's will in spiritual wisdom, yielding God-pleasing lives (Col. 1:9–12). Paul explicitly mentions the Spirit in his prayer for the believers in Ephesus:

> I do not cease to give thanks for you, remembering you in my prayers, that the God of our Lord Jesus Christ, the Father of glory, may give you the Spirit of wisdom and of revelation in the knowledge of him, having the eyes of your hearts enlightened, that you may know what is the hope to which he has called you, what are the riches of his glorious inheritance in the saints, and what is the immeasurable greatness of his power toward us who believe, according to the working of his great might. (Eph. 1:16–19)

Paul has profound realities to explain, "every spiritual blessing in the heavenly places" in Christ (Eph. 1:3). In order for the saints to "see" their hope, their identity as God's inheritance, and the divine power exerted in Christ for them, they need illumination from God's "Spirit of wisdom and of revelation" (v. 17). So Pastor Paul prays for them. Of course, they are not devoid of God's Spirit. When they trusted Christ, they were "sealed" with the Holy Spirit (vv. 13–14). Because the Spirit had made them one, they must preserve the Spirit's unity through humility, gentleness, and patience (4:1–6; see 2:14–18). Yet they are always dependent on the Spirit's enlightening grace, in order to receive and respond to the glorious good news. That consciousness must compel and shape pastors' prayers for God's people.

Conclusion

For good reason Paul characterizes the ministry of gospel proclamation and pastoral care as "the ministry of the Spirit." Pastors need the ongoing presence and power of the Holy Spirit in our own persons, unmasking our needy weakness and displaying his power through our frailty. We need the Spirit to open our own eyes to see Jesus' glory in the pages of the Bible. We need the Spirit to open our mouths to proclaim his grace boldly, so that others see Christ, too. We need the Spirit's wisdom and compassion to care well for Jesus' wounded, wayward, stumbling, stubborn sheep. So we ask the Father for the Holy Spirit, knowing that he can be trusted to give us, constantly and in increasing measure, the Spirit of the Son, through whom we cry out, "Abba, Father" (Rom. 8:15; Gal. 4:6). And we rejoice to watch the Spirit bear his beautiful fruit in others' lives through his life-giving Word, to the glory of God the Father and Jesus Christ, his only Son, our Lord.

Key Terms

adoption
exegesis
glorification
justification
regeneration
sanctification

Recommendations for Further Reading

Azurdia, Arturo G., III. *Spirit Empowered Mission: Aligning the Church's Mission to the Mission of Jesus.* Fearn, Scotland: Christian Focus, 2016.

Clowney, Edmund P. *The Church*. Contours of Christian Theology. Downers Grove, IL: InterVarsity Press, 1995.

Ferguson, Sinclair B. *The Holy Spirit*. Contours of Christian Theology. Downers Grove, IL: InterVarsity Press, 1996.

Gaffin, Richard B., Jr. *Perspectives on Pentecost: New Testament Teaching on the Gifts of the Holy Spirit*. Phillipsburg, NJ: Presbyterian and Reformed, 1979.

Johnson, Dennis E. *The Message of Acts in the History of Redemption*. Phillipsburg, NJ: P&R Publishing, 1997.

Discussion Questions

1. What is new about Pentecost?
   a. Discuss continuity in the salvific work of the Spirit as Christ's accomplishment of redemption moved redemptive history forward from "promise" into "fulfillment."
   b. Discuss continuity and development in the ministerial empowering work of the Spirit as redemptive history advanced from "promise" into "fulfillment."
2. What textual support is offered for the claim that "Old Testament texts anticipate a future escalation of the Holy Spirit's ministry-empowering activity in two directions, an individual concentration and a corporate expansion"?
   a. How does the "individual concentration" in the promised Servant of the Lord find fulfillment in the ministry of Jesus himself?
   b. How does the "corporate expansion" desired by Moses and promised through Joel work out in the distribution of ministry gifting and activity throughout Christ's new covenant community?
3. How should we understand these complementary New Testament teachings?
   a. The Spirit *distinctively* empowers special officers in the church (apostle, prophet, evangelist, pastor, elder, teacher, deacon) to fulfill particular ministries (Word, rule, mercy); and
   b. The Spirit *universally* empowers every believer to serve the rest of the body.

   c. How should the Spirit's complementary bestowals of gifts (to special officers, to all members of Christ) practically form and reform the way that our congregations function?

4. What biblical evidence supports the claim that we need the sanctifying presence of the Spirit in the person of the pastor, and not only the Spirit's ministry-empowering abilities in the practice of the pastorate? Can an abundance of the Spirit's ministry gifts compensate for an absence of the Spirit's fruit (love, joy, peace, patience, kindness, goodness, faithfulness, gentleness, self-control, Gal. 5:22–23)? Have you witnessed this "disconnect" in yourself or others? Without breaching confidentiality, discuss the outcomes that you have observed when "fruit" is lacking though "gifting" is present.

5. The author claims that Bible-believing pastors may lapse into "practical deism" as we prepare and deliver sermons, provide pastoral care, carry out leadership and governance, and perform other aspects of ministry.

   a. What may be symptoms of our failure to depend on the presence and power of God's Spirit?

   b. What may be remedies to our bias toward self-reliance and independence?

6. How should awareness of our own weakness and of the Spirit's life-giving power form and transform pastors' prayer lives—frequency/consistency, what we ask for, our expectations? Get specific about changes that you purpose to pursue!

12

JUSTIFICATION

The Declaration of Righteousness
That Shapes Our Present Ministry[1]

JOHN C. A. FERGUSON

Justification has been referred to as the subjective, or material, doctrine giving rise to the Reformation.[2] As such, it has abiding significance in life and ministry and has a vital role in the present and future life of the church. J. I. Packer describes its pivotal role in the gospel: "The gospel centres upon justification; that is, upon the remission of sins and acceptance of our persons that goes with it."[3] Sinclair Ferguson comments on its place at the heart of theology: "Justification by grace alone (*sola gratia*) through faith alone (*sola fide*) has stood at the centre of evangelical theology ever since Martin Luther's famous insistence that the church stands or falls with this doctrine."[4]

1. Written in honor of Sinclair Ferguson, who has taught me, as my minister, as my professor, and most of all as my father, salvation by grace alone, through faith alone, in Christ alone, according to Scripture alone, for the glory of God alone.
2. Philip Schaff, *Creeds of Christendom*, 3 vols. (New York: Harper & Row, 1931; repr., Grand Rapids: Baker, 2007), 1:206; the formal or objective principle, according to Schaff, is Scripture.
3. J. I. Packer, *Knowing God* (London: Hodder & Stoughton, 2013), 151.
4. Sinclair B. Ferguson, *Some Pastors and Teachers: Reflecting a Biblical Vision of What Every Minister Is Called to Be* (Edinburgh: Banner of Truth, 2017), 487.

Martyn Lloyd-Jones wrote of the vital need of justification by faith alone for the life of the church: "There has never been a revival but that this has always come back into great prominence."[5] The doctrine has tremendous significance for the present day as well as in the history of the church. For "this doctrine means the end of all thinking about ourselves and our goodness, and our good deeds, and our morality, and all our works."[6]

Before discussing how justification bears on the preacher and preaching, we must consider what the Bible teaches about the doctrine. Doing so will help us focus on challenges that preachers face with respect to justification from a biblical perspective. Personal challenges that preachers face will be explored in light of justification and suggestions offered about how difficulties may be overcome.

Justification and the Bible

We discover the doctrine of justification through Scripture's teaching. Although the language of "justification" is rare in the Old Testament (Job 32:2; 33:32; Ps. 51:4; Prov. 17:15; Isa. 45:25), there is abundant material relating to it. John Murray observed that closely related themes such as *righteousness* and *justice* are frequently discussed in the Old Testament.[7] And most significantly, the foundation blocks that inform the doctrine of justification are all found in the Old Testament: the problem of sin, the relationship between God and man, the remedy for this broken relationship, and the means by which the relationship is restored. These teachings are found within the traditional division of the Old Testament as Law, Prophets, and Writings: The Law describes creation and the subsequent fall of humanity as bearing on justification (Gen. 1–3; see also Rom. 5–6), as does Abraham's call (Gen. 12–17; see also Rom. 4; Gal. 4), the provision of the law on Sinai (Ex. 20), and the development of the ceremonial law (all of Leviticus).

5. D. Martyn Lloyd-Jones, *Revival* (London: Marshall Pickering, 1986), 55.
6. Lloyd-Jones, *Revival*, 55.
7. See John Murray, *The Epistle to the Romans*, 2 vols., NICNT (Grand Rapids: Eerdmans, 1997), 1:336–47.

Prophets are universally concerned with the sins of the people and how they may be forgiven. The Old Testament sacrifices are considered an abomination in God's sight (Isa. 1). Yet God's mercy is also demonstrated toward his people by the prophets' notice of the new covenant and pouring out of the Holy Spirit. The prophets looked ahead to Christ's coming and fulfillment of God's covenant promises (1 Peter 1:10–12). The Writings also have justification in view, for they are broadly concerned with mercy and salvation. This can be seen in the instruction on righteousness (e.g., Ps. 1; Prov. 1:3) and forgiveness (e.g., Pss. 32; 51; 103; 130).

These themes set the scene for Christ in the New Testament. Justification is directly discussed in relation to acceptance by God, forgiveness of sins, eternal life, grace, sacrifice, and faith in him. Old Testament teachings are brought into view in Christ's earthly ministry in the Gospels. As we will see below, Jesus focuses attention on justification, reflected by his more frequent use of the terminology. On several occasions, Jesus either uses language of justification or speaks with reference to it.

When he exposed the Pharisees' hardened hearts, Jesus said, "Wisdom is justified by all her children" (Luke 7:35; see Matt. 11:19). Here "justified" means "vindicated." Wisdom is proved by what it produces. The Pharisees' offense at Jesus and John the Baptist was evidence of their spiritual deadness. On the other hand, those who accepted John's and Jesus' ministries declared God just (Luke 7:29). Today also, Christ is rejected and his name taken in vain. But those who trust in him declare God righteous.

Declaring God as righteous is a theme found in other passages where Jesus uses justification language. He spoke of how all will give an account to God on the day of judgment for their words (Matt. 12:36). Thereafter he described the place of our words in justification: "For by your words you will be justified, and by your words you will be condemned" (v. 37). Plainly, justification is pivotal in a person's future, eternal relationship to God. Christ's words have reference to God's judgment, shown by the antithesis of condemnation.[8] Regard-

8. John Owen, *The Doctrine of Justification by Faith*, vol. 5 of *The Works of John Owen*, ed. William H. Goold (Edinburgh: Banner of Truth, 1965), 5:129.

ing words, he did not say that a person will justify himself by them. He did not identify words as a cause of justification. God is the one who justifies (Rom. 8:33). The preposition "by" (*ek*) indicates that it is not the words themselves that justify, but words are inseparable from the relationship that a person has with God, whether justified or under condemnation. Hence there is a binding effect, such that the words can be described as though they are justifying. As our words are taken into account in God's judgment, they are described as having an effect, issuing in justification or condemnation. Christ's analysis of the sins of the tongue demonstrates our need of his righteousness for justification. In application, J. C. Ryle writes:

> Our words are the evidence of the state of our hearts, as surely as the taste of the water is an evidence of the state of the spring. "Out of the abundance of the heart the mouth speaketh." The lips only utter what the mind conceives. Our words will form one subject of inquiry at the day of judgment: we shall have to give account of our sayings, as well as of our doings. Truly these are very solemn considerations. If there were no other text in the Bible, this passage ought to convince us, that we are all "guilty before God," and need a righteousness better than our own, even the righteousness of Christ (*Phil.* 3:9).[9]

The Pharisees' sin was their desire to justify themselves (Luke 16:15). This self-exalting is an affront to God and results in condemnation. God's judgment, therefore, issues in either a person's justification or condemnation. His provision of justification in Christ received by faith averts condemnation.

Justification is God's work. A sinner who cannot offer any defense of himself and instead depends on God's mercy is declared righteous in God's sight. Two stories in the Gospels demonstrate this dependence on God for justification—the parable of the good Samaritan and the parable of the tax collector.

The lawyer with whom Jesus conversed in the parable of the good

---

9. J. C. Ryle, *Expository Thoughts on Matthew* (Edinburgh: Banner of Truth, 2012), 107–8.

Samaritan is described as "desiring to justify himself" (Luke 10:29). Jesus' parable demonstrates fallen humanity's inability to self-justify. The parable teaches that for the lawyer to fulfill the law himself, he must be merciful to the person most offensive to him. He must show kindness to the one to whom he is least inclined to show it. Ultimately, his righteousness must exceed what his fallen nature is able to accomplish. By contrast, Christ perfects the way of righteousness. The Holy One of God, who had the sins of the world imputed to him, declared, "Father, forgive them, for they know not what they do" (23:34).

Dependence on God for justification is also evident in the parable of the tax collector. Jesus contrasted the self-righteousness of the Pharisee that leads to condemnation with the tax collector's dependence on God that leads to justification. He said, "I tell you, this man went down to his house justified, rather than the other" (Luke 18:14). God justified the tax collector. He considered himself unworthy of God and asked God for mercy. He was accepted by God. The proud Pharisee looked down on the tax collector and counted himself righteous, but Jesus taught that his self-righteousness was irreconcilable with justification. He was, in fact, under God's wrath.

We also learn in this parable the timing of the tax collector's justification. He was justified by God's mercy there and then. When viewed together with his saying in Matthew 12:37 concerning the future implications of justification, we can observe Jesus teaching that justification has an "already-not yet" aspect. Justification is a present reality for a Christian. The man was justified that day. It is also a future reality. It ensures deliverance from condemnation for sin on the day of judgment. Further, Jesus' use of the perfect tense expresses that this justification has ongoing as well as present validity.

Through studying these instances when Jesus used justification language, we find key components of the doctrine in his teaching. It has an eschatological character. The antithesis of justification is condemnation. It concerns God's judgment. It has present-day application and eternal consequences. It finds its origin in God's mercy and is a gift received, not an award earned. While the words of a repentant sinner do not justify, they are so bound to God's mercy that the words can appear in themselves to have a justifying effect.

Jesus' concern, though, was not only to teach about justification, but also to accomplish it. He did this in his life, death, and resurrection. He was "raised for our justification" (Rom. 4:25). Accordingly, justification is brought into full view in the apostolic writings, particularly in Paul, the former Pharisee, with his treatments of the subject in Romans 1–8 and Galatians 2–5. James's comments are also well known. There are twenty-seven direct references to justification in Paul's letters and three in James. Language of justification also appears twice in Acts and is attributed to Paul on both occasions.

Although the balance is heavily weighted toward Paul's writings, we should resist presenting the doctrine as merely Pauline. It is, in the first place, Christian doctrine. Justification is Paul's interest because it is Christ's interest, as we have seen. He develops Christ's teaching on the subject and the truth that Christ is our justification. For the benefit is not found apart from him but in him. "The benefits of the gospel are *in Christ. They do not exist apart from him.* They are *ours* only *in him.* They cannot be abstracted from him as if we ourselves could possess them independently of him."[10]

Focusing our attention on the three figures around whom Paul discusses justification—Adam, Abraham, and Christ—will allow us to view how justification is brought to bear in Christ.

Adam

The fall in Genesis 3 introduces an epochal change in the human relationship to God. At creation, mankind is able to sin and able not to sin. Adam's decision to eat from the tree of knowledge of good and evil set the trajectory for all of humanity. After the fall, Adam and his posterity's situation is changed, and they are unable not to sin. As sin entered, so also did the need for salvation if any were to live before a holy God. For Adam's disobedience resulted in God's curse and death.

All are related to Adam (Acts 17:26). Therefore, his transgression in the garden of Eden led to death for all (see Rom. 5:17). John Owen commented, "As he was after the fall, so are we by nature, in the very same state and condition."[11] Mankind is entrapped in sin, unable to

10. Sinclair B. Ferguson, *The Whole Christ: Legalism, Antinomianism, and Gospel Assurance—Why the Marrow Controversy Still Matters* (Wheaton, IL: Crossway, 2016), 44 (italics original).

11. Owen, *Justification by Faith*, 5:76.

save himself from it and unable to relieve himself of responsibility for committing it. Man has had no excuse "ever since the creation of the world" (Rom. 1:20). This point of enduring responsibility that continues throughout the generations is sealed by Romans 3:19, which states that all are accountable to God's law, and not only those to whom it was first given. For those who are "under the law" are identified as "the whole world." John Murray concludes, "There can be no question but here is the note of all-inclusive universality."[12] God has therefore held the world to account for sin ever since the fall. "In Adam," the only possible verdict is "guilty." Hence, even before the law was given, death reigned from Adam to Moses (Rom. 5:14).[13]

Relevant biblical material for the doctrine of justification is therefore traced to creation. Paul's references to Adam serve to demonstrate the universal need for justification, establishing the antithesis that Christ's justification addresses. His focus is on God's grace to us in Christ. In keeping with this, Murray elicits the gracious character of the gospel from the Adam-Christ comparison in Romans 5:12–21: "It is eminently germane to the whole argument of this passage that death reigned over those who did not sin after the similitude of Adam's transgression. For the apostle is chiefly interested in demonstrating that men are justified who do not act righteously after the similitude of Christ's obedience."[14] Justification is the remedy for condemnation. So "the judgment following one trespass brought condemnation, but the free gift following many trespasses brought justification" (Rom. 5:16). The first indication of justification in Christ was made in the garden in Adam's hearing (Gen. 3:15). Indeed, as John Owen said, this justification was proposed to Adam: "In this lost, forlorn, hopeless condition, God proposeth the promise of redemption by Christ unto him. And this was the object of that faith whereby he was to be justified."[15] Already in promissory form, this doctrine is present in God's response to the first sin.

---

12. Murray, *Romans*, 1:106.

13. Moral law in creation is often overlooked today in theology but was a subject of much interest in the development of federal theology in Scotland. See John Colquhoun, *A Treatise on the Law and the Gospel* (Morgan, PA: Soli Deo Gloria, 1999), 1–25; Hugh Martin, *The Atonement* (Edinburgh: Knox Press, 1976), 255–66.

14. Murray, *Romans*, 1:188.

15. Owen, *Justification by Faith*, 5:76.

Abraham

God's calling of Abraham focuses our attention on the manner in which justification is delivered—that is, through promise. When Paul describes justification by faith and not by works of the law, he uses the pre-Sinai example of Abraham.

Before the law was given (i.e., the written law at Sinai), "death reigned from Adam to Moses" (Rom. 5:14). Abraham was therefore in need of justification. His justification came through God's promise. It is traced back to God's eternal counsel and brought about through his provision of the Lord Jesus Christ. Abraham's story reveals the means by which we are saved. Romans 3–4 and Galatians 3 provide comment on Abraham and how he was justified not by his works but by faith.

While law demonstrates the need for justification, justification itself does not proceed from law, but from promise, hence grace (Rom. 4:13; Gal. 3:18). Law cannot perfect (Heb. 10:1) and so does not offer justification. So justification is attained not by our works of the law but rather through faith in Christ. Faith is the means by which we are raised out of condemnation into justification. It is a gift that does not proceed from law, yet it meets the demands of law. In Christ "the righteousness of God has been manifested apart from the law" (Rom. 3:21). He is our righteousness and therefore our justification (1 Cor. 1:30).

Abraham was justified because he believed in God's promise. God graciously credited his belief with righteousness. Today, a Christian is justified because of belief in Christ, his death, and his resurrection (Rom. 4:23–25). The credit of Christ's righteousness and the faith by which the credit is attained are both gifts of God's gracious will toward us. Accordingly, the means by which Abraham in the Old Testament and Christians today are justified is the same—by faith.

Abraham is the father of the faithful (Rom. 4:16), and so there is a paradigm in his relationship to God for all who believe. James Buchanan wrote, "The Apostles made use of the case of Abraham to prove all the most important points of the doctrine of Justification . . . and that it was not singular, but similar, in all essential respects, to the justification of every other sinner."[16] Therefore, as for Abraham,

---

16. James Buchanan, *The Doctrine of Justification* (Birmingham, AL: Solid Ground Christian Books, 2006), 35.

so also for us: justification is the fruit and fulfillment of promise and not obtained through works of the flesh (see Gal. 3–5). Accounts of Abraham in the New Testament thus serve to demonstrate the necessity of turning to Christ in faith (Rom. 4:23–24).

Here we must briefly comment on James's exposition of justification. He is sometimes understood as teaching that the means of justification is works and not faith. On the contrary, he, too, recognizes that Abraham was justified by faith (James 2:23). When he says that "a person is justified by works and not by faith alone" (v. 24), he should most likely be understood as making a similar point as Jesus does in Matthew 12:37. Jesus is not arguing that words justify (see Matt. 7:22–23), but rather is stating that justification cannot be separated from words. Similarly, in the Christian life, faith is bound together with works in a manner such that it is impossible to conceive of the former without there being evidence of the latter.[17]

Christ

Our studies of Adam and Abraham lead us to Christ, who fulfills the justification anticipated in the Old Testament. Whereas Adam and Abraham teach us about justification, Christ provides justification: "But now the righteousness of God has been manifested apart from the law, although the Law and the Prophets bear witness to it—the righteousness of God through faith in Jesus Christ for all who believe" (Rom. 3:21–22). Christ has fulfilled the obligations of the old covenant through his obedience to God. John Calvin wrote, "Justified by faith is he who, excluded from the righteousness of works, grasps the righteousness of Christ through faith, and clothed in it, appears in God's sight not as a sinner but as a righteous man."[18] God justifies us in Christ and effects that justification by the Holy Spirit. It is necessary to receive his Son for justification because in him all the promises of God are "Yes" and "Amen" (2 Cor. 1:20). In him they are all confirmed, and our interest in them sealed.

---

17. For further discussion on the relationship between James and Paul on justification, see Ferguson, *Some Pastors and Teachers*, 500–503.

18. John Calvin, *Institutes of the Christian Religion*, ed. John T. McNeill, trans. Ford Lewis Battles, 2 vols., Library of Christian Classics 20–21 (Philadelphia: Westminster, 1960), 3.11.2.

The statement that "one act of righteousness leads to justification and life for all" (Rom. 5:18) simultaneously exalts Christ's perfect work and exposes the corruption of sin. One righteous act is needed for salvation, and Christ alone offers it. No one else can accomplish it.

God in Christ brings a sinner into a new relationship with himself. He provides his Son as the sacrifice for our sins. Christ lived in full and perfect obedience to the Father, and his Father was pleased with him. Yet for our sake, he numbered him among the transgressors (Isa. 53:12; Luke 22:37). Christ suffered the penalty of death—but not because he deserved penalty, for he is righteous. Rather, he graciously agreed to the imputation of sin for our salvation, assuming the curse resulting from the first Adam's sin in his own death. In justification, Christ is counted first as sin. Not that he sinned (Heb. 4:15), but because he had his covenant people's sins credited to his account.

His death is the most powerful of works (John 12:32). He is a priest "by the power of an indestructible life" (Heb. 7:16). "He was always the Living One . . . and never more gloriously so than in his death-destroying death."[19] He swallowed death up in victory (1 Cor. 15:54).

He is justified in his resurrection, declared to be the Son of God (Rom. 1:4) and raised from the dead for our justification (4:25). He rose from the dead, never to die again (6:9). Death is now behind him. Consequently, the sinner who comes to faith in Christ is declared innocent and righteous (counted as having positively fulfilled the law). Christ's righteousness is imputed to those he saves.

Justification is not only the revoking of penalty; it is the gift of Christ's righteousness. God's grace is shown again in that he provides the perfect righteousness of his Son in return for the corruption of our sin. What we receive in Christ (justification) is the very antithesis of what we would expect to receive outside Christ (condemnation).

The sinner is helpless and depends on the free grace of Christ. In that grace she finds the justification needed before the holy God. The remedy for sin is provided through Christ's death on the cross and expressed well in Toplady's hymn "Rock of Ages":

---

19. Hugh Martin, *Christ for Us: Sermons of Hugh Martin* (Edinburgh: Banner of Truth, 1998), 53.

Let the water and the blood,
From thy riven side which flowed,
Be of sin the double cure,
Cleanse me from its guilt and pow'r.[20]

In focusing on this particular benefit in Christ of justification, we find that it affects a person's status before God, rather than a person's moral condition. It is distinct from sanctification. The righteousness imputed does not describe a person's moral condition, any more than sin describes Christ's moral condition when it was imputed to him in his humiliation. It describes a person's status, or standing, before God. Christ's standing by imputation was one of sin and guilt, and so he was condemned to death, even while his moral condition was (and is) holy and righteous. The sinner's standing, by imputation, is one of obedience and righteousness. Hence the sinner is justified. The renewing of the mind and daily conforming to Christ's character—the moral condition—is addressed in sanctification.

Imputed righteousness is not automatically conferred on the whole of the human race in Adam. It must be brought to bear in a person's life. The means by which that is done is the gift of faith in Christ (Eph. 2:8). Without this faith, a person remains "in Adam" and under the curse of sin and death. We are saved, therefore, not because of anything inherent in our human nature that makes us worthy of justification, but solely according to God's gracious will, through the free provision of Christ's righteousness. In him a sinner finds God's acceptance.

Summary

The curse of sin and the fall is reversed in justification. Justification through Christ cancels the power of death as a means for eternal separation from God's mercies. Death for the believer is now a translation into the heavenly kingdom, to be with Christ.

The need for Christ's justification is demonstrated in the Old Testament. None is righteous, save for Christ, who is God. He is the "one mediator between God and men" (1 Tim. 2:5). Scripture focuses our

---

20. Augustus Montague Toplady, "Rock of Ages" (1776).

attention on Christ. The gospel is offered from Jerusalem to the end of the earth (Acts 1:8). No person is able to justify him- or herself, but justification is offered to all freely through Christ: "He is able to save to the uttermost those who draw near to God through him" (Heb. 7:25). Justification of sinners lies at the heart of Jesus Christ's ministry and mission. Hence, he calls preachers to preach the message to the world.

Preacher and Preaching

How does justification affect a preacher? How does it affect his preaching? What challenges are there, and how may they be overcome? We turn now to practical applications.

Theology and the Preacher

We depend on God's Word to know that Adam's sin entails a universal need of justification. The Word is also our guide for acquiring this grace. While general revelation tells of the law and our need for justification, our fallen condition is such that we need special revelation—the written Word—and the help of the Holy Spirit to perceive these truths aright.[21] The minister and congregation alike, therefore, sit underneath the authority of the Word.

The gospel message has an objective aspect that is reflected in preaching. The sinful condition is universal, and the preacher is not excluded from this number. In this regard, the preacher can consider himself a member of the congregation, also in need of the offer of grace that follows in Christ Jesus. For the message that is faithfully conveyed to the congregation does not originate in the preacher; it originates in God, is preached to all, and applies to all, including the preacher.

This universal aspect of justification is advantageous to the preacher in communicating it. For he has the same fallen nature as the congregation. He can minister, having had personal experience of how the flesh and Spirit work and wage war against each other. The preacher, as the congregation, is wholly dependent on the grace of God.

21. Calvin, *Institutes*, 3.1.1.

The doctrine of imputation, which is a feature of justification, also has applications for gospel ministers. Imputation is the assignment of one person's righteousness (or sinfulness) to another. In Adam, sin is imputed to all born of the flesh, and death is the result. Through the lens of Abraham's relationship to God, we discover imputation as a means by which people are justified. "Abraham believed God, and it was counted to him as righteousness" (Rom. 4:3; James 2:23; see Gen. 15:6). Similarly, today, to be justified by faith in Christ is to have Christ's righteousness imputed, or credited to one's account, leading to eternal life. Christ's righteousness is imputed to all born of the Spirit. Abraham shows the way by which one is transferred to eternal life in the Lord—through faith in him. There are significant implications for the preacher when this doctrine of imputation is applied. This is especially the case with respect to status and condition, as discussed earlier.

Preachers proclaim divine truths, but as fallen human beings. The whole man is fallen—the body, soul, and mind. The old man is condemned under the wrath of God. But in Christ we are made a new creation. The new status that we have before God in Christ is perfect, for Christ's righteousness is credited to us through faith in him. But our condition has some way to go. For it to be fully rectified, "this perishable body must put on the imperishable, and this mortal body must put on immortality" (1 Cor. 15:53). Romans 7 provides insight to life while the gospel is at work. The Christian lives with the flesh and Spirit opposing each other and experiences the daily battle within. Since our sin means that we can be justified only by God's gracious imputation of Christ's righteousness and not our works, justification refers to our status before God, not our moral condition. A Christian is justified, fully accepted by God on the basis of Christ's righteousness, but still sins. Our moral condition is in need of continual improvement.

Observing the distinction between status and condition is key for a preacher. There are faults on either side to contend with when it is not observed. These are not limited to preachers—for they are common to Christians—but they may be keenly felt by them.

Spiritual pride develops if we attribute the righteous status we have to our condition. A preacher is not wholly sanctified. Yet through faith in Christ, he is wholly justified. But if we believe that our condition is complete, as our status is, we arrive at a false view of ourselves—and may be tempted to think of ourselves more highly than we ought (cf. Rom. 12:3).

Another danger emerges from the reverse problem of confusing our fallen condition with our newfound status before God in Christ. Despite being justified by God in Christ, one might be tempted to avert eyes away from him, forget the credit that his righteousness provides, and seek it elsewhere. This can lead to despair through vain effort to attain justification by works, but needlessly so, for in Christ the sin-stained garments of our own works have already been exchanged for the new and perpetually stainless robes of Christ's righteousness.

Both errors may be repaired through a correct grasp of the relationship between faith and works. Since Christ's righteousness is received by faith, there is no room for our own works to enter into justification. As a professional golfer or tennis player periodically checks his or her grip on a golf club or tennis racquet in order to strike the ball in the intended direction, so also the pastor does well to revisit his understanding of these doctrines in his aim of entering the kingdom through the narrow gate and leading others with him.

Preachers have many duties to fulfill, including preparing sermons, visiting the congregation, and chairing meetings. It may be tempting to think that good works, valuable in the church community, have some import into justification before God. Closely related to this is a self-assessment of judicial standing before God according to how I am doing those works, or what works I am doing. This is corrected by taking into account first what has been done for me in justification and that God in Christ has done it. This is evident in Paul, who lived this out in an exemplary fashion, as he counted his righteousness under the law as loss, "because of the surpassing worth of knowing Christ" (Phil. 3:6–8). The doctrine of justification thereby revitalizes the church by turning it from a false evaluation of its own works to a right evaluation of God and his work:

> Look at the history of revivals, and you will find men and women
> feeling desperate. They know that all their goodness is but filthy

rags, and that all their righteousness is of no value at all. And there they are, feeling that they can do nothing, and crying out to God for mercy and compassion. Justification by faith. God's act. "If God does not do it to us," they say, "then we are lost." And so they wait in utter helplessness before him. They pay no attention, and attach no significance to all their own past religiosity, and all their faithfulness in church attendance, and many, many other things. They see it is all no good, even their religion is of no value, there is nothing that is of value. God must justify the ungodly. And that is the great message that comes out, therefore, in every period of revival.

And, of course, it is important for this reason: holding to this doctrine, people are always very conscious, at such times, of the immediate possibility of salvation.[22]

The implications of justification in Christ are thus far-ranging and glorify God. But if we assess our relationship to him by our works, including works of service in ministry, then we vainly attempt to supplant God's justification by grace. Similar to a "to-do" list that isn't completed, justification is never accomplished. Luther expressed the problem and its solution well: "The law says, 'Do this,' and it is never done. Grace says, 'Believe in this,' and everything is already done."[23]

Theology and Preaching

Justification concerns our relationship to God. It concerns a person's eternal standing and day-to-day living before him. Preachers should seek ways by which to illustrate biblical doctrines, including justification.[24] Biblical metaphors include clothing (Isa. 61:10), counting (Gen. 15:6), finance (Matt. 20:1–16), and geography (Ps. 103:12).

The best approach to preaching the doctrine is by regular exposition of the Scriptures. Scripture's teaching is contrary not only

22. Lloyd-Jones, *Revival*, 55–56.
23. Heidelberg Disputation, 26. See Timothy F. Lull and William R. Russell, eds., *Martin Luther's Basic Theological Writings*, 3rd ed. (Minneapolis: Fortress Press, 2012), 16.
24. For an example of illustrating justification and other doctrines, see Timothy Keller, *Preaching: Communicating Faith in an Age of Scepticism* (London: Hodder & Stoughton, 2017), 169–75.

externally to the secular spirit of the day, but internally to the heart of the natural man. Application of the whole Word is best fitted to break down the old ways. The whole Word is fitted to do that because the whole of God's Word is gospel.[25]

Justification is one aspect of Christ's salvation communicated to us in the Word. A preacher should therefore consider its setting in preaching the gospel. Tone in delivery also has a bearing in application.

Setting

Perhaps as a result of justification as the "material cause"[26] of the Reformation, other doctrines (such as adoption and sanctification) have been eclipsed among teachers of Reformed theology. But when we read the Reformers, especially John Calvin, we find them a help to address the balance. Their focus in communicating the gospel was not primarily justification, but Jesus Christ in whom we find our justification. Therefore, the subject of preaching is Christ. The benefits that come from him, including justification, derive from him. In order to have a clear focus on the doctrine of justification, we must simultaneously, and primarily, look to the one from whom justification comes.

Calvin taught that Christ is primary and his benefits are secondary: "as long as Christ remains outside of us, and we are separated from him, all that he has suffered and done for the salvation of the human race remains useless and of no value for us."[27] Regarding the relationship of justification to other benefits in Christ, he would say that justification apart from sanctification is impossible, "for he cannot be divided into pieces."[28] Sinclair Ferguson has described the doctrine of adoption as a theme in Calvin's *Institutes* that "undergirds everything he writes."[29] We want to keep these observations in mind when communicating the doctrine of justification.

In Christ, there is no justification apart from sanctification or

---

25. Colquhoun, *Treatise on the Law and the Gospel*, 99–102.
26. Schaff, *Creeds of Christendom*, 1:206.
27. Calvin, *Institutes*, 3.1.1.
28. Calvin, *Institutes*, 3.16.1.
29. Sinclair B. Ferguson, "The Reformed Doctrine of Sonship," in *Pulpit and People: Essays in Honour of William Still on His 75th Birthday*, ed. Nigel M. de S. Cameron and Sinclair B. Ferguson (Edinburgh: Rutherford House, 1986), 82.

adoption. A Christian cannot be justified without also being sanctified or becoming a child of God. None of these benefits are received apart from union with Christ. Our primary concern, then, must be that he abides in us, and we in him (John 15:4–11). Christ is God's chief gift to us (Rom. 5:15). Justification is one of many blessings we receive from him as a result.

Tone

The fragmented world into which a preacher communicates the Word is portrayed well in Martin Luther's preface to the New Testament:

> It would be right and proper for this book to go forth without any prefaces or extraneous names attached and simply have its own say under its own name. However many unfounded interpretations and prefaces have scattered the thought of Christians to a point where no one any longer knows what is gospel or law, New Testament or Old. Necessity demands, therefore, that there should be a notice or preface, by which the ordinary man can be rescued from his former delusions, set on the right track, and taught what he is to look for in this book, so that he may not seek laws and commandments where he ought to be seeking the gospel and promises of God.[30]

Luther taught that human nature is such that the Word is not always easily received. Each person, including the preacher, has his or her own preconceived ideas. There can be resistance to the Word and disagreement with it; at times the Scriptures are interpreted as though they taught something contrary to what they actually express (see 2 Peter 3:16).

Hugh Martin described the pastoral difficulty in communicating the doctrine of justification: "In the matter of justification the great difficulty is to prevent men from seeking to co-operate with God, their desire, while not yet fully humbled, being, at least partly, to justify themselves."[31] The preacher is not immune from this difficulty. Accordingly, justification should be preached with humility.

30. Lull and Russell, *Martin Luther's Basic Theological Writings*, 93.

31. Hugh Martin, "Co-Ordination of Grace and Duty," *British and Foreign Evangelical Review* 32 (1883): 321.

When God gave the Ten Commandments, he referred to himself by his covenantal name, "the LORD" (Ex. 20:2). He thereby revealed himself as the God of the covenant of grace. His revelation of law proceeded from his grace. Justification involves absolution from the curse of breaking the law and has also been communicated graciously to us in Christ. Therefore, a gracious note should be evident in the preacher's tone, delivery, and message when expounding truths relating to God's law and his remedy of justification in Christ, delivering us from our transgressions.

Conclusion

The doctrine of justification is a vital truth for the church and its message to the world. It is a biblical truth taught in the Old and New Testaments, raised in profile as it is accomplished in Jesus' ministry. For a Christian preacher of the gospel, it is personal truth. It is not abstract to him but one that he has personally come to know.

Our survey of the passages in Scripture shows that the theological framework relating to justification is established in the Old Testament. In the New Testament, the doctrine is brought into full bloom because of Christ and his accomplishments. New Testament studies of Adam and Abraham provide the biblical-theological perspective for understanding Christ's justifying work.

In proclaiming the gospel, the faithful preacher seeks to be faithful to the Word, conscious of his own faults and the "old man" who desires self-justification. The manner in which the gospel is preached is in itself an effective means of witness to its truth. Preachers help bring the truth of justification to bear on congregational life by encouraging their flocks to fix their eyes on the Lord Jesus, who is their justification.

Key Terms

imputation
justification

Recommendations for Further Reading

Calvin, John. *Institutes of the Christian Religion*, edited by John T. McNeill. Translated by Ford Lewis Battles. 2 vols. Philadelphia: Westminster, 1960. Bk. 3, chaps. 11–18.

Ferguson, Sinclair B. *Some Pastors and Teachers: Reflecting a Biblical Vision of What Every Minister Is Called to Be*. Edinburgh: Banner of Truth, 2018. Pp. 505–19.

Macleod, Donald. *A Faith to Live By: Understanding Christian Doctrine*. Fearn, Scotland: Christian Focus, 1998. Pp. 157–72.

Martin, Hugh. "Justification." *British and Foreign Evangelical Review* 29 (1880): 393–408.

Owen, John. *The Doctrine of Justification by Faith*. In *The Works of John Owen*, edited by William H. Goold, 5:1–400. Edinburgh: Banner of Truth, 1965.

Discussion Questions

1. What effect does justification have on congregational life?
2. Why should a pastor periodically give attention to the doctrine of justification?
3. How may justification be illustrated in a sermon?
4. How does the fact that justification is found only in Christ affect how the doctrine is preached?
5. What pastoral issues are faced with respect to justification today, and how may they be addressed?

13

ADOPTION

Sons of the Father, in the Son, by the Spirit

LIGON DUNCAN

Adoption is the name that Paul gave to a multifaceted biblical reality, rooted in the eternal purposes of God, revealed in the Scriptures, accomplished in Jesus Christ, applied by the Holy Spirit, crowning the Christian life with joy and confidence, and energizing our living for God in the totality of life. John Murray famously calls adoption "the apex of grace and privilege."[1] J. I. Packer likewise says that adoption is "the highest privilege that the gospel offers."[2] Sinclair Ferguson adds that "of all biblical pictures of what it means to be a Christian, this one is as crucial for our times as it is central to the Christian gospel."[3] Few truths are more important for a minister to understand

---

1. John Murray, *Redemption: Accomplished and Applied* (Grand Rapids: Eerdmans, 1955), 134.

2. J. I. Packer, *Knowing God* (London: Hodder & Stoughton, 2013), 232.

3. Sinclair B. Ferguson, *Children of the Living God* (Edinburgh: Banner of Truth, 1989), xiii. I have had the privilege of knowing Sinclair Ferguson since my teenage years. My pastor at the time, Paul G. Settle, a longtime Westminster Seminary board member, brought Sinclair to preach a Bible conference at my home church. Ever since then, I have read him with appreciation, sat under his preaching ministry often, and considered him a father in the Lord (though he is old enough only to be my older brother). Our connections are many, and our friendship has grown

and to deploy in the work of gathering and perfecting the saints. Few truths are more encouraging for a Christian life of glorifying God and enjoying him forever.

What exactly do we mean by *adoption*? Simply put, *adoption* means that God graciously takes us for his own children. He welcomes us into his family. Packer treats the subject under the heading "God makes his people his children."[4] When God saves us, he gives us a new heart (regeneration), a free pardon (justification), and a son's relationship (adoption), and he begins a moral transformation (sanctification). God's redeeming work thus addresses everything lost in the fall. Adoption is at the very heart of that recovery because of its close and obvious connection to communion with God as Father. Christianity is the true and saving knowledge of the gracious and holy Father, through Christ, by the Spirit—a description close to Calvin's definition of *piety*: "a sincere feeling which loves God as Father as much as it fears and reverences him as Lord, embraces his righteousness, and dreads offending him worse than death"[5] and "that reverence joined with love of God which the knowledge of his benefits induces."[6] Adoption is the doctrine that mirrors this truth of God's redemptive fatherhood, and its reality implants it in our experience. The Westminster Shorter Catechism explains it this way: "Adoption is an act of God's free grace, whereby we are received into the number, and have a right to all the privileges of the sons of God" (WSC 34). The Westminster Larger Catechism helpfully elaborates: "Adoption is an act of the free grace of God, in and for his only Son Jesus Christ, whereby all those that are justified are received into the number of his

---

over the years. I have been privileged to be a faculty colleague of Sinclair's for these last many years here at Reformed Theological Seminary, where he now serves as Chancellor's Professor of Theology and where he has regularly been teaching for around thirty years.

4. J. I. Packer, *Concise Theology: A Guide to Historic Christian Beliefs* (Wheaton, IL: Tyndale, 1993), 167.

5. I. John Hesselink, *Calvin's First Catechism: A Commentary: Featuring Ford Lewis Battles's Translation of the 1538 Catechism* (Louisville: Westminster John Knox, 1997), 8.

6. John Calvin, *Institutes of the Christian Religion*, ed. John T. McNeill, trans. Ford Lewis Battles, 2 vols., Library of Christian Classics 20–21 (Philadelphia: Westminster, 1960), 1.2.1.

children, have his name put upon them, the Spirit of his Son given to them, are under his fatherly care and dispensations, admitted to all the liberties and privileges of the sons of God, made heirs of all the promises, and fellow heirs with Christ in glory" (WLC 74).

So adoption, like justification, is a covenantal legal act of God. In justification, we are pardoned and accepted and declared right with God. In adoption, we are enfolded into God's family and made sons and heirs of God. In justification, God bestows an acquittal and acceptance. In adoption, he bestows a royal and filial relationship.

The Importance of Adoption for Pastoral Ministry

Modern Reformed theologians, Sinclair Ferguson, Douglas Kelly, David Garner, and Chad Van Dixhoorn among them, have lamented the lack of dogmatic development and appreciation of this doctrine in our tradition.[7] Our focus here is on the massive pastoral importance of this truth for ministry. In short, adoption is close to the heart of what it means to be a Christian. This is why Packer notes that "the entire Christian life has to be understood in terms of it" and can summarize the gospel in three words: "adoption through propitiation."[8]

This means, among other very important things, that adoption is

---

7. Sinclair B. Ferguson, "The Reformed Doctrine of Sonship," in *Pulpit and People: Essays in Honour of William Still on His 75th Birthday*, ed. Nigel M. de S. Cameron and Sinclair B. Ferguson (Edinburgh: Rutherford House, 1986), 81–88; Douglas F. Kelly, "Adoption: An Underdeveloped Heritage of the Westminster Standards," *Reformed Theological Review* 52, no. 3 (1993): 110–20; David B. Garner, "Adoption in Christ" (PhD diss., Westminster Theological Seminary, 2002); Chad Van Dixhoorn, *Confessing the Faith: A Reader's Guide to the Westminster Confession of Faith* (Edinburgh: Banner of Truth, 2014). Van Dixhoorn says of the confession's chapter on adoption: "The most noteworthy fact about this chapter is that there is a chapter at all. Biblical sonship is the Cinderella of Christian theology and has only recently been recognized as the royal topic that it really is" (171). See also Tim Trumper, "Adoption: The Forgotten Doctrine of Westminster Soteriology," in *Reformed Theology in Contemporary Perspective*, ed. Lynn Quigley (Edinburgh: Rutherford House, 2006), 87–123; Tim Trumper, "An Historical Study of Adoption in the Calvinistic Tradition" (PhD diss., University of Edinburgh, 2001). Joel R. Beeke offers pushback to these estimations in his *Heirs with Christ: The Puritans on Adoption* (Grand Rapids: Reformation Heritage Books, 2008) (see chapter 1, "Introduction: Correcting a Caricature," 1–14).

8. Packer, *Knowing God*, 226.

vital to the pastoral work of a confessional Reformed minister. If we aim at bringing those given by the Father to the Son, into the love of the Father for the Son, which we experience in coming to the Father by the Father's drawing, through the Son whom the Father sent, by the Holy Spirit sent by the Father in the name of the Son—and that is precisely what we aim to do in ministry if we understand John 17:14–26—then we will need to teach them to believe and understand, and pray for their experience and expression of, the reality of adoption. The words of Scott Swain aptly express this reality: "All that the triune God has done in creation and redemption, and all that the triune God will do in consummating all things, are aimed at bringing those given by the Father to the Son into the love of the Father for the Son."[9]

To put it another way, if the gospel minister wants to see sinners from every tribe, tongue, people, and nation brought into a communion of love with the triune God, he will direct them to look in faith to Jesus. And if healthy piety and maturity in the Christian life is the response of believers to the theology and experience of God's love in Christ, that response is expressed in their love to and for Christ.[10] Then understanding the significance of the doctrine of adoption, the truth and reality that by God's grace God is our Father and we are God's sons in God's Son by God's Spirit, is indispensably imperative for Christian ministry. The benefit of Christ's work, applied to us by the Spirit, grounds us in the reality and experience of the Father's love, which his Son, Jesus, asked the Father that all his disciples would know (John 17:23, 26).

So what are some of the important ways that the truth and reality of adoption shape our preaching and aims in pastoral ministry? We could organize our reflection on this topic in a number of ways.

We could, of course, look at the term *adoption* (Greek υἱοθεσία, *huiothesia*) in its five occurrences in Paul's writings and expound

---

9. Scott Swain (@scottrswain), "John 17:24 Paraphrased," Twitter, May 29, 2020, accessed November 21, 2020, https://twitter.com/scottrswain/status/126634 8380000866308.

10. This is pure Robert Murray M'Cheyne. See Jordan Stone's *A Communion of Love: The Christian-Centered Spirituality of Robert Murray M'Cheyne* (Eugene, OR: Wipf & Stock, 2019) and *Love to Christ: Robert Murray M'Cheyne and the Pursuit of Holiness* (Grand Rapids: Reformation Heritage Books, 2020).

Paul's application of it there (Rom. 8:15, 23; 9:4; Gal. 4:5; Eph. 1:5). But the theological idea, the doctrinal truth, of adoption has massive, transcanonical, and biblical and systematic theological underpinnings, even when the term is not used, and we would miss some of those emphases. For our purposes, the dogmatic summary of the biblical doctrine in the Westminster Confession of Faith provides a helpful framework for its pastoral application, so we will begin there.

Applying the Doctrine of Adoption with the Help of the Westminster Confession

The Westminster Confession of Faith outlines the subjects, basis, definition, and (six specific) blessings of adoption as follows:

> All those that are justified, God vouchsafeth, in and for his only Son Jesus Christ, to make partakers of the grace of adoption, by which they are taken into the number, and enjoy the liberties and privileges of the children of God, have his name put upon them, receive the spirit of adoption, have access to the throne of grace with boldness, are enabled to cry, Abba, Father, are pitied, protected, provided for, and chastened by him, as by a Father: yet never cast off, but sealed to the day of redemption; and inherit the promises, as heirs of everlasting salvation. (WCF 12)

To recapitulate and paraphrase, the confession says that all those who are justified are also freely granted the grace of adoption by God. This is done in their union with and on account of God's only Son, Jesus Christ. By adoption, they are numbered among God's children and enjoy the freedoms and privileges of the sons of God. They have God's name given to them. They receive the spirit of adoption. They have access to the throne of grace. They are pitied, protected, provided for, and disciplined by the Father. They are never cast off but sealed. They inherit the promises of God as heirs of everlasting salvation.

The confession's shortest chapter is packed full of truth with profound significance for the Christian life and ministry. Indeed, the confession's chapter on adoption contains several distinct assertions. Recounting them will give us a feel for the reach of this truth, as well as suggest important pastoral applications and implications of the doctrine.

The Subjects of Adoption

The confession first identifies the subjects of adoption: "All those that are justified, God vouchsafeth . . . to make partakers of the grace of adoption." In other words, all the justified are also freely or graciously granted ("vouchsafed") the favor and status of adoption by God. The justified are adopted, and the adopted are justified. In our preaching and ministry, then, we will want to make sure that both these coordinate truths of justification and adoption are paired and featured in our preaching and teaching (along with the doctrine of sanctification, too, of course). We will want our people to understand and appreciate them both, and we will want to see evidence of the expression of both in their Christian experience. As R. A. Webb once observed: "Justification recovers his lost citizenship; Adoption recovers his lost sonship."[11] The Reformed minister will want his people to appreciate the unique and distinct witness to the mercy and love of God in justification and adoption.

Another thing to be said in relation to the topic of the subjects of adoption is that the Confession's definition of adoption points us to the significance of specifying the kind of sonship we are talking about when we use the term "children of God." Thomas Ridgeley, for instance, in his discussion of adoption in *A Body of Divinity* (a massive commentary on the Larger Catechism) observes six ways in which sonship is deployed in the Bible: First, "Some are called the sons of God, as they are invested with many honours or prerogatives from God as a part of his image. Thus magistrates are called 'the children of the Most High'" (see Ps. 82:6). Second, "Others are called God's children, by an external federal relation, as members of the visible church. In this sense we are to understand the scripture in which it is said, 'the sons of God saw the daughters of men,' &c. When Moses went in to Pharaoh to demand liberty for the Israelites, he was ordered to say, 'Israel is my son, even my first-born'" (see Ex.

---

11. R. A. Webb, *Christian Salvation: Its Doctrine and Experience* (Richmond, VA: Presbyterian Committee of Publication, 1921), 398.

4:22). Third, "The name 'sons of God' is sometimes taken in a more large sense, as applicable to all mankind. Thus the prophet says, 'Have we not all one father? hath not one God created us?'" (see Mal. 2:10; cf. Acts 17:25, 28). Fourth, "Those are called the sons of God who are endowed with his supernatural image, and admitted to the highest honours and privileges conferred upon creatures. Thus the angels are called 'the sons of God'" (see Job 38:7). Fifth, "Our Lord Jesus Christ is called the Son of God, in a sense not applicable to any other. His Sonship includes his deity, and his having, in his human nature, received a commission from the Father, to engage in the great work of our redemption." Sixth, "Believers are called the sons of God, by a special adoption. . . . The practice which it denotes was much in use among the Romans in the apostles' time; in which it was a custom for persons who had no children of their own . . . to make choice of such as were agreeable to them and beloved by them, . . . obliging them to take their name upon them and to pay respect to them as if they had been their natural parents, engaging to deal with them as if they had been so." Thus, "this new relation" establishes "a bond of affection; and the privilege arising from it" so "that he who is in this sense a father, takes care of and provides for the person whom he adopts, as if he were his son by nature. Hence, civilians call adoption an act of legitimation, imitating nature, or supplying the place of it."[12]

Ridgeley notes that it is this latter sense that the confession explicates in its chapter on adoption and in its corresponding catechism questions. The preacher should thus be clear in specifying that he is speaking of this special redemptive sonship when he expounds and applies the doctrine of adoption. This is a part of what the Puritans called *discriminating preaching*—that is, being crystal clear about who exactly is (and is not) the subject or beneficiary of a particular biblical blessing.

The Basis of Adoption

The confession in the second place points out the basis on or by which we are adopted, indicating that adoption is enjoyed in union

---

12. Thomas Ridgeley, *A Body of Divinity*, 2 vols. (New York: Robert Carter, 1855), 2:131–32.

with Christ and because of his person and work: it is "in and for his only Son Jesus Christ." In other words, adoption is enjoyed as one of the benefits we receive by virtue of our being "in Christ" and on the basis of who Christ is and what he has done on our behalf.

Just as the confession enumerates benefits of adoption in this section, so also is adoption one of the benefits of union with Christ. Like justification, its basis is outside us. It is "the grace of adoption," and we are made partakers of this grace in our union with Christ, and for his sake. Just as the Father's merciful and just forgiveness of us is grounded in the righteousness of Christ, so also the Father's loving bestowal of the status of sons on us is rooted in our union with his Son. This truth allows the preacher the joy of proclaiming to the believer a wondrous truth: the glorious objective basis of our being children of the heavenly Father. We are justified by grace alone through faith alone in Christ alone, and we are adopted by grace alone in Christ alone.

This also allows the preacher to emphasize both the mercy (justification) and love (adoption) of the Father to the believer in a unique way. Francis R. Beattie observes: "In the Scriptures justification is related to the law of God, and adoption to the love of God." He goes on to explain that by distinguishing the doctrine of adoption from that of justification (instead of grouping them in the same locus), the confession gives due prominence "to the love of God in the system of doctrine, and the fact of the sonship of believers . . . [is] put in its proper place" and "plants the fact of the spiritual fatherhood of God and the divine sonship of the believer, as distinct from that which is merely natural, upon the redemptive work of Christ."[13]

The Definition of Adoption

Only after establishing the subjects of and basis for adoption does the Westminster Confession, in the third place, define *adoption*: adoption entails our being counted as God's own children, with all the freedoms and privileges thereof, which is indicated when the confession says that by adoption "they are taken into the number, and enjoy the liberties and privileges of the children of God." In other words,

---

13. Francis R. Beattie, *The Presbyterian Standards* (Brevard, NC: Southern Presbyterian Press, 1997), 213.

adoption means being numbered among and enjoying the freedoms and accompanying benefits of being God's children, members of his household. The great Thomas Boston explains:

> Adoption, in the general, is a legal act, whereby one doth, to all intents and purposes in law, become wholly the child of another, than him whose child he was by nature. Adoption, then, is not a change of our nature, but of our state. Neither is it a work carried on by degrees, but an act perfected in an instant: 1 John 3:2, "Beloved, now are we the sons of God," &c. But the full enjoyment of the benefits thereby coming unto us, will not be till the last day: Rom. 8:23.[14]

It is one of the joys of the minister of the gospel to proclaim, explain, and apply the Bible's teaching about the freedoms and privileges of believers by virtue of their adoption. Many Christians struggle to grasp this reality. And plenty of bad teaching confuses Christians on these things. On the one hand, various kinds of petty legalisms plague the experience of many Christians, and they do indeed need to be liberated from those shackles. On the other hand, well-meaning preachers can be heard relating a view of Christian freedom alien to the Bible's teaching. The so-called free-grace teaching that emanated from the dispensational Bible church world into the wider evangelical scene asserted that believers are freed from obedience, and some in the Reformed world have articulated something like this, too: "God didn't save you so that you would be holy; he saved you so that you would be free."

But the Bible never opposes freedom and obedience. And the freedom of adoption is not antinomianism. The right experience of the reality of our status as adopted ones actually sets us free to obey, not as under a covenant of works, but as under the covenant of grace. Christian obedience is simply being and doing what God created and redeemed us to be and do. Freedom is wanting to be and do what we were created to be and do.

Thus, one of the confessional Reformed minister's challenges in

14. Thomas Boston, *An Explication of the Assembly's Shorter Catechism*, in *The Whole Works of the Late Reverend Thomas Boston of Ettrick*, ed. Samuel M'Millan, 12 vols. (Aberdeen: George and Robert King, 1848–52), 7:100–101.

teaching adoption will be to help get this clear and straight in the hearts, minds, and lives of his congregation. Adoption doesn't free us from obedience. It frees us to and for a glad and willing obedience, precisely because of the relation we sustain to the loving Father as his loved children. God's adopting love sets us free to exercise duty and obedience with joy. It is easy to want to please someone who you know already loves you. It is deadly to try to please someone in order to get that person to love you. Adoption works into the Christian's experience the reality that we love because he first loved us. This is vital to living the Christian life.

The fundamental freedom of adoption is being freed from slavery to sin and Satan. Sin is not freedom; it is slavery. Evangelical obedience is not slavery; it is freedom. As the old hymn puts it:

> Out of my bondage, sorrow, and night,
>   Jesus, I come! Jesus, I come!
> Into Thy freedom, gladness, and light,
>   Jesus, I come to Thee!
> Out of my sickness into Thy health,
> Out of my want and into Thy wealth,
> Out of my sin and into Thyself,
>   Jesus, I come to Thee![15]

Thomas Ridgeley explains that in adoption, "They are all emancipated, or freed from the slavery which they were before under either to sin or Satan. They who were once 'the servants of sin,' are, by adoption, 'made free from sin, and become the servants of righteousness,' or become 'servants to God, have their fruit unto holiness, and the end everlasting life.' 'The Son makes them free;' and therefore, 'they are free indeed.'" He adds: "They are described as having formerly . . . to have been 'of their father, the devil,' and to 'have done his works,' or followed his suggestions, ensnared and 'taken captive by him at his will' . . . . But they have now deliverance from these evils; which cannot but be reckoned a glorious privilege."[16]

---

15. William True Sleeper, "Out of My Bondage, Sorrow, and Night" (1887).
16. Ridgeley, *Body of Divinity*, 2:134.

This celebration of freedom sounds very much like the sentiment of the epitaph of John Newton on the wall of St. Mary Woolnoth in London: "John Newton, clerk, once an infidel and libertine, a servant of slaves in Africa, was by the rich mercy of our Lord and Saviour Jesus Christ, preserved, restored, pardoned, and appointed to preach the faith he had long laboured to destroy."[17]

Libertines are not free, even if they think they are. Freedom is found only for sons in the Son, who said: "My food is to do the will of Him who sent Me and to accomplish His work" (John 4:34 NASB). And it is this that the Reformed minister has the glorious privilege of explaining to God's people,[18] and praying and laboring to see formed in them, and also of explaining to those who are still lost, so that, by the Spirit's use of his Word, they may come to realize their blindness and slavery and come to him who alone can make them free indeed.

The Blessings of Adoption Enumerated

Having explained the doctrine itself, the confession, in the fourth and final place, spends the greater part of the paragraph enumerating a half-dozen key blessings of adoption, beginning with the fact that to be adopted, for the Christian, means that God's name is given to us: "they . . . have his name put upon them." In other words, in adoption, God gives believers his own name. As God gave his name to Jacob and called him Israel, and as he explained his name to Moses and told him to tell the people who their God is, and called them by his own name, so also does he give us his name. Chad Van Dixhoorn comments, "Consider what it means to be called by God's name—to have the Lord God Almighty give us his family name (Jer. 14:9; 2 Cor. 6:18; Rev. 3:12)."[19]

Thomas Ridgeley amplifies the point: "God's adopted children have also Christ's name put on them. 'Of him the whole family in heaven and earth is named.' . . . They are also styled his children, when he says, 'Behold I and the children which God hath given me.'

---

17. John Newton, *The Works of John Newton*, new ed., 4 vols. (Edinburgh: Banner of Truth, 2015), 1:cvii–cviii.

18. Westminster Confession chapter 20, and 20.1 in particular, is a superb help in explaining the freedom of adoption.

19. Van Dixhoorn, *Confessing the Faith*, 173.

Indeed, when he is called a surety, or an advocate, or is said to execute certain offices as a Saviour or Redeemer, these are all relative terms; and whatever he does in the capacities which they denote is in the name of his people, and for their advantage."[20]

This is an enormous privilege, and the preacher should make much of it, but we should also not forget that it comes with an explicit command and responsibility that we not take up God's name in vain (Ex. 20:7; cf. WLC 112). This does not mean that we qualify or mitigate this blessing and privilege to true believers. Rather, it means that we should be mindful of the importance of distinguishing in our preaching those who may be outwardly numbered among God's people, but who are not so inwardly (Rom. 2:28–29).

Second, adoption involves receiving the Spirit/spirit of adoption: they "receive the spirit of adoption." In other words, by the work of the Holy Spirit, who testifies to and with our spirit of our adoption by God, we live like we are sons. As Thomas Boston memorably explains: "The spirit of adoption is the spirit of his Son, sealing them with the Son's image, and working in them a son-like disposition and affection towards God."[21] We relate to God as sons, not slaves—we fully realize that we are sons of his household, but we don't merely revel in our privilege and status and rest on our rights; we serve like the Son. Understanding this is the key to the minister's preaching of all the privileges of adoption. The right preaching of those privileges should prompt comfort and energy, assurance and service, gratitude and activity, self-giving and self-denial.

After all, if we have the disposition and affection toward God in us, by virtue of the spirit of adoption, that Jesus has to the Father, then we, too, will delight to deny ourselves and do the Father's will. "The Son of Man came not to be served but to serve" (Matt. 20:28); and if we are like him in our disposition, we, too, will serve as those with the mind of Christ, in humility counting others more significant than ourselves, looking not only to our own interests but also to the interests of others (Phil. 2:3–7).

Those who truly have the spirit of adoption have the disposition

20. Ridgeley, *Body of Divinity*, 2:135.
21. Boston, *Explication of the Assembly's Shorter Catechism*, 7:104.

of the Son to be a servant. This is important. If we preach only privilege and never emphasize responsibility in the blessings of adoption, then we are deploying our doctrine of adoption without reference to the way in which the only-begotten Son of God deployed his sonship in willing, costly service. True sons of God serve.

Here again we see the nexus of blessing and obligation in the Christian life. The realization of the privileges of God's gracious blessing of adoption gives us an affection for God that disposes us to willing, joyful obedience. This reality is important to the discipleship of every Christian.

Third, adoption gives us access to the throne of grace *as sons*: believers "have access to the throne of grace with boldness, are enabled to cry, Abba, Father." In other words, Christians are enabled to boldly approach the throne of grace in prayer, crying out in time of need, naming God "our Father" as his adopted sons. Again, Thomas Ridgeley beautifully explains what it is that we want our people to get from this benefit of adoption: "Another privilege which they enjoy, is access to God, as a reconciled Father, through Christ. They have liberty to 'come boldly to the throne of grace, that they may obtain mercy, and find grace to help in time of need.'" This means that

> whatever their straits and difficulties are, God holds forth his golden sceptre, invites them to come to him, asks, "What is thy petition?" and gives them ground to hope that it shall be granted, so far as it may redound to his glory and their good. And inasmuch as they are often straitened in their spirits, and unprepared to draw nigh to him, they have the promise of the Spirit to assist them; on which account he is called "the Spirit of adoption, whereby they cry, Abba, Father." This privilege is said to be a consequence of their being sons.[22]

So in our ministry, we long for our people to grow in their knowledge, understanding, belief, experience, and expression of (1) suitable, appropriate, generous, becoming conceptions of the Divine Majesty, (2) a reverential fear of God, (3) a love for God, (4) earnest desires of

22. Ridgeley, *Body of Divinity*, 2:135.

communion with God, and (5) a sense that they are recipients, bene-factors, partakers of the blessings he has imparted. The doctrine of adoption allows us to put these things before the eyes of their hearts.

Here, even before we move on to consider the next blessing, a word of pastoral counsel for pastors is in order. Remember, despite all the wonderful things that the doctrine of adoption is, it is not a silver bullet. The doctrine of adoption is not a panacea. It can't fix everything in the Christian life or church. We shouldn't make it bear that freight. Actually, there is no silver bullet in the Christian life and ministry at all. Everything we do is utterly dependent on the sover-eign purposes and providence and grace of God, and no doctrine guarantees our pastoral "success" or our people's transformation. Why do I say this? Because some well-meaning attempts at Christian discipleship have (perhaps unintentionally) led Christians to believe that grasping the doctrine of adoption is something akin to a "second blessing" or "higher life."

But we don't need to make that demand of the doctrine or to abstract it from the other blessings of the Christian life. We don't need to make the doctrine of adoption the dogmatic center of our doctrinal system, or the solution to every theological and pastoral problem in the world, in order to appreciate its profundity and usefulness. All Scripture is inspired. All of it is profitable. All needful. What we need to do is to make sure that we are not neglecting adoption (especially in connection with our expositions of justification and sanctification), and that as pastors we have as our aim and are praying that the doc-trines of the redemptive fatherhood of God and our adoption as sons of God are manifesting themselves in at least some healthy ways in the Christian experience and life of our people. In the end, this is the work of the Holy Spirit, for which we are his mere instruments, but we will still want to be pastorally vigilant and aspire to our own and our people's growth in grace in this area of the Christian life.

The fourth blessing of adoption is that believers are mercifully treated, powerfully protected, providentially supplied, and lovingly disciplined by the Father: Christians "are pitied, protected, provided for, and chastened by him, as by a Father." In other words, the Father's pity, protection, provision, and correction are on and over them. Each of these is vital to the Christian's sense of being in a state of grace.

Robert Shaw explains each of these four blessings-in-one: believers "are the objects of God's fatherly sympathy and pity. He knows their frame, and remembers that they are but dust," citing Psalm 103:14. "They enjoy the protection of their heavenly Father. Numerous are their spiritual enemies, and manifold the dangers to which they are exposed; but he who neither slumbers nor sleeps, watches over them with unwearied care. He gives his angels charge concerning them, who encamp around them, and, in ways unknown to us, perform many kind offices for them"—and here Shaw has in view Psalm 34:7 and Hebrews 1:14. "They are provided for by their heavenly Father. He knows they need his providential favours in this world, and these he does not withhold"—as we read in Psalm 34:9–10, Matthew 6:30–32, and Philippians 4:19. Finally, "paternal correction is not withheld when necessary" (see Heb. 12:6), and even though we "are apt to regard as a punishment rather than a privilege," it remains "the fruit of paternal love" (see Ps. 89:30–34).[23]

Pastors must stress that if Christians understand these things, they will have a doctrine of a God who is compassionate, understanding, and sympathetic, who protects and cares for them in his providence, and who lovingly corrects them in his goodness. So as a preacher who is rightly preaching adoption, you are also forming your people's doctrine of God. It should also be said that there is no trial so severe in the Christian life as to feel that God has stopped disciplining you for your sin. God's fatherly correction, far from being a discouragement, is one of the very greatest blessings of the Christian life. Just as it is true that when a man loses his belief in the providence of God, he is not many steps from abandoning his belief in God at all, so also it is true that a loss of a sense of the Lord's discipline may be a precursor to a step into unbelief. As painful as God's corrections can sometimes be, every true believer knows, and eventually feels, the powerful reality of the love of God behind him.

If we are still counting our blessings, the fifth is that adopted believers will never be cast off by God, but are confirmed as secure by the Spirit until the consummation. We are "never cast off, but

---

23. Robert Shaw, *The Reformed Faith: An Exposition of the Westminster Confession of Faith*, 8th ed. (Edinburgh: Blackie and Son, 1857), 140.

sealed to the day of redemption." In other words, we are preserved and marked as God's, and thus we persevere. This is what Shaw calls the blessing of "unfailing establishment in their state of sonship."[24] The connection of adoption to the doctrines of perseverance and assurance here is close and obvious (see WCF 17–18). "All that the Father giveth me shall come to me; and him that cometh to me I will in no wise cast out" (John 6:37 KJV). We are sealed by "the promised Holy Spirit, who is the guarantee of our inheritance until we acquire possession of it" (Eph. 1:13–14) in "the day of redemption" (4:30).

This kind of assurance is a distinctive Reformational Protestant teaching. As Sinclair Ferguson has often reminded us, Cardinal Robert Bellarmine (1542–1621), Pope Clement VIII's personal theologian and one of the ablest figures in the sixteenth-century Roman Catholic Counter-Reformation movement, asserted: "The greatest of all Protestant heresies is assurance."[25] Bellarmine feared that the Protestant doctrine of assurance would lead to antinomianism. But Dr. Ferguson points out that Hebrews 10:22 exhorts us to "draw near with . . . full assurance of faith," which, according to the logic of Hebrews 10, leads to "an unwavering faithfulness to our confession of faith in Jesus Christ alone as our hope (v.23); second, a careful consideration of how we can encourage each other to 'love and good works' (v.24); third, an ongoing communion with other Christians in worship and every aspect of our fellowship (v.25a); fourth, a life in which we exhort one another to keep looking to Christ and to be faithful to him, as the time of his return draws ever nearer (v.25b)."[26]

That is, Christian assurance doesn't lead to disobedience and antinomianism; it leads to fruitful godliness that is faithful to Jesus, and that encourages us to love and good deeds, to communion with fellow believers in worship, and to mutual exhortation to faithfulness to Christ. And, the confession reminds us, the doctrine of adoption is one part of the theological foundation of this kind of assurance. So in preaching adoption rightly, you are helping your people's assurance of salvation, helping them to understand its biblical foundation,

24. Shaw, *The Reformed Faith*, 140.

25. Quoted in Sinclair B. Ferguson, *In Christ Alone: Living the Gospel-Centered Life* (Orlando, FL: Reformation Trust, 2007), 149.

26. Ferguson, *In Christ Alone*, 149.

and helping them to see what assurance will actually look like in a Christian's life.

Sixth, and last in the Westminster Confession's enumeration of adoption's blessings, we remember that to be adopted means to be inheritors of the promises of God and joint heirs with Christ of everlasting salvation, for we "inherit the promises, as heirs of everlasting salvation." In other words, believers inherit all the covenantal promises of God and are heirs of everlasting salvation. Ridgeley's description of this is breathtaking: "Hence, all the blessings which we have either in hand or in hope, the blessings of both worlds, the blessings which are conferred upon us from our conversion to our glorification, are the privileges which God bestows on those who are his adopted children."[27]

To borrow Paul's words, "the God and Father of our Lord Jesus Christ . . . has blessed us in Christ with every spiritual blessing in the heavenly places" (Eph. 1:3). Charles Simeon states, "God has *adopted us into his family—dealt with us as children—and given to us the inheritance of children*,"[28] and that means every single spiritual blessing ever promised by God, in Christ. Simeon continues: "All of them without exception are the purchase of his blood, the fruit of his intercession, and the gifts of his grace. They are all treasured up in him; and when He is given to us, they are made over to us, as the ore in the mine." And since we are in him, we also inherit in him. "Are we chosen? it is 'in him.' Are we predestinated to the adoption of children? it is 'in him.' Are we accepted? it is 'in him.' Are we forgiven? it is 'in him.' Are we brought into one body? it is 'in him.' Have we obtained an inheritance? it is 'in him.' Are we 'sealed with the Holy Spirit of promise, as the earnest of that inheritance?' it is 'in him.' Are we blessed with all spiritual blessings? it is 'in him,' and in him alone."[29]

The doctrine of adoption allows the preacher to set forth the panoply of God's blessings, the fullness of his inheritance, the scope of his promises, all of which are "yea" and "Amen" in Christ (2 Cor. 1:20 KJV). And as Shaw reminds us, "they are adapted to every

27. Ridgeley, *Body of Divinity*, 2:136.

28. Charles Simeon, *Galatians–Ephesians*, vol. 17 of *Horae Homileticae* (London: Holdsworth and Ball, 1833), 267.

29. Simeon, *Galatians–Ephesians*, 267–68.

condition in which the children of God can be placed" and "reserved for them in heaven."[30] One can readily see the application of this truth to suffering saints, and those who have lost loved ones in Christ. But expounding this blessing of adoption is also a way to wean saints who are too much at home in this present world from their love of this lesser blessing and to set their hearts on things above.

A Different Kind of Happiness

This sketch of the rich biblical doctrine of adoption and these brief suggestions for its application perhaps are indicative of the richness and usefulness of this truth as we think together about theology for ministry. As Van Dixhoorn has observed:

Many Christians experience this gift of adoption into God's family most keenly, and treasure it most deeply. Admittedly, there are few greater joys than knowing that one is justified before God, to hear the verdict that we are forgiven and as righteous in the sight of our judge as any man could ever be. Likewise, it is a great thing to be sanctified. To know that the great physician is at work, to know that our wounds are healing, the disease is leaving, the mortal illness of sin is mortal no longer. But neither of these pieces of news is fully realized and enjoyed outside the context of adoption.

The happiness we find in a family is different from that found in a courtroom or a doctor's surgery. Those who have been blessed with good parents can imagine the qualitative difference between leaving the judge in the courtroom without fear, and going home to a father with great joy. There is nothing like being a child of God and enjoying all the liberties and privileges of God's own family. What a freedom it is to be able to address God as our Father even though he is in heaven and we on earth! What a privilege it is to have brothers and sisters in every corner of the globe! What an honour it is to even have the power to be joint heirs with God's own Son! (Rom. 8:17, John 1:12).[31]

30. Shaw, *Reformed Faith*, 140.
31. Van Dixhoorn, *Confessing the Faith*, 173–74.

No wonder Sinclair Ferguson speaks of adoption "as crucial for our times as it is central to the Christian gospel."[32]

Key Terms

adoption
sonship
spirit of adoption

Recommendations for Further Reading

Ferguson, Sinclair B. *Children of the Living God*. Edinburgh: Banner of Truth, 1989.

Girardeau, John L. "The Doctrine of Adoption." In *Discussions of Theological Questions*. Harrisonburg, VA: Sprinkle, 1986. Pp. 428–521.

Murray, John. *Redemption: Accomplished and Applied*. Grand Rapids: Eerdmans, 1955. Pp. 132–40.

Packer, J. I. *Knowing God*. London: Hodder & Stoughton, 2013. Pp. 225–60.

Ridgeley, Thomas. *A Body of Divinity*. 2 vols. New York: Robert Carter, 1855. Pp. 2:131–37.

Discussion Questions

1. Discuss differences between justification and adoption.
2. What does it mean for a Christian to be called by God's name?
3. What practical applications does adoption have for Christians?
4. How does the doctrine of adoption affect our understanding of God?
5. How may a pastor effectively communicate the doctrine of adoption through his ministry?
6. Describe ways in which the doctrines of adoption and the fatherhood of God may be manifested through a pastor's life.

---

32. Ferguson, *Children of the Living God*, xiii.

14

SANCTIFICATION

A Pastor's Labor for the
Obedience of Faith[1]

WILLIAM R. EDWARDS

The matter of sanctification can be simply stated. It has been defined as "the work of God's free grace, whereby we are renewed in the whole man after the image of God, and are enabled more and more to die unto sin and live unto righteousness" (WSC 35). The manner in which this work progresses in a person's life, however, is more difficult to fathom. This is evident in Paul's description of his own experience: "For I do not *understand* my own actions. For I do not do what I want, but I do the very thing I hate" (Rom. 7:15). With consternation he continues, "For I do not do the good I want, but the evil I do not want is what I keep on doing" (v. 19). He questions with deep conviction, "Wretched man that I am! Who will deliver me from this body of death?" (v. 24), yet concludes with confidence, "Thanks be to God through Jesus Christ our Lord!" (v. 25). While the doctrine

---

1. It was my privilege to have Dr. Ferguson as a professor during my MDiv studies at Westminster Theological Seminary. As it happened, during those years, I had him for more classes than any other professor, taking his courses on the Doctrine of God, Doctrine of Man, Doctrine of the Holy Spirit, and Doctrine of the Sacraments. Dr. Ferguson was a model of learning and piety in his lectures, sermons, and prayers. He was kind to me, as I know all his other students would affirm.

of sanctification may be simply stated, understanding our personal experience as we continue to struggle with sin is another matter. And personal confusion in our experience may cloud our comprehension of the doctrine itself.

Perplexity concerning sanctification is not surprising in part because it is not new. Historically, the word *mystery* has been commonly used. The seventeenth-century pastor Walter Marshall wrote a treatise, stemming in part from his own personal struggle, entitled *The Gospel Mystery of Sanctification*, taken from Paul's statement in 1 Timothy 3:16, "Great is the mystery of godliness."[2] Another well-known pastor-theologian from the seventeenth century, John Owen, repeatedly uses the word *mystery* in speaking of sanctification in his treatise on the Holy Spirit, claiming, "The work itself, as hath been before declared at large, is secret and mysterious."[3] Later, he confesses: "The sense of what the Scripture proposeth, what I believe, and what I desire an experience of, that I shall endeavor to declare. But as we are not in this life perfect in the duties of holiness, no more are we in the knowledge of its nature."[4]

Despite these difficulties, Marshall and Owen, along with many other Reformed pastors and theologians, have labored to explain the pattern of sanctification and its application as taught in Scripture.[5] In my experience, however, those entering ministry speak with greater clarity about the doctrine of justification than they do

2. Joel R. Beeke, in his introduction, describes the context for Marshall's treatise, prompted by his own perceived lack of progress in sanctification. Marshall visited Thomas Goodwin to seek help, confessing his ongoing struggle with particular sins. According to Beeke, "Goodwin's response was that Marshall had forgotten to mention the greatest sin of all, of not believing on the Lord Jesus Christ for the remission of his sins and the sanctifying of his nature." Joel R. Beeke, introduction to *The Gospel Mystery of Sanctification*, by Walter Marshall (Grand Rapids: Reformation Heritage Books, 1999), vi.

3. John Owen, *A Discourse concerning the Holy Spirit*, in *The Works of John Owen*, ed. William H. Goold (Edinburgh: Banner of Truth, 1994), 3:402.

4. Owen, *Discourse concerning the Holy Spirit*, 3:473.

5. Surely Sinclair B. Ferguson is at the forefront of contemporary pastor-theologians to richly explicate the doctrine of sanctification biblically, theologically, historically, and pastorally. This is evident throughout his preaching and writing, and more recently in his book *Devoted to God: Blueprints for Sanctification* (Edinburgh: Banner of Truth, 2016).

sanctification. While confident concerning the necessity of Christ's death and resurrection for pardon of sin, there may be unease in describing the efficacy of the same for our being conformed to the image of Christ through the work of the Spirit.[6] The question is whether Scripture teaches a clearer pattern of sanctification than we seem able to articulate.

Paul declares that the purpose of the apostleship in which he shares is "to bring about the obedience of faith," a statement he uses to bookend his epistle to the Romans (Rom. 1:5; 16:26). According to John Murray, in this instance, faith itself is the act of obedience to which Paul refers.[7] Here, faith in Christ comprehends the whole of the obedience to which we are called, for "the righteousness of God is revealed from faith for faith" (1:17). Yet as Paul later explains, it is both a faith that justifies, receiving righteousness as a gift through Christ Jesus (3:22–25), and also a faith that sanctifies, through which we count ourselves dead to sin and alive to God in Christ Jesus, as we present ourselves to him in obedience leading to righteousness (6:16). This dynamic role of faith is expounded in the Westminster Confession of Faith, which describes "the principal acts of saving faith" as "accepting, receiving, and resting upon Christ alone for justification, sanctification, and eternal life, by virtue of the covenant of grace"; faith functions in "yielding obedience to the commands" as well as "embracing the promises of God for this life, and that which is to come" (WCF 14.2). Sanctification, no less than justification, is a matter of faith in Christ Jesus.

The pastor, therefore, must labor for the obedience of faith in the fullest sense. Paul describes a parental-like concern for those to whom he ministers, telling the Galatians that he is "in the anguish of childbirth until Christ is formed in you" (Gal. 4:19). In Colossians, he describes the aim of his ministry: "that we may present everyone mature in Christ" (Col. 1:28). He reminds the Ephesians of how they had "learned Christ" as they were "taught in him, as the truth is in Jesus," explaining again the putting off of the old self and the putting

---

6. These observations come from twenty years of participating in the examination of candidates for ordination.

7. John Murray, *The Epistle to the Romans*, 2 vols., NICNT (Grand Rapids: Eerdmans, 1968), 1:13.

on of the new, "created after the likeness of God in true righteousness and holiness" (Eph. 4:20–24). Telling Titus to "teach what accords with sound doctrine" (Titus 2:1), he continues:

> For the grace of God has appeared, bringing salvation for all people, training us to renounce ungodliness and worldly passions, and to live self-controlled, upright, and godly lives in the present age, waiting for our blessed hope, the appearing of the glory of our great God and Savior Jesus Christ, who gave himself for us to redeem us from all lawlessness and to purify for himself a people for his own possession who are zealous for good works. (Titus 2:11–14)

"Declare these things," Paul exhorts (Titus 2:15). The grace of God does not simply tell us to say no to ungodliness, but trains us, teaches us. And this training is not merely negative, but positively presents a new pattern for our lives, with a focus on Christ Jesus. The question for those engaged in ministry is whether we ourselves have learned Christ as Paul describes, and can then teach others the grace of God in such a way that leads to sanctification in those who have faith in Christ Jesus. Paul tells Timothy, "Keep a close watch on yourself and on the teaching. Persist in this, for by so doing you will save both yourself and your hearers" (1 Tim. 4:16). In our labor for the obedience of faith, then, we must be able to teach the pattern of sanctification while also portraying it in our lives. In what follows, we will examine the framework of sanctification, with the aim of incorporating its central themes more thoroughly within our ministry, while also exploring the impact of the pastor's own sanctification in his labors.

Every Struggle with Sin Is Part of a Much Larger Story

If we are to teach Christ in a way that leads to sanctification, we must first help others see that every struggle with sin is part of a much larger story found in Scripture. Jesus prays for his disciples, "Sanctify them in the truth; your word is truth" (John 17:17). Thus, we will not be sanctified apart from Scripture. Yet as Geerhardus Vos reminds us, "The Bible is not a dogmatic handbook [nor, we might add, an ethical handbook] but a historical book full of dramatic interest."[8] The Bible does not simply reveal what is right and wrong, and therefore what we should do and not do. Sanctification is not simply a matter of understanding the Bible's imperatives. Instead, Scripture reveals the drama that makes sense of our own experience while also drawing us to Jesus Christ as the one who saves us fully from our sins.

This points to our deeper struggle. Individual sins are not what most threaten progress in sanctification. The greater danger is framing our lives with a false narrative, or an alternative story that stands in opposition to Scripture. In his exhortation to Timothy to preach the Word, Paul describes the danger in this way: "having itching ears they will accumulate for themselves teachers to suit their own passions, and will turn away from listening to the truth and wander off into myths" (2 Tim. 4:3–4). A myth is a story full of dramatic interest that is at odds with the truth of Scripture. In our teaching, therefore, we must challenge the false narratives that shape people's lives while orienting them to the truth as it is in Jesus.

The myths to which Paul refers are propagated so that those who inhabit them can suit their own passions. This is the backstory behind every sin: placing myself and my desires at the center of the story. Grasping this is essential for sanctification. We must examine the storyline of our lives. Who are the main characters? What are the driving themes? What role does Jesus play in the drama? We must ask these questions as we consider the narrative of our own ministries. Could it be that I am seeking to make a name for myself even as I proclaim the name of Jesus? There are ultimately only two metanarratives: the story of Scripture in which Christ is central, and a fictitious myth in which I lay claim to the leading role. Pastors must heed Count Zinzendorf's exhortation to the missionary, who "must seek nothing for himself: no seat of honor, no report of fame"; instead, "he must be content to suffer, to die, and to be forgotten."[9] We will not make

8. Geerhardus Vos, *Biblical Theology: Old and New Testaments* (Grand Rapids: Eerdmans, 1991), 17.

9. A. J. Lewis, *Zinzendorf, the Ecumenical Pioneer: A Study in the Moravian Contribution to Christian Mission and Unity* (London: SCM Press, 1962), 92. A similar, though unsubstantiated, quote is frequently attributed to Zinzendorf: "Preach

progress in sanctification while clinging to our self-centered stories. Rather, we must profess with Paul, "I do not account my life of any value nor as precious to myself, if only I may finish my course and the ministry that I received from the Lord Jesus, to testify to the gospel of the grace of God" (Acts 20:24). Christ himself must be presented as the protagonist in the sweep of redemptive history to which our own lives must be oriented, as we teach toward this conclusion: "that one has died for all, therefore all have died; and he died for all, that those who live might no longer live for themselves but for him who for their sake died and was raised" (2 Cor. 5:14–15). Only as attention is drawn to Jesus will sanctification progress (3:18).

In the drama of Scripture, Adam and Jesus are the historical figures of prime importance. The account of Adam and Eve's fall into sin is the source of our own sinful nature and provides the type for every temptation that follows. They decide to believe a different story about God, put forward by the serpent, and to take a different role, looking at the world apart from God's word, deciding for themselves what is good and desirable (Gen. 3:1–6). The need, therefore, is for another Adam-like individual who possesses a similar far-reaching impact. Jesus is this person. Scripture refers to him as the "last Adam" (1 Cor. 15:45). These two are compared side by side in Romans 5:19: "For as by the one man's disobedience the many were made sinners, so by the one man's obedience the many will be made righteous." As Adam's disobedience is the source for all our struggles with sin, Jesus' own obedience is our only hope for sanctification, the "one who in every respect has been tempted as we are, yet without sin" (Heb. 4:15).

This comparison between Adam and Jesus is dramatized in the opening chapters of the Gospels when Jesus comes face to face with Satan, the tempter, not in a garden as did Adam and Eve, but in the wilderness, a barren world under the curse because of sin (Matt. 4:1–11; cf. Mark 1:12–13; Luke 4:1–13). The substance of Satan's temptation, as it was for Adam and Eve, was that Jesus should live for himself. "Satisfy *your* hunger, Jesus. Call upon others to deliver *you*, Jesus. Take the kingdoms of the world for *yourself*, Jesus." Yet Jesus refuses, responding with Scripture, as he takes upon himself the role that the

---

Christ, die, and be forgotten."

Father gave him as a servant to others, who through his own death and resurrection comes to deliver the descendants of Adam and Eve, the heirs of those who had decided to live for themselves.

As Jesus became a servant and submitted himself in obedience, he became the source of sanctification. Jesus himself said, "For them I sanctify myself, that they too may be truly sanctified" (John 17:19 NIV). Jesus is the main character, however, not as he exalts himself but as he humbles himself. It is this mind, according to Scripture, that we must share (Phil. 2:3–11). And as we read Scripture, we must continually be drawn to him, turning from our self-centered stories and placing our hope, our faith, in him, if we are to be transformed into his image. As J. C. Ryle observes, "If we would be sanctified, our course is clear and plain: we must begin with Christit. . . . The very first step towards sanctification, no less than justification, is to come with faith to Christ."[10]

Death and Resurrection Are the
Central Themes in Sanctification

If Jesus Christ is the principal protagonist in all of Scripture, then his death and resurrection are central to the entire account. Paul refers to his death and resurrection together as the matter of "first importance" (1 Cor. 15:3–4). They are the climactic moments of redemptive history. Yet they are important not simply as past events. Jesus' death and resurrection are the source of the Christian life, serving as the dynamic of sanctification in the power of the Holy Spirit. According to Ryle, "He, who supposes that Jesus Christ only lived and died and rose again in order to provide justification and forgiveness of sins for His people, has yet much to learn."[11] The fullness of salvation is sourced in Jesus' death and resurrection, sanctification included.[12]

---

10. J. C. Ryle, *Holiness* (Darlington, UK: Evangelical Press, 2001), 30–31.

11. Ryle, *Holiness*, 16.

12. As the Westminster Confession of Faith states, sanctification occurs "through the virtue of Christ's death and resurrection, by his Word and Spirit dwelling in them; the dominion of the whole body of sin is destroyed, and the several lusts thereof are more and more weakened and mortified; and they more and more quickened and strengthened in all saving graces, to the practice of true holiness,

This is the pattern of New Testament teaching. In Romans 6, Paul repeatedly relates Christ's death and resurrection to our present lives. In verse 4, he says, "We were buried therefore with him . . . , in order that, just as Christ was raised . . . , we too might walk in newness of life." In verse 5, Paul describes being "united with him in a death like his" as well as being "united with him in a resurrection like his." In verse 6, he speaks definitively: "our old self was crucified with him"; and in verse 8: "we have died with Christ," and "we will also live with him." These are indicatives: statements of fact for the one in Christ Jesus. A relationship to Christ, who died and was raised, dramatically changes our relationship with sin.[13] Paul's indicative statements describing what is true for us in Christ then become imperatives for how we are to live by faith in Christ, outlined in verses 10–11: "For the death he died he died to sin, once for all, but the life he lives he lives to God. So you also must consider yourselves dead to sin and alive to God in Christ Jesus." What is true for Christ must be counted as true for us through our relationship with him.

A difficulty we face in ministry is that personal experience seems to diminish these striking truths. Owen, with great pastoral wisdom, notes that "there are two things hard and difficult." The first: "To convince those in whom sin evidently hath the dominion that such indeed is their state and condition." The second: "To satisfy some that sin hath not the dominion over them notwithstanding its restless acting itself in them and warring against their souls."[14] Though hard

---

without which no man shall see the Lord" (WCF 13.1). According to John Murray, "The bearing of Jesus' death and resurrection upon our justification has been in the forefront of Protestant teaching. But its bearing upon sanctification has not been sufficiently appreciated." John Murray, "The Agency in Definitive Sanctification," in *Collected Writings of John Murray*, vol. 2, *Systematic Theology* (Edinburgh: Banner of Truth, 1977), 286. For a rich biblical and theological analysis of the role of Christ's death and resurrection in sanctification, see John Murray, "The Dynamic of the Biblical Ethic," in *Principles of Conduct* (Grand Rapids: Eerdmans, 1997), 202–28.

13. John Murray asserts, "No fact is of more basic importance in connection with the death to sin and commitment to holiness than that of identification with Christ in his death and resurrection." John Murray, "Agency in Definitive Sanctification," 286. See also John Murray, "Definitive Sanctification," in *Collected Works of John Murray*, vol. 2, *Systematic Theology* (Edinburgh: Banner of Truth, 1977), 277–84.

14. John Owen, *On the Dominion of Sin and Grace*, in *The Works of John Owen*, ed. William H. Goold (Edinburgh: Banner of Truth, 1994), 7:517.

and difficult, this is our task as we labor for the obedience of a faith that looks to Christ Jesus, who died and was raised. John Murray says perceptively, "We are too ready to give heed to what we deem to be the hard, empirical facts of Christian profession," speaking of the hesitation to fully embrace this teaching of Scripture, and we thus fail to teach in our ministry the defining truths of Christ's death and resurrection for sanctification.[15]

Considering ourselves dead to sin and alive to God is an essential aspect of what it means to live by faith in Christ Jesus. Though apparently apocryphal, an account of Augustine provides an example of what this looks like in practice.[16] Before becoming a Christian, Augustine was admittedly sexually promiscuous.[17] The story goes that years later, after he had become bishop of Carthage, his former mistress passed him in the street, calling out, "Augustine, it is I." He stopped, turned, and responded, "Yes, but it is no longer I, Augustine." What does he mean? Augustine's brief response is grounded in this conviction: "The Augustine you once knew is no more. That Augustine is now dead. This Augustine standing before you is alive to God in Christ Jesus." The account is intended to teach that the life of faith requires such a response in the face of temptation that appeals to our old self.

This by no means suggests that this is an easy thing to do. If we were to run further with the story, we might wonder how Augustine felt at the time, how powerful the temptation was as he recalled his past relationship with this woman. The point of the story, however, is that Augustine responded in faith as he identified himself with Christ, his death, and his resurrection, despite what may have been a strong allure to a previous life. This is what it looks like to have "learned Christ," as Paul says in Ephesians 4:20.

---

15. Murray, "Dynamic of the Biblical Ethic," 205.

16. I first heard this account from Sinclair Ferguson while a student at Westminster Theological Seminary. The story is found in a sermon by Charles Haddon Spurgeon, "The Way to Honor," Christian Classics Ethereal Library, accessed March 7, 2018, https://www.ccel.org/ccel/spurgeon/sermons19.xxx.html. It likely originates from an illustration given by Ambrose, who describes a similar encounter while not naming Augustine. Ambrose, *Concerning Repentance*, 2.10.96.

17. Augustine, *Confessions*, 2.1–3.

Pastors and theologians have termed the application of Christ's death and resurrection in practice as *mortification* and *vivification*. This is the sum of repentance. As John Calvin describes it, "repentance consists of two parts: namely, mortification of the flesh and vivification of the spirit."[18] He continues: "Both things happen to us by participation in Christ."[19] Many to whom we minister may think repentance is simply ceasing one behavior and replacing it with another. If this were all there was to repentance, however, it would have nothing to do with Jesus. Christian repentance entails much more. Owen distinguishes *"moral duties"* from an *"evangelical obedience,"* the difference being that the latter "grafts all duties of moral obedience on this stock of faith in Christ Jesus."[20] He must remain the focus in every aspect of sanctification. If we are to learn Christ, we must ask in the face of every struggle, "What does the death and resurrection of Jesus Christ require in this situation, as I look in faith to him?" As Peter exhorts us: "arm yourselves with the same way of thinking" (1 Peter 4:1–3).

Paul describes the practice of this pattern of mortification and vivification in Ephesians 4:21–32. He indicates that the substance of his teaching here is basic to his apostolic instruction, describing it as what it means to be "taught in him, as the truth is in Jesus" (Eph. 4:21). He contrasts the "old self, which belongs to your former manner of life and is corrupt through deceitful desires," and "the new self, created after the likeness of God in true righteousness and holiness" (vv. 22–24). He calls us to "put away" practices associated with the "old self," such as lying, stealing, sexual immorality, anger, and obscene talk, to be replaced by patterns of behavior in keeping with the "new self," such as speaking the truth, laboring to provide for

18. John Calvin, *Institutes of the Christian Religion*, ed. John T. McNeill, trans. Ford Lewis Battles, 2 vols., Library of Christian Classics 20–21 (Philadelphia: Westminster, 1960), 3.3.8.

19. Calvin, *Institutes*, 3.3.9.

20. Owen, *Holy Spirit*, 279 (emphasis original). See also Sinclair B. Ferguson, *John Owen on the Christian Life* (Edinburgh: Banner of Truth, 1987), 67–69. Ralph Erskine succinctly outlines this difference within a sermon: Ralph Erskine, "The Difference between Legal and Gospel Mortification," *Monergism*, accessed October 15, 2020, https://www.monergism.com/blog/difference-between-legal-gospel-mortification.

others, compassion, kindness, and humility (vv. 25–32).[21] Mortification and vivification must address the details. They are opportunities to exercise faith in Christ, who died and was raised unto personal sanctification.

An example from ministry may help in considering what this looks like in practice. Years ago, when I was engaged in campus ministry, a young woman came to me with roommate problems. Although living in the same house, she and her roommate had not spoken with each other in over a month. At the same time, each had been saying plenty about the other to friends. The details concerned money, bills, and who would keep the refrigerator they had bought at the start of the year. A very typical conflict was an opportunity to learn Christ.

In our conversation, I read Ephesians 4:31–32: "Let all bitterness and wrath and anger and clamor and slander be put away from you, along with all malice. Be kind to one another, tenderhearted, forgiving one another, as God in Christ forgave you." Notice how the first sentence describes mortification and the second vivification. As I read, the young woman began to cry. I soon realized, however, that these were not tears of conviction. They were flowing from a hard heart. She responded, "But I can't do that!" Of course, in one sense she was exactly right. It was not within her power to rid herself of anger and instead be tenderhearted. She needed to turn to Christ, to call out to him who died and was raised for her, and then move toward her roommate, trusting that God would be present, providing the grace needed in what appeared to be an impossible situation. The problem, of course, was that she did not want to do it because it would mean dying to pride, to being right, and going humbly to the other person. It would mean listening with a willingness to put the other's interests above her own. It would have required nothing less than death and resurrection through looking to Christ in faith.

---

21. Whereas in Ephesians 4:22 and 25, Paul uses the verb ἀποτίθημι, "put away," in a parallel passage, Colossians 3:1–17, Paul uses the verb νεκρόω, "put to death," in verse 5. Similarly, in Romans 8:13, Paul uses the synonym θανατόω. In these instances, the language of mortification is made explicit. See F. F. Bruce, *The Epistles to the Colossians, to Philemon, and to the Ephesians*, NICNT 12 (Grand Rapids: Eerdmans, 1984), 140n49.

The Aim of Sanctification Is Complete Renewal

The scenario above illustrates the deeper dimensions of sanctification. It concerns more than changed behavior. It must reach the heart. As Walter Marshall explains, "Our work is not only to alter vicious customs, but to mortify corrupt natural affections, which bred those corruptions; and not only to deny the fulfilling of sinful lusts, but to be full of holy love and desire."[22] The reach of sanctification requires us to consider the depth of sin. If love for God and love for neighbor underlie true obedience to God's law (Matt. 22:37–39), we must trace sinful behavior to other affections at work in our hearts. As discussed above, Paul provides the apostolic pattern of sanctification in Ephesians 4, with the imperative to put away particular sins that are replaced with behaviors in keeping with the new life that we have through Christ's resurrection. The sinful patterns to be put off have their source in what Paul calls the "old self" or "old man": our prior identity in Adam. He further describes this "old self" as "corrupt through deceitful desires" (Eph. 4:22). Every sin is ultimately sourced in these deceitful desires, which must be addressed if we're to make genuine progress in sanctification. Otherwise, while there may be success in changing certain behaviors, the deceitful desires that underlie sin will continue to manifest themselves in other ways.

Let me provide a personal example from when I first began to learn the depths of sin's working in my life. Although I grew up in the church, my life reflected little of the gospel I professed to believe as I entered college. Greater freedom allowed for more opportunities to pursue sensuality and various kinds of impurity, to use Paul's language in Ephesians 4. After a time, however, I became tired of the typical routine of indulging these desires. I sensed their emptiness and experienced a measure of conviction. I decided instead to give myself to my studies. I worked diligently. I had ambitions. I did well. Outwardly, much had changed. No one thought to question how I lived now. Yet I came to realize that I was actually no different from before. None of my new behaviors came from a love for God or a love for my neighbor. They all flowed from a great love for myself, as had my

22. Marshall, *Gospel Mystery of Sanctification*, 25.

previous patterns of indulgence. The only difference was that my aim was not immediate gratification but a desire for acclaim and recognition for my intelligence and ability. Though refined, sin it remained, stemming from self-centered desires that needed to be exposed.

Paul's description of sin's source in "deceitful desires" is instructive. The true working of sin is not evident at the surface. To pursue sanctification, we must have a growing awareness of the workings of these deeper desires. The following chart, adapted from David Powlison, portrays this dynamic of sin and sanctification:[23]

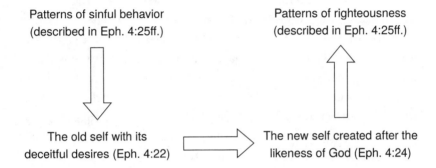

Patterns of sinful behavior (described in Eph. 4:25ff.)

Patterns of righteousness (described in Eph. 4:25ff.)

The old self with its deceitful desires (Eph. 4:22)

The new self created after the likeness of God (Eph. 4:24)

Fig. 14.1. The Dynamic of Sin and Sanctification

The top boxes contain outward behaviors, while those below are the deeper dynamic from which they are derived. In ministry, we must stress that sanctification does not occur simply through exchanging patterns of sinful behavior for patterns of righteous living. Gospel obedience includes much more. Sinful behaviors must be traced to deeper desires, and their corresponding identity, at work below.

At that deeper level we find the "old self," who is always for himself or herself. For example, in considering various patterns of sexual immorality (whether manifest in a relationship, through pornography, or simply in our imagination), we find the "old self" driven by desires for self-centered pleasure, self-centered security, or perhaps an expression of self-pity. Sanctification occurs through first embracing our new identity in Christ Jesus, who came not to gratify himself but

23. David Powlison, "Crucial Issues in Contemporary Biblical Counseling," in *Counsel the Word*, 2nd ed. (Glenside, PA: Christian Counseling & Educational Foundation, 2002), 111.

to sacrificially serve others. Once again, as Paul reminds the Corinthians, "For the love of Christ controls us, because we have concluded this: that one has died for all, therefore all have died; and he died for all, that those who live might no longer live for themselves but for him who for their sake died and was raised" (2 Cor. 5:14–15). This then provides a completely different agenda in our relationships. "From now on, therefore, we regard no one according to the flesh," Paul concludes (v. 16). This "new self," being transformed into the image of Jesus, looks for ways to love God and our neighbor, producing new patterns of living, no longer centered on myself but on others.

Although the love of Christ is to control us, we are not to wait until we feel the right way before we act consistently with God's love shown to us in Christ. Once again, we are not to live at the whim of our desires. We must act in faith. Much of the time, what we feel as Christians is great conflict. According to Herman Bavinck, "The life of the Christian is not a quiet growth, but a continuous struggle against enemies without, and no less a struggle against the enemy who dwells within our own bosoms."[24] As Paul reminds us in Galatians 5:17, "the desires of the flesh are against the Spirit, and the desires of the Spirit are against the flesh." In the midst of this struggle, the power of the gospel is evident as we take hold of who we now are in Christ and strive against the "old self," no longer allowing our former identity in Adam to dictate how we live. Rather, as those who live by faith in Christ, who died and was raised, we strive to put on "the new self, created after the likeness of God in true righteousness and holiness" (Eph. 4:24).

This striving in sanctification inevitably leads to a greater personal awareness of sin's presence in our lives. The sense of struggle will increase. But as Owen writes, "Your state is not at all to be measured by the opposition sin makes to you, but by the opposition you make to it."[25] Once again, we must remember Paul's description of his own experience: "Wretched man that I am! Who will deliver me from this body of death? Thanks be to God through Jesus Christ

---

24. Herman Bavinck, *The Wonderful Works of God: Instruction in the Christian Religion according to the Reformed Confessions*, trans. Henry Zylstra (Glenside, PA: Westminster Seminary Press, 2019), 474.

25. John Owen, *An Exposition upon Psalm CXXX*, in *The Works of John Owen*, ed. William H. Goold (Edinburgh: Banner of Truth, 1995), 6:605.

our Lord!" (Rom. 7:24–25). We must never forget that Christ is our righteousness as we pursue sanctification. This assurance frees us to look honestly and deeply at how sin works in our lives without fear. A growing awareness of sin must always be accompanied by an increasing conviction concerning the depths of God's grace.

Others Are Essential for Progress in Sanctification

If the heart of sanctification is love for God and love for neighbor, then our relationships play a significant role in sanctification. We may be tempted to make sanctification a private study, not wanting others to know about our personal struggles with sin due to shame. Yet this betrays what we profess: that Christ alone is our righteousness. And Scripture is clear that we will not make progress in sanctification if we are working to keep our sins a secret. James exhorts us to "confess your sins to one another and pray for one another, that you may be healed" (James 5:16). It is difficult to imagine a better way to die to ourselves than to confess our sins in humility to others. Thus, death and resurrection, both mortification and vivification, are not individual activities but a collective pursuit.

Scripture clearly calls us to participate in one another's sanctification. Our willingness to do so itself evidences genuine progress:

If your brother sins against you, go and *tell him his fault*, between you and him alone. If he listens to you, you have gained your brother. (Matt. 18:15)

Let the word of Christ dwell in you richly, teaching and *admonishing* one another in all wisdom. (Col. 3:16)

Take care, brothers, lest there be in any of you an evil, unbelieving heart, leading you to fall away from the living God. But *exhort* one another every day, as long as it is called "today," that none of you may be hardened by the deceitfulness of sin. (Heb. 3:12–13)

Graciously confronting, exhorting, and admonishing is participation in one another's mortification. The clear implication is that if we are not involved in one another's lives in this way, we are allowing one another to be hardened by sin. We need others to bring insight and clarity into our self-deception, and we are likewise called to do the same for others. Overlooking one another's sin simply allows the pattern to be reinforced.

While the death of Christ must shape our relationships, so must his resurrection. We are called not only to confront and exhort but to encourage as well:

> Rather, *speaking the truth in love*, we are to grow up in every way into him who is the head, into Christ. (Eph. 4:15)

> Therefore *encourage* one another and build one another up, just as you are doing. (1 Thess. 5:11)

> And let us consider how to *stir up one another* to love and good works, . . . encouraging one another, and all the more as you see the Day drawing near. (Heb. 10:24–25)

Through such words the Spirit imparts new life. We are to be adept not simply at seeing one another's sin but also at envisioning what resurrection will look like in one another's lives. Both mortification and vivification, death and resurrection, must shape how we relate.

Scripture uses the image of the athlete to describe the work of ministry (Phil. 2:16; 2 Tim. 4:7) as well as the Christian life (1 Cor. 9:24–27; Gal. 5:7). As Hebrews reminds us, "since we are surrounded by so great a cloud of witnesses, let us also lay aside every weight, and sin which clings so closely, and let us run with endurance the race that is set before us" (Heb. 12:1). Yet it is difficult to run alone. Motivation comes when we are surrounded by others, keeping pace, moving toward the same end. The same is true in sanctification, as together we are "looking to Jesus, the founder and perfecter of our faith, who for the joy that was set before him endured the cross, despising the shame" (v. 2). Momentum is built as we join with others, striving together against sin and moving closer to the image of Christ, encouraging one another as we go.

Involvement in the lives of others requires that we think less of ourselves, which is the very thing that sanctification entails. According to Tim Lane and Paul Tripp:

> Living in community pushes us to die to ourselves. There will be times when loving others and allowing others to serve and love us will feel like death, but this is the pathway to real life in Christ. The more we understand our own hearts, the more we see that it takes a work of God's grace to transform self-absorbed individuals into a community of love.[26]

If we are to effectively labor for the obedience of faith, we must encourage such a setting for sanctification through our ministry within the life of the church. We will not witness genuine progress apart from such relationships.

The Pastor's Life Is a Portrayal of Sanctification

Recalling again Paul's charge to Timothy, the pastor must also embrace the role of his own sanctification in the work of ministry: "Keep a close watch on yourself and on the teaching. Persist in this, for by so doing you will save both yourself and your hearers" (1 Tim. 4:16). In an ordination sermon, Robert Murray M'Cheyne exhorts the new minister: "But, oh! Study universal holiness of life. Your whole usefulness depends on this."[27] Similarly, Charles Spurgeon tells young ministers: "It is not great talents God blesses so much as likeness to Jesus. A holy minister is an awful weapon in the hand of God."[28] A danger, however, arises when the one engaged in ministry feels compelled to put on a show of personal righteousness that does not correspond with the realities of remaining sin in his life, or with the gospel of Christ's death and resurrection that he proclaims.

---

26. Timothy S. Lane and Paul David Tripp, *How People Change* (Winston-Salem, NC: Punch Press, 2006), 83.

27. Robert Murray McCheyne, "Sermon XI: Ordination Sermon," in *The Works of the Late Rev. Robert Murray McCheyne*, vol. 2 (New York: Robert Carter, 1847), 85–86.

28. Charles H. Spurgeon, "The Minister's Self-Watch," in *Lectures to My Students* (Edinburgh: Banner of Truth, 2008), 2.

The pastor, too, is laboring to learn the obedience of faith and experiences the same conflict between the flesh and the Spirit as those to whom he ministers. We must not pretend otherwise. In his longing for the final resurrection and the full righteousness it entails, Paul confesses, "Not that I have already obtained this or am already perfect, but I press on to make it my own, because Christ Jesus has made me his own" (Phil. 3:12). This confession, he indicates, underlies true maturity in Christ (v. 15).

As seen above, Paul is not afraid to intensely personalize the ongoing conflict with sin (Rom. 7:14–25). In fact, he portrays this as an essential aspect of his ministry. With his characteristic formula identifying apostolic doctrine to be maintained within the church, Paul tells Timothy, "The saying is trustworthy and deserving of full acceptance, that Christ Jesus came into the world to save sinners" (1 Tim. 1:15).[29] And yet he continues the sentence, applying the same to himself: "of whom I am the foremost." Paul magnifies his identity as a sinner before those to whom he ministers. He then further reflects on the import of this in his ministry, concluding, "But I received mercy for this reason, that in me, as the foremost, Jesus Christ might display his perfect patience as an example to those who were to believe in him for eternal life" (v. 16). The value of his ministry, he indicates, is that he serves as a type for others, that they, too, might learn what it means to trust Christ and know his continued patience even with the foremost of sinners. If we resist this role in ministry, the inevitable result, in some measure, will be to subtly proclaim ourselves rather than "Jesus Christ as Lord, with ourselves as your servants for Jesus' sake" (2 Cor. 4:5). In his labor for the obedience of faith, the pastor must be willing to humbly serve as such an example.

Ministry itself provides plenty of opportunities. In pastoring those who suffer, we, too, bear a measure of their burdens, multiplied across the congregation, while also enduring other hardships unique to ministry. These provide their own temptations to seek solace apart

29. As explained by George W. Knight, πιστὸς ὁ λόγος is a quotation formula unique to the Pastoral Epistles (1 Tim. 1:15; 3:1; 4:9; 2 Tim. 2:11; Titus 3:8), identifying established statements that faithfully represent apostolic teaching. George W. Knight III, *The Pastoral Epistles: A Commentary on the Greek Text*, NIGTC (Grand Rapids: Eerdmans, 1992), 99–100.

from Christ, rather than carrying our cross as we follow him. The demand to die to self will be impressed on all who are engaged in gospel ministry.

Paul vividly describes this in his role as an apostle in 1 Corinthians 4:9: "I think that God has exhibited us apostles as last of all, like men sentenced to death, because we have become a spectacle to the world, to angels, and to men." The Greek word translated as "spectacle" is θέατρον, the word for "theater." In his following letter to the Corinthians, Paul describes this show in greater detail. Contrasting his own weakness with the glory of Christ, he says, "But we have this treasure in jars of clay, to show that the surpassing power belongs to God and not to us" (2 Cor. 4:7). He provides a list that captures how this is exhibited in his own life: "afflicted in every way, but not crushed; perplexed, but not driven to despair; persecuted, but not forsaken; struck down, but not destroyed" (v. 9). The whole of his experience is then condensed in these words: "always carrying in the body the death of Jesus, so that the life of Jesus may also be manifested in our bodies" (v. 10).[30] Although the uniqueness of the apostles' role should be noted, surely there is a similar experience in all ministry built on this foundation (Eph. 2:20). The life of the minister is a theater for Christ's death and resurrection.[31] Though foremost a message to be told, Christ's death and resurrection must also be shown in our lives, a portrayal that is part of the pastor's sanctification. Paul takes courage as he concludes, "Though our outer self

30. The Greek text reads τὴν νέκρωσιν τοῦ Ἰησοῦ, which may be translated as "the dying of Jesus." Philip Edgcumbe Hughes comments that "νέκρωσιν here retains its proper significance of an actual *process*, of dying," as opposed to "a *state* of deadness." Philip Edgcumbe Hughes, *The Second Epistle to the Corinthians*, NICNT (Grand Rapids: Eerdmans, 1962), 141n12 (emphasis original). This corresponds to the ongoing experience that Paul describes. This death is yet unfinished in him. John Owen applies this to sanctification in a vivid description, captured in our experience, as he compares mortification to a man dying on a cross. Even as his life is coming to a certain end, he struggles and strains at times with the appearance of great strength, as does our flesh in our striving to put it to death. John Owen, *The Mortification of Sin*, in *The Works of John Owen*, ed. William H. Goold (Edinburgh: Banner of Truth, 1995), 6:30.

31. For a fuller development of this theme, see William R. Edwards, "Participants in What We Proclaim: Recovering Paul's Narrative of Pastoral Ministry," *Themelios* 39, no. 3 (2014): 455–69.

is wasting away, our inner self is being renewed day by day" (2 Cor. 4:16). The trials of ministry are used to conform us to the image of Christ, even as they display the mighty works of Christ before others.

If we fail to take this to heart, we cannot remain faithful. Ministry is a stage, but we ourselves are not the show. Instead, within our ministries we are to play a supporting role in a much greater story that focuses others on Christ. As John the Baptist understood of his own ministry, we must likewise confess, "He must increase, but I must decrease" (John 3:30). All who stand on the stage of ministry can "no longer live for themselves but for him who for their sake died and was raised" (2 Cor. 5:15). A pastor's sanctification requires nothing less.

Conclusion

The pastor himself must learn Christ if he is to labor for the obedience of faith in the lives of those to whom he ministers. Could it be that the prevailing difficulty in explaining this doctrine stems from a failure to pursue sanctification in our own lives? Surely this is true in part. God's Word is clear. Sin, however, always brings confusion. The articulation of sanctification cannot be separated from its exemplification in the pastor's life. We will not sincerely toil to present others mature in Christ if we are not personally concerned for the same (Col. 1:28–29).

In the final chapter of *The Mortification of Sin*, Owen describes all that he has written to this point in the treatise as "*preparatory* to the work aimed at than such as will *effect* it."[32] Indeed, he provides only one conclusive direction, followed by assurances that arise from the work of the Spirit. It is this:

> Set faith at work in Christ for the killing of thy sin. His blood is the great sovereign remedy for sin-sick souls. Live in this, and thou wilt die a conqueror; yea, thou wilt, through the good providence of God, live to see thy lust dead at thy feet.[33]

32. Owen, *Mortification of Sin*, 78 (emphasis original).
33. Owen, *Mortification of Sin*, 79.

Every prior direction provided by Owen aims to convince us of the necessity of the work, and that there is no other way but through faith in Christ. In laboring for the obedience of faith, we must constantly provide such focus with its corresponding assurance.

Paul speaks of the Philippians' obedience, calling them to continue to "work out your own salvation with fear and trembling," and yet encourages them that "it is God who works in you, both to will and to work for his good pleasure" (Phil. 2:12–13). The start of his letter includes similar assurance: "And I am sure of this, that he who began a good work in you will bring it to completion at the day of Jesus Christ" (1:6). Likewise, he concludes his letter to the Thessalonians with a benediction that expresses this confidence: "Now may the God of peace himself sanctify you completely, and may your whole spirit and soul and body be kept blameless at the coming of our Lord Jesus Christ. He who calls you is faithful; he will surely do it" (1 Thess. 5:23–24). Sanctification is a work of God's grace even as we strive strenuously through faith for the full obedience that shows forth the glorious likeness of Christ. As Marshall concludes, "Sanctification in Christ, is glorification begun; as glorification is sanctification perfected."[34] In our labor of ministry, this is our final hope that we must also confidently hold before others.

Key Terms

 mortification
 repentance
 sanctification
 vivification

Recommendations for Further Reading

Ferguson, Sinclair B. *Devoted to God: Blueprints for Sanctification*. Edinburgh: Banner of Truth, 2016.

Marshall, Walter. *The Gospel Mystery of Sanctification*. Grand Rapids: Reformation Heritage Books, 2013.

---

34. Marshall, *Gospel Mystery of Sanctification*, 227.

Murray, John. "Definitive Sanctification." In *Collected Works of John Murray*. Vol. 2, *Systematic Theology*, 277–84. Edinburgh: Banner of Truth, 1977. Also see his other essays on sanctification in this volume.

———. "The Dynamic of the Biblical Ethic." In *Principles of Conduct*, 202–28. Grand Rapids: Eerdmans, 1997.

Owen, John. *The Mortification of Sin*. Edinburgh: Banner of Truth, 2004.

Ryle, J. C. *Holiness*. Darlington, UK: Evangelical Press, 2014.

Discussion Questions

1. Do you find it easier to grasp the role of faith in relation to justification than to sanctification? Why?
2. What are the myths or false narratives that you believe, that tend to shape your life, and that stand in opposition to the truth of Scripture focused on Christ Jesus?
3. In our ministries, how might we more effectively draw attention to Jesus in such a way that encourages progress in sanctification?
4. Both mortification and vivification are necessary for genuine repentance. But how have you attempted half-measures, attempting one without the other, or either apart from Christ? How is the result less than biblical sanctification?
5. Walter Marshall says, "Our work is not only to alter vicious customs [behaviors], but to mortify corrupt natural affections, which bred those corruptions." How does sanctification progress at the level of the affections?
6. How can we encourage a corporate setting for sanctification in our own lives as well as through our ministries, fostering the relationships required for genuine progress?
7. How is a pastor's own sanctification an essential component of his ministry? And what are some unique challenges and dangers that he may face?

15

FAITH AND REPENTANCE

Implications for the Gospel
Call in Preaching[1]

CORNELIS P. VENEMA

As stewards of the gospel and ambassadors of Christ (1 Cor. 4:1; 2 Cor. 5:20), ministers have as their principal task the extending of the gracious summons of the gospel to lost sinners, calling them to faith and repentance. If Christ is pleased to gather his people to himself through the ministry of his Spirit and Word, the minister of Christ has no greater task than to proclaim the joyful message of the gospel that whoever believes in Christ will not perish but have eternal life (John 3:16). Those who proclaim this gospel must always be mindful of the apostle Paul's teaching in Romans 10:14–15:

> How then will they call on him in whom they have not believed? And how are they to believe in him of whom they have never heard? And how are they to hear without someone preaching? And how are they to preach unless they are sent? As it is written, "How beautiful are the feet of those who preach the good news!"

1. I count it a privilege to write this chapter for a book that honors Sinclair Ferguson's contributions to biblical and Reformed theology over several decades. Sinclair is a model of a pastor-theologian who has helped the church to "follow the pattern of . . . sound words" (2 Tim. 1:13).

In the course of gospel ministers' extending the call of the gospel, it is critically important that they properly understand what they are calling their hearers to do. Misunderstanding the nature of faith and repentance can easily lead to serious problems in the ministry. If a minister calls people to faith, but not to repentance, he might encourage a form of "easy believism" or an antinomian view of the Christian life.[2] Or if a minister calls people to repentance, but without undergirding this call with a clear presentation of the gospel of salvation by grace alone through the work of Christ alone, and received by faith alone, he might unwittingly encourage a form of legalism that views repentance as the ground for God's favor. A misconstrual of gospel faith and repentance can lead to serious errors in the way that the gospel is proclaimed and the way that lost sinners seek assurance of salvation.

I was reminded of this in an unexpected way early in the course of my pastoral ministry in a Reformed church in Southern California. Several months after my ministry began, I discovered to my surprise that a stalwart member of the congregation (I will refer to him as Henry) had never professed his faith in Christ and become a communicant member of the church. Though Henry had been baptized as an infant and gave every impression that he was a believer in Christ, he was unwilling to publicly embrace the promise of the gospel. He was unable to acknowledge and find assurance that the gospel promise of salvation in Christ was for him. Upon learning this, I began to visit with him regularly, seeking to find out why he was not a communicant member of the church and to encourage him to publicly profess his faith in Christ. No matter how hard I tried to convince him to do so, however, I found myself running up against a brick wall, which, as I discovered, had been built out of a misguided presentation of the gospel in the church of his youth.

The gospel presentation in the church in which Henry had been raised characterized the assurance of salvation through faith in the

---

2. For critical assessments of gospel presentations that neglect the call to repentance and lead to antinomianism, see Walter J. Chantry, *Today's Gospel: Authentic or Synthetic?* (London: Banner of Truth, 1970); Mark Jones, *Antinomianism: Reformed Theology's Unwelcome Guest?* (Phillipsburg, NJ: P&R Publishing, 2013); Wayne Grudem, *"Free Grace" Theology: 5 Ways It Diminishes the Gospel* (Wheaton, IL: Crossway, 2016).

gospel promise as a rare jewel. Only a small number of the church's members were able to gain any assurance of their election and salvation. Unless and until the experience of God's grace was so compelling as to confirm beyond any doubt the genuineness of their conversion, they could find no sure footing for confidence regarding God's favor for them in Christ. Henry repeatedly said to me, "How can I be sure that I am not self-deceived regarding my salvation? If I were to profess faith in Christ, would I not run the risk of pretending to acknowledge the depths of my unworthiness or the genuineness of my professed repentance for my sins?"

Though it took a long time, God used the apostle Paul's words to the Philippian jailer's question, "What must I do to be saved?"—to which Paul immediately and directly responded, "Believe in the Lord Jesus, and you will be saved, you and your household" (Acts 16:30–31)—to bring Henry to confidently profess his faith. This passage brought Henry to recognize that he was crippled by the perverse notion that the depth of his own experience of his sinfulness was a precondition for coming to Christ in faith. Happily, the Holy Spirit used the simple command to believe to persuade Henry to look away from himself and focus his faith on Christ and the spiritual blessings that are granted to all who trust him.

While further examples could be provided of distortions of the gospel call, Henry's case illustrates the need for a clear understanding of the Bible's teaching regarding faith and repentance. Otherwise, ministers run the risk of misrepresenting the gospel when they call their hearers to believe and repent. For this reason, I will begin this chapter with a summary of the Scripture's teaching regarding the gospel call to faith and repentance. Only then will we be able to identify some of the pastoral implications of the Scripture's teaching for presenting the gospel call.

Faith and Repentance: Inseparable, yet Distinct Responses to the Gospel Call

In the teaching of the Scriptures, particularly in the New Testament, faith and repentance are clearly identified as the proper, indispensable responses to the gospel message. Some passages emphasize the call to faith, while others specifically emphasize the summons to repentance. While these distinct emphases might suggest that there are two separate responses to the gospel call, it is evident from the testimony of the New Testament that faith and repentance belong together. They represent distinct, yet inseparable ways in which those to whom the gospel message is proclaimed are called to respond. Faith implies repentance, and repentance does not occur when faith is absent. When believers embrace the gospel promise in faith, they do so by way of a penitent faith. When believers turn from their sins in repentance, they also do so as those who trust in Christ and his saving work on their behalf.

Before we offer a closer exposition of the distinctive character of faith and repentance, several illustrations of their role as indispensable responses to the gospel will prove instructive. When Jesus preached the "gospel of God" in Galilee, he encouraged his hearers by saying, "The time is fulfilled, and the kingdom of God is at hand; repent and believe in the gospel" (Mark 1:14–15). In one of several warning passages in the book of Hebrews, the author urges his readers to "leave the elementary doctrine of Christ and go on to maturity, not laying again a foundation of *repentance* from dead works and of *faith* toward God" (Heb. 6:1). The gospel message that the apostle Paul preached in Ephesus is described in the book of Acts as a call to "repentance toward God and of faith in our Lord Jesus Christ" (Acts 20:21). In these passages, faith and repentance are joined together as inseparable components of a comprehensive response to the presentation of the gospel.

Yet there are other passages that speak distinctly of faith or repentance, as though either response included all that the gospel message summons its hearers to do. In the well-known account of the conversion of the Philippian jailer, mentioned above, Paul answered his question about what he must do to be saved by simply urging faith, saying, "Believe in the Lord Jesus, and you will be saved, you and your household" (Acts 16:31). In the next chapter in Acts, however, Paul's preaching in Athens on the Areopagus concludes with a call to repentance: "The times of ignorance God overlooked, but now he commands all people everywhere to repent, because he has fixed a day on which he will judge the world in righteousness by a man whom he has appointed" (17:30–31). Shortly after this summary of Paul's preaching as a call to repentance, we are told that some of the Athenians who heard him "believed" the message. Similarly, at several other points in the book of Acts, the preaching of the gospel is summarized as a call to repentance (2:38; 3:19; 5:31; 11:18).

At the end of the Gospel of Mark, the commission that Jesus gives to his disciples includes the promise, "Whoever believes and is baptized will be saved, but whoever does not believe will be condemned" (Mark 16:16). This language is echoed in the well-known words of John 3:16—"For God so loved the world, that he gave his only Son, that whoever believes in him should not perish but have eternal life"—and other passages in the Gospel of John (3:18; 6:35, 47; 7:31; 11:25–26; 14:1; 20:28–31).[3] Throughout the epistles of the apostle Paul, the gospel of Jesus Christ is often presented as a summons to salvation through faith in the Word concerning Christ (e.g., Rom. 10:9; Gal. 2:16; Eph. 2:8). But it is also a gospel that calls its recipients to repentance (e.g., 2 Cor. 7:9–11; 1 Thess. 1:9). Clearly, it would be a mistake to conclude from these passages that faith and repentance are not only distinct but even alternative ways in which sinners may respond to the gospel message. A better conclusion would be to recognize that when faith or repentance is distinctly identified as an appropriate response to the gospel, it is viewed by synecdoche to refer to the entirety of what the gospel requires of its recipients.

In the light of this clear testimony that the gospel call to conversion requires the response of faith and repentance, the question has arisen within Reformed theology regarding the relative priority of faith and repentance. Within the framework of the *ordo salutis* ("order of salvation"), this question is usually posed in terms of the logical, rather than chronological, order between faith and repentance. Does repentance logically precede or follow faith? Among

---

3. Though it is sometimes argued that the Gospel of John does not include repentance as a requisite response to the gospel call, it should be noted that this Gospel does speak of the Spirit's role in "convict[ing] the world concerning sin and righteousness and judgment" (John 16:8). Furthermore, the Gospel of John teaches that all true believers love the light (3:19), obey the Son (3:36), worship in spirit and truth (4:23–24), follow Jesus (10:26–28), and obey Jesus' commandments (10:26–28). For a critical treatment of this argument, see Grudem, *"Free Grace" Theology*, 51–55.

Reformed theologians, three primary answers are typically given to this question. First, there are those who follow John Calvin by insisting that repentance follows or is born out of faith. According to Calvin, "it ought to be a fact beyond controversy that repentance not only constantly follows faith, but is also born of faith."[4] While Calvin emphasizes the inseparability of faith and repentance, he places faith before repentance in order to stave off the idea that repentance can occur without a prior awareness of God's mercy or that it is motivated simply by an awareness of the legal consequences of disobedience.[5] Second, there are others, such as Louis Berkhof, who maintain that repentance is logically prior to faith. Berkhof believes that there can be no disputing that "repentance and the knowledge of sin precede the faith that yields to Christ in trusting love."[6] And third, there are those, such as John Murray, who maintain that the question is in some respects pointless. Since faith and repentance are inseparable, Murray argues that they are mutual or conjoined in such a way that the one permeates the other:

> It is an unnecessary question and the insistence that one is prior to the other futile. There is no priority. The faith that is unto salvation is a penitent faith and the repentance that is unto life is a believing repentance. . . . Saving faith is permeated with repentance and repentance is permeated with faith.[7]

Though I wholeheartedly concur with Murray that faith and repentance are inseparable responses to the gospel, I am sympathetic with

4. John Calvin, *Institutes of the Christian Religion*, ed. John T. McNeill, trans. Ford Lewis Battles, 2 vols., Library of Christian Classics 20–21 (Philadelphia: Westminster, 1960), 3.3.1. For an extensive argument for the priority of faith to repentance, see John Colquhoun, *Repentance* (1826; repr., London: Banner of Truth, 1965), 105–18.

5. Cf. W. G. Shedd, *Dogmatic Theology*, ed. Alan W. Gomes, 3rd ed. (Phillipsburg, NJ: P&R Publishing, 2003), 791, who argues for the precedence of faith for similar reasons.

6. Louis Berkhof, *Systematic Theology*, 4th ed. (Grand Rapids: Eerdmans, 1960), 492.

7. John Murray, *Redemption Accomplished and Applied* (Grand Rapids: Eerdmans, 2015), 118–19. Cf. Anthony Hoekema, *Saved by Grace* (Grand Rapids: Eerdmans, 1989), 123.

Calvin's view that they must be distinguished, and that a certain priority belongs to faith as the ground for the believer's union with Christ and repentance from sin.[8]

While faith and repentance together comprise the necessary response to the gospel message, we also need to consider what especially distinguishes these two features in this response. For the sake of conciseness, I will summarize the Scriptures' teaching regarding faith and repentance by making use of the Westminster Confession of Faith's descriptions in chapters 14 ("Of Saving Faith") and 15 ("Of Repentance unto Life").

Saving Faith

1. The grace of faith, whereby the elect are enabled to believe to the saving of their souls, is the work of the Spirit of Christ in their hearts, and is ordinarily wrought by the ministry of the Word, by which also, and by the administration of the sacraments, and prayer, it is increased and strengthened.

2. By this faith, a Christian believeth to be true whatsoever is revealed in the Word, for the authority of God himself speaking therein; and acteth differently upon that which each particular passage thereof containeth; yielding obedience to the commands, trembling at the threatenings, and embracing the promises of God for this life, and that which is to come. But the principal acts of saving faith are accepting, receiving, and resting upon Christ alone for justification, sanctification, and eternal life, by virtue of the covenant of grace.

3. This faith is different in degrees, weak or strong; may be often and many ways assailed, and weakened, but gets the victory; growing up in many to the attainment of a full assurance, through Christ, who is both the author and finisher of our faith. (WCF, chap. 14)

---

8. This seems to be the view reflected in the Heidelberg Catechism and the Belgic Confession. In the Heidelberg Catechism's treatment of conversion or repentance, the good works that repentance produces are said to "be done from true faith" (answer 91). The Belgic Confession also insists that the good works "proceed from the good root of faith" (art. 24).

The first article of the Westminster Confession of Faith's treatment of saving faith emphasizes that faith is graciously granted to believers through the ministry of the Holy Spirit, who uses the means of grace—the preaching of the gospel, the administration of the sacraments, and prayer—to produce, increase, and strengthen faith. Though faith is a genuine act on the part of those who respond to the call of the gospel, it is not a human work that merits God's grace or is performed apart from the Spirit's work in regeneration. When sinners embrace the gospel call to believe in Jesus Christ for salvation, they do so as the Holy Spirit works with the Word to illumine their minds, to soften their hearts, to enliven their wills, and to renew their affections. Faith is, accordingly, a gift of God's grace and not a human achievement that merits God's favor.

That faith is God's gracious gift is clearly taught in Scripture. We are told that when Paul and Barnabas began to preach to the Gentiles in Pisidian Antioch, "as many as were appointed to eternal life believed" (Acts 13:48). The verb used in this passage, "appointed," has the strong sense of "ordained" or "destined." The Gentiles who believed did so not because they were disposed to believe but because they were graciously enabled to do so according to God's purpose. The apostle John states, "Everyone who believes that Jesus is the Christ has been born of God" (1 John 5:1). The verb used for the idea of regeneration or new birth in this passage is in the perfect tense, describing an action in the past that has an abiding result. This passage teaches, then, that the one who believes does so because of God's act granting that person the new birth. In the Gospel of John, those who believe and acknowledge Jesus Christ are described as doing so in accordance with the Father's purpose. Those who come to Jesus in faith are granted the ability to do so by the Father (John 6:65; cf. 6:37; 17:6–9, 20–21). The author of Hebrews describes Christ as the "founder [author] and perfecter of our faith" (Heb. 12:2). Two passages in the epistles of the apostle Paul are particularly instructive. In Philippians 1:29, we read: "For it has been granted to you that for the sake of Christ you should not only believe in him but also suffer for his sake." In this passage, the faith of those who embrace Christ, as well as the sufferings that accompany such faith, is granted to believers by God. Perhaps the most striking expression of faith as God's gracious gift is found in Ephesians 2:8: "For by grace you have been saved through faith. And this is not your own doing; it is the gift of God." Though there is some question about the antecedent of "And this," there is no question that Paul is emphasizing that the whole of the believer's salvation in Christ is a fruit of God's grace, and not based in any way on works.[9] This includes the gift of faith whereby believers receive Christ and his saving benefits.

Although faith is a gift granted to believers by the ministry of the Spirit through the Word, it is simultaneously a distinct act on the part of those who embrace the gospel message. Even though God graciously grants faith, his gracious work does not diminish the responsibility of those who are called to faith through the gospel message. As John Murray observes, "It is by God's grace that a person is able to believe but faith is an activity on the part of the person and of him alone. In faith we receive and rest upon Christ alone for salvation."[10]

After emphasizing that faith is God's gracious gift, the Westminster Confession of Faith turns in its second article to describe the nature of this faith. In this article, there is a clear distinction between what is often termed faith in its general sense (*fides generalis*) and faith in its more special sense (*fides specialis*). In its general sense, faith is an acceptance of all that God reveals in his Word. Faith is the acknowledgment and conviction that the testimony of the Word of God is altogether true and unassailable. Because God, who is truth, speaks in his Word, the appropriate response to the Word is to recognize its divine authority and embrace its teaching (John 17:17). In its special sense, however, saving faith is the acceptance of, reception of, and resting upon Christ and the promise of the saving benefits of his comprehensive work as Mediator and Redeemer. For this reason, the Westminster Confession of Faith especially emphasizes that the "principal acts of saving faith are accepting, receiving, and resting on Christ alone for justification, sanctification, and eternal life, by virtue of the covenant of grace" (WCF 14.2). Because the testimony of the Word of God finds its focus and center in the person and work of

9. For helpful treatments of this question, see Hoekema, *Saved by Grace*, 144–45; S. M. Baugh, *Ephesians*, ed. H. Wayne House, Evangelical Exegetical Commentary (Bellingham, WA: Lexham Press, 2016), 160–61.

10. Murray, *Redemption Accomplished and Applied*, 111.

Jesus Christ, saving faith is the wholehearted acknowledgment and acceptance of the good news that all the blessings of salvation are ours in him.[11]

In the history of theological reflection on the nature of saving faith, a helpful distinction is drawn between three distinct, yet inseparable aspects of such faith: knowledge (*notitia*), conviction or assent (*assensus*), and trust (*fiducia*).

Faith as Knowledge

Though it may seem strange to modern ears to say that knowledge belongs to faith, it is clear that faith must include a knowledge or apprehension of the testimony provided in the Word of God, particularly the gospel testimony to the person and work of Jesus Christ. When the gospel message is proclaimed, hearers are called to believe in Jesus Christ for salvation. But no one can believe in Jesus Christ in any meaningful sense unless the person knows something about who Jesus is and what he has done to procure the person's salvation. As the apostle Paul declares in Romans 10:13–14:

> For "everyone who calls on the name of the Lord will be saved."
> How then will they call on him in whom they have not believed?
> And how are they to believe in him of whom they have never heard?
> And how are they to hear without someone preaching?

The testimony to the gospel that is found in the Scriptures includes at least three fundamental components: that all human beings are sinners in Adam, who by virtue of their original and actual sins are justly liable to condemnation and death; that Jesus Christ, the Son of God, who assumed our human nature, is the only Mediator, whose

11. The Heidelberg Catechism's definition of true faith also distinguishes faith in its general sense from faith in its special sense: "Q. 21. What is true faith? A. True faith is not only a sure knowledge, whereby I hold for truth all that God has revealed to us in His Word, but also a firm confidence which the Holy Spirit works in my heart by the gospel, that not only to others, but to me also, remission of sins, everlasting righteousness and salvation are freely given by God, merely of grace, only for the sake of Christ's merits." In this definition, the three aspects of true faith—knowledge, conviction or assent, and trust—are also clearly identified.

atoning death and redeeming work are able to restore fallen sinners to favor with God; and that the Christian life of gratitude is lived in the power of the Spirit, who renews believers after his image and will ultimately perfect them in holy obedience to God's will. While it is futile to try to identify exactly how much believers need to know in order to believe, it is certainly impossible for true faith to exist without a rudimentary knowledge of the gospel message in its principal parts.[12] Saving faith must not be confused with credulity or a willingness to believe what is neither known nor warranted by the testimony of God's Word.

In the history of theological reflection on the doctrine of faith, there are at least two ways in which the knowledge of faith has come into clear focus. First, a common distinction is drawn between "the faith by which we believe" (*fides qua creditur*) and "the faith which is believed" (*fides quae creditur*). "The faith by which we believe" is the act whereby believers embrace the promises of the gospel. The preponderance of biblical references describe faith in this way. But in some instances, the language of faith is used to refer to the content of the gospel attested in Scripture. Perhaps the clearest instance of this usage is Jude 3, which appeals to those whom God has called through the gospel "to contend for the faith that was once for all delivered to the saints" (cf. Gal. 1:23; 1 Tim. 4:1). Even though the second usage is less frequent, it offers compelling testimony to the fact that faith exists only by virtue of the testimony of the gospel, and that without some acquaintance with the gospel's teaching, believers would have no occasion to believe. And second, the traditional Roman Catholic doctrine of "implicit faith" (*fides implicitas*) seriously misrepresents what belongs to saving faith. According to this doctrine, members of the church may be regarded as true believers, even though they may not know much, if anything, about the church's official teaching. So

12. Cf. Hoekema, *Saved by Grace*, 141–42: "At this point we may ask, How much knowledge is necessary? Faith . . . must embrace the truth of the gospel and Christ's redemptive work for us. But how much of the gospel must one know to be saved? That is not easy to say. We must have enough knowledge to realize that we are sinners who need redemption, that we cannot save ourselves but that only Christ can redeem us from sin and from the wrath of God, and that Christ died and arose for us."

long as the church's members implicitly assume that whatever the church teaches is true, they do not need to have an explicit knowledge of that teaching.[13]

Faith as Conviction or Assent

The second aspect of faith is conviction or assent, the firm persuasion that the gospel message is true. It is not enough to know merely what the gospel teaches. Faith also requires the heartfelt conviction that the gospel promise of salvation on the basis of Christ's redeeming work is altogether trustworthy, and a matter of ultimate importance. When the apostle Paul speaks of faith in Romans 10, he not only affirms that it comes "through hearing" the Word of Christ. He also speaks of those who respond to the Word by confessing with their mouths and believing the gospel message in their hearts (Rom. 10:9). Saving faith is more, but not less, than believing the gospel. It is one thing to know the teachings that belong to the gospel message. But it is quite another thing to consent to these teachings, to embrace them from the heart and out of the conviction that all the promises of the gospel are reliable.

Faith as Confidence or Trust

One of the most important emphases of the Reformation's understanding of saving faith is that it produces trust in the gospel promise that Christ is able to save to the uttermost those who draw near to God through him (Heb. 7:25). Contrary to the Roman Catholic teaching that faith is merely an "intellectual" assent to the truths of the gospel, which needs to be "formed through love" by the sacraments, the Reformers especially emphasized the heartfelt confidence and assurance of God's favor that belongs to saving faith.[14] Saving

13. In his criticism of the Roman Catholic affirmation of "implicit faith," Calvin does not deny that believers remain ignorant of many things that God has revealed in his Word. But Calvin also insists that faith is not "heedless gullibility" but rests on a "knowledge not only of God but of the divine will" revealed in the gospel (*Institutes*, 3.2.2–3).

14. This Reformation emphasis is especially evident in the Heidelberg Catechism's definition of faith. But it is not absent from the Westminster Standards, which affirm that faith properly brings assurance while pastorally acknowledging the struggles that believers sometimes have in obtaining full assurance. For a

faith is more than mere knowledge of and assent to the truth of the gospel. As the apostle James notes, even the demons believe that God is one (James 2:19). They know and are even convinced of it, but such faith is not saving faith. Saving faith involves a personal and whole-hearted confidence in Christ himself, who believers are convinced has fully satisfied for all their sins. For this reason, the verb for "to believe," *pisteuo*, is ordinarily used in the New Testament with the prepositions "upon" (*epi*, e.g., Acts 16:31; 1 Tim. 1:16), "into" (*eis*, e.g., Gal. 2:16), and "in" (*en*, e.g., Mark 1:15). Faith believes "upon," "into," and "in" Christ. Through faith, believers enter into a life-embracing, mysterious union with Jesus Christ, which produces the confidence that he truly does save to the uttermost those who entrust themselves wholly to him.[15] Even though there may be circumstances that some-times diminish a believer's assurance of salvation, the consensus view of the Reformation is that saving faith includes confidence of God's grace in Christ.

Interestingly, the third article of chapter 14 in the Westminster Confession of Faith addresses in a pastoral way the confidence or trust that belongs to saving faith. While acknowledging that faith may be "different in degrees," sometimes weak, sometimes strong, and may often be "assailed [or] weakened" for a variety of reasons, it affirms nonetheless that saving faith will prevail. Believers, who place their trust in Christ for salvation, knowing that he is the "author and finisher" of their faith, will find their faith growing and increasing, even to the point of full assurance. Because faith rests in Christ and the promise of every spiritual blessing in him, it derives its strength not from itself but from him. Thus, even though it may be weak or small, the Savior in whom faith trusts is strong and great. B. B. War-field expresses this eloquently:

---

compelling defense of the continuity between the Heidelberg Catechism's empha-sis on assurance (following Calvin) and the Westminster Standards, see Sinclair B. Ferguson, *The Whole Christ: Legalism, Antinomianism, and Gospel Assurance—Why the Marrow Controversy Still Matters* (Wheaton, IL: Crossway, 2016), 185–94.

15. James Hope Moulton, *A Grammar of New Testament Greek* (Edinburgh: T. & T. Clark, 1949), 1:67–68: "To repose one's trust *upon* God or Christ was well expressed by *pisteuein epi*, the dative suggesting more of the state, and the accusa-tive more of the initial act of faith; while *eis* recalls at once the bringing of the soul *into* that mystical union which Paul loved to express by *en Christo*."

The *saving power* of faith resides thus not in itself, but in the Almighty Saviour on whom it rests. . . . It is not, strictly speaking, even faith in Christ that saves, but Christ that saves through faith. The saving power resides exclusively, not in the act of faith or the attitude of faith or the nature of faith, but in the object of faith.[16]

Repentance unto Life

1. Repentance unto life is an evangelical grace, the doctrine whereof is to be preached by every minister of the gospel, as well as that of faith in Christ.

2. By it, a sinner, out of the sight and sense not only of the danger, but also of the filthiness and odiousness of his sins, as contrary to the holy nature, and righteous law of God; and upon the apprehension of his mercy in Christ to such as are penitent, so grieves for, and hates his sins, as to turn from them all unto God, purposing and endeavouring to walk with him in all the ways of his commandments.

3. Although repentance be not to be rested in, as any satisfaction for sin, or any cause of the pardon thereof, which is the act of God's free grace in Christ; yet it is of such necessity to all sinners, that none may expect pardon without it. (WCF, chap. 15)

The Westminster Confession of Faith begins its treatment of repentance on the same note with which it began its description of saving faith: repentance is an "evangelical grace" because it, too, is worked by the Spirit of Christ through the gospel. The gospel call to repentance depends for its efficacy on the work of the Spirit. While repentance shares with faith the obligation that the hearer respond appropriately to the gospel call, it, too, is a grace granted through the ministry of the Holy Spirit. Every gospel minister must call his hearers to repentance, and he does so with the confidence that what the gospel demands God will grant. That repentance is an evangelical grace is explicitly confirmed in the book of Acts. When the apostle Peter reports to the church in Jerusalem that the Gentiles had "received the Word of

16. Benjamin B. Warfield, "The Biblical Doctrine of Faith," in *The Works of Benjamin B. Warfield*, vol. 2, *Biblical Doctrines* (1929; repr., Grand Rapids: Baker, 1981), 504.

God" and believed (Acts 11:1), he was obliged to answer the criticism of the circumcision party. Upon Peter's account of the way that the Holy Spirit had fallen on the Gentiles, his critics were silenced, and they glorified God, saying: "Then to the Gentiles also God has granted repentance that leads to life" (v. 18). Because repentance is God's gracious work, the apostle Paul urges Timothy to reprove his opponents in a spirit of gentleness in the hope that "God may perhaps grant them repentance leading to a knowledge of the truth" (2 Tim. 2:25).

Though repentance is as much an evangelical grace as faith, it involves a distinct response to the message of the gospel. Whereas faith is a heartfelt acknowledgment, conviction, and confidence that receives and rests in Christ for salvation, repentance is simultaneously a heartfelt sorrow for having provoked God by my sins and a heartfelt "joy in God through Christ" for his mercy.[17] "Repentance," as one of the two primary terms used in Scripture (*metanoeō*, "to change one's mind") suggests, involves a change of heart and mind with respect to my sins. On the one hand, repentance expresses itself in a heartfelt sorrow that my sins are an offense against God's holiness and the claims of his righteous law. Genuine repentance is rooted in what the apostle Paul describes as a "godly grief" for sin (2 Cor. 7:9–11). On the other hand, repentance is also rooted in an apprehension of God's mercy and grace in Christ. When sinners are called to repentance through the gospel, they are not merely called to repent through the ministry of the law, which exposes our sins for what they are and reminds us that we justly deserve condemnation and death on their account. Without sinners' having any understanding of God's mercy and grace, the law's exposure of our sinfulness and liability to God's just punishment, condemnation and death, could leave sinners only in a state of despair and fear. The gospel's announcement of God's grace and mercy in Christ toward undeserving sinners, however, produces a heartfelt delight and joy in turning from sin and seeking to live in a way that pleases God in Christ Jesus.[18]

17. I am here using language from the Heidelberg Catechism, which speaks of true conversion or repentance as being rooted in "heartfelt sorrow" for sin and "heartfelt joy in God through Christ" (89–90).

18. To emphasize this positive motivation for true repentance, Reformed theologians have often distinguished *legal* from *gospel* repentance. In his treatment of

The twin roots of such godly sorrow for sin and heartfelt joy in God's mercy bear two corresponding fruits. True repentance expresses itself negatively in the mortification of the old self, and positively in the quickening or vivification of the new self. For this reason, the second common term for "repentance" in the New Testament, *epistrephō* ("to turn around"), emphasizes the way in which godly sorrow and gospel joy produce the beginnings of new obedience. Such obedience involves turning away from sinful habits and a turning toward God and others in loving obedience. When sinners are sorry for their sins, they no longer find pleasure in them, but rather turn away from them, "purposing and endeavouring to walk with him [God] in all the ways of his commandments." When sinners find their joy in the grace of God in Christ, they earnestly desire to live a life that is pleasing to him. While repentance may in some cases take the form of a sudden and radical change of heart and life, the nature of true repentance is such that it involves a lifetime of continuous dying to sin and living more and more in a way that exhibits the fruits of repentance. In Luther's Ninety-five Theses, the first declares: "Our Lord and Master Jesus Christ, when he said, *Poenitentiam agite*, willed that the whole life of believers should be repentance."[19] As Anthony Hoekema remarks, "The fact that repentance is a lifelong activity has some important implications. First, it suggests that we must distinguish between an initial repentance at the beginning of the Christian life and a repentance which continues throughout that life. There is indeed a turning from sin to God that begins a person's Christian pilgrimage, but there is also one that characterizes the entire journey."[20]

---

this distinction, Calvin notes that gospel repentance surpasses a mere awareness of the gravity of sin and its consequences, and occurs only when sinners "aroused and refreshed by trust in God's mercy" turn to the Lord (*Institutes*, 3.3.4).

19. Martin Luther, *The Works of Martin Luther*, trans. Henry Eyster Jacobs (Philadelphia: Muhlenberg Press, 1943), 1:29. Cf. Calvin, *Institutes*, 3.3.20: "Indeed, this restoration [of the image of God] does not take place in one moment or one day or one year; but through continual and sometimes even slow advances God wipes out in his elect the corruptions of the flesh, cleanses them of guilt, consecrates them to himself as temples, renewing all their minds to true purity, that they may practice repentance throughout their lives and know that this warfare will end only at death."

20. Hoekema, *Saved by Grace*, 131.

Because repentance is inseparable from faith as an indispensable component of a proper response to the gospel, the Westminster Confession of Faith concludes by noting that no sinner may expect to enjoy God's gracious pardon without it. Though repentance is not the basis for a believer's confidence in God's free grace in Christ, it always accompanies faith. While faith alone receives and rests in Christ, such faith is never alone but always joined with true repentance.

Pastoral Implications of the Gospel Call to Faith and Repentance

In the light of my summary of the gospel call to faith and repentance, I will conclude with some pastoral observations for those who are called to gospel ministry.

First, ministers must proclaim the gospel call with joyful confidence. When you preach the gospel, calling lost sinners to faith and repentance, never forget that these are *evangelical graces*. God is pleased to use the presentation of the gospel to grant faith and repentance, and therefore you do not need to fear that what you call sinners to do in response to the message lies beyond their reach. Indeed, the gospel call does ask sinners to do what they cannot do of themselves. But God is pleased to grant the very thing he demands and promises to bless your ministry when you faithfully call sinners to salvation in Jesus Christ. The call of the gospel is a gracious summons that invites sinners to embrace Christ for salvation in the way of faith and repentance. Both faith and repentance spring from a ministry of the Word in the power of the Spirit that testifies to the truth that Christ will save to the uttermost all those who come to God through him.

Second, pastors must beware of confusing the gospel call with a doctrine of cheap grace. The second implication of the biblical doctrine of faith and repentance is that it warns all ministers of the gospel to beware of the temptation to avoid preaching repentance for fear of legalism or moralism. This temptation is particularly pressing within the evangelical church in our day. Within some circles, particularly dispensationalism, a categorical distinction is drawn between "carnal" and "spiritual" Christians. Carnal Christians are said to be those who embrace the gospel promise of free justification and forgiveness, but who have not yet turned from their sins in true repentance. They believe in Christ for salvation, but have not yielded or surrendered their lives to him in new obedience. A similar view is taught by those who hold to what is often called a "nonlordship" or "free-grace" view of salvation.[21] Those holding this view believe that the gospel promise of God's free acceptance through faith in Christ alone is compromised when the gospel call includes an emphasis on the necessity of repentance.[22] Faith alone is required for salvation, but repentance is in effect optional.[23]

The antidote to the fear of legalism, however, is not found in a form of gospel preaching that diminishes the call to repentance. As we have seen, faith and repentance are inseparable graces, and belong to any biblically faithful presentation of the gospel. No doubt it is possible to preach repentance in a legalistic manner, insinuating that such repentance is a kind of precondition to, and even a basis for, a sinner's acceptance with God. There is a type of preaching that confuses gospel repentance with legal repentance. In such preaching, repentance is exclusively grounded in the fearful apprehension of the law's exposure of my sin and God's just judgment upon it. When the gospel of Christ's saving work is properly presented in all its fullness and richness, however, it invites sinners to rest in Christ alone for salvation and at the same time moves them, out of an awareness of the costliness of their redemption through the atoning sacrifice of Christ, to view their sin with sorrow and to find delight in turning to God. The law alone does not bring any sinner to true repentance. Only the

21. Cf., e.g., Zane Hodges, *Harmony with God: A Fresh Look at Repentance* (Dallas: Redencion Viva, 2001), 57: "So far we have reached two fundamental conclusions about repentance. These are: (1) that repentance is not in any way a condition for eternal salvation; and (2) repentance is the decision to turn from sin to avoid, or bring to an end, God's temporal judgment."

22. See, e.g., David R. Anderson, *Free Grace Soteriology*, ed. James S. Reitman, rev. ed. (The Woodlands, TX: Grace Theology Press, 2012), 137–38.

23. For good summaries and critical assessments of these views, see Grudem, *"Free Grace" Theology*; Kenneth L. Gentry, *Lord of the Saved* (Chesnee, SC: Victorious Hope, 2010); Michael Horton, ed., *Christ the Lord: The Reformation and Lordship Salvation* (Grand Rapids: Baker, 1992); Ernst C. Reisinger, *What Should We Think of the Carnal Christian?* (Edinburgh: Banner of Truth, 1978); Ernst C. Reisinger, *Lord and Christ: The Implications of Lordship for Faith and Life* (Phillipsburg, NJ: P&R Publishing, 1994).

gospel, and a believing apprehension of God's rich mercy toward us in Christ, ultimately moves sinners to serve God with glad-hearted thankfulness. True repentance is suffused with faith, even as faith enjoys no life without repentance.

"Why the Marrow Controversy Still Matters"

Since this essay is included in a collection that aims to honor Sinclair Ferguson, it seems fitting to conclude with an encouragement to pastors to be familiar with a lesson about faith and repentance that can be gleaned from the Marrow Controversy. In his wonderful book *The Whole Christ*, Ferguson treats the Marrow Controversy as an illustration of how the grace of the gospel can be perverted when sinners are required to forsake their sin as a kind of "pre-requisite" or "precursor" to receiving Christ in faith.[24] Though Ferguson rightly emphasizes the inseparability of faith and repentance, he deftly analyzes the various ways in which the preaching of repentance can fall into legalism. When we forget that faith brings us into union with the "whole Christ" and all his saving benefits—which invariably include the evangelical graces of faith and repentance—we run the risk of preaching cheap grace on the one hand and legalism on the other. For fear of cheap grace, we call sinners to do something, namely, repent, in order to fit themselves for embracing Christ by faith. The warrant for receiving Christ by faith, then, becomes some subjective condition that we must first experience. Or for fear of legalism or moralism, we neglect to call sinners to repentance, as though this would compromise the gospel of God's free acceptance of sinners on the basis of Christ's work alone. The proper presentation of the gospel, however, aims to present Christ in all his fullness, as the Savior who has fully satisfied for all our sins and who by his Spirit brings us to a repentance that is born out of an awareness of his abounding grace toward unworthy sinners.

The lesson here for would-be gospel ministers is a simple one. It was the same lesson that Henry, the parishioner whom I mentioned in my introduction, had to learn.[25] Henry could not come to Christ

24. Ferguson, *Whole Christ*, 43. The terms "pre-requisite" and "precursor" are Ferguson's.
25. In addition to the pastoral implications I have identified, Henry's case also

in faith because he doubted the sincerity of his repentance and true conviction of sin. What he failed to see (but eventually did by God's grace) was that, as Ferguson so finely puts it, "neither conviction nor the forsaking of sin constitutes the warrant for the gospel offer. Christ himself is the warrant, since he is able to save all who come to him. He is offered without conditions. We are to go straight to him! It is not necessary to have any money in order to be able to buy Christ."[26] May this gospel truth inform the preaching of all those who are granted stewardship of the gospel of Jesus Christ.

Key Terms

antinomian
fides generalis
fides implicitas
fides qua creditur
fides quae creditur
fides specialis
legalism
ordo salutis

Recommendations for Further Reading

Bavinck, Herman. *Reformed Dogmatics*. Edited by John Bolt. Translated by John Vriend. Vol. 4, *Holy Spirit, Church, and New Creation*. Grand Rapids: Baker Academic, 2008. Pp. 96–175.

Ferguson, Sinclair B. *The Whole Christ: Legalism, Antinomianism, and Gospel Assurance—Why the Marrow Controversy Still Matters*. Wheaton, IL: Crossway, 2016. Pp. 177–229.

---

illustrates the danger of making a particular kind of conversion experience or narrative of grace the norm for all genuine believers. Though faith and repentance must be understood normatively in terms of their biblical profile, the actual experience of conversion by individual believers takes many different forms and comes to expression in a diversity of ways. For a good treatment of this point, see Herman Bavinck, *Reformed Dogmatics*, ed. John Bolt, trans. John Vriend (Grand Rapids: Baker Academic, 2008), 4:153–58.

26. Ferguson, *The Whole Christ*, 59–60.

Grudem, Wayne. *"Free Grace" Theology: 5 Ways It Diminishes the Gospel*. Wheaton, IL: Crossway, 2016.

Hoekema, Anthony. *Saved by Grace*. Grand Rapids: Eerdmans, 1989. Pp. 113–51.

Murray, John. *Redemption Accomplished and Applied*. Grand Rapids: Eerdmans, 2015. Pp. 111–22.

Discussion Questions

1. Why does the Westminster Confession of Faith describe faith and repentance as "evangelical" graces (chap. 14)? Explain why this is an important emphasis.

2. Identify three views of the relation between faith and repentance among Reformed theologians.

3. If faith and repentance are inseparable aspects of conversion, what difference might it make to say that one (logically) "precedes" or "follows" the other?

4. At the time of the Reformation, Calvin and others distinguished *gospel* from *legal* repentance. Define these two types of repentance, and explain why this distinction is important.

5. Describe and evaluate the so-called nonlordship view of salvation from the standpoint of a biblical understanding of the relation between faith and repentance.

6. In what way is the gospel compromised when repentance is regarded as a "pre-requisite" or "precursor" to receiving Christ in faith (cf. Ferguson on the "Marrow Controversy")?

16

PERSEVERANCE

The Hope-Full Gospel That
Encourages Abiding Faith

PAUL D. WOLFE

It was the spring of 1999. I was in my third year of study at Westminster Theological Seminary in Philadelphia, and my lineup of courses that spring semester was an embarrassment of riches.[1] Professor Alan Groves, teaching on the books of the Old Testament prophets. Dr. Richard Gaffin, teaching on the book of Acts and the letters of Paul. Dr. Gaffin *also* teaching on the person and work of Christ. (Yes, a Gaffin double-dose that semester.) And finally (fitting for this volume), Dr. Sinclair Ferguson, teaching on the ministry of the Holy Spirit, including the Spirit's ministry to preserve believers so that they persevere. "The Perseverance of the Saints" was heading number XI in the syllabus that semester. (Copies of my nearly illegible handwritten notes are available upon request. Yes, I still have them twenty years later. I may be the only one who can read them, but I'm glad I can. Recently I did again, to my profit.)

---

1. It was during those seminary days when I first met Sinclair Ferguson. I'm exceedingly grateful for the blessing that his ministry and friendship have been in my own life, and for the chance in this chapter to repay some of the debt.

The perseverance of the saints, which has to do with believers' abiding, is itself an abiding doctrine—it must be, since Scripture teaches it—which is why we can consult ancient class notes (from 1999) and historic creedal formulations (from centuries ago) and find ourselves instructed, edified, and challenged all over again. This is a truth whose origins are from of old, and yet that proves mercifully new every morning. Let us consider this doctrine, and the way in which it rightly shapes pastoral ministry to this day.

The Biblical and Confessional Basis of Perseverance

Reformed Affirmations

Since this chapter is the contribution of one Presbyterian minister to a volume in honor of another, I, like other contributors to this volume, have thought that the Westminster Confession of Faith of the 1640s seems a very good place to start. Chapter 17 in the confession is entitled "Of the Perseverance of the Saints," and its three sections affirm the doctrine admirably:

> 1. They, whom God hath accepted in his Beloved, effectually called, and sanctified by his Spirit, can neither totally nor finally fall away from the state of grace, but shall certainly persevere therein to the end, and be eternally saved.

There the Westminster divines make it clear whom they have in mind in this chapter: not anyone and everyone who claims or is claimed to be a Christian, but only those "accepted . . . , effectually called, and sanctified" by God. This means that even the term *saints* in the expression "the perseverance of the saints" needs to be clarified: those in view are not all those who are numbered among the members of God's visible church (though this membership is itself a saintliness of a sort, for this is to belong to the body that belongs to God in the world), but only those who have been saved and set apart unto God by regenerating, justifying grace. Sadly, there are church members who remain strangers to that grace. Happily, those who have known it "can neither totally nor finally fall away" from it. Though burdened with trials, and beset with temptations, and perhaps even wandering far as a result of those temptations, in their souls the seed of faith will ever remain. Thus the promise of perseverance.

> 2. This perseverance of the saints depends not upon their own free will, but upon the immutability of the decree of election, flowing from the free and unchangeable love of God the Father; upon the efficacy of the merit and intercession of Jesus Christ, the abiding of the Spirit, and of the seed of God within them, and the nature of the covenant of grace: from all which ariseth also the certainty and infallibility thereof.

There the divines give all the glory for believers' perseverance to the one who truly deserves it: the triune God, who chose them, and redeemed them, and abides with them, bringing them to life with a life that is truly eternal, and even binding himself to them with unbreakable cords of covenant love. The Bible does insist on perseverance, and calls believers to persevere, and this call and related warnings are genuine (e.g., "the one who endures to the end will be saved," Matt. 24:13); the promise is that God by his Spirit will enable his own to hear and heed that call.

> 3. Nevertheless, they may, through the temptations of Satan and of the world, the prevalency of corruption remaining in them, and the neglect of the means of their preservation, fall into grievous sins; and, for a time, continue therein: whereby they incur God's displeasure, and grieve his Holy Spirit, come to be deprived of some measure of their graces and comforts, have their hearts hardened, and their consciences wounded; hurt and scandalize others, and bring temporal judgments upon themselves.

Admittedly, for a doctrine designed to give comfort and encouragement, that final section may seem a rather dour note to end on. Temptation. Corruption. Neglect. Grievous sin. Divine displeasure. Deprivation. Hardening. Wounding. Scandal. Judgment. But those sobering lines bring much-needed clarification to this doctrine. After all, believers need to be warned as well as comforted. Wandering from God, and wandering far, is a very real prospect. The

Christian who reads those lines rightly falls to his knees, crying out to God for mercy to be guarded from that prospect, and then rises up with new wariness.

At the same time, we should notice the implication of grace in those lines. The people who may experience the sins and sorrows described there are those "accepted . . . , effectually called, and sanctified" by God (recall section 1). Indeed, it is precisely in response to sinful falls, and their fallout, that the genuine believer again puts perseverance on display: instead of totally and finally bailing out on the God he has grieved, he repents, and trusts, and rises up, and presses on, because the same God who accepted, called, and sanctified him in the first place remains ever faithful and just to forgive and restore him. So it turns out that the clarifying language in that third section proves doubly pastoral after all: it warns us of fearful spiritual possibilities, to be sure, but it also magnifies the grace of God, which is greater than all the sin and backsliding of his children. Here the possibility of wandering from God is acknowledged in the context of an affirmation of divine grace, and not the other way around.

When we glance at that Westminster language from the 1640s, the theological conflicts that raged among Dutch Calvinists a generation beforehand come to mind, when the proponents of Jacobus Arminius's theology called into question several tenets of prevailing Calvinist orthodoxy. Famously, their theological challenge was five-fold, eliciting from their opponents the so-called five points of Calvinism, of which the last was indeed the perseverance of the saints. It is noteworthy that of the five theological issues discussed in those debates, perseverance was the one that the Arminians admitted they needed to study more fully before they could be dogmatic about it. Speaking of "those who are incorporated into Christ by a true faith, and have thereby become partakers of his life-giving Spirit," the Arminian Remonstrants held back on any final pronouncement about perseverance:

> whether they are capable, through negligence, of forsaking again the first beginnings of their life in Christ, of again returning to this present evil world, of turning away from the holy doctrine which was delivered them, of losing a good conscience, of becom-

ing devoid of grace, that must be more particularly determined out of the Holy Scripture, before we ourselves can teach it with the full persuasion of our minds.[2]

The Calvinists who responded with their own five points harbored no such hesitancy on this subject! In the Canons of the Synod of Dort, Fifth Head, we find (as in Westminster) a candid acknowledgment of the reality of remaining sin in the lives of believers, but then comes this affirmation:

> By reason of these remains of indwelling sin, and the temptations of sin and of the world, those who are converted could not persevere in a state of grace if left to their own strength. But God is faithful, who having conferred grace, mercifully confirms and powerfully preserves them therein, even to the end.[3]

Here, too, credit is given where credit is due. Yes, the saints do persevere, but they do so because their faithful God "powerfully preserves them," and not because they are sufficiently strong on their own to pull it off.

Scripture Foundations

So the Calvinists of Dort affirmed the doctrine of perseverance. The divines of Westminster affirmed it after them. Generations of Reformed-minded believers have affirmed it ever since. But of course, the big question is, does Scripture affirm it?

Indeed it does!

The Perseverance of the Saints

We might turn to a host of places in Scripture where this doctrine is taught, whether explicitly or implicitly. (Which is why, for example,

---

2. "The Five Arminian Articles," in *The Creeds of Christendom, With a History and Critical Notes*, vol. 3, *The Evangelical Protestant Creeds*, ed. Philip Schaff, rev. David S. Schaff, 6th ed. (Grand Rapids: Baker, 1998), 548–49.

3. "The Canons of the Synod of Dort," in *The Creeds of Christendom, With a History and Critical Notes*, vol. 3, *The Evangelical Protestant Creeds*, ed. Philip Schaff, rev. David S. Schaff, 6th ed. (Grand Rapids: Baker, 1998), 593.

there is no paucity of Scripture proofs that the Westminster divines appended to their affirmations on perseverance that we noted above.) Space permits us to note only a few.

A fruitful—and thrilling—place to start is with the words of our Savior in John 10. Speaking of those who are his "sheep," he says: "I give them eternal life, and they will never perish, and no one will snatch them out of my hand. My Father, who has given them to me, is greater than all, and no one is able to snatch them out of the Father's hand" (John 10:28–29). Surely it would amount to just such a "snatching" if somebody who truly believed in Christ later repudiated Christ just as truly. In that case, the evil one would have won. Jesus speaks here of "eternal life." *Eternal.* Apart from the promise of perseverance, the life that Jesus gives is hardly worthy of that descriptor. "Present life," perhaps. But not "eternal life."

Consider as well Paul's testimony in Philippians 1: "And I am sure of this, that he who began a good work in you will bring it to completion at the day of Jesus Christ" (Phil. 1:6). Paul was sure, and he wanted the Philippians to be sure as well: the very fact that they had come to believe in Christ was evidence that God had begun a good work in them, and that work would remain eternally *in*complete if any of them later traded in their genuine faith for the genuine unbelief of their pagan past. And God is not one to leave his good works unfinished. Paul makes the same point in his benediction at the end of 1 Thessalonians: "Now may the God of peace himself sanctify you completely, and may your whole spirit and soul and body be kept blameless at the coming of our Lord Jesus Christ. He who calls you is faithful; he will surely do it" (1 Thess. 5:23–24). The implication is plain: for Paul, it was a matter of divine faithfulness that those who had come to believe in Christ would be kept for the *day* of Christ and presented thoroughly blameless on that day. Will God prove faithless in the end? By no means!

Paul's words at the climax of Romans 8 are, if anything, even more dramatic. He poses the crucial rhetorical question: "Who shall separate us from the love of Christ? Shall tribulation, or distress, or persecution, or famine, or nakedness, or danger, or sword?" (Rom. 8:35). Then he wonderfully answers his own question: "No, in all these things we are more than conquerors through him who loved us.

For I am sure that neither death nor life, nor angels nor rulers, nor things present nor things to come, nor powers, nor height nor depth, nor anything else in all creation, will be able to separate us from the love of God in Christ Jesus our Lord" (vv. 37–39). If someone who has been converted to Christ later reverts to unbelief, that person has been separated from the love of God in Christ Jesus our Lord, and it is precisely that prospect that Paul here resoundingly rules out.

One more. Consider Peter's praise at the beginning of his first epistle: "Blessed be the God and Father of our Lord Jesus Christ! According to his great mercy, he has caused us to be born again to a living hope through the resurrection of Jesus Christ from the dead, to an inheritance that is imperishable, undefiled, and unfading, kept in heaven for you, who by God's power are being guarded through faith for a salvation ready to be revealed in the last time" (1 Peter 1:3–5). The believer's faith is instrumental in the divine work of guarding him in this life until the reception of his everlasting inheritance in the life to come. And that's just it: it is a *divine* work, accomplished by divine power. Not only is the inheritance being kept; the heir is, too.

What we must appreciate about all these passages—the words of Jesus, and of Paul, and of Peter (and of course, these passages are just a sampler)—is that they all come crashing to the ground if we try to hold on to some notion that the genuine believer might totally and finally revert to unbelief. Imagine Jesus as meaning, "No one will snatch them out of my hand . . . although they might snatch themselves by a failure to persevere." Or imagine Paul as meaning, "Nothing in all creation will be able to separate us from the love of God in Christ Jesus our Lord . . . except for our own weakness." Or imagine Peter as meaning, "God's power is guarding us through faith for a salvation ready to be revealed in the last time . . . although he's not guarding us from the prospect of the failure of that faith." At that point, if Jesus or Paul or Peter meant anything like that, then those passages would be practically pointless—even cruel—because the implication would be that believers are left unguarded against the one enemy that is closest to home: namely, their own sinful nature. No, it cannot be. Instead, it must be that the divine promise to preserve and protect and defend is all-encompassing. And if it is, then the perseverance of the saints is guaranteed.

The Perseverance of the Saint

To reinforce this point, we may contemplate Christ as the one who himself persevered in the calling that his Father had given him. (I'm confident that this is a fruitful theological avenue to pursue, because my 1999 class notes tell me that the perseverance of the saints is the "realization of union with Christ in permanent form." Indeed it is. Were those the exact words of the Scottish lecturer or the American notetaker? Likely the former.)

Consider that Christ was and is "the Holy One of God." The disciples understood this, and said so (John 6:69), and the demons did, too: "What have you to do with us, Jesus of Nazareth? Have you come to destroy us? I know who you are—the Holy One of God" (Mark 1:24). Disciples *and* demons. Apparently, this truth was widely grasped! Christ was God's Holy One. What did that mean? It meant that he was set apart unto God: he belonged to God, and he demonstrated his belonging in devoted service. "The Holy One of God." And this is just what the word *saint* means. It means "someone set apart unto God in order to serve God."

We would blanch—for many reasons—at the suggestion that we might refer to our Savior as "Saint Jesus"! The term simply bears too much baggage to be used that way. But there is some vital truth in that admittedly strange-sounding manner of speaking. Understanding the term rightly, we can say that Jesus Christ was and is *the* preeminent "Saint."

And the point is this: as the Holy One of God, as the preeminent Saint in the whole of human history, Jesus persevered. He was set apart unto God in order to serve God, and he followed through on that service to the very end. Loved by the Father, who chose and ordained him, and endowed with the Spirit above measure, Jesus pressed on and finished.

This is precisely what made him the Adam that we sinners needed. The first Adam disobeyed God in the garden, and that disobedience was, among other things, a failure to persevere. Our original representative head had been called to love the Lord his God, and to keep going in that love, but he didn't make it. His obedience came to an end. Soon afterward, salvation was promised (Gen. 3:15), and surely that salvation would require a second Adam, a last Adam, who, unlike the first, would keep going in his love for God, and who would do so to the end, "to the point of death, even death on a cross" (Phil. 2:8). And he did!

A beautiful picture of Christ's perseverance is painted for us in John 13. A remarkable episode unfolds before our eyes: the incarnate divine Son kneels down to wash his disciples' feet. John introduces the account this way: "Now before the Feast of the Passover, when Jesus knew that his hour had come to depart out of this world to the Father, having loved his own who were in the world, he loved them to the end" (John 13:1). Notice that last phrase: "to the end." That might have a chronological meaning: as in "until the conclusion of his earthly sojourn." Or it might have a qualitative meaning, as in "to the uttermost of sacrifice, to the deepest depths of human need." Or it might deliberately mean both! In any case, it certainly captures the truth of our Savior's persevering, loving service. Whereas the first Adam did not love to the end when put to the test, this last Adam will. No matter how long it takes, no matter how deep he must go, no matter what it will require of him to kneel down and serve and save, he must, and will, press on. And he did. To the end.

What does this truth about Christ have to do with the perseverance of believers? Much in every way! First, we may be reassured that Christ, who persevered to the end of his earthly mission, will also persevere in his heavenly ministry at his Father's right hand. As nineteenth-century Dutch theologian Herman Bavinck put it, "In his state of exaltation there still remains much for Christ to do,"[4] and surely that includes the work of guarding believers and getting them to glory. Again, Bavinck: "Because Christ is a perfect Savior, who brings not only the possibility but also the actuality of salvation, He cannot and may not and will not rest before those who are His own have been bought by His blood, been renewed by His Spirit, and brought where He is, there to be the spectators and sharers of His glory (John 14:3 and 17:24)."[5] If a believer departs from the faith and fails to reach the world to come, it can only mean that Christ was not

---

4. Herman Bavinck, *Reformed Dogmatics*, ed. John Bolt, trans. John Vriend, vol. 3, *Sin and Salvation in Christ* (Grand Rapids: Baker Academic, 2006), 568.

5. Herman Bavinck, *Our Reasonable Faith*, trans. Henry Zylstra (Grand Rapids: Baker, 1977), 553.

a perfect Savior after all, because in that case Christ himself would have failed to follow through on his own ministry to the end of the age. The Christian can take heart: Jesus, the Holy One of God, *still* perseveres! He holds on to us, and he will never let go.

Second, Christ's perseverance connects to our own in that God's great, overarching purpose for the redemption of his people is that we should be "conformed to the image of his Son, in order that he might be the firstborn among many brothers" (Rom. 8:29). In other words, God's purpose is that the character of Christ should be reproduced in us, and thus the very pattern of Christ's experience replayed in our own. Our Elder Brother, loved by the Father and endowed with the Spirit, showed himself to be a Son who held on to his Father's Word to the end, and now that same character must be true of those who are united with him by that same Spirit. Our Elder Brother persevered in suffering on the way to glory, and now it shines as a mark of our adoption into God's family that that same pattern becomes our own: "The Spirit himself bears witness with our spirit that we are children of God, and if children, then heirs—heirs of God and fellow heirs with Christ, provided we suffer with him in order that we may also be glorified with him" (vv. 16–17). As Peter puts it, "And after you have suffered a little while, the God of all grace, who has called you to his eternal glory in Christ, will himself restore, confirm, strengthen, and establish you" (1 Peter 5:10). It is an aspect of our perseverance in union with Christ that we persevere *like* Christ. No, the perseverance is not identical: he pressed on as the Redeemer; we do so as the redeemed. But it is certainly a Christlike steadfastness that the Spirit works in us and brings out of us.

The truth of Christ's own perseverance helps us to understand the tragic phenomenon that is apostasy from the faith: some who claim to trust in Christ forsake him down the road, repudiating the faith altogether and never returning to it. As grievous as this is—and many of us have known the heartbreak of seeing it happen—apostasy is hardly a stumbling block to the doctrine of perseverance, since we have already noticed what that doctrine does and does not assert: not that everyone who claims to be a Christian will certainly persevere in that claim, but that those who have known true saving grace will certainly remain in it. The apostle John, referring to apostates, puts it this way: "They went out from us, but they were not of us; for if they had been of us, they would have continued with us. But they went out, that it might become plain that they all are not of us" (1 John 2:19).

Thus, we can add this dimension as well: those who finally depart from the faith must never have been savingly united with Jesus in the first place, because Christ is the one who perseveringly holds on to believers and reproduces his own steadfastness in their lives. To depart from the faith altogether is to show oneself to have been a stranger to Christ all along. In effect, Christ can say to them, "I never knew you, for those I know I grasp and never let go, and they become like me, and walk like me, and persevere like me." To be sure, it is a hard word to imagine. The believer, however, can take comfort that he will never hear it. Faith looks to Christ and finds in him the steadfast Savior that we need. We continue with God's people, as John puts it, and this is because Christ continues with us first.

Perseverance and Pastoral Ministry

Having briefly considered the perseverance of the saints in union with Christ as we find it in Scripture, we turn now to its impact in the work of pastoral ministry. What difference does it make for ministers who embrace this doctrine?

Purpose in Preaching

One of the fruits that the doctrine of perseverance bears in ministry is the sense of purpose it adds to preaching. Charles Spurgeon said so, and, since Spurgeon has been named the "Prince of Preachers," his testimony definitely gets our attention!

Of course, Spurgeon loved to preach the gospel. "Tell me the day I do not preach," he said: "I will tell you the day in which I am not happy."[6] Thus, it is jarring to hear Spurgeon remark that any consideration could have caused him to "renounce the pulpit." What prospect provoked such strong language from him? It was, he explained, the prospect of preaching the gospel with the doctrine of perseverance

---

6. Charles H. Spurgeon, "Foretastes of the Heavenly Life," in *Spurgeon's Sermons*, vol. 3 (Grand Rapids: Baker, 2004), 142.

removed from it. Deny that doctrine, he said, and preaching proves pointless and the gospel is gutted of good news. Spurgeon put it this way:

> O how I love that doctrine of the perseverance of the saints. I renounce the pulpit when I can not preach it, for the gospel seems to be a blank desert and a howling wilderness—a gospel as unworthy of God as it would be beneath even my acceptance, frail worm as I am—a gospel which saves me to-day and rejects me to-morrow—a gospel which puts me in Christ's family one hour, and makes me a child of the devil the next—a gospel which justifies and then condemns me—a gospel which pardons me, and afterward casts me to hell. Such a gospel is abhorrent to reason itself, much more to the God of the whole earth. But on the other ground of faith, that "He to the end must endure, As sure as the earnest is given," we do enjoy a sense of perfect security even as we dwell in this land of wars and fightings.[7]

Once again, Prince Charles put it powerfully. The Bible's teaching that believers endure makes the good news truly, thoroughly good, and thus gives the preacher a gospel worthy of preaching, one that encourages his own perseverance in its faithful proclamation.

Such encouragement is needed because preaching requires the personal, sacrificial investment of the preacher himself—perhaps like few other aspects of pastoral ministry. The man who mounts the pulpit to declare God's Word does so as one who "spend[s] and [is] spent" for the task (2 Cor. 12:15). The words he speaks during those few minutes on Sunday have hours behind them of study, and prayer, and wrestling with the Word, and seeking wisdom. (Indeed, not just hours, but years.) As Paul reminded the Thessalonians concerning his ministry among them, he and his fellow servants "were ready to share with you not only the gospel of God but also our own selves" (1 Thess. 2:8). Preaching is intensely personal, not in the sense that the minister preaches himself (God forbid!), but in the sense that the minister pours himself into his preaching. "For what we proclaim is not ourselves, but

7. Spurgeon, "Foretastes of the Heavenly Life," 140.

Jesus Christ as Lord, with ourselves as your servants for Jesus' sake" (2 Cor. 4:5). Paul and those with him did not proclaim themselves; instead, they were servants, and that service was profoundly sacrificial, preaching included. And so it has been for preachers ever since.

Not only so, but preaching is a task to be carried on "in season and out of season," and at times in the face of overt opposition: "For the time is coming when people will not endure sound teaching, but having itching ears they will accumulate for themselves teachers to suit their own passions, and will turn away from listening to the truth and wander off into myths" (2 Tim. 4:2–4). There are Sundays when the preacher steps up to the pulpit, keenly aware of the fact that his message that day runs counter to prevailing cultural moods, and perhaps moods within the congregation as well. And even on those Sundays when that reality is not quite so acute, still the world, the flesh, and the devil are always arrayed against the truth he has to proclaim.

So the question becomes: what sustains a man in this work that requires such perseverance of his own, and that might otherwise wear him down and make him quit? What motivates a man to spend himself, and to do so when it feels out of season, and when strong winds are blowing against him? The answer, in part, is the knowledge that the gospel he preaches is just that—gospel, good news—and it is the biblical doctrine of perseverance that makes it so. We say that ours is a religion of hope, but if the best the believer can say about himself is "I believe today, but who knows about tomorrow?," then we have inadvertently taken away with one hand the hope we first gave with the other. Thanks to the doctrine of perseverance, the preacher has a message that is truly hope-*full*, which is just what he needs to get out of bed in the morning and rise up and pour himself into the labor of love that is Christian ministry.

And because it is a message of such hopefulness, it is also powerfully used by God to accomplish his own saving purposes. Take the doctrine of perseverance away, says Spurgeon, and the preacher is left with a message of divine vacillation, and come-and-go Christian confidence, and such a message as that is useful . . . to do what, exactly? Though God deals mercifully with his children whose grasp of the gospel is foggy, and often does not give them over to the logical consequences of their foggy thinking (every single one of us should be grateful for that), still it must be said that a Christianity in which the perseverance of the saints is denied is a message that has the potential to make for fearful Christians who are especially vulnerable to the winds and waves of fashionable doctrine and moral temptation.

This is because the gospel itself as they have come to grasp it has a major hole in it—a hole where strong hope ought to be—and people often go looking for something else, somewhere, anywhere, to fill in the hole and remedy the deficit. On the other hand, a Christianity with the perseverance of the saints affirmed, and embraced, and celebrated—in other words, a truly biblical Christianity—is especially mighty in the hands of God to reassure and strengthen his people, as well as to rescue lost souls who ache deeply for "a sure and steadfast anchor" (Heb. 6:19). Of course, God is able to do great things by means of all sorts of instruments (again, every one of us should be grateful for that)—including flawed men and women and sermons and books and hymns and prayers—and yet should the preacher not desire to wield the sharpest of swords? Imagine the difference it makes for a man to take in hand a sword engraved with this inscription: "I am sure of this, that he who began a good work in you will bring it to completion at the day of Jesus Christ."

Resting in God's Will

Another blessing that flows from a right understanding of the doctrine of perseverance is the reassurance it provides the minister when dealing with difficult pastoral cases.

We noticed above that there are sobering realities that we need to come to grips with when it comes to perseverance. First, there is the prospect that even genuine believers may wander far from God. At first glance, that might seem only disheartening, but here we can highlight the encouraging side as well: the minister who's in the position of caring for such a wayward Christian need not conclude that grace is absent in that person's life, and always was. The minister, even then, can appeal to that person's knowledge of Christ and experience of the grace of Christ as a way of winning the person back to a place of strength and standing.

Second, we recognized the reality of apostasy among members of the visible church. Some who profess faith later reject it and never return. We have noted that this phenomenon does not contradict the doctrine of perseverance, but here we can keep going and positively encourage the minister to rest in the goodness, wisdom, and power of God. The minister can trust that the purposes of God will surely come to fruition, including the everlasting salvation of all those chosen, redeemed, and regenerated, even if, for now, there remains an element of mystery—and even heartbreak—about those purposes. God will certainly get his chosen ones home.

In this connection, Paul's words in 2 Timothy 2:19 are crucial: having named Hymenaeus and Philetus as those "who have swerved from the truth" (v. 18), Paul adds, "But God's firm foundation stands, bearing this seal: 'The Lord knows those who are his,' and, 'Let everyone who names the name of the Lord depart from iniquity.'" No question, apostasy is a bitter reality, but those words of Paul are sweet: "The Lord knows those who are his." The Lord knows infallibly, though we do not. He sees people's hearts, though we do not. And he knows his own savingly, and eternally. He knows them in such a way as to preserve them and get them to glory. He rescues them so that they depart from iniquity and reach the world to come. In that truth, the minister may always rest. In fact, there he *must* rest.

Reflecting on Paul's words in that 2 Timothy verse, John Calvin writes, "We know too well, by experience how much scandal is produced by the apostasy of those who at one time professed the same faith with ourselves"—especially when they were "Christians" of some reputation and prominence.[8] He continues: "This is the subject which Paul has now in hand; for he declares that there is no reason why believers should lose heart, although they see those persons fall, whom they were wont to reckon the strongest. He makes use of this consolation, that the levity or treachery of men cannot hinder God from preserving his Church to the last."[9] Paul's statement ("The Lord knows those who are his") "reminds us," Calvin says, "that we must not judge, by our own opinion, whether the number of the elect is great or small; for what God hath sealed he wishes to be, in some respect, shut up from us. Besides, if it is the prerogative of God to

8. John Calvin, *Commentaries on the Second Epistle to Timothy*, in *Calvin's Commentaries*, vol. 21, trans. William Pringle (Grand Rapids: Baker, 1998), 226.

9. Calvin, *Commentaries on the Second Epistle to Timothy*, 226.

know who are his, we need not wonder if a great number of them are often unknown to us, or even if we fall into mistakes in making the selection."[10] Finally, Calvin concludes:

> Hence arises a twofold advantage. First, our faith will not be shaken, as if it depended on men; nor shall we be even dismayed, as often happens, when unexpected events take place. Secondly, being convinced that the Church shall nevertheless be safe, we shall more patiently endure that the reprobate go away into their own lot, to which they were appointed; because there will remain the full number, with which God is satisfied. Therefore, whenever any sudden change happens among men, contrary to our opinion and expectation, let us immediately call to remembrance, "The Lord knoweth who are his."[11]

Paul's words, and Calvin's words explaining them, certainly have the effect of putting the minister in his place, do they not?—mindful of his own limitations, lacking access to a list of the elect, powerless to prevent the apostasy of some, and, when it happens, grieving what feels like a death in the family—and yet it is precisely in that humble place that abundant consolation may be found. We need not lose heart. Nothing can hinder God from preserving his chosen ones so that they persevere. Our faith need not be shaken. God will be satisfied, and therefore so may we. For any minister, to see a Christian depart from the faith and eventually excommunicated is as bad as it gets. But in those moments, when we remember that "the Lord knows those who are his," when we bring to mind the sure promise that he will preserve his elect so that they persevere, when we cast our gaze upward again at his infinite goodness and unsearchable wisdom and almighty power, then we find strength to rise up and persevere in our own calling after all. In short, it's OK that we don't know everything, and can't do everything, because it's enough to know that God does, and God can, and he will get his true children home.

10. Calvin, *Commentaries on the Second Epistle to Timothy*, 227.
11. Calvin, *Commentaries on the Second Epistle to Timothy*, 227–28.

The Perseverance of the Minister

Finally, we may note that the perseverance of the saints touches down in a minister's life most personally, in the sense that he himself is numbered among those saints and can rest in the knowledge that Christ is preserving *him.*

I had this point driven home not long ago in a remarkable conversation with a beloved Christian brother and fellow minister who knew that his time on earth was quickly drawing to a close. Dr. Howard Griffith, longtime pastor of All Saints Reformed Presbyterian Church in Richmond, Virginia, and then professor of systematic theology and academic dean at Reformed Theological Seminary in Washington, D.C., was diagnosed with cancer in 2018. Howard and his wife, Jackie, fought a brave, faithful, prayer-full battle against his disease for nearly a year. Then in March 2019, Howard and Jackie were advised by his doctors that his illness had progressed to such a degree that further treatment would not be wise. Their response was to heed that advice, and to make preparations for his homegoing.

I visited with Howard less than a week before his death. It was the last lengthy conversation I would enjoy with him in this life. Remarkably, in those potent, poignant moments, our conversation turned to the topic . . . of this chapter! Caring brother that he was, Howard asked me how *I* was doing (he often did), and I mentioned the opportunity to write this chapter about the perseverance of the saints and its payoff in pastoral ministry (I knew he'd be interested), and the mere mention of it caused him to light up, and sit up, and share with me what the doctrine of perseverance meant to him. He even gave me Scripture reading recommendations! "Read John 10," he said. I did. And as you surely noticed, it is included in this chapter. "Read Romans 8," he said. I did. I put that passage in, too.

Finally, Howard summed up the doctrine of perseverance in just a few words. What it boils down to, he said, is this:

"God's going to get you through this. It's not you."

I doubt that I'll ever forget that conversation, and that summation.

"God's going to get you through this. It's not you."

So said Howard Griffith, knowing that he'd soon be going home to Jesus.

In those moments, the doctrine of the perseverance of the saints came down off the bookshelf, arose from the pages of the systematic theology textbooks, emerged from the handwritten notes from seminary theology lectures, and landed squarely in the living room—and make no mistake, it was a *living* room, indeed, for even then Howard was so full of *life*—and touched down in the most powerful, practical way. Howard Griffith had served the Lord faithfully for decades as a minister himself, pastoring, and then teaching. In March 2019, he could look back and see how the Lord had mercifully preserved him in faith all those years, and he could also look forward and trust that the Lord would keep preserving him when his calling would soon become the calling to close his eyes. "God's going to get you through this," he said. "It's not you," he said. This man who had preached and taught that the saints persevere because God preserves them had clearly internalized that truth.

Howard so loved the doctrine of the believer's union with Christ. Over the years, we had talked a lot about that one, too. So he knew that he was bound to Christ by the Spirit through faith, and that Christ would never let him go. He knew that Christ's character was being forged in him. He knew that Christ's storyline of suffering unto glory had become his own. He knew that Christ, who had persevered to the end, and still does, would make sure that Howard did, too. And he did. On March 20, 2019, Howard closed his eyes. And Christ loved him to the end. Christ held him to the end, and then ushered him into the most glorious new beginning.

What makes Howard's testimony fitting to share in this volume is that Howard, like so many of us, enjoyed the opportunity to study God's truth under Sinclair's instruction. Howard had even hoped to contribute a chapter of his own to this work. Sadly, that was not to be. (It would have been a very good chapter, no doubt.) But perhaps, in this different way, Howard has made a contribution after all in honor of a beloved professor and friend. Howard's testimony spoke volumes. I pray that the record of it here will prove a blessing in this one.

So with gratitude for Sinclair's own persevering faith and faithfulness, and for that of so many, like Howard, who learned from him, may we say: thanks be to our triune God. My fellow ministers, take heart. It's not you. It's God. And he's going to get you through this. He's going to get you home.

Key Terms

apostasy
Arminianism
backsliding
perseverance
union with Christ

Recommendations for Further Reading

Cunningham, William. *Historical Theology*. Edinburgh: Banner of Truth, 1960. See chap. 25, "The Arminian Controversy," esp. sec. 14, "Perseverance of Saints."
Murray, John. *Redemption Accomplished and Applied*. Grand Rapids: Eerdmans, 2015. See chap. 8, "Perseverance."
Turretin, Francis. *Institutes of Elenctic Theology*. Phillipsburg, NJ: P&R Publishing, 1992. Chap. 15, sec. 16.

Discussion Questions

1. Where in Scripture do we see the doctrine of the perseverance of the saints taught, whether explicitly or implicitly?
2. In what ways do we see perseverance in Jesus' life and ministry? What difference does it make to know that Jesus himself persevered, and still does?
3. Marshal the most plausible arguments you can think of *against* this doctrine. How might you biblically answer those challenges?
4. How might you counsel a fellow believer who struggles with fears about the prospect of apostasy? Have you wrestled with such fears yourself?
5. Think of a believer you know whose persevering faith has shone in the midst of trials. What stands out about that person's example?
6. What difference does the doctrine of perseverance make for the pastor in his preaching? In his private counseling?

17

ASSURANCE OF FAITH

Pastoral Wisdom for
Struggling Christians[1]

JOEL R. BEEKE

We live in a day in which many people mistakenly assure themselves that they are Christians, usually based on some form of presumption or "easy believism." But they do not evince the marks of a true work of grace. How dreadful it will be for the self-deceived on judgment day when Christ denies to have known them (Matt. 7:21–23)! On the other hand, there are those who embrace a kind of "hard believism." There may be solid biblical evidence that they are children of God, but they set the bar too high or look for evidences that they have no right to expect. A proper understanding of assurance will demonstrate that the fruit of the new birth in one's life is indispensable evidence of salvation, but also show that true, albeit small, marks

---

1. I am honored to write in this volume for Sinclair Ferguson, who has been one of my best friends and mentors for the last four decades. From the days I sat under his superlative teaching and moving prayers as a PhD student at Westminster Seminary, to the numerous talks we've had in sharing each other's conversion and spiritual experiences as well as on a variety of theological subjects, to the many favors he has done for me until today in writing sterling forewords and endorsements for my books, I owe him an incalculable debt. Sinclair, thanks so much for your multifaceted friendship: it is one of my most treasured gifts on earth, and I pray that it will be an eternal friendship around the Lamb's throne!

of grace should not be despised (Zech. 4:10). How are pastors to consider these challenges?

Scripture speaks of a "full assurance of understanding"; "full assurance of hope"; "full assurance of faith" (Col. 2:2; Heb. 6:11, 18–19; 10:22).[2] There are a number of important reasons for seeking to attain to and grow in assurance, not the least of which is the fact that our understanding of assurance of faith determines the soundness of our understanding of spiritual life. We can be orthodox in many areas, yet be unsound in our understanding of this key doctrine of Scripture. "Assurance is the conscious confidence that we are in a right relationship with God through Christ," writes Sinclair Ferguson. "It is the confidence that we have been justified and accepted by God in Christ, regenerated by the Spirit, and adopted into his family, and that through faith in him we will be kept for the day when our justification and adoption are consummated in the regeneration of all things."[3]

Thomas Brooks (1608–80) titled his book on assurance *Heaven on Earth*,[4] partly because having assurance greatly enriches our lives with peace and hope and joy even now, while it hastens our longing for heaven hereafter. It enriches our communion with God, enhances our zeal in Christian service, accelerates our sanctification, and emboldens us in our confession of the gospel before a dying world. Assurance is the nerve center of doctrine put in *use*, as the Puritans would say—that is, God's truth applied to our own lives and to the life of the world. It entwines itself with the work of the Spirit in every link in the chain of salvation, touching every facet of salvation as we come to experience it and live it out. Assurance is broad in scope, profound in depth, and glorious in height.

How important this whole question of assurance is! Full assurance is not essential to the being of faith, but it is vital for the well-being

2. Scripture quotations in this chapter are from the KJV.

3. Sinclair B. Ferguson, "The Reformation and Assurance," *Banner of Truth* 643 (April 2017): 20; cf. 30n1. This paper is largely an abridgment of Joel R. Beeke, *Knowing and Growing in Assurance of Faith* (Fearn, Scotland: Christian Focus, 2017), and Joel R. Beeke, *The Quest for Full Assurance: The Legacy of Calvin and His Successors* (Edinburgh: Banner of Truth, 1999). Used with permission.

4. Thomas Brooks, *Heaven on Earth: A Treatise on Christian Assurance* (London: Banner of Truth, 1961).

of our faith. Though it is possible to be saved without assurance, it is scarcely possible to be a healthy Christian without assurance.

In this chapter, after addressing a few introductory questions, I will address a variety of issues related to assurance of salvation by expounding and applying to pastoral life and ministry the most important Reformed confessional chapter ever written on this subject: Westminster Confession of Faith, chapter 18.

Why Do Many Christians Lack Assurance?

Despite its importance, many Christians lack assurance. Some claim to never struggle with assurance even though their lives show little, if any, marks of true Christianity. They think they have it when their lives show that they do not. Their presumption may very well pave the road to hell for them. Other people say that they long to have assurance, but cannot ever seem to find or embrace it. It is a painfully personal matter for them, for they have struggled desperately with assurance, sometimes for many years.

Some reasons that a genuine believer may struggle with assurance include:

- Conscious awareness of sin, especially indwelling sin;
- False conceptions of God's character and of his gospel;
- Lack of clarity on justification by faith;
- Lack of confessing Christ;
- Disobedience and backsliding;
- Ignorance of satisfying evidences of grace;
- Possessing a doubting or negative disposition;
- Lack of clarity concerning the circumstances of conversion;
- Looking for the wrong kind of experience;
- Lack of acknowledging what God has done; and
- Being attacked by Satan.

This is a rather formidable list and urgently calls for us as shepherds to preach on these matters for our sheep, as well as on the whole doctrine of assurance of salvation. As a pastor, I have encountered all these reasons for believers' lacking assurance on numerous occasions—some more than others. I have not only spent many hours counseling believers who could not seem to rise above low levels of assurance at best, but often discovered that when I preach from Scripture on one or more of these reasons for lacking assurance, attention is rapt in the church. Preaching from Scripture about why Christians lack assurance, and then stressing how the Word of God—such as many of the passages in 1 John that deal with assurance—can deliver believers from the bondage of these reasons, is not only soul-liberating for the believer but also pastorally rewarding for the minister. One of my greatest joys in ministry is witnessing my dear sheep grow in assurance of faith and become robust and zealous Christians for the triune God. As I often say to my students, that is a minister's real wages—to see believers grow in the grace and knowledge of Christ and in personal assurance of their own salvation.

When we preach from chapters such as Romans 8 and 1 John 2 on how believers may gain assurance by prayerfully meditating on the promises of God, appropriating them by faith, and examining our lives by the marks that he has given us in his Word, the Holy Spirit often uses such messages to lift up the downcast so that they are delivered from the bondage of doubts and fears. As the Puritans were fond of emphasizing, we need a Word-guided, Spirit-assisted self-examination that arrives at a conclusion: yes or no. Too much or too little self-examination arrives at no safe conclusion. It stops short of certainty, and leaves us in despair, or with a mere "perhaps" or "maybe." We should never rest satisfied with bare conjectures or presumption. By the Spirit's co-witnessing with the believer's own conscience that he is a child of God under the faithful preaching of God's Word (and the faithful administration of the sacraments), the believer can grow immensely in assurance of salvation.

Is Assurance of Faith Biblical and Normative?

True Christians yearn for divine affirmation that they are saved in and by Christ. Thankfully, Scripture abounds with testimonies of God's servants' being assured of his saving mercies toward them. There is, however, direct proportionality between faith and assurance. Strong faith tends to embrace strong assurance, and weak faith tends to embrace weak assurance. All Scripture affirms that assurance is rooted in faith that receives God's gracious redemption in Christ and rests in his Word of promise.[5]

In the Old Testament, faith is often related to assurance. At the call of God, Abram ("by faith," Heb. 11:8) set out from Ur of the Chaldees in search of an unknown country. From this beginning, his faith grew in both depth of conviction and scope of vision, until he became "strong in faith, giving glory to God; and being fully persuaded that, what he had promised, he was able also to perform" (Rom. 4:20–21).

The concept of faith as resting or relying on "the LORD" runs throughout the entire Old Testament (2 Kings 18:5, 22; 1 Chron. 5:20; Pss. 86:2; 143:8; Prov. 3:5; 16:20; 28:25; Jer. 49:11; Zeph. 3:2). The prophets often spoke with assurance of a future-oriented hope that God will rule the nations and punish the wicked (Isa. 2; 11; 13–25; 46–47; Jer. 25; 43; 46–51; Ezek. 25–32; 38–39). And the Psalms revel in assurance of faith, even in the midst of the turmoil of battling for faith in the midst of intense struggles of soul (Pss. 78; 106; 121; 136).

In the New Testament, God's new utterance in the words and deeds of Christ brings fuller assurance of present salvation (Heb. 1:1–2). Types, shadows, prophecies, promises, and expectations are fulfilled through its inaugurated Christocentric eschatology as the Spirit's work in his people intensifies (cf. Joel 2:28; Acts 2:16–21). Believers may know that they know God (John 17:3), "are the children of God" (Rom. 8:14–16), currently possess eternal life (1 John 5:13), and are eternally secure (John 10:28–29; 2 Tim. 1:12).

Assurance is a constitutive element of saving faith, even if it is only in seed form (Heb. 11:1). Scripture shows that assurance of salvation is the normal possession of Christians in principle, despite varying measures of conscious enjoyment of it. Though some degree of assurance for believers is normal, that normativity does not make assurance essential for salvation (see Heb. 10:22; 2 Peter 1:10; 1 John 5:13). From the testimony of the Scriptures, it is clear that it is our duty to sincerely and earnestly seek to attain to large measures of assurance of faith.

---

5. Much of this section is gleaned and summarized from Robert Letham's helpful thesis, "The Relationship between Saving Faith and Assurance of Salvation" (ThM thesis, Westminster Theological Seminary, 1976).

This is particularly true for us as pastors engaged in the daily challenges of ministry. Over the last four decades of ministry, I have repeatedly experienced that this precious truth of the assurance of my own salvation, being grounded in God's promises and evidenced by the Spirit's saving and witnessing work in my own heart and life, has given me the staying power I needed to avoid becoming a hireling who abandons the sheep entrusted to my care. Without assurance of my own salvation and of my internal call to the ministry, I would certainly have resigned from the ministry on several occasions over the decades. In spite of my sin and suffering, as well as challenges from personal critics, the assurance that Christ is mine and that I belong to him has provided me with confidence and comfort in the grueling work of sermon preparation, the needy work of pulpit proclamation, and the challenging work of leading both my personal family and my larger church family. The more we know and grow as pastors in assurance of our own salvation, the more we experience stability and joy in Christ in our personal, domestic, and church life.

Relative to this duty of seeking to know and grow in assurance, it is helpful to consider which of the possible three situations we may find ourselves in.

Three Possibilities concerning Assurance

No group of theologians worked harder or were better at spelling out the biblical doctrine of assurance of faith than did the seventeenth-century Puritans. The Puritan doctrine of assurance was formally codified by the Westminster Confession of Faith in chapter 18, "Of the Assurance of Grace and Salvation"—the most important chapter devoted to assurance in any Reformed confession. It is a biblical, experiential, pastoral, and practical masterpiece spelled out for us in four short paragraphs. Under several headings I want to unpack these four paragraphs, since I believe there is no better way to explain the basics of assurance of faith than to expound chapter 18 of the Westminster Confession.

The first paragraph presents the three possibilities we have in relation to assurance:

Although hypocrites, and other unregenerate men, may vainly deceive themselves with false hopes and carnal presumptions of being in the favour of God, and estate of salvation (which hope of theirs shall perish): yet such as truly believe in the Lord Jesus and love him in sincerity, endeavouring to walk in all good conscience before him, may, in this life, be certainly assured that they are in the state of grace, and may rejoice in the hope of the glory of God, which hope shall never make them ashamed.

The confession begins its explanation of the doctrine of assurance by addressing the first possibility: the issue of "false hopes and carnal presumptions." *False assurance*, the Puritans believed, is a real danger. This is one of the ways that the deceitfulness of sin and the fallen human heart express themselves. People are prone to deceive themselves into a false peace, based on an assurance grounded only on their favorable opinion of themselves. Anthony Burgess (d. 1664), who served ably at the Westminster Assembly, wrote, "We are possessed with self-love and carnal confidence, and upon this foundation it is impossible to build a good superstructure."[6]

The next possibility is *true assurance*. Chapter 18.1 of the confession clearly says that assurance is possible for Christians, but it also stresses that assurance cannot be obtained apart from Christ. Every part of 18.1 connects assurance with Christ in saying: believe in *him*; love *him*; walk before *him*. Assurance is interwoven with Christian believing, Christian loving, and fruits of faith in Christ. The essence of assurance is living in Christ.

Finally, chapter 18.1 of the Westminster Confession emphasizes a third possibility: *believers may possess saving faith without the joy and full assurance that they possess it.* Burgess said that assurance is "not of absolute necessity to salvation: it's not a necessary effect of our calling and election at all times."[7] Assurance augments the joy of faith, but it is not essential to salvation. Faith *alone* justifies through Christ

6. Anthony Burgess, *Faith Seeking Assurance* (Grand Rapids: Reformation Heritage Books, 2015), 24–25. See Anthony Burgess, *Spiritual Refining* (1662; repr., Ames, IA: International Outreach, 1996); see esp. 1–60 (sermons 1–11) and 670–86 (sermons 116–18).

7. Burgess, *Spiritual Refining*, 672.

alone; assurance is the conscious enjoyment of that justification and salvation. A genuine believer may feel as though he abides in darkness (Isa. 50:10).[8] Burgess acknowledged that this is agonizing, more painful than broken bones.[9] It is certainly not an ideal condition. The Word offers much practical help to those who are in this state by specifying three major sources of assurance.

The Foundations of Assurance

The Westminster Confession gets to the heart of how to obtain personal assurance of salvation when it identifies the foundations of assurance in chapter 18.2:

> This certainty is not a bare conjectural and probable persuasion grounded upon a fallible hope; but an infallible assurance of faith founded upon the divine truth of the promises of salvation, the inward evidence of those graces unto which these promises are made, the testimony of the Spirit of adoption witnessing with our spirits that we are the children of God, which Spirit is the earnest of our inheritance, whereby we are sealed to the day of redemption.

It is important here not to confuse the foundations or grounds of *assurance* with the foundations or grounds of *salvation*.[10] As John Murray said: "When we speak of the grounds of assurance, we are thinking of the ways in which a believer comes to entertain this assurance, not of the grounds on which his salvation rests. The grounds of salvation are as secure for the person who does not have full assurance as for the person who has."[11]

In this sense, Westminster Confession 18.2 presents a complex ground of assurance,[12] which includes a primary, objective ground

8. Sinclair B. Ferguson, *The Whole Christ: Legalism, Antinomianism, and Gospel Assurance—Why the Marrow Controversy Still Matters* (Wheaton, IL: Crossway, 2016), 178.

9. Burgess, *Spiritual Refining*, 26.

10. Paul Helm, *Calvin and the Calvinists* (Edinburgh: Banner of Truth, 1982), 28, 75.

11. John Murray, *Collected Writings* (Edinburgh: Banner of Truth, 1980), 2:270.

12. James Buchanan, *The Doctrine of Justification: An Outline of Its History in the*

("the divine truth of the promises of salvation") and two secondary, subjective grounds ("the inward evidence of those graces unto which these promises are made" and "the testimony of the Spirit of adoption witnessing with our spirits"). Let us look at all three of these under separate headings, beginning here with the objective ground of assurance.

Divine Promises in Christ

The Puritans believed that God's promises in Christ are the primary ground for a believer's assurance. Thomas Brooks wrote:

> The promises of God are a Christian's *magna charta*, his chiefest evidences for heaven. Divine promises are God's deed of gift; they are the only assurance which the saints must show for their right and title to Christ, to His blood, and to all the happiness and blessedness that comes by Him. . . . The promises are not only the food of faith, but also the very life and soul of faith; they are a mine of rich treasures, a garden full of the choicest and sweetest flowers; in them are wrapped up all celestial contentments and delights.[13]

Burgess said that it "is a more noble and excellent way" to find assurance of faith by relying on God's promise in Christ outside us than it is to come to assurance by being assured of the evidences of grace within us.[14] That emphasis on God's promises in Christ implies several things for our own and our people's experience of assurance.

First, neither we as pastors nor our parishioners gain assurance by looking at ourselves or anything we have produced apart from God's promises; rather, first and foremost, we gain assurance by looking to God's faithfulness in Christ as he is revealed in the promises of the gospel. Paul tells us in 2 Corinthians 1:18–20: "But as God is true, our word toward you was not yea and nay. For the Son of God, Jesus Christ, who was preached among you . . . , was not yea

Church and of Its Exposition from Scripture (Edinburgh: T. & T. Clark, 1867), 184. Cf. Louis Berkhof, *The Assurance of Faith* (Grand Rapids: Eerdmans, 1939), 49–68.

13. Thomas Brooks, *A Cabinet of Jewels*, in *The Works of Thomas Brooks*, ed. Alexander B. Grosart (1864; repr., Edinburgh: Banner of Truth, 1980), 3:254–55.

14. Burgess, *Faith Seeking Assurance*, 140 (Burgess, *Spiritual Refining*, 51).

and nay, but in him was yea. For all the promises of God in him are yea, and in him Amen, unto the glory of God by us." God doesn't speak out of both sides of his mouth. God's gospel promises in Christ cannot fail because God's character is true and faithful. Thus, our assurance for our personal salvation as well as for our daily ministry lies in the character of our faithful God, who manifests himself in the unchangeable person and finished work of his Son. The same offers of grace and gospel promises that lead us to salvation are sufficient to lead us to assurance.

Second, as assurance grows, God's promises become increasingly real to us personally and experientially. The promises of God and assurance of faith reinforce each other. This is because God's promises are the pathways on which Christ meets the soul. So Thomas Goodwin wrote, "If one promise belongs to thee, then all do; for every one conveys [the] whole Christ in whom all the promises are made and who is the matter of them."[15] Another Puritan, William Spurstowe (c. 1605–66), wrote, "The promises are instrumental in the coming of Christ and the soul together; they are the warrant by which faith is emboldened to come to him, and take hold of him; but the union which faith makes is not between a believer and the promise, but between a believer and Christ."[16] The promises ground our assurance, and our assurance emboldens our faith to make further appropriation of the promises, which brings us into fuller, personal communion with Christ. That sweet, personal communion with Christ provides incalculable strength and joy in persevering in ministry even in discouraging times when we feel as though we cannot preach or pastor, and when impasses in ministry seem insurmountable.

Third, the Christ-centeredness of personal assurance is accented in God's promises, for Jesus Christ himself is the "sum, foundation, seal, treasury of all the promises" of God.[17] "Let thy eye and heart,

15. Thomas Goodwin, *The Works of Thomas Goodwin*, 12 vols. (Grand Rapids: Reformation Heritage Books, 2006), 3:321.

16. William Spurstowe, *The Wells of Salvation Opened: or, A Treatise Discerning the Nature, Preciousness, and Usefulness of the Gospel Promises and Rules for the Right Application of Them* (London: T. R. & E. M. for Ralph Smith, 1655), 44–45.

17. Edward Reynolds, *Three Treatises: Of the Vanity of the Creature. The Sinfulness of Sinne. The Life of Christ* (London: B. B. for Rob Bastocke and George Badger, 1642), 365.

first, most, and last, be fixed upon Christ, then will assurance bed and board with thee," said Brooks.[18] Burgess wisely counseled his readers to beware of an obsessive and overambitious "introspectionism" when he wrote: "We should not so gaze upon ourselves to find graces in our hearts that we forget those acts of faith whereby we immediately close with Christ and rely upon Him only for our justification."[19]

Let us particularly use God's promises in our own lives and in our preaching to focus on Jesus Christ and to enhance our people's knowledge of him—knowledge about his person, names, offices, states, and natures; knowledge about his relationship to the Father and the Spirit, as well as to us as his adopted brothers and sisters. I pray that minds and hearts might be so moved as we preach and teach about our "altogether lovely" Savior, who is the substance of all of God's promises, that we might move our people to worship him in Spirit and truth as they attend on the means of grace. Let us never forget that we are most near to Christ when we are overwhelmed with a sense of his stupendous promises and love for hell-worthy sinners like us. Then we will be so lost in the wonder of divine love that, with Paul, we will confess that its depth, height, and breadth goes beyond our understanding. This ought to be the hallmark of all our preaching, teaching, and pastoring: our delight and assurance in the love of Christ, from which nothing will be able to separate us (Rom. 8:38–39). Ultimately, the goal of Christian ministry must be to lead our people, by the Spirit's grace, to find their total salvation in Christ, both here and forever, so that they might cry out from the experiential depth of their souls, with Paul, "For to me to live is Christ, and to die is gain" (Phil. 1:21).

Finally, though subjective phenomena may sometimes *feel* more real than faith in God's promises, such experiences give less glory to God than divine promises apprehended directly by faith. Burgess said: "Trusting in God and in Christ when we feel nothing but guilt and destruction in ourselves is the greatest honor we can give to God. Therefore, though living by signs is more comfortable to us, living by faith is a greater honor to God."[20]

18. Brooks, *Heaven on Earth*, 307.
19. Burgess, *Faith Seeking Assurance*, 114 (Burgess, *Spiritual Refining*, 41).
20. Burgess, *Faith Seeking Assurance*, 156 (Burgess, *Spiritual Refining*, 57).

When Christian was confined in Doubting Castle in *The Pilgrim's Progress*, Giant Despair beat him and threatened to kill him the next day. But that night, Christian remembered that he had "the key of promise" in his pocket. Using that key, he quickly opened all of the castle's locks and escaped. John Bunyan's message is unmistakable: the key was there all along! We need not fear, since God loves to see his children scoop up his promises and put them to good use. They are always available, always in our "pocket," so to speak. We need not be shy to simply embrace and believe them, that is, to believe in Jesus Christ, who is the content of these promises. As we do so, we discover to our astonishment and joy that Giant Despair is powerless to keep us as his prisoner. How liberating that is for us as ministers but also for our sheep! Brothers in the ministry, do we who preach often on God's promises use this key to deliver ourselves from Giant Despair?

Here is our comfort: The objective promise embraced by faith is infallible because it is *God's* comprehensive and faithful covenant promise. Consequently, subjective evidence, though necessary, must always be regarded as secondary, for it is often mixed with human convictions and feelings even when it gazes on the work of God. All exercises of saving faith apprehend to some degree the primary ground of divine promises in Christ.

Assurance from Evidences of Grace

While God's promises are the primary ground of assurance, they are not the only ground. It is true that if we examine ourselves apart from resting in the promises by faith, we may become lifted up with pride or be brought to despair when we realize how much sin still lives within us.[21] But there are also many "Christians" who claim assurance of grace because they trust in the promises of God alone for salvation, but whose lives do not bear the fruit of their profession. Jesus himself said, "Ye shall know them by their fruits" (Matt. 7:16). And the apostle John repeatedly identified the fruits that we need to possess if we would have assurance that we are true believers (1 John 2:3, 5; 3:14; 5:2).

21. John Calvin even said that such self-examination will only lead us to sure damnation. For an explanation of Calvin's views on self-examination, see Beeke, *Quest for Full Assurance*, 59–60.

So how must self-examination be done today? What are the fruits that we are to look for? How are we to engage in that search? How can we be sure that our search is accurate? These are the kinds of questions that thoughtful Christians have asked in the past and are still asking today, and we must answer these questions in our preaching—clearly, lovingly, patiently, and repetitively—both in preaching and in pastoring.

The Westminster Confession addresses such questions as these when it says in the last half of 18.2 that assurance of faith is grounded not only on the promises of God embraced by faith, but also on "the inward evidence of those graces unto which these promises are made."

The Logic of Assurance

The Puritans were convinced that the grace of God within believers confirms the reality of faith. William Ames (1576–1633) wrote, "He that rightly understands the promise of the covenant, cannot be sure of his salvation, unless he perceives in himself true faith and repentance."[22] They searched for the grace of God at work in believers by means of logical arguments called *syllogisms*, based on the so-called reflex or reflective act of faith.[23] What it amounts to is simply this: By the reflective act of faith, the Holy Spirit sheds light on his work in the believer, enabling him to conclude that his faith is saving because its exercises have a saving character. Thus, the logic of assurance involves the act of faith looking at itself or viewing its reflection in its acts in response to God and his Word. Burgess put it this way:

> First, there are the *direct acts* of the soul, whereby the soul immediately and directly responds to some object. Second, there are *reflex acts* of the soul, by which the soul considers and observes what acts it does. It's as if the eye is turned inward to see itself. The Apostle John expresses this fully, saying, "We do know that we know" (1 John 2:3). So, when we believe in God, that is a direct act of the soul; when we repent of sin, because God is dishonored, that is a

22. William Ames, *The Marrow of Theology*, trans. John D. Eusden (Boston: Pilgrim Press, 1968), 1.3.22.

23. John Flavel, *The Works of John Flavel* (repr., London: Banner of Truth, 1968), 2:330.

direct act; but when we know that we do believe, and that we do repent of our sin, that is a reflex act.[24]

The syllogism was based on the believer's sanctification and good works in daily life. It emphasized the believer's internal and external life of obedience that confirmed his experience of grace. It went something like this. *Major premise*: According to Scripture, only those who possess saving faith will receive the Spirit's testimony that their lives manifest fruits of sanctification and good works. *Minor premise*: I cannot deny that by the grace of God I have received the Spirit's testimony that I manifest fruits of sanctification and good works. *Conclusion*: I am a partaker of saving faith.

A clear biblical example is 1 John, which often uses the syllogism in a succinct form. For example: "Hereby we do know that we know him, if we keep his commandments" (1 John 2:3); that is, those who know him keep his commandments; I keep his commandments; therefore, I know that I know him (cf. 3:14; 5:2).

Putting the Syllogism and Reflective Act of Faith into Practice

So how does all this work in practice both for you as a pastor and for your people? Let's say that you are spiritually distressed on a given day because you feel very unspiritual, distant from God, and lukewarm in your faith. In fact, you can scarcely pray, which makes you wonder whether you truly have faith at all. You turn to the Scriptures, but even special promises of God, which have been made very precious to you in the past, such as 1 John 1:9—"If we confess our sins, he is faithful and just to forgive us our sins, and to cleanse us from all unrighteousness"—now seem empty and distant. What do you do?

The Puritans would say that you should turn to some of the evidences of grace that are laid out for us in Scripture, ask the Spirit to shed light on them for you, and then, as you reflect on your life, if you can say with assurance that one of these evidences is your experience, you can be assured that you are a child of God—even if you can't see other evidences in you. So for example, continuing with 1 John, you turn to 1 John 3:14, "We know that we have passed from death unto

---

24. Burgess, *Spiritual Refining*, 672.

life, because we love the brethren." You ask yourself syllogistically: Since only those who are true children of God have a true love for the brethren, do I have a true love for the people of God? Perhaps you can answer: Yes, I certainly can't deny that I have a special love for the people of God. I love to fellowship with them; they are real brothers and sisters to me. I love to see Christ in them. Your conclusion, then, is: Therefore, I must be a child of God.

The point is this: If you can grasp one of these marks of grace (such as love for the brethren), then you may know that since God does a complete work of salvation in his people, you also possess all the other marks of grace, including 1 John 2:5, even though you can't see that today. Though these evidences have an experientially discriminatory effect in exposing counterfeit "Christians," the Puritan employment of them was normally pastoral also—they were meant to confirm, to console, and to strengthen the believer's faith and assurance, not drive him to despair.

Assurance from the Holy Spirit's Witnessing Testimony

Westminster Confession 18.2 teaches us that we also gain our assurance as Christians by the witnessing testimony of the Holy Spirit himself. In the words of the confession:

> the testimony of the Spirit of adoption witnessing with our spirits that we are the children of God, which Spirit is the earnest of our inheritance, whereby we are sealed to the day of redemption.

The writers of the Westminster Confession knew that the most difficult part of assurance to understand was the testimony or witness of the Holy Spirit. They confessed that vast mysteries confronted them when they spoke of that subject. No doubt one reason that the assembly did not detail more specifically the Spirit's role in assurance was to allow for the freedom of the Spirit. A second reason was that the assembly wanted to allow freedom of conscience to those who differed about the finer details of the Spirit's testimony.

Most of the members of the assembly had one of two emphases. Some believed that the Spirit's witness referred to in Westminster Confession 18.2 was simply the Spirit's witnessing with our spirit that the inward evidences of grace are true so that we may be assured that we are children of God. According to these divines, there is then only one secondary ground of assurance: the evidences of grace, co-witnessed with our spirits by the Spirit of God.[25]

Other Puritans said that though that may be part of the meaning here, there can also be a direct witness of the Holy Spirit to our souls through the Word that can give a substantial increase to our assurance and comfort, especially in times of great need.[26] For example, when the Spirit applies to us a special promise, such as "I have loved thee with an everlasting love: therefore with lovingkindness have I drawn thee" (Jer. 31:3), with considerable power and sweetness—such that we enjoy a profound experience of communion with God and of his love and a profound sight of the beauty and glory of Christ—that immediate or direct witness of the Spirit to us can give a large boost to our assurance. At such times, we might feel that the intimately personal application of the Word to our own soul seems to be the most suitable text in the entire Bible for our particular need!

In every sense, however, the assembly's divines unitedly asserted that the Spirit's testimony is always tied to, and may never contradict, the Word of God. We must preach this truth avidly to our congregations as well. We must teach them that the activity of the Spirit in conjunction with the Word is essential in every part of assurance. Without the application of the Spirit, the promises of God may lead to self-deceit, carnal presumption, and fruitless lives. Without the illumination of the Spirit, self-examination tends to introspection, bondage, and legalism. The witness of the Spirit, divorced from the promises of God and from scriptural inward evidences, can lead to unbiblical mysticism, antinomianism, and excessive emotionalism.

Whatever view one takes, it is important to maintain that the Spirit bears testimony with and through the Word. We must never separate the Spirit from the Word or affirm one at the expense of the

---

25. See Burgess, *Faith Seeking Assurance*, 122 (Burgess, *Spiritual Refining*, 44).

26. Samuel Rutherford, *A Survey of the Spirituall Antichrist* (London: by J. D. & R. I. for Andrew Crooke, 1648), 238–39; Henry Scudder, *The Christian's Daily Walk* (repr., Harrisonburg, VA: Sprinkle, 1984), 338; Goodwin, *Of the Creatures*, in *Works*, 7:66; Goodwin, *Of the Object and Acts of Justifying Faith*, in *Works*, 8:362–63, 366–67.

other. And we must never separate the three grounds of assurance. The promises of God, the evidences of grace, and the testimony of the Holy Spirit all work in tandem to produce a true and well-grounded assurance. Coming into greater and greater realization of these truths helps us to grow in assurance.

How to Cultivate Assurance

Second Peter 1:10 says, "Give diligence to make your calling and election sure." But just how do you make "your calling and election sure"? How do you cultivate assurance? That is the burden of Westminster Confession 18.3, which touches on five practical issues on assurance:

> This infallible assurance doth not so belong to the essence of faith, but that a true believer may wait long, and conflict with many difficulties, before he be partaker of it: yet, being enabled by the Spirit to know the things which are freely given him of God, he may, without extraordinary revelation, in the right use of ordinary means, attain thereunto. And therefore it is the duty of every one to give all diligence to make his calling and election sure, that thereby his heart may be enlarged in peace and joy in the Holy Ghost, in love and thankfulness to God, and in strength and cheerfulness in the duties of obedience, the proper fruits of this assurance; so far is it from inclining men to looseness.

First of all, there is the relation of faith to assurance. A commonly debated question in church history is this: Is the seed of assurance embedded in faith? Most Puritans and their contemporary Scottish divines argued yes. And yet they distinguished faith from assurance of faith. "It is one thing for me to believe, and another thing for me to believe that I believe," said Brooks.[27] Assurance of salvation is not the same thing as saving faith, but it is its fruit.[28] As such, assurance is related to faith, and the degree to which one enjoys it depends on

---

27. Brooks, *Heaven on Earth*, 14.
28. Ames, *Marrow of Theology*, 167 (I.xxviii.24).

the health, vigor, and maturity of faith.[29] But justification is by faith alone—even frail, feeble faith—not by assurance.[30] Whether assurance is strong or weak, the righteousness of Christ that is appropriated by the weakest faith is still perfect and sufficient to save.[31]

Second, according to the Westminster Confession, "a true believer may wait long, and conflict with many difficulties, before he be partaker of" assurance (18.3), but the relationship between faith and assurance usually strengthens over time, "growing up in many to the attainment of a full assurance" (14.3). It is important to preach to our people that grace usually grows with age, and that as faith increases, other graces increase. Age and experience do not guarantee assurance, however, nor is it impossible for God to plant faith and full assurance simultaneously. As in conversion, God remains sovereign in the dispensing of assurance. Typically, however, "He works it by degrees,"[32] so that our doubts about our own salvation generally diminish as we grow in grace (2 Peter 1:5–10).

Third, Westminster Confession 18.3 goes on to say that "[the believer] may, without extraordinary revelation, *in the right use of ordinary means,* attain" to assurance. We must preach to the children of God that they have a lifelong call to make diligent use of the means of grace in pursuit of ever greater degrees of assurance, because God uses both sovereignty and means to bequeath assurance.[33] We must proclaim to them that four means are predominant: God's Word,[34] the

29. William Ames, *Medulla SS. Theologiae, ex sacris literis, earumque interpretibus, extracts & methodice disposita* (Amstelodami: Joannem Janssonium, 1627), 1.27.19.

30. John Downe, *A Treatise of the True Nature and Definition of Justifying Faith* (Oxford: I. Lichfield for E. Forrest, 1635), 12–13.

31. John Rogers, *The Doctrine of Faith: Wherein Are Particularly Handled Twelve Principall Points, Which Explaine the Nature and Use of It* (London: N. Newbery and H. Overton, 1629), 201.

32. Anthony Burgess, *The True Doctrine of Justification Asserted and Vindicated, from the Errors of Papists, Arminians, Socinians, and More Especially Antinomians* (London: by Robert White, for Thomas Underhill, 1648), 152.

33. Anthony Burgess, *CXLV Expository Sermons upon the Whole 17th Chapter of the Gospel according to St. John* (London: Abraham Miller for Thomas Underhill, 1656), 356.

34. Thomas Watson, *Heaven Taken by Storm* (Morgan, PA: Soli Deo Gloria, 1994), 12–15.

sacraments,[35] prayer,[36] and affliction (including conflicts, doubts, trials, and temptations).[37] We must explain how God uses these means to increase our and their assurance.

Fourth, it is our duty to pursue assurance diligently. In short, God commands us to pursue assurance prayerfully and fervently, promising that he will bless it. "A good improvement of what we have of the grace of God at present, pleases God, and engages him to give us more," Bunyan wrote. "Therefore, get more grace."[38] The Puritan stress on duty reinforced the conviction that assurance must never be regarded as only the privilege of exceptional saints, but that at least some degree of it is normative for the believer.

Finally, Westminster Confession 18.3 stresses that assurance produces God-glorifying, delightful fruit, so that our "heart may be enlarged in peace and joy in the Holy Ghost, in love and thankfulness to God, and in strength and cheerfulness in the duties of obedience, the proper fruits of this assurance; so far is it from inclining men to looseness." Assurance elevates God-glorifying and soul-satisfying affections. We must preach how that assurance produces holy living marked by spiritual peace, joyful love, humble gratitude, cheerful obedience, and heartfelt mortification of sin.[39] We must show our people from the Scriptures how that assurance enables faith to reach greater heights, from which all other aspects of Christian character flow. We must teach them that this invigoration of faith results in a new release of spiritual energy in their Christian life at every point.[40]

---

35. Burgess, *Faith Seeking Assurance*, 145–46 (Burgess, *Spiritual Refining*, 53); Robert Bruce, *The Mystery of the Lord's Supper*, ed. and trans. Thomas F. Torrance (Richmond, VA: John Knox Press, 1958), 82.

36. Burgess, *Faith Seeking Assurance*, 174–75 (Burgess, *Spiritual Refining*, 673); cf. Burgess, *True Doctrine of Justification*, 273.

37. Burgess, *Faith Seeking Assurance*, 97 (Burgess, *Spiritual Refining*, 35).

38. Quoted in Richard L. Greaves, *John Bunyan* (Grand Rapids: Eerdmans, 1969), 149.

39. See John Owen, *Of the Mortification of Sin*, in *The Works of John Owen*, ed. William H. Goold (Edinburgh: T. & T. Clark, n.d.), 6:33–53.

40. Thomas Brooks, *The Crown and Glory of Christianity, or Holiness, the Only Way to Happiness*, in *The Works of Thomas Brooks*, ed. Alexander B. Grosart (1864; repr., Edinburgh: Banner of Truth, 1980), 4:235.

Assurance Lost and Renewed

As faithful Puritan pastors, the Westminster divines concluded their historic chapter on assurance with a succinct but comprehensive paragraph (18.4) both on how believers can temporarily lose their assurance of faith and on how they can renew and revive it:

> True believers may have the assurance of their salvation divers ways shaken, diminished, and intermitted; as, by negligence in preserving of it, by falling into some special sin which woundeth the conscience and grieveth the Spirit; by some sudden or vehement temptation, by God's withdrawing the light of His countenance, and suffering even such as fear Him to walk in darkness and have no light: yet are they never utterly destitute of that seed of God, and life of faith, that love of Christ and the brethren, that sincerity of heart, and conscience of duty, out of which, by the operation of the Spirit, this assurance may, in due time, be revived; and by the which, in the meantime, they are supported from utter despair.

This section of the confession offers a magnificent link between Reformed theology and Puritan piety. It says that the reasons for a loss of assurance are found primarily in the believer. They include negligence and spiritual slothfulness, falling into sin, or yielding to some temptation. What it is teaching is quite clear: *The Christian cannot enjoy high levels of assurance while he persists in low levels of obedience.*[41] Burgess concluded, "It is therefore an unworthy thing to complain about the loss of God's favor and assurance if all your duties and performances are careless and withered."[42]

It is critical that we apply this lesson home to our own heart and to the hearts of our parishioners. I once had an elder call me in great personal agony just before I had to leave for a pastor's conference. He said that he was in a bad way with God, and felt that he was a reprobate. "Could you come over right away?" he asked. I told him

---

41. This is a common Reformed emphasis, as the German and Dutch family of Reformed standards make clear. Cf. Belgic Confession, art. 24; Heidelberg Catechism, Lord's Day 24; Canons of Dort, Head V.

42. Burgess, *Faith Seeking Assurance*, 95 (Burgess, *Spiritual Refining*, 34–35).

that I was so sorry that I could not, but I would visit him as soon as I returned. "Meanwhile," I advised, "spend thirty minutes alone with God each day—reading Scripture, meditating, and praying." "I can't do that," he said, "because my very prayers are an abomination in God's sight." I persisted: "Your lack of prayer is a double abomination in God's sight. You must return into the path of obedience if you want to regain your lost assurance." "I will try," he said. Three days later when I returned home, there was a note on my study chair: "No need to visit your elder; all is well with his soul."

Another reason for the loss of assurance is not in the believer as such but in God. According to his sovereign and mysterious will, he may withdraw the light of his countenance, or permit a believer to be tried with vehement temptations or intensified afflictions that do violence to his peace and joy. This may have the purpose of allowing the believer to "taste and see how bitter sin is," or to "keep us low and humble," or to treasure assurance more greatly, or to depend more fully on the grace of Christ and endeavor to pursue a closer walk with God.[43] God's withdrawals and his placing of trials in the path of the believer are motivated by his *fatherly discipline*, which teaches "right walking"; by his *fatherly sovereignty*, which teaches dependence; and by his *fatherly wisdom*, which teaches that he knows and does what is best for his own.[44] God ordains these trials for his glory and the benefit of his elect. Hence, as William Gurnall wrote, "The Christian must trust in a withdrawing God."[45]

Whatever the reason(s) for the loss of assurance, the confession rightfully stresses that it can be revived in due time. Even in the believer's darkest struggles, the Holy Spirit abides within him and bears him up, keeping him from "utter despair." Indeed, the child of God may be losing assurance even while he advances in grace.[46]

---

43. Burgess, *Faith Seeking Assurance*, 97–101 (Burgess, *Spiritual Refining*, 35–36). See *Works of Thomas Brooks*, 2:330–34, and *Works of Thomas Goodwin*, 3:298–99, for similar lists.

44. Samuel Rutherford, *The Trial and Triumph of Faith* (Edinburgh: Collins, 1845), 326–29; Goodwin, *Works*, 3:231–36.

45. William Gurnall, *The Christian in Complete Armour* (repr., Edinburgh: Banner of Truth, 1974), 2:145.

46. Rutherford, *Trial and Triumph of Faith*, 139–40.

This is because the *grace* and *essence* of faith abides with the believer even though he is blind to the *acts* and *practice* of faith. This gracious preservation of faith offers hope for the revival of assurance, for the flame of God's life within the soul can never be completely snuffed out. The embers burn, although barely and subtly at times, but can be fanned into the full flame of assurance by the persevering use of God's appointed means. Assurance is revived in the same way that it was obtained the first time. Believers should review their lives, confess their backsliding, and humbly cast themselves on their covenant-keeping God and his gracious promises in Christ, being sure to engage continually in fresh acts of ongoing conversion through faith and repentance.[47] If Job and David recovered their loss of assurance, why shouldn't the believer (Job 19:25–27; 23:8–9; Pss. 30:6–7; 42:5–8; 51:12; 71:20–21)? We should remember that the loss here is for only a short time; soon we will have perfect assurance and perfect enjoyment of God forever in the eternal Celestial City.[48]

Conclusion

The Westminster divines fleshed out the doctrine of assurance of salvation in chapter 18 of the Westminster Confession of Faith with precision to undeceive the false professor of faith, to awaken the unsaved, to mature the young in grace, and to comfort the mature in faith. The terminology they developed, their treatises on assurance, their pastoral overtones of compassion for the weak in faith, and their pressing admonitions and invitations to grow in faith showed their great appreciation for vital union and communion with Christ. We can learn a great deal from them as we strive to preach and pastor ourselves and our people into greater measures of assurance.

Scholars today who attribute morbid introspection and man-centeredness to seventeenth-century Puritans have missed the mark. Most Puritan divines examined spiritual experience microscopically because they were eager to trace the faithful track record of God in their lives so that they could attribute glory to the Father who elects

47. Burgess, *Spiritual Refining*, 34–35, 673–75; Joel R. Beeke, *A Tocha Dos Puritanos: Evangelização Biblica* (São Paulo: Evangélicas Selecionadas, 1996), 42–68.
48. Cf. Brooks, *Heaven on Earth*, 311–14.

and provides, the Son who redeems and intercedes, and the Spirit who applies and sanctifies. This, too, is an important part of preaching today. If we can move our parishioners to see how faithful God has always been in their lives from the moment they were regenerated, they will usually grow in assurance of their own salvation.

Let us teach our people to live out each day the lessons that the Puritans teach us: Our primary ground of assurance is in the promises of God in Christ. Those promises must be applied to our hearts, must bear fruit in our lives, and help us experience the Spirit's corroborating witness with our spirit that we are indeed sons of God. Daily we are called to live fruitful lives, to speak well of our great assuring God, and to serve as salt in the earth.

The practical message for us as pastors and parishioners is simply this: Faith must ultimately triumph because it comes from the triune God and rests on his Word; let us therefore not despair when, for a time, we do not feel its triumph. Let us more fully embrace God's promise in Christ, recognizing that our certainty, both objective and subjective, lies wholly in Christ, for faith is of Christ and rests in him.

Christ will ultimately win the day in us and all the rest of his children. Let us take courage and seek grace to honor Christ—and, through Christ, God triune—in our entire life and in all our preaching and pastoring, for ultimately, our assurance is not about self-confidence but about confidence in the Father, the Son, and the Spirit. That is what faith and assurance—yes, Scripture and life itself—are all about: honoring the triune God through Jesus Christ. "For of him, and through him, and to him, are all things: to whom be glory for ever. Amen" (Rom. 11:36).

Key Terms

assurance
mortification

Recommendations for Further Reading

Beeke, Joel R. *Knowing and Growing in Assurance of Faith*. Fearn, Scotland: Christian Focus, 2017.

Brooks, Thomas. *Heaven on Earth: A Treatise on Christian Assurance.* London: Banner of Truth, 1961.

Ferguson, Sinclair B. *The Whole Christ: Legalism, Antinomianism, and Gospel Assurance—Why the Marrow Controversy Still Matters.* Wheaton, IL: Crossway, 2016.

Lloyd-Jones, D. Martyn. *The Assurance of Our Salvation.* Wheaton, IL: Crossway, 2013.

Discussion Questions

1. How can true assurance be distinguished from false assurance?
2. What Bible passages might a pastor include in a series of sermons on assurance?
3. Why do many Christians struggle to have assurance?
4. How can a pastor help a person find assurance?
5. Explain how a pastor's experience of his own assurance can be helpful in pastoring others on the subject.
6. What wisdom can be supplied from Puritan theology in pastoring Christians lacking assurance?

18

THE LAW OF GOD

Preaching the Law as Competent
Ministers of a New Covenant

PHILIP S. ROSS

I was very hard-headed. I felt like I was almost the last person who covered in the music ministry. . . . After a month I have read everything; I have read the Scriptures . . . ten times in this first Corinthians 11. . . .

My prayer was this, "Lord, if you really want—if this is a very important thing that I must do, that pleases you, that I should cover my hair, I want you to speak to me. . . ."

That night I knew that the Holy Spirit is speaking to me about the head covering and I am convinced in my heart that I should do it. . . . I wept for 30 minutes; I just said thank you, Lord, that you are speaking to me. . . .

It's my own personal choice, and it's your own personal choice, but we have a different conviction in our heart, and I decided to obey that voice inside me. And I want to obey God in everything, and surrender my life to him, so this afternoon I want to rededicate my life.

Thank you, and God bless you.[1]

1. "Analyn's Head Covering Testimony: I Was One of the Last to Cover," The Head Covering Movement, 5:32, June 3, 2017, https://www.headcoveringmovement .com/christian-covering-videos/analyns-head-covering-testimony-one-last-cover.

So says Analyn to a round of applause in a video found on the website of The Head Covering Movement—"a community of Christians who are sparking a return to the biblical practice of head covering (1 Cor. 11:2–16)."[2] The website has a catalogue of on-message sermons and testimonies from women who have covered their heads.

What should Christian ministers make of this—not so much of Analyn's tearful testimony as of an organization that promotes head coverings and teaches that if women will obey God, they must cover their heads? Must we urge the women in our congregations to do so? Or can we dismiss those who preach head covering as bearded eccentrics? And what about other debated practices, such as tithing? Is it a sin not to tithe?

Debates about such issues might not be what most people connect with the doctrine of the law of God as defined in chapter 19 of the Westminster Confession of Faith, but if we classify anything as sin, we are bound to relate it to the law. This means that we should at least consider how our teaching on the law relates to such issues. I cannot feign an interest in every historical controversy or contemporary (and often parochial) debate about the confession's teaching that may spring to mind when one hears the word *law*. Nor can I imagine why anyone would want me to regurgitate what others have covered elsewhere.[3] I will therefore focus instead on some implications of teaching and applying the confession's doctrine of law, categorized as moral, ceremonial, and judicial,[4] using three case studies: the first on the issue of head coverings, the second on tithing, and the third on the preaching of the moral law.

---

2. www.headcoveringmovement.com.

3. J. V. Fesko, *The Theology of the Westminster Standards: Historical Context & Theological Insights* (Wheaton, IL: Crossway, 2014), 267–98; Whitney G. Gamble, *Christ and the Law: Antinomianism at the Westminster Assembly* (Grand Rapids: Reformation Heritage Books, 2018); Mark Jones, *Antinomianism: Reformed Theology's Unwelcome Guest?* (Phillipsburg, NJ: P&R Publishing, 2013); Robert Letham, *The Westminster Assembly: Reading Its Theology in Historical Context* (Phillipsburg, NJ: P&R Publishing, 2009), 293–98.

4. I have argued in another place that those categories have a biblical basis and defended many of the underlying assumptions in this chapter. See Philip S. Ross, *From the Finger of God: The Biblical and Theological Basis for the Threefold Division of the Law* (Fearn, Scotland: Mentor, 2010).

Obeying God in Everything?

Analyn believed that to obey God in everything, she had to cover her head. Is that so? Was the voice inside her from God? How should we settle such issues? Most of us will want to examine the exegetical and theological arguments. According to The Head Covering Movement, that should begin with recognizing how much the spirit of the age has shaped our perspectives.

The Myth of Millinery and Exegetical Uniformity

The narrative is that "until fifty years ago, every woman in every church covered her head. . . . What has happened in the last fifty years? We've had a feminist movement."[5] No doubt women have been on the march, but the idea that until the rise of feminism, all women throughout history covered their heads in submission, while men did not, is false.

The abandonment of head coverings is common to both sexes and may have as much to do with fashion or infrastructure as the rise of feminism. A woman in Regency Britain, for example, might have worn a bonnet inside because of her drafty drawing room and outside because she wished to preserve the pale complexion of the genteel classes. In the postwar twentieth century, her great-great-granddaughter ditched her bonnet because she now had central heating and even the upper-middle classes wanted to look as though they had spent August in Antibes.

The hat was never simply a sign of submission when found on a woman's head, but a fashion statement, a symbol of social superiority, or even authority. Well before the feminist era, Matthew Henry observed that "it was a signification either of shame or subjection for persons to be veiled, or covered, in the eastern countries, contrary to the custom of ours, where the being bare-headed betokens subjection, and being covered superiority and dominion."[6] Even something as basic as portraiture from the Reformation undermines the narrative

---

5. R. C. Sproul Jr., quoted in Jeremy Gardiner, *Head Covering: A Forgotten Christian Practice* (Edmonton, AB: Head Covering Movement, 2016), 9.

6. Matthew Henry, *An Exposition of the New Testament*, vol. 2 (Edinburgh: J. Wood, 1759), 292.

of modern head-covering advocates. Did the Reformers preach bare-headed? On the contrary, male clerics or others often wore head coverings to indicate authority, even in the church. In congregations of that era, were male worshipers always bareheaded? Again, they routinely kept their heads covered in cold churches and where permitted to do so, judging, as John Lee Thompson summarizes it, that "decorum is amply served if a man removes his hat at the beginning or end of the sermon."[7]

This myth of millinery uniformity in church before the 1950s also feeds the view that the entire church had a single interpretation of 1 Corinthians 11 until radical feminists came along and made a bonfire of head coverings.[8] It is, however, oversimplification to say that the idea that Paul refers to hair as a covering is "different from how the church understood this passage for nineteen hundred years"[9] (with appeals to church history that are characterized by slender quotation and that do not even consider conflicting evidence from the same author).[10]

In any case, even if there were nineteen centuries of exegetical uniformity, identifying the covering in 1 Corinthians as fabric would still not be trouble-free. Arguments that insert κάλυμμα into the text of 1 Corinthians 11 amount to a futile emendation. κάλυμμα is not the only noun that may be implied by various cognates of καλύπτω (cf. Ex. 29:22; Lev. 3:3, "fat"; Num. 22:5, "people"; Hab. 2:14, "sea"; Isa. 6:2, "wings"). And if the face is left uncovered, as head-covering advocates permit, unfortunately all the New Testament and Septuagint uses of κάλυμμα suggest a covering that impedes vision (e.g., Ex. 27:16; 2 Cor. 3:13–16). Some advocates of a material covering like to think that the argument for hair as a covering is too puerile to even consider, but arguments for hair as the covering are at least as persuasive.[11] In gen-

---

7. John Lee Thompson, *John Calvin and the Daughters of Sarah: Women in Regular and Exceptional Roles in the Exegesis of Calvin, His Predecessors, and His Contemporaries* (Genève: Librairie Droz S.A., 1992), 211.

8. Gardiner, *Head Covering*, 15–17.

9. Gardiner, *Head Covering*, 65.

10. For example, Gardiner's appeal to Augustine's letter to Possidius does not consider his comments in "Of the Work of Monks," 39, where "long hair is also instead of a veil." Gardiner, *Head Covering*, 11.

11. For example, Philip B. Payne, *Man and Woman, One in Christ: An Exegetical and Theological Study of Paul's Letters* (Grand Rapids: Zondervan, 2009).

eral, the passage has too often become a testing ground for desperate exegetical measures, such as Lucy Peppiatt's proposal that the passage is a quotation of a view that Paul rejects.[12]

Historical practice and exegesis cannot settle the matter, and narrow investigations into the text of 1 Corinthians 11 only prove that it is always possible to wade deeper into an exegetical quagmire. Can we step back from that? Or does faithfulness to the Word of God require us to specify the covering and bring the women of our congregations into line—whatever the consequences?

Could an Apostle Make a Law?

The Westminster doctrine of the law not only allows us to step back from that bog, but requires us to do so, having implications for several other doctrines. In the nineteenth century, Hugh Martin highlighted its relevance to atonement: "So long as philosophy and theology shall conserve the distinctive peculiarity of Moral Law, . . . the Westminster doctrine, which is the Catholic doctrine, of Atonement is impregnable."[13] I will let the man explain himself:

> Accepting the fundamental beliefs of all Christian theology, we recognise the Incarnation of the Eternal Word as exhibiting the union of divine and human natures in the one divine person of the Son of God; and the immediate design of this great mystery of godliness, God manifest in the flesh, we believe to have been accomplished by this God-man putting Himself in the room of those whom the Father hath given Him, under an authoritative and unchangeable, but by them violated Moral Law, to fulfil, as their representative, all its commandments, and endure, as their substitute, all its curse.
>
> But what instrumentality or efficiency towards anything like this can possibly be ascribed to the Incarnation of God's Son, if there be no strictly moral and authoritative juridical law?[14]

---

12. Lucy Peppiatt, *Women and Worship at Corinth: Paul's Rhetorical Arguments in 1 Corinthians* (Cambridge: James Clarke & Co., 2017).

13. Hugh Martin, *The Atonement: In Its Relations to the Covenant, the Priesthood, the Intercession of Our Lord* (Edinburgh: Lyon and Gemmell, 1877), 255.

14. Martin, *The Atonement*, 265–66.

None. Everything begins to unravel. Moral law cannot be vague or variable.

The doctrine of sin is also related to the doctrine of law, "every sin, both original and actual, being a transgression of the righteous law of God" (WCF 6.6). Sin is not defined by a fluctuating standard. In every era, a sin is a transgression of moral law. If it was once a sin to go up by steps to God's altar (Ex. 20:26), but it is not so now, it is because that law had in-built temporal validity as a particular application of moral law under the Mosaic administration, not because the definition of sin has changed. The temporal validity of a law is not necessarily defined only by the impermanence of the old covenant. Even under the Mosaic administration, the "statutes and ordinances" (חֻקִּים וּמִשְׁפָּטִים) were to be observed "in the land" (Deut. 4:5, 14; 5:31; 6:1; 12:1), yet as Georg Braulik points out, this "does not, however, imply any difference of degree in the binding force of the law." The difference is "in the range of validity: the Decalogue and in particular the first commandment remain binding for YHWH's people always and everywhere."[15] The fundamental sin in any case is a transgression of the Decalogue, which remains a sin.

One implication of this is that there can never be an expansion of the sin base, so that things that were not sin become sin. If the Lord "added no more" (Deut. 5:22) to the Decalogue, should anyone else propose an addendum? Could Jesus have done that? Despite rumors to the contrary from some New Testament scholars, Jesus' teaching did not advance, intensify, or supplement moral law, but upheld its full scope and intent.[16]

What about an apostle? Once Christ's work was done so that ceremonial law was abrogated and judicial law expired, could an apostle formulate a new law, causing something that had not been

---

15. Georg Braulik, "Wisdom, Divine Presence and Law" (German title: *Weisheit, Gottesnähe und Gesetz*), in *The Theology of Deuteronomy: Collected Essays of Georg Braulik*, trans. Ulrika Lindblad (North Richland Hills, TX: BIBAL Press, 1994), 7. See also Ross, *From the Finger of God*, 92–106, for further discussion of the Decalogue as the foundation of all other law.

16. I argue for this position in *From the Finger of God* (145–264). The sacraments should also be viewed within that framework and not classified as new ceremonial law, although I recognize that this point requires further argument and definition.

a sin to become forevermore a sin? The approach that some interpreters take to Paul's instructions in 1 Corinthians 11:2–16 suggests
exactly that. To insist that Paul requires women to wear a head covering in public worship, and that not to do so is always sin, makes
Paul a lawgiver.

The idea that the "traditions" or "ordinances" of 1 Corinthians
11:2 are ever-binding rules about worship, "delivered with apostolic
authority,"[17] is difficult to reconcile with the confessional view of law.
If Paul teaches that women must wear cloth head coverings in worship, but men must not, and that to do otherwise is a sin in all generations, he contradicts the law. His statement that "every man who
prays or prophesies with his head covered dishonors his head" (v. 4)
makes little sense as a perpetual truth, since it would suggest that the
law obliged priests to practice this dishonor (Ex. 28:4).

The greater problem, however, is that the law of God does not
require men to uncover their heads and women to cover theirs as
the perpetual application of any statute. For Paul to create such a
permanent ordinance would mean that he had added to the law, making something to be sin that was not sin before. Is there any other
example of an apostle's adding to the law of God? Could he do what
not even Christ had done—add to or subtract from the law? To say
that he did so also unravels the Westminster doctrine of worship and
what we know as the regulative principle. Was Paul's approach to the
worship of God not "limited by His own revealed will" (WCF 21.1)?
Could he impose on the Corinthian worshipers something that God
had not commanded?[18]

Those who do not understand the law within the framework of
Reformed theology may embrace such new commandments. Though

17. Gardiner, *Head Covering*, 56.
18. Although I am aware of Parliament's unwelcome imposition of proof texts
on the Westminster divines, the reference to 1 Corinthians 11:13–14 in WCF 1.6
is consistent with this view when it refers to "some circumstances concerning the
worship of God, and government of the Church, common to human actions and
societies, which are to be ordered by the light of nature, and Christian prudence,
according to the general rules of the word, which are always to be observed." Had
they regarded Paul's teaching in 1 Corinthians as a new law requiring a fabric head
covering, not only would it have undermined their teaching in WCF 19, with wide
implications, they could not have cited this text at 1.6.

writing "within the framework of confessional evangelicalism,"[19] Brian Rosner claims that "according to Paul, if Jews are obliged to obey the Law of Moses, believers in Christ are not. Instead, they are to obey apostolic instructions."[20] Since "confessional evangelicalism" has yet to produce a confession of faith, perhaps it can accommodate such a statement, but within a Reformed and catholic framework I think there are at least two possibilities about how we interpret 1 Corinthians 11:2–16.

"It Seemed Good . . ."

The first possibility is that if Paul speaks of cloth head coverings, he does so in line with apostolic teaching about how Christians should relate to one another. He is not making a new ceremonial law but setting out how the Corinthians should fulfill the obligations of the second-greatest commandment in their context. Rather than cast off their head coverings and despise cultural norms (if there were such norms), scandalizing one another, and perhaps even those outside the church (as in 1 Cor. 5:1), by implying that their women were insubordinate, they were to conform to this norm. By doing so, they were not obeying an apostolic extralegal tradition but applying the commandment to love one another. This makes the underlying dynamic somewhat like that operating in Acts 15, which, despite scholarly efforts to prove the opposite, is not based on Mosaic ceremonial laws. For more general reasons, shaped by the fundamental principles of the law, Paul could also have said in 1 Corinthians 11, "It . . . seemed good to the Holy Spirit and to us" (Acts 15:28).

What the General Equity Requires

The second possibility, which I think more plausible, is that Paul applies specific Mosaic laws to the situation in Corinth. In his exposition of 1 Corinthians 11:2, Chrysostom asks "what sort of crime it was for the woman to be uncovered, or the man covered?" His answer is that both "disturb the proper order, and transgress the disposition

---

19. D. A. Carson, "Series Preface" to Brian S. Rosner, *Paul and the Law: Keeping the Commandments of God* (Nottingham, UK: Apollos, 2013), 11.
20. Rosner, *Paul and the Law*, 96.

of God, and their own proper limits," by their clothing.[21] For support, he turns to Deuteronomy 22:5. Thompson mentions this in a footnote and also Heinrich Bullinger's similar appeal to Deuteronomy.[22] The connection that those two historical figures make between 1 Corinthians 11 and Deuteronomy 22:5 is reasonable. Deuteronomy has been woven into Paul's text,[23] so it would not be surprising to find a link here. In this case, Paul applies what we know as the "general equity" of an identifiable judicial law (WCF 19.4), undergirding which is the moral law of the seventh commandment. In some way, the Corinthians were embracing sexual ambiguity, which they displayed in their outward appearance, even before the face of God in public worship. By this behavior, they adopted the fashions of the sexually immoral, and failed to recognize how that affected their practice in worship.

This second possibility does not preclude the possibility that the Corinthians were laying aside a fabric head covering. Were that a universal norm, such that for a woman to cast it aside was the equivalent of cross-dressing, then that would make sense. It is, however, easier to see that hair, rather than a material head covering, might be a distinguishing characteristic of the sexes, woven into the fabric of creation, so that manly hair on a woman, or effeminate hair on a man, would point to the kind of gender-bending that Deuteronomy 22:5 forbids. Again, I think Matthew Henry had the right idea when he said that the female lock-shearing of which Paul speaks suggests that she is "desirous of changing sexes." Switching to manly or effeminate coiffure may be only one of many practices adopted by those who disregard gender boundaries, but it is often prominent, and one that Christians may thoughtlessly mimic.

If such biblical thinking lies behind Paul's argument, 1 Corinthians 11:2–16 has never been more significant. To apply it exclusively

21. *Homilies of St. John Chrysostom, Archbishop of Constantinople, on the First Epistle of St. Paul the Apostle to the Corinthians*, Homily 26, ed. Philip Schaff, Nicene and Post-Nicene Fathers of the Christian Church 12 (New York: Christian Literature Company, 1889), 151.

22. Thompson, *John Calvin and the Daughters of Sarah*, 208.

23. These are some of the suggested references or allusions: Deut. 17:7/1 Cor. 5:13; Deut. 6:4/1 Cor. 8:4; Deut. 20:6/1 Cor. 9:7; Deut. 25:4/1 Cor. 9:9; Deut. 18:1–3/1 Cor. 9:13; Deut. 8:3/1 Cor. 10:3; Deut. 10:17/1 Cor. 10:20; Deut. 10:21/1 Cor. 10:22; Deut. 10:14/1 Cor. 10:26–28.

to material head coverings or to hair minimizes its significance. First Corinthians still addresses the trivialization and transgression of boundaries between the sexes. Those boundaries were established in creation, assumed in the moral law, and protected in the judicial law. Society has no right to abandon them, but it is particularly obnoxious for the church to do so in worship, rejecting the order that God has established to his face.

The idea of a link between 1 Corinthians 11 and Deuteronomy 22 may merit further detailed investigation, but whichever of those two possibilities seems more convincing, we ought to consider how the doctrine of the law relates to such issues. Preaching the law to our congregations is not just proclaiming what it requires, but also not demanding what it does not require and focusing instead on the principles that such a New Testament passage upholds. Ministers who make Paul a lawgiver in 1 Corinthians undermine the Reformed and catholic doctrines of law, along with atonement, sin, good works, worship, and whatever else depends on the doctrine of law.

Tithe and Grow Rich?

If Reformed theology cannot make Paul or Jesus lawgivers, it also cannot make Moses a lawgiver beyond his time and treat laws outside the Decalogue as ever-binding moral law. One of the marvels of the modern church is that some within it set aside the fourth commandment in the Decalogue while insisting on the abiding validity of tithing. While no Reformed church will want to slim down the Decalogue, it is puzzling that some impose tithing on their congregations, or assume the abiding legitimacy of the practice. Even a superficial reading of chapter 19 of the Westminster Confession should raise questions about such an assumption.

The moral law "doth for ever bind all" (WCF 19.5), but all else is "abrogated" (19.3), "not obliging any other now" (19.4). The abrogated ceremonial laws do hold forth various "instructions of moral duties" (19.3). Likewise, the judicial laws that "expired" with the ancient Israelite state still contain "general equity" that we are obliged to follow (19.4). Giving a tenth of one's income is, however, neither such a moral duty nor abiding general equity; it is an attempt at literal application of the tithing laws. Paul's reference to cleansing out the old leaven in 1 Corinthians 5 is an example of a moral duty held forth in a ceremonial law, while his reference to treading oxen in 1 Corinthians 9 is an example of general equity.

The example of 1 Corinthians 9 might also be slightly troubling to those who endorse tithing. What was Paul thinking? At the very point when he should have laid down the law on tithing, he drags a hungry ox out of the stable. If only he had thought to say to the Corinthians, "Embrace the tithe and the church will never go short." Or even better, "Send in a check and an even bigger one will miraculously turn up in the mail." To make matters worse, even when he refers to the priests' getting their food from the temple in 1 Corinthians 9:13, he makes no direct reference to tithes. Nor does 1 Corinthians 16:2—"something . . . as he may prosper" allows for a range of circumstances and proportions. Paul also forgets about tithing in 1 Timothy 5:18. It seems that he has no interest in a literal application of laws about tithing, only in applying general principles of justice and fairness found in the law.

Should we be surprised at this? Not if the statements in the Westminster Confession of Faith about ceremonial and judicial law reflect biblical teaching. Had Paul taken the opportunity to reaffirm a literal application of the laws about tithing, we would be bound to excise those sections of the confession.

In any case, what is assumed to be a literal application of the laws about tithing in the call to give 10 percent of one's income is not even a literal application, since the combined tithes required under Mosaic law came to more than 20 percent. It is perplexing that someone arguing for tithing should recognize this and then write, as R. T. Kendall does: "Are Christians bound to tithe like this today? No. This elaborate system was a part of the Mosaic law. . . . I am satisfied that the Christian obligation is a basic 10% of his income."[24]

Other arguments for sustaining tithing are also weak in the context of the Westminster doctrine of the law. Even assuming that Jesus endorsed the Pharisees' tithing when he said, "These you ought to have done, without neglecting the others" (Matt. 23:23), it is a

24. R. T. Kendall, *Tithing: A Call to Serious Biblical Giving* (Grand Rapids: Zondervan, 1983), 79.

nonpoint. What else would he have done? He did not approve of disobedience to any law, and it is essential to our beliefs about Jesus Christ that "He was made under the law, and did perfectly fulfil it" (WCF 8.4). His comment in Matthew 23:23 is no more significant for Christian practice than his instruction to the cleansed leper to "offer the gift that Moses commanded" (Matt. 8:4).

Similarly, even assuming that Abram's tithe to Melchizedek was a pre-Mosaic tithe, it does not give the tithe the same status as the Sabbath. It is correct that the Pentateuch presupposes the existence of all the laws in the Decalogue before its promulgation at Sinai, which supports the view that what was "written in two tables," God also "gave to Adam [as] a law" (WCF 19.1–2). Their prior existence highlights their ever-binding constitutional status, yet prior existence does not make them constitutional. By that measure, we would be obliged to append to the Decalogue not only tithing, but also laws about sacrifice and, on some interpretations of Genesis 26:5, every law of Moses.[25] The key factor that establishes a pre-Mosaic law as ever-binding is its inclusion in the Decalogue as one of those God-uttered words that would be inscribed in stone as the foundation of all other laws. Tithing does not meet those criteria. It therefore has no abiding jurisdiction beyond "the people of Israel, as a church under age" (WCF 19.3) and "as a body politick" (19.4).

"Yee Must Have Compassion of Your Brethren . . ."

It is our duty as teachers to set people free from this burden rather than to "tie up heavy burdens, hard to bear, and lay them on people's shoulders" (Matt. 23:4). For some poor Christians, even the undercalculated 10 percent is an intolerable burden. To tell them that if they give a tenth of their meager income God will surely make up for it is to peddle false hope.[26] Why should God reward obedience to laws that have expired, whether tithing, circumcision, or anything else?

25. Ephraim E. Urbach, *The Sages: Their Concepts and Beliefs*, trans. Israel Abrahams (Jerusalem: Magnes Press, Hebrew University of Jerusalem, 1990), 318.

26. For example, Kendall, *Tithing*, 92: "What if one cannot afford to tithe? The answer is, we cannot afford not to tithe." Similarly, in the case of *Christians v. Crystal Evangelical Free Church (In re Young)*, "the Youngs felt they could *not* afford to not tithe to their church." See Troy S. Anderson, "*Christians v. Crystal Evangelical*

It is especially perverse for church leaders to argue that Christians facing sequestration or bankruptcy should give to the church ahead of their creditors.[27] Does God no longer desire mercy and not sacrifice? For churches to argue for such "giving" is again to give a law that no longer binds priority over the eighth commandment, which is ever-binding.

In such circumstances, we should approve of the sentiments expressed by John Knox and his five fellow Johns in *The First Book of Discipline* (1560) concerning the patrimony of the church: "If yee will have God authour and approver of this reformation, ye must not follow their foot-steps [Papists], but yee must have compassion of your brethren, appointing them to pay reasonable teinds [tithes], that they may finde some benefit of Christ Jesus now preached unto them."[28] Let us be the first to set people free as we call them to the Christ whose yoke is easy and whose burden is light.

How Much Is Enough?

What, then, should we teach people about giving if a straightforward instruction to give a 10 percent cut to the church is not required? We have probably all heard scolding demands from the pulpit that Christians open their wallets. That can be avoided only if the call to give comes to us from Christ, not Moses—a subject to which we will turn in a moment. The Savior's free and cheerful giving of himself is the foundation and motivation for all our giving (2 Cor. 8:9). If we have not embraced him to the extent that we have begun to emulate his giving, how can we call anyone else to give with authenticity? If we

---

Free Church (*In re Young*): Why Would 'Christians' Take Money Out of the Church Offering Plate?," *Regent University Law Review* 4 (1994): 209.

27. See John J. Dyer and Gregory T. Jones, "Judicial Treatment of Charitable Donations in Bankruptcy before and after the Religious Liberty and Charitable Contribution Protection Act of 1998," *DePaul Business & Commercial Law Journal* 2, no. 2 (2004): 265–94.

28. John Knox et al., *The First Book of Discipline* (1560), in *The Government of the Church of Scotland Fully Declared* (London: Sold by John Sweeting at the Angel in Popes-head-Alley, 1647), 51. For a survey of how tithing was viewed in church history, see David A. Croteau, "A Biblical and Theological Analysis of Tithing: Toward a Theology of Giving in the New Covenant Era" (PhD diss., Southeastern Baptist Theological Seminary, 2005), 8–23.

have never done anything for his sake that bore a cost, even though it be a hidden cost, will it not show somehow?

It must begin like that because Jesus has more admiration for a poor widow who gives all she has to live on than for rich benefactors giving out of their abundance (Luke 21:4). The only percentage he ever mentioned was "all that you have" (18:22), though he offered no corrective to a man who went only halfway (19:8). We honor Christ not by setting tariffs, but by proclaiming his glory and humility, by seeking to follow him and calling others to do likewise. If we share his intense commitment to the kingdom of God, the call to give "all that you have" is not a terrible demand that makes tithing look attractive, but our heart's desire. We want to understand what it means to obey it in our circumstances. If we find our own hearts opened in that way, we know that it will be enough to proclaim Christ, so that when we present the biblical reminders to support the ministry of the church and to care for poor brethren, Christian people will excel in the grace of giving (2 Cor. 8:7). Moses cannot open hearts; Christ does.

Who Should Be a Christian's Teacher?

If angry demands do not make Christians give, they also will not make Christians obedient, and if a minister is adversarial in his preaching, the congregation might begin to wonder what has possessed him. If he likes to preach the moral law as summarized in the Decalogue, they may attribute his aggression to the law. But the law did not make the preacher that way. Nor does his rage reflect God's purposes as lawgiver toward mankind or his people. The fury normally comes from within, expressing turbulent personality rather than righteous anger springing from a sense of affronted divine majesty.

Discussing preaching on the moral law as summarized in the Decalogue is not the same as discussing the distinction between law and gospel, or discussing "legal preaching." Some homiletical statutes want to make legal preachers of us all, to reduce every Scripture to an imperative, and to suppose that unless our hearers exit the building knowing exactly what they must do on Monday morning, we have failed. Legal preaching may in fact pay little attention to biblical law. It does not need to identify 365 negative commandments in the Torah to leave congregations straining a spiritual sinew for every day of the year; legal preaching can even exploit the gospel of grace to divert Christian out of his way and toward Mr. Legality's house.

Preaching the moral law does not mean only those occasions when we might preach on Exodus 20 or Deuteronomy 5. The Ten Words permeate the whole of Scripture, so we may find ourselves preaching the moral law from any of 1,187 other chapters in the Bible. The moral law "doth for ever bind all." Being justified does not justify disobedience. Christ in the gospel strengthens our obligation to obey (WCF 19.5). Nor does being unjustified justify disobedience. The moral law, which is "of great use" to the regenerate, is also useful "to others . . . as a rule of life" and to show them their need of Christ (19.6). Its distinct uses for both classes are not "contrary to the grace of the gospel, but do sweetly comply with it" (19.7).

It is therefore somewhat jarring for anyone to preach the moral law with severity that empties it of all sweetness. That cannot express God's goodness in giving it to all men as a "perfect rule of righteousness" (WCF 19.2), nor the Spirit of Christ's readiness to subdue and enable our wills to freely and cheerfully do what it requires (19.7). How can I learn to preach God's law with sweetness, or even just without censoriousness and contrived solemnity?

I could try to develop the psalmist's spiritual tastes, meditating on the law of God all the day (Ps. 119:97) until, having gained more understanding than all my teachers (v. 99), his words are sweet to my taste (v. 103). It should be hard, then, to preach his commandments as if they were burdensome. I could also remind myself of my own miserable failures in keeping the law, and ask myself a few pointed questions such as: "Do you suppose, O man—you who judge those who practice such things and yet do them yourself—that you will escape the judgment of God?" (Rom. 2:3), or "While you preach against stealing, do you steal? You who say that one must not commit adultery, do you commit adultery?" (vv. 21–22). That, too, should make for a gentler proclamation from anyone who has found that the law of God discovered the "sinful pollutions of their nature, hearts, and lives" (WCF 19.6).

Useful, however, as all that is, it may not be enough to give my preaching the taste of sweet compliance. That will come down to how I receive the law. Ireful preaching of the law comes from within. Though it may come from God insofar as it proclaims bald precepts, it does not come from God insofar as my demeanor lets slip that I have been saying to God in private, "I knew you to be a hard man, reaping where you did not sow, and gathering where you scattered no seed" (Matt. 25:24). It is the same law of God I preach, but how I receive it from God shapes my delivery of the message.

Only at the Hands of Christ

In *The Marrow of Modern Divinity*, Evangelista, having explained to Nomista that the "law of Christ, in regard of substance and matter, is all one with the law of works, or covenant of works," goes on to respond to Nomista's observation that "their forms do differ."[29] "The one," says Evangelista, "is to be delivered by God as he is Creator out of Christ, only to such as are out of Christ; the other is to be delivered by God, as he is a Redeemer in Christ, only to such as are in Christ. Wherefore, neighbor Neophytus, seeing that you are now in Christ, beware that you receive not the Ten Commandments at the hands of God out of Christ, nor yet at the hands of Moses, but only at the hands of Christ; and so shall you be sure to receive them as the law of Christ."[30]

If I receive the law of God from the hands of God out of Christ, I will, as Thomas Boston points out in his note, "receive them as the law (or covenant) of works,"[31] which means that my preaching of the law will never rise above a frantic effort to secure in others the "conviction of, humiliation for, and hatred against sin" (WCF 19.6), which I am struggling to secure in myself. The anger toward the transgressions of others comes from within because Christ is not within, since I have not received the law from his hands. Receiving the law out of Christ may make me punctilious, but it will be of limited use to me and to others. It is a path that we are liable to follow if we forget that "Christ should be a Christian's teacher, and not Moses."[32]

---

29. Edward Fisher, *The Marrow of Modern Divinity* (Fearn, Scotland: Christian Focus, 2015), 185.
30. Fisher, *The Marrow of Modern Divinity*, 186.
31. Fisher, *The Marrow of Modern Divinity*, 186n4.
32. Fisher, *The Marrow of Modern Divinity*, 187.

Helpful preaching of the law must begin with our own reception of the law from the hands of Christ, with his Spirit enabling us to display free and cheerful obedience, which adorns the sweet compliance of the moral law as a rule of life with the grace of the gospel. Such obedience will in principle be no different in a minister than it is in anyone else. That he must be above reproach (1 Tim. 3:2), or that the moral law applies to him and his household (vv. 2–5), does not mean that there is a uniquely ministerial way not to take the Lord's name in vain or not to commit adultery. Perhaps free and cheerful obedience will mean deleting your Twitter account[33] to keep the second commandment, taking physical rest to honor the fourth, or not entangling yourself in the "sinful snares" bound up in extrabiblical ordination vows to fulfill the ninth.

Only like Christ

The best example of what free and cheerful obedience to the Decalogue will look like in a preacher filled with the Spirit of Christ must be Christ Jesus. Though Jesus was accused of transgressing the moral law (John 5:18; 8:13; 19:7), no one can uphold those accusations without also rejecting Jesus and the gospel. His obedience, however, was not the mere absence of transgression, but many acts of consecration flowing from a pure and undivided heart. Despite keeping him under constant watch to accuse him, his opponents could never accuse him of hypocrisy. Unlike them, his love for the law leaves no area of his life untouched. Single-minded devotion to God (I) frees him from seeking security apart from God (II) so that he is a true worshiper (III) who enjoys the Sabbath as made for man (IV). That devotion makes him a wise son (V) and a preserver of life (VI). He treats the women around him as mothers and sisters in all purity (VII), rendering what was due to whom it was due (VIII), always speaking the truth (IX), and exhibiting complete disentanglement from things (X).

Before Jesus ever preached on the law, his life displayed the law's true intent, which Judaism had obscured. When he said, "You have heard. . . . But I say to you . . ." (Matt. 5:21–30), his was not the

---

33. Visit https://help.twitter.com/en/managing-your-account/how-to-deactivate -twitter-account (and stay away for at least thirty-one days).

preaching without practice that he saw in the scribes and the Pharisees (23:2). Like their master, the Lord's apostles must not emulate the preaching and practice of the camel-swallowers, but exceed their righteousness (5:20). The apostolic preaching, including ours, will be credible only if we emulate Christ, following God's directions and teaching his commandments in a way that displays their intent, never limiting their jurisdiction to outward behavior or ceasing to pursue the unreserved devotion to God and his kingdom to which they call us.

Proclaiming the True Intent

The contrast between Jesus and the Pharisees stands out in their approaches to several of the Ten Words. He accused them of making "void the word of God" because their tradition justified disobeying the fifth commandment (Matt. 15:3–6). The sixth commandment would also have to yield to "Jews" of whom Jesus said "none of you keeps the law" (John 7:19). But it was the fourth commandment that most often revealed that they had received the law as from a tyrannical master rather than Israel's fatherly God (Ps. 89:26–34). That reinforced their tendency to focus on outward conformity and confirmed their inability to grasp the true intent of the commandment. Their Sabbath was a spiritual minefield—move an inch and you'd be blown to bits. The Mishnah, which sees itself as transmitting "an essential part of the revelation of the Torah at Sinai,"[34] records where some of the mines had been laid. The first situation in its section on Shabbat addresses the moral conundrum of finding a beggar outside one's house on the Sabbath. If this Lazarus stuck his hand inside the house to get something, then he would be liable, but what if the householder stuck his hand outside and put something into the beggar's bowl? Then the householder would be guilty.[35] Another law forbids the roasting of "meat, onions, and eggs, unless there is time for them to be roasted while it is still day [Friday]."[36]

---

34. Jacob Neusner, *Making God's Word Work: A Guide to the Mishnah* (New York: Continuum, 2004), 33.

35. *The Mishnah: A New Translation*, trans. Jacob Neusner (New Haven, CT: Yale University Press, 1988), 179.

36. *Mishnah*, 180.

Were such regulations absurd? To some Christians they may sound absurd, but to others they will sound strangely familiar because they have lived under a Sabbath regime that owes more to the spirit of rabbinic Judaism than to the Spirit of Christ. Legalistic Sabbatarianism may largely have given way to disregard for the pattern of rest and work that God established, yet when preachers seek to reverse that disregard and to make practical applications of the fourth commandment, there is always a risk of sounding as though we found the Mishnah more helpful than the Gospels. But the memoirs and remains of the Pharisees are still at odds with Jesus Christ.

Jesus never disregarded the Sabbath day. He may have trampled over Judaic legal tradition, but in all his conflicts with the scribes and Pharisees over Sabbath, he proclaimed the true intent of the fourth commandment, just as he did for the fifth and sixth. That never amounted to a similar but more intense application: "You have heard it said that you shall not roast onions on the Sabbath, but I say to you, whoever thinks about a favorite recipe on the Sabbath has desecrated the seventh day." Jesus brings out the intent of the law in a different way.

The Gospels offer many examples, one of which is in the account of the woman bent double (Luke 13:10–17). Whatever the medical description of her awkward posture, Jesus put it down to Satan, from whose bind he freed her with the laying on of his hands and a declaration of freedom. Then, while she glorified God for her release, the synagogue ruler had a meltdown, insisting that there are six days for work, including healing, and the Sabbath is not one of them.

Jesus' first response exposes the hypocrisy of the synagogue congregation—they disapprove of his healing on the Sabbath, yet they care for their beasts. Their hypocrisy, however, goes beyond double standards. It includes a refusal to see what God is doing (Luke 12:56), which also affects their reading of the fourth commandment. They see that the fourth commandment deals with labor and work, but they should also see that Sabbath rest points to a greater rest, which has implications for them:

- They are in the middle of a war between Satan and the angels of God;

- The Sabbath rest that God promised Israel will come when Satan is defeated;
- When a daughter of Abraham is set free from Satan's fetters, God strikes a blow to Satan that declares his imminent defeat;
- God strikes that blow through Jesus.

That makes Jesus' healing acts necessary. It was not necessary to heal the woman on the Sabbath just because she was disabled. Healing her of her stoop could wait one more day. It was necessary (δεῖ) that she be healed because the fourth commandment required it. This was its true intent. The Sabbath commandment does not just permit such liberation; it demands it. Jesus' healing act proclaimed it, and it remains the chief end of the Sabbath to deliver to God's people the rest that Christ's work has secured for them.

When the kingdom of God comes in its fullness, that rest will be delivered to us as complete physical and spiritual renewal, which will seal Satan's defeat. It is the minister's task in the meantime to deliver as much of that rest as we can to God's people through the preaching of the gospel and the ministry of the church. In doing so, we obey the fourth commandment and teach them to do likewise. That does not dissolve its practical requirements but does "much strengthen" them (WCF 19.3), though not by way of exhaustive codification. If we have received the commandment from Christ and had him as our teacher, obedience to it is neither a restriction nor a bare duty, but an opportunity to taste the rest and liberty of all that is yet to come in the kingdom of God.

Conclusion

One goal for this volume has been to set out how the doctrines in each chapter should shape a pastor's life and ministry. I have mentioned several ways in which our understanding of biblical law affects what we preach and how we preach. I have also suggested that the moral law should shape a minister's life just as it should shape anyone else's life. But how should the law shape our ministry? Should it? There is always a risk that in my hands, the law will produce a "ministry of death, carved in letters on stone" (2 Cor. 3:7), only without the glory. So when I ask, "How should the law shape our ministry?," I want to answer, "It shouldn't; Christ should." My priority is to have a life and ministry shaped by Jesus Christ. Such a life and ministry will not be at odds with the confessional teaching on law; it will incorporate it by default, and in the only way that enables me to deliver it to others with the glory of the life-giving Spirit.

Only Jesus Christ can teach us how these applications and uses of the law "sweetly comply" with the "grace of the Gospel" (WCF 19.7). They comply because, as Sinclair Ferguson writes, "it was not legalism for Jesus to do everything his Father commanded him. Nor is it for us."[37] Likewise, they comply because it is not antinomianism for us to set people free from additions to the law, or from literal application of laws that are now abrogated or expired because Christ Jesus has done everything his Father commanded.

"We appreciate the clarity of the law only when we gaze fully into Christ's face. But when we do gaze there, we see the face of the one who said, 'Oh how I love your law; it is my meditation all the day'— and we want to be like him."[38]

Key Terms

atonement
ceremonial law
Decalogue
judicial law
moral law
Sabbath
tithing

Recommendations for Further Reading

Ferguson, Sinclair B. *The Whole Christ: Legalism, Antinomianism, and Gospel Assurance—Why the Marrow Controversy Still Matters.* Wheaton, IL: Crossway, 2016.

37. Sinclair B. Ferguson, *The Whole Christ: Legalism, Antinomianism, and Gospel Assurance—Why the Marrow Controversy Still Matters* (Wheaton, IL: Crossway, 2016), 173.
38. Ferguson, *The Whole Christ,* 172.

Fisher, Edward. *The Marrow of Modern Divinity*. Fearn, Scotland: Christian Focus, 2015.

Martin, Hugh. *The Atonement: In Its Relations to the Covenant, the Priesthood, the Intercession of Our Lord*. Edinburgh: Lyon and Gemmell, 1877.

Discussion Questions

1. Thinking of the various subjects addressed in this book or in the Westminster Confession of Faith, think about how those subjects depend on and relate to the view of law expressed in the confession. For example, sin (WCF 6.6), covenants (7), Christ's active obedience (8.4), good works (16), liberty of conscience (20), worship (21).

2. "Good works are only such as God has commanded in his holy word" (WCF 16.1). Could one of Christ's apostles demand a previously unlegislated good work?

3. How would you characterize the two sacraments in relation to biblical law? Is "Do this in remembrance of me" (Luke 22:19) a law? If so, how could Christ be under the law, yet proclaim new law, and what are the implications of your characterization for the Reformed view of the law?

4. What is the foundation of Christian giving—law or grace?

5. What ten passages in the Gospels would you choose to highlight Christ's obedience to each of the Ten Commandments?

6. Jesus Christ brought out the true intent of the fourth commandment. What implications does that have for how we seek to obey it?

7. How can we receive the law "only at the hands of Christ," yet still preach the law with proper sensitivity to the context of its delivery "at the hands of Moses"?

19

CHRISTIAN LIBERTY

The Pastor as the Guardian of Freedom[1]

DAVID STRAIN

The recovery and defense of the doctrine of Christian liberty is at once among the most important achievements of the Protestant Reformation and one of the most precious possessions of the Christian believer. John Calvin wrote that Christian freedom is "a thing of prime necessity, and apart from a knowledge of it consciences dare undertake almost nothing without doubting."[2] In view of the complex ethical questions facing the contemporary church, however, a nuanced re-presentation of the doctrine of Christian liberty presents a unique challenge:

1. Though I doubt he knows it, Sinclair B. Ferguson has had a profound effect on my life and ministry since I first heard him preach at St. George's Tron in Glasgow as a recently converted teenager. When I began training for the ministry, someone gave me cassette tapes of messages he had preached on various subjects related to the call and work of the ministry. I wore those tapes out, and God used them to sustain me through some very dry times in a liberal seminary context in Scotland. Sinclair's blend of pastoral warmth, penetrating exegesis, and theological depth has been a model to me throughout my ministry, and I owe him an incalculable debt.

2. John Calvin, *Institutes of the Christian Religion*, ed. John T. McNeill, trans. Ford Lewis Battles, 2 vols., Library of Christian Classics 20–21 (Philadelphia: Westminster, 1960), 3.19.1.

367

Like a coin handled for too long by too many hands, "freedom" has lost its clear imprint. We still circulate the coin—the more quickly and the more frequently the less it's worth. Yet we no longer know what "freedom" means. Is it what is realized when we create the meaning and the values of our own lives? Is it what is brought about when we exercise the right of making our own choices without being answerable to anyone? Is it what is mandated by political liberation and self-determination? Is it what is presupposed by moral responsibility? Is it what comes about when we receive the gospel of God's free grace? Is it several of these? Or all of them? Or is "freedom" simply an equivocal term that covers fundamentally different and ultimately incompatible things?[3]

In an effort to eradicate moral ambiguities, it is all too easy to adopt needlessly narrow restrictions on Christian behavior or, in an attempt to stay relevant, to give way to the spirit of the age entirely ("times change, after all, and the church must change with them!"). Given these challenges, it has never been more important to understand and clearly articulate the main contours of Christian liberty. Fidelity requires the minister of the gospel to navigate these waters with care and compassion, but without compromise.

The Theme of Freedom in Redemptive History

As we will see, the New Testament explains Christian freedom as a fruit of Christ's redemptive ministry. We note, however, that the basic "grammar and syntax" of freedom from bondage, in which the New Testament is so fluent, is drawn from the redemptive themes of the Hebrew Bible. Christ's earthly ministry is explained in light of the history of Israel, especially her deliverance from bondage in the exodus. As Moisés Silva points out, Israel's "long period of Egyptian slavery became a powerful symbol of oppression, and so the deliverance of the Israelites through Moses spoke to them of freedom in a more profound sense—indeed, of spiritual redemption."[4] Thus, Isra-

3. Reinhard Hütter, *Bound to Be Free: Evangelical Catholic Engagements in Ecclesiology, Ethics, and Ecumenism* (Grand Rapids: Eerdmans, 2004), 112.

4. Moisés Silva, *The Evangelical Dictionary of Biblical Theology*, ed. Walter A.

el's deliverance foreshadows and anticipates a much fuller liberation that Christ would accomplish.

The annual Passover celebration reminded Israel that by means of the blood of a lamb, the people were delivered from death and redeemed from Egyptian bondage (Ex. 12; Num. 9; Deut. 16). Their freedom is blood-bought. Subsequently, the exodus event itself serves as the gracious indicative that grounds all the imperatives of the Decalogue as a whole (Ex. 20:2; Deut. 5:6), and of the Sabbath command in particular (Deut. 5:12–15), demonstrating that redemption from bondage was understood to issue in obedience to God. According to Deuteronomy 15, slaves were to be released and debts were to be canceled every seventh year because "you shall remember that you were a slave in the land of Egypt, and the LORD your God redeemed you" (Deut. 15:15). Leviticus 25:1–7 provides for a Sabbath for the land, and in verses 8–22, the Year of Jubilee required Israel to "consecrate the fiftieth year, and proclaim liberty throughout the land to all its inhabitants" (Lev. 25:10). Thus, built into the liturgical rhythms of the Hebrew calendar and into the civil laws of the nation were regular reminders of deliverance from slavery by the grace of the Lord. The very fabric of Israel's faith and culture was to bear witness to the freedom that God had provided.

Israel's subsequent history was marked by cycles of covenant faithfulness and decline into idolatry, leading in turn to oppression by pagan nations, climaxing in exile, in accordance with the covenant curse of the Lord (Deut. 28:25–40; 2 Chron. 7:22; cf. Jer. 7:21–34; Dan. 9:11–15; Neh. 1:8–9). Throughout Israel's history, the theme of exodus liberation features prominently in the praise and prayers of the faithful (e.g., 1 Chron. 17:21; Neh. 9; Pss. 77:16–20; 78; 81; 99:6–7; 103:6–7; 105:26–45). And the redemption of the people from bondage, together with the motif of a new exodus, came to play a significant role in the ministry of the prophets (see Isa. 63:11–12; Mic. 5:1–4; 6:4). Isaiah 61:1–2, for example, develops the language of the Year of Jubilee from Leviticus 25. The prophet looks to a day when the Servant of the Lord will establish true freedom:

Elwell, s.v. "Freedom" (Grand Rapids: Baker, 1996), 270.

The Spirit of the Lord God is upon me,
  because the Lord has anointed me
to bring good news to the poor;
  he has sent me to bind up the brokenhearted,
to proclaim liberty to the captives,
  and the opening of the prison to those who are bound;
to proclaim the year of the Lord's favor,
  and the day of vengeance of our God. (Isa. 61:1–2)

As redemptive history progresses, these themes coalesce with the coming of Jesus Christ. Mary's song in Luke 1:46–55 concludes by placing the advent of Christ into the context of the fulfillment of the covenant promise, echoing the words spoken to Moses before the exodus (Ex. 3:6–9). The same themes reappear in the song of Zechariah, whose son, John, would call Israel to a new exodus (Luke 1:68–75). Luke 3:4–6 quotes Isaiah 40:3–5, in which, as Darrell Bock points out:

Isaiah declares that God is repeating the fundamental pattern of his salvation, an exodus like that which formed the nation. . . . Isaiah discusses how God repeatedly saves his people in a pattern like the exodus. God did it in the Babylonian period, but the language of these texts looks for a more complete vindication that Luke now proclaims is about to be fulfilled.[5]

When John baptized Jesus, he alluded to the significance of the Paschal Lamb, declaring of Christ, "Behold, the Lamb of God, who takes away the sin of the world!" (John 1:29). Likewise, when Jesus celebrated his last Passover with his disciples, he told them that the bread was his body, and the cup the new covenant in his blood (Matt. 26:26–29; Mark 14:22–25; Luke 22:19–20; 1 Cor. 11:23–25). The liberation from Egyptian bondage, effected by the blood of the Passover lamb, is understood by the New Testament authors to point to the blood of Christ, the Lamb of God, who brings liberation from sin's curse. "Christ, our Passover lamb, has been sacrificed" (1 Cor. 5:7).

---

5. Darrell L. Bock, *Luke 1:1–9:50*, BECNT 3A (Grand Rapids: Baker, 1994), 292.

Likewise, in Luke 4, Christ read the Isaiah scroll in the synagogue at Capernaum. His text was Isaiah 61:1–2, quoted above, in which the prophet takes up the Levitical language of the Year of Jubilee, which recalls Israel's liberation from slavery, and applies it to a future day of deliverance. After reading, Jesus sat down and said, "Today this Scripture has been fulfilled in your hearing" (Luke 4:21). The message is unambiguous: in Christ the true liberation of captives has come. Similarly, 1 Corinthians 7:22–23 declares that "he who was called in the Lord as a bondservant is a freedman of the Lord. Likewise, he who was free when called is a bondservant of Christ. You were bought with a price; do not become bondservants of men." Here again, we note the echoes of the Year of Jubilee and the manumission of slaves. Jesus sets captives free.

In view of this brief survey, it is clear that the scriptural theme of liberation is a central artery in the biblical corpus, leading to the very heart of the message of redemption in Jesus Christ.

Christian Freedom Is "in Christ"

We have noted the importance of freedom imagery throughout Scripture. Now, as we proceed to trace the contours of the doctrine more systematically, it is crucial not to lose sight of the central soteriological affirmation of the New Testament: that believers enjoy all the benefits of redemption "in Christ" (John 15:1–11; Rom. 5:12–20; 6:1–11; Eph. 1:3–14; etc.). Christians are free, but that freedom is a facet of their union with Jesus Christ. We are free only because we are "in him." This becomes clear when we notice that the New Testament regularly coordinates these two truths and brings them into the closest possible connection. For example, Paul warns of false brothers secretly brought in to spy out the "freedom that we have *in Christ*" (Gal. 2:4). In Romans 6, Paul expounds the theme of union with Christ in his death and resurrection, which results in our being "set free from sin" (Rom. 6:7, 18, 22). In the death Christ died, we died to sin. The resurrection life into which he entered is the new life of freedom from the wages of sin that comes to us. In the resurrection, the Father pronounced himself satisfied with the atonement Christ had made. On the third day, Jesus was vindicated. He was "justified."

By virtue of our union with Christ in his resurrection, the vindication of Christ—the verdict of the Father pronounced over him—is pronounced over us. Thus, we are free forever from condemnation, for "the law of the Spirit of life has set [us] free *in Christ Jesus* from the law of sin and death" (Rom. 8:1–2). Christian freedom is one important way in which Scripture describes the blessedness of the believer's union with Christ. This means that we must not conceive of Christian freedom as an abstraction. The freedom in view cannot be found outside Christ. Not only is Christ our liberator, but he is himself the realm and sphere of our liberty. We are free *in him*. Apart from him, we are not free. Christ, therefore, completely defines the bounds of this liberty, both soteriologically and ethically.

Christian Freedom Is "Freedom From . . ."

From what, then, are those who are united to Christ set free? First, the Christian believer is *free from the condemnation of the law*. Paul's succinct declarative statement of freedom from condemnation in Romans 8:1 has already been noted. Similarly, 1 Thessalonians 1:10 urges us to wait for the Son from heaven, whom God raised from the dead, even Jesus, "who delivers us from the wrath to come." Likewise, Galatians 3:13 rehearses the good news that "Christ redeemed us from the curse of the law by becoming a curse for us." To be in Christ, who was condemned and vindicated, necessarily entails the freedom of the Christian from the condemnation that our sins deserve. The debt is paid in full. It is finished. We are freed.

Second, we are *free from the obligations of the ceremonial law*. Galatians 4:1–3 asserts that God's people, under the Mosaic administration, while "sons," are nonetheless "no different from a slave" until their majority. This majority has come with the redemption won in Christ (Gal. 4:4). Similarly, the allegory of Galatians 4:21–31 contrasts those who still wished to live as "children of the slave" woman, understood as those who wish to live under the now-obsolete Mosaic economy, with those who are "children . . . of the free woman," those who, through Christ, are free from its obligations. The ceremonial law finds its antitype in the person and work of Christ, and its demands no longer constrain believers.

Third, Christians are *free from the bondage of sin*. Romans 6:12 urges Christians not to allow sin to have dominion in their mortal bodies. In verse 14, Paul supplies the reason: "For sin will have no dominion over you, since you are not under law but under grace." Romans 8:2 says that the "law of the Spirit of life has set you free in Christ Jesus from the law of sin and death." Paul's thought here, according to John Murray, "moves in the realm of internal operation and not in that of objective accomplishment."[6] In other words, the freedom in view is a deliverance from sin's dominion in the life of the believer. We have been transferred from the tyranny of sin under which we are unable, in our natural condition, to please God, and brought instead under the governance of a new principle of grace implanted in the heart.

Fourth, those who are in Christ are set *free from the bondage of Satan*. The Father, Paul tells us, "has delivered us from the domain of darkness and transferred us to the kingdom of his beloved Son, in whom we have redemption, the forgiveness of sins" (Col. 1:13–14). Jesus, in calling Saul of Tarsus, commissions him to go to the Gentiles to "open their eyes, so that they may turn from darkness to light and from the power of Satan to God, that they may receive forgiveness of sins and a place among those who are sanctified by faith in me" (Acts 26:18). Once we were "dead in the trespasses and sins in which [we] once walked, following the course of this world, following the prince of the power of the air, the spirit that is now at work in the sons of disobedience," but now, since by grace alone we have been "made . . . alive together with Christ," the prince of the power of the air no longer holds sway (Eph. 2:1–10).

And fifth, Christians are *free from the commandments of men*. The Christian's freedom from doctrines or practices that are not taught in Holy Scripture is part of the genius of the Protestant conception of the Christian life. In articulating this, texts such as Matthew 15:6–9 are frequently appealed to: "for the sake of your tradition you have made void the word of God. . . . 'In vain do they worship me, teaching as doctrines the commandments of men.'" In Acts 4:19–20, Peter and John answer the Sanhedrin, "Whether it is right in the sight of God

---

6. John Murray, *The Epistle to the Romans*, NICNT (Grand Rapids: Eerdmans, 1959), 1:277.

to listen to you rather than to God, you must judge, for we cannot but speak of what we have seen and heard." And in Acts 5:29, the apostles tell the church, "We must obey God rather than men." Similarly, in Colossians 2:20–23, Paul states that binding the conscience by man-made regulations is incompatible with the freedom we have in Christ: "If with Christ you died to the elemental spirits of the world, why, as if you were still alive in the world, do you submit to regulations—'Do not handle, Do not taste, Do not touch' (referring to things that all perish as they are used)—according to human precepts and teachings? These have indeed an appearance of wisdom in promoting self-made religion and asceticism and severity to the body, but they are of no value in stopping the indulgence of the flesh."

Few summaries of this part of the doctrine surpass the Westminster Confession of Faith's masterful statement:

> God alone is Lord of the conscience, and hath left it free from the doctrines and commandments of men which are in anything contrary to his word; or beside it, if matters of faith, or worship. So that to believe such doctrines, or to obey such commandments out of conscience, is to betray true liberty of conscience: and the requiring of an implicit faith, and an absolute and blind obedience, is to destroy liberty of conscience, and reason also. (WCF 20.2)

A detailed exposition of this paragraph is beyond the scope of this chapter. It is worth noting, however, that the confession is applying its earlier statement concerning the sufficiency of Scripture to the question of conscience:

> The whole counsel of God, concerning all things necessary for his own glory, man's salvation, faith, and life, is either expressly set down in Scripture, or by good and necessary consequence may be deduced from Scripture; unto which nothing at any time is to be added, whether by new revelations of the Spirit, or traditions of men. (WCF 1.6)

If Scripture is sufficient for faith and life, to believe or obey merely human commands "out of conscience" is ruled out. The sufficiency of Scripture is the guarantor of Christian liberty. Nothing can be imposed on the believer's free conscience without a clear "thus saith the LORD." This is not to naively suggest that the Bible speaks in explicit terms to every subject or offers direction for every conceivable circumstance. Instead, as Calvin affirms, believers have the right to use "outward things that are of themselves 'indifferent.'"[7] Similarly, the Westminster Confession allows for Christian liberty in the use of human traditions, as long as these are not observed "out of conscience." Those things that are contrary to the Word are clearly forbidden. We are *not* free to do them. But there are some things that are "beside" the Word in matters of faith or worship. These indifferent things, governed by "Christian prudence, according to the general rules of the word, which are always to be observed" (WCF 1.6), may be made use of, or refrained from, by Christians in the due exercise of their liberty. Thus Calvin:

> We should use God's gifts for the purpose for which he gave them to us, with no scruple of conscience, no trouble of mind. With such confidence our minds will be at peace with him, and will recognize his liberality toward us. For here are included all ceremonies whose observance is optional, that our consciences may not be constrained by any necessity to observe them but may remember that by God's beneficence their use is for edification made subject to him.[8]

Christian Freedom Is "Freedom For . . ."

Christian liberty is not merely negative, focused on the removal of constraint. It is also positive. It is the freedom to do and act, to live and be, in accordance with the will of God.

Thus, the New Testament asserts that Christians are *free for obedience to the law*. Earlier we noted that the freedom Christ grants delivers us from the condemnation of the moral law, and from the ceremonial obligations of the Mosaic economy. But this is not at all

7. Calvin, *Institutes*, 3.19.7.
8. Calvin, *Institutes*, 3.19.8.

to suggest that Christians are free from the requirement to keep the moral law. To be sure, they do so now without any regard to their justification. Law-keeping, the Christian understands, cannot result in acceptance before God: "For by works of the law no human being will be justified" (Rom. 3:20). And yet, having been adopted and counted righteous in Christ, and having had our wills renewed by his grace, believers desire to please God and live in accordance with his commandments. In Galatians 5:13–14, Paul reminds the Galatians that they "were called to freedom" and then exhorts them: "Only do not use your freedom as an opportunity for the flesh, but through love serve one another. For the whole law is fulfilled in one word: 'You shall love your neighbor as yourself.'" Fulfilling the law is the purpose for which they have been set free. Similarly, in 1 Corinthians 9:20–21, the apostle explains his missionary strategy in relation to Jews and Gentiles: "To those under the law I became as one under the law (though not being myself under the law) that I might win those under the law. To those outside the law I became as one outside the law (not being outside the law of God but under the law of Christ) that I might win those outside the law." Paul makes use of his liberty to adopt certain Mosaic ceremonial customs, which no longer bind him in the new covenant, in order to avoid giving offense to Jews when ministering to them. Yet this he does freely, without submitting to the ceremonial law as a matter of conscience. On the other hand, knowing himself to be free of such restrictions, he gladly lives without concern for dietary or ceremonial obligations among Gentiles. This does not make him an antinomian, however. He is "under the law of Christ," understood to refer to the same moral law found in the Ten Commandments and summed up by Christ as love to God and love to neighbor (Matt. 22:37–39). Paul never conceives of freedom as the removal of moral constraint, but sees it as freedom to serve God and keep his commandments. Animated by the power of the Spirit of sonship, not slavery, and as a fruit of our adoption, and a great evidence of it, we put to death the deeds of the body and live anew (Rom. 8:13–15). Thus, freed by grace for obedience, Christians do not use their liberty to indulge sin but to live as servants of God (1 Peter 2:16).

Before we move on, however, we must account for the fact that in this life, Christian obedience is always, of necessity, imperfect obedience. In Hebrews 6:10, the author reminds those to whom he writes that "God is not unjust so as to overlook your work and the love that you have shown for his name in serving the saints." But *how* is God just to reward the imperfect obedience of a Christian that, in a non-Christian, would be damnable? In a beautiful passage, Calvin contrasts the partial obedience of servants, who dread appearing before their masters until their task is perfectly performed, with sons, whose father understands their desire to please him, and who therefore accepts their imperfect obedience, and so they do not hesitate to bring their imperfect works to him: "Such sons ought we to be, firmly trusting that our services will be approved by our most merciful Father, however small, rude, and imperfect these may be."[9] God accepts our imperfect obedience *in Christ*. While Christians are enabled to obey God from the heart in a way that they could not do before, by virtue of their union with Christ the demerits of their imperfect obedience are not counted against them. We are justified in Christ by his grace and not by our works. Yet because we have been justified without works, our imperfect works are *themselves* now justified in Christ. Thus God, looking upon the Christian's obedience "in his Son, is pleased to accept and reward that which is sincere" (WCF 16.6).

Second, Christians are *free for access to God*. One of the great benefits of the new covenant is the full access and communion with God in Jesus Christ. At the death of Christ, the tearing from top to bottom of the temple curtain that blocked access to the *sanctum sanctorum* signified the opening of access to God for all for whom Christ shed his blood (Matt. 27:51). Thus, Hebrews 9:7–8 reminds us that into the most holy place "only the high priest goes, and he but once a year, and not without taking blood, which he offers for himself and for the unintentional sins of the people. By this the Holy Spirit indicates that the way into the holy places is not yet opened." But when Christ appeared as a high priest "of the good things that have come," he entered into the antitypical holy place, the heavenly presence of God, by means of his own blood (Heb. 9:11–12). Thus, now Christians "have confidence to enter the holy places by the blood of Jesus,

---

9. Calvin, *Institutes*, 3.19.5.

by the new and living way that he opened for us through the curtain, that is, through his flesh." Because Jesus is our High Priest, we can "draw near with a true heart in full assurance of faith" (10:19–22). New covenant believers have freedom of access to God flowing to them from the cross of Jesus Christ.

Third, Christians are set *free for the new creation*. In Romans 8:20–25, Paul explains that freedom is a feature of the life of the world to come. The world has been subjected to futility in hope, "that the creation itself will be set free from its bondage to corruption and obtain the freedom of the glory of the children of God. . . . And not only the creation, but we ourselves, who have the firstfruits of the Spirit, groan inwardly as we wait eagerly for adoption as sons, the redemption of our bodies." The freedom of the Christian, purchased by Christ, is consummated in the age to come and experienced by the whole creation. The "subjection," the "futility," and the "groaning" will give way to "the freedom of the glory of the children of God."

Christian Freedom Is Precious

Christian freedom, then, is a precious gift of grace. But as the letter to the Galatians makes clear, like many other precious things, Christian freedom is fragile. It needs to be carefully preserved. "For freedom Christ has set us free; stand firm therefore, and do not submit again to a yoke of slavery" (Gal. 5:1). We entitled this chapter "Christian Liberty: The Pastor as the Guardian of Freedom." Given our survey of the main contours of the doctrine of Christian liberty, what conclusions can we draw for the work of the pastor? We will focus on three areas.

First, and perhaps most obviously, the pastor *must teach Christian freedom*. Paul's repeated example here reminds us that it is the pastor's task to inform consciences, rebuke sin, and train believers for maturity. Understanding the nature and limits of Christian freedom is vital if a new generation of Christians is to faithfully navigate the complex ethical dilemmas of the contemporary scene.

Increasingly, it is becoming common in popular preaching to speak of the law of God in wholly negative terms: "The law is our enemy. We can't keep the law. The law only shows us our sin and then condemns us. But . . . good news! Jesus saves us from the law." Such sentiments, when left unqualified by an insistence that, in Christ, the law is now also our rule of life, are half-truths at best. They serve only to reinforce an aversion in some contemporary models of discipleship to the thoroughly biblical categories of duty, obedience, and the keeping of the commandments. But as Romans 8:4 makes clear, Paul believed that "the righteous requirement of the law [is] fulfilled in us, who walk not according to the flesh but according to the Spirit." Our pulpit labors are less than Pauline, then, if we do not insist on the law's righteous requirements, not simply as a tool to awaken slumbering consciences to the need of forgiveness, but as a warm encouragement to live the life of Christian liberty "under the law of Christ" (1 Cor. 9:21). Reformed pastors must not be shy to preach the law as the Christian's friend. It is the perfect law of liberty (James 1:25). In this connection, we warmly commend the Westminster Larger Catechism's exposition of the Ten Commandments as a most useful model and guide for the faithful, positive application of the principles and limits of Christian freedom.

In the second place, the pastor *must exercise Christian freedom.* Here we mention three areas in particular. First, he must exercise Christian freedom in the conduct of public worship. The sufficiency of Scripture, applied to the worship and government of the church, often called the *regulative principle*, must be carefully observed in order to protect the consciences of the people of God. Pressure to impose on the congregation elements of worship foreign to the simplicity of the New Testament, all in the service of tradition, or relevance, or outreach, can be enormous. Yet the pastor must never forget that he is charged with the care of the flock, and their tender consciences must not be violated by demanding of them what God has not commanded. Second, he must exercise Christian freedom in his own pursuit of holiness. In his private life, the pastor must remember that the liberty to which he has been called in Christ is a liberty from sin's entanglements. Godliness is an implicate of Christian freedom, and the pastor must exemplify the pursuit of holiness, that the church may see in him the potency of the liberation from sin's dominion that Christ has won for them all. And third, the pastor must exercise Christian freedom in the use he makes of the access given to us in the new covenant to the throne of grace. The bold liberty with which we may enter the most holy place is no small part of our freedom, and it belongs to the office of the pastor to be devoted "to prayer and to the ministry of the word" (Acts 6:4). Prayer, both for himself and for the flock of God, is a vital pastoral priority, and the freedom of access to God that is ours in Christ by the Spirit should be a great encouragement to pursue it diligently. Moreover, a church that rejoices in the liberty won for it at Calvary will be a praying church. Is it too much to see a connection between the widespread disappearance of the prayer meeting in American churches on the one hand and widespread confusion about Christian liberty on the other? The pastor can, by example and leadership, help to change that.

And finally, the pastor *must be ready to relinquish Christian freedom.* Here we remember the two criteria according to which Paul restricts the believer's legitimate freedom. The first is concern for the "weaker brother." Addressing the issue of idol meats in Corinth, Paul declares, "If food makes my brother stumble, I will never eat meat, lest I make my brother stumble" (1 Cor. 8:13; cf. Rom. 14:20–23). A pastor is to be a tender shepherd of the sheep, and his liberties should be readily relinquished if there is a possibility that, in exercising them, he might lead one of Christ's people to betray his or her (as yet uninformed) conscience. I was once given a tour of a Southern town by a pugnacious Presbyterian ruling elder. Fixing me with a suspicious eye, he informed me as we drove past a local Episcopal church, "We call them the Whiskey-palians, on account of how *they* believe in drinking!" To his mind, the vital distinction in his community between Presbyterians and Episcopalians was that the former did not imbibe. The hook carefully baited, he sat back to see whether I would bite. I smiled and nodded and, mercifully, managed to say nothing. However trivial or wrongheaded the firmly held hang-ups of our people may be, a faithful shepherd must know and take pains to accommodate his flock (Rom. 14:20; 1 Cor. 10:32). Yes, he must work to inform their consciences by faithful preaching and teaching, but he must not cause any to stumble needlessly by the unthinking exercise of his liberty in the process.

And the second criterion for restricting our freedom is mission. In 1 Corinthians 9:19–23, Paul explains how he exercised or curtailed his freedom for the sake of those to whom he ministered, concluding: "To the weak I became weak, that I might win the weak. I have become all things to all people, that by all means I might save some. I do it all for the sake of the gospel, that I may share with them in its blessings." Christian liberty is a blessing at the very heart of the gospel. But it is a mark of a faithful pastor that he gladly surrenders lesser liberties in regard to indifferent matters of human custom and behavior, that he might lead people into the far greater liberty from sin's slavery that Christ has won for them by his cross.

By way of illustration, one thinks of the example of Hudson Taylor. Shortly after the formation of the China Inland Mission, in the year 1866, he returned to Shanghai, at the head of the largest party of missionaries to arrive in China to date. Almost immediately their methods sparked controversy. In a move considered scandalous in the European settlement in Shanghai, everyone in the group— men and women alike—adopted Chinese dress and customs. Taylor devoted himself to learning several Chinese languages and dialects. He was proficient enough to preach in many of them and helped translate the New Testament into one of them. In an echo of Paul's principle above, Taylor said: "Let us in everything not sinful become like the Chinese." All told, he would spend fifty-one years in China, pouring out his life for Christ and the salvation of the Chinese people. He returned one last time, at the age of seventy-three. It was his eleventh visit, and there he finally laid down his life and went to his eternal reward. He is buried near the Yangtze River, awaiting the resurrection.

Through all the sacrifices and deprivations he endured, Taylor expressed a delight in seeing Chinese people come to faith in Jesus: "If I had a thousand pounds China should have it—if I had a thousand lives, China should have them. No! Not China, but Christ. Can we do too much for Him? Can we do enough for such a precious Saviour?"[10]

While sometimes extensive, the voluntary limits that a pastor will be called on to place on his liberties in the ordinary course of

---

10. Howard Taylor, *Hudson Taylor in the Early Years: The Growth of a Soul*, 6th ed. (London: China Inland Mission, 1923), 503.

his ministry are more than compensated for by the joy of being the instrument in Christ's hand as he builds his church.

In this brief survey I have endeavored to show that the biblical doctrine of Christian liberty has a pervasive influence on the life of the believer, and on the ministry of the pastor in particular. It is my conviction that a widespread failure to understand the character and limits of the doctrine contributes to many of the liabilities to which the witness of the church is exposed. Restoring the doctrine of Christian liberty to its rightful place as the guardian of the conscience and the custodian of our privileges is therefore greatly to be desired.

Key Terms

    antinomian
    ceremonial law
    Decalogue
    judicial law
    moral law
    regulative principle

Recommendations for Further Reading

Calvin, John. *Institutes of the Christian Religion*. Edited by John T. McNeill. Translated by Ford Lewis Battles. 2 vols. Library of Christian Classics 20–21. Philadelphia: Westminster, 1960. Bk. 3, chap. 19.

Ferguson, Sinclair B. "Eating Black Pudding." Chap. 4 in *In Christ Alone: Living the Gospel-Centered Life*. Orlando, FL: Reformation Trust, 2007.

Luther, Martin. *On Christian Liberty*. Minneapolis: Fortress Press, 2003.

Discussion Questions

1. What biblical principles concerning the nature of Christian freedom help to guard against the pitfalls of adding to God's moral law (legalism) or setting aside the moral law along with the ceremonial (antinomianism)?

2. What might be some common sacrifices of freedom that pastors need to make, and what biblical principles should inform why and how they should do so?
3. What are some practical ways that a pastor could both explain and model Christian liberty in his own church context?

20

WORSHIP

Grounding Our Practice in God's Word[1]

W. ROBERT GODFREY

Reformed Christianity gave great attention to the matter of worship in the sixteenth century. As John Calvin stated in his remarkable defense of the Reformation, *The Necessity of Reforming the Church*, "If it be inquired, then, by what things chiefly the Christian religion has standing existence amongst us, and maintains its truth, it will be found that the following two not only occupy the principal place, but comprehend under them all the other parts, and consequently the whole substance of Christianity, viz., a knowledge, *first*, of the mode in which God is duly worshipped; and, *secondly*, of the source from which salvation is to be obtained."[2] For Calvin, worship was the aim of theology (knowing, meeting, communing with God) and the center of Christian life (where Christians gather, learn, fellowship, serve, and prepare to live). In worship, theology comes to expression and God is encountered in practice.

For Calvin, the theology of worship, as indeed all theology, must be learned from the Scriptures. When one understands the Scriptures

---

1. Sinclair Ferguson for many years has been a faithful servant of Jesus as an extraordinary pastor, preacher, teacher, and writer. I am delighted to join in honoring Sinclair and Dorothy Ferguson, whom I count as dear friends.
2. John Calvin, "The Necessity of Reforming the Church," in *Selected Works*, ed. Henry Beveridge, vol. 1 (Grand Rapids: Baker, 1983), 26.

on worship, that understanding *must* be incorporated into the public worship of God. That was not easy in the sixteenth century. Again, Calvin wrote: "I know how difficult it is to persuade the world that God disapproves all modes of worship not expressly sanctioned by His Word."[3] Yet Calvin, in his writing and practical reforms, labored to introduce biblical worship.

The greatest obstacle to fully reforming worship for Calvin arose from the need to persuade the civil government to implement the truth that the ministers had found in the Bible. Calvin never fully succeeded in Geneva. While the medieval superstitions were thoroughly removed, the disciplinary desires of Calvin to educate members and guard the Lord's Supper were not fully enacted. The city council in Geneva believed in church discipline for common people, but not for important people like themselves. On this point, at least, Calvin was a democrat.

The reforms that Calvin and other leaders of the Reformed churches introduced in worship remained largely in place over the following centuries. In the area of music, though, some changes were made over time—hymns supplemented or replaced psalms, musical instruments were introduced, and choirs were added. In fact, one problem with Reformed stability was that the character and order of worship came to be taken for granted. Even leaders in the church may forget why we do what we do. Particularly when theological battles are being waged in other fields, years of peace in the worship wars may lead to neglect or disarmament (to press the war analogy too far). The explosion of change in worship across Protestantism during the second half of the twentieth century largely rested on (1) the claim that Christians were free to do in worship whatever was not forbidden, and (2) the culturally appealing enthusiasm of Pentecostal worship. By the time these changes were in progress, Reformed influence had already been greatly diminished, particularly in American evangelicalism, and many Reformed leaders had forgotten their theology of worship.

In the theological and liturgical confusion in which we find ourselves, we need to rebuild our Reformed theology and practice of

---

3. Calvin, "The Necessity of Reforming the Church," 128.

worship on a sure foundation. We need to return to a careful study of the Bible, not just to gather together some "proof texts," but to look with fresh eyes at text and context. As Reformed Christians, we need to show that we are not driven by theological preconceptions or by an excessive use of the Old Testament. If we are to convince those outside our own tradition, we can and need to show that worship is a genuine and extensive concern of the New Testament and that historic Reformed worship correctly understood its teaching.

Obviously, we cannot undertake such a study in the short compass of this essay, but we can indicate how it might be done and where it might begin. By looking at two of the teachings of Jesus, we can taste the foundational importance and sharp clarity of the issue of worship for him. We will use two key texts, one from John 4 and the other from Matthew 15, to anticipate the character of such a study.

Jesus on the Centrality of Worship: John 4

The meeting of Jesus with the Samaritan woman at Sychar is very familiar to Bible students. Jesus' teaching there—on living water, worship in spirit and truth, and the fields white for the harvest—has been frequently cited and recognized as vitally important. Yet the words of Jesus here on worship (John 4:21–24) are seldom carefully examined as a window on the Bible's foundational teaching on worship. Let us carefully track John's account to see what may be learned from it.

The fourth chapter of John's Gospel begins somewhat awkwardly. Jesus had been in Jerusalem for the Feast of the Passover, where he cleansed the temple and met with Nicodemus. He then withdrew with his disciples into the Judean countryside to continue his work of making disciples and baptizing. We are not told how long he was there or exactly where he was. But then without much elaboration, John records that Jesus left Judea for Galilee. Yet the focus on Jesus' making disciples continues. Of course, this is exactly what Jesus does in Sychar, not only with the woman he meets at the well but also with many other inhabitants there.

Another notable feature at the beginning of this chapter is the specific, detailed description of the setting for the meeting. Often John offers little detail about the sites of Jesus' actions, but he seems here to underscore the importance of this meeting. This detail encourages us to think about the historic character of this place. Sychar was on or very near the site of the ancient city of Shechem. There Abraham paused at the oak of Moreh after he left Haran, and there the Lord appeared to him, promising to give him the land that he was crossing (Gen. 12:4–9). Abraham built an altar to the Lord at Shechem. There, too, Jacob and Joseph were buried (Acts 7:15–16; Josh. 24:32). Nearby stood Mount Gerizim, where Moses had taught that Israel was to be blessed after the people entered the promised land (Deut. 11:29). After Rehoboam, Solomon's son, was crowned king in Shechem, there he provoked Jeroboam's rebellion by his intransigence (1 Kings 12), leading to the formation of the land and religion that became Samaritan. The Samaritans much later built a temple for themselves on Mount Gerizim, which the Jews had destroyed in 128 B.C. So when John refers to the field that Jacob gave to Joseph and to Jacob's well, he is drawing the minds of his readers back to critical historical events that had occurred there for about two thousand years. Sychar is a remarkable place to reflect on the meaning of the patriarchs, the land of promise, the division of the people, and true worship. It is an ideal place to show the fulfillment of the old covenant and the introduction of the worship of the new covenant.

John highlights not only the significance of the place, but also the unusual character of the conversation to underscore its importance. Jesus takes the initiative in the conversation at the well with the local woman from Sychar who came to draw water. He asks her for a drink of water. This request was unusual in several ways. A rabbi did not speak to an unknown woman when they were alone. A Jew would not drink from a Samaritan cup lest he be made ritually unclean. The woman knew that this was unusual, expressing her surprise that a Jew would make such a request.

We do not know how she knew that Jesus was a Jew. Perhaps it was the way he dressed or the accent with which he spoke. Her statement certainly introduces a major theme of this chapter, namely, the identity of Jesus. At the beginning he is called a Jew. Then she asks if he is greater than Jacob. Later she concludes that he is a prophet. When she refers to the Christ who will reliably answer her question on the place of worship, Jesus declares that he is the Christ. She begins to ask herself and others: "Can this be the Christ?" (John 4:29). At the end of this episode, the Samaritans of Sychar who have believed declare: "we know that this is indeed the Savior of the world" (v. 42). This is indeed the identity of Jesus: Jew, greater than Jacob, prophet, Christ, and Savior of the world.

The identity of Jesus is intimately connected to his mission. As we have seen, ultimately the mission of Jesus was to make disciples—followers of Jesus. Another way of expressing that mission was to provide living water that would give eternal life, to gather the harvest for eternal life, to gather believers, to be the Savior of the world. Jesus makes disciples as he helps them to see who he truly is. In this setting, we also see Jesus leading his new disciple toward a fuller understanding of worship.

The woman responds with a question: where should we worship—in Jerusalem, as you Jews say, or on this mountain, as our fathers taught? Some commentators on this passage have suggested that the question is an embarrassed effort to change the subject from her moral condition to a theological distraction. The implication of this observation is that morality is important and that theology and worship are at best peripheral. But Jesus does not treat the question as a distraction or an irrelevance. He certainly never allows himself to be distracted from his purpose in conversations. He takes the woman's question with the greatest seriousness and as genuinely important. Whether she realized it or not, this was the correct trajectory for their conversation, and Jesus provides a very profound answer.

His statement on worship makes three key points: first, worship is central to the life of the new covenant; second, worship in the new covenant has strong continuities with worship in the old covenant; and third, worship in the new covenant has significant changes from the old.

Worship is central to the mission of Jesus. One of the ways of speaking of the totality of his mission is seeking true worshipers of God (John 4:23). Far from worship's becoming peripheral or irrelevant, it is the fulfillment of God's purpose in Jesus. But he is not seeking just any kind of worshipers; he is seeking true worshipers. Jesus is telling us that we must pursue the kind of worship that God requires of us. Here indeed is a call to study and then to faithfulness.

Jesus also shows the centrality of worship in his teaching on its necessity. As it was necessary in the old covenant to worship in Jerusalem (John 4:20), so now it will be necessary to worship in Spirit and in truth (v. 24). Worship is not optional but will be as necessary to the faithful Christian as worship in Jerusalem was to the faithful Jew. Jesus puts his seal of approval on Old Testament worship both by his teaching here and by his consistent practice as described in the Gospels, where he is recorded as regularly worshiping in synagogue on the Sabbath and attending in Jerusalem the great feasts appointed for Israel (Luke 4:16; John 18:20). Indeed, John makes such a point of Jesus' attending the feasts in Jerusalem that he seems to organize his Gospel around them.

The worship of which Jesus speaks here has strong continuities with the worship of the old covenant. The centrality of worship is, of course, one of the continuities, but Jesus also makes it clear that God must teach his people how to worship by revelation. In the old covenant, the Jews worshiped what they knew as taught by God, whereas the worship of the Samaritans was based on ignorance (John 4:22). Beyond the need for revelation, Jesus also shows that true worship is tied to salvation. Salvation was God's gift to the Jews, and that salvation was tied to their faithfulness in worship (see, for example, Deut. 4). Jesus implies here that the same is true in the new covenant (John 4:22). That is made explicit in Hebrews 12:28–29.

Jesus also makes it clear that he is bringing significant changes to worship in the new covenant. Jerusalem and its temple will no longer be the center and focus of worship for God's people. From our perspective today, that may not seem so remarkable, but from the time of David, a thousand years before, the center and focus of the worship of God's people had been Jerusalem. The temple in Jerusalem has contained the Most Holy Place, where God dwells with his people. To say that this whole system of worship is coming to an end is a radical and dramatic announcement. The great change is that worship will no longer have a local focus on earth. Jesus is the Savior of the world, and the world will not be required to look to the land of Israel or to an earthly temple.

Christians are not bound to any place for their worship, not Jerusalem or Rome or Constantinople. Worship in the new covenant is universal. Jerusalem, the temple, the priesthood, the sacrifices were always pointers to the things to come in Christ, and as they are fulfilled in him, they pass away.[4]

In the old covenant, the Jerusalem temple in a basic way was the connection between God and his people. In the new covenant, the Spirit and truth (or perhaps this is a hendiadys meaning "the Spirit of truth," as we find in John 14:17 and 16:13) connect the people of God. The Spirit is the other Helper whom Jesus promised to send (14:15–17) to be his presence with us. The Spirit brings the truth of Jesus to us (14:26; 15:26) and gives the truth life in our minds and hearts. The Spirit makes the church (Eph. 2:21–22; 1 Peter 2:5) and individual Christians (1 Cor. 6:19) into the temple of God.

Jesus also introduces a new intimacy of fellowship between God and his true worshipers in the new covenant. Obviously, Jesus is not introducing a new deity to the people of God. The God of the Old Testament is the God of the New Testament. Jesus certainly assumes that what we learned about the character and ways of God in the Old Testament will continue to be true. Yet in this short space he focuses on two particular aspects of God: God is spirit and God is Father. Neither of these points, clearly, is brand-new. Jesus stresses that God is spirit to underscore that the worship he is introducing will reflect the omnipresent spiritual character of God more fully than was true in the Old Testament. Second, he stresses that God is Father. This approach to God is not unknown in the Old Testament, but Jesus (see John 20:17) stresses that in the new covenant the characteristic way for Christians to think of God is as Father. That is new and wonderful.

Jesus on Worship and the Word: Matthew 15

As Jesus taught in John 4 that true worshipers must worship in Spirit and in truth, so in Matthew 15 he teaches that true worshipers must worship from the heart according to the Word. This text may not initially seem to yield much on worship, but its significance for

4. As the Westminster Confession of Faith clearly states, "Neither prayer, nor any other part of religious worship, is now, under the gospel, either tied unto, or made more acceptable by any place in which it is performed, or towards which it is directed: but God is to be worshiped everywhere, in spirit and truth" (WCF 21.6).

worship is nonetheless great. Jesus has a confrontation with the Pharisees and scribes over the tradition of the ritual washing of hands before eating. While not focused on worship in a narrow sense, Jesus introduces the subject by his quotation of Isaiah 29:13. So what can we learn about worship from this text?

As we approach Matthew 15:1–20, recognizing its literary form will be very helpful. The passage is organized as a chiasm, formed of three parts, each marked by the audience that Jesus addresses. Jesus first speaks to unfaithful teachers in the form of the Pharisees and scribes (Matt. 15:1–9), then to the people (vv. 10–11), and finally to those who are to be faithful teachers in the form of his disciples (vv. 12–20). This chiasm helps us see that Jesus' words in Matthew 15:10–11 are the center of his teaching here.

In the first part of this text, the Pharisees and scribes, representing part of the religious establishment in Jerusalem, come to Galilee to criticize Jesus through the practices of his disciples. The focus of the criticism is the failure of the disciples to keep the tradition of the elders that required the ritual washing of the hands before eating bread.[5] It is surely strange that the Pharisees would travel about a hundred miles not to ask Jesus about the great things that he was doing—preaching the kingdom, healing, and feeding thousands. Instead, they want to lay a trap in terms of their traditions.

Jesus answers their question with a question that is very pointedly critical and confrontational, turning their words back on them. The sharp nature of Jesus' response shows his evaluation of the real character of the Pharisees' seemingly innocent question. Jesus' statement presents his conviction that the Pharisees have valued their traditions over the Word of God and indeed have allowed their traditions to contradict and reject the commandments of God. As Jesus pointedly says, "So for the sake of your tradition you have made void the word of God" (Matt. 15:6).

Jesus' forceful words regarding the Word of God and tradition (Matt. 15:1–20) are very compact, and we need to follow them

---

5. The esv translation of Matthew 15:2 reads, "For they do not wash their hands when they eat." The Greek here literally reads, "For they do not wash their hands when they eat bread." The presence of "bread" in the text is very important to its interconnections with surrounding texts.

carefully. He certainly implies that these traditions of the elders are not morally binding, but he explicitly attacks the Pharisees at a more basic level by declaring that they break the true commandments of God for the sake of their invented traditions.

At first glance, Jesus' citing the fifth commandment may seem strange and even irrelevant. The connection seems to be that the Pharisees have claimed to honor their forebears, "the elders," but have neglected their prime forebears, their fathers and mothers. Jesus shows the importance of the fifth commandment by also citing Moses' elaboration on it in Exodus 21:17 ("Whoever curses his father or his mother shall be put to death"), showing that honoring one's true elders, father and mother, is the basic requirement. The Pharisees have created traditions that allow them to protect their money and to neglect their parents.

The Pharisees, of course, would insist that their traditions are applications of and supplements to the commandments of God. But Jesus sees through such rationalizations, recognizing that such traditions in reality always lead to voiding the Word of God. In the history of the people of God, the reality is rarely Word and tradition, but typically tradition against the Word.

Next Jesus declares that he is not surprised by tradition's voiding the Word of God because Isaiah (Isa. 29:13) had prophesied that this was a recurring problem for God's people. Isaiah had declared that judgment was coming on Israel because its worship had come to be controlled by the commandments of men, not the commandments of God. Throughout its history, Israel had replaced God's Word with its own ideas and practices. Isaiah seems to prophesy against the Pharisees when he goes on to state that "the wisdom of their wise men shall perish, and the discernment of their discerning men shall be hidden" (Isa. 29:14). Jesus does seem to apply this to the Pharisees, as we will see below in the third part of the chiasm.

In the second part (Matt. 15:10–11), we come to the immediate center of this chiasm in Matthew 15 (which is also the center, as we will see, of the larger chiasm of Matthew 13–17). Jesus turns to the crowds following him and speaks a word that seems to be almost a proverb, a word that Peter calls a "parable" (15:15). Jesus calls the people to hear and understand a most basic and vital truth: "it is not what goes into the mouth that defiles a person, but what comes out of the mouth; this defiles a person" (v. 11). Jesus moves beyond the specifics of the elders and washing to the deeper meaning of the law. The law is really concerned not primarily with external ceremonial requirements, but with the heart and what comes out of the mouth from the heart. True religion is not in the first place a matter of externals, but a matter of the internal.

This statement is radical indeed. Mark in his Gospel makes this explicit: "Thus he declared all foods clean" (Mark 7:19). The whole complex of dietary restrictions in the law of Moses is eliminated by Jesus. Is Jesus, then, the one who is rejecting the law of God? No. Rather, his teaching reveals him as the fulfiller of the Old Testament and as the Lawgiver in the new covenant. As Isaiah prophesies of Jesus, "behold, I will again do wonderful things with this people, with wonder upon wonder" (Isa. 29:14).

The Pharisees might well have responded to this teaching by saying: "Well, who is really rejecting the law? The law clearly declares that some foods are unclean. If Jesus is declaring all foods clean, then he is the one who is rejecting and contradicting the law!" Jesus would have been wrong and the Pharisees would be right if the whole law of Moses were unchanging and the ultimate fulfillment of the purpose and revelation of God. Jesus rejects that contention. He is showing himself to be not only the true interpreter of the Old Testament but also the founder and Lawgiver of the new covenant. Jesus' right to act and teach in this way is supported and validated by the elements of the chiasm that surround this teaching, which we will examine shortly.

In the third part of this chiasm (Matt. 15:12–20), the disciples of Jesus report that the Pharisees were offended, or scandalized, by Jesus' teaching on food. Jesus is indignant in response. His strong language shows that all must decide whether Jesus or the Pharisees are the correct interpreters of the law of Moses. Jesus, throughout his ministry, is showing in a variety of ways that the law of Moses—especially the ceremonial law—is temporary and will be fulfilled by the Messiah and altered by the new covenant that he brings.

The ceremonial law of Moses was given as a daily reminder to the people of God that they were holy and must keep themselves separate from the profane world: "You are to distinguish between the holy and the common, and between the unclean and the clean" (Lev. 10:10). "The LORD will establish you as a people holy to himself, as he has sworn to you, if you keep the commandments of the LORD your God and walk in his ways. And all the peoples of the earth shall see that you are called by the name of the LORD" (Deut. 28:9–10). Now Messiah is coming to bring true holiness to the hearts of his people and to tear down the wall that had divided Jews from Gentiles (Eph. 2:14–15). By making the law of Moses forever binding in its totality, the Pharisees are blind teachers and guides who will lead their followers to fall into a ditch. In fact, they are not sent by God or serving God, but are hypocrites as those who talk about the law but do not keep it.

Jesus continues to show that real defilement and unholiness come out of the heart. To support this point, he marshals all the sins against the second table of the Ten Commandments (Matt. 15:19), those sins that are all manifestations of the violation of the command to love your neighbor. Jesus sees the hypocrisy of the Pharisees' claim to care passionately for God and his law when they repeatedly fail to love their neighbor. Their hatred of him and of others violates the law that they need to follow: "If anyone says, 'I love God,' and hates his brother, he is a liar; for he who does not love his brother whom he has seen cannot love God whom he has not seen. And this commandment we have from him: whoever loves God must also love his brother" (1 John 4:20–21). If they do not love their neighbor, then they do not love God.

The fundamental points that Jesus is making in Matthew 15:1–20 on the heart, the Word, and tradition are strongly reinforced by the chiasm in which it is the center. It is as if Matthew has surrounded this section with pointers or signals saying: "See how important this is!" The importance of that teaching is heightened by seeing the context that Matthew has shaped for that teaching. Jesus' presentation here seems to stand at the center of a chiasm that runs from Matthew 13:1 to Matthew 17:13. We could diagram this chiasm in the following way:

A. Jesus speaks of hearing and understanding the Word (13:1–52)
B. Jesus is rejected in Nazareth (13:53–58)
   C. The identity of Jesus: Herod and John (14:1–12)
      D. Jesus feeds five thousand (14:13–21)

       E. Jesus walks on water (14:22–33)

         F. Jesus heals many in Gennesaret (14:34–36)

           X. Jesus on commandments and traditions (15:1–20)

       E'.Jesus and the Canaanite woman (15:21–28)

         F'. Jesus heals many in Galilee (15:29–31)

     D'. Jesus feeds four thousand (15:32–39)

   C'. The identity of Jesus: Pharisees, Sadducees, and Peter (16:1–20)

 B'. Jesus will be rejected in Jerusalem (16:21–23)

A'. Jesus speaks of hearing and understanding the Word (16:24–17:13)[6]

The chiasm is bracketed by the call of Jesus to hear and understand his Word (Matt. 13:1–52 and 16:24–17:13). Jesus, like Isaiah, knows that many will hear and not understand (13:14) but that some will hear and understand (13:23) and that his disciples are gradually coming to understand his teaching (17:13). The center of the chiasm, "hear and understand" (15:10), reiterates the beginning and end of the chiasm.

The next part of the chiasm (Matt. 13:53–58 and 16:21–23) points to how Jesus will be rejected by many as he comes as God's Messiah. Isaiah had prophesied, "He was despised and rejected by men, a man of sorrows and acquainted with grief; and as one from whom men hide their faces he was despised, and we esteemed him not" (Isa. 53:3). The rejection of Jesus by many of Israel's religious leaders does not prove that Jesus was wrong.

The chiasm next stresses the identity of Jesus (Matt. 14:1–12 and 16:1–20). He is not John the Baptist or one of the prophets, but rather he is the Christ, the Son of the living God.

The chiasm then shows that Jesus is the one who feeds and provides life-giving bread to his people (Matt. 14:13–21 and 15:32–39). Indeed, there are striking parallels in these stories with Moses and the people of Israel in the wilderness. The people then ate manna, "the bread of the angels" (Ps. 78:25), which God gave from heaven.

6. This chiasm is rather clear in its balance and its parallels except that it is broken or varied on the E and F, which are reversed in the second part of the chiasm. Such artful variations in a literary structure such as a chiasm are not unusual.

Now Jesus, God come in the flesh, is feeding his people both physical bread and the Bread of Life. He gives life as God with us. While the Pharisees focus on washing before eating bread, Jesus gives himself as the Bread of Heaven.

Then we see Jesus walking on water to his disciples and Jesus responding to the appeal of a Canaanite woman (Matt. 14:22–33 and 15:21–28). In both episodes, the issue of faith is central, specifically Peter's struggle of faith and the strong faith of the Canaanite woman. Peter appealed, "Lord, save me" (14:30), and Jesus reached out his hand and took hold of him. The woman appealed, "Lord, help me" (15:25), and asked for the crumbs of bread from the table of the children. Jesus commended her great faith and healed her daughter. Here the hand and bread of Jesus are saving.

Next in order are the brief general statements on healings in Gennesaret and in Galilee (Matt. 14:34–36 and 15:29–31). Here we see the divine power of Jesus at work and the demonstration that he is the divine deliverer of his people. Always implicit in healings is the touch of Jesus' hand.

The elements of the chiasm that surround the central teaching of Jesus on the heart, tradition, and the Word of God show that Jesus is not simply a teacher who vindicates the Word, but is indeed God's Son and Messiah who brings the Word. He is the one who delivers, heals, saves, and feeds his people. His hand is the hand of salvation, and his bread is the Bread of Life. Faith in him and in his Word is the essential response to him. While some will hear him and reject him, at the center of his work is his call to hear and understand, to believe and follow from the heart.

Jesus insists that the true religious life must conform to his Word and to it alone. Human wisdom, traditions, and creativity have no place. He has the clear right to demand such a response to his Word and, as God has always done, show his zeal to defend and maintain his Word. We see clearly that "man shall not live by bread alone, but by every word that comes from the mouth of God" (Matt. 4:4, quoting Deut. 8:3). If the Word governs worship in the broad sense, then *a fortiori* it governs public worship more narrowly defined. And if an emphasis on worship is built into the very structure of biblical books, how significant this topic must be in both theology and practice.

Our two New Testament texts on worship show the dangers of failing to see the ways in which the Messiah fulfills the Old Testament and the ways in which the dead hand of tradition can distort or destroy worship according to the Word of God. They direct us to true worship, which is from hearts renewed by the Spirit and according to the Word of truth.

For the Pastor

If a pastor has read this brief introduction to a study of biblical teaching on worship and is persuaded that the Bible must undergird and direct our worship, what is he then to do?

First, in light of the importance of worship, he must continue to study the Scriptures on this subject. A faithful pastor is a student of the Word of God. In the worship wilderness of our time, a minister must give serious study to worship until he has reached a settled conviction on what the Scriptures teach. He should, of course, make use of the historical, theological, and biblical studies of others.[7] But he must have biblical convictions about worship for himself. If ministers are to teach "them to observe all that I have commanded you" (Matt. 28:20), then they must know what Christ has commanded.

The study of the Word on worship and on all other subjects is a

---

7. See, for example, Sinclair B. Ferguson and Mark E. Dever, eds., *The Westminster Directory of Public Worship* (Fearn, Scotland: Christian Focus, 2008); Jonathan Gibson and Mark Earngey, eds., *Reformation Worship: Liturgies from the Past for the Present* (Greensboro, NC: New Growth Press, 2018); Bard Thompson, *Liturgies of the Western Church* (Minneapolis: Fortress Press, 1980). See also studies such as Hughes Oliphant Old, *Worship: Reformed according to Scripture*, rev. ed. (Louisville: Westminster John Knox, 2002); Richard A. Muller and Rowland S. Ward, *Scripture and Worship: Biblical Interpretation and the Directory for Worship* (Phillipsburg, NJ: P&R Publishing, 2007); D. G. Hart and John R. Muether, *With Reverence and Awe: Returning to the Basics of Reformed Worship* (Phillipsburg, NJ: P&R Publishing, 2002); and early polemical works in defense of Reformed worship such as George Gillespie, *A Dispute against the English-Popish Ceremonies, Obtruded upon the Church of Scotland* ([Leiden], 1637); Robert Baillie, *Ladensium autokatakrisis, the Canterburians Self-Conviction* ([Glasgow], 1640); "Smectymnuus," *An Answer to a Booke Entituled, An Humble Remonstrance. In Which, the Original of Liturgy and Episcopacy Is Discussed* (London, 1641); Jeremiah Burroughs, *Gospel-Worship* (London: Printed for Peter Cole, 1648).

duty for ministers. Pastors will have different abilities, but they must apply themselves diligently to that study. Such study must be more than a duty, however; it must be a delight. The Word of God is one of God's greatest gifts to his people, and its study is a great privilege, which should lead the student not just to greater knowledge, but also to greater love for the Word. Too often today, ministers declare their devotion to the authority of the Word but spend little time studying it, loving it, or teaching it.

Second, on the basis of his worship convictions, a pastor must set worship goals for himself and his congregation. Those goals should be pastoral goals, which is to say that they should be the goals not of an individualist firebrand, but of a loving and gentle pastor who with the concurrence of his elders seeks patiently to lead his congregation to deeper understanding and better practice. In Calvin's day, the minister only had to convince the civil government in order to make the most sweeping changes to public worship. But today the task is equally challenging because the pastor must persuade his congregation to accept and approve changes to public worship. Remember, Calvin defined the church as the gathering where the Word is preached and heard. If no one hears because they have all been driven away by a foolish minister, there is no church.

Pastoral goals will be prioritized goals. Some issues are so basic and necessary that they must not be compromised. The Bible and the confessional standards of the church (which are the collected wisdom of the church on the teaching of the Bible) will help us see that level of priority.[8] Other issues may be important but will leave some room for difference of opinion. Still others may have value but still permit diversity of practice.

These goals should be established with a good measure of humility and in the community of the office-bearers of the church. As Paul reminds us: "Put on then, as God's chosen ones, holy and beloved, compassionate hearts, kindness, humility, meekness, and patience,

---

8. For the summation of biblical teaching on worship and related matters in Reformed confessions and catechisms, see the appropriate sections in Joel R. Beeke and Sinclair B. Ferguson, eds., *Reformed Confessions Harmonized* (Grand Rapids: Baker, 1999), as well as the following: Belgic Confession arts. 25, 29, 32; Heidelberg Catechism 96–98; WCF 19–21; WLC 103–110, 116–117; and WSC 45–52, 57–62.

bearing with one another. . . . And let the peace of Christ rule in your hearts, to which indeed you were called in one body. And be thankful" (Col. 3:12–15). Peace as well as purity must be our goal.

Third, a wise pastor will realize that he cannot convince everyone, and that in the spiritual environment in which we live his congregation will probably lose members if he upholds biblical standards of worship. Some will choose traditional, medieval forms of worship. Others will choose Pentecostal excitement for their worship. It will be surprising and frustrating to experience such losses—although as one very wise pastor said years ago, there are also "blessed subtractions" in the ministry. The calling of the minister is not ultimately to please men, but to please the Lord. Often where biblical worship is wisely promoted, the church will see gains as well as losses.

Fourth, the minister should pray diligently that the Spirit of the Lord would lead him and the congregation to joy in the truth of worship. A minister cannot do any of the work of the ministry in his own strength apart from the blessing of God by his Spirit. The Lord remarkably in his Word appeals to us again and again to pray. He directed even his own Son: "Ask of me, and I will make the nations your heritage, and the ends of the earth your possession" (Ps. 2:8). To his ministers and people Jesus says, "Ask, and it will be given to you; seek, and you will find; knock, and it will be opened to you" (Matt. 7:7). When we pray, he has promised to bless.

Fifth, the minister must model something of his ministerial goals in his ministerial practice. If the minister wants his people to pray and to improve prayer in public worship, he must give time and thought to prayer in public worship. I know of churches where the minister preaches on the vital importance of prayer in the life of Christians and then spends almost no time in prayer in the service. His example cancels his precept. Similarly, the minister must show the importance of Bible reading by reading significant portions of the Bible in public worship. Reading only a verse or two will not model for worshipers the central vitality of Bible reading. The same is true in choosing the sung praise for the congregation. Lifting our minds, hearts, and voices to the living God is a great privilege and solemn responsibility. The content of that praise must not be shallow or vain repetition, but be serious and thoughtful. Praise is not for the people, but for God.

Obviously, pastoral wisdom and care is particularly needed in this area, but here, too, the pastor must model in his choices and leadership the goals he is pursuing.

If we are children of the Reformation, we must have a passion for the Word of God and an eagerness to know its teaching on the vital topic of worship. We must pursue worship that is acceptable to God (Heb. 12:28), worship from the heart that follows the Word of God. The very small beginning we have made here should encourage all of us to continue our study of the Scriptures. In worship as in everything else, we must follow the godly example of George Wishart, the Scottish martyr, who declared, "Except it be the Word of God, I darre affirme nothing."[9]

Key Term

worship

Recommendations for Further Reading

Ferguson, Sinclair B., and Mark E. Dever, eds. *The Westminster Directory of Public Worship*. Fearn, Scotland: Christian Focus, 2008.

Gibson, Jonathan, and Mark Earngey, eds. *Reformation Worship: Liturgies from the Past for the Present*. Greensboro, NC: New Growth Press, 2018.

Hart, D. G., and John R. Muether. *With Reverence and Awe: Returning to the Basics of Reformed Worship*. Phillipsburg, NJ: P&R Publishing, 2002.

Muller, Richard A., and Rowland S. Ward. *Scripture and Worship: Biblical Interpretation and the Directory for Worship*. Phillipsburg, NJ: P&R Publishing, 2007.

Old, Hughes Oliphant. *Worship: Reformed according to Scripture*. Rev. ed. Louisville: Westminster John Knox, 2002.

9. Quoted in Donald Macleod, *Therefore the Truth I Speak: Scottish Theology 1500–1700* (Fearn, Scotland: Mentor, 2020), 25.

Discussion Questions

1. What does Jesus' interaction with the Samaritan woman in John 4 teach us about the continuities and/or discontinuities between old covenant and new covenant worship?
2. How might Jesus' teachings in Matthew 15 be applied in churches that struggle to avoid the ditches of either overvaluing their worship tradition or overvaluing their subjective experience of worship?
3. What are some common unhelpful or unbiblical preconceptions about worship that church congregation members might have that pastors will need to wrestle with and answer in order to help their churches conform to a biblical paradigm of worship?
4. What might be some guiding, methodological principles for a pastor or group of elders who are seeking to develop a faithful form of worship, persuade their congregations of it, and implement it lovingly?

21

THE CHURCH

The Well-Ordered Church in
a World of Distrust[1]

MARK A. GARCIA

"We Believe in Christ, Not the Church"

Among the songs of the sons of Korah we read, "Glorious things of you are spoken, O city of God" (Ps. 87:3). At the close of Holy Scripture, an angel invites the servant of the Lord: "'Come, I will show you the Bride, the wife of the Lamb.' And he carried me away in the Spirit to a great, high mountain, and showed me the holy city Jerusalem coming down out of heaven from God, having the glory of God, its radiance like a most rare jewel, like a jasper, clear as crystal" (Rev. 21:9–11). The city who is a bride, a glorious bride who is the church of the Lamb: these images are anchored in something more that the sons of Korah say: she is *loved*. "The Lord loves the gates of Zion more than all the dwelling places of Jacob" (Ps. 87:2). This love is easy to miss in reflections on church order, but it is the ardor at work in the order. And yet pastors know from hard experience that love and glorious things are not always what come to mind regarding the church's governance.

1. I write with profound appreciation for Dr. Ferguson's devotion to the church and his eminent and effective service to her. I hope in doing so that he might finally forgive me for attending Edinburgh rather than Glasgow for my PhD.

403

Trust is, as the saying goes, hard won and easily lost. For this reason, these are difficult days for the doctrine of the church, particularly its government. To be sure, other factors also play a role. When the "gospel" of some gospel-centered movements is disembodied—that is, shorn of traditional liturgical, sacramental, and ordering elements—earnest interest in matters of church government seems unduly scrupulous, peripheral to the church's mission, and unnecessarily divisive. Alongside this unwieldy challenge, however, is the more poignant one, namely, that the church as an institution, or certain of its leaders, also sometimes bruises and breaks the trust of those under her care. Within the church we hear of spousal and child abuse, sexual exploitation, abuses of church power, and fearful neglect of hard responsibilities. These are not days in which "glorious things" are spoken of the church.[2]

Marveling at the church's identity as glorious does not displace the need for an honest consideration of the church's faults and sins. Instead, only when we properly grasp the glorious identity and vocation of the church can we begin to appreciate the tragedy of the church's sin, as well as the urgency of her faithfulness. R. B. Kuiper puts the matter well in the very first words of his highly useful and edifying work *The Glorious Body of Christ*. He writes: "The Word of God tells us that Christ's Church is glorious. Not only does history ascribe to it a past that is in many respects glorious and does prophecy predict for it a glorious future, it is *essentially* glorious. The Christian Church is glorious *in its very nature*." But Kuiper then immediately adds these sober words: "Today the glory of the Church is thickly veiled. It is no exaggeration to assert that in the main it presents a picture of advanced decadence and extreme feebleness."[3]

---

2. It is sadly easy to find representative examples. In addition to many studies of domestic violence and the church, note the ecclesiastical aspects of the dark stories recounted in Rachael Denhollander, *What Is a Girl Worth? My Story of Breaking the Silence and Exposing the Truth about Larry Nassar and USA Gymnastics* (Carol Stream, IL: Tyndale, 2019); and Rachel Louise Snyder, *No Visible Bruises: What We Don't Know about Domestic Violence Can Kill Us* (New York: Bloomsbury, 2019). Denhollander is a professing Christian. Snyder profiles abusive men who use Christianity or the Bible as a warrant for their violence, and the author faults Christianity and the Bible for the abuse.

3. R. B. Kuiper, *The Glorious Body of Christ* (Grand Rapids: Eerdmans, 1966; repr., London: Banner of Truth, 1967), 13 (original emphases).

At the same time, we must allow that our expectations of the church may at times be at fault. In the emotionally high days of a recent conversion experience, or in times of great spiritual vitality and encouragement, we may be tempted toward a kind of church utopia, an idealistic but false vision of the church. Similarly, in times of great difficulty, particularly when a church body or officer is at fault in harming us or our loved ones in some way, we may find ourselves yielding to church dystopia, a cynical but equally false rejection of the church on account of her sins. Neither disposition can survive the biblical testimony concerning the real church.

We may restate our question in more classic terms. The late sociologist Peter Berger, reflecting on the line in the Apostles' Creed, "I believe in . . . the holy catholic church," captures the situation in his characteristically mordant way:

> The empirical reality is one of emphatically non-holy activities and of all sorts of sometimes vicious tribalism. . . . Their clergy can be fanatical, greedy, hungry, and exploitative. Their members can be narrow, petty, and prejudiced. . . . A holy institution? Not likely. . . . The empirical picture, most of the time, is devastatingly uninspiring.[4]

It may be that the perceived failures of the church are her most conspicuous feature in the public eye.[5] For decades, prognosticators have feared the effects of broken trust on the stability and growth of the church, the way that economists have argued for the importance of social trust to the emerging global economic order.[6] As a result,

4. Peter Berger, *Questions of Faith: A Skeptical Affirmation of Christianity* (Malden, MA: Blackwell Publishing, 2004), 131.

5. To be sure, especially in a social media world, the church is also often innocent of the accusations leveled against her, both institutionally and regarding certain leaders. For our purposes, however, I leave unjust or erroneous accusations to the side in order not to distract our focus from those failures that undeniably *do* take place. With that reality in view, I ask what presbyterian polity may have to say about how things ought to be.

6. Cf. the concerns raised in Bernard Iddings Bell's 1942 essay, "Will the Christian Church Survive?," *Atlantic*, October 1942, 106–12, with the socioeconomic version of similar concerns in Francis Fukuyama, *Trust: The Social Virtues and the Creation of Prosperity* (New York: Free Press/Simon & Schuster Inc., 1995).

many today are more likely to stumble at "I believe in . . . the holy catholic church" than at statements on the Trinity or Christology. The latter doctrines may be dismissed as quaint, but the former are viscerally rejected, while affirming the general moral importance of Jesus of Nazareth. Modern people are, in short, more comfortable believing in (a version of) Jesus than his church.[7]

In fact, the sentiment "We believe in Christ, not the church" has a long pedigree. The Donatist controversy of the early church may be reduced to just this question: when the church's ministers fail, and the church seems to fail with them, may we choose Jesus by leaving or rejecting his church? Augustine was deeply grieved by the Donatist schism and preached movingly against its dangerous errors.[8] But the Donatist question has repeatedly returned in the story of Christian difficulties with an imperfect church ministry. Later in that story, it was the late-medieval theologian Wessel Gansfort (d. 1489) who used the words "We believe in God and in Christ, not in the Church" as a way of interpreting Augustine against the Donatists. Gansfort in turn influenced the great Reformer of Strasbourg, Martin Bucer (d. 1551).[9]

In this essay, our interest is neither in the proper interpretation of Augustine nor in the history of this tension, but in this question: how might the distinctive principles of church order find practical expression in such a way that this tension is minimized or eliminated among God's people?

The Christ of Church Order

If church order will serve us here, we must begin with the order to be observed in considering the church. First, we must be clear about the gospel as it illuminates what, or rather who, the church is. Only then may we proceed to speak of its order. This is because, as

---

7. The enduring value of J. Gresham Machen's 1923 work *Christianity and Liberalism*, rev. ed. (Grand Rapids: Eerdmans, 2009), is perhaps most visible here.

8. See Adam Ployd, *Augustine, the Trinity, and the Church: A Reading of the Anti-Donatist Sermons* (Oxford: Oxford University Press, 2015).

9. Marijn de Kroon, *We Believe in God and in Christ. Not in the Church: The Influence of Wessel Gansfort on Martin Bucer* (Louisville: Westminster John Knox, 2009).

one writer has put it, "the Church precedes the ministry in the logic of grace."[10]

What, then, is the identity and vocation of the church in relation to the gospel? The church is the *glory* of the eternal Son made flesh and the *Bride-gift* from the Father to the Son in the Spirit (John 6:35–40). We will happily never exhaust the rich profundity of these two descriptors. They establish that the church's identity is fundamentally, essentially glorious, not because of an abstract principle of necessity but because of the inviolable, free, effective love that the Father has for his Son and his determination to glorify the Son in this way. The church is glorious, then, not in the abstract but as the glory *of the Son*. Thus, the church's very existence arises from the mysteries of superlative intra-Trinitarian love. Remembering this will help us to understand much of what the Scriptures say of the church's servants.

We press further: what might it mean that all things outside God himself have been created *for* the Son? Paul's epistle to the Colossians commends to the eye of faith a supremely preeminent Lord Jesus Christ. He is the very image of the invisible God, firstborn of all creation by whom, through whom, and for whom all things have been created. He is the one before all things, their very fount or head, and everything subsists in and because of him. This one, in whom the whole fullness of God dwells bodily, is the head of his body, the church. He is, as the one raised by the Father in the Spirit, the firstborn of the dead so that in everything he might be preeminent. In him, where all wisdom and knowledge are hidden, we are ourselves raised to new life in the sacrament of baptism, and from him his body draws all vitality, nourishment, and growth and is, like the cosmos itself, held or knit together in him (Col. 1:15–20; 2:3, 9, 12, 15, 19; 3:1–4). The church is thus united to the Son, lives because of the Son, and exists for the Son.

In this Pauline panorama, we perceive a universe of rich theology at work in those simple words of John 6:39, "all that the [Father] has given me," a theology that accounts, I suggest, for *everything* outside

10. Paul D. L. Avis, speaking of Luther in *The Church in the Theology of the Reformers* (London: Marshall, Morgan & Scott, 1981), 111, quoted in John Webster, "The Self-Organizing Power of the Gospel: Episcopacy and Community Formation," in *Word and Church: Essays in Christian Dogmatics* (Edinburgh: T. & T. Clark, 2001), 195.

God himself, including the *who* and *why* of the church. Underlying all things, the Scriptures seem repeatedly to suggest, is a mysterious act of divine love: the Father determined to glorify his Son in the Spirit through the gift of this bride, and thus the cosmos, history, humanity, *everything.*

With Bonaventure, then, we may see the universe as the *macrocosm* of which God's image-bearers—men and women—are the *microcosm.* As the Incarnate One in whom all things hold together, Christ personally unites the Godhead not only to the macrocosm (by creation and providence) but also to the microcosm, that is, to people (by incarnation and redemption). Which people? The people of his own possession, who are those gifted to him by the Father in the mystery of Trinitarian love (John 6).

What, then, do we call this visible and intermediate reality, this entity or sphere between the macrocosm and the microcosm? This elect body, the church, we may say, is the *mediocosm.*[11] The churchly mediocosm is that intermediate reality between the expanse of creation (maximally considered) and the particularity of the individual person. In this intermediate reality, the eschatological bridal and motherly City of God is progressively formed and built in history. Eternally, it was the Father's purpose that the Son would be head of a body, which would be his glory. But this glorious bride would be formed and readied by way of history, and not apart from it—a history that, on account of the fall into sin, would include the redemptive mission of the head himself to secure the welfare of his bride.

The final, climactic vision of the church provided in Scripture is of a thoroughly glorious bridal and motherly city (Rev. 21:9–22:5). It is an image in which various deep-running and interwoven biblical strands converge, most prominently the strands of woman, garden, city, land, and temple. A biblically faithful understanding of church structure and ministry in the present must be ordered to this vision of the church's future. This appears to be the conviction of the biblical

11. The term suggested by Marilyn McCord Adams, *Christ and Horrors: The Coherence of Christology* (Cambridge: Cambridge University Press, 2006), 200. The reference to Bonaventure is also based on Adams's discussion. While stimulating and useful, Adams's approach to this topic diverges from the one taken here in many important ways that go well beyond the scope of the present discussion.

writers themselves when they address matters of church governance and life.

Yet isn't this the idealism from which our modern problem of distrust springs, the notion that the church is otherworldly in importance and glory, perhaps beyond the reach of justice and beyond reproach, unassailable in its judgments and behavior? To the contrary! The foundation of the church in the mysteries of intra-Trinitarian love is precisely why the church's *order* follows from her *identity* as a matter of vocation, of calling. It may be helpful to consider church order as a temporary ordering provision by which Jesus Christ, the true Shepherd of souls, preserves and secures his church's future. The church's order safeguards, reflects, and advances the ardor of the Father's love for the Son, and of the Son's love for his bride, in the Spirit. Church polity may seem to some like dreary stuff, but when seen this way, meditation on the ordering of the church can lead the saint's heart to sing rather than slumber.

Presbyterian Principles for Practice

How, then, is this body of Christ ordered in relation to her head so as to safeguard the concerns of Trinitarian and Christological love? Unsurprisingly, the Lord has not left such an important matter to the whims of his creatures. But to say that the government of the church is divinely ordered is to say much more than, for instance, *here* are some big biblical principles for running the church, or *there* are some biblical passages that detail matters of polity. It is to say that it is ordered by and with a view to *this* Christ and his final glory, and by the triune God whose purpose is being realized by way of this same Christ. We discover, importantly, that the church's order is not the reflex of an interest in order or law as such; nor is it limited to the interests of responsibility, management, or efficiency. Critically, *the ordering of the church is not designed to fund but to restrain our natural thirst for power.* The concerns for the flock's welfare are advanced rather than compromised by the ordering of the church.

The Lord Jesus Christ, as head, holds all government within and under himself. By his free determination and through his free gifts,[12]

12. On church officers as gifts acquired through Christ's warfare against his and our enemies, see Michael Horton, "Ephesians 4:1–16: The Ascension, the

he appoints servants through whom his church is to be ordered and cared for. In subjection at every point to the will of Christ the head, these servants have derivative and ministerial but real authority. When stepping away from that revealed will of the head, these men have no authority whatsoever.

The authority of that government is real, not pedantic or illusory, but it is clearly and strictly circumscribed by the Word of God in which the true Shepherd cares for his sheep. On the one hand, this derivative authority secures the ability of ministerial servants to carry out their vocation in and for Christ; on the other hand, this model secures the liberty of the sheep not to be governed by someone other than their true Shepherd himself. Some forms of church government embody these concerns more fully than others.[13] Put simply, at work in presbyterian principles and polity is *a conviction that the nature of the church as Christ's possession must find expression in the care of that church.* His prerogative is the church officer's command, and the Lord is unflinching in his insistence that ministers and elders never forget that the church is his and not theirs.

These principal features and commitments of presbyterian government are familiar, and upon reflection, they bring Christological and eschatological concerns to expression. They may be found in many church constitutions and manuals and were most famously articulated in the dramatic development of presbyterianism in the seventeenth century. A late-nineteenth-century effort at definition captures the matter succinctly for our purposes. Instructed by "expedience, the nature of the Church, the Scriptures and the practice of the early Church," presbyterians hold that

> the Church should be governed by courts composed of Ministers, all of the same order, and of Elders, representing the people, chosen by them, ordained to their office and having an equal voice in all questions with the Ministers; and that these courts should be congregational, presbyterial and synodical assemblies, the smaller

---

Church, and the Spoils of War," in *Theological Commentary: Evangelical Perspectives*, ed. R. Michael Allen (London: T. & T. Clark, 2011), 129–53.

13. Edmund P. Clowney, *The Church*, Contours of Christian Theology (Downers Grove, IL: InterVarsity Press, 1995), 202.

being subject to the larger, and all to that body which represents the whole Church (Matt. 18:15–20; Acts 15:2–28; 1 Cor. 5:4; 1 Tim. 4:14).[14]

Note certain important features of that definition: the presbyterian model of church governance is grounded, in part, in "the nature of the Church," and ministers are "of the same order," while ruling elders, representing the people who have selected them, have "equal voice" with the ministers. Presbyterianism seeks to avoid the vulnerabilities both of a hierarchical model, in which power focuses on individual leaders and there is no real involvement in the matter of rule by the congregation, and of a purely democratic (congregational and independent) model, in which there is no real connectionalism with or accountability to a regional or general church.

In his edifying 1858 work *The Church of God as an Essential Element of the Gospel,* Stuart Robinson provides a useful chart comparing features of presbyterian, independent, and prelatic church polities.[15] Carefully considering the relationship of the nature of the church to the gospel it proclaims, the power it exercises, and the organic nature of its assembled form, we cannot help but hear the summons to faithful practice contained within presbyterian distinctives.

For our purposes, we may take special note of the concern for accountability and imagine how a rogue church officer might fare in the alternative models: in a top-down hierarchical model, the bishop (in forms of episcopacy in which his office is regarded as ontologically distinct from ministers or priests)[16] may be subject to the censure of

14. From "The Form of Government and Forms of Process of the Presbyterian Church in the United States of America, as Amended 1805–1895," in J. Aspinwall Hodge, *What Is Presbyterian Law as Defined by the Church Courts? Containing the Decision of the General Assembly to 1894, Inclusive,* 7th rev. ed. (Philadelphia: Presbyterian Board of Publication and Sabbath-School Work, 1894), 118.

15. Stuart Robinson, *The Church of God as an Essential Element of the Gospel, and the Idea, Structure, and Functions Thereof. A Discourse in Four Parts* (Philadelphia: Joseph M. Wilson, 1858; repr. [and ed. with a foreword by A. Craig Troxel], Willow Grove, PA: Committee on Christian Education of the Orthodox Presbyterian Church, 2009), 88–92.

16. As Reformed Anglicans are keen to remind us, not all forms of episcopal order include this ontological commitment. Arguably, the historic form does not,

other bishops but only to them (or, in earlier times, his metropolitan or archbishop). He is not subject to other priests or ministers. In the congregational model, in which connections with other churches are voluntary, there is no accountability beyond the particular congregation itself, and in many cases the congregation is utterly at the mercy of the pastor's power and prerogative. In either situation, the possibilities are disastrous for the vulnerable in those congregations.

The presbyterian model, in contrast, requires forms and degrees of real accountability regardless of experience, reputation, accomplishments, or popularity, while also focusing church power in bodies rather than individuals. For these reasons and others, the dignity, importance, and synodical or general-assembly service of the *ruling* elder—chosen by the congregation whom he represents in his service, laboring alongside the pastor as his equal in matters of congregational oversight, and involved in ordination and discipline—has sometimes been regarded as the key distinguishing mark of properly functioning presbyterianism.[17] Among the lessons here is the need to encourage ruling elders in their unique relationship to the congregation, as well as the need to avoid the temptation toward an inordinate dependence on individuals

---

and the result is a more administrative or pastoral oversight for the bishop alongside real parity. J. B. Lightfoot's work on the question is a standard and effective way into the topic. Lightfoot (1828–89) was an Anglican clergyman, a canon of St. Paul's, and bishop of Durham. He is justly famous for his discussion of church ministry and officers in his meticulous and dense but spiritually moving "Essay on the Christian Ministry," first published as a "dissertation" in his highly regarded Philippians commentary. See J. B. Lightfoot, *Saint Paul's Epistle to the Philippians: A Revised Text with Introduction, Notes and Dissertations* (1913; repr., Grand Rapids: Zondervan, 1953), 181–269.

17. Robert J. Breckinridge forcefully insisted on this in his October 20 speech at the 1843 Synod of Philadelphia, meeting in Baltimore, which was later printed as "Presbyterian Government Not a Hierarchy, but a Commonwealth," *Southern Presbyterian Review* 33, no. 2 (April 1882): 258–90; cf. David W. Hall and Joseph H. Hall, eds., *Paradigms in Polity* (Grand Rapids: Eerdmans, 1994), 505–23. His chief concern was to maintain the right of ruling elders to lay hands on men in their ordination to the ministry. Breckinridge argued "that the right and necessity of this presence of ruling elders in Church assemblies, distinguishes Presbyterianism from Erastianism and Independency, as well as from Prelacy, as completely as the existence of the assemblies themselves does; . . . the two grand powers residing in these assemblies, called by Henderson the powers 'of ordination and ecclesiastical jurisdiction,' must at last place the Church . . . helpless and prostrate at the feet of a hierarchy" (509).

or nonrepresentative committees to do the work of the church, which must remain, meaningfully, the work of the church as a whole.

To be sure, no form of church government guarantees orthodoxy of theology or of pastoral care. This does not render church government peripheral, however. We now go on to identify biblical ways in which intra-Trinitarian love, the church's nature, and order find—or ought to find—expression in church practice. In short, we wish to accent that what the Scriptures do say about the particulars of the church's ordering are meaningful only as they belong to this Christological and eschatological reality of the church's glorious identity, and not as they scratch the proverbial itch that some may have for power, organization, or even good order per se.

Biblical Aspects of a "Glorious" Church in Practice

It is illuminating to approach biblical teaching about the church's order and servants by way of the most conspicuous exemplars of how those servants must *not* be. Chief of these is the Pharaoh of Exodus, whose structural and personal oppression of the Hebrews, taskmaster mode of operation, and destructive refusal of rest and mercy make him the most paradigmatic of "anti-Christs" in Holy Scripture. This deepest of covenant historical images of the false or counterfeit shepherd also serves to clarify the nature of the exodus in a way that helps us understand our topic. The exodus is the deliverance of the oppressed Hebrews from the hand of an abusive husband in order to join them to Yahweh in a (re)marriage ceremony at Sinai's mountain,[18] just as the Lord Jesus Christ, as second and last Adam, would climactically join to himself in marital union a body once enslaved by a union, in the first Adam, to sin and death.[19] Alongside Pharaoh as the antichrist of oppression and harm, the Scriptures also give us the

18. For a helpful study that brings many of these facets of the exodus together, see Nicholas P. Lunn, "'Let My People Go!' The Exodus as Israel's Metaphorical Divorce from Egypt," *Evangelical Quarterly* 86, no. 3 (2014): 239–51.

19. See, e.g., Tom Holland, *Contours of Pauline Theology: A Radical New Survey of the Influences on Paul's Biblical Writings* (Fearn, Scotland: Mentor/Christian Focus, 2004), 85–154; Tom Holland, *Romans: The Divine Marriage: A Biblical Theological Commentary* (Eugene, OR: Wipf & Stock, 2011).

false, exploitative shepherds roundly condemned by Israel's prophets, the Pharisees and other religious leaders attached to misuses of Torah and empty of mercy, the Simon Magus of ministerial exploitation, and more. By way of such antichrist examples, the Scriptures outline the profile of the faithful Shepherd that Christ is, and establish concrete forms of faithful ministry for those who serve in his name. Further, the church is, in this way, best understood in relation to the gospel of this Christ and the Christ of this gospel.

Glorious Discernment: Matthean Mercy and Ministry

The Gospel of Matthew reflects this concern in the way in which Jesus opposed the presumed righteousness of the Jewish religious leaders. These leaders routinely misused biblical law in ways that reflected a lack of discernment, and thus compromised the actual concerns of justice. This is particularly relevant for our purposes, for in Matthew a disordered use of biblical (and constitutional) procedure may be seen as analogous to the disorderliness condemned in Scripture in relation to sacrifices. Here is something on which every church officer must meditate.

The point is brought home in Jesus' definition of mercy not merely as consistent with justice, or permitted by it, but *as* justice. In Matthew, Jesus says twice, quoting Hosea 6:6, "I desire mercy, and not sacrifice" (Matt. 9:13; 12:7). Importantly, when Jesus quotes this line, it is in the context of a dispute with the religious leaders. Further, in both instances the issue is the real intention of the law (eating with the unclean in Matthew 9; the Sabbath laws in Matthew 12). In Matthew, Jesus uses Hosea to defend his and his disciples' activities against accusations. The issue is hermeneutical and practical. Jesus introduces his quotation from Hosea with the stinging, sober words, *"Go and learn what this means,* 'I desire mercy, and not sacrifice'" (9:13). Finally, even when the other Synoptic Gospels include the same scenes, only Matthew includes Jesus' clearly strategic refrain-like use of Hosea, suggesting that it is quite important to the overall message of Matthew's Gospel.[20] In a Gospel punctuated with the most

---

20. Mary Hinkle Edin, "Learning What Righteousness Means: Hosea 6:6 and the Ethic of Mercy in Matthew's Gospel," *Word and World* 18, no. 4 (Fall 1998): 355–63.

conspicuous possible concern for the "higher righteousness" that must be found among Jesus' disciple-shepherds, this distinctive feature of Matthew's presentation of Jesus' ethic is not surprising.

Matthew's message is simple but poignant. It concerns true law-keeping *and* law-use, and Hosea's words serve that end powerfully. The *hesed* ("faithfulness," "steadfastness") of Hosea is present as *eleos* ("mercy") in Matthew, a term limited in Matthew to these same two scenes with the addition of a "woe" to the scribes and Pharisees regarding the "weightier matters of the law" (Matt. 23:23). Like the leaders in Hosea's day, the religious leaders in Jesus' day are not steadfast. As Mary Hinkle Edin remarks:

> The Pharisees appear to be concerned with righteousness—at least they are concerned with law observance—yet Jesus argues that their understanding of righteousness is at odds with what God desires. Their teaching is internally inconsistent (Matt 23:16–22) and their practice is inconsistent with even those elements of their teaching that are true (Matt 23:3). . . . They have failed to recognize the connection between law observance and mercy. . . . In short, the Pharisees' righteousness exhibits neither of the defining characteristics of *hesed*, and so is not the righteousness of God at all.[21]

What difference does this make in the interplay of church order and faithful ministry? The mercy priority of true righteousness requires that we ask what the ultimately righteous *why* is behind every procedural *what*, and be directed by the former. Thus, procedural fidelity is not the whole picture of actual fidelity to Christ. The books of order used by many presbyterian communions in our day are quite detailed about policies and procedure. This is proper and good. While detailed polities may put off some Christians in our day, particularly those who are concerned about (and have perhaps experienced) abuses of power *as* abuses of procedure, Jesus does not critique the Law or laws any more than Hosea condemned sacrifices as such. No, when we are tempted to confuse the written regulations

---

21. Edin, "Learning What Righteousness Means," 359–60.

with the *whole* of ultimate righteousness, we must grasp Jesus' whole point in Matthew that *it must not be this way* among his disciples.

Presbyterian polity is an aid rather than a vulnerability in this context. In fact, a rich history of thoughtful pastoral care has given rise to the present form(s) of presbyterian order, including disciplinary procedures.[22] A church officer would do well to acquaint himself with that history, but more importantly with how law, especially biblical law, is designed to work (and how it is not).[23] Presbyterians using our good procedures must always remain attentive to the Lord's summons to "go and learn what this means": God desires mercy, not sacrifice.

Glorious Leadership: Petrine Shepherding Ministry

To desire mercy requires recognizing the need for it. Shepherds know mercy better than hirelings do, because shepherds care for their sheep. Such attentive love and understanding appear to be of concern in Jesus' indictment of the Jewish leaders in Matthew. And the shepherd motif for a church leader, found throughout Scripture, is a useful way to connect who the church is to church officers (undershepherds) and to Christ himself, the true Shepherd.[24]

In 1 Peter 5, the apostle unpacks the Shepherd-shepherd dynamic along the very lines that concern us here. But we will hear these words

22. Readers might begin with the "Prologue to the Ecclesiastical Canons" by Ivo of Chartres in *Prefaces to Canon Law Books in Latin Christianity: Selected Translations, 500–1245*, commentary and trans. Robert Sommerville and Bruce C. Brasington (New Haven, CT/London: Yale University Press, 1998), 133–58; and then proceed through the Reformed casuistic manuals of William Perkins and William Ames, into the relevant portions of the Westminster Larger Catechism and early Reformed polities, noting the continuity of concerns and procedures when discerning righteousness in complicated cases.

23. On the development of law and how its use changed over time, see Harold J. Berman, *The Law and Revolution: The Formation of the Western Legal Tradition* (Cambridge, MA: Harvard University Press, 1983); Harold J. Berman, *Faith and Order: The Reconciliation of Law and Religion* (Grand Rapids: Eerdmans, 1993). For how biblical law works in light of the concerns raised above, see esp. Michael LeFebvre, *Collections, Codes, and Torah: The Re-Characterization of Israel's Written Law* (New York: T. & T. Clark/Bloomsbury, 2006).

24. For an excellent study, see Timothy S. Laniak, *Shepherds after My Own Heart: Pastoral Traditions and Leadership in the Bible* (Downers Grove, IL: IVP Academic, 2006).

best when we hear them in light of what the author himself once heard from the risen Shepherd: "Feed my sheep" (John 21:15–17). When Peter here tells church leaders to "feed the flock of God," he "is giving to others the very same command which he was himself given by the risen Lord" (v. 16).[25]

In doing so, the apostle certainly identifies himself with the local church leaders. "I exhort the *presbyteroi* among you, as a fellow *presbuteros* . . ." (1 Peter 5:1). Peter's words contain no trace of a self-consciousness of his belonging to a superior order of officer; instead, we see evidence that suggests the opposite. He is a presbyter speaking to fellow presbyters, but with the apostolic authority of one who has witnessed the sufferings of Christ (v. 1).

While this coheres well with the presbyterian distinctive of the parity of ministers (as Peter gives to other church leaders a command once given only to himself), there is more to his teaching than this. To his fellow presbyters, Peter then says, "Shepherd the flock of God that is among you, exercising oversight" (1 Peter 5:2). We should note that there is real authority or power that presbyters exercise, a real "oversight," to use Peter's language. "Servant leadership" is thus not less than real leadership and authority. But we also note that the flock of God with regard to whom this rule is exercised is just that: the flock *of God*. This reality provokes Peter's immediately subsequent admonitions: faithful shepherds do not serve under compulsion, but willingly, as God would have us; not for shameful gain, but eagerly; not domineering over those in our charge, but being examples to the flock. Returning to the opening theme of whose flock this is, Peter then closes his admonitions to presbyters with a perfectly fitting reference to Christ himself as the "chief Shepherd" (v. 4). Peter's concerns could have been directly lifted from any number of recent church scandals, but they also reflect enduring temptations reflecting sin's proclivity to distort and misuse—the apostle's admonitions are timely.

A final observation on Peter's list is necessary here. The shepherd who is no mere hireling is also the shepherd willing to pay a great cost, perhaps the greatest cost, for the welfare of the true Shepherd's

---

25. Alan M. Stibbs, *The First Epistle General of Peter*, Tyndale New Testament Commentaries (Grand Rapids: Eerdmans, 1959), 167.

sheep. It is easy enough to write about the need to be willing to lay one's life down for the sheep; it is quite another to face the decision itself. But it happens. Why, though, would a minister or elder sacrifice his reputation, maybe even his ministry, livelihood, friendships, and more, in order to "get in the way" of the enemy's missiles to shield one little lamb? What kind of logic can this be?

It is the logic of the church as the glory of the Son, and of the ferocity of his own cross-shaped devotion to her good. When we consider who the bridal church really is in the economy of Trinitarian love, we dare not get in the way of the Father's love for his Son, which takes the form of the church. Grounding presbyterian commitments to representation, the eldership, and so on in the love of the Father for the Son in the Spirit, we begin to understand, though feebly, why Christ's little ones *must* be guarded, *must* be cared for, *must* be ministered to, and at any earthly price, *for they are Christ's and not our own*, and he *must* be glorified. "Feed my sheep," said our Lord three times to Peter—three times, like the trihagion, the thrice "holy, holy, holy" of God himself (Isa. 6:3; Rev. 4:8). Perhaps we are to read "*feed, feed, feed*" of John 21 similarly, as a testimony to the superlative urgency that Christ's sheep be faithfully fed, an urgency arising from the superlative glory of the thrice-holy Son: "You, minister, must feed *my* sheep."

Glorious Humility: Pauline Recessive Ministry

I suggest that we have a special example of this very point in the apostle Paul's words to the Corinthian church, words that we can now consider in brief compass. Presbyterian polity yields a "recessive" ministry in which Christ the true Pastor is relentlessly put forward as his servants relentlessly recede into the background.

In 1 Corinthians 3:5–23, addressing factionalism and rivalry in a young church, the apostle provides "the longest discussion in the New Testament of how the leaders of the church and its members relate to each other."[26] Throughout the passage, we discover that the driver of Paul's correction of disorder is his theology of the church's *identity*:

---

26. Roy E. Ciampa and Brian S. Rosner, *The First Letter to the Corinthians*, Pillar New Testament Commentary (Grand Rapids: Eerdmans, 2010), 142.

again, who the church *is* carries the force of command regarding how the church must *be*. His core point is that ministers exercise a "recessive" sort of ministry, receding happily into the background so that the true Minister's Word and work remain at the fore. There are many excellent treatments of the passage.[27] I offer only a few remarks.

Paul's message proceeds through a series of metaphors, deploying a few deeply rooted images for God's people to great effect, telling the Corinthians that the church is God's field-edifice (1 Cor. 3:5–9), his building (vv. 10–15), and his temple (vv. 16–17). Each of these images is, of course, drawn from the Old Testament, each receives feminine characterization in the Old Testament, and each is enlisted in—and gives rise to—Paul's argument regarding proper ministerial and congregational conduct.

Paul takes to task those members of the congregation who see themselves as "belonging" to certain of their leaders. No, Paul argues, the reverse is true: your leaders belong to you. "Paul or Apollos or Cephas . . .—all are yours" (1 Cor. 3:22). The congregation is not the possession of the minister or bishop. No, if anything, the minister "belongs" to the congregation because he serves in the name and at the pleasure of the true Bishop, and thus labors utterly for their good (not his own). In this way at least, the minister is theirs, not vice versa. But this does not reflect congregationalism; instead, it exposes the basis of Paul's most conspicuous and driving concern: the church's only ultimate allegiance must be to God in Christ, for *"you belong to Christ, and Christ belongs to God"* (v. 23 NASB).

Paul would appear to echo here what the apostle John said in the words noted earlier: "All that the Father gives me" (John 6:35–40). With these few words, we seem to have arrived at the core gospel mystery of the church that yields not only John's theology but also Peter's and Paul's governmental instruction. In short, Paul evidently believes that if the church is the field-edifice, building, and temple of God, and if the church is therefore Christ's in God, then certain order and ministerial consequences follow necessarily.

---

27. Ciampa and Rosner are particularly helpful. See also David W. Kuck, *Judgment and Community Conflict: Paul's Use of Apocalyptic Judgment Language in 1 Corinthians 3:5–4:5*, NovTSup 66 (Leiden: Brill, 1992); Anthony C. Thiselton, *The First Epistle to the Corinthians*, NIGTC (Grand Rapids: Eerdmans, 2000), 295–335.

The feminine nature of Paul's Old Testament metaphors may also aid us in understanding the link, in context, between the urgency of the Corinthian church's driving out sin (the unclean thing) from her midst on the one hand, and her leaders' mirroring Christ faithfully on the other. The apostle evidently understands the mystery of the church as the environment and expression of the mystery of the gospel: God the Son becomes man, the second-last Adam of a new Edenic sanctuary, who, in love for his Father's gift, the bride, cultivates the garden to be fruitful, drives out the unclean thing(s), and guards—with priestly fervor and a husband's jealousy—his beloved.

Indeed, perhaps this link helps us to better appreciate why there is such holy vehemence and rage when the Lord, through his Old Testament prophets, sometimes threatened judgment against his false, counterfeit shepherds: forgetting who their own Master is, in whose name they are called to serve, they are harming not merely other people but *his* bride. Like any good husband, but infinitely better than the best of men, the Lord strongly protects his beloved and cares for her. And how could he not? This bride is nothing less than the loving gift of the Father to the Son in the Spirit, created to be his glory, and redeemed at the cost of his own sacrificial blood. The faithful servant of the church will allow this truth of the church's identity to inform and shape—even determine—the practical content of his vocation. In fact, we may go further to suggest that it is perhaps the worst form of inconsistency when a man operates on presbyterian principles when on the floor of a presbytery meeting and in the session meeting room but is either a detached puppet or an authoritarian tyrant at home.

On the other hand, Christ's true service as the church's Prophet-Priest-King also implies a *temporary* and *provisional* ministry on the part of every human pastor or elder in this age. Paul pushes Christ forward and his servants backward in reflection of eschatological reality. In the final order of things, when grace finds full expression in glory, there will be only one Pastor, one Shepherd, not many. All who are currently ministers and elders in the church will step back from their roles and find their place within the glorified body of Christ, the church, alongside their brothers and sisters in the holy household. This "recessive" reality, in which leaders of the church will "recede" into the background when Jesus' shepherding is finally and fully visible, anchors a deep-running humility on our part in all our churchly endeavors.

This "recessive" conviction accents several important features of presbyterian polity, including the exclusively ministerial, declarative nature of church power and the critical concern for Christian liberty, by which no Christian may be obliged to do something that Christ in his Word has not obliged us to do. The faithful minister brings only Christ's Word, not his own, both positively, in that the Word of Christ may be confidently declared as true precisely because it is Christ's, and negatively, in that Christ exercises his rule in an exclusive way, shielding his little ones and their consciences from the commands of mere men by securing for them a true liberty bounded normatively by his Word.

These relativizing considerations ought not to trouble but delight us. In a sense, the church is not the point. The love of the Father for the Son in the Spirit—that's the Trinitarian, doxological point of everything. Regaining a sense of proportion regarding the church's identity and mission, in which this Trinitarian love occupies the central place, ironically ensures the meaning, value, and eternal glory of our proper devotion to the church. And if such a reordering makes the minister smaller in stature, if the "recessive" nature of ministry in Christ's name threatens to push our presence and skills and prerogatives from center stage, then this is wonderful news, not only for the minister himself but for those to whom he is called to minister.

A Better Presbyterianism

At the foundation of the proper theological ordering of the church, I have suggested, is the vigorous, vital, and relentless love of the Father for the Son and, in its wake, the love of Christ for his church, which is the Father's gift to him. At the heart of why the church is ordered as she is, and especially why her ministers fulfill a recessive ministry, is not a love for order or procedure as such, but the safeguarding of the divine love that will not be frustrated.

If, then, the order of the church enables its ardor for the broken, the answer to the unrest in our day is not Christ without his church,

421

or an ardor without order. Churches fail. Church bodies and officers fail. Again, no form of church government is able, per se, to guarantee the welfare, security, and well-being of any member. If Cicero was right that a true republic is that place where true justice is found, then Augustine was right to warn his readers that even the best version of the Roman republic fails to satisfy. No, only another "republic" can provide that: "But the fact is, true justice has no existence save in that republic whose founder and ruler is Christ[;] . . . we may at all events say that in this city is true justice; the city of which Holy Scripture says, 'Glorious things are said of thee, O city of God.'"[28]

If this is true, then our word to pastors is this: the answer to our contemporary crisis of broken trust is not the abandonment of presbyterianism, but a better presbyterianism, a church that loves what Christ loves and hates what Christ hates, and thus enjoys and glorifies him in fellowship with the triune God. In a world of broken trusts, the simple words of the ancient psalmist (Ps. 87:3) and of the eminent church father sound eerily contemporary: a city that lasts, ordered and ruled by Christ, where true justice is found—glorious things indeed.

Key Terms

macrocosm
mediocosm
microcosm
presbyterianism

Recommendations for Further Reading

Huber, Lynn R. *Like a Bride Adorned: Reading Metaphor in John's Apocalypse*. Emory Studies in Early Christianity 10. New York: T. & T. Clark/Bloomsbury, 2007.

Kuiper, R. B. *The Glorious Body of Christ*. Grand Rapids: Eerdmans, 1966. Reprint, London: Banner of Truth, 1967.

28. Augustine, *City of God*, 2.21, NPNF ser. 1, 2:36. Augustine interacts with Cicero here.

Laniak, Timothy S. *Shepherds after My Own Heart: Pastoral Traditions and Leadership in the Bible.* Downers Grove, IL: IVP Academic, 2006.

LeFebvre, Michael. *Collections, Codes, and Torah: The Re-Characterization of Israel's Written Law.* New York: T. & T. Clark/Bloomsbury, 2006.

Robinson, Stuart. *The Church of God as an Essential Element of the Gospel, and the Idea, Structure, and Functions Thereof. A Discourse in Four Parts.* Philadelphia: Joseph M. Wilson, 1858. Reprint (and edited with a foreword by A. Craig Troxel), Willow Grove, PA: Committee on Christian Education of the Orthodox Presbyterian Church, 2009.

Westminster Confession of Faith, chap. 25.

Discussion Questions

1. Why is it important to explore the order of the church by way of the nature of the church, rather than as a separate consideration?

2. What are some distinctive principles and priorities of presbyterianism in distinction from other forms of church government?

3. In what ways does faithful presbyterian church polity restrain rather than indulge our sinful quest for power?

4. How might the topic of biblical and faithful church government serve as good news for the vulnerable in the church?

5. Relate the love of a church officer for the church to the love of Christ for his church and the love of the Father for the Son. How do these loves help shape faithful church practice?

6. In what way does the biblical teaching regarding "mercy, and not sacrifice" (Matt. 9:13; 12:7) help to protect a church officer from misusing good and orderly church procedure?

7. How would you respond to someone who claims to love Christ but not his church?

22

COMMUNION OF THE SAINTS

Sharing the Spirit-Endowed Riches

of Christ's Gifts and Graces[1]

A. CRAIG TROXEL

Ecclesiology is no less immune to contracting the latest cultural trend than the other loci of theology. Perhaps it is even more susceptible because of its penchant for (rightly) bridging theory with practice. Such is seen in the idea of *building community*, which not only is popular in business leadership forums or discussions among sociologists, but is in vogue among churches of every persuasion. Local churches give it star billing in mission statements. Some church movements define themselves by it.[2] Some theologians promote community as the integrating motif of all theology.[3] Being communal has been eagerly

1. Those who've been blessed with a godly mentor understand why Elisha called Elijah his "father." In addition to spoon-feeding me theology that oriented my heart, you, Dr. Ferguson, nurtured by pastoral example that helped to orient my ministry. *Tapadh leibh!*

2. Representatives of the "emerging church" movement refer to their groups as "communities that practice the way of Jesus" and see the formation of community itself as being of highest importance. Eddie Gibbs and Ryan K. Bolger, *Emerging Churches: Creating Christian Community in Postmodern Cultures* (Grand Rapids: Baker, 2005), 44.

3. Stanley Grenz and John Franke, *Beyond Foundationalism* (Louisville: Westminster John Knox, 2001), 53.

425

welcomed as the newest inductee into the halls of church relevancy, right alongside "missional" and "incarnational" ministries.

And why not? Who can deny the importance of community? Parents underscore the importance of their children's school community every time they attend a sports event, a band concert, or a (dreaded) parent-teacher conference. We prioritize our neighborhood communities with play dates, block parties, and watching out for our friends next door. The significance of civic and political communities is regularly measured by our petitions and votes that hold governing officials accountable. Our workplaces, fitness clubs, hobby groups, book clubs, and scout troops all have their respective places in our lives, because they are the communities with which we identify. The motto "building community" is not only pervasive in the business world and among social groups. It is also finding its way into church strategies in particular and practical ways.

Is this a healthy trend? One way to get at this is by asking a rather pointed question: Is the idea and practice of building community in the church consistent with, or the same as, the doctrine that Christians have confessed for almost two millennia: "I believe in . . . the communion of saints"? The answer depends on how we understand these phrases, *communion of saints* and *building community*. And that same answer provides a bearing to orient the principles and practice of a pastor who ministers among the holy community that Christ is building.

Current Ideas about Community

The idea of building community is a practical principle that stresses the importance of investing in relationships and in one's community (whatever it may be) for the welfare of both the individual and members of the community. But this simple idea is actually the practical outworking of earlier and deeper intellectual currents, typically labeled as *communitarianism*. The central theme to this movement is that someone's identity and sense of meaning are shaped by the surrounding community in which the person lives. Although much communitarian thought began in political philosophy, it has now branched off into different disciplines (philosophy and sociology, among others), traditions, and schools of thought (Marxists, social conservatives, postmoderns); and it unites voices (Alasdair MacIntyre, Robert Bellah, Charles Taylor) that would not otherwise be associated with one another. A pertinent example of this is the book *Community and Society* by Ferdinand Tönnies. His work has inspired or provoked much of contemporary communitarian thought, which emphasizes that humanity unfolds its essence only by living in communities of kinship.[4] This book is particularly relevant for our purposes because some postmodern theologians have leaned heavily on Tönnies and his insights for their proposals regarding community. They insist that "community" is theology's "integrative motif" and should operate as the organizing concept of all theological construction. This is especially true for postmodern theology, since it asserts that all knowledge is a social construct and is situated in a specific community. Because one cannot know the truth absolutely, he or she must learn the language (semiotics) of a particular community and meaning within that community. All theology is the "world-constructing, knowledge-forming, identity-forming 'language' of the Christian community."[5]

Wittingly or not, the postmodern commitment to community as a central idea for theology is replicating a previous theological ancestry. Friedrich Schleiermacher, the father of modern theology, held that the church was "above all a fellowship" that exists through the voluntary actions of men. Schleiermacher insisted that the whole nature and idea of the church must be derived from this assumption.[6] The existential theologian Emil Brunner agreed. He stated that the essence of the New Testament church was seen in its "oneness of communion" and its "brotherhood in love."[7] Similarly, one evangelical theologian suggests that we should rid ourselves of the word *church* altogether and replace it with the term *community*.[8] Other strains of

4. Ferdinand Tönnies, *Community and Society*, ed. and trans. Charles P. Loomis (1887; repr., Lansing, MI: Michigan State University Press, 1957).

5. Grenz and Franke, *Beyond Foundationalism*, 53.

6. Werner Elert, *Eucharist and Church Fellowship in the First Four Centuries*, trans. N. E. Nagel (St. Louis: Concordia, 1966), 2.

7. Emil Brunner, *The Misunderstanding of the Church* (Philadelphia: Westminster, 1953), 117.

8. See Roger E. Olson, "Free Church Ecclesiology and Evangelical Spirituality," in *Evangelical Ecclesiology: Reality or Illusion?*, ed. John G. Stackhouse Jr. (Grand

theological descent have laid claim to the same conviction. Ecumenical theology is surely responsible, in part, for the resurgence of the idea of *fellowship* in modern ecclesiology. It has been suggested that the church's relevancy for the third millennium will be determined by how well churches follow in the footsteps of ecumenical ecclesiologists and fulfill "the basic task" of what it means for the church to embody *koinonia*.[9] Or, as another has speculated, only those groups that adopt "participative models" and congregational government will be the churches of the future.[10] It is evident that *community* has come to enjoy wide appeal as an article of faith for churches and theologians, whether their theological convictions could be categorized as modern, postmodern, or evangelical. But how does this compare to the doctrine of the communion of saints?

Historical Ideas about *Communion of Saints*

"*credo . . . sanctorum communionem*" (Apostles' Creed)

The History of *Communion of Saints*

The "Old Roman Creed" (or "Shorter Roman Symbol") is the undisputed and formal progenitor of the Apostles' Creed.[11] The Roman Creed was a baptismal formula from the late second century that is preserved in early statements of faith.[12] The Roman Symbol spread to the four various areas under the influence of the Roman Empire (northern Italy, Spain, North Africa, and the Balkans and

---

Rapids: Baker, 2003), 161–78.

9. Veli-Matti Karkkainen, *An Introduction to Ecclesiology: Ecumenical, Historical & Global Perspectives* (Downers Grove, IL: InterVarsity Press, 2002), 231. One also sees the same basic commitment to community as being central to theology in process theology (Teilhard de Chardin, John Cobb), liberation theology (Gustavo Gutiérrez, Leonardo Boff, Juan Luis Segundo), and the social gospel (Walter Rauschenbusch).

10. Miroslav Volf, *After Our Likeness: The Church as the Image of the Trinity* (Grand Rapids: Eerdmans, 1998), 13.

11. John H. Leith, ed., *Creeds of the Churches*, 3rd ed. (Atlanta: John Knox Press, 1982), 22.

12. E.g., "Interrogatory Creed of Hippolytus" (215); "Creed of Marcellus" (340); "Creed of Rufinus" (404). J. N. D. Kelly, *Early Christian Creeds*, 3rd ed. (New York: Longman, 1972), 127; Leith, *Creeds of the Churches*, 23.

Gaul ["Gallican" region]). These areas produced modified "daughter creeds," which all retained the core marks of their maternal archetype.[13] From the Gallican line we trace the present-day version, the *textus receptus* of the Apostles' Creed, which is dated around A.D. 700–724.[14] This is the form that Martin Luther, John Calvin, and Huldrych Zwingli recognized as being among the accepted doctrinal norms.[15]

The phrase *sanctorum communionem* ("communion of saints") is a late addition to the creed. It does not appear before the fifth century.[16] It is not found in any of the confessional treatments of Ignatius of Antioch, Justin Martyr, Irenaeus, or Tertullian, and the words do not appear in the creeds of Caesarea (325), Nicea (325), and Constantinople (381).[17] Ambrose and Augustine instructed their flocks to memorize and recite the creed, but it was a creed without the words *sanctorum communionem*.[18] It does not appear in any of the Eastern creeds.[19] But what does the phrase actually mean?

The Meaning of *Communion of Saints*

There are two schools of thought on what the phrase *communion of saints* means. Do the words suggest a "communion of holy persons (saints)" or a "participation in holy things"? Is it about Christian fellowship, or is it about sacramental communion? The reason for these alternative interpretations is due to a grammatical issue. What is the root of the word *sanctorum* (which in Latin is a genitive plural)? Is it masculine (*sancti*) or neuter (*sancta*)? Which idea was originally intended?[20]

---

13. Kelly, *Creeds*, 369; Leith, *Creeds of the Churches*, 24.

14. Kelly, *Creeds*, 411–20.

15. Kelly, *Creeds*, 368.

16. F. Q. Gouvea, "The Communion of the Saints," in *The Evangelical Dictionary of Theology*, ed. Daniel J. Treier and Walter A. Elwell (Grand Rapids: Baker, 2017), 257.

17. Leith, *Creeds of the Churches*, 16, 18, 21–22, 27–31.

18. Kelly, *Creeds*, 370; Philip Schaff, *The Creeds of Christendom*, 3 vols. (Grand Rapids: Baker, 1993), 1:55; Herman Witsius, *The Apostles' Creed*, 2 vols. (1823; repr., Escondido, CA: den Dulk Christian Foundation, 1993), 2:376–77.

19. Henry B. Swete, *The Holy Catholic Church: The Communion of Saints* (London: Macmillan, 1916), 157. When representatives from the East appeared at the Council of Florence (1438–45), they said that they knew nothing about a so-called Apostles' Creed. Kelly, *Creeds*, 4; Leith, *Creeds of the Churches*, 24.

20. Silke-Petra Bergjan, "Ecclesiology in Faith and Order Texts," *Ecumenical*

If *sancti* is in view, then the phrase refers to the fellowship of Christians of all ages in their union with Christ and their fellowship with one another through him. It "signifieth not holy things, but holy ones, that is, persons holy."[21] Speaking broadly, this was the prevailing view from the fifth to the eighth centuries, and then again from the sixteenth century up until the late nineteenth century.[22] The Roman Catholic Church has used this phrase to defend the veneration of the saints.[23] As Rome's ecclesiastical influence ascended, so also did its stress on the mysterious union between the church *militant* on earth, the church *triumphant* in heaven, and the church *expectant* in purgatory. For example, the Creed of the Council of Trent (1565) affirmed that "there is a purgatory" and that "the souls detained there are helped by the prayers of the faithful," that "the saints reigning together with Christ should be honored and invoked," and that their "relics should be venerated."[24] The First Dogmatic Constitution on the Church of Christ of the Vatican Council (1870) stated that communion entailed a believer's affectionately associating with the Roman See in order that the person might receive all "the rights of communion."[25] The Dogmatic Constitution on the Church from the Vatican Council II (1964) stated the same, but also affirmed that the church was "a kind of Sacrament of intimate union with God" and that she is "a sign and an instrument of such union and unity," and thus laid special emphasis on the importance of believers' sharing goods and graces together as an expression of this unity and fellowship.[26]

If *sancta* is in view, then the phrase refers to a participation in holy things, namely, the sacraments (thus, the "sacramental view").

Review 46, no. 1 (January 1994): 55.

21. John Pearson, *An Exposition of the Creed*, 6th ed. (Oxford: Clarendon, 1877), 621–22.

22. Berard L. Marthaler, *The Creed* (Mystic, CT: Twenty-Third Publications, 1987), 362; Kelly, *Creeds*, 394. Peter Lombard and Bernard of Clairvaux held to this view.

23. Kelly, *Creeds*, 391.

24. Leith, *Creeds of the Churches*, 441; *The Catechism of the Catholic Church* (Collegeville, MN: Liturgical Press, 1994), nos. 946, 948–59, 961.

25. Leith, *Creeds of the Churches*, 451.

26. Leith, *Creeds of the Churches*, 459, 463–64.

This view arose in later medieval theology.[27] It has become increasingly popular ever since the late nineteenth century.[28] Abelard and Jerome assume this position. The Fourth Lateran Council (1215) did not address communion of the saints per se, but it did state in Canon 1 that a believer partakes of the transubstantiated elements of the Lord's Supper in order "to accomplish the mystery of our union" and "receive of Him what He has received of us."[29] In one sense, the sacramental view believes that the phrase can refer to both, things and persons.[30] This is reified in the liturgical words *Sancta sanctis!* ("Holy gifts [things] for [God's] holy people"). This was the view of Albert the Great, Ivo of Chartres, Jocelin of Soissons, and Alexander of Hales.[31] Believers commune with the sacrament and with those in purgatory, and have the right to venerate and pray to deceased saints.

An example of how this can get complicated is seen in how people have interpreted the words of Thomas Aquinas, who wrote: "Because all the faithful form one body, the benefits belonging to one are communicated to the others. There is thus a sharing of benefits (*communio bonorum*) in the Church, and this is what we mean by *sanctorum communio.*"[32] Some suggest that Thomas's words—like medieval theology at large—clearly allude to a participation in the good benefits of holy things, the Eucharist.[33] Whereas J. N. D. Kelly states that "it should be evident" that Thomas refers to "that sharing or participation which saints enjoy."[34] These conflicting views would seem to embody what one has said: "The history of the interpretation of *sanctorum communio* is the history of the Western interpretation of the Church."[35]

27. Kelly, *Creeds*, 394.
28. Kelly, *Creeds*, 390.
29. Leith, *Creeds of the Churches*, 58.
30. G. C. Berkouwer, *The Church*, trans. James E. Davison (Grand Rapids: Eerdmans, 1976), 92; Henry Wheeler, *The Apostles' Creed: An Examination of Its History and an Exposition of Its Contents* (New York: Eaton & Mains, 1912), 150–51. This is obviously the Eastern Orthodox view as well. See Timothy Ware, *The Orthodox Church* (New York: Penguin, 1997), 242; Marthaler, *Creed*, 347.
31. Kelly, *Creeds*, 393.
32. Kelly, *Creeds*, 394.
33. Gouvea, "Communion of the Saints," 257.
34. Kelly, *Creeds*, 394.
35. Elert, *Eucharist*, 8.

The Historic Reformed View

Churches in the tradition of the Reformation have long affirmed the church as the fellowship of God's people, or as the communion of saints. The Augsburg Confession (1530) affirms that the church is an "assembly of the saints" (*congregatio sanctorum*) or the "assembly of believers" (*congregatio fidelium*).[36] In its "Collect for All Saints' Day," the Book of Common Prayer (1549) affirms that Christians are "in one communion and fellowship in the mystical body of Christ our Lord," with this "mystical body" defined as "the blessed company of all faithful people." It is significant that the same wording appears in the prayer before the blessing of holy communion.[37] The Second Helvetic Confession (1566) asserts that the church is

> a company of the faithful called and gathered out of the world; a communion . . . of all saints, that is, of them who truly know and rightly worship and serve the true God, in Jesus Christ the Saviour, by the word and the Holy Spirit, and who by faith are partakers of all those good graces which are freely offered through Christ. . . . These all are citizens of one and the same city, living under one Lord, under the same laws, and in the same fellowship of all good things; for the apostle calls them "fellow citizens with the saints and members of the household of God" (Eph. 2:19); terming the faithful upon the earth saints (1 Cor. 4:1), who are sanctified by the blood of the Son of God. Of these is that article of our Creed wholly to be understood, "I believe in the holy Catholic Church, the communion of saints."[38]

The Belgic Confession (1561) assumes the same: "The Church . . . is joined and united with heart and will, by the power of faith, in one and the same spirit."[39] The Cambridge Platform (1648) says that the members of the militant visible church enjoy a "spiritual union, and communion, common to all believers," and in churches "are all

---

36. Or the "Versammlung aller Gläubigen." Leith, *Creeds of the Churches*, 64.

37. As noted in Swete, *Communion*, 167.

38. Leith, *Creeds of the Churches*, 141.

39. Schaff, *Creeds of Christendom*, 3:417, art. 27 ("Of the Catholic Christian Church").

united unto Christ, not only as a mystical, but as a political head; whence is derived a communion suitable thereunto."[40] Perhaps the clearest expression of this view is provided by the Heidelberg Catechism: "What dost thou understand by the *communion of saints*?" (Q. 55). The answer states: "First, that believers, all and every one, as members of Christ, have part in him and in all his treasures and gifts. Secondly, that each one must feel himself bound to use his gifts, readily and cheerfully, for the advantage and welfare of other members."[41]

Chapter 26 ("Of the Communion of Saints") of the Westminster Confession of Faith describes the communion that exists as being between persons, not things: "All saints that are united to Jesus Christ their Head by His Spirit and by faith, have fellowship with Him in His graces, sufferings, death, resurrection, and glory: and, being united to one another in love, they have communion in each other's gifts and graces" (WCF 26.1). There is nothing here about purgatory or about the necessity of a believer's union with the Roman See. Neither does the confession say anything about sacramental union. The Lord's Supper is "a bond and pledge" of the church's communion with Christ, and with each other as "members of his mystical body" (WCF 29.2). John Calvin affirmed that although "the communion of saints" was a late addition to the creed, it "very well" expresses what the church is, because it so much as says that by joining the church, "the saints are gathered into the society of Christ on the principle that whatever benefits God confers upon them, they should in turn share with one another." This is a community of heart and soul that rules out neither the diversity of graces and gifts nor the right of civic order and private ownership of property.[42] James Bannerman expresses the same in his *Church of Christ*: "The Christian Church was established in the world, to realize the superior advantages of a social over an individual Christianity, and to set up and maintain the communion of saints."[43]

---

40. Leith, *Creeds of the Churches*, 387–88. The latter quote comes from chapter 14, entitled "Of the Communion of Churches One with Another."

41. Schaff, *Creeds of Christendom*, 3:325.

42. John Calvin, *Institutes of the Christian Religion*, ed. John T. McNeill, trans. Ford Lewis Battles, 2 vols., Library of Christian Classics 20–21 (Philadelphia: Westminster, 1960), 4.1.3 (cf. 4.1.7).

43. James Bannerman, *The Church of Christ: A Treatise on the Nature, Powers,*

The Reformed creedal tradition denies that *sanctorum communionem* has anything to do with the veneration of or prayers to deceased saints. The Augsburg Confession (1530) states in article 21 ("The Cult of Saints") that although Scripture encourages us to imitate the faith and example of deceased brothers and sisters, we should not invoke them or seek their help, because Christ is the Christian's "only high priest, advocate, and intercessor before God."[44] In the Second Helvetic Confession (1566), Heinrich Bullinger strikes the same balance as Philipp Melanchthon by stating that although the faith of departed saints ought to be emulated, the church cannot approve of festival days ordained for men or departed saints. It also teaches that the church militant and the church triumphant exhaust the parties in the communion of the saints, with no mention of those in purgatory ("church expectant").[45] Prayers and vigils for the dead are opposed by the Ten Conclusions of Berne (1528).[46] Calvin criticizes the veneration of dead saints and our praying to them.[47] Furthermore, the Reformed tradition would deny that communion of saints necessitates one's acceptance of the Roman See.[48]

According to Reformed theology, *communion of saints* should be understood not as referring to a participation of things, but as a fellowship among persons, namely, God's holy people. So how does this interpretation relate to popular practices of "building community" or historic theories of communitarianism?

Building Community vs. Communion of Saints

All saints that are united to Jesus Christ their Head by His Spirit and by faith, have fellowship with Him in His graces, sufferings, death, resurrection, and glory: and, being united to one another in love, they have communion in each other's gifts and graces, and are

---

Ordinances, Discipline, and Government of the Christian Church, 2 vols. (Edinburgh: Banner of Truth, 1960), 1:91.

44. Leith, *Creeds of the Churches*, 77–78.

45. Leith, *Creeds of the Churches*, 142.

46. Leith, *Creeds of the Churches*, 129–30.

47. Calvin, *Institutes*, 3.20.21–3.20.27.

48. Second Helvetic Confession, chap. 17; Leith, *Creeds of the Churches*, 142.

obliged to the performance of such duties, public and private, as do conduce to their mutual good, both in the inward and outward man. (WCF 26.1)

Chapter 26 of the Westminster Confession of Faith ("Of the Communion of Saints") provides a key insight into how we should approach the meaning of *communion of saints*. The confession appears to have an agenda, and that agenda is reflected in the order by which it addresses the subject. First, it addresses the communion ("fellowship") that believers have with Christ in his work and the benefits they enjoy by right of their union with Christ, and then it proceeds to address the consequent communion that believers have with one another in their gifts and graces. This order reflects precedence. What believers share together in their mutual communion stems from the more fundamental communion they have with Christ. The communion between believers is built on the communion that believers have with Christ and have together in Christ. Because Christians are united to Christ by faith and the Spirit, they are united to one another in love. Because believers commune with Christ in his gifts and graces, they commune with one another in their mutual gifts and graces. For example, the Lord's Supper functions first as a bond and pledge of the believer's union and communion with Christ, and then it is consequently a bond and pledge of our union and communion with one another (as members of Christ's body). By this method, the confession establishes a Christ-centered understanding of the communion of saints. To put it another way, it gives us the proper starting point for approaching the meaning of *communion of saints*. It also helps us to discern what *building community* and *communion of saints* have in common and how they differ.

The difference between the two ideas is brought out by asking the question: from where does the communion of saints gain its life? This question exposes one essential problem with some postmodern and ecumenical expressions of community, namely, that just like modern theology, they are devoid of biblical supernaturalism. They talk about community. But in substance and practice, they set forth a demythologized view of community. This is a horizontal understanding of the church, without much, if any, emphasis on the vertical. By *vertical* we are referring to God's supernatural activity in the church's life and ministry. Any view of the church that understates or ignores supernaturalism will inevitably misconstrue the meaning of *communion of saints* (not to mention every other core doctrine in Scripture). The vitality of the church's communal life comes by the Spirit as he connects believers to Christ in a living union. The communion of saints is above all else the outworking of a deeper union and communion, in which believers partake in the world above and gain a foretaste of the life to come in which God's people will fellowship with the triune God in glory. Any conception or practice of community that doesn't build on a supernatural foundation will inevitably construct a man-made community. Such a community lacks a soul. It is a distortion of the real thing. It is a "non-mediated community of souls."[49]

Christ said: "I am the vine; you are the branches. Whoever abides in me and I in him, he it is that bears much fruit, for apart from me you can do nothing" (John 15:5). The communion of saints begins and is sustained here. The body of Christ, which is "called into the fellowship" of Jesus Christ, finds all that it needs in connection to its living head (1 Cor. 1:9). Christian community must be a "community mediated through Christ."[50]

In his book *Life Together*, Dietrich Bonhoeffer states: "Christian community means community through Jesus Christ and in Jesus Christ. There is no Christian community that is more than this, and none that is less than this. . . . We belong to one another only through and in Jesus Christ."[51] The church's ongoing life is inseparably bound up with its Mediator. We have "access to one another, joy in one another, community with one another through Christ alone."[52] Christian community is founded on and animated by Christ, and this is what makes it different from any other community.[53] Berard Marthaler makes essentially the same point: "The solidarity of the saints with one another rests on their communion with Jesus, the Lord. It

---

49. Dietrich Bonhoeffer, *Life Together*, trans. Daniel W. Bloesch and James H. Burtness (Minneapolis: Fortress Press, 2005), 41.

50. Bonhoeffer, *Life Together*, 41.

51. Bonhoeffer, *Life Together*, 31; see 33–34, 41.

52. Bonhoeffer, *Life Together*, 47, 34.

53. Bonhoeffer, *Life Together*, 38.

is his presence that transforms a thanksgiving meal into a eucharist. It is his communion with the Godhead that makes the COMMUNION OF SAINTS, in spite of human sinfulness, the source and sacrament of holiness in the world."[54] Similarly, James Bannerman wrote that when we speak of Christ as the head of his church, we do not merely mean that he is the *establishing* head of the church, but also mean that he is the *presiding* head of the church.[55] Or, as he puts it, "Christ . . . [is] personally present, governs and administers ordinances and blessing through the Church. The Church has no store of life apart from Christ being in it; the ordinances of the Church have no deposit of grace apart from Christ present with them; the office-bearers of the Church have no gift of power, or authority, or action, apart from Christ ruling and acting by them."[56] Without him we can do nothing. In him we can do all things.

The importance of prioritizing the supernatural foundation for the communion of saints is also seen in the Christian community's highest privilege, worship. Worship is communing with God, and it is this foremost: "An assembly of public worship is not merely a gathering of God's children with each other, but is, before all else, a meeting of the triune God with his covenant people."[57] When God's people gather together in Christ's name, two things are taking place simultaneously. Christ gathers in the presence of his people, and God's people gather in his presence. God's people draw near to Christ by faith, and Christ draws near to his people by the Spirit (Matt. 18:20; John 4:23–24; Phil. 3:3; Heb. 12:22–24). The efficacy and benefit of worship build on the assumption that the church really is the "dwelling place of God" (see 2 Cor. 6:16; Eph. 2:19; 1 Peter 2:5). The lifeblood of worship is found in its vertical connection, not in its horizontal dimension. The presence of Christ among his worshiping people supplies the backbone to the *dialogical principle* of public worship—the idea that when God's people worship corporately, a dialogue between God and his people is carried out in worship: "As

54. Marthaler, *Creed*, 365.
55. Bannerman, *Church of Christ*, 1:198–200.
56. Bannerman, *Church of Christ*, 1:199.
57. *The Book of Church Order of the Orthodox Presbyterian Church*, "The Directory for the Public Worship of God," I.B.1.

a service of public worship is in its essence a meeting of God and his people, the parts of the service are of two kinds: those which are performed on behalf of God, and those which are performed by the congregation. In the former the worshippers are receptive, in the latter they are active. It is reasonable that these two elements be made to alternate as far as possible."[58] None of this dialogue will be truly effective unless the Spirit of God is at work and animating the hearts of God's people, applying the truth of the gospel with conviction and comfort according to their needs. This also underscores the necessity of God's people's exercising faith in Christ's promise to manifest his power among his people and to supply his grace, which is so desperately needed and cannot be received from anyone else. This faith waits, watches, and listens expectantly in worship for what neither humanity nor the world can supply. By this faith, and the ensuing blessings of God's presence, those congregated are separated from the world as God's holy people. It is more than a gathering of people. It is a communion of *saints* who are being set apart for sacred privileges and equipped for consecrated purposes.

The priority of the supernatural activity of Christ for the communion of saints is also seen in how this fellowship is maintained. The gospel is intended to draw people into this fellowship: "That which we have seen and heard we proclaim also to you, so that you too may have fellowship with us; and indeed our fellowship is with the Father and with his Son Jesus Christ" (1 John 1:3). It is a "communion in each other's gifts and graces." But how are such gifts and graces sustained? Every gift that a believer has is given by the Spirit (1 Cor. 12:4–7). And such gifts are not only Spirit-endowed, but also Spirit-empowered. The sustenance of the church's entire spiritual repertoire is lodged where the church's spiritual life began, in the sovereign Spirit of Christ. The presence of Christ's Spirit empowers all the activity of fellowship and mutual service in the church:

> Now there are varieties of gifts, but the same Spirit; and there are varieties of service, but the same Lord; and there are varieties of activities, but it is the same God who empowers them all in

58. OPC, "Directory," III.1.

everyone. To each is given the manifestation of the Spirit for the common good. For to one is given through the Spirit the utterance of wisdom, and to another the utterance of knowledge according to the same Spirit, to another faith by the same Spirit, to another gifts of healing by the one Spirit, to another the working of miracles, to another prophecy, to another the ability to distinguish between spirits, to another various kinds of tongues, to another the interpretation of tongues. All these are empowered by one and the same Spirit, who apportions to each one individually as he wills. (1 Cor. 12:4–11)

When Paul tells Timothy to "fan into flame the gift of God" that he has received for ministry, he grounds his exhortation in the promise that "God gave us a spirit not of fear but of power and love and self-control" (2 Tim. 1:6–7). It is the work of the Spirit, not human effort, that inflames spiritual gifts for their intended efficacy in the body. Peter supposes the same reality when he reminds believers about their gifts: "As each has received a gift, use it to serve one another, as good stewards of God's varied grace . . . by the strength that God supplies" (1 Peter 4:10–11). Gifts are not just Spirit-endowed; they are Spirit-empowered. Whether the increase is the external growth in numbers or it is an internal growth in grace, it is God that gives the growth (1 Cor. 3:6). When Paul urges the Philippians in the grace of humility, he begins with the assumption, "So if there is any encouragement in Christ, any comfort from love, any participation in the Spirit" (Phil. 2:1). The life-giving "participation in the Spirit" and "encouragement in Christ" supply the power for Christian growth and maturity.

Every command that Christ gives his church to practice Christian community requires the sustaining grace that he alone can supply. As fellow believers seek to welcome, encourage, comfort, admonish, serve, forbear with, build up, pray for, and speak the truth to one another, they are in constant need of his strength. This is especially true in light of the formidable standards of the commands to show mercy *as* God has shown mercy to us, to forgive *as* God has forgiven us in Christ, and most of all, to love our brothers and sisters *as* God has loved us in Christ (Matt. 18:33; Col. 3:13; John 13:34). Who is sufficient for these things? What community is capable of such noble devotion? Only those who are empowered by the Holy Spirit and the grace of God can embody the virtues that Christ requires of his church. Whether we are meeting the inner needs of the heart or outward needs of the body, Christian service calls out for spiritual strength and wisdom that are beyond our natural powers. And this service demands the work of the Spirit in a Christian's heart so that service and good deeds will be done with righteous motives and for righteous ends. For the body of Christ to build itself up in love, it must be built up by Christ's grace and truth (Eph. 4:16, 21). The ideals of the communion of saints are not within the reach of mere community-building.[59] What is taking place in the church body can be built and sustained only by its living head, who indwells it by his Spirit.

How does this Reformed understanding of the communion of saints impact the principles and practices of a pastor among his flock? Specifically, how does it shape his responsibility to shepherd, intercede, and exhort; and in particular, how does it impact the way that he leads the fellowship of God's holy people in their gathering for public worship?

Ministry Shaped by the Communion of Saints

A pastor understands that in order for the church to be a living fellowship, it must be blessed by the Holy Spirit—who must never be relegated to being a mere instrument of God's gracious activity, but rather be relied on as its source. This conviction reminds the pastor to "get out of the way" and not impede the direct connection between the members of the church and the person of the Holy Spirit.[60] Their immediate communion and dependence on the Spirit is as indispensable for their gifts as it is for his. The Holy Spirit is not an impersonal force that is "kept on tap," but the one who inhabits his people, inflames their hearts, and empowers their gifts.[61] His work is

59. This thought was inspired by John Piper, *Brothers, We Are Not Professionals: A Plea to Pastors for Radical Ministry* (Nashville: B&H Publishing, 2013), 54–55.

60. Benjamin B. Warfield, *The Plan of Salvation* (1915; repr., Avinger, TX: Simpson Publishing, 1989), 63.

61. Warfield, *The Plan of Salvation*, 64.

not sequestered to the ordained class. He has been set loose on the communion of saints to do as he sovereignly pleases.[62] The faithful pastor preaches and teaches this. He models it. He regularly points the congregation to the source of their strength and help, which is not their pastor. It is their God—with whom they fellowship.

A pastor also appreciates that for the church to be a thriving fellowship, each member of the body should employ his or her gifts and graces in service to one another, by the strength that the Spirit supplies. The scope of a pastor's duties provides him with ample opportunities to encourage God's people in their callings and gifts. It is the rule, not the exception, that when a pastor visits a church member, he will inquire about that member's service. Ordinarily, the person's service will be well known. But other gifts and graces might be hidden from sight (and for good reason), yet these, too, need to be fanned into flame. A pastoral visit offers a discreet occasion to affirm abilities that the pastor and others have noted. What an opportunity to urge a member to bless the wider community. There are other moments in the life of the church when skills, aptitude, potential, and (most important of all) character are openly displayed before the observant shepherd. He makes mental notes as he matches gifts and needs among the flock. Underneath all this is his conviction that just as the body cannot be built up without the ministry of the Word, so also it cannot be built up unless "each part is working properly" (Eph. 4:12, 16). He seizes every favorable moment to spur a member on to do his or her part and pursue the person's unique forms of service. He further points the member to look to the Spirit for the grace to fulfill these callings "by the strength that God supplies" (1 Peter 4:11).

A pastor shepherds a flock that does not belong to him. Nevertheless, Christ requires his steward to bear spiritual fruit, which he cannot produce in and of himself. As John Piper has written, "a pastor who feels competent in himself to produce eternal fruit—which is the only kind that matters—. . . must have his sights only on what man can achieve. But brothers, the proper goals of the life of a pastor are unquestionably beyond our reach. . . . We are called to labor for that which is God's alone to give. The essence of the Christian

---

62. Warfield, *The Plan of Salvation*, 64.

ministry is that its success is not within our reach."[63] For some pastors, this insight comes in the flash of a moment. For others, it is a gradual realization. But at some point, an honest pastor becomes acutely aware of his helplessness, emptiness, and neediness. He even wonders why this did not occur to him (long) before. Such awareness recasts every attitude he has held of his ministry, and it inevitably forms the frequency and fervency of his prayers, how he steps into the pulpit, and the mode of his leading worship, notably when he administers the Lord's Supper.

As ministers, we instinctively pray when we come to the end of our confidence, wisdom, or ability. We pray when we sense that the results we labor for will not come from our doing—despite our talents and hard work. We pray when it sinks in that we are completely outmatched by the world and our adversary the devil—whose powers we always appraised, but as Strider would instruct us, "You fear them, but you do not fear them enough."[64] Prayer is our coming to terms with these limitations because prayer is the act of a desperate man, not one who feels in control. This is why Charles Bridges stated that even though prayer is only "one half of our ministry," it is what "gives to the other half all its power and success."[65] Ole Hallesby put it in stronger terms: "Prayer is the most important work in the kingdom of God."[66] It is the most important, he reasoned, because "it is prerequisite to all the rest of the work we have to do in the kingdom of God: preaching, pastoral work, meetings, societies, administrative groups, organization, and solicitation of funds."[67] Unqualified comments such as these acknowledge that there will be little efficacy to what we do as ministers if we do not ask, seek, or knock (Matt. 7:7). If we do not request the blessing of God's Spirit on our preaching, our shepherding, and even our praying, then where do we think this help is going to come from? From us, in our emptiness? Or from Christ,

63. Piper, *Brothers, We Are Not Professionals*, 54–55.
64. J. R. R. Tolkien, *The Fellowship of the Ring* (New York: Houghton Mifflin, 2014), 162.
65. Charles Bridges, *The Christian Ministry* (1830; repr., Edinburgh: Banner of Truth, 1991), 148.
66. Ole Hallesby, *Prayer* (Minneapolis: Augsburg Publishing House, 1931), 72.
67. Hallesby, *Prayer*, 85.

in his fullness? The pastor's heart turns to Christ. The pastor's heart also beats in rhythm with the needs of God's people (not just his own), and his prayers flow into varied streams of regular intercession on their behalf as he lays all the needs of "his" flock before the throne of Christ.

The same holds true when a pastor looks to the rest of his duties. Like a farmer who gazes across his fields, his stock, and his buildings, and sees all the work that needs to be done, a pastor looks to his labor and sees more than his two hands can attend: the visits that are overdue, the reluctant member who is quietly eluding him, the wounded and weak, the mismanaged exchange that he must rectify, the incomplete sermon that weighs on him, the longing for deeper study *and* for wider witnessing, and the wife who understands but who is exhausted. All this draws him to bend his knees and ask for seasons of refreshment—both for himself and for God's people. The horizontal needs discourage him, and they are many; but his hope is set on the vertical provision, which is more abundant than all he could ask or think.

The pulpit is the appropriate context from which a pastor shows how God's Word touches upon the duties of his people. As a younger minister, I, too, often found this to be *one* of my sins of omission. Too seldom did I rally my brothers and sisters in Christ to what they were equipped to do in the mutual bonds of love. Accepting, serving, forgiving, and loving one another ought to be heard as constant refrains in our preaching, not unlike our repeated emphases on justification, adoption, perseverance, and assurance. Both the fundamentals of the Christian faith and the fundamentals of community living call for frequent recitals. Christ's ambassador must regularly focus on the "one another" commands, the forms of mutual service, the fruit, gifts, and graces of the Spirit, and especially the cream of all graces, love.

As the pastor's weekly appointment in the pulpit approaches, the pressure builds as time slips away. No matter how strongly he has grasped its truth or how strongly it has grasped him, he still feels inadequate. He will scatter seed and water, but the growth must come from God. He will plead with all his heart, but the hearts of his people will not be reached unless the Spirit of truth brings himself to bear on them. The best thing this preacher can do for the communion of saints is, again, to "get out of the way" and let the people hear the voice of Christ, unrivaled. The Savior must increase, and the servant must decrease. This is a preacher's noble goal, but it is not always his attitude. There are moments when he secretly craves applause. But when he is in his right mind, he sincerely desires to fade into the background and die to self. Staying true to this commitment will require the Spirit's help. But this should not surprise us. Christ said that the "true worshipers" worship God "in spirit and truth" (John 4:23). True worship is undergirded by the work of the Spirit, even in the hearts of those who lead in that worship.

This is no less true when the pastor administers the Lord's Supper. He believes that Christ is present by his Spirit, and so he oversees the meal accordingly—not just as a sign to remember what Christ has done but also as a seal to remind us of what Christ is doing. Just as he expounds the meaning of the Supper, so also he explains the benefits of the Supper. In plain words, he exhorts the congregation to eat and drink in faith in order to receive its spiritual nourishment. Just as a pastor prays before he preaches, hoping that all who hear the Word of God will receive it by faith, so also he prays before he distributes the sacrament, hoping that all who handle the elements will receive them with an active and lively faith. The Supper is akin to the Word of God as a means of grace, and yet it is distinct. As one of my seminary professors would say, "It is not a different grace that is ministered, but the same grace ministered differently." The pastor's expectation is that the Spirit of Christ will work in the hearts of believers according to their need—whether it concerns their forgiveness, adoption, assurance, conviction, humility, strength, peace, comfort, or simply resting in God's sufficient love. Few moments in the life of the church picture the communion of saints more dramatically or emotionally than when we fellowship at the table. Sometimes it is nearly impossible to describe the exact nature of God's grace that meets us there. The gospel comes to us with terrific force in the Supper. We feel our unworthiness as we cling to our acceptance. Our sin abounds, but the Savior's love abounds all the more. Not every doubt is silenced, but our assurance grows. The sobriety of our joy can be overwhelming. The pastor who senses these things would be wise not to rush at this point (even if communion *is* often needlessly prolonged). God's people welcome thoughtful and silent pauses in a worship service, especially in these prized minutes. Here is the communion of saints, communing with the living God by the Spirit and through faith. And it anticipates a greater meal when our faith will become sight, and the communion of saints will become consummated in heavenly eternity. Truly there is no community on earth that rivals the blessings that the church of Jesus Christ enjoys in this world, and nothing compares to the inheritance of glory that awaits her saints in the world to come.

Conclusions about Communion

The communion of saints is a doctrine that "accords with godliness" (Titus 1:1). Like all other sound Christian doctrine, it works itself out into healthy Christian living, if one begins at the right place and proceeds with the right priorities. As for the beginning point, the communion of saints is not a participation in things. It is a fellowship between people. As for proceeding with the right priorities, the communion of saints is first and fundamentally a communion between Christ and his people. This is important to bear in mind as the church considers her ministry—with regard to both the basis and the ongoing vitality of her communion. If Christ ceases to function as the center of its mission and the source of its life, then the church will descend into something resembling a mere man-made community. It will become too horizontal. But when the church honors Christ as its source for life, power, and sustaining grace, then the benefits of the church's communion with God flow to and through the communion of the body. Words and deeds of love and truth will bear the hallmark of Christ's Spirit and bear fruit to Christ's glory.

These conclusions engender tremendous hope when we consider the communion of God's people inwardly. Christ promised to build and to protect his church (Matt. 16:18), but he also promised to indwell and empower his church (1 Cor. 3:16; 1 Peter 2:5). The Spirit of Christ distributes gifts to every member, and he also invigorates those gifts for the common good (1 Cor. 12:7; 14:4–5, 17). As gifts of the Spirit, they are means of Christ's grace and power to bring about greater and greater transformation, individually and corporately. The Spirit blesses every believer with maturity and the sanctifying fruit of love, joy, peace, patience, kindness, goodness, faithfulness, gentleness, and self-control—which strengthen the faith of others and revitalize the communion's purity, peace, and unity. This growth in grace will be much needed when the bonds of communion are tested in seasons of suffering, inward strife, or outward oppression. As the fellowship perseveres together, they reap the spiritual benefits of what they have faithfully sown in prayer, mutual service, trust, and love—most especially love. For it is love that sets them apart from any other community of people, proving that they are a communion of saints.

This is exactly what Christ said would take place when the world observes his communion of saints outwardly. Christ commanded his disciples to "love one another: just as I have loved you, you also are to love one another." And then he promised his disciples, "By this all people will know that you are my disciples, if you have love for one another" (John 13:34–35). When God's people show the genuine nature of their spiritual gifts and godly love, the true source of their life is unveiled. The horizontal gives testimony to the vertical. The communion of brothers and sisters reveals their communion with the living God. Such graciousness, kindness, gentleness, selflessness, humility is utterly uncommon. It is holy. And when those of the world watch the communion of saints flourish with life and beauty, they behold something that transcends their own efforts and experience. They sense something higher, something greater, something that smacks of another world. The appeal is undeniable, and there is even a wish to contract whatever it is that has infected the hearts of these Christians, who are so obviously a communion of saints.

Key Terms

communitarianism
communion of saints
community
dialogical principle of worship
ecclesiology
koinonia

Recommendations for Further Reading

Bonhoeffer, Dietrich. *Life Together*. Translated by Daniel W. Bloesch and James H. Burtness. Minneapolis: Fortress Press, 2005.

Hallesby, Ole. *Prayer*. Minneapolis: Augsburg Publishing House, 1931.

Owen, John. *Communion with God*. Edinburgh: Banner of Truth, 1991.

Witsius, Herman. *The Apostles' Creed*. 2 vols. 1823. Reprint, Escondido, CA: den Dulk Christian Foundation, 1993.

Discussion Questions

1. As a pastor, do you consistently pray and think about your dependence on the Holy Spirit for your ministry's vitality and success?

2. As a worship leader, how regularly are you leading in public worship in a way that reflects your sensitivity to God's presence among his gathered people?

3. Paul says in Ephesians 4 that the church grows and is built up as each member does his or her part. What are the areas in which your congregation needs further growth or development? How could you equip your congregation to develop in these areas? Are there ways in which you could do a better job of leading by example?

4. Are there obvious areas in which the purity, peace, and unity of your congregation are vulnerable, weak, or threatened? How can you address those areas?

5. As a pastor, think about those who lead and serve in your congregation (whether openly or covertly). How can you encourage them in their gifts and service (whether openly or covertly)?

6. What are the legitimate ways in which you can help to instill true community in and among the members of your congregation? Are there ways that you could improve by setting an example?

23

THE SACRAMENTS

Communion with God in
Union with Christ[1]

CHAD VAN DIXHOORN

Reformed churches ordain their pastors as ministers of Word, sacrament, and prayer. All three ordinances are important to us. Indeed, as William Strong once argued, "The communion that the saints have with God, it is with all the persons in the Trinity," and "this communion in this life is chiefly in ordinances."[2] While a Reformed ministry is supposed to be characterized by this triad of ordinances, a case could be made that of these three, we are least attentive to the sacramental side of our ministries. While neither a sociologist nor a demographer, I venture to say as a historian that in the past century the Protestant church has expended more energy perfecting its preaching and thinking about prayer than studying the sacraments. Indeed, situated as evangelicals are in the Reformation's afterglow rather than its full light, the sacraments appear to be an afterthought,

---

1. This essay is dedicated to Sinclair Ferguson, the professor who taught the majority of my systematics courses, and to Dorothy, who charmed a young couple when we met at graduation, and who blessed us in the moments when our paths have crossed since.

2. William Strong, *The Saints Communion with God, and God's Communion with Them in Ordinances* (London: for George Sawbridge, 1656), 16.

with an increasing number of churches simply making things up as they go along. We evidence our lack of thoughtfulness in the way in which we borrow practices from other Christian communions without considering in any depth whether those practices have meanings complementary to a Reformed understanding of the sacraments. For example, in many churches, ministers lead frequent celebrations of the Lord's Supper but teach their members little about the meal. Still other pastors administer the Lord's Supper infrequently, supposing that their congregations will understand that if we do something less often, we will imbue it with more meaning. (It is just this kind of thinking that leads me to kiss my wife only three times a year.)

In an effort to reflect on the meaning and practice of the sacraments, this chapter tackles three related topics. First, it outlines a biblically informed and confessionally shaped understanding of the sacraments. Second, it describes in broad brushstrokes different approaches to administering the sacraments and reflects on the wisdom of those different approaches. It concludes with a series of reflections on the Lord's Supper in particular, offering some theology for ministry by considering the message that the Supper preaches to the pastors who administer this meal.

The Master of the Sacraments

In my early twenties, I joined a Reformed church that, after a two- or three-year hiatus (itself a story!), had just resumed celebrating the Lord's Supper. Since I was a newly conscious believer in a small, low-energy church, my elders tapped my enthusiasm by tasking me with teaching the Shorter Catechism to a group of children. Reading ahead for class and memorizing the proof texts as we went along, I began to appreciate through the tutelage of the catechism how to assemble a doctrine by paying attention to key texts and terms.

Building a doctrine from the Bible's own teaching, we learn that, most basically, sacraments are both signs and seals of the gospel or of the covenant of grace (see WCF 7; 14.2; 17.2). We can glean this information, for example, from the sacrament of circumcision. It is called a "sign" in Scripture. Besides, it was a "seal" of the righteousness that comes from God alone (Rom. 4:11). The sacrament of circumcision was gracious, representing God's undeserved favor to sinners who believed in Another. Moreover, it was covenantal, cementing God's promises to his people (Gen. 17:7, 10).

Once we began to celebrate the Supper, and especially once I was permitted to participate in that sacrament myself, I found a renewed interest in understanding baptism and the Lord's Supper as illuminated by the whole of the Bible. It is clear from the inspired writings of Moses, Matthew, and Paul that the sacramental signs and seals of the Old and New Testaments were given directly by the Lord. We see this when the great covenant was made with Abraham, when the Great Commission was given to the apostles, and when our Lord, on the night when he was betrayed, instituted a new sacrament for his disciples (Gen. 17:7, 10; Matt. 28:19; 1 Cor. 11:23). Indeed, the last two references remind us that the sacraments of the New Testament, baptism and the Lord's Supper, are given directly by Christ himself, the Lord of the church, which is why they are often called the *dominical sacraments*. Christ is the Master of the sacraments.

The Shorter Catechism is helpful for summarizing biblical teaching. So, too, is the Westminster Confession of Faith. As the opening lines of WCF 27.1 indicate, the sacraments have at least four functions. In the first place, they "represent Christ, and his benefits." They point to the Savior and to the blessings that flow from a vital relationship with him. They proclaim Christ (1 Cor. 11:26). Second, the sacraments confirm our God-given share in or title to our Redeemer. They confirm that we belong to Jesus or, as Paul puts it with reference to baptism, that we have "put on Christ" (Gal. 3:27). Third, the sacraments "put a visible difference between those that belong unto the Church" and "the rest of the world." This difference is perhaps not easy to see in the state of Alabama or on Scotland's Isle of Lewis, but there is no mistaking the distinguishing significance of baptism in India or Indonesia. When the triune God names us as his own, the world does not let go of us without a fuss. Fourth, the sacraments "solemnly . . . engage" us "to the service of God in Christ, according to His Word." They remind us that we cannot have it both ways: our commitment is either to Christ or to the devil, but not to both (1 Cor. 10:21). Understanding this is critical for pastoral ministry: we serve brothers and sisters who have a declared allegiance and thus an identifiable enemy. It is a joy to be a

Christian partaking of these symbols. At the same time, in fact every time we administer the sacraments, we are at once engaging ourselves to Christ and inviting opposition from the enemy.

The substance of these sacraments is the Master of the sacraments himself. This is true of any sacrament of the covenant of grace, Old Testament or New: Christ himself with all his benefits is the substance promised, exhibited, conferred. We receive him in baptism and the Lord's Supper, as they "become effectual means of salvation" to us, "by the blessing of Christ, and the working of his Spirit" (WSC 91). And nothing else does this in the same way. There is something special about ordination and marriage and even foot-washing, but no other action and symbol in the New Testament has the same center and substance as do the two dominical sacraments and their respective signs.

This is not to suggest that Christ is the substance of the Lord's Supper in a crass, corporeal sense. But that being said, the symbols of the Lord's Supper do represent well the substance of the gospel: Jesus uses a loaf of bread and a cup of wine for a reason. Throughout the Old Testament, bread symbolized God's provision for his undeserving people (e.g., Ex. 16:4). Jesus Christ is that provision. And in the writings of the Old Testament prophets, the cup symbolized the cup of God's wrath and the judgments that sinners were to drink for rebelling against God (Isa. 51:17). Jesus Christ drank that cup of wrath that we deserved to drink. The symbols are meaningful, and we must continue to use the symbols that he provides, both the bread and the cup.

We must also consider the actions of our Lord: look what Jesus does with the bread and wine. Perhaps he poured the wine in front of the Twelve, to picture his blood pouring out. It is not pleasant to remember that the wine symbolizes his spilled or splattered blood, and then to drink it. But that is how horrible sin is. When God covenanted to save us, that blood was always in view. Certainly, Jesus took the loaf and broke it in order to picture the violent tearing of his body that was to take place with whips, thorns, nails, and a spear. It is, in a way, terrible to think of. It is, in some sense, shocking to consider that this bread symbolizes Christ's torn body and then to put it into our mouths and chew it. But that is the horror of sin. It required a real man and a real death. When Christ commands us to remember his sacrifice, it is no mere principle we are to remember. We are to remember our Savior's death.

Notice as well the words that Jesus used. *There are words.* We are not to simply eat bread and drink wine without explanation. That would make the Supper an empty ritual. Christ gives words of explanation, and that makes the Supper a rich and full symbol. As Augustine put it (referring to baptism, but equally true for the Supper), "The Word is added to the element, and there results the Sacrament."[3]

Then, too, we must consider the words themselves: "This is my body"; "this is my blood, poured out for you." We should be ready to say that since Jesus was standing in front of his disciples, the bread in his hands and the wine in his cup were obviously not his physical body. We should be just as quick to say this today. Christ is in heaven today with a real body. To say that he is physically present in the bread and the wine across the world today denies the reality of his humanity; the doctrine of the real physical presence of Christ in the Supper is a very grave error indeed, if we mean that he is present bodily.

But when Christ says that we are to eat this bread that is his body and drink this wine that is his blood, he is obviously not emphasizing his *distance* from the disciples. He is not leaving his disciples with a doctrine of real absence any more than he is leaving them with a doctrine of real presence. Christ is present in the Supper, but not in the elements of solid bread and liquid wine. He is not the elements themselves; it is intended that we distinguish between the sign and the one who is signified. Nonetheless, the reality signified is communicated to us by means of the sign. Christ is most certainly present in the message of the elements and the reception of the elements, as the Reformers used to say. Christ is in the message preached by the broken bread and poured wine, and Christ is the blessing that is received from the Supper. We can even say that Christ is present by his Holy Spirit. New pastors can feel very much alone as they face the congregation and administer the sacrament for the first time. He is not alone; no one in the room is alone. Matthew Henry and

---

3. Augustine, *Lectures or Tractates on the Gospel according to St. John*, trans. John Gibb and James Innes, in *Nicene and Post-Nicene Fathers*, 1st ser. (hereafter NPNF 1), ed. Philip Schaff (1888; repr., Peabody, MA: Hendrickson, 1994), 7:344 (tract. 80).

Simon Browne state that we are "his guests to whom the sacrifice was offered."[4] And we can say more: Christ is with us as we worship God in the Savior's Supper, and for this reason Reformed people like to speak of the spiritual presence of Christ in the Supper.

Augustine called the sacraments "visible words" because the same principles apply to the sermon and to the Supper, or baptism.[5] Does Christ speak of preaching as the Word, and does he call himself the Word? Yes. In the same way, Christ calls the bread and the wine his body. Can Christ be present by his Spirit in the preaching of his Word? Yes. So, too, he can be present by his Spirit in the Lord's Supper. Is grace automatically received in preaching? Does every person who walks into a church and hears a sermon instantly become a Christian? No. Does every person who preaches a sermon automatically benefit from it? No. So, too, with the Lord's Supper. We need the blessing of the Holy Spirit, and we need to receive the preaching and the Supper by faith. Can a sermon be spiritual food for you? Yes. And so, too, can this Supper feed your soul. As "low" a churchman as Charles Hodge would insist that the sacraments are real means or channels of grace. "They are not, as Romanists teach, the exclusive channels; but they are channels."[6]

But what is the grace that we receive? Lecturing on the Westminster Standards two decades ago, Sinclair Ferguson noted that "Christ is received by faith, as we might say, in the Word, not because the pages of your NIV turn into the body and blood of Christ. . . . He is present in the Word as his presence is communicated to us by the power of the Holy Spirit and [as] faith is evoked in our hearts towards him." The reality is that Christ calls the bread and the wine his body and blood because he wishes to be closely, but not crassly, identified with his Supper. And as Professor Ferguson said more than once in class, quoting Robert Bruce, "you don't get a different Christ in the

4. Matthew Henry, *Matthew Henry's Commentary*, vol. 6, *Acts to Revelation* (1723; repr., Peabody, MA: Hendrickson, 2003), 449 (sub loc., 1 Cor. 10:16).

5. E.g., Augustine, *John*, 7:344 (tract. 80); see also John Calvin, *Institutes of the Christian Religion*, ed. John T. McNeill, trans. Ford Lewis Battles, Library of Christian Classics 20–21 (Louisville: Westminster John Knox, 2006), 4.14.4.

6. Charles Hodge, *Systematic Theology* (1873; repr., Peabody, MA: Hendrickson, 2003), 3:499.

Supper from the Christ you get in the Word, but you may get the same Christ better."[7]

It becomes evident in studying the Scriptures that the faith evoked by the Holy Spirit is essential for a profitable reception of the sacraments. As John Calvin explained the Lord's Supper, when Jesus "uses the word eat, he exhorts us to faith."[8] That is not to say that "to eat is only to believe; I say that we eat Christ's flesh in believing."[9] By faith the Spirit helps us to see that the water of baptism pictures the accomplishment of great redemptive events. Water is a sign of God's righteous punishment, and a sign of his great mercy. In the great flood, God punished a disobedient world, and in the Red Sea he drowned Pharaoh's army. And yet in that same flood God saved Noah and his family, and God led his people through the Red Sea on dry ground. Water baptism pictures the application of those events through our union with Christ in his death and resurrection. It signifies that we are cleansed by the blood of Jesus and accepted for Christ's goodness and Christ's perfection and not our own.

Ministering the Sacraments

For the honor of Christ and for the benefit of our flocks, Reformed ministers are trained to explain our privileges, including the meaning of God's gifts to us in the sacraments. That is one way of saying that there is a ministry of the Word that frames the ministry of sacraments. In practice, as already mentioned, Reformed churches often function in very different ways. Many of us are sacramental minimalists of one kind or another. Others of us see ourselves as sacramental maximalists. Sometimes we manage to be both at the same time.

There is a place in ministry for a proper minimalism. In fact, when my presbytery examines men for ministry, I sometimes ask a candidate, "What is the least that needs to be said and done for the

7. Sinclair Ferguson, "The Westminster Standards," Westminster Theological Seminary Media, tape 14.

8. John Calvin, *Commentary on the Gospel according to John: Volume First*, trans. William Pringle (1553; repr., Grand Rapids: Baker, 2003), 261.

9. Calvin, *Institutes*, 4.17.5.

Lord's Supper to be the Lord's Supper and not a small snack?" A presbytery or congregation should want men to know more than this! But we should not want them to know less than this. When explaining the Lord's Supper or baptism to children, or to new believers, ministers need to be able to state simply the message of each sacrament. It sounds too clinical to put it this way, but there are other practical reasons for being able to summarize succinctly the message of each sacrament in a few sentences. These include the needs of itinerant ministers, decisions on family vacations, and the practicalities of weekly communion.

I have been invited to serve as a guest preacher, only to see the communion table readied for the Lord's Supper and be asked by the elders if I would not mind serving the Supper to the congregation. Separately, I have also been asked to baptize someone in a church without a pastor (on one occasion, the parents of the child being presented for baptism changed their minds while I was posing the baptismal questions!). In moments like these—when one is unexpectedly asked to administer a sacrament—it is important to have in mind what must be said and done for the sacrament to be a sacrament. We want to know (1) that the sacrament must be framed by words spoken by a minister of Christ, (2) that our words should explain what the sacramental actions and elements represent, (3) that our prayers should include a request that these ordinary elements be used by God's Spirit for his extraordinary purposes, (4) who should partake of the sacrament, and (5) how we might benefit from it.

We also want ministers to be able to offer a bare-bones understanding of the sacrament because families go visit other churches, and are sometimes invited to join in the celebration of the Lord's Supper. It is helpful in these cases for our flocks to know essentials that need to be said and done. I have even had to whisper to my family that what is taking place does not appear to be the Lord's Supper at all. A well-meaning member discussing what he learned about life from his cat, followed by "Let's eat and drink," offered our family an easy decision. But sometimes a congregation's celebration of the Supper is simply different from our own, and we don't want the perfect (possibly our perception of our own congregation's way of celebrating the Supper) to be the enemy of the good (any other church's celebration of the Supper). Ministers love their members when they enable them to see the most important things that must be done in a celebration of the Supper, thus assisting their decisions when they are away from home.

Finally, a knowledge of what must be said and done about the Supper is helpful for ministers serving churches that celebrate the sacrament frequently. Of course, by frequent celebration of "the sacrament," I am not referring to baptism. Even churches with parking lots populated by minivans will not likely celebrate baptism with the frequency that some churches celebrate the Lord's Supper. In places where the Lord's Supper is celebrated weekly, it would be a mistake to say everything we know about the Lord's Supper every time it is celebrated. Here, too, a clear understanding of what must be said and done will keep before us our core ideas and actions, to which we can then add a circulating set of other ideas to leaven the Lord's Supper on a given week.

In speaking about frequency, I believe that a biblical case for a weekly celebration of the Lord's Supper has yet to be made. True, the Lord's Supper is clearly a normal part of Christian corporate worship (Acts 20:7; 1 Cor. 11:25; perhaps Acts 2:42). But passages such as these evidence only a regular, perhaps frequent pattern of eucharistic observance, and do not rise as high as a requirement for weekly communion (let alone the practice of daily communion mentioned in passing by church fathers).[10] Indeed, if such passages did prove that the Supper must be celebrated when the church gathers for worship, then a "weekly" requirement would be too soft: the church should celebrate the Supper in its every service, and not in its morning or main service only.

The weakness of biblical evidence inevitably brings other considerations, such as the pattern of the early church, into play. Justin Martyr, for example, famously describes what looks like communion as a component part of a weekly service of worship: "when our prayer is ended, bread and wine and water are brought, and the president in like manner offers prayers and thanksgivings, according to his ability, and the people assent, saying Amen; and there is a distribution to

---

10. E.g., Augustine, *John*, 7:173 (tract. 26).

each, and a participation of that over which thanks have been given, and to those who are absent a portion is sent by the deacons."[11]

But we are selective in our use of the church fathers. After all, Justin's description of the worship of the early church makes no reference to singing. And writing centuries after the last of the apostles, Augustine notes that singing in the services of the Latin, Western church was a recent innovation.[12] Thus, the practice of singing offers an instructive parallel to the celebration of the Lord's Supper. With singing, as with the Lord's Supper, we find at most some New Testament evidence that singing constitutes a key element of worship. With singing, as with the Lord's Supper, it appears that some important elements of worship can be part of the regular worship of the church without being part of every worship service.

I think that a requirement for a weekly administration of the Supper cannot be sustained. But that does not mean that a minimalistic approach must be the order of the day. Historically, in many Reformed churches, the Lord's Supper was celebrated quarterly or semiannually. Continued practices of sacramental infrequency sometimes simply mimic these traditional patterns. Nonetheless, there are also those who seek to supply infrequency with a theoretical defense. The arguments here tend not to be biblically based (except insofar as they argue against the requirement for weekly celebration). The usual arguments in favor of infrequent celebration of the Lord's Supper are (1) that it makes it more special and (2) that infrequent celebration permits more extensive treatment of the subject of the Supper, thus giving it the solemnity that it deserves.

The initial assumption is that common sense dictates that infrequency itself makes an important point in the sacrament's celebration. Within a given tradition and culture, this in fact may be the case. In these traditions, the solemnity of the Supper is often emphasized, and the infrequency of the Supper encourages solemnity. John Flavel argues that none of us beholding the torture and death of a friend or father taking a punishment on our behalf could do so with "dry eyes"

---

11. Justin Martyr, *First Apology*, in *The Apostolic Fathers with Justin Martyr and Irenaeus*, ed. Alexander Roberts, James Donaldson, and A. Cleveland Coxe, in *Ante-Nicene Fathers* (1885; repr., Peabody, MA: Hendrickson, 1994), chap. 67 (1:185).

12. Augustine, *Confessions*, 9.7 (15).

or "unaffected" hearts. Thus, he approved of the old saying, "The sacrament of the Lord's Supper, and the very point of death, require equal seriousness." For Flavel, "a man's spirit should be as deeply solemn and composed at the Lord's Table, as upon a death-bed. We should go to that ordinance, as if we were then going into another world." If this is the case, might not a weekly event dilute the communication of such an important point? Again, Flavel argues that in the Supper we sense a special nearness to Christ and to heaven. For those who fellowship with Christ in his Supper, "Heaven is no dream or night vision: It is sensibly tasted and felt by thousands of witnesses in this world; they are sure it is no mistake. God is with them of a truth, in the way of their duties: They do not only read of a glorified eye, but they have something of it, or like it in this world."[13] If this is what one takes away from the Supper, why rush the meal? Might not a weekly meal rush such a precious moment?

But this cuts two ways. If life is so hard, and this glimpse of eternity so powerful, might we not benefit from a more frequent reminder of such glorious realities? Family dinners at Easter, Mother's Day, Thanksgiving, and Christmas are indeed special in many homes. But do they offer an adequate replacement for weekly dinners on Sunday afternoons? Arguments for infrequency, in other words, enjoy plausibility in certain contexts but find equally plausible rebuttals, for infrequency can inadvertently send the wrong message, too. Indeed, a pastor might be making his ministry more difficult by depriving needy Christians of a means of grace that could help them grow by failing to offer regularly clear tokens and experiences of God's love.

Infrequency, in the second place, allows the minister a substantial amount of time to teach church members about the Supper. Pastors can equip their congregations with a fuller understanding of the depth and importance of the Lord's Supper. They can do so by speaking at length, or by offering preparatory sermons, or by reading a lengthy set form of words. In offering a directory or form to guide administrators of both sacraments, they usually provide rich, gospel-filled explanations of both sacraments, warm invitations to

---

13. John Flavel, *The Works of John Flavel* (1820; repr., Edinburgh: Banner of Truth, 1997), 6:383, 390–91.

the Lord's Supper, and reasoned warnings to the morally lax and to nonmembers. Many churches in the Continental and Scottish traditions of the Reformed faith draw on confessional material to explain the sacraments, some of it dating to the Reformation. The advantage of these forms is that they guide ministers in a profitable framing of a sacrament that is almost guaranteed to fully cover the essentials in a manner that is both clear and properly qualified at all the key points. The language employed has been carefully considered by thoughtful men and approved by ecclesiastical assemblies.

The disadvantage of these forms or directories, if followed in full every time a sacrament is used, is that it takes a considerable amount of time. Insistence on the full form almost guarantees an infrequent communion. It has long been the case that as with sermons, so with sacraments: a subset of ministers tend to say everything that *can* be said instead of what *must* be said. We enable this kind of habit through infrequent communion. Of course, a corresponding lack of creativity is possible with weekly communion, but we can at least address the malady by teaching young ministers to identify what must *always* be said, and then help them create lists of what can *eventually* be said, one or two points at a time, as the weeks and months roll on in a man's ministry.

In most basic terms, less can be more when it comes to words spoken before the Supper. Unless trained and accompanied by the most gifted of ministers, few congregations (and few people within those few congregations) have the maturity to make it, with full attention, through to the end of the spiritual marathon typical of infrequent celebrations of the Supper.

On the other hand, the challenge with a move toward increased frequency of celebration lies, of course, with the need for relative brevity. Some restraint must be shown in the ministry of the Word accompanying the Supper if it is celebrated more frequently. In some circles, there is also a worry about a slippery slope leading to mere ceremony, a communion with sacraments rather than with the Savior. If there are excess words at some celebrations of the Supper, there is also a verbal minimalism that can attach itself to frequent celebrations. Many ministers seem to be enforcing austerity measures, barely feeding, and never feasting with, their hungry congregations.

What is more, frequent celebration with few words may fail to provide adequate clarity. In order to run an efficient service, or to include as many servers as possible, or to avoid controversy by saying too much, the message is streamlined. In these circumstances, ministers tend to speak of the presence of Christ, or to announce the benefits received in the sacraments, but (1) without the careful qualification used by our fathers in the faith when they addressed these subjects and (2) without any verbal fencing of the Table. This offers a kind of sacramental fuzziness friendly for high-church tastes or high-speed services. But in addition to its theological failings, it is no friend to the true cure of souls. As many ministers realize, sometimes too late, those lobbying for few words and frequent celebration can move all too easily from a vaguely Reformed church to a clearly Roman one. Qualifications and clarifications are important.

But if there are dangers in the ditch on one side of the road, there are troubles awaiting the traveler on the other side, too. In some Reformed churches, the minister spends so much time qualifying and defending the "Reformed" view from all detractors that he leaves little time for a positive explication of the sacrament at all, or so fully explicates what it means for a Christian to be worthy or in good standing that he renders the invitation to the Table of little effect. Clarifications of what infant baptism is not are so thorough that one is left with something like a wet-baby dedication. Administrations of the Lord's Supper are so clearly not Catholic that they come across as belated memorial services for Jesus.

Howard Griffith, who died before he could write this chapter, realized one day that the number of contented Baptist members in his Presbyterian congregation beautifully reflected the warmth of his elders and his congregation but problematically reflected a muffled Reformed teaching evident in his administration of the sacraments. He began to explain more clearly what baptism and the Lord's Supper do mean for God's people instead of explaining what they do not mean. As he told me years later, many more members came to understand and to embrace what the church as a whole believed, and Baptist members came to embrace the whole of Reformed teaching about the church and its sacraments, thus enriching the church with greater unity and expanding the number of persons eligible for leadership positions.

A mere memorialism is perhaps the most common theological malaise that attends the Lord's Supper in Reformed churches. As a general rule, church members will generally hold a memorialist form of sacramental minimalism if the Supper is always explained from 1 Corinthians 11. Only when 1 Corinthians 10 is incorporated into the celebration of the Supper will church members (and ministers!) understand communion with Christ, our mystical union with him, and the fellowship in the Supper about which Calvin writes so vividly in his *Institutes*,[14] and that Ferguson returned to appreciatively in his teaching on the subject.[15] It is to this topic, and other key themes, that we now turn.

Sacraments for Ministers

The Reformed minister must know what the sacraments mean and know how to administer them, but in his ministry to the congregation he is also to seek to benefit from the sacraments himself. The sacraments are intended to lead us into communion with God through union with Christ, who leads us by the hand—his sacraments, if you will—into his Father's presence. But as William Strong, a member of the Westminster Assembly, often stressed, we seek communion with God and not with the ordinances themselves. The sacraments, as a means to an end, help to lift us to heaven while our bodies remain on earth.[16]

The history of the church has shown that it is not hard for ministers to be caught up with the elements themselves instead of the Christ whom they represent. At the same time, a minister of the gospel is in a unique position vis-à-vis the sacraments. He feels the water running through his hands, he breaks the bread, he pours the wine. The liveliness of these emblems is perhaps most apparent to him. He

14. Calvin, *Institutes*, 4.17.

15. See Sinclair B. Ferguson, *Some Pastors and Teachers: Reflecting a Biblical Vision of What Every Minister Is Called to Be* (Edinburgh: Banner of Truth, 2018), chap. 9.

16. William Strong mourns those whose "business is with the ordinance alone, and with that he goes away satisfied." Strong, *Communion with God in Ordinances, The Saints Priviledge and Duty* (London: by R. W. for Fra. Tryton, 1656), 24.

462

is also the one administering both sacraments, framing them with the ministry of the Word. Usually a minister has a heightened consciousness regarding the words he uses to introduce these signs and seals. As a disciple of the kingdom of heaven, he will self-consciously be considering how best to bring out from his storehouse treasures new and old, and be benefiting himself as he does so.

Sinclair Ferguson once commented, "Ministers of the gospel often have the privilege of occupying 'the best seat in the house.'"[17] As the one who has prepared in advance to serve this meal, the minister is in a unique position to profit from the sacraments—and how he needs its lessons and benefits! Indeed, when one considers the Lord's Supper and its establishment by Christ, we are reminded of ten cardinal truths about the Supper, all of which have implications for those who administer this meal.[18]

First, it was our Lord Jesus who instituted this new sacrament.[19] As Paul explained to the Corinthians, this meal is "the table of the Lord" and "the cup of the Lord"; it is "the Lord's supper" (1 Cor. 10:21; 11:20). Knowing this allows ministers to administer the Supper with confidence and urgency. And it reminds us, as we lead the congregation, that we are servants of the Master, ministering in his name.

Second, the presence of one of the guests at the Table sounds a note of caution, for the Gospels recall that there was one "disciple" at the meal who did not believe any of these things. He did not love or serve the Savior. His partaking of this meal did him only harm. Yes, recalling the betrayal makes our hearts "softer than wax," as Chrysostom says.[20] But at the same time, the Lord loves his servants so much that he keeps before us this betrayal as a warning (1 Cor. 11:23), not least to pastors.

Third, the other eleven guests at the Table send us a message of hope. We are reminded that one person's unfaithfulness is not

17. Sinclair B. Ferguson, *Devoted to God: Blueprints for Sanctification* (Edinburgh: Banner of Truth, 2016), 3.

18. Many are identified in WCF 29.1.

19. Some phraseology is drawn from Chad Van Dixhoorn, *Confessing the Faith: A Reader's Guide to the Westminster Confession of Faith* (Edinburgh: Banner of Truth, 2014), 384–86.

20. John Chrysostom, *Homilies on the Epistles of Paul to the Corinthians* (1889; repr., Peabody, MA: Hendrickson, 2004), NPNF 1, 12:161 (Homily 27).

meant to drive the poor in spirit away from the kingdom of heaven, or to tell those who mourn for their sin that they cannot be comforted—including the one serving the elements. When we consider the Lord's Supper in the light of the first Supper, we get a sense of the wide range of people who are called to come feast with Christ and on Christ. There we see the relatively unimportant disciples about whom history knows nothing, much like it will be for you and me. We see Thomas, who doubted when he should have trusted. We see the servants of Jesus who would argue about who was the greatest almost as soon as the Supper was finished. There we find the Sons of Thunder, too much given to temper and tempest. We see Peter, who was not nearly as strong as he thought.[21] Jesus welcomed them all to his Table. Perhaps you see their sin and weakness exhibited in yourself. Maybe you see in yourself a temper, or pride, or doubts, or maybe you see nothing interesting in yourself at all and your very insignificance troubles you. What matters in this meal is what your Father in heaven sees, and he sees every justified sinner in the arms of his Son, clothed in his righteousness, welcomed at his Table. What minister has not had a Sunday when he feels utterly unworthy to be leading in worship, preaching the Word, or administering the sacraments? This minister has! And yet week by week or month by month (or quarter by quarter!), we are reminded that the feast that Jesus spreads is a meal for baptized disciples of all sorts, for every faithful member of an evangelical church that preaches and loves the gospel, and for the ministers that lead them. This is a meal for any who have publicly professed faith in Jesus, submit to his rule, and await the final wedding supper of the Lamb.

Fourth, Jesus instituted a sacrament of his "body" and "blood" (1 Cor. 11:24–25; cf. Matt. 26:26–28; Mark 14:2–24; Luke 22:19–20). The realities of body and blood remind us that Christ has given his very self for us. Ministers are often blessed to remember this at the end of a service, not least because many worship services place the Supper at the end of the worship service, after we have preached and have been reminded of our own failings and inadequacies, yet his

---

21. This train of thought was generated by reading Andrew A. Bonar, *Andrew A. Bonar: Diary and Life*, ed. Marjory Bonar (Edinburgh: Banner of Truth, 1960), 441.

sufficiency. How good it is to remember that the Lamb of God was given for both sheep and undershepherds, weak and failing as we are.

Fifth, this Supper is to be observed until the end of the world. This is why the apostle Paul repeated both of Jesus' calls to remembrance, and then concluded by saying that "as often as you eat this bread and drink the cup, you proclaim the Lord's death until he comes" (1 Cor. 11:24–26). This insistence helps ministers remember the core of their message, preaching a Savior who gave us these lively emblems of his sacrifice, presence, and love. It also helps each servant of the gospel to remember that our good Master will return—the one whose yoke is easy, whose burdens are light, and whose word of commendation is sure for those who proclaim the Savior instead of themselves.

Sixth, we see that Jesus was promising real benefits to true believers. Here we begin to see the critical importance of 1 Corinthians 10 for understanding the Supper. It is because the Supper serves as a seal of the benefits and treasures of redemption that Paul refers to the wine as "the cup of blessing" (1 Cor. 10:16). Ministers need these benefits also. How many over the years have turned to the bottle who needed the cup! Let us seek our blessings from Christ and his enduring gifts.

Seventh, this Supper is to be observed for our spiritual, not bodily, nourishment and growth in Christ. Paul had to remind the Corinthians of this because they were treating it like fast food (1 Cor. 11:17–22). And this is one reason why we need to remember that Jesus took the symbolic cup and used it as an emblem of his own sacrifice "*after* supper" (Luke 22:20; 1 Cor. 11:25). The Lord's Supper is like a good sermon: it is intended as food for the soul. And like the sermon, it is intended to feed the minister and not simply church members.

Eighth, participation in this meal is also a profession of exclusive loyalty to Jesus Christ that implies submission to his lordship alone. As Paul warned the Corinthians, "You cannot drink the cup of the Lord and the cup of demons. You cannot partake of the table of the Lord and the table of demons" (1 Cor. 10:21). Each time we participate in the Lord's Supper, we are saying that we are on the Lord's side; it is a moment when pastors who train disciples remember that we ourselves are disciples, that we leaders are also followers.

Ninth, and as we have discussed above, the Lord's Supper is to be observed in the church as a powerful symbol of our communion with

Christ by his Holy Spirit. As Ferguson notes, "The objective channels through which this communion and assurance come are the word of God . . . and the sacraments."[22] "Even by" this "external profession," we "maintain that unity that subsists between us and Christ."[23] This is where inadequate men and women, including men who are ministers, commune with the Master of the feast.

Tenth and finally, recollection of that first Supper and reflection on 1 Corinthians 10 are both clearly calculated by God to underscore the closeness of our communion not only with Christ, but with Christians. Here as elsewhere, ministers are reminded that we are not a priestly class. Far from it: we may serve the elements, but we partake of them with everyone else, for we are all part of one family. The disciples communed with Christ at the Last Supper, but they also communed with one another. And while 1 Corinthians 10:16 stresses our union with Christ in this Supper, 1 Corinthians 10:17 stresses our union with other believers in this same Supper: "Because there is one bread, we who are many are one body, for we all partake of the one bread." This unity with one another in Christ, reinforced in this Supper, is also a unity with one another in the Spirit. Just as "in one Spirit we were all baptized into one body," so also, now with reference to the Lord's Supper, "all were made to drink of one Spirit" (1 Cor. 12:13). No wonder the Westminster Assembly concluded that the sacrament of Christ's body and blood is to be observed as "a bond and pledge of their communion with Him, and with each other, as members of His mystical body" (WCF 29.1). If we as ministers really grasped the richness of this fellowship, I wonder how it would transform the churches that we lead. Should we say more on a Sunday morning about what it means for us to share a meal as one Christian family? Should we speak more of the privilege of being united around one meal as people of different backgrounds, interests, personalities, skills, and skin colors, but all part of Christ's body? Surely the Lord's Supper is an important part of a ministry of reconciliation within the body of Christ.

From time to time, Sinclair Ferguson allows himself flights of pastoral fancy in his lectures. Once, while considering this communion

---

22. Ferguson, *Some Pastors and Teachers*, 154.

23. Calvin, *Commentary on the Epistles of Paul the Apostle to the Corinthians*, trans. John Pringle, vol. 1 (1546; repr., Grand Rapids: Baker, 2003), 336.

of Christians with one another in the Lord's Supper, he remarked (while playfully inverting a famous saying) that if Muhammad won't come to the mountain, then perhaps the mountain must come to Muhammad. "There are ways of getting most people to church. Why shouldn't we have beds at communion? If we have ambulances to take the housebound to hospital, it strikes me that it would be a singular benediction in the church where people were actually carried into it. Few people are quite so housebound that they cannot be carried to the Table." He went on to note: "Communion is always a corporate occasion, and therefore, if there are logistical problems, you solve them corporately and imaginatively. Roll in the beds, I say! If you need to knock over a few pews to do it, well and good. It will do the congregation a world of good to have some people in beds and [lounge] chairs taking the Lord's Supper." Going to the shut-in is possible. "You can take the elders along or take a few people along. My own feeling is that that's the cheap answer because it's the easy answer. The last thing we want to do is be inconvenienced so Mrs. Smith can come, bed and all. It strikes me that the best thing we can do as a congregation is not to underline to Mrs. Smith, 'We're coming to you because you are never going to be able to come to us.'" Much "better to do what the men in the Gospels did, and that is to knock a hole in the church roof and let her down among the people, where she really belongs, if she really belongs to Christ. By that you are saying—in what may be a quasi-dramatic way—you are saying that this sacrament is a sacrament of the body of Christ." And then the clincher (even if the verb of the sentence, as is so often the case with Sinclair Ferguson, is reserved to the end): "This old woman in her bed, and this woman in her wheelchair, just as much as 7-foot-11-inch Joe Smith—the great basketball player who has all the health and energy in the world—are equally members of the body of Christ, and [thus] meet with each other."[24]

The reason that such considerations are commendable is that, as William Strong explained, "communion in this life is chiefly in ordinances." Our communion now is not yet what it will be. "All the communion wee have in this world, it is a mediate communion, there

---

24. Ferguson, "Westminster Standards," tape 14.

are mediums betwixt us and God, through which God conveyes grace unto us, and drawes us up unto him." "Immediate communion is reserved for another world."[25] God so loves us that he gave us his Word, prayer, and sacraments through which, by Spirit-given faith, we fellowship with Father, Son, and Holy Spirit. May he give us the fidelity, boldness, and wisdom that we need to make the best use of these gifts and deepen our communion with him until the day he takes us home, or until the hour that he returns.

Key Terms

administration
benefits
elements
fencing the Table
memorialism
ordinances
seal
sign
spiritual presence

Recommendations for Further Reading

Bavinck, Herman. *Reformed Dogmatics*. Edited by John Bolt. Translated by John Vriend. Vol. 4, *Holy Spirit, Church, and New Creation*. Grand Rapids: Baker Academic, 2008. Pp. 441–585.

Blocher, Henri A. G. "Calvin on the Lord's Supper: Revisiting an Intriguing Diversity." *WTJ* 76, no. 1 (Spring 2014): 55–93 (pt. 1). *WTJ* 76, no. 2 (Fall 2014): 411–29 (pt. 2).

Calvin, John. *Institutes of the Christian Religion*. Edited by John T. McNeill. Translated by Ford Lewis Battles. Louisville: Westminster John Knox, 2006. Bk. 4, chaps. 14–17.

Ferguson, Sinclair B. *Some Pastors and Teachers: Reflecting a Biblical Vision of What Every Minister Is Called to Be*. Edinburgh: Banner of Truth, 2018. Pp. 153–64.

---

25. Strong, *Saints Communion with God*, 27.

Griffith, Howard. *Spreading the Feast: Instruction and Meditations for Ministry at the Lord's Table.* Phillipsburg, NJ: P&R Publishing, 2015.

Discussion Questions

1. What is the least that needs to be said and done for the Lord's Supper to be the Lord's Supper and not a small snack?
2. What issues are most helpful or important for considering the frequency with which churches should celebrate the Lord's Supper? How frequently do you believe it should be celebrated in your context?
3. What is the practical importance of considering 1 Corinthians 10 and 11 in our development of a theology of the Lord's Supper?
4. What might be some guiding principles for when and how pastors should clarify and qualify the sacraments? What are the pitfalls to avoid?

24

MISSIONS

The Magnetic Person of Jesus Christ[1]

DANIEL STRANGE

When we read the Bible, we can identify with almost every character. Some of them are better than us, others worse. Yet we can project ourselves into either persona. But there is one singular and surpassing exception. In Christ we encounter a figure who is at once one with us and yet apart from us, who inspires admiration and defies emulation. He has fellow feeling without loss of firmness, and familiarity without hint of complicity. He can speak at the level of a child, yet with a reserve of subtlety that leaves the keenest listener out of his depth. No other figure, in either fact or fiction, covers such a range and or strikes such a balance, for in him we witness perfect manhood and perfect Godhood conjoined in one peerless person.[2] (Steve Hays)

Regardless of what anyone may personally think or believe about him, Jesus of Nazareth has been the dominant figure in the history

1. I first encountered the ministry of Sinclair Ferguson through reading his IVP book on the Holy Spirit while studying theology as an undergraduate in a liberal department. It was a lifeline, and from then on I was hooked.
2. Steve Hays, "Why I Believe: A Positive Apologetic," *Third Millennium Magazine Online* 5, no. 27 (2003), accessed July 30, 2019, https://www.thirdmill.org/new files/ste_hays/PT.Hays.Why.Believe.apologetics.1.html.

471

of Western culture for almost twenty centuries. If it were possible, with some sort of super magnet, to pull up out of that history every scrap of metal bearing at least a trace of his name, how much would be left?[3] (Jaroslav Pelikan)

Introduction

It was given as an introductory observation declared to be so "obvious" that the speaker was worried that he would appear foolish: a preparatory waggling on the tee, a methodological clearing of the throat. For me, it was gold dust. In 2010, I had the privilege of speaking at the same conference as Sinclair Ferguson, who was giving the plenary addresses. The theme of this conference for evangelists was "Preaching Jesus," and Sinclair's first talk was entitled "Behold the Man."[4] Having noted with his customary clarity, first, the Christ-centeredness of the apostolic and Holy Spirit witness, and second, the largeness of the cosmic Christ presented to us in Scripture, Sinclair hovered for a few moments on the significance of the conference title, "Preaching Jesus." Preaching Jesus, he argued, cannot be reduced to learning scriptural exegesis or exposition, however good and faithful. One can do both these things and be capable of missing this point: *it was not simply what Jesus did that the apostles preached; it was Jesus that the apostles preached.* He illustrated this difference by turning to the account of Philip and the Ethiopian in Acts chapter 8. Comparing translations of Acts 8:35,[5] he noted that in his opinion many modern translations get the verb right but the point wrong, having something like this:

> Then Philip opened his mouth, and beginning with this Scripture he told him the good news about Jesus. (ESV)

---

3. Jaroslav Pelikan, *Jesus through the Centuries: His Place in the History of Culture* (New Haven, CT: Yale University Press, 1985), 1.

4. The audio of Ferguson's address at the 2010 Evangelists Conference in Leyland, UK, can still be found here: http://www.evangelists-conference.org.uk/Behold theMan.mp3 (accessed July 25, 2019).

5. "ἀνοίξας δὲ ὁ Φίλιππος τὸ στόμα αὐτοῦ καὶ ἀρξάμενος ἀπὸ τῆς γραφῆς ταύτης εὐηγγελίσατο αὐτῷ τὸν Ἰησοῦν."

It is the older translations, however, that actually get the point:

> Then Philip opened his mouth, and began at the same scripture, *and preached unto him Jesus.* (KJV)

As Philip literally "evangelized him Jesus," so authentic preaching and teaching *is offering other people a person.* The Bible describes Jesus; the Scriptures must be ransacked in order to understand his person, and if we love him we will certainly do this to know him better. But we do not offer commodities or even forgiveness and peace. We are in the business of offering people the Lord Jesus, who brings forgiveness and who gives peace. The more we are riveted on the person of Jesus, so the more vibrant our personal conversations and public preaching and teaching will be. This is what has always marked the authentic messenger of Jesus Christ. We come from a person and offer to other persons the person of Jesus Christ, as John Calvin described, "clothed in the gospel."[6] So we are not offering people justification apart from their coming to faith in the Lord Jesus Christ, in whom alone justification and forgiveness and new life are to be found. The simple profundity of this observation has stayed with me ever since, waiting for an opportunity to be unpacked further.

In an increasingly complex and bewildering Western culture, we daily encounter fearfulness, fragility, and frustration not just outside our Christian communities but within. Indeed, if we are being honest, these conditions are not just found "outside" us in the people to whom we minister, but can be found within our own person. Looking for ministerial traction, we are revving loudly and spinning furiously, but through all the smoke and smell of burning rubber, rather than advancing forward, we wonder whether we're just slipping back.

Faced with this situation, it can be disheartening that discussions and debates surrounding the disciplines of apologetics, evangelism, and mission often seem to become increasingly complex and bewildering— and I say that as a professional theologian and theological educator. Indeed, I have no doubt contributed to this: I have skin in the game!

6. John Calvin, *Institutes of the Christian Religion*, ed. John T. McNeill, trans. Ford Lewis Battles, Library of Christian Classics 20–21 (Louisville: Westminster John Knox, 2006), 3.2.6.

Such academic discourse is, of course, necessary and (culturally) mandated as we seek to more accurately and more faithfully define, describe, delineate, and deepen our understanding according to the whole counsel of the scriptural norm. A simplistic biblicism is certainly not the answer; indeed, it is a dereliction of duty. Pastorally, however, when we, and those under our care, are caught like rabbits in the headlights when it comes to understanding not only our world, but also *our mission* in the world, maybe we need a way to cut through, and a lodestar to guide us. I would like to suggest that in our evangelism, apologetics, and mission, *offering Jesus* is such a guide. To adapt Gregory the Great's much-quoted aphorism, Jesus "is, as it were, a kind of river, if I may so liken it, which is both shallow and deep, wherein both the lamb may find a footing, and the elephant float at large."[7] All our much-needed whirling, swirling discussions about the Christian faith in terms of philosophy (ontology, epistemology, ethics, and aesthetics), in terms of worldview, narrative, cultural liturgies, and social imaginaries, in terms of plausibility structures and defeaters should be supporting and leading us to persons offering other persons a Person. *We offer Jesus.*

It is in the spirit of "offering Jesus" that I would like to practice what I preach by beginning to explore how Jesus is the *telos* of an anthropological framework that I have mentioned in previous work: the so-called magnetic points as conceived by the Reformed missiologist and pastor J. H. Bavinck.[8] In terms of applied Reformed missiology, apologetics, cultural analysis, and engagement, I have found Bavinck's work here immensely helpful and pregnant for further development. Moreover, Bavinck's life and evident love for people exemplify the pastor-theologian and the essence of theology for ministry.[9] In what follows, I will summarize the theological anthropology out of which the magnetic points are fashioned, describe the points themselves, and suggest how offering Jesus subversively fulfills these points.

7. Gregory the Great's commentary on Job (*Moral.* inscr. 4 [CCL 143:6]).

8. See Daniel Strange, *Their Rock Is Not like Our Rock: A Theology of Religions* (Grand Rapids: Zondervan, 2014), 251–54.

9. For a full biography, see Paul J. Visser, *Heart for the Gospel, Heart for the World: The Life and Thought of a Reformed Pioneer Missiologist, Johan Herman Bavinck (1895–1964)* (Eugene, OR: Wipf & Stock, 2003). A shorter account of Bavinck's life and work can be found in John Bolt, James D. Bratt, and Paul J. Visser, eds., *The J. H. Bavinck Reader* (Grand Rapids: Eerdmans, 2013), 1–92.

The Magnetic Points

The theological anthropology out of which Bavinck's magnetic points arise lies comfortably within the Dutch neo-Calvinist tradition, with Bavinck's famous uncle Herman an obvious influence.[10] One could summarize Bavinck's exegesis of Romans 1:18–32 as nothing more than a faithful yet creative restatement of Calvin's notions of the *sensus divinitatis*, *semen religionis*, and *fabrica idolorum*, refracted through a somewhat psychoanalytic prism.[11] In the cosmic game of hide-and-seek played between the uncreated Creator and the created creature, and contrary to popular imagination, God is not the one hiding; *we are*.[12] God's dynamic and relational revelation is clear and present in us and around us. It overwhelms us. As image-bearers (Gen. 1:27), we are made to relate to God and made to cultivate for God (v. 28). The "invisible qualities" of God's "eternal power" and "divine nature" (Rom. 1:20)[13] are for Bavinck to do with our dependence on God and our accountability to him.[14] This revelation "does not simply slide past people like a drop of rain does off a waxy leaf of a tree."[15] It penetrates with a result that in a juridical sense all humanity knows God and is without excuse.[16]

Our response to this revelation is one of suppression (or repression) and substitution, which creates its own "religious consciousness." The suppression can never be total, however, and the

10. See Visser, *Heart for the Gospel*, 8–11.

11. Bavinck's expositions of Romans 1:18–32 can be found in his book *Religious Consciousness and Christian Faith*, available in English as part of Bolt, Bratt, and Visser, *J. H. Bavinck Reader*, 241–48, 277–90; and in J. H. Bavinck, *The Church between Temple and Mosque* (Grand Rapids: Eerdmans, 1966), 117–28.

12. As evidenced in the postlapsarian scene in Genesis 3 where Adam and Eve hide from God. Helmut Thielicke makes much of this scene and God's question, "Where are you?," demonstrating for him the divine initiative of questions in the apologetic encounter. See Jeffrey L. Hamm, *Turning the Tables of Apologetics: Helmut Thielicke's Reformation of Christian Conversation* (Eugene, OR: Pickwick Publications, 2018), 127–29.

13. Unless otherwise indicated, Scripture quotations in this chapter are from the NIV.

14. Bavinck, *Religious Consciousness*, 243.

15. Bavinck, *Religious Consciousness*, 283.

16. Bavinck, *Religious Consciousness*, 283–84.

counterfeit idol substitutes are parasitic on the truth even though they are lies. Bavinck uses the evocative illustration of dreaming to describe this process in the non-Christian: "that revelation impinges on them and compels them to listen, but it is at the same time pushed down and repressed. And the only aspects of it that remain connected to human consciousness, even while torn from their original context, become seeds of an entirely different sequence of ideas around which they crystallize."[17] As a result, sinful human beings are a messy epistemological mix of knowing and not knowing, of running away and searching for. This is precisely the theological anthropology undergirding Paul's apologetic adventures at the Areopagus in Acts 17.[18]

At this point, however, and in what could be called a Reformed comparative religion, Bavinck detects a morphology in the messiness:

> It appears that humanity always and everywhere has fallen back on definite ideas and presumptions, and that these ideas and presumptions always resurface in surprising ways whenever they may have been temporarily repressed for various reasons. . . . This is a universal religious consciousness that remains indestructible in the midst of all disturbing and confusing developments.[19]

> There seems to be a kind of framework within which human religions need to operate. There appear to be definite points of contact around which all kinds of ideas crystallize. There seem to be quite vague feelings—one might better call them direction signals—that have been actively brooding everywhere. . . . Perhaps this can be expressed thus: there seem to be definite magnetic points that time and again irresistibly compel human religious thought. Human beings cannot escape their power but must provide an answer to those basic questions posed to them.[20]

17. Bavinck, *Religious Consciousness*, 290.

18. See Strange, *Their Rock*, 285–94. See also Flavien Pardigon, *Paul against the Idols: A Contextual Reading of the Areopagus Speech* (Eugene, OR: Pickwick Publications, 2019).

19. Bavinck, *Religious Consciousness*, 150–51.

20. Bavinck, *Religious Consciousness*, 226–27.

These "magnetic points" are aspects of or perspectives on the one religious consciousness and, while noting individual, cultural, and religious variegation, are as perennial, fixed, and universal as both the *imago Dei* and the suppression and substitution of truth. As we will see, the revelation out of which these points are idolatrously fashioned in the religious consciousness is none other than the eternal power (our dependence on God) and divine nature (our accountability to God) manifest in creation. In various writings Bavinck describes these points, demonstrating their presence largely from the great world religions.[21] My interest most recently has been to start applying the magnetic points to "secular" disenchanted (or, better, "differently" enchanted) Western culture.[22] These magnetic points can be summarized as follows:[23]

The first can be called *totality* and is concerned about *a way to connect.* As humans, we have an innate sense of totality, that we are connected and part of something much bigger, "the feeling of communion with the cosmic whole."[24] This gives us the understanding that we do not stand alone as islands in the universe but sense that we somehow belong. With this, though, comes a tension as in the face of the cosmos we simultaneously experience that we are insignificant nothings but also "so powerful as to experience all things converging and uniting within oneself."[25] We crave connection, feel abandoned after we've experienced it, and crave for it again and again.

The second can be called *norm* and is concerned about *a way to live.* We have a vague sense that there are rules to be obeyed. We know and accept that there are moral standards and codes that come from outside us but to which we must adhere. There is an appreciation of transcendent norms of behavior that apply to all people and

21. See Bavinck, *Religious Consciousness*, 151–98; Bavinck, *Church between Temple and Mosque*, 37–106.

22. See, for example, Daniel Strange, "Never Say 'The Phones Are Quiet,'" *Themelios* 44, no. 2 (2019): 216–25. See also Daniel Strange, *Plugged In: Connecting Your Faith with What You Watch, Read, and Play* (Epsom, UK: Good Book Company, 2019), 69.

23. In what follows I have adapted Bavinck's own nomenclature and added my own subdescriptions.

24. Bavinck, *Religious Consciousness*, 160.

25. Bavinck, *Religious Consciousness*, 162.

that are cosmically ordered. This brings with it a sense of responsibility to live up to those norms: "life is a dialogue between law and reality, between natural self-fulfillment and the moral demand for self-restraint. People chafe against the law and they want to be enveloped by it, carried by it."[26]

The third can be called *deliverance* and is concerned about *a way out*. We know that something is not right with the world. There is finitude, brokenness, and wrongdoing in the world, and the problem of suffering and death consistently confronts us. We mourn for a "paradise lost" and yearn for deliverance from these evils, craving redemption. And so we ask: Is redemption an act? Can we bring it about ourselves? Are we saved from the world or with it? What is this redeemed state we long for? How are we both part of the universe and yet free and responsible to be able to sin, to be able to be saved?

The fourth can be called *destiny* and asks whether there is a *way we control*. Although we know ourselves to be active players in the world, we have that nagging feeling that we are also passive participants in somebody else's world. This creates an existential tension between human freedom and boundedness. Life courses between action and fate, like actors on a stage, aware that though they act out their part, they are working from someone else's script:

> A person is only master of his or her life up to a certain point. A power exists that repeatedly reaches into a person's existence, that pushes him or her forward with compelling force, and from whose grip the person finds it impossible to struggle loose. Sometimes people can despair that they can lead their own life. Sometimes they gradually achieve the insight, in the school of life's hard knocks, that it is more appropriate to say that they suffer or undergo events that develop in and around them.[27]

The fifth and final point can be called *higher power* and asks whether there is *a way—a way above* in terms of transcendence or *a way beneath* in terms of a transcendental. People everywhere

26. Bavinck, *Religious Consciousness*, 293–94.
27. Bavinck, *Religious Consciousness*, 192–93.

perceive that behind all realities stands a greater reality. This greater reality is variously conceived but is always a superior power. There is also a sense that humans stand in some sort of relationship to this higher power, or at least they should. This understanding creates the expressed desire to seek connection with this power, but what is it? Who is it?

As already noted, these five magnetic points are all connected and demonstrate a particular interrelationship in that *totality* and *destiny* focus on human insignificance and boundedness, while *norm* and *deliverance* focus on human significance and freedom: "at the intersection of these two lines of thoughts . . . lies the awareness of being related to a higher power. The higher power is at the same time the deepest meaning of the whole, the bearer of cosmic laws, the energizer of the norm, the helper toward salvation. That intersection of these two lines is obviously the heart of religious consciousness."[28]

With the spectacles to see the world through this magnetic morphology, we can take great encouragement in our engagement, especially in a climate where we often experience the missiological pain of banging our head against a brick wall, wondering how we are ever going to break through. It is imperative that we trust our theological anthropology, knowing that "people are always more than as people they actually are. . . . Missionary proclamation does not proceed as mere teaching, but in the knowledge that God has already been busy with people long before we came to them, and that God already began the discussion with them before we have spoken even one word to them."[29] As we walk around and carefully observe our neighbors' and our culture's objects of worship (cf. Acts 17:23), these magnetic points are flashing left, right, and center. They are ripe for engagement.

The Magnetic Person

And so now in the twenty-first century, as has been the case in the first century, the fifth, or the fifteenth, we come as persons offering

28. Bavinck, *Religious Consciousness*, 203.
29. Bavinck, *Religious Consciousness*, 287–88.

other persons a Person. *We offer Jesus.* To return to an earlier illustration, in the cosmic game of hide-and-seek:

God is not hiding. We are.

God is not hiding. Indeed, like a little child who does not get the game of hide-and-seek and in his excitement always reveals his location, so God is jumping up and down, saying, "Here I am!" "No one has ever seen God, but the one and only Son, who is himself God and is in closest relationship with the Father, has made him known" (John 1:18).

God is not hiding . . . but he is the greatest seeker: "For the Son of Man came to seek and to save the lost" (Luke 19:10).

Just as God spoke to Adam, "Jesus Christ too is calling to us, saying the same words. He too is searching behind the bushes and calling, 'Man—my brother and sister—where are you?'"[30]

> In the darkness of human existence, where repressing and replacing focus their empty work day and night, only the proclamation of the gospel of Jesus Christ can bring light. Truth is found in him. This is the complete and living power for people, the power long repressed and rejected. Contained in his words is always something of the "I was always with you, but you were not with me." "I am the Christ whom you have repressed." "I am the one with whom you have struggled and whom you have assaulted." "It is hard for you to kick against the pricks."[31]

Such an approach recognizes that in our teaching, preaching, discipling, indeed in everything we do, we offer Jesus in both "zoom

30. Helmut Thielicke, *Man in God's World*, trans. John W. Doberstein (New York: Harper & Row, 1963), 167, quoted in Hamm, *Turning the Tables*, 130.

31. Bavinck, *Religious Consciousness*, 290. Note also: "The only basis we can ground our message upon is the certainty that God was concerning Himself with these Gentiles before we met them. God was occupying Himself with them before we came to them. We do not open the discussion, but we need only make it clear that the God who has already revealed His eternal power and Godhead to them now addresses them in a new way, through our words. It is always God who takes the initiative. He turns His face towards this wretched world and reveals His majesty to all his creatures." J. H. Bavinck, *The Impact of Christianity on the Non-Christian World* (Grand Rapids: Eerdmans, 1949), 109.

focus" and "wide angle" to individuals, families, nations, and cultures.[32] Offering Jesus is saying both "no" and "yes."[33] Offering Jesus entails both subversion and fulfillment. Offering Jesus means both connection and confrontation. Offering Jesus means that a missiological "point of contact" is a "point of attack."[34] Offering Jesus means demonstrating *both* his magnetic *appealingness* in the living water he offers and the *appallingness* of idolatry with its cracked cisterns that cannot hold water (cf. Jer. 2:13). Offering Jesus calls for faith and repentance. And because all this entails persons offering other persons a Person, it means communication that engages holistically,

32. I am adapting the terms "zoom focus" and "wide angle" from Kevin DeYoung and Greg Gilbert, who speak of two "lenses" on the gospel. See *What Is the Mission of the Church? Making Sense of Social Justice, Shalom, and the Great Commission* (Wheaton, IL: Crossway, 2011), 91–113. The "wide-angle lens" is the good news that Jesus is going to remake the world, and that Jesus Christ through his death and resurrection is the down payment on that transformation and renewal (Isa. 9:1; 61; Matt. 4:15–16, 23). The "zoom-focus lens" is the good news that God has acted to save sinners through the death of Jesus in their place and his subsequent resurrection (Acts 10:36–43; Rom. 1:16–17; 1 Cor. 1:17–18).

33. This is how Bavinck ends *Religious Consciousness*: "The missionary calling of the church is to preach the gospel in service to Jesus Christ. That involves speaking an emphatic and convicted 'no' to all human religious consciousness. . . . But mission work is far more than simply saying 'no.' Its heart and core are much more about saying 'yes.' It is to say 'yes' to the voiceless speech of God's self-manifestation in this world that even the pagans 'know,' even though they do not really know it because they have suppressed and exchanged it. Mission work is to be involved, using weak human muscles—no, using the strong arm of Christ himself—with all the mechanisms of repression's machinery that never shuts down but runs day and night. It is to command them to stop, on the basis of Christ's gospel. It is to say 'yes' to that unceasing and inscrutable work of God's mercy that has been active through all generations since the beginning of time. It is never to say 'yes' to human effort, but always to say 'yes' to God and to his work of mercy. It is to unfurl the gospel to blinded human hearts. It is to bring that always-new revelation of the measureless depth of God's love, seen in the cross of Jesus Christ" (299).

34. "We would like to distinguish, therefore, a 'point of attack' (*aangrijpingspunt*) from a 'point of contact' (*aanknopingspunt*). The point of attack signifies for the awareness of need, poverty, and inability, which we frequently encounter in non-Christian nations, as well as in our own surroundings. This universal feeling of need or of anxiety is not in itself a thirsting for Christ, but we can use it in our preaching to bring to light the deeper need of man, the need for God." J. H. Bavinck, *An Introduction to the Science of Missions* (Philadelphia: Presbyterian and Reformed, 1960), 140–41.

kardioptically, embodily, and humanely. Offering Jesus is relationality cubed. It demands patience and a "bearing with" tolerance, which in the current climate is so countercultural. It requires the skills of listening carefully, of questioning incisively, of building trust incrementally.[35] It calls for the emotional and contextual intelligence to recognize how we hear and how we are heard.

The challenge of offering Jesus will drive us to our knees in prayer, as we seek to discern in those we encounter the magnetic points that sinful humans have attempted to hide behind, but that have continued to haunt and frustrate, leaving them itching, restless, haunted, and dissonant. We offer a Jesus who says, "Come to me, all you who are weary and burdened, and I will give you rest" (Matt. 11:28–30). Such offering is certainly not smooth or pain-free:

> The gospel of Christ addresses people and rips open their religious consciousness. People want to suppress and push away the gospel in the worst way, just as they have repeatedly done with God. But it can happen that God causes their heart to submit. Then all the engines of resistance are switched off and people listen. Then the King of Glory makes his entrance, and the everlasting doors of the understanding are thrown open. And this is what we call the new birth.[36]

And so to the point of totality, *we offer Jesus*. He says: "I am the vine; you are the branches. If you remain in me and I in you, you will bear much fruit; apart from me you can do nothing" (John 15:5). Being made in God's image means both a recognition of our insignificance because we are only images and not divine, and at the same time a unique significance and royalty because we are images *of God*. As created ones "from the earth," we can affirm our desire to crave connection. But something has gone wrong: we are not connected. We are disconnected in ourselves, in our relationships, with our environment, and all because we are disconnected and alienated

---

35. On these areas I recommend Gregory Koukl, *Tactics: A Game Plan for Discussing Your Christian Convictions* (Grand Rapids: Zondervan, 2009); Randy Newman, *Bringing the Gospel Home* (Downers Grove, IL: InterVarsity Press, 2011); Jerram Barrs, *Learning Evangelism from Jesus* (Wheaton, IL: Crossway, 2009).

36. Bavinck, *Religious Consciousness*, 291.

from our Creator. Desiring to be connected to this world is a tragedy because it means a connection to a world that is perishing. It means ultimately futility and darkness and death. But *"Ecce Homo."* Jesus is the true Image, the second Adam who both proclaims and ushers in another world, an amazing kingdom to be entered into by repentance and faith; "it is the kingdom that is coming and that is also already present, and it gathers up people into its indescribable rest."[37] By grace, nature is restored and perfected so that people commune with God and other human beings so that the common good is realized in a way that does not suppress but enables the flourishing or happiness of the individual. In this kingdom we are cosmically connected, but without losing our individuality or responsibility. "Taking one's stand within the new kingdom definitely does mean dying. But it also means finding oneself anew in the resurrection of the Lord Jesus Christ. This is the ultimate dying and the ultimate rising to eternal life."[38] It means not simply connection but also, through union with Christ by the Spirit, communion with the living God and true community in the body of Christ.

To the point of norm, *we offer Jesus*. He says, "Do not think that I have come to abolish the Law or the Prophets; I have not come to abolish them but to fulfill them" (Matt. 5:17). Jesus says that we are right, the world is not as it should be, but you can't fix it. Jesus offers himself both as a standard and as the Savior. His authority is magnetic as time and again he demonstrates the knowledge, ethical character, and effectiveness that command both love and obedience. He offers a way of life within the fixed and constraining boundaries of God's holy law—there for human flourishing, not human withering. Yes, he offers the dependability and fixity that conservatives crave, and yet he offers compassion to the outcast, courage to stand up against those who advocate sterile and deadly rules for rules' sake. In this way he is radically progressive and authentically "real."

To the point of deliverance, *we offer Jesus*. He says: "I am the way and the truth and the life. No one comes to the Father except through me" (John 14:6). The enmity within ourselves, between ourselves and

37. Bavinck, *Religious Consciousness*, 292.
38. Bavinck, *Religious Consciousness*, 293.

with the spiritual and natural realms that we long to be rescued from, has to be understood to be symptom rather than cause or as fruit rather than root. It is our enmity with God, his righteous wrath, and an eternity in hell that we need deliverance from and that can be dealt with only through a work outside ourselves, through one Mediator, the God-man Jesus Christ *and him alone* (*solus Christus*). Outside this, there is no hope. Such deliverance will mean a life of sacrifice: "Whoever wants to be my disciple must deny themselves and take up their cross and follow me" (Mark 8:34). But it also means a life of blessing and the breaking in of a new cosmic world order, for "no one who has left home or brothers or sisters or mother or father or children or fields for me and the gospel will fail to receive a hundred times as much in this present age: homes, brothers, sisters, mothers, children and fields—along with persecutions—and in the age to come eternal life" (10:29–30). The resurrection of Christ means that our deliverance is not about escape but about restoration.

To the point of destiny, *we offer Jesus.* He says: "I am the good shepherd. The good shepherd lays down his life for the sheep" (John 10:11). The world is not chaotic and meaningless. It is not governed by capricious finite "gods" or a grinding impersonal fate that makes us automatons. Jesus said to the superpower of his day, "You would have no power over me if it were not given to you from above" (19:11). The interplay between divine sovereignty and human responsibility, while never fully explained or comprehended by our finite minds, has been graciously revealed to us in space and time in the death of Christ: "This man was handed over to you by God's deliberate plan and foreknowledge; and you, with the help of wicked men, put him to death by nailing him to the cross" (Acts 2:23). There is a Christian destiny that is so liberating and joyful:

> The lot that is assigned a person is not some dark fate, nor is it cosmic determinism. But in the deepest sense it is the unfolding plan of God. The dialogue that a person experiences between his or her activity and his or her destiny increasingly takes on the character of a dialogue between a child and its father.[39]

39. Bavinck, *Religious Consciousness*, 296.

Finally, to the point of the higher power, *we offer Jesus*. He says: "I am the light of the world. Whoever follows me will never walk in darkness, but will have the light of life" (John 8:12). Humans are made for worship and don't have to scrabble around in the darkness, making up gods of their own imagination, gods that are nothing but the works of human hands. We do not worship a something or an "It" but a Someone, maximally absolute and maximally personal, one who is both transcendent and immanent. We worship one who has reached down to us in grace, the Word made flesh: "That Higher Power is the one that came into the world in the form of Jesus Christ and removed the veil over his face so that we might know the Son and the Father. 'Whoever has seen me has seen the Father.'"[40] *We offer Jesus.*

Conclusion: The Magnetic People

On Sunday evening, March 11, 1883, Charles Spurgeon offered Jesus at the Metropolitan Tabernacle, "on an evening when the regular hearers left their seats to be occupied by strangers."[41] His text was "And I, when I am lifted up from the earth, will draw all people to myself" (John 12:32). The sermon was entitled "The Marvelous Magnet":

It is the Spirit of God who puts power into the Truth of God about Christ. And then men [and women] feel that Truth and come to Christ and live. But our blessed Lord and Master uses instruments. The force of Christ's love is sometimes shown to men by those who already love Him. One Christian makes many. One Believer leads others to faith. To come back to my metaphor of a magnet—you have sometimes seen a battery attached to a coil and then, if you take a nail and put it on the coil, the nail has become a strong magnet. You notice that the nail turns into a magnet, for you take another nail and you put it on the end of it and it holds the second nail fast.

40. Bavinck, *Religious Consciousness*, 294.
41. Charles H. Spurgeon, "The Marvelous Magnet," *Spurgeon's Sermons (1717)*, vol. 29 (1883), accessed July 30, 2019, https://www.ccel.org/ccel/spurgeon/sermons 29.xx.html.

... All the magnetism comes from the first place from which it started—and when it ceases at the fountainhead, there is an end of it altogether.

Indeed, Jesus Christ is the great attractive magnet and all must begin and end with Him! ... Thus from one to another, the mystic influence proceeds—but the whole of the force abides in Jesus. More and more the Kingdom grows, "ever mighty to prevail," but all the growing and the prevailing come out of Him! So it is that Jesus works—first by Himself—and then by all who are in Him. May the Lord make us all magnets for Himself.[42]

As we continue to come to terms with what it means for post-Christendom "strangers" to occupy the seats of the "regular hearers" of Christendom, we can be bold and joyful, knowing that the Lord Jesus Christ "subversively fulfils"[43] the magnetic points of the human heart and the cultures we build on our common objects of love. While I have given only a sketch of what this might begin to look like, I hope it will spark our imaginations to go bigger and bolder as we creatively offer Christ in our pastoring, and in the vocational callings of those to whom we pastor. More than that, though, I hope such an exposition warms our hearts to love Jesus Christ more deeply as we are overwhelmed by his majestic magnetism, thus transforming us into a magnetized people who will be an attractive and not a repellent presence.

May the Lord make us all magnets for himself.

Key Terms

fabrica idolorum
semen religionis
sensus divinitatis

---

42. Spurgeon, "The Marvelous Magnet."

43. The notion of *subversive fulfillment* (a term coined by Hendrik Kraemer) is one that I have explored in detail in previous work. See Strange, *Their Rock*, 266–73; Strange, *Plugged In*, 102–3.

Recommendations for Further Reading

Bavinck, J. H. *An Introduction to the Science of Missions*. Philadelphia: Presbyterian and Reformed, 1960.

Bolt, John, James D. Bratt, and Paul J. Visser, eds. *The J. H. Bavinck Reader*. Grand Rapids: Eerdmans, 2013.

Strange, Daniel. *Plugged In: Connecting Your Faith with What You Watch, Read, and Play*. Epsom, UK: Good Book Company, 2019.

———. *Their Rock Is Not like Our Rock: A Theology of Religions*. Grand Rapids: Zondervan, 2014.

Discussion Questions

1. How can we more clearly offer the person of Jesus in our preaching rather than merely focusing on the benefits of the gospel?

2. Discuss the various "magnetic points," described by J. H. Bavinck, and their value in identifying a culture's religious awareness.

3. Daniel Strange claims, "God is not hiding . . . but he is the greatest seeker." Rather, it is we who hide from him. Discuss various ways that evidence of God's existence or presence is thought to be lacking. How might this be challenged?

4. According to Daniel Strange, Jesus himself is the ultimate magnetic point, or rather the magnetic person. What are various ways that Jesus subversively fulfills the magnetic points of the human heart?

25

ESCHATOLOGY

How the Telos *of Humanity Must Inform Pastoral Ministry*

MICHAEL HORTON

"The chief end of man is to glorify God and to enjoy him forever." This famous opening answer of the Westminster Shorter Catechism identifies the goal of the triune God for our existence, and hints at an eschatology that should inform pastoral ministry. Indeed, one could say without exaggeration that this goal lies at the heart of the whole Bible with its plot of creation, fall, redemption, and consummation. Not even the fall can finally defeat God's purposes to unite his image-bearers to himself in the most intimate bonds of familial love.[1]

The Eschatological Impulse

Created with this *telos*, human beings are by nature eschatological creatures. We recognize this in the natural desire to mature, to

---

1. This intrinsic purpose, with redemption in Christ as the basis for reaching it, is a leitmotif throughout Sinclair Ferguson's ministry of preaching, teaching, and writing. A friend of many years, Sinclair has also been and remains a mentor—the model pastor-scholar. Having learned much from him in writing and in person on this as on many other points, I am very grateful to be included in a volume praising our covenant Lord for this especially gifted servant and friend.

achieve milestones, and especially to find a calling that contributes a sense of meaning and purpose for our lives and others'. And when human beings anticipate death, it is typical across all times and cultures to inquire, "What comes next?" It is the eschatological impulse that explains in part why we are *homo religionis*, groping in confused and inchoate ways for a god to make sense of our ineradicable hope. Yet it is Scripture that provides the only framework for understanding the nature, source, and justification for this impulse. What we're made *for* gives us a metric for life now, which is why this *telos* that is nuclear to the image of God can be crushing and condemning for fallen creatures. Yet in Christ, it becomes a fulfilled goal and a gospel that justifies and renews us.

Eschatology is the study of "last things" (*ta eschata*), so it is natural that many Christians think its exclusive focus is on things to come. Yet with the incarnation, life, death, resurrection, and ascension of Christ, the new creation has already begun, the kingdom inaugurated, and the Spirit poured on all flesh. With Christ as the prototype and pioneer, the future has penetrated into the present. While awaiting the consummation, we have even now been "enlightened," "have tasted the heavenly gift, and have shared in the Holy Spirit, and have tasted the goodness of the word of God and the powers of the age to come" (Heb. 6:4–5). This reality must thoroughly inform a pastor's life and ministry. The gospel minister must envision all his labors in relation to God's kingdom now come in Christ, as unfolded in Scripture, that he might exhibit its arrival in his proclamation and explain its significance for our present lives.

Although biblical eschatology has many implications for pastoral theology, I will focus on its significance for personal identity as we minister to those created in the image of God, in relationship with him and others, as we either realize or resist the purpose for which we are made. Every week we face men and women and children, searching for significance, questioning their sense of self, wondering whether they and their actions really matter. Numerous questions are raised. Why do we find our callings fulfilling, or vain repetition, or something in between? How do we respond to the growing crisis of mental health in our society? Are we defined *ultimately* by our sex and gender or by our creation and redemption in Christ? Is identity something we choose or something that we are born—and reborn—with? These and a host of other pastoral issues are addressed at least in part by a biblical understanding of the eschatological character of human identity.

The notions of covenant and eschatology are closely intertwined in biblical theology. Covenant provides the *context* for the unfolding story, while eschatology indicates the *direction* of the plot. Both are oriented toward promise and fulfillment. This promise-fulfillment pattern does not begin after the fall, but begins with creation itself.

This eschatological perspective, in continuity with Irenaeus and the Cappadocians, extends the logic of Reformed (covenant) theology. As Geerhardus Vos reminds us, "The universe, as created, was only a beginning, the meaning of which was *not perpetuation, but attainment*."[2] Creation began with a greater destiny lying before it. Creation was the stage—the "beautiful theater"—for God's drama, not an end in itself. Life in the garden was not intended to simply go on in perpetuity, but was merely the point of departure for the great march of creation behind God's vice-regent into the everlasting life of God's own Sabbath rest.

The Self as Servant: What Is the "Image of God"?

One of the obstacles to a biblical-eschatological perspective is the Western inheritance of concepts alien to Scripture. Platonism in particular teaches a cyclical view of time as an image of eternity. Therefore, "the end is like the beginning," a maxim often found in the church father Origen of Alexandria, who tried unsuccessfully to interpret the Christ event within a Platonist framework.[3] How does the Platonic idea of the soul's escape from the body comport with the biblical promise of the resurrection? For Philo of Alexandria, the

2. Geerhardus Vos, *The Eschatology of the Old Testament*, ed. James T. Dennison Jr. (Phillipsburg, NJ: P&R Publishing, 2001), 73–74 (emphasis added). Vos continues: "Eschatology aims at consummation rather than restoration. . . . It does not aim at the original state, but at a transcendental state of man."

3. See Michael Horton, "Atonement and Ascension," in *Locating Atonement: Explorations in Constructive Dogmatics*, ed. Oliver Crisp and Fred Sanders, Proceedings of the Los Angeles Theology Conference 3 (Grand Rapids: Zondervan Academic, 2015), 226–50.

great Jewish-Platonist thinker of Jesus' day, and a host of Christian theologians after him, the *imago Dei* is the highest (rational) part of the soul. It is reason that separates humans from the rest of the animals with whom they share their bodily nature; in fact, the rational soul itself is a spark of the divine Soul.

Where Platonism regards the union of the soul with the body as an evil and the separation of the soul from the body as deliverance, the Bible treats the former as intrinsic to God's good creation and the latter as the result of God's judgment on fallen humanity. A biblical anthropology has nothing to lose—in fact, everything to gain—from the dissolution of such a radical mind-body dualism, whether ancient or modern.

Nowhere in the Bible is the soul identified with the mind. More often, in fact, it is identified with the heart or even the bowels, in a self-consciously figurative manner, and the center of agency is the *person*, not a particular faculty abstracted from others. Nothing is threatened, much less lost, in Christian teaching when we learn that much of what we once attributed to the mysterious soul can be explained by the inner workings of the brain, a bodily organ. One wonders today how many godly Christians have had to suffer not only from mental illnesses but from so little understanding about them. Even today, the physiochemical and other physical aspects of such maladies are sometimes insufficiently treated because these matters are considered spiritual issues. Often, however, a sufferer cannot even recognize properly, much less deal with, moral and spiritual responsibilities until there is a medical diagnosis and treatment. On the other side, the beliefs and obligations that we take seriously as believers are sometimes undermined by the opposite extreme of treating these matters as medical *rather* than spiritual issues. Even cancer is a spiritual issue, and even depression is a physical issue. A robust doctrine of the biblical representation of humans as psycho-somatic (soul-body) creatures is of immense pastoral consequence, today more than ever. As with physical maladies, there are spiritual causes and effects that lie beyond the expertise of physicians. Scripture addresses human beings in their wholeness as persons responsible before him, rather than simply as mind, soul, or spirit.

Biblical faith differs from pagan dualism as much as it does from materialism. According to Scripture, the soul is not divine. Death is not our salvation from the bodily prison but God's sentence for sin and the last enemy to be destroyed, so that we may be raised bodily as whole persons forever. The soul is not in its very nature eternally immortal (immortality being a divine attribute, 1 Tim. 1:17), but is created in time. In fact, as Herman Bavinck points out:

> Adam's body was formed from the dust of the earth and then the breath of life is breathed into him. He is called "Adam" after the ground from which he was formed; he is "from the earth, a man of dust" (1 Cor. 15:47). The body is not a prison, but a marvelous piece of art from the hand of God Almighty, and just as constitutive for the essence of humanity as the soul (Job 10:8–12; Pss. 8; 139:13–17; Eccl. 12:2–7; Isa. 64:8). . . . Now, this body, which is so intimately bound up with the soul, also belongs to the image of God. . . . The incarnation of God is proof that the human body is an essential component of that image.[4]

Immortality is not an attribute of the soul any more than the body; it is God's gift of resurrection-glorification in Jesus Christ (1 Cor. 15:53; 2 Tim. 1:10).

To put it more simply, Platonism sees *embodiment* as a curse, while Christianity understands *disembodiment* to be a result of the curse. While the body and soul *can* be separated, and are at death, they are not *meant* to be, and our salvation is not complete until we are bodily raised as whole persons (Rom. 8:23). There is an intermediate state, following death and before Christ's return, but this is not the final state.[5] John Murray summarizes this consensus: "Man

4. Herman Bavinck, *Reformed Dogmatics: Abridged in One Volume*, ed. John Bolt (Grand Rapids: Baker Academic, 2011), 327.
5. In reaction against the Platonist perspective, we can go too far in the opposite direction, as G. C. Berkouwer did in denying the intermediate state. See G. C. Berkouwer, *Man: The Image of God* (Grand Rapids: Eerdmans, 1962), 194–233. Scripture affirms that even as the body lies in the grave, the soul is present with the Lord until that glorious day of reunion. One who dies in the Lord "is taken away from calamity, he enters into peace" (Isa. 57:2). Jesus promised the believing thief on the cross that he would be present with him in paradise upon his death (Luke 23:43). The moment the soul is absent from the body, it is present with the Lord

is bodily, and, therefore, the scriptural way of expressing this truth is not that man has a body but that man *is* body. . . . Scripture does not represent the soul or spirit of man as created first and then put into a body. . . . The bodily is not an appendage."[6] In brief, Christian theology offers a richer and more complex anthropology, and it is determined not by speculation about essences but by an unfolding drama that leads from creation to consummation.[7]

Having summarized these matters, we turn our attention to the biblical motifs of covenant and eschatology, which as stated above provide the setting and direction for human life. The image of God

---

(2 Cor. 5:8). "Blessed are the dead who die in the Lord from now on. . . . They may rest from their labors" (Rev. 14:13). But there is a reason why it is called the *intermediate* state: *final* salvation comes with "the resurrection of the body, and the life everlasting," as stated in the Apostles' Creed. Even in their relative blessedness, the souls of the martyrs cry out from the altar, "O Sovereign Lord, . . . how long . . . ?" (Rev. 6:10), as they long for the final judgment and restoration of all things, including the resurrection and glorification of their complete humanity, body and soul in perfect union. An eschatology that culminates in the soul's separation from the body is Platonic, not Christian, looking away from the risen and glorified Christ, who has gone before us. Earlier Reformed theologians were more judicious in this matter. Peter Martyr Vermigli observes the close identification in the Old Testament of the soul (*nephesh*, "life") with the blood, highlighting the soul-body integration. Based on Genesis 9:4, he argues that "the blood is the soul." This represents a metonymy: "Since the blood is a sign of the soul's presence, it may be called the soul itself. . . . I do not offer this as if I accept it as the reason why God gave that commandment [against eating the blood of animals], but to indicate the communion of man's soul with the body." Joseph C. McLelland, ed. and trans., *The Peter Martyr Library*, vol. 4, *Philosophical Works*, Sixteenth Century Essays and Studies (Kirksville, MO: Sixteenth Century Journal Publishers, 1996), 42. "As flesh and spirit (taken physically) are *disparates, not contraries*," explains Francis Turretin, "so also are the appetites, inclinations and habits of both in themselves. The repugnancy now found in them arises accidentally from sin." Quoted in Heinrich Heppe, *Reformed Dogmatics*, ed. Ernst Bizer, rev. ed. (Eugene, OR: Wipf & Stock, 2008), 468 (emphasis added).

6. John Murray, *Collected Writings of John Murray*, vol. 2 (Edinburgh: Banner of Truth, 1977), 14.

7. John W. Cooper, *Body, Soul, and Life Everlasting: Biblical Anthropology and the Monism-Dualism Debate* (Grand Rapids: Eerdmans, 1989). I agree with Cooper that "anthropological dualism" expresses the Christian conviction insofar as it affirms the distinction between body and soul. At the same time, I prefer a term such as *psychosomatic holism*, since *dualism* suggests that the distinction between soul and body is more basic than its unity.

(*imago Dei*) is not something *in* us that is semidivine but something *between* us and God that constitutes a covenantal relationship. To put it a little differently, the image of God is not something that we *have* somewhere inside us; it is what we *are*. "The whole being, the whole human person and not just 'something' in us is the image of God," notes Bavinck. "Thus, a human being does not *bear* or *have* the image of God but *is* the image of God."[8]

Before turning to eschatology, we need to understand how our identity—the *imago Dei*—is determined covenantally. The stock of metaphors in biblical revelation for Israel's relationship to God is taken not from religion but from politics. The surrounding civilizations had developed elaborate mythopoeic religious cults, but this was idolatry in Israel. Yahweh was not just another god, lending transcendent authority to the earthly ruler, but the Ruler himself—the Suzerain or Great King. The idea of a covenant of a people *with their God* has no parallels in the ancient world. Yahweh delivered his people and made them his nation. Israel's relationship to God was founded on a covenant, similar to the vassal-suzerain treaties of secular kingdoms. Significantly, the holiest part of the holy of holies in the temple was the ark of the covenant. In ancient Near Eastern politics, two copies of the covenant would be made and deposited in the archive of both partners. There is something similar in many modern nations. For example, visitors to Washington, D.C., can see the U.S. Constitution in the National Archives. At the center of Israel's holiest shrine was not an image of the chief deity, as in pagan temples, but the ark (archive) of the covenant: a box in which God's covenant law was placed. So the concept of human beings as the image of God is not drawn from the typical stock of pagan religion (viz., the idol as the replica of the deity). Rather, it is a political image. Just as the crown prince is the image of his imperial father, human beings are God's viceroys, his representatives among the creatures that God has made.

Biblical faith differs from its rivals not just in a few doctrines here or there, but in the offer of a radically different paradigm. In addition to providing a different understanding of God and the God-world relationship generally, a covenantal paradigm grounds a

8. Bavinck, *Reformed Dogmatics: Abridged*, 324.

fundamentally different view of human personhood. We do not meet God in the inner realm of our spirit or at sacred rivers, trees, or mountains. Rather, God hallows common places as historical events of his *discourse*. Places are special in biblical faith because God met with his people there and spoke his covenant word. As covenantal, then, this faith is always social: meeting with God and others he has gathered, in public spaces, where we are constituted the people of God.

The triune God is not a collection of individuals entering into a social contract, but united in essence: a distinguishable but inseparable communion of persons, defined not by an autonomous individualism but by their relations to one another. Even before creation, the covenant of redemption highlights this intra-Trinitarian fellowship. Creating us in his image, God made human beings finite analogies of this intimate communion. What defines human personhood, on this account, is not so much what happens within the self, or in the cycles of nature, but what happens between persons (God and human beings) in history.

Our covenantal identity as God's analogies is evident also in the fact that we imitate his pattern of work and rest. Significantly, this workweek is crowned by the Sabbath: the eschatological sign par excellence. "Under the sun"—that is, within a fallen, purely immanent perspective—our days are a cycle of one vain thing after another, as the Preacher tells us in Ecclesiastes. Or in a Platonist outlook, we end up where we started, that is, before we descended into a body. The biblical *telos*, however, is something that "no eye has seen, nor ear heard, nor the heart of man imagined" (1 Cor. 2:9), our sharing in the prize of consummation, the right to eat from the Tree of Life, which Adam forfeited.

The creation week itself establishes a point of departure and a destination, already giving birth to the very notion of history that is essential to human identity. The first man, Adam, forfeited his destiny of leading creation into the consummated form of its natural existence. Creation is currently filled with strife and sin, not because of an unfortunate ontological descent from an eternal state of being, but because of a historical fall from covenantal obedience. Only with the last Adam do we see the firstfruits of the consummation. This consummation is not yet fully realized. "But we see him who for a little while was made lower than the angels, namely Jesus, crowned with glory and honor because of the suffering of death, so that by the grace of God he might taste death for everyone" (Heb. 2:8–9). We come to a proper understanding of the nature of creation only when we recognize its end as well as its origin, and Jesus Christ as the one person who brings them together.

This covenantal relationship is not something added to human nature, but is essential to it. To exist as a human being is not to be a "thinking thing," a disembodied and unrelated ego, but is already to be enmeshed in a web of relationships: a society. From the beginning, "It is not good that the man should be alone" (Gen. 2:18). Strikingly, Descartes arrived at his concept of the autonomous *res cogitans* ("thinking thing") by a double act of contemplative solitude: first, by abstracting himself from the world (isolating himself from contact with others as much as possible) and then by disengaging his body from his mind. A. N. Whitehead's famous quip "Religion is what the individual does with his own solitariness" is far removed from any view of the self as oriented covenantally.[9]

The Bible places human beings in a dramatic narrative that defines their existence as inherently covenantal—fully engaged with God, with one another, and with the nonhuman creation. Instead of drawing us within ourselves in order to draw our contemplation upward from our lived experience in the world, a covenantal anthropology draws us outward, where we find ourselves responsible to God and our neighbors.

The Covenant of Creation

Because the covenant is not something added later, but is intrinsic to our creation in God's image, and the original covenant was a legal command to love God and neighbor and to subdue any ethical threat to this reign of God, all people retain some sense of God as their Lawgiver and Judge and of the obligation to love (as Paul argues in Romans 1–3). It is not that this religious and moral sense is lost in the fall, but it has been gravely distorted and depraved. Thus, even

---

9. Alfred North Whitehead, *Religion in the Making* (New York: Meridian, 1960), 16.

after the fall, human existence remains intrinsically covenantal, even though it is divided between Cain's proud city (Gen. 4:17–24) and the City of God represented by Seth, whose descendants are distinguished by their invocation of the Great King for their salvation: "At that time people began to call upon the name of the LORD" (v. 26). Those who do not invoke God or embrace his covenant of grace are "in Adam" under the *original* covenant, yet upheld by common grace despite their being strangers to the divine promises announced in the covenant of grace. Adam and Eve could declare independence from God but possessed no power to re-create themselves as autonomous beings. Their created covenantal identity, together with the *telos* it entails, remained, though now lived out under the curse.

Intrinsic to humanness, particularly the *imago*, is a covenantal office or commission into which every person is born. This covenantal identity is therefore a universal phenomenon, shared equally by all, and the basis for God's righteous judgment of humankind even apart from special revelation. This is to say that "law"—in particular, the divine covenant law—is natural, a *verbum internum* ("internal word") that rings in (yet is not identical to) the conscience. The covenant of creation renders every person a dignified, and therefore accountable, image-bearer of God. "So they are without excuse" (Rom. 1:20b). This is why human rights derive not from the authority of the individual or the state, but from God alone. Ultimately, it is God's claim on us and our neighbors, not individual autonomy, that is determinative here—which is why, in a covenantal scheme, responsibilities (to others) are more basic than rights (for ourselves).[10] It is noteworthy in Reformed catechism summaries of the second table of the Law that murder is assigned not only to what I *do*, but to what I leave *undone*, and the emphasis is not only on my rights or my neighbor's rights to be unharmed, but on my responsibility before God to preserve my neighbor's life, goods, and reputation. Imagine a society in which love of God and neighbor, rather than laws and courts, defined relationships. Yet because we do not live in such a society since the fall,

---

10. This covenantal view of personhood represents an important area of convergence between Jewish and Christian theologies, as can be seen especially in David Novak, *Covenantal Rights: A Study in Jewish Political Theory* (Princeton, NJ: Princeton University Press, 2000).

the securing of rights remains necessary. In anticipation of Christ's consummated kingdom, we might hope that Christians at least consider such legalistic relationships necessary but not sufficient. God is the original rights-holder, and this grounds justice; and he is the Redeemer, and this grounds our hope even here and now that the church at least can be a place where we see one another as a gift rather than a burden or threat.

This original covenant is also intrinsic to that eschatological character of human hope mentioned at the beginning.[11] The internal alarm clock of our shared covenant consciousness that awakened unfallen Adam and Eve to a new day's quest to "glorify God, and to enjoy Him forever" (WSC 1) becomes a cause of stress and anxiety after the fall. We have not loved God and our neighbor, but each of us has gone his or her own way, suffering the loneliness of an illusory autonomy. "Now we know that whatever the law says," whether written on the conscience or on tablets, "it speaks to those who are under the law, so that every mouth may be stopped, and the whole world may be held accountable to God" (Rom. 3:19). The law brings no hope of relief, but only the knowledge of breach (v. 20). The gospel, by contrast, is entirely foreign to the human person in this natural state. It comes as a free decision on God's part in view of the fall and can be known only by a *verbum externum* ("external Word"), an astounding proclamation that brings hope and confidence in our standing before God (vv. 21–26). As Paul points out in the opening chapters of Romans, however, the original revelation continues to speak, holding all of humanity accountable for suppressing its ultimate claims, even when these lead unmistakably to the judgment of a personal God.

It is within the covenant framework of creation that Jesus appears as the new federal head to fulfill in righteousness all that the Adamic commission required, as well as to bear the covenant curse of those

---

11. Bavinck notes that the covenant of works is assumed in the Belgic Confession (arts. 14–15), in the Heidelberg Catechism (6–11), and in the Canons of Dort (III/IV), and is explicit in the Irish Articles, the Westminster Confession, the Helvetic Consensus Formula, and the Walcheren Articles. "Although the doctrine of the covenant of works also found acceptance with some Roman Catholic and Lutheran theologians," notes Bavinck, "it was vigorously opposed by Remonstrants [Arminians] and Rationalists." Bavinck, *Reformed Dogmatics: Abridged*, 330.

whom he represents as covenant head. At his temptation by the serpent, Jesus does not determine for himself who he will be and how he will respond; he receives his identity as the gift of God's speech (Matt. 4:4). He does this as our example, to be sure, but more importantly, as our covenantal head, as Paul explains in Romans 5. Humanity was not finished at creation, since Adam had yet to secure the fullness of life promised through his obedience. Jesus, however, not only is completing the proper ethical orientation where Adam failed, but is undoing Adam's fateful decision even as he will bear the guilt of Adamic treason for his people.

Although refined by later Reformed theologians, the seeds of the covenantal approach can be easily discerned in the likes of Philipp Melanchthon, Heinrich Bullinger, Martin Bucer, and John Calvin.[12] "Now that inward law (*lex interior*), which we have described as written, even engraved, upon the hearts of all," says Calvin, "in a sense asserts the very same things that are to be learned from the two Tables."[13] In contrast to Stoicism (and much of medieval natural-law

12. For a definitive survey, see John T. McNeill, "Natural Law in the Teaching of the Reformers," *Journal of Religion* 26, no. 3 (1946): 168–82. See also Philipp Melanchthon, *Loci communes* (1555), chap. 7. See also, more recently, David VanDrunen, *Natural Law and the Two Kingdoms: A Study in the Development of Reformed Social Thought*, Emory University Studies in Law and Religion (Grand Rapids: Eerdmans, 2009). In fact, ancient theologians, including Irenaeus and Augustine, referred to this original relationship as a covenant. Irenaeus, "Against Heresies," bk. 4, chap. 25, in *The Ante-Nicene Fathers*, ed. Alexander Roberts and James Donaldson (repr., Grand Rapids: Eerdmans, 1989), 5.16.3; 4.13.1; 4.15.1; 4.16.3. See also Ligon Duncan, "The Covenant Idea in Irenaeus of Lyons," paper presented at the North American Patristics Society annual meeting, May 29, 1997 (Greenville, SC: Reformed Academic Press, 1998); Everett Ferguson, "The Covenant Idea in the Second Century," in *Texts and Testaments: Critical Essays on the Bible and the Early Church Fathers*, ed. W. Eugene March (San Antonio: Trinity University Press, 1980), 135–62. Augustine writes, "The *first covenant* was this, unto Adam: 'Whensoever thou eatest thereof, thou shalt die the death,'" and this is why all his children "are breakers of God's covenant made with Adam in paradise." Augustine, *City of God* (16.27), trans. Henry Bettenson, ed. David Knowles (New York: Penguin, 1972), 688–89 (emphasis added). Augustine elaborates this point in considerable detail in these two pages, contrasting the creation covenant with the covenant of grace as we find it in the promise to Abraham.

13. John Calvin, *Institutes of the Christian Religion*, ed. John T. McNeill, trans. Ford Lewis Battles, 2 vols., Library of Christian Classics 20–21 (Philadelphia: Westminster, 1960), 2.8.1.

thinking), then, the law of nature is the product not of our participation in divine reason, but of our being summoned in every moment as covenant creatures made in God's image and likeness. Of Romans 2:14–15, Calvin observes, "There is nothing more commonly recognized than that man is sufficiently instructed in a right rule of life by natural law (concerning which the apostle speaks here)."[14] In fact, Calvin praises "the sagacity" of the great scientists, philosophers, and jurists "in things earthly," scolding sectarians for insulting the Holy Spirit, who gives such common gifts to humanity.[15]

Law is not opposed to love. God created us to love him and our neighbor—that is intrinsic to our identity as human beings, as the *imago Dei*. We begin to truly understand love only when we come to know God in this history of the covenant, as *hesed—covenant* love. And in this state Adam could expect—for himself and his covenant heirs—royal entrance into the consummation, the Sabbath rest of God himself, and everlasting confirmation in righteousness. In the words of the Formula Consensus Helvetica, "the promise annexed to the covenant of works was not just the continuation of earthly life and felicity," but a confirmation in righteousness and everlasting heavenly joy.[16]

Because of this covenant of creation, I am responsible for what happens to my neighbors. The universality of this covenant (unlike the covenant of grace) is evident in its implicit recognition beyond the circle of Christianity. In his excellent book *Covenantal Rights*, Jewish scholar David Novak argues that a covenantal approach differs from Greek philosophical theories of natural law on one side and modern autonomy on the other. It is, after all, a personal God and not an abstract concept of the *good* that ultimately grounds a biblical sense of justice (equity). God establishes by his command the rights and duties that are reciprocally related in all human relationships.[17]

Although the Mosaic covenant is unique to Israel, according to Novak, the original claim of righteousness is grounded in creation and encompasses all human beings. Through the cries of victims, we

---

14. Calvin, *Institutes*, 2.2.22.
15. Calvin, *Institutes*, 2.2.15.
16. Heppe, *Reformed Dogmatics*, 295.
17. Novak, *Covenantal Rights*, 20.

may hear God's own claim, yet it is not individuals or communities that establish their rights and claims, often over against other groups. Rather, all of us are bound to one another by God's claim on us. Novak concludes, "The general claims on that world, which the rabbinic tradition sees going back to Noah, even to Adam and Eve, are not overcome by the [Mosaic] covenant; instead, they are subsumed into the covenant intact."[18] Thus, human solidarity is always more basic than national, racial, or cultural solidarity. It is based not on a social contract, but on a divine covenant.[19] Humans are on the receiving end of their identity and obligations, founded by a word that they did not and could not speak to themselves. It is precisely because *God* created us different, male and female, and "made from one man every nation of mankind to live on all the face of the earth" (Acts 17:26)—yet all "in the image of God" (Gen. 1:27) that is reconstituted redemptively in a kingdom consisting of the elect of every race (Rev. 5:9)—that there is a genuine justice and peace that autonomous grounding for human dignity can only parody. If we as Christians and churches better exhibited this truth ourselves, perhaps secularist alternatives would not seem so attractive.

Every religion and culture professes some commitment to that which the Bible identifies as the law written on the human conscience in creation. Whether it is called the Tao, dharma, Karma, Torah, the Universal Declaration of Human Rights, or "the little voice within," the most ineradicable report of general revelation is our moral accountability before a holy God for how we treat one another. This is the law above all positive laws of nations and international bodies. No matter how we try to suppress, distort, and deny it, our sense of being personally responsible for our sin is universal and natural. Even if Scripture did not teach it, experience would require something like the covenant of creation to account for this moral sensibility.

The implications of the covenant of creation for our concept of human personhood are many. First, it underscores the point that all human beings are created in God's image: believer and unbeliever alike. Every human being has a personal relationship with God—and

18. Novak, *Covenantal Rights*, 86.
19. David Novak, *Jewish-Christian Dialogue: A Jewish Justification* (New York: Oxford University Press, 1989), 27.

with one another. The question is whether it is a relationship of enmity or friendship. Second, the covenant of works establishes a proper basis for working alongside non-Christians in common society. The law is written on their conscience, and they are given particular callings and gifts by God for the mutual benefit of society. Third, the covenant of works provides a biblical paradigm for understanding human personhood that contrasts at important points with dominant paradigms that we have inherited even in Christian theology.

The Convergence of Human Personhood and the *Imago*: "Here I Am"

Persons in Communion

The covenant of creation provides the context now for drawing conclusions about what it means to be human, especially to be created in God's image. To be created in God's image is to be persons in communion: with God and one another, as well as with the whole creation.[20] There was no moment when a human being was actually a solitary, autonomous, unrelated entity; self-consciousness always included consciousness of one's relation to God, to one another, and to one's place in the wider created environment.

First, this interpretation strikes at the heart of attempts to ground the image of God in any dualistic opposition between mind/spirit and body. Cornelius Van Til observed:

> Man is not in Plato's cave. . . . Man had originally not merely a capacity for receiving the truth; he was in actual possession of the truth. The world of truth was not found in some realm far distant from him; it was right before him. That which spoke to his senses no less than that which spoke to his intellect was the voice of God. . . . Man's first sense of self-awareness implied the awareness of

20. See Colin E. Gunton, "Trinity, Ontology and Anthropology," in *Persons: Divine and Human*, ed. Christoph Schwobel and Colin E. Gunton (Edinburgh: T. & T. Clark, 1991), 47–61. At the same time, I find such arguments as those employed by Harriet A. Harris (against a purely relational ontology of person) compelling; "Should We Say That Personhood Is Relational?," *Scottish Journal of Theology* 51, no. 2 (1998): 222.

the presence of God as the one for whom he had a great task to accomplish.[21]

One cannot contemplate this covenantal consciousness within ourselves; it is not a *telos* that some arrive at but not others. Rather, it is the common property of every human being, not as a goal but as a fact. Truth is a covenantal and therefore an ethical concept. It is communicated between persons, within a context of hearing and answering.

If we extend this reflection, we could say—and this brings us in line with an argument below—that human beings are those who reflect God's image not chiefly in *what they are essentially* but in *how they reply ethically*. Though determined *as* human persons by the mere fact of their creation as God's image, their *realization of the purpose* of their personhood depends on whether they correspond to God's intentions. We could interject Aristotle for a moment: *good* is teleologically defined. A good watch is one that tells time well. A broken watch is still a watch, but it is not a good one. Similarly, the creation was pronounced good by God at every stage precisely because it "answered back" appropriately. When God said, "Let there be lights in the expanse of the heavens to separate the day from the night" and to serve as "signs and for seasons" (Gen. 1:14), summer was warmer and winter was colder. When God said, "Let the waters swarm with swarms of living creatures, and let birds fly above the earth across the expanse of the heavens" (v. 20), the fish did not despise their lot by trying to become birds, nor did birds covet the sea. So when humans were created, the superlative benediction was God's evaluation of the "answering back" that he heard.

An obvious liturgical motif is at work here, with the divine melody issuing in the antiphonal reply of the creaturely chorus: "'Let there be *x*!' And there was *x*"; "'Let the earth bring forth *y*.' And the earth brought forth *y*." Humanity was created as the cantor, to conduct the choir and symphony in celebration of God's creation-work (see, for example, Ps. 29:1–11). Throughout the Psalter, creation imagery blends with God's enthronement in Israel: "Clap your hands,

21. Cornelius Van Til, *The Defense of the Faith* (Philadelphia: Presbyterian and Reformed, 1955), 90.

504

all peoples! Shout to God with loud songs of joy! For the LORD, the Most High, is to be feared, a great king over all the earth." Just as he subdued the watery chaos in the beginning to create space for covenant fellowship with his vice-regent, "he subdued peoples under us, and nations under our feet. . . . For God is the King of all the earth; sing praises with a psalm!" (47:1–7). In the history of redemption, Israel interprets its exodus from the waters of destruction, conquest of the defiling serpent, and entrance into the promised land for its mission of extending God's glory from Zion as fulfilling the original intention of creation.

The Image-Bearer's Covenant Response

Throughout the biblical narrative, the human servant of Yahweh is the one who answers back to the commission of the Great King, "Here I am." The Hebrew idiom "Here I am" (*hinah*, "behold," plus *ni*, "me"), and its New Testament Greek equivalent (*idou*, "behold," plus *ego*, "me"), is the typical marker of covenantal response on the part of God's servants. In fact, the flight of Adam and Eve from the divine call, "Where are you?" (Gen. 3:9), is contrasted with the "Here I am" of Abraham, Moses, Samuel, Isaiah, Mary, and Jesus. The focus in Genesis 1–3 is not on *what* Adam is in his inner essence, but on *who* he is and *where* he is in relation (ethically) to his Maker. By replying, "Here I am," the covenant servant acknowledges the Suzerain's authority. The servant nails himself down, so to speak, vis-à-vis the covenant Lord. That is why the silence of Adam and Eve is so sinister when God called. By contrast, after the angel's auspicious announcement, Mary declares, "Here am I, the servant of the Lord; let it be with me according to your word" (Luke 1:38 NRSV). It is noteworthy that Jesus announces his triumphant arrival in heaven with the words, "Here am I [*idou ego*], and the children whom God has given me" (Heb. 2:13b NRSV). As humanity was created as a word from God, it was intended to respond to God's speaking by repeating back God's Word as its own. The "answering back" in the first instance was the creation itself, but it was meant to be the continual response, though expressed in countlessly diverse ways.

Thus, human existence is *human* regardless, but it is "very good" insofar as humans answer back according to the purpose of their existence. In his first two chapters of Romans, Paul does not claim that the wicked are no longer human persons but stresses that, precisely because they are human persons, they stand under judgment for having forsaken their office. "Here I am," as an answer to the other, is diametrically opposed to the autonomous self that is the product of one's own introspective reflection. We cannot begin to think that we really know ourselves until we know someone other than ourselves. We do not possess ourselves, but were spoken into existence by our covenant Lord. Because we were spoken by the Father *in the Son*, our personhood has a definite content, analogous to (but, of course, not identical with) the Father's begetting of the Son. Human beings are the created effect of God's speech, but the Son is the eternally begotten Word. Furthermore, it is only the Spirit who can open us up to the Father's summons in the brilliance of the Son's glory, so that we answer back according to his Word (Ps. 143:10; Isa. 32:15; 63:14; Ezek. 3:12; Acts 1:8; 2:17; 4:8; Rom. 8:16, 26–27; 1 Cor. 12:3; Gal. 4:6).

The covenantal relationality that is integral to human nature opens us up to say, "Here I am," not only to our Creator but also to our creaturely neighbors. At her creation, Eve is greeted by Adam in a way analogous to God's greeting of Adam. Hence Paul's statement that Eve is Adam's image because she is consubstantial with him in humanity: "In the image of God he created *them; male and female*" (Gen 1:27 NRSV). "This at last is bone of my bones and flesh of my flesh" (Gen. 2:23) is analogous (anthropomorphic) to God's joyful response to his creation of Adam. As Stanley Grenz observes, "Adam's cry of elation resembles the traditional kinship formula, 'my bone and (my) flesh' (cf. Gen. 29:14; Judg. 9:3; 2 Sam. 5:1; 19:12–13), which Walter Brueggemann suggests is actually a covenant formula that speaks of a common, reciprocal loyalty."[22]

This relational—which is to say, covenantal—pattern is undermined by the identification of human identity in general and the *imago* in particular with something in the individual, such as a mind or soul. The mind-body dualism leads us "into the problems of individualism and ecology," as Colin Gunton warns.[23] The tradition from Augustine

22. Stanley Grenz, *The Social God and the Relational Self* (Louisville: Westminster John Knox, 2001), 276.

23. Colin E. Gunton, *The Promise of Trinitarian Theology* (Edinburgh: T. & T.

to Aquinas deepens this tendency and further draws reflection away from the relational aspect of humanness. Stressing "the inner dimensions of the person" and then identifying the vestiges of the Trinity within the human soul (especially in Augustine's psychological analogy), "God's relatedness is construed in terms of self-relatedness, with the result that it is as an individual that the human being is in the image of God, and therefore truly human."[24] The biblical emphasis on the image of God as constituted chiefly in the relatedness of persons to God and to one another (and to the nonhuman world) recedes into the background of an anthropology that is basically oriented toward the inmost being of the individual self (i.e., the soul).

Further Qualifications concerning God's Image

Though hardly an intentional innovator, Calvin broke away from this trajectory at important points. His contributions have enormous significance for how we understand our calling as ministers and how we articulate and apply scriptural teaching on human identity in a society that has no conception of an origin in creation and a goal in the new creation. First, he rejected any theological distinction between "image" and "likeness" in Genesis; they are used as synonyms, for emphasis. From there he turns to a discussion of "the faculties of the soul," and here he is apparently more circumspect than the tradition—his suspicion of speculation once more awakened: "For that speculation of Augustine, that the soul is the reflection of the Trinity because in it reside the understanding, will, and memory, is by no means sound. Nor is there any probability in the opinion of those who locate God's likeness in the dominion given to man, as if in this mark alone he resembled God, that he was established as heir and possessor of all things."[25] Calvin has here rather sharply reduced the traditional list—including the rather widespread consensus that it included humans' dominion. Nor is the image of God an "emanation," he says, "as if some portion of immeasurable divinity had flowed into man."[26]

Clark, 1997), 101.

24. Gunton, *The Promise of Trinitarian Theology*, 49.
25. Calvin, *Institutes*, 1.15.4.
26. Calvin, *Institutes*, 1.15.5.

Second, Calvin argues that the proper seat of the image-likeness is the soul, but he goes beyond the earlier tradition in attributing its glory to the whole person, encompassing both moral perfections and the "goodly beauty" of the body.[27] This is in contrast to Augustine, who asserted that "surely not in the body, but in that same mind, was man made after the image of God."[28] Calvin, instead, held that "there was no part of man, not even the body itself, in which some sparks did not glow."[29] For this reason, "it would be foolish to seek a definition of 'soul' from the philosophers," he says, and then to make this definition the basis for our understanding of the *imago*.[30] At least implicitly, Calvin was criticizing the tradition, represented by Augustine's statement, "For not in the body but in the mind was man made in the image of God."[31]

Third, the true nature of this image "can be nowhere better recognized than from the restoration of his corrupted nature."[32] Rather than speculate about essences and faculties, we should be guided in our reflections on what human beings are by what or who they will be as a result of redemption and the consummation. Eschatology for Calvin does not come later, after the fall, but is already the goal of fulfilled creation. From the redemption of humanity, we discern that "God's image was not totally annihilated," but was grossly disfigured. "Consequently, the beginning of our recovery of salvation is in that restoration that we obtain through Christ, who also is called the Second Adam for the reason that he restores us to true and complete integrity."[33] Thus, redemption is at least in part understood in terms of "putting on" Christ: "Put on the new man, who has been created according to God" (Eph. 4:24).[34] Christ is the eternal Image of the

27. Calvin, *Institutes*, 1.15.5; see also 1.15.3.

28. Augustine, *Homilies on John's Gospel*, in *Lectures or Tractates on the Gospel according to St. John*, ed. Philip Schaff, trans. John Gibb and James Innes, Select Library of the Nicene and Post-Nicene Fathers of the Christian Church 7, 1st ser. (Grand Rapids: Eerdmans, 1956), 155.

29. Calvin, *Institutes*, 1.15.3.

30. Calvin, *Institutes*, 1.15.6.

31. Augustine, *Homilies on John's Gospel*, 19.

32. Calvin, *Institutes*, 1.15.4.

33. Calvin, *Institutes*, 1.15.4.

34. Calvin, *Institutes*, 1.15.4.

Father by nature, while in him we are the Father's image by creation, fulfilled eschatologically by adoption (and the justification, sanctification, and glorification that belong to it). The understanding of *image* is therefore to be sought not through speculation concerning a distinctive faculty within us, but by learning from eschatology the identity of the second Adam in whom the image is fully expressed: "Now we see how Christ is the most perfect image of God; if we are conformed to it, we are so restored that with true piety, righteousness, purity and intelligence we bear God's image."[35] Calvin rejects both Augustinian speculations concerning a "trinity" of the soul as well as Neoplatonic emanation.[36] Even the restoration of the image does not consist of a divine "inflowing of substance, but the grace and power of the Spirit. For he says that by 'beholding Christ's glory, we are being transformed into his very image . . . as through the Spirit of the Lord' [2 Cor. 3:18], who surely works in us without rendering us consubstantial with God."[37] Inevitably, this shift from locating the image of God in a part or faculty (i.e., spirit or intellect) to the covenant and commission given to humanity by God marked a significant transition in anthropology from what humans are in their inner essence to their identity before God as responsible creatures in history.

God's Image: Gift and Task

So according to the biblical account, the image of God is not something that human beings possess somewhere within, but is the office that they hold together with the attributes appropriate to that office—namely, "true righteousness and holiness" (Eph. 4:24; cf. Luke 1:75).[38] It is a gift, but also a task. Confirmation in this status was held out as the future glorification of the victorious servant. Human beings

35. Calvin, *Institutes*, 1.15.4.
36. Calvin, *Institutes*, 1.15.5.
37. Calvin, *Institutes*, 1.15.5.
38. See also WCF 4.2: In Adam, human beings were "endued with knowledge, righteousness, and true holiness, after His own image; having the law of God written in their hearts, and power to fulfil it: and yet under a possibility of transgressing, being left to the liberty of their own will, which was subject unto change. Beside this law written in their hearts, they received a command, not to eat of the tree of the knowledge of good and evil; which while they kept, they were happy in their communion with God, and had dominion over the creatures."

are more advanced in problem-solving, evaluating, communicating, and creating societies, but piles of scientific data suggest that our fellow creatures, from octopuses to orangutans, possess intelligence. We are creatures in time, and not even the highest creature, since God made us "a little lower than the heavenly beings" (Ps. 8:5a). Contemplating merely that part of the vast universe evident to the naked eye, the psalmist felt small and insignificant (vv. 3–4). Yet in spite of his apparently slight place in nature, God has consecrated him for a great task: "You . . . *crowned* him with glory and honor. You have *given him* dominion over the works of your hands; you have *put* all things under his feet" (vv. 5b–6). The uniqueness of humankind is a gift, not a given. Our true uniqueness can be discovered only in relation to God, as we are covenantal servants and ambassadors, created to lead the vast choir of creation in its "Hallelujah" chorus.

The marks of the image of God may be expressed in terms of what is usually connected with the threefold office of *prophet*, *priest*, and *king*. Bavinck explains concerning this original calling: "As prophet, man explains God and proclaims his excellence; as priest, he consecrates all that is created to God as a holy offering; as king, he guides and governs all things in justice and rectitude. In all this he points to One who in a still higher and richer sense, is the revelation and image of God, to him who is the only begotten of the Father, and the firstborn of all creatures. Adam, the son of God, was a type of Christ."[39] And it is now the image of the glorified Son, our Savior, that becomes both the template that we set before our congregations and the present reality that challenges despair. Like ourselves, those whom we shepherd remain simultaneously justified and sinful, and we can pastor with patience and hope only because we know that God brings to completion every good work that he has begun (Phil. 1:6).

None of these aspects of the image-office was left unscathed by the fall, and at the same time, none has been entirely lost. No one can escape the reality of God in his or her experience, because no human existence is possible or actual apart from the ineradicable covenant identity that belongs to us all, whether we flee the summons or reply, "Here I am."

---

39. Bavinck, *Reformed Dogmatics: Abridged*, 328.

Key Terms

covenant
eschatology
image of God
telos

Recommendations for Further Reading

Hoekema, Anthony A. *The Bible and the Future*. Grand Rapids: Eerdmans, 1994.

Horton, Michael S. *Covenant and Eschatology: The Divine Drama*. Louisville: Westminster John Knox, 2002.

Ridderbos, Herman N. "Fundamental Structures." In *Paul: An Outline of His Theology*, translated by John Richard de Witt, 44–90. Grand Rapids: Eerdmans, 1975.

Vos, Geerhardus. "Eschatology in the New Testament." In *Redemptive History and Biblical Interpretation*, 25–58. Phillipsburg, NJ: Presbyterian and Reformed, 1980.

———. "The Structure of the Pauline Eschatology." In *The Pauline Eschatology*, 1–41. Phillipsburg, NJ: Presbyterian and Reformed, 1991.

Discussion Questions

1. Although eschatology's scope is frequently limited to events yet to come, how does Scripture present an eschatological orientation from the very beginning?

2. How do the unique roles of Adam and Christ orient a thoroughly biblical eschatology? See Romans 5:12–21 and 1 Corinthians 15:20–49.

3. How does eschatology inform the way that we think about humanity and the image of God, as well as the covenant?

4. Discuss the significance of expanding our notion of eschatology for pastoral ministry, including matters such as human identity, purpose, and significance.

5. How does eschatology inform biblical ethics, beyond the law, with a notion of the *good*?
6. How should the offices of prophet, priest, and king, fulfilled by Christ, shape our eschatological calling?

26

SINCLAIR B. FERGUSON

Teacher, Pastor, Preacher, Author

CHAD VAN DIXHOORN

Sinclair Buchanan Ferguson, born February 21, 1948, to Robert and Emma, was raised in Glasgow, Scotland's largest and friendliest city.[1] Sinclair's parents were hardworking people who offered a caring

1. I have limited this biographical sketch to those details that Sinclair Ferguson has offered in print and in public interviews. While Ferguson's writings are not self-referential, he offers a smattering of personal recollections as illustrations in his essays and more popular books. His least explicitly autobiographical works are his study of the Holy Spirit and four New Testament commentaries, although here especially his doctrinal and biblical expositions of the Christian life exemplify the spiritual dynamics of his own life and thought, and here, too, he smuggles in a few references to topics close to his heart, such as Scotland and golf, e.g., Sinclair B. Ferguson, *Let's Study Ephesians* (Edinburgh: Banner of Truth, 2005), 2, 10. Oral sources included two interviews: "In Conversation with Sinclair Ferguson," an interview with Dan Pugh, 2018, accessed August 14, 2020, https://www.youtube.com/watch?v=AEJJDNXqFhw (hereafter "Interview with Pugh"); and a two-part autobiographical reflection by Sinclair at the Charlotte campus of Reformed Theological Seminary, "Preaching the Word: Reflections at Sixty" as an installment in the RTS "Special Seminars in Pastoral Ministry," accessed August 14, 2020, https://podcasts.apple.com/us/podcast/preaching-the-word-reflections-at-sixty/id378879868 (hereafter "RTS Reflection 1" and "2"). My own interviews in June and July 2020 with two generous friends, Steven J. Lawson and Derek Thomas (about his writing and public ministry), and Sinclair's second son, Peter Ferguson, chiefly address matters relating to Ferguson's public ministry. Sinclair's own help was not solicited because this volume was designed as a surprise.

home for their two boys. Sinclair recalls playing conkers with other young friends and reading books by the family's "electric fire."[2] His was "a relatively sheltered life" in a morally ordered environment with clear, if unwritten, household rules.[3] One rule was that he and his elder brother, Kenneth, were forbidden to attend the "Old Firm" football games, for the renowned Glaswegian friendliness was sometimes suspended during these important sporting events.[4]

It was not a home untouched by hardship. Sinclair's parents had no real opportunities for social or economic advancement. Their "formal education . . . had ended around the age of fourteen." Indeed, no one in his "family tree . . . had ever gone to university."[5] This did not hinder originality, however, and Sinclair would remember some of his father's more memorable homemade lines, including the sharp comment that his son's head was "full of broken glass," clearly a reflection on Sinclair's at-times-fragmented thoughts.[6] But Robert Ferguson had had a harrowing childhood, and even as an adult he found speaking difficult and conversation awkward.[7] The family was of very modest means, and Sinclair recalls his mother's care of the home, washing laundry by hand,[8] while ensuring, with her husband, that their sons had the basic resources to follow their more important interests—in Sinclair's case, providing the few pounds per year necessary to play golf.[9]

Christian influence came to Sinclair at an early age. Like many of their neighbors, the family kept a Sunday Sabbath—a joyless, tedious affair for Sinclair until he became a Christian, at which point the first

---

2. Sinclair B. Ferguson, *From the Mouth of God: Trusting, Reading, and Applying the Bible* (Edinburgh: Banner of Truth, 2014), 177; Sinclair B. Ferguson, *Faithful God: An Exposition of the Book of Ruth* (Bridgend, Wales: Bryntirion Press, 2005), 110–11.

3. Sinclair B. Ferguson, *Child in the Manger: The True Meaning of Christmas* (Edinburgh: Banner of Truth, 2016), 16; RTS Reflection 1; Sinclair B. Ferguson, *In Christ Alone: Living the Gospel-Centered Life* (Orlando, FL: Reformation Trust, 2007), 175.

4. Ferguson, *Child in the Manger*, 16.

5. Ferguson, *Child in the Manger*, 62.

6. Sinclair B. Ferguson, *To Seek and to Save: Daily Reflections on the Road to the Cross* (N.p.: Good Book Company, 2020), 17.

7. RTS Reflection 1.

8. Sinclair B. Ferguson, *The Grace of Repentance* (Wheaton, IL: Crossway, 2010), 32.

9. RTS Reflection 1.

day was transformed into his favorite day of the week.[10] The family also had his grandmother's Bible, and when "scarcely able to read," Ferguson would hunt through the pages to find the life stories of exciting figures such as Joseph and Daniel.[11] He was exposed at age seven to some details of the story of Ruth in a woman's magazine to which his mother subscribed.[12] These were hints of a life to come—Sinclair's reading everything he could get his hands on: the few books in the house, the magazines and newspapers that the postman delivered, and shelves of books in the local library.[13]

Significantly, his parents thought it "part of a 'decent upbringing' to send" him to the Sunday school of the church at the end of the street.[14] He behaved badly. But he enjoyed the songs and in time was impacted by the character of some of his teachers.[15] During the week, Scripture was read in morning assembly in the state primary school,[16] and children learned inspiring passages such as the Beatitudes by heart at age seven.[17] Indeed, religious instruction in the public schools at the time would "sometimes amount to no more than memorizing passages of Scripture."[18] Ferguson found it hard to sit still in class, but there was evidence of thoughtfulness beneath the restlessness.[19] He recalls that from the time he "was a little boy," nothing fascinated him "more than the knowledge of God."[20] And "as a young boy, when capital punishment was still administered in the United Kingdom," he "used to waken with a sense of horror on the rare morning when an execution was to take place," reflecting on what it might be like to

---

10. Sinclair B. Ferguson, *Devoted to God: Blueprints for Sanctification* (Edinburgh: Banner of Truth, 2016), 49–50, 269.

11. Sinclair B. Ferguson, *Daniel*, Preacher's Commentary 21 (Nashville: Thomas Nelson, 1988), 23.

12. Ferguson, *Faithful God*, 49–50.

13. Ferguson, *In Christ Alone*, 123; Ferguson, *Faithful God*, 50.

14. Ferguson, *Faithful God*, 49; Interview with Pugh.

15. RTS Reflection 1; Ferguson, *Daniel*, 23.

16. Ferguson, *Child in the Manger*, 83.

17. Sinclair B. Ferguson, *The Sermon on the Mount: Kingdom Life in a Fallen World* (Edinburgh: Banner of Truth, 1987), 11.

18. Sinclair B. Ferguson and Derek W. H. Thomas, *Ichthus: Jesus Christ, God's Son, the Saviour* (Edinburgh: Banner of Truth, 2015), 57.

19. Ferguson, *To Seek and to Save*, 31.

20. Sinclair B. Ferguson, *A Heart for God* (Edinburgh: Banner of Truth, 1997), ix.

wake as a prisoner facing such a sentence on that day.[21] With encouragement, Ferguson joined the Scripture Union and began to read the Bible regularly. He was nine years old. For the next five years, he operated on the assumption "that reading the Bible and being a Christian were one and the same thing."[22]

This continued until a series of events changed the direction of his life. As he tells it, in the regular course of daily reading "I was arrested by these words: 'You search the Scriptures because you think that in them you have eternal life; and it is they that bear witness about me, yet you refuse to come near to me that you may have life'" (John 5:39–40).[23] Sinclair realized to his horror that he was not only a person who committed sins, but an actual sinner, and one who had not come to Christ. It was also about this time that he slipped while walking down the street, only to recover his balance and find himself facing a complete stranger who, seeing Sinclair's Bible, challenged him: "Are you saved, son? Are you saved?"[24]

Soon after, he was invited to St. George's-Tron, a city-center church, to hear the gospel preached. Ferguson heard a businessman tell the story of his own testimony (it had to do with good typing!), and Ferguson encountered powerful preaching that penetrated any remaining defenses. He came to Christ shortly before his fifteenth birthday.[25] Ferguson struggled like other young believers at his age about what family and friends might say in response to his profession of faith, and how he might be treated at school—but his path was set.[26] By the time he was sixteen, he had a clear sense that he needed to be a minister (although he was equally clear that he should not teach in a theological seminary!).[27]

---

21. Sinclair B. Ferguson, *The Christian Life: A Doctrinal Introduction* (Edinburgh: Banner of Truth, 1989), 39, first published as *Know Your Christian Life: A Theological Introduction* (Downers Grove, IL: InterVarsity Press, 1981).

22. Ferguson, *From the Mouth of God*, 54.

23. Ferguson, *From the Mouth of God*, 54.

24. Ferguson, *To Seek and to Save*, 55–56.

25. Interview with Pugh; Ferguson, *Faithful God*, 76. The "component parts" of Ferguson's conversion are similar to that of Augustine: reading the Gospel of John, hearing a believer's testimony, and an encounter with impressive preaching.

26. Ferguson, *Child in the Manger*, 2, 150.

27. RTS Reflection 1; Interview with Pugh.

Ferguson's earliest moments as a self-conscious Christian in the public eye were owed to the game of golf. By the time he was an early teen, he was playing as many as twenty rounds of golf per week, and after a period of ambivalence toward the game as a new Christian, he returned to the links.[28] Now a new believer, Ferguson had his character noted in Scottish newspapers. As expected from those who have joined him on the golf course, he featured in headlines ("Ferguson shines at Cowglen"),[29] in photos ("Sinclair Ferguson lines up a putt"),[30] and in glowing commendations ("Sinclair Ferguson . . . emerged as the outstanding home player," "played the course intelligently," "did not falter").[31] But in another column, a commentator saw something more. On a day of personal victories over future professional golfers, a sportswriter noted Ferguson's modesty, for he was "peculiarly lacking in the exaggerated mannerism of his fellow golfers."[32]

Ferguson's character was being shaped by friends, by continual Bible reading, and by his local church. Friends presented a picture of the Christian life that emphasized realistically the path of hard obedience. Studying Romans led to a personal discovery that there was a shape to the Bible as a whole.[33] And he was overjoyed to hear in a sermon that Christ was *in him*! After one such discovery (first making sure that no one was looking), he skipped and danced all the way home.[34] So great was his desire to see Jesus that he began to dream of heaven—only to awaken on one occasion with the embarrassing realization that in his dream he had been rude, pushing past welcoming friends in his eagerness to be near Jesus.[35]

Ferguson was also impacted by the books he was reading. He had been reading everything that the library could offer on golf.[36] Now he devoured books about the Bible and the Christian faith. Sinclair was

---

28. RTS Reflection 1.

29. *Glasgow Herald*, August 4, 1965, 6; *Evening Times*, April 16, 1965, 32.

30. *Evening Times*, August 4, 1965, 20.

31. *Evening Times*, August 16, 1965, 18; April 16, 1965, 32.

32. *Glasgow Herald*, August 16, 1965, 4.

33. Ferguson, *In Christ Alone*, 39.

34. Ferguson, *Devoted to God*, 67–68.

35. Sinclair B. Ferguson, *Love Came Down at Christmas: Daily Readings for Advent* ([Epsom, UK]: Good Book Company, 2018), 135.

36. RTS Reflection 1.

deeply moved by one of the first Christian books he ever read, and here, as elsewhere, his heavenly Father's guiding hand was on him.[37] In the 1960s, evangelical Christians had far fewer reading choices than do Christians today, and with Ferguson's voracious appetite for books, he could easily have selected less helpful and more readily available material.[38] But he did not. He spent his whole allowance on J. B. Phillips's paraphrase of the book of Revelation.[39] He read Elisabeth Elliot, Howard Guinness,[40] the Scots Confession,[41] and Bonhoeffer's *Cost of Discipleship*, the last a parting gift from a Christian high-school teacher.[42] He bought a "Promise box" with Bible verses to memorize on encouraging themes.[43] By his later teen years, he was reading John Newton,[44] John Murray, and John Calvin, and, of course, he was continuing to read John the apostle.[45]

He met John Owen at age seventeen, the same year that he met Dorothy May Allan.[46] The latter, in all likelihood, starred as the imaginary young woman whom an imaginary young man falls in love with in one of Ferguson's illustrations of the saints' love for God: "You are a young student who has just fallen in love. You return to your dorm. Your friends, who know the name of the girl you were with, want to know where you have been and what you have been doing for the past four hours. You say, 'We haven't actually been doing anything.' Then they say, 'You can't spend four hours not doing anything.'" To which the young man responds inwardly, "I have never experienced anything quite like this! I feel I could explore her mind and soul without intermission. And even then I feel there would be more to know and adore."[47]

---

37. Ferguson, *In Christ Alone*, 18.

38. RTS Reflection 2.

39. Ferguson, *From the Mouth of God*, 177.

40. Ferguson, *Love Came Down*, 25.

41. Ferguson, *From the Mouth of God*, ix.

42. Ferguson, *To Seek and to Save*, 57.

43. Ferguson, *In Christ Alone*, 141.

44. Sinclair B. Ferguson, *Some Pastors and Teachers: Reflecting a Biblical Vision of What Every Minister Is Called to Be* (Edinburgh: Banner of Truth, 2017), xiii.

45. RTS Reflection 2.

46. Sinclair B. Ferguson, *The Trinitarian Devotion of John Owen*, Long Line of Godly Men Profile (Orlando, FL: Reformation Trust, 2014), preface.

47. Ferguson, *Some Pastors and Teachers*, 459.

Ferguson's parents had been preparing him for further education from the time he was a child. He spent "five (miserable) years studying French."[48] And from the age of eleven he learned Latin—a more obvious blessing to him once he began to read Owen, who not only included Latin quotations in his works, but wrote even his English sentences in a Latinate style.[49]

At age seventeen, Ferguson went to Aberdeen. The University of Aberdeen, founded in 1495, offered the only choice, by process of elimination, for someone with Ferguson's background intent on attending one of Scotland's ancient universities: Glasgow University was too close to home and would not broaden his experience; the golf at St. Andrews might distract him from his calling as a student; and Edinburgh was not Glasgow (reason enough for any Glaswegian).

It was thrilling to be at Aberdeen, studying subjects of interest and being loved by Christians intent on mentoring young persons such as himself.[50] But most significantly, it was at Aberdeen that Ferguson entered the orbit of William Still. In God's "divine strategy" for his life, the young student was drawn to the ministry of a man who, for the next thirty years, would find opportunities to pour himself into Ferguson.[51] Still's model for ministry—prayerfulness and devotion to the Word—solidified Ferguson's own priorities for the Christian life and ministry. Ferguson not only encountered Still, but also heard John Murray ("a kind of Alice in Wonderland experience"), John Stott (a superb "exegetical homiletician"), Eric Alexander (an "awesome" address on revival), and Martyn Lloyd-Jones. Murray was the most impressive living theologian that Ferguson had ever met, and the preaching of all these men was powerful. Later, as a young minister, Ferguson was to relish the privilege of spending a few days with Stott (who appreciated Ferguson's preaching as well), hearing Alexander pray for his congregation before a service, and ministering at a conference in Wales with Lloyd-Jones ("one of the high privileges

48. Ferguson, *Love Came Down*, 14.

49. Ferguson, *Trinitarian Devotion of John Owen*, preface.

50. Sinclair B. Ferguson, *Undaunted Spirit: The Life and Testimony of Gordon Anderson-Smith* (Edinburgh: Rutherford House, 1988), 13; Ferguson, *Some Pastors and Teachers*, 458; Ferguson, *In Christ Alone*, 167.

51. RTS Reflection 2.

of my life").[52] Ferguson noticed in Still the same apostolic priorities that he witnessed in the other great men he admired: they "devoted" themselves "to prayer and to the ministry of the word" (Acts 6:4).[53] Although it took a shy young Ferguson eighteen months before he had his first conversation with his new pastor, the influence of William Still on Ferguson's life would rank second only to Dorothy's.[54]

Ferguson earned an MA at age twenty from the University of Aberdeen. Three years later, in busy 1971, he earned a BD at Aberdeen (with a fistful of prizes), and began serving as assistant minister at St. George's-Tron Church, the church in which he had been converted. There, among other tasks, he preached at daily morning services before the start of the workday.[55] Best of all, it was in 1971 that he married Dorothy, the much-praised wife given special honor in four decades of published prefaces and introductions. Prize money paid for the honeymoon.[56]

The Rev. Ferguson's first solo pastoral charge was as minister at St. John's, Baltasound, meeting in a small nineteenth-century church building about the same size as a larger American home. Baltasound is a northern settlement and former fishing town on the windswept isle of Unst, itself in the very north of the ruggedly beautiful Shetland Islands. Unst is far enough north that the sun does not quite set in the height of summer or quite rise in the dead of winter. When darkness did descend in the winter, "it was impossible to see the fingers on one's hand, or the features of someone near enough to touch." Ferguson notes that "conversation in the dark could be an eerie experience."[57]

A family member observed that Unst is not in the middle of nowhere; it is the end of nowhere—and for that reason it appeared to be a surprising choice for a first parish. But Unst offered a quiet space to grow in ministerial gifts, to read John Owen, and, in time, to commence doctoral research at the University of Aberdeen. Reading

---

52. Ferguson, *Child in the Manger*, 62–63; RTS Reflection 2; Ferguson, *Some Pastors and Teachers*, 613; Ferguson, *Grace of Repentance*, 48.
53. RTS Reflection 2.
54. RTS Reflection 1.
55. Ferguson, *Daniel*, 89.
56. Personal communication with family.
57. Ferguson, *Sermon on the Mount*, 63.

became Ferguson's profession for some years: from 1976, he served on the editorial staff of the Banner of Truth Trust, based in Edinburgh. During this time, the Ferguson family faced losses and moved several times, but Ferguson's work on his favorite Puritan culminated in the award of a PhD from the university in 1979 for his more than five-hundred-page thesis on John Owen. These were still relatively early days for the academic study of Puritan theologians, and the subtitle shrewdly implied the importance of the subject by appealing to Owen's own political and academic accomplishments.[58] Ferguson was still at the Trust in 1982 when he was called to serve as a professor of systematic theology at Westminster Theological Seminary, where he labored for sixteen years—his longest tenure in any one place.

It was a plausible time to move a family, although challenging with four children under ten or eleven years of age. Philadelphia's sports teams were having a rare good year, and the older children were impressed with their new city. But Sinclair's mother had a stroke while visiting, and it soon became clear that with no other surviving relatives to care for her,[59] the family would need to move back to Scotland. Sinclair would remain in Philadelphia for weeks at a time during term time, hurrying off campus in late afternoons to speak with Dorothy on the telephone before she went to bed, and "commuting" back to Glasgow as often as possible. While stateside, he became a fixture in the Edgar home, discussing theology with Bill over dishes each night after enjoying Barbara's cooking. Out of term he would return home to Glasgow, preaching, playing golf, writing, and spending time with the family. Dorothy and the children, benefiting from a strong ministry at St. George's-Tron, continued under the arrangement with courage and forbearance. As one child recalls these years, the foundations of faith were persuasively presented as unshakable, helping them manage life with a father often an ocean away.

---

58. Sinclair B. Ferguson, "The Doctrine of the Christian Life in the Teaching of Dr. John Owen (1616–83)—Chaplain to Oliver Cromwell and Sometime Vice-Chancellor of the University of Oxford" (PhD diss., University of Aberdeen, 1979).

59. Both father and brother passed away while Ferguson was writing his thesis on Owen. See Ferguson, "Doctrine of the Christian Life in the Teaching of Dr. John Owen," ii. Also on the loss of Kenneth, Sinclair B. Ferguson with Alistair Begg, *Name above All Names* (Wheaton, IL: Crossway, 2013), 12.

Since those days, Ferguson's family has grown, with the addition of three daughters- and one son-in-law, and grandchildren. Over the years he has served as a visiting lecturer or guest professor at dozens of seminaries as well as Reformation Bible College, where he developed a special friendship with R. C. Sproul. Ferguson has also since served as senior minister of two other churches: as minister of St. George's-Tron (1998–2003), following Eric Alexander, and again at First Presbyterian Church in Columbia, South Carolina (2005–13). Ferguson has also had two more stints as a professor of systematic theology: first, and for much of it bivocationally, at Westminster (later Redeemer) Theological Seminary in Dallas (2003–16), and more recently at Reformed Theological Seminary, with campuses ranging from Mississippi to Washington, D.C. So, having retired from his pastoral ministry in Columbia, he has maintained North American connections with RTS and as a Ligonier Teaching Fellow, while also returning to teach for Westminster Seminary. But it was in Glasgow and Baltasound, and then at Westminster Theological Seminary, that Ferguson had his first opportunities to flourish as a preacher and teacher of the Word.

As this "résumé" suggests, and as readers will be reminded in what follows, Ferguson has proved to be a very productive servant. This may have something to do with his caffeine consumption (mention of coffee comes up in many stories and varied settings), and with his commitment not only to work but to rest. Sometimes books were written on overnight flights.[60] At other times, novels and nonfiction were read and vacations enjoyed in Scotland.[61] But Sinclair has also always been consciously committed to writing (and, we might add, speaking) amid the pressures of other ministry demands, trusting that the Lord would use these opportunities to stretch him and bless others.[62]

A study of Ferguson's life and thought is a real desideratum. What follows is an impressionistic portrait of a man's ministry, a man who

60. Ferguson, *Some Pastors and Teachers*, 754; Sinclair B. Ferguson, *By Grace Alone: How the Grace of God Amazes Me* (Orlando, FL: Reformation Trust, 2010), 15–16.

61. Ferguson, *By Grace Alone*, 7, 109; Ferguson, *Daniel*, 13; Lynn Nickles, "The Only Thing That Matters," *Reach Out Columbia*, November 2009, 6.

62. Ferguson, *Some Pastors and Teachers*, xii–xiv.

is at once a teacher, pastor, preacher, and author (and all of that without a modern "ministry monetizing mentor"!).[63] Family and friends may conclude that this sketch does not do true justice to its subject; I myself feel keenly its inadequacies. But sometimes a picture poorly drawn provokes a gifted artist to pick up a pencil or brush and offer a truer likeness. Perhaps this essay will prompt Sinclair, or a scholar who better understands him, to write the intellectual biography that his life and ministry deserve, and that those who have learned from him desire.

Teacher

Generations of members and ministers have now sat under Professor Ferguson's ministry, and for those who received training for the pastorate under his watch, the experience was unforgettable. First, there was prayer at the beginning of each class. Praise and petition were offered to our Father in heaven, with assurance that it would be heard. A holy God who is wholly other was addressed in these prayers. And yet this communion with God evidenced a confidence that God is both a mighty Savior and a compassionate Father who understands the weakness of his children. Together we approached the throne of grace in Jesus' name and the Spirit's power, finding Christ sufficient not only for our sin, but also for our faults, for our foolishness, and in all our suffering. I have found Sinclair all too willing to announce that he was never a great classroom teacher, and it must be admitted that he toted only a modest bag of tricks when it came to holding the attention of students. But he did not need techniques to teach us about God. He had us halfway to heaven in the opening prayer. More than one student thought that to be so led into the presence of God was itself worth the price of tuition.[64]

63. Note his horror of the idea in Sinclair B. Ferguson, *In the Year of Our Lord: Reflections on Twenty Centuries of Church History* (Orlando, FL: Reformation Trust, 2018), 216n4.

64. Ferguson was (at least) once asked to write a book on prayer. He recalls feeling "flattered" but opting to offer a roster of better-qualified authors to perform the task. He was then amused to hear that they had all been approached first, before the publisher came to Ferguson himself. Ferguson, *In Christ Alone*, 145.

This was not true for everyone. A subset of students for whom English was a second language sometimes lost their way in the opening prayer. The Scottish dialect envied by preachers felt like one more language to master after Hebrew and Greek for a few foreign nationals, especially for those who, in refining their spoken English, had made the common mistake of watching television produced in Hollywood instead of Glasgow.

Ferguson could be mischievous about his accent, and in the classroom it could afford comic relief as he attempted to pronounce a repeatedly misunderstood word in his best American accent. But it was his true delight if, when teaching and preaching, his hearers would "cease to notice the accent and hear only *His* accent."[65] It was a hope, and perhaps a prayer, that was often answered. Nonetheless, for some students "underground" lecture transcripts were essential: collections of word-for-word transcriptions of past Ferguson lectures circulated among the student body, thus guiding generations of first-years into patterns of theology and occasional heresy set by the typists, many of them admired more for the length than for the accuracy of their transcriptions.

In dealing with students from all quarters, Ferguson was gentle, and whenever possible would call on students by name. I took six or seven courses with Ferguson, and I do not recall his ever rebuking a student, even though there seemed to be one or two each year who needed remedial assistance with their manners, and even though an eyebrow may have lifted slightly when students began with an innocent "I feel . . ." instead of the preferred "I think."

Professor Ferguson was also patient with those who relished theological controversy. He himself was reluctant to engage in conflict, but not unwilling. When a defense of the truth was needed, he would rise to the task. His sustained, intelligent opposition to the New Perspectives on Paul in his classroom lectures is a case in point. But he had to be sure that the conflict served a constructive purpose. When students sniffed the faint odor of a distant skirmish, or spotted a shade of difference between Ferguson and another theologian (past or present), there were always some who were eager to find fodder

---

65. Ferguson, *Some Pastors and Teachers*, 649 (uppercase added for clarity).

for lunchtime debate. The professor's response disarmed whole tribes of would-be polemicists by helping them consider texts and persons with charity and modesty. Should the Westminster Confession of Faith be revised because of its awkward reference to the "regenerate part" of a believer? No, because we need to read each statement in the context of the larger work, as we would want done for ourselves: "I don't think so myself, Jonathan, because I'm capable of reading the statement—'the regenerate part doth overcome'—in the light of what has preceded it: namely, that there isn't a part that is unregenerate."[66] Would the world have been a better place if we had been around to teach our forebears? No, because even our professor did his best work while seated on their shoulders: "It was no loss to the Westminster divines that Sinclair Ferguson was not one of them, saying, 'Excuse me, brethren, but can't we just change this a bit, because I think it's a slightly infelicitous way of putting it'!"[67] When an error had to be identified, it was discussed with care and understanding and humanity, thus modeling thoughtful criticism of opposing views. And when observations about the modern church were raised, they were offered with modesty: "My own feeling (!) about what is going on . . ."

Of course, as every student came to discover, question periods with Ferguson came few and far between. Indeed, in one series of lectures the first question came at the end of the third week! Ferguson's lectures tended to be packed with students and auditors, and perhaps began to feel like the conferences at which he spoke. As one would not interrupt a conference speaker mid-address, so few students would dare interrupt Ferguson, who, if not speaking, usually appeared to be deep in thought.

At key junctures in a lecture series, questions were eventually permitted. It was here that the tricks came out of the bag, for what the professor gave with his right hand, he took away with his left. Soon after Q&A began, an answer would end with a mild, "Any more questions, or can we go on?" An answer to a demanding or tangentially relevant question would conclude with, "If anyone was interested in a PhD topic . . . ," and the lecture would soon resume. These were his

66. Sinclair Ferguson, "The Westminster Standards," Westminster Theological Seminary Media, tape 9.

67. Ferguson, "Westminster Standards," tape 9.

standard get-out-of-jail cards, and his students will recognize them immediately. But the reason for limiting questions had everything to do with the quantity of material that the professor wanted to impart and nothing to do with his comfort level in answering questions. (In fact, fellow panelists in conferences confess to studying ways to defer to Ferguson because he has the extraordinary ability to pull answers out of his hat and crack the hard nuts with one good tap.) Other more subtle devices kept the question from being voiced in the first instance, such as his wildly optimistic line, "I think you will remember . . . ," even for a matter so obscure that only the most widely read person could have known it and only a photographic memory recall it.

Pride of place among the professor's favorite theologians went to the troika of John Calvin, John Owen, and John Murray—fittingly, each the subject of essays by Ferguson and reprinted in a recent work.[68] While Owen constituted his research focus, Ferguson had clearly absorbed the corpus of the three Johns and utilized this learning in the classroom with remarkable ability. Ferguson's careful use of historical figures, their lives, and their writings resembles his approach to preaching biblical figures, and follows a pattern that he saw in Calvin himself. Calvin "does not say: Look at the passage, see yourself. Rather the dynamic of his application is: Look at the passage, see Jesus; understand the Spirit's ministry: now see yourself." And then Ferguson's observation: "This is a helpful hermeneutical safeguard against unhealthy aspects of a tendency to either moralism or naked exemplarism."[69]

Instruction in theology was enriched by choice quotations and informed by useful concepts—quotes and ideas loaned to the lecturer by Gregory Nazianzen, Anselm of Canterbury, Thomas Boston, Louis Berkhof, Dietrich Bonhoeffer, and C. S. Lewis. Dr. Ferguson also attempted to improve lectures with choice Latin words and phrases. He tended to be more successful in his use of apt illustrations and the deployment of his active imagination.

A UK commercial for a cleaning fluid (Domestos) serves to

---

68. Ferguson, *Some Pastors and Teachers*, chaps. 1–16.
69. Ferguson, *Some Pastors and Teachers*, 105.

illustrate the experience of sanctification, for according to the advertisement, it "reached the parts that other domestic cleaners couldn't reach." Then comes the doctrine: "In a way, this is the picture. . . . The power of sanctification has not yet radically, finally, cleansed every aspect of the individual's life, and will not do so until the resurrection. That's the meaning of the resurrection: it's the consummation of not only redemption and justification; it's the consummation of regeneration and sanctification." And: "Now, if that's true (there is no part of me which is unaffected by sanctification, but correspondingly, there is no part of me in which the germs of defilement have been finally destroyed), then there arises one of the most memorable phrases in the confession: 'there abideth still some remnants of corruption in every part, whence ariseth a continual and irreconcilable war.'" And then comes Ferguson's comment on the Christian's experience—that final, memorable touch in which the professor is also the pastor: "the basic principle that's being underlined here, I think, is fairly patent for all of us: until the believer is finally perfected, it is inevitable that there be irreconcilable war. . . . So what the divines are wanting to emphasize here is the true nature of sanctification. Sanctification is a battle, and believers ought not, therefore, to be surprised that the Christian life is portrayed in Scripture as being a warfare."[70]

Alternatively, a kidnapping imaginatively illuminates the relative freedom of the will: "I might put a gun in your ribs after the class tonight and say, 'Take me to Friendly's and buy me an ice cream,' and you might say, 'I want you to know that I do this only against my will.' (By which you really mean, 'I'm doing this against my better judgment because if I do this, my wife's going to kill me when I get home at eleven o'clock at night.') But you do it willingly." The professor continues, imagination blending with explication: "Yes, there is an external constraint which affects your judgment and leads you to believe that to do this is *wise* willing, but the *will itself* wills to do it, and in that sense, you don't take me to Friendly's for an ice cream against your will; you take me to Friendly's for an ice cream against your better judgment." That said, "you do actually will to do it under all the circumstances that there are. To will to take me to Friendly's

---

70. Ferguson, "Westminster Standards," tape 9.

seems better than getting a bullet between your shoulder blades. That, of course, is only an illustration of the point."[71] It was a good illustration, and no one dared to ask how the professor, having stuck a gun into a student's ribs, could be so poor a shot as to hit him between the shoulder blades!

While the professor offered little by way of useful tips on criminality or self-defense, undeniable strengths and interests of Ferguson's are explications of redemptive-historical realities and applications to church life. Indeed, this is what we came to appreciate as students: a redemptive-historical grounding of a theological topic, moving to an exegetically shaped and historically informed discussion of a given doctrine, and then application. And not just the doctrine, but the glory of the doctrine.[72] Every class offered theology for ministry.

Ferguson became increasingly interested in "the individual's experience in the course of redemptive history" and "the 'already-not yet' dimension of the New Testament's teaching. Christ has won the battle, Christ is still to return, and we live in between the times." Borrowing an illustration from Oscar Cullmann, Ferguson argued that this can be understood "in terms of the difference between D-Day and V-Day at the end of the Second World War. To all intents and purposes, the war was over at D-Day. That was when the decisive battle, from which the enemy forces never could recover, was fought. But in between that D-Day and V-Day when, one might say, the victory was celebrated and universally recognized, there was a lot of bloodshed. But the blood that was shed was shed in the light of the victory that had been won." We must remember that it was, on the Axis part, "resistance against the inevitable, not the conflict of two forces that were equal and opposite."[73] The lesson for Christians is obvious.

Ferguson taught doctrine from the Word, but he also had a special interest in the theology that we ought to learn from God's created order, and from the imprint of the Creator left on the creature. He would sometimes soliloquize on the whole new view of the world

71. Sinclair Ferguson, "The Westminster Standards," Westminster Theological Seminary Media, tape 8.
72. Ferguson, *Heart for God*, 15.
73. Ferguson, "Westminster Standards," tape 9.

that he gained when he came to the realization that the whole of creation is his Father's world. He also taught about the significance of the light of nature and Christian prudence: neither "mandate[s] that the church service in every place in a given country should be at 11 o'clock in the morning, although it's fairly obvious that it should be at 11 o'clock in the morning! But it can be at 9 o'clock in the morning if you're all business executives, and if you're all milking the cows it better be at 11."[74]

Occasionally the professor appeared to descend into pure silliness, but even then, there was a point. I recall a time when laptops were a new addition to Ferguson's classroom experience and keyboards had not yet learned how to be quiet. Ferguson would speak, and then pause; the keyboards would clatter, and then pause. Unable to ignore the strange rhythm, he abruptly began to reflect in a future past tense about a small Midwestern college town where everyone, having been subject to four years of antiphonal response between lecturers and typists, picked up a strange cadence of speech in which they continually uttered half-sentences, paused, spoke, paused. This was only the beginning, and by the time Ferguson was done, world chaos seemed inevitable, all because of the loud computers in those unfortunate classrooms. We were astonished, delighted, and, for those who had typed with reckless oblivion to those around them, chastened. A few people switched to pen and paper. Others plucked at the keys more gingerly than before.

God's gifts of godliness, gentleness, learning, and humorous imagination have combined to make Ferguson not only a treasure to his family, colleagues, and students, but a blessing to a wider Christian public outside the classroom, for he has taught or preached in many countries and on almost every continent. Even before teaching in a theological seminary, he served as a public teacher of the church at large, and it is no secret that securing Dr. Ferguson as a speaker is a prize for any conference. Unquestionably, he is a good speaker. Steve Lawson notes that Ferguson is pastoral in his approach, even disarming. He speaks in a voice that lulls the listener into thinking that

---

74. Sinclair Ferguson, "The Westminster Standards," Westminster Theological Seminary Media, tape 4.

he is speaking just to you, seated in your living room. This engaging personality is aided by the filing system he has between his ears, the scant notes brought to the pulpit, strong eye contact with the pew, and a message that is at once accessible and profound.

Clever people do not always like other people. Thankfully, Ferguson likes people and not simply ideas. In fact, he is an effective conference personality, in part, because he cares about others: those he speaks to, and those he speaks with. Conference speakers who get to know him find that he helps them to relax. Part of this is work: he draws in other speakers and makes them feel at home. Part of this is his mere presence: there is a sense that there is a grown-up in the room, that things cannot get too bad, that even the most unruly Q&A periods will not prove too intimidating, since one can always turn to Ferguson, ask for his thoughts, and reasonably expect to be edified. It is no secret that postconference dinners are equally a highlight for other speakers, as Sinclair relaxes and amuses. R. C. Sproul loved to tell about the time when he was laughing so hard at a Ferguson story that he thought he was having a heart attack and a cardiologist had to be summoned.

Pastor

Ferguson's service as a seminary professor and public teacher has always been interrupted or accompanied by spells as a pastor. Derek Thomas recalls that Ferguson—a friend of many years and fellow pastor of two years[75]—tended to lead from the rear, not the front. He was a peacemaking pastor, apolitical, cheerful, a shepherd both in elders' meetings and with the congregation. Members of congregations where Ferguson served still remember sermon series, personal greetings, prayers, and especially the funerals.

Ferguson has also had a lifelong pastoral concern about doctrine and the "preconditions" needed for the absorption of truth. It was his observation that many people find that a sermon has too much to take in. And yet the problem may actually be that they have nowhere to put what they've received. A preacher can pour down good content,

75. Ferguson and Thomas, *Ichthus*, x.

but the hearers are without the rain barrels to hold it. They hear solid expository sermons, but a preaching ministry can have limited effect without a framework of doctrine to undergird it. A good catechism, or some kind of doctrinal instruction, offers people that structure; to change the metaphor, it offers them the Velcro strips to hold what is thrown at them.[76]

Sinclair cares about doctrinal instruction. He has also had a life-long love for and commitment to evening services. As long ago as his days in Aberdeen, he saw that it was only by the evening service that Christians had put off enough of the worries of the week, and were sufficiently reoriented as pilgrims on the way, that they were finally ready to worship![77] Actually, in Aberdeen, the Saturday evening prayer service was so well attended that the Sunday morning service in Rev. Still's church felt like the Sunday evening service everywhere else.

This kind of ministry and these kinds of concerns bring tangible blessings to a church. There is also the intangible. Ferguson writes that "there are few richer blessings than being in the presence of someone who obviously lives for Christ."[78] This blessing, too, the Lord has extended through Ferguson to the churches where he was placed as a pastor.

Ferguson's pastorates were most obviously focused on the sheep under his care. Nonetheless, he has also long served as a help to other shepherds, offering an informal mobile mentoring service to his peers. Ferguson is a teacher with direct pastoral experience of the challenges of ministry; he experienced difficulties, drew lessons from them, and uses them to help others, sometimes mentioning these lessons in books or sermons.[79] (My own favorite is the parishioner who often encouraged Ferguson to continue his ministry of writing—routinely delivering his comment soon after Ferguson had preached!)[80]

But there is something more. Arguably, it is the years of studying

76. RTS Reflection 2.
77. Ferguson, *Devoted to God*, 49–50.
78. Sinclair B. Ferguson, *Let's Study Philippians* (Edinburgh: Banner of Truth, 1997), 32.
79. Ferguson mentions how the experience of teaching God's Word showed him that the greatest need for Christians is not to understand "'deeper truths' of the gospel" but to grasp the "basic truths of the gospel." Ferguson, *Christian Life*, 1.
80. Ferguson, *Love Came Down*, 115–16.

the Word in order to preach and teach the Word that has had an evident shaping influence on Ferguson's life and thought, offering a spiritual value far exceeding the benefits of mere experience. It was not just the years in the manse, but the miles in the Word that have helped to shape the man himself and to set him apart not only as a pastor among pastors, but as a pastor to pastors. Indeed, if one were to label leaders in the late twentieth century, many would recognize Billy Graham as the evangelist of the evangelicals, John Stott as their public spokesman, and Sinclair Ferguson as their pastor (with Reformed churches functioning as his "core group").

Preacher

At some of the larger churches he served, and even more so at Christian conferences, many people chiefly encountered Ferguson as a preacher—an irony for Ferguson himself, since he finds public speaking hard, and does it only when he must (which is often).[81] Ferguson has preached around the world. His preaching is mentioned in a Christian hip-hop song, and he himself has preached before Queen Elizabeth II, once spending a weekend with the royal family at Balmoral Castle in Scotland: "like watching a TV program all your life, and then discovering you're actually in it. And it turns out not to be a TV program after all, but real life."[82]

Derek Thomas, who has heard countless Ferguson sermons, considers his friend to be a kind of Directory for Public Worship preacher. Following William Perkins's and the Westminster Assembly's guides to preaching, Thomas hears Ferguson expounding a passage, considering its doctrines, and applying it to the hearer. In his study of Ferguson's preaching, David Vanbrugge offers a different take, arguing that Ferguson "does not embrace the entire style of William Perkins . . . nor the homiletical structure of doctrine, explanation, and uses," but rather "reanimates" the Puritan plain style of preaching "by applying the principles of plain preaching to his own context."[83]

81. RTS Reflection 2.
82. Nickles, "The Only Thing That Matters," 6–7.
83. David Vanbrugge, "Sinclair Ferguson: A Plain Preacher," *PRJ* 10, no. 1 (January 2018): 228, 243.

Certainly Ferguson's use of the Puritan sermon style is adaptive, not imitative. The Puritans themselves, as Ferguson sees it, were not clones of William Perkins,[84] and he himself stresses the importance of imagination in preaching.[85] On a more pedestrian note, Ferguson also differs from some of his forebears in that he tends to preach paragraphs where many Puritans would preach verses. And it appears that he turns to the New Testament more often than to the Old (although a short piece on preaching the Old Testament is prized among students and pastors).[86] Ferguson himself is inimitable in his style. But his ability to give his passage the right amount of context, his knack for finding the center of a passage, his ability to help Christian people not only understand but appreciate hard passages—these are the aspects of his exegetical and homiletical endeavors that students seek to imitate.

As a preacher of the Word, Ferguson is also a teacher of doctrine; and as a teacher of doctrine, Ferguson is practical. He applies theology to the mind. Those sitting under his preaching feel like amateur theologians, routinely learning something in each sermon that they did not know before it began. But these are not doctrinal lectures abstracted from life; they are presented as matters of critical importance for one's own life, as well as the lives of others. Most of all, this is doctrine so wonderful that as one follows the preacher, one feels that he or she is getting a momentary glimpse of the glory of God.

In his preaching, Ferguson's "experimental" applications feel natural; they are creative, fluid, and unforced. Unlike the preaching of some admirers of Puritans, there is no guilt in the air after his sermons. The hearer is struck by the strong security of being in Christ, by wonder, joy, and the true privilege of being a Christian. Ferguson preaches the gospel and loves the law, but the law—even something as unpopular as the Sabbath—is presented not as a Christian's burden but as a Christian's delight.[87] Arguably, what is commonly understood as an explosive tension between law and gospel is defused in his mode

84. Ferguson, *Some Pastors and Teachers*, 760.

85. Ferguson, *Some Pastors and Teachers*, 757–58.

86. Sinclair B. Ferguson, *Preaching Christ from the Old Testament* (London: Proclamation Trust, 2002).

87. See esp. Ferguson, *Devoted to God*, 261–70; Ferguson, *In Christ Alone*, 227–29.

of application by the persistence of two doctrinal features. First is an adherence to the indicative-imperative dynamic of the Bible's teaching—what Ferguson often calls the "grammar" of the gospel.[88] This includes how the gospel orders Christian theology and the Christian life: what we must be and do (the imperative) is in response to who God is, what he has done, and what he is doing (the indicative).[89] The second "defuser" is the centrality of the doctrine of union with Christ in Ferguson's thought, evident in his preaching and his writing.[90]

Author

If many Christians know him as a preacher, the widest number know Ferguson as an author, for his essays and books have gone to countless places where the blue blazer and diagonally striped ties have not. A few of these works cover topics that Ferguson taught in class, such as the doctrine of God[91] and the application of redemption.[92] But there is no easy way to categorize the whole of Ferguson's writings or the range of topics they cover. Nor is there an obvious way to keep up with his writing. Ferguson seems to produce printed pages more quickly than many of us can read them.

These pages include scores of short pieces in journals, magazines, and websites, some of them hammered out amid the busyness of an active pastoral ministry. These bite-sized pieces invariably contain nuggets of exegetical, doctrinal, or practical insight—ideas hot from the oven of a busy kitchen, such as the tapestry of topics now

---

88. Ferguson, *To Seek and to Save*, 45–47; Ferguson, *Devoted to God*, 33–34.

89. For the importance of the indicative-imperative for preachers, see Sinclair B. Ferguson, "Exegesis," in *The Preacher and Preaching: Reviving the Art in the Twentieth Century*, ed. Samuel T. Logan (Phillipsburg, NJ: Presbyterian and Reformed, 1986), 193.

90. Abiding in Christ appears as a leading theme already in Ferguson's first book. See *Add to Your Faith: Biblical Teaching on Christian Maturity* (London: Pickering & Inglis, 1980), chap. 3. See also below.

91. Ferguson, *Heart for God*.

92. Ferguson, *Christian Life*; Sinclair B. Ferguson, *Children of the Living God* (Edinburgh: Banner of Truth, 1989); Sinclair B. Ferguson, *The Holy Spirit*, Contours of Christian Theology (Downers Grove, IL: InterVarsity Press, 1996); Ferguson, *Devoted to God*.

presented in *In Christ Alone* (2007), providing a ten-minute read for almost every Sunday evening of the year.

Ferguson is also an accomplished essayist, and his writings include around fifty essays or chapters in books in the last fifty years, the first of which was published in 1971. Many of these are famous in their own right, and are still referenced decades later by those considering topics such as preaching, hermeneutics, and the law.[93] These are some of his best essays, perhaps most worth reading for pastors, since Ferguson was himself bearing the burden and the cares of a shepherd while writing on behalf of fellow shepherds and their flocks. Some of these shorter writings and essays are now being given a renewed lease on life as they are collected, arranged, and published in volumes such as *In Christ Alone* (2007) and *Some Pastors and Teachers* (2017). Readers can only hope that both author and publishers will see the value in such volumes and that the trend will continue.

Ferguson's willingness to assist editors who ask for his contributions to their journals and books speaks to the cooperative side of his writing ministry. The greatest visible monument to his collaborative commitments was his participation, with J. I. Packer and David Wright, in editing *The New Dictionary of Theology*. The most frequent reminder of Ferguson's willingness to promote the research and writing of others is found in the countless forewords, introductions, and book endorsements that bear his name. These short pieces especially exhibit Ferguson's work as a servant to others, as well as the difficulty he finds in saying no when he has the opportunity to advance someone else's work, whether it be a saint in heaven or a young pastor or scholar just beginning to make his way on earth. The least visible work that Ferguson performs with his pen is his continued work with the Banner of Truth Trust, for even after he ceased to be a paid editor for the Trust, he has continued to play a part in guiding books and series of books (such as the devotional Let's Study series) through the press, polishing stronger pieces and more constructively editing the others.

---

93. Sinclair B. Ferguson chapters in *Inerrancy and Hermeneutic*, ed. Harvie M. Conn (Grand Rapids: Baker, 1988); *Theonomy: A Reformed Critique*, ed. William S. Barker and W. Robert Godfrey (Grand Rapids: Zondervan, 1990); Logan, *The Preacher and Preaching*.

Ferguson's own books began to arrive in the 1980s, including *Add to Your Faith* (in place of a book on the Trinity that Sinclair had first suggested!),[94] *The Christian Life, Grow in Grace*, and his enormously helpful *Discovering God's Will*, of all his books the one perhaps most frequently reprinted and translated. Thirteen volumes appeared in that decade (not including the *New Dictionary of Theology*), and twelve in the next. It was in the 1990s that his first coauthored books appeared, as did his most scholarly monograph (*The Holy Spirit* in 1996) and his first children's book. The first decade of the new millennium saw fifteen books, ten of them for children, and the decade that is winding down as I write this chapter has been equally productive, including major new books such as *The Whole Christ* (2016), *Devoted to God* (2016), and a survey of church history, *In the Year of Our Lord* (2018)—so many books in total that Ferguson himself has not managed to keep a copy of each title he has written.[95]

As indicated, the Christian appetite for these books extends well beyond English-language readers. Croatians were the first to have Ferguson translated, but over the years Koreans have been the most insistent on reading him in their own language. Translations in Slovakian, Portuguese, and Chinese lead the way among the approximately twenty languages in which Ferguson's books are known to have appeared thus far. Ferguson once commented, "In some ways it's more moving to see a translation of a book I wrote years ago than to see the first copy of a new book," for a translation offers "the privilege of encouraging people to whom you could never ordinarily minister."[96]

Why is Ferguson so honored as an author? It seems to me that one reason has to do with the admirable clarity of his prose. Chapters make arguments, sections support chapters, paragraphs find their homes in the right places, and sentences have an obvious purpose just where they are. The author does not make the rookie mistake of offering headings in place of transition sentences. Indeed, reading Ferguson makes writing look effortless. Sentences are read twice not because they are unclear but because they are profound.

Structural clarity is further supplemented by a healthy mix of

94. Ferguson, *From the Mouth of God*, xi.
95. Ferguson, *From the Mouth of God*, 42.
96. Nickles, "The Only Thing That Matters," 7.

shorter and longer paragraphs, pithy aphorisms (but not too many), some brief sentences, and well-placed interrogative—the latter often at the beginning of a paragraph or the end of his shorter essays. Each device helps each page to speak to the reader. Questions are anticipated, often put more clearly and pointedly by the author than the reader might have done for him- or herself. All this care makes for user-friendly reading. As J. I. Packer put it, Ferguson feeds sheep, not giraffes.[97]

The effect of this hard work by the author is that key points are driven home, and then lodge with the reader. I can clearly recall the specific occasions when various truths taught by Ferguson struck me for the first time or with renewed force. Some of these points were simple, others profound. Some were doctrinal, others exegetical: I must live with and relate to other Christians as a child of God first, as a Presbyterian second. Legalism and antinomianism are "nonidentical twins from the same womb." John 20 and Acts 2? The one is a sprinkling and the other an outpouring of the Spirit.

In the second place, Ferguson writes with refreshing creativity. It is not that he is without a repository of preferred words ("existential," "literally," "privilege," "extraordinary") and phrases ("warp and woof," "*mutatis mutandis*," "reflect a little," "began to understand," "didn't know him from Adam," "really dawned on me"). He does have them, and they seem to emerge more often in conference settings when he is giving a couple of addresses or in an intensive seminary setting in which the last third of a course is always a little more spontaneous because it is always a little more rushed. He may also have a few go-to illustrations ("where's Waldo?"), favorite passages (perhaps 2 Corinthians 4), and historical themes (the first of Luther's Ninety-five Theses, the opening reflections of book 3 of Calvin's *Institutes*, or stories from *The Pilgrim's Progress* and the tales of Narnia). While I'm at it, there are also familiar gestures while preaching (moving his hands forward at his side with his arms down, as though whacking the door of a car) and meaningless habits (playing with his watch as though he might wind down a sermon in the next ten minutes or so).

97. J. I. Packer, preface to *The Christian Life: A Doctrinal Introduction*, by Sinclair B. Ferguson (Edinburgh: Banner of Truth, 1989), x.

Ferguson's creativity can be seen by comparing his preached expositions to his published commentary. One hears echoes of his famous sermon on Mark 4:35–41, for example, in his *Let's Study Mark*. But Ferguson's associate minister at St. George's-Tron, the Rev. Murdo Maclean, once remarked to me how surprised he was that Ferguson's preached exposition of Mark was entirely independent of what he published, for Ferguson's *Let's Study Mark* had come out at the same time. (The Let's Study volume was itself a light revision of *Understanding the Gospel*, a little-known book destroyed in a warehouse fire in 1989[98] and, at the time of the writing of this essay, ranked as the 6,434,331st most popular book on Amazon—a rare problem for a Ferguson title, but still an achievement for lesser authors.)

Although Christian people will often comment that what they read in Ferguson's books is profound, his pages are not filled with unremitting expositions of texts and truths, all food for the strong. When he offers meat, there is sauce to accompany it. Readers find themselves swimming with the current of the author, not against or across it. Each chapter or sermon, and sometimes each page, is colored with fresh expositions infused with oxygen in the form of a nice turn of phrase or extended metaphor. Ferguson does not see in himself a special facility in generating apt illustrations, but they can hardly be missed by readers.[99] From the Philadelphia Orchestra to the Rolling Stones, from tuning in to the radio to speaking on the radio, Ferguson relates brief stories in tune with people from every walk of life.[100] What is more, these illustrations are truly useful, for the point remains securely attached to the picture, just as the author intends.[101] We hardly have space to mention his use of Christian poetry and hymns (one of which structures a whole book),[102] the smatterings of Latin and Greek for learned readers, and the curious combination of simple book titles with sometimes startling or playful chapter titles:

98. Sinclair B. Ferguson, *Let's Study Mark* (Edinburgh: Banner of Truth, 1999), xii; Sinclair B. Ferguson, *Understanding the Gospel* (Eastbourne, UK: Kingsway, 1989).

99. Ferguson, *Some Pastors and Teachers*, 660.

100. Ferguson, *To Seek and to Save*, 34; Ferguson, *By Grace Alone*, 19–20; Ferguson, *Daniel*, 104; Ferguson, *To Seek and to Save*, 94.

101. Ferguson, *Devoted to God*, 189.

102. Ferguson, *By Grace Alone*.

"The Holy Spirit and his story," "A hidden revival," "Santa Christ?," and "Guess who is out of jail?"

This clarity and creativity is perhaps what makes his occasional critiques of evangelical culture more palatable. But more to the point is the fact that his critiques, his deconstructions and surgeries, always appear to be reconstructive and healing—the third aspect of Ferguson's writing that stands out to me as a reader. There is no heavy-handedness to his assessments of the more questionable trends, unhelpful emphases, or unsanctified practices of the church. Even his little pokes at American Christianity—a practice so common among British authors, not least those conscious of their status as resident aliens[103]—recognize in part that Americans seem to enjoy having their pet foibles lampooned publicly, and in part that they will sometimes listen to a tall Scotsman on points on which they will not hear midsized Americans. And even these critiques soften in time, perhaps because Ferguson self-consciously tries to resist being cynical and clever at the expense of others.[104]

Perhaps Ferguson's earlier work is a little more edgy, vocalizing on the page what might later be reserved for a lecture. It seems to me that in early writing we see more straightforward critique about matters on which later works are oblique. But these are at most shades of change in a ministry of remarkable kindness, in which challenges are not divisive, not intended to help us better critique others or enlarge our tribe; instead, critique is convicting, edifying, helping us to better understand ourselves and follow Christ.

Aside from some disarming charm, what is it that makes Ferguson's call to holiness in life and thought more compelling than threatening? It seems to me that one part of the answer has much to do with his understanding of Spirit-impelled motivations for godliness. As I see it, Ferguson believes that Scripture's most basic motivation for sanctification is identity. We are united to the risen Christ by Spirit-worked faith, and thus we should be what we are. As he explains

103. Ferguson, *Sermon on the Mount*, 9.

104. E.g., Ferguson, *Add to Your Faith*, 3–4. The rewrite of the story omits to specify that an unwise teacher was an American; see Sinclair B. Ferguson, *Maturity: Growing Up and Going On in the Christian Life* (Edinburgh: Banner of Truth, 2019), 3. For caution against cynicism, Ferguson, *In Christ Alone*, 101.

in his chapter "Become what you are," this is "the logic that always marks his [Paul's] teaching on growing in holiness. Our new identity has come through union with Christ in his death and resurrection. The new life, which flows from it, involves putting away . . . everything which is unlike Christ, and putting on . . . the resurrection power of the Lord."[105] This is "a great principle of Pauline theology: union with Christ should lead to the imitation of Christ."[106]

There are, of course, other biblically sanctioned drives toward sanctification (gratitude is one!). And each properly founded biblical impulse toward holiness recognizes the indicative-imperative dynamic already noted as being so pervasively present in Sinclair's preaching. But concentration on our new identity in Christ is particularly helpful in focusing the mind not only on past graces but on present privileges and lived realities. We are new creatures, adopted children, so we must live out the new life that is already ours, no longer living under the shadow of a guilty conscience when we can bask in the full sunshine of our Father's face. But even that is not quite it, for a mere understanding of this structure can still leave hearers unmoved. For many ministers, too often myself included, it is as though we plop a little pile of gospel fact on one end of a lever, and are surprised at the lack of movement at the other end. Ferguson, on the other hand, drops such an enormous view of God on the one end of the seesaw that godliness is propelled with enormous force from the other.

If we are still counting, this consciousness of the privilege of being a Christian—awareness of being sons and daughters of such a God, of being inheritors of this extraordinary self-revelation of God—is the fourth feature that pervades Ferguson's writings. Here we see the Lord working in a life that is all of a piece: in prayer, as a professor separated from his family, as a pastor and preacher, Ferguson exudes an outsized confidence in what God has done, is doing, and will do.

Quite apart from the content of his writing, the very playfulness of some of his prose exhibits joy and thankfulness for the triune God. His celebration of the life of adopted sons and daughters, his gratitude for the Christian's union with Christ,[107] his confidence in

105. Ferguson, *Ephesians*, 122.
106. Ferguson, *Philippians*, 45.
107. For adoption, see Ferguson, *Children of the Living God*. For union with

the eventual triumph of the Holy Spirit in every life that he savingly touches—all of this shouts out to the reader that Ferguson knows, and wants us to know, that it is a great privilege to be a Christian! For the blessings that come from being in Christ "are not benefits to which faith works up, but blessings which are bestowed upon us the moment we belong to Christ. If we are Christians, all of this is true of all of us all of the time!"[108]

Finally, Ferguson deliberately grounds his teaching in the Word of God. His New Testament commentaries (Mark, Ephesians, Philippians, James) are tightly written and keyed carefully to specific paragraphs. His Old Testament studies closely resemble his preached expositions and tend to be "suggestive rather than exhaustive."[109] But no matter what the subject, Ferguson evidences an unembarrassed reliance on Scripture and offers abundant biblical reflection throughout his writings. As Ferguson explained in the introduction to his first book, there are "no short-cuts or instant packages for the Christian life," and so his instructions and exhortations are "based on various important and relevant passages of the Bible."[110] This does not mean that biblical passages are always quoted, are quoted constantly, or when quoted are always quoted in full. Ferguson, along with Calvin, knows how to use biblical paraphrase, for sometimes a restatement or summary of a passage presents a point forcibly and memorably.

Arguably, passages cited are all the more useful because Ferguson does not pile up scriptural proofs like stones without mortar. Instead, like John Murray, he builds with the best bricks for the project at hand, selecting each one with care. Of course, his sentences are often punctuated with scriptural support (most often in his shorter

---

Christ, see Ferguson, *Holy Spirit*, chap. 7. Curiously, and perhaps following John Murray, in expounding the application of redemption in a 1981 work, Ferguson argues for centrality of this doctrine ("union with Christ is the foundation of all our spiritual experience and all spiritual blessings"), but places union in chapter 11, following after his treatment of justification and adoption (but before his chapter on election!). See Ferguson, *Christian Life*, 111. Usefully, in this Ferguson also raises the little-asked question of why or how Paul came to see union with Christ as foundational.

108. Ferguson, *Christian Life*, 110.
109. Ferguson, *Daniel*, 11.
110. Ferguson, *Add to Your Faith*, ix.

essays?), but Ferguson will not infrequently quote relevant parts of a key verse, or explicitly urge the reader to "look it up" or "notice" some feature of the text (more often in his books?).

Aside from biblical poetry, Ferguson avoids the use of block quotations in his later writings. This is no doubt due to a recognition that while writers may indent scriptural passages in order to highlight their importance, readers often skip over these sections, hoping for a summary of the passage in a following line. Presenting scriptural passages in block quotations has the inadvertent effect of minimizing the impact of a biblical passage, and thus Ferguson commonly integrates his quotations in the flow of his prose, forcing the reader to read the words and grasp the meaning of Scripture as expounded by the author. The exceptions to the rule include quotations of biblical poetry and passages that require more extensive exposition (most often in his expositions of biblical books or chapters). A similar restraint with and use of block quotations can be seen in his historical studies of Calvin and others.

But the effect is greater than these various parts. Reading Ferguson, one is left with a growing appreciation for the Scriptures. And as he grew as a theologian and writer, it seems to me, Ferguson increasingly brought into focus the larger sweep of Scripture, leading us through whole books and connecting both Testaments. Reader rejoices with writer that our Father in heaven has given us his Book, a volume that is holy and set apart from all other writings. Reader, following writer, finds new reason to praise God for a Book that bears the Spirit's signature on every line.

Ferguson helps us to see that it is in the Scriptures that we find our true story. It is in this Book that we meet the Creator, the Architect, the Builder of all things. Hard as it is to read (and this, too, is not hidden from the readers of Ferguson's writings), it is in these holy pages that light is shed on the darkness that has overcome every fallen human heart.

If this is who God is, and what we have become, then how great is the story of redemption that we find in Holy Scripture! This is what Ferguson unfolds in one book after another. From the record of Genesis to the prophecy of Malachi, and from the Gospel of Matthew to the Revelation of John, we are taught to see in this Book first a plan and then a history of our salvation. We meet Abraham and Aaron, Samuel and Jehoshaphat, Solomon and Jeremiah. Each of these is a gift to us, presented in God's Word, but pointing to something later and better.

We discover the patriarchs, and yet in reading their history, we do not find in them the spouse for which we yearn. We are presented with priests, but they do not offer the presence we long for, or the one sacrifice we need. We meet judges, but they prove to be unjust kings who were only shadows of the Ruler who must subdue us, rule over us, and protect us from all his and our enemies. Next we encounter the gift of wise men, the greatest pundit of whom fell into the folly against which he warned. Last came the prophets, but they could not persuade a people to turn from their sins. In fact, Jonah could hardly be convinced to preach at all. All of these are given by inspiration to warn us in this life, and to direct us to faith. By God's grace, one of Ferguson's most valuable skills is found in opening up the Scriptures and helping us to see this for ourselves.

But what makes us love Ferguson's writing most of all? Is it not that in leading his readership through this library of books that we call the Bible, he invariably shows us Jesus? Whether it be in expounding the Sermon on the Mount, the Gospel of Mark, or an epistle to the Ephesians or Philippians, or by James, Ferguson introduces us at every turn to the effective Prophet who called us to repentance, the Teacher who astonishes us with his insight, the Bringer of the kingdom, and the Judge of all the world. It is here that we learn of a God coming among us, a High Priest offering himself for us.

When we look at Sinclair Ferguson as a man and minister, the publisher of and contributors to this book see a servant of Christ who has helped us to see the Master. Ferguson takes us through his published pages to much the same spot where we are brought through his prayers. Thankful for the work that God has done in and through our friend, we pray that Christ will teach us by his Holy Spirit to ever live for the same Lord who made Sinclair what he is, and will help us to persevere until the day when we will feast with our Savior, and with every saved sinner, at the wedding feast of the Lamb.

AFTERWORD

Theological Reflections on the True Nature of Friendship

WILLIAM EDGAR

"I wonder what Piglet is doing," thought Pooh. "I wish I were
there to be doing it, too." (A. A. Milne, Winnie-the-Pooh*)*

Sinclair Ferguson has been my dear friend for now nearly three decades.[1] Friendship is without a doubt one of God's greatest gifts. It is opportune, then, in this brief conclusion to the many contributions in honor of our revered mentor and friend to reflect a little on the true nature of friendship.

There is abundant literature on the subject, and the Scripture is replete with examples and directives about friendship. David and Jonathan, Ruth and Naomi, Paul and Barnabas, Jesus and John . . . these friends exhibit the truths that truly "two are better than one" (Eccl.

---

1. When Barbara and I were in Aix-en-Provence at the Reformed Seminary (now called Jean Calvin), someone sent us *Man Overboard*, a series of reflections on Jonah. We were hooked. We started ordering all of Dr. Ferguson's books and would read them after meals. Little did we imagine that we would be moving to Glenside, Pennsylvania, and become not only colleagues but very dear friends. After hearing him preach on Isaiah 6 at Tenth Presbyterian Church, we decided that we didn't want to listen to him anymore. It was so deeply moving and soul-stirring that we weren't sure that we wanted to subject ourselves to such a blessing. Well, we got over it and have listened to him perhaps hundreds of times. Even though the Fergusons and the Edgars now live on different continents, we are still close, and truly love each other.

4:9) and that "there is a friend who sticks closer than a brother" (Prov. 18:24). Not surprisingly, some of the best poets have rhapsodized about friendship. Most of us know the opening lines from Shakespeare's Sonnet 104:

> To me, fair friend, you never can be old,
> For as you were, when first your eye I ey'd,
> Such seems your beauty still.

Enduring friendship in this case will outlast beauty itself, which fades:

> So your sweet hue, which methinks still doth stand,
> Hath motion and mine eye may be deceiv'd:
> For fear of which, hear this, thou age unbred;
> Ere you were born, was beauty's summer dead.

Or we may remember Cicero's *Ode to Friendship*:

> He that is thy friend indeed,
> He will help thee in thy need:
> If thou sorrow, he will weep;
> If thou wake, he cannot sleep:
> Thus of every grief in heart
> He with thee doth bear a part.
> These are certain signs to know
> Faithful friend from flattering foe.

These lines are remarkably prescient of Paul's admonitions to his Roman readers: "Rejoice with those who rejoice, weep with those who weep" (Rom. 12:15), though they lack the apostle's full context, as we will see a little further on.

It seems to me in our world of advanced modernity that one of the victims of the secularization process is the loss of the loftier ideal of friendship. The subject is broad and elusive. Yet I believe there are certain signposts along the way that help illuminate not only where we are, but also how to recapture what has been lost. So here is what I propose. I want to begin with a brief look at one of the hinge figures in the development of secularization, as he reflects on friendship. Then I would like us to look at the reaction of one of his chief critics. And then a few words on where we have gone since, with a final appeal to recover the biblical standard of friendship.

* * *

The literary pioneer of the French Renaissance, Michel de Montaigne (1533–92), wrote one of his most powerful *essais*, titled *De l'amitié*.[2] The essay contains reflections on one of the most famous friendships of the sixteenth century, between the author and Étienne de La Boétie. La Boétie (1530–63) is considered, among other things, the founder of modern French political theory. Tragedy surrounds the friendship, since La Boétie died, not having reached his thirty-third birthday, so that this friendship lasted, at least in the flesh, only two years. How, then, did it become the stuff of legends, which it did?

La Boétie wrote an influential text, *Discours sur la servitude volontaire ou Contr'un*, in 1548, and was soon after made judge in the prominent court system of Bordeaux.[3] Montaigne himself had been a judge in Périgueux, whose court merged with Bordeaux in 1561 (Montaigne eventually became mayor of the city). It is through these circumstances, being thrust together in the government of a local city, that they actually met, although Montaigne had known of La Boétie before meeting him, and had always felt they were kindred spirits. La Boétie contracted dysentery and succumbed in August 1563, having willed all his papers to Montaigne. It is of no small historical interest that the *Discours sur la servitude volontaire* was influential on the cause of religious tolerance in France. Though a Roman Catholic, and in fact never openly favorable to complete religious pluralism, La Boétie called for freedom from tyranny, and his views unintentionally contributed to the desire among many Protestants to rise up in revolt after the Saint Bartholomew's Day massacre of the Huguenots in 1572. Oddly, Montaigne sought to suppress the essay, in order

2. Michel de Montaigne, *Les Essais, livre Ier, chapitre XXVIII*. "On Affectionate Relationships" can be found in an elegant modern translation (except for the title!) by M. A. Screech (New York: Penguin, 1993), 205–19.

3. La Boétie's tract was widely read. An English translation, *The Anti-Dictator*, is available from Columbia University Press, 1942.

to protect his deceased friend's memory from being associated with sedition. In the event, numerous clandestine copies, not all of them faithful to the original, circulated.

Thus, when he arrived in Bordeaux, Montaigne did not hesitate to go and call on La Boétie, already his hero and a model to him (though only two years his elder). In *De l'amitié* he is extravagant:

> If I am urged to say why I loved him, I feel that it cannot be put into words; there is beyond any observation of mine a mysterious, inexplicable and predestined force in this union. We sought each other before we had met through reports each had heard about the other, which attracted our affections more singularly than the nature of the situation can suggest. I believe it was some dispensation from Heaven. When we met we embraced each other as soon as we heard the other's name. . . . We found we were so captivated, so revealed to each other, so drawn together, that nothing ever since has been closer than one to the other.[4]

We are in the sixteenth century, not the nineteenth! The language of "romantic" love has not escaped a host of commentators who would wish to turn this friendship into what it decidedly was not. Montaigne spoke of two souls' being knit together, never of anything indecent. What could have been the source of their genuine mutual attraction? In the rather fanciful series *Le roman des grandes existences*, André Lamandé suggests that this friendship was something like that of an older and a younger brother.[5] Montaigne, he tells us, was at "the age of passions." Driven by voluptuousness and ambition, he wanted to safeguard his liberty in a world of religious hatred and corruption. La Boétie sought to bridle him. Montaigne might have become cynical had he not encountered this wise and virtuous mentor.[6]

The subsequent meetings and conversations, according to Lamandé, revolved around Montaigne's unprincipled love for women, and La Boétie's gentle but firm reproaches for his misadventures.

4. Estienne de La Boétie, *Œvres Complètes* (Bordeaux: C. Gounouihou, 1892), 385.

5. André Lamandé, *La vie gaillarde et sage de Montaigne* (Paris: Librairie Plon, 1927).

6. Lamandé, *La vie gaillarde et sage de Montaigne*, 70–71.

Why does he have to chase after loose women? Why would he even dare go after a married woman? Besides hearing the voice of reason in matters of morals, Montaigne was genuinely drawn to the political views of La Boétie, who tried to steer a balance between a degree of toleration and at the same time promote a Roman Catholic Church in need of purification. Although La Boétie's untimely death deprived Montaigne of the presence of his dearest soulmate, he would continue to celebrate his views and his memory until his own death.

Going deeper, there must be other reasons why this particular friendship stirs the hearts of people even to this day. One of them is surely its modernity. Montaigne's language is decidedly from a world very different from the medieval world he was leaving behind. One of the central portions of the essay is telling:

> Au demeurant, ce que nous appelons ordinairement amis et amitiés, ne sont qu'accointances et familiarités nouées par quelque occasion ou commodité par le moyen de laquelle nos âmes s'entretiennent. En l'amitié de quoi je parle, elles se mêlent et se confondent l'une en l'autre, d'un mélange si universel qu'elles s'effacent et ne retrouvent plus la couture qui les a jointes. Si l'on me presse de dire pourquoi je l'aimais, je sens que cela ne se peut exprimer qu'en répondant: "Parce que c'était lui, parce que c'était moi."[7]

Where can we situate this sentiment within the history of ideas? As the philosopher Jean Brun puts it, whereas Copernicus was extricating man from the center of the cosmos, Montaigne was busy placing him at the very heart of philosophical reflection.[8] In his decidedly modern appeals for tolerance, Montaigne asks his readers to see that truth is primarily a matter of customs, not absolutes derived from

---

7. "In the end, what we ordinarily call friends and friendships, are in reality merely acquaintances and familiarities bound together in certain occasions or conveniences by means of which our souls converse. In the friendship of which I am speaking, they mix and are intermingled one with the other, in a combination so universal that they become effaced, never again to find the seam which has joined them. If someone presses me to say why I love him, I sense that it cannot be expressed except by saying, 'Because it was he, because it was I.'" Montaigne, *Essais*, 144.

8. Jean Brun, *L'Europe Philosophe: 25 siècles de pensée occidentale* (Paris: Stock, 1988), 160.

nature. In a famous essay on education, Montaigne exclaims that what we need is children with beautiful heads, not filled heads.

He was the first to have made his very self the subject of greatest interest. Though a believer in divine intervention, fascinated by freakish events and people, and a critic of the cold scholastic method of antiquity, Montaigne determined that the self is of even greater significance than either *monsters* or *miracles*. He was interested in the forces that shape the human subject: "I do not depict being, I depict the pathway." This radical turn, Jean Brun argues, is the source of the modern jargon about guiltlessness, about authenticity, and about the aesthetics of pathology, exemplified by Maurice Barrès, André Gide, Henry de Montherlant, and even Jean-Paul Sartre. Montaigne's approach may be subjective, but it is light-years away from Augustine's *Confessions*, which understands the self only in relation to God's presence.[9]

The incisive literary critic Erich Auerbach devotes a chapter to Montaigne in his classic, *Mimesis*.[10] He acknowledges in Montaigne a vestige of the Christian awareness of human significance because of being made after the image of God, but places him nevertheless in a modern idea of the human condition. Like the modern scientist, Montaigne subjects the self to innumerable experiments, illuminating the self from every direction. "The result of this is not, however, a mass of unrelated snapshots, but a spontaneous apprehension of the unity of his person emerging from the multiplicity of his observations."[11] The most famous phrase of Montaigne's is likely the most misunderstood: *Que sais-je?* ("What do I know?"). He said it in an extended essay about the Catalan theologian Raymond de Sebond.[12] The title is ironic, for Montaigne is fiercely critical of the pedantic arguments set forth by Sebond, which, he said, amount only to a foolish appeal to a putatively all-wise human being. Instead, how do we really know? It

---

9. Brun, *L'Europe Philosophe*, 161–62.

10. Erich Auerbach, *Mimesis: The Representation of Reality in Western Literature*, trans. Willard R. Trask (New York: Doubleday/Anchor Books, 1957), 249–73.

11. Auerbach, *Mimesis*, 257.

12. Michel de Montaigne, *Apologie de Raymond Sebond* (1573), republished in English as *In Defense of Raymond Sebond*, trans. Arthur H. Beattie, Milestones of Thought in the History of Ideas (New York: Frederick Ungar, 1959).

is most important not to view this as relativism or as raw skepticism. Later, Pierre Bayle could be labeled a skeptic, although even his is not Pyrrhonist. In the event, Montaigne did believe in a good number of the Christian principles from his heritage in the Roman Catholic Church. But he was wary of any kind of human arrogance.

The form of Montaigne's *Essays* is the key to their content. He compares his writing to a musical composition that features variations, surprises, and new developments. As a Renaissance man, he loved quotes, aphorisms, and sources far more than carefully reasoned arguments. In true humanist fashion, he appealed to Plato and other authors of antiquity. And yet, "No philosopher of antiquity, not even Plato in his presentation of the discoursing Socratic style, could write directly out of the will of his own concrete existence, so juicily, so animally, so spontaneously."[13]

We are beginning to get the full picture. What is the world that undergirds Montaigne's extravagant statements on friendship? While surely based on his experience with La Boétie, the paragraphs in the *Essay* go far beyond what could be contained in a single friendship. Montaigne is depicting *la condition humaine*, the world of the subject, eschewing the world of the givenness of revelation. Charles Taylor sees him as enabling the passage from the medieval "porous self" to the modern "buffered self."[14] According to Taylor's historiography, there was a time when it was virtually impossible not to believe in God or the Christian message, because it penetrated our porous selves, whereas the secular age is one in which the Christian faith is only one of many options because the self is buffered, able to withstand the forcefulness of revelation and make its own choices. "Because it was he, because it was I" is the ultimate reason for this particular affection.

* * *

Montaigne's earliest commentators were René Descartes and Blaise Pascal. To the question, *Que sais-je?*, Descartes (1596–1650) answered, "I know what I understand," whereas Pascal (1623–62) would say, in effect, "I know what I believe," or even "I know what is revealed." The

13. Montaigne, *In Defense of Raymond Sebond*, 259.
14. Charles Taylor, *A Secular Age* (Cambridge, MA: Belknap/Harvard University Press, 2007), 539–40.

famous *cogito ergo sum* from the former's *Discourse on Method* is said to have launched modern philosophy. The book's subtitle is telling: *For Conducting Reason and Telling the Truth in the Sciences* (1635). The latter, Pascal, had very few kind words for Descartes. "*Inutile et incertain*," he wrote about him in the *Pensées*. To which he added, "Je ne puis pardonner à Descartes: Il voudrait bien, dans toute la philosophie, se pouvoir passer de Dieu; mais il n'a pu s'empêcher de lui donner une chiquenaude pour mettre le monde en mouvement; après cela, il n'a plus que faire de Dieu."[15]

But of Montaigne, Pascal is more respectful. He does say, frankly, "Les défauts de Montaigne sont grands," because he takes salvation lightly.[16] More pointedly, he criticizes Montaigne's "sot projet qu'il a de se peindre," that is, the foolish project of describing himself.[17] Yet he adds that the foolishness is based on a confused method, rather than simply on selfishness. He otherwise has at least guarded praise for Montaigne. He notes his wisdom, which can be acquired only with difficulty. His faults are easily dealt with. What are they? That he speaks too often of himself.[18] Thus, Pascal could be sharply critical of Montaigne while at the same time appreciating many of his insights. It is likely that Pascal was frustrated by the casual way in which Montaigne could speak of religion, as exemplified in both his content and his style, while at the same time praising his defense of such notions as miracle, and the mystery of God over against rationalism.[19] He also deeply appreciated Montaigne's realism in the face of death. The *Pensées* are full of quotes from the early essay of Montaigne, *Que philosopher c'est apprendre à mourir*. A person ready to face death is

---

15. "Montaigne's faults are great." Nos. 887 ("useless and uncertain"); 1001 ("I cannot forgive Descartes: he would love, in all philosophy, to do without God; but he couldn't help himself from attributing to him a final nudge in order to set the world in motion; after that he had nothing more to do with God"). Several editions of the *Pensées* exist. For our purposes, we refer to the Port-Royal collection, numbered by Léon Brunschvicg, revised by Louis Lafuma, found in *Pascal Oeuvres Completes* (Paris: Seuil, 1963), 501–641.

16. Pascal, *Pensées*, 680.

17. Pascal, *Pensées*, 780.

18. Pascal, *Pensées*, 649.

19. Frank M. Chambers, "Pascal's Montaigne," *PMLA* 65, no. 5 (September 1950): 794–97.

a person who is capable of great piety. Still, in the end, Pascal is not on the same boat as Montaigne. For Montaigne is too easygoing, too nonchalant when faced with life's great looming threats.

What are Pascal's views of friendship? Like Montaigne, he recognizes the mystery of love. Yet he puzzles over how often love can misguide the soul. He says of some love, "la cause est un je ne sais quoi."[20] Yet its effects are "effroyables" capable of shaking the entire earth.[21] Often, the love of neighbor is merely a safe kind of love, an affection for people just like us.[22] At the same time, Pascal heartily recommends true love, love within the bounds of God's own grace. In a spirit very different from Montaigne's, he confesses a love for every redeemed creature. He loves his neighbor in his sinfulness, in his poverty, and not simply in his grandeur. In a magnificent passage, he describes his love for a neighbor as he is, in his need:

> J'aime la pauvreté parce qu'il l'a aimée. J'aime les biens parce qu'ils me donnent le moyen d'en assister les misérables. Je garde fidélité à tout le monde. Je ne rends point le mal à ceux qui m'en font, mais je leur souhaite une condition pareille à la mienne où l'on ne reçoit point de mal ni de bien de la part des hommes. J'essaye d'être juste, véritable, sincère et fidèle à tous les hommes et j'ai une tendresse de cœur pour ceux à qui Dieu m'a uni plus étroitement.
>
> Et soit que je sois seul ou à la vue des hommes j'ai en toutes mes actions la vue de Dieu, qui les doit juger et à qui je les ai toutes consacrées.
>
> Voilà quels sont mes sentiments.
>
> Et je bénis tous les jours de ma vie mon Rédempteur qui les a mis en moi et qui d'un homme plein de faiblesse, de misère, de concupiscence, d'orgueil et d'ambition a fait un homme exempt de tous ces maux par la force de la grâce, à laquelle toute la gloire en est due, n'ayant de moi que la misère et l'erreur.[23]

---

20. Literally, "the cause is I don't know what," or prosaically, "the cause is a mystery."

21. Pascal, *Pensées*, 413.

22. Pascal, *Pensées*, 355.

23. Pascal, *Pensées*, 931. "I love poverty because [God] loved it. I love wealth because it enables me to help the destitute. I stay faithful to everyone. I do not return evil for those who do evil to me, but I wish for them a condition similar to

Here we have a very different vision for friendship from what Montaigne has set forth. It is full of biblical insights. It appears that Pascal has drawn much of this from Paul's appeal to the Romans, mentioned above. At the same time, he has made them personal. And he has expressed Paul's injunctive by wearing his soul on his sleeve. In that way, he has kept Montaigne's subjective sensitivity without slouching into his subjectivism. Indeed, he far more resembles Augustine than Montaigne.

The passage from Romans is worth quoting somewhat fully, as it represents a unity of thought and not simply assembled aphorisms:

> Let love be genuine. Abhor what is evil; hold fast to what is good. Love one another with brotherly affection. Outdo one another in showing honor. Do not be slothful in zeal, be fervent in spirit, serve the Lord. Rejoice in hope, be patient in tribulation, be constant in prayer. Contribute to the needs of the saints and seek to show hospitality.
>
> Bless those who persecute you; bless and do not curse them. Rejoice with those who rejoice, weep with those who weep. Live in harmony with one another. Do not be haughty, but associate with the lowly. Never be wise in your own sight. Repay no one evil for evil, but give thought to do what is honorable in the sight of all. If possible, so far as it depends on you, live peaceably with all. Beloved, never avenge yourselves, but leave it to the wrath of God, for it is written, "Vengeance is mine, I will repay, says the Lord." To the contrary, "if your enemy is hungry, feed him; if he is thirsty, give him something to drink; for by so doing you will heap burning coals on his head." Do not be overcome by evil, but overcome evil with good. (Rom. 12:9–21)

---

my own, where I don't count either on good or evil from men. I try to be just, truthful, sincere and faithful to every human, and I have a tenderness of heart for those whom God has united to me more closely. And whether I be alone or in the sight of other people, I behave entirely as before the gaze of the Lord, who will judge them and to whom I have consecrated them all. These are my sentiments. And every day of my life I bless my Redeemer who has put them in me, and who, out of a man full of weakness, of misery, of concupiscence, pride and ambition, has made a man exempt from all these evils by the strength of his grace, to whom all glory for it is due, contributing from myself only misery and error."

While it is the case that Paul is addressing the Christian community as a whole, and not commenting on individual friendship,
it is instructive to consider that these rules for Christian friendship
should apply to the entire church. As everyone knows, it is easy (or
easier) to love those who love us. Paul himself enjoyed that kind of
love. Indeed, he had a few precious friends and did not mind admit-
ting so. We know a few of them by name, since he mentions them in
the greetings spread around his letters. At the end of Colossians, he
calls Tychicus his "beloved brother" (Col. 4:7). He then names Aris-
tarchus, John Mark, and Justus as those who have been a comfort to
him (vv. 10–11). His friendship with John Mark is the more poignant
in that they parted company over a disagreement about strategy, but
yet later had become reconciled (Acts 12:12).

But the love that Paul is calling for is more universal. It is grander.
Pascal believes Paul with all his heart, the Paul of love's principles,
more than the love from his example of ministry partners. Pascal per-
sonalizes those principles in a way that does recall Augustine. Instead
of simply weeping with those who weep, he loves poverty because
that allows him to reflect God's own condescension toward the poor.
Not only does he contribute to the needs of the saints, but he loves
wealth because that allows him to be generous to those in need. Not
only will he show honor, but he is impervious to the attacks of others,
and wants them to have the same dignity he enjoys. And not only
is he not overcome by evil, but he lives before the face of God, who
alone gives sufficient grace for such friendship.

It may be a stretch, but not by much, to say with Jean Brun that
Montaigne's approach to affection is linked to our advanced modern sense, whereas Pascal's sets the tone for the more rare kinds of
friendships rooted in the love of God. The biblical view is deeper,
even better, than one of its cobelligerents, the classical view. Sensing the impoverishment of friendship because of the secularization
process, many would try to revive this more classical model. Studies
such as Richard Godbeer's and Ivy Schweitzer's document the close
connection between friendship, loyalty, and civic duty in the early
American Republic.[24] But these kinds of loyalties, noble as they may

---

24. Richard Godbeer, *The Overflowing of Friendship: Love between Men and*

be, fall short of the love that stems from the full understanding of a loving God. They tout virtue, strength, resolve, but not Pascal's love of poverty. As Robert Bellah comments, the classical view of friendship depended on three interwoven components: friends must enjoy each other's company, they must be useful to each other, and they must share a common commitment to the good. Today, he surmises, we have the first, but not so much the second and third.[25] Bellah is citing Aristotle. Good as the virtue approach may be, it falls far short of the biblical model.

The utter uniqueness of our Christian faith is that it begins with the love of God, a love that has no motive other than . . . love. As Sinclair's mentor John Owen puts it, "The greatest sorrow and burden you can lay on the Father, the greatest unkindness you can do to him is not to believe that he loves you."[26] Thus, the biblical way is deeper, more genuine than even the classical way. That is because it centers on self-giving, on mercy. True friendship is to lay down one's life. It is to share everything, good things, dirty laundry, time and energy, with our neighbor. Enjoyment is a by-product, good in itself. There are many other by-products, including Bellah's mutual usefulness and working for a common cause. Yet they are not the center. They are not the *principium*.

Not surprisingly, the greatest model of friendship ever to grace the pathways of earth is the Lord Jesus Christ. One of his last sayings to the disciples before going to the cross (John 15:12–15) should astonish anyone who has a sense for who Jesus really is:

> This is my commandment, that you love one another as I have loved you. Greater love has no one than this, that someone lay down his life for his friends. You are my friends if you do what I command you. No longer do I call you servants, for the servant does not

---

the *Creation of the American Republic* (Baltimore: Johns Hopkins University Press, 2009); Ivy Schweitzer, *Perfecting Friendship: Politics and Affiliation in Early American Literature* (Chapel Hill, NC: University of North Carolina Press, 2006).

25. Danielle L. Blackburn, "Transcending Private Friendships to Public Hearts: Implications of Interracial Friendships for Public Life" (PhD diss., Duquesne University, 2010), 5.

26. John Owen, *Communion with God* (Edinburgh: Banner of Truth, 1991), 16.

know what his master is doing; but I have called you friends, for all that I have heard from my Father I have made known to you.

Light-years beyond Montaigne, and even Aristotle, Jesus summarizes friendship as the gift of what is most precious to us: our own life. Jesus would do this in ways that the disciples at this point could not fully know. He would not hold back. Everything he received from the Father, he freely gave them. But then he concludes his thoughts simply, powerfully, by saying, "These things I command you, so that you will love one another" (John 15:17).

True friendship is not an investment; it does not profit us. C. S. Lewis once said: "I have no duty to be anyone's friend and no man in the world has a duty to be mine. No claims, no shadow of necessity. Friendship is unnecessary, like philosophy, like art, like the universe itself. . . . It has no survival value; rather it is one of those things which gave value to survival."[27] This is almost right. Of course, we have a duty to love others, since Jesus commanded it. But what Lewis is getting at is that true love should not be utilitarian. Loving undeserving wretches is not a good investment by our Lord. Yes, he gained "rewards" for his sacrificial love, the "joy" that was set before him (Heb. 12:2): fellowship with us! We are the host of captives he led (2 Cor. 2:14). He even experienced, mysteriously, a deeper manifestation of the Father's love for himself (John 10:17). But precisely because it is not necessary, his love is resplendent. And so may ours be, our love for him and for one another, by his grace.

Sinclair and Dorothy have been remarkable friends to many of us. It is in considerable part because they have so generously given us what is most precious, their very selves. Thank you!

Recommendations for Further Reading

Auerbach, Erich. *Mimesis: The Representation of Reality in Western Literature.* Translated by Willard R. Trask. New and expanded ed. Princeton, NJ: Princeton University Press, 2003.
Augustine. *Confessions.*

27. C. S. Lewis, *The Four Loves* (New York: Harcourt, 1960), 71.

Brun, Jean. *L'Europe Philosophe: 25 siècles de pensée occidentale*. Paris: Stock, 1988.

Cicero. *Ode to Friendship*.

Lewis, C. S. *The Four Loves*. New York: Harcourt, 1960.

Owen, John. *Communion with God*. Edinburgh: Banner of Truth, 1991.

Shakespeare, William. *Sonnet 104*.

Taylor, Charles. *A Secular Age*. Cambridge, MA: Belknap/Harvard University Press, 2007.

Discussion Questions

1. What is implied in Montaigne's expression *Que sais-je?*
2. What overlap is there and what are the contrasts between these famous literary friendships and friendship in the Bible?
3. What was the heart of Pascal's criticisms of Descartes and Montaigne?
4. Describe as best you know it the developments leading to the modern view of the self.
5. What does Montaigne mean by "to philosophize is to learn to die"?
6. Explain the apostle Paul's description of friendship in Romans 12:9–21.
7. Though he was God's own Son, how was it that Jesus could have special friends?
8. Describe a friendship that is precious to you.

GLOSSARY

Definitions of the following terms, found in the various chapters, are provided by the contributors. Some are taken from the Westminster Confession of Faith and catechisms and other sources as noted. Italic terms within definitions are defined in the glossary.

administration. The dispensing of a sacrament—in the Reformed tradition, always with words of explanation.

adoption. "An act of the free grace of God, in and for his only Son Jesus Christ, whereby all those who are justified are received into the number of his children, have his name put upon them, the Spirit of his Son given to them, are under his fatherly care and dispensations, admitted to all the liberties and privileges of the sons of God, made heirs of all the promises, and fellow-heirs with Christ in glory" (WLC 74). See *benefits*; *sonship*; *spirit of adoption*.

anthropocentric. Pertaining to a pattern of thought and practice centered on the primacy or experience of humans as opposed to God.

antinomian. Relating to the view that believers are released by grace from the obligation of observing the *moral law*.

apostasy. A formal or functional renunciation of the Christian faith, by all appearances permanent. Cf. *backsliding*.

Arminianism. In its modern usage, the modifications of Jacobus Arminius to Reformed understandings of the doctrine of predestination, the human will, the extent of the *atonement*, and the role of the Holy Spirit in human salvation. See *perseverance*.

assurance. A Christian's grounded confidence of "grace and salvation" or of his or her own faith. Within the Reformed tradition, Christians have debated what constitutes the best grounds for

assurance and whether the Christian life ought to be characterized by confidence rather than doubt as the norm.

atonement. Christ's bloody sacrifice on behalf of his elect. Sometimes
used as an umbrella term for various aspects of the saving work
of Christ, such as his sacrifice and suffering. See *Arminianism;
penal substitution.*

backsliding. A temporary, rather than permanent, falling away from
the Christian faith. Cf. *apostasy.*

benefits. The spiritual blessings that flow from a vital relationship
with Christ, or the blessings that flow from or accompany justification, adoption, and sanctification. See *sonship.*

blind faith. See *fides implicitas.*

ceremonial law. That aspect of the Mosaic law code that required ceremonies, sacrifices, and other religious rites unique to the Mosaic
administration of the *covenant* of grace. The ceremonial law finds
its fulfillment in the person and work of Christ, and its demands
no longer constrain believers. Cf. *judicial law; moral law.*

Christocentricity. The teaching that Jesus Christ is the centerpiece of
Scripture, from creation to consummation.

civil law. See *judicial law.*

communion of saints *(sanctorum communionem).* On account of
believers' *union with Christ,* the saints' communion with God
himself and the saints' communion with one another. See *community.*

communitarianism. The idea that personal identity and meaning are
shaped by the surrounding community in which people live.

community. For some, an integrating motif for theology; Reformed
theologians assert that community must have a supernatural
foundation, lest it be a merely horizontal and man-made imitation of the much richer reality of the *communion of saints.*

concurrence. The relationship between God as Primary Cause and
creatures as secondary causes.

covenant. God's condescending fellowship with man first by way of
works and, after the fall of man, by way of grace, and mediated
through Christ alone. Covenant is a pervasive concept in Scripture and is both Trinitarian and redemptive in its orientation. See
ceremonial law; eschatology; federal Calvinism; image of God; seal.

Decalogue. The Ten Commandments as first issued in Exodus 20 and later summarized in Deuteronomy 5. See *moral law*.

decrees of God. God's "eternal purpose, according to the counsel of his will, whereby, for his own glory, he hath foreordained whatsoever comes to pass" (WSC 7). See *infralapsarian*; *supralapsarian*.

dialogical principle of worship. The idea that since public or corporate *worship* is essentially a meeting of God and his people, worship is a dialogue between God and those gathered to worship him. Some elements of that worship are performed on behalf of God, and some are performed by the congregation.

ecclesiology. The doctrine of the church; principles of church government rather than particular points of practice (the latter is often called "church polity").

election. God's eternal choice in Christ to save some sinners.

elements. The physical sacramental *signs*, namely, water in baptism, and bread and wine in the Lord's Supper.

eschatology. Traditionally, a study of the "last things," focusing on the inauguration of Christ's kingdom. In Reformed theology, eschatology orders all of human history covenantally, giving it a forward and heavenly orientation. See *covenant*.

eternal generation. The unique property of the Son in relation to the Father. Since God is eternal, the relation between the Father and the Son is eternal. This is not to be understood on the basis of human generation or begetting, since God is spiritual.

exaltation of Christ. In contrast to the *humiliation of Christ* (beginning with his birth to his burial), the state of Christ that consists in his resurrection, his ascension to heaven, and his present reign, or *session*, at the right hand of God the Father, as well as his future coming in judgment. See *historia salutis*.

exegesis. The discipline of interpreting a passage of the Bible, taking into account its linguistic and literary features, historical context and situation (including human author and original audience), structure and flow of thought, and canonical context within the unfolding history of redemption and the completed canon of Scripture. See *historia salutis*.

ex nihilo **creation.** Creation out of nothing by God's word of power and purpose.

fabrica idolorum ("factory of idols"). A phrase used by John Calvin
in *Institutes*, 1.11.8 to describe man's sinful nature.

federal Calvinism. A development of John Calvin's theology that views
covenant *union with Christ* as a leading theological category for
understanding a Christian's relationship to God. This theology is
articulated in the Westminster Standards. See *covenant*.

fencing the Table. In the Reformed tradition, inviting saved sinners to the Lord's Table, while reminding a congregation that
the Supper is for Christians who understand its meaning and
who are themselves repentant members in good standing of an
orthodox (or in some cases a Reformed) church.

fides generalis ("general faith"). The general knowledge and conviction that what God has revealed in his Word is true.

fides implicitas ("implicit faith"). A faith that is mere assent without certain knowledge—for example, a faith that accepts as true
"what the church teaches," without knowing the objective contents of the faith. Sometimes called *blind faith*.

fides qua creditur ("faith which believes"). The faith by which it
is believed, that is, the faith of the believer that receives and
embraces the revelation of God; faith subjectively considered.

fides quae creditur ("faith which is believed"). The faith that is
believed, that is, the content of faith as revealed by God; faith
objectively considered.

fides specialis ("special faith"). The knowledge, conviction, and confidence that rests in Christ and the gospel promise of forgiveness
and salvation in him.

glorification. The completion of the Holy Spirit's application of
Christ's redemptive accomplishment to the elect, in which, at
Christ's return, all who are his are set free from the presence of
all sin and all its consequences, receive incorruptible new bodies
like his glorious body, and are publicly vindicated as righteous,
on the ground of the perfect obedience of Christ imputed to
them by grace alone through faith alone.

historia salutis. Literally, "history of salvation." The term refers to the
unfolding of salvation history from the fall until its climax in
the humiliation and exaltation of Jesus Christ and brings into
view specifically the accomplishment of salvation by the triune

God in redemptive history through the humiliation and *exaltation of Christ*. See *exegesis*; *humiliation of Christ*.

humiliation of Christ. In contrast to the *exaltation of Christ* (beginning with his resurrection), the state of Christ that consists in his birth, his taking our humanity, his living under the curse, and his suffering and dying for sin, culminating with his burial. See *historia salutis*.

hypostasis (pl.: hypostases). Greek for "something with a concrete existence." In terms of the Trinity, it came to mean "person." Thus, by the end of the fourth-century controversy, it referred to what is distinct in God, the way in which he is three.

image of God. The concept of man's creation in God's image. This concept has been central to recent discussions of *theological anthropology* and is central to Reformed theology. As argued in this volume, the relations of the Godhead anchor conceptually the character of Adam as the created image of God in *covenant* with God (Gen. 1:27; 2:7–17). See *sanctification*; *semen religionis*.

imputation. Associated with the act of *justification*, wherein the status of one is legally ascribed or credited to another. Thus, in justification, the righteousness of Christ is credited to the sinner, while on the cross the sins of the elect are ascribed to Christ.

infralapsarian. Pertaining to the order of God's decrees, particularly the relationship between God's decree of the fall into sin and his decree of election to salvation in Christ. Infralapsarians hold that God first decreed the fall and then decreed to save some in Christ and to condemn others for their sins. Historically, this has been the position of the majority within Reformed theology.[1] See *decrees of God*. Cf. *supralapsarian*.

inspiration. The influence of the Holy Spirit on the human writers of the Bible and the text they wrote such that their contribution to the biblical canon is "breathed out" by God as his very Word written (2 Tim. 3:16).

judicial law. That aspect of the Mosaic law code pertaining to the nation of Israel's public polity. It includes specific penalties for

1. From W. Robert Godfrey, "Predestination," in *New Dictionary of Theology*, ed. Sinclair B. Ferguson and David F. Wright (Downers Grove, IL: InterVarsity Press, 1988), 529.

breaches of the *moral law* and *ceremonial law*; once Christ's work was done, the judicial law expired with the ancient Israelite state. Also called *civil law*.

justification. "An act of God's free grace to sinners, in which he pardons all their sins, accepts and accounts their persons righteous in his sight; not for anything wrought in them, or done by them, but only for the perfect obedience and full satisfaction of Christ, by God imputed to them and received by faith alone" (WLC 70). See *benefits*; *imputation*.

koinonia (κοινωνία). Greek for "communion" or "fellowship."

legalism. The teaching that believers find favor with God, or maintain their status as acceptable to God, wholly or partly on the basis of their obedience to the law of God.

macrocosm. The whole of a complex structure, ordinarily the world, universe, or cosmos, contrasted with a small or representative part of it. Cf. *mediocosm*; *microcosm*.

mediocosm. A neologism referring to that intermediate reality between *macrocosm* and *microcosm*, i.e., between the expanse of creation (maximally considered) and the particularity of the individual person.

memorialism. An understanding of the Lord's Supper that stresses the sacrament's function as a remembrance of Christ's death. Memorialism is associated with Zurich rather than Geneva.

microcosm. A community, place, or situation regarded as encapsulating in miniature the characteristic qualities or features of something much larger. Cf. *macrocosm*; *mediocosm*.

moral law. A reflection of the holy character of God himself, demanding of all creatures perfect, personal, and perpetual obedience. The essence of the moral law is summarized in the *Decalogue*. See *antinomian*. Cf. *ceremonial law*; *judicial law*.

mortification. The Christian activity of addressing sin and putting it to death. See *vivification*.

new relation. The relation between the immutable Creator and the mutable creature established in the work of creation.

ordinances. Religious observances commanded by God; the term is thus broader in scope than *sacraments*. In the New Testament, ordinances include the reading and preaching of the Word, as well as baptism and the Lord's Supper.

ordo salutis ("order of salvation"). The logical order of the Holy Spirit's application of the work of redemption to those who are brought into fellowship with Christ.

Pelagianism. The idea taught by Pelagius in the early fifth century, and his followers, that fallen humans could of themselves respond to the gospel, without the help of divine grace. This was rejected as heresy at the Council of Carthage in A.D. 418.

penal substitution. Christ's representative role in his death for sin, resulting in *atonement*, bearing judgment (the penalty, hence *penal*) in the place of sinners.

perseverance. The Reformed doctrine that Christians continue in the faith as they are continually striving after holiness. To be distinguished from an Arminian doctrine of mere preservation, which asserts only that Christians will remain in a state of salvation and which does not have *sanctification* in view. See *Arminianism*.

piety. The reverence and love toward God that exists in the soul by *regeneration*, expressed in devotion and personal communion with God.

pluralism and polytheism. Diversity of ideas and many gods.

presbyterianism. An understanding of church government that asserts the importance of the visible unity of the church of Christ. That unity is expressed in a connectional form of church government and diaconal care through regional presbyteries, or meetings of elders; local churches are led by a plurality of elders, who enjoy a parity in their authority.

providence. Works of God that are "his most holy, wise, and powerful preserving and governing all his creatures, and all their actions" (WSC 11). See *semen religionis; sensus divinitatis*.

psychosomatic. Pertaining to the union of body and soul in human beings.

redemptive history. See *historia salutis*.

regeneration. A gracious act of God's initiative in which he imparts spiritual life to those who, apart from his merciful intervention, would remain dead in trespasses and sins (Eph. 2:1), both unwilling and unable to respond to his call to *repentance* and faith through the gospel. The Westminster Standards speak of regeneration in terms of effectual calling, "the work of God's

Spirit, whereby, convincing us of our sin and misery, enlightening our minds in the knowledge of Christ, and renewing our wills, he persuades and enables us to embrace Jesus Christ, freely offered to us in the gospel" (WSC 31). See *piety*.

regulative principle. The idea that the church is to worship only in ways that are commanded in Scripture. According to the Westminster Confession, "the acceptable way of worshipping the true God is instituted by himself, and so limited to his own revealed will, that he may not be worshipped according to the imaginations and devices of men, or the suggestions of Satan, under any visible representations or any other way not prescribed in the Holy Scripture" (WCF 21.1). See *worship*.

relation of coinherence. The inter-Trinitarian relation wherein each person of the Trinity exhaustively indwells the person of the other, each being fully God.

relation of origin. The inter-Trinitarian relation wherein the Father is unbegotten, the Son is begotten of the Father, and the Holy Spirit proceeds from the Father and Son.

relation of subsistence. The inter-Trinitarian relation wherein each Trinitarian person is the possessor of the entire and undivided essence of God, so that the Father is God, the Son is God, and the Holy Spirit is God.

repentance. A turning from sin and to God; in Reformed theology, a lifelong practice rather than a one-time event. See *regeneration*; *sanctification*.

Sabbath. In Reformed theology, the eschatological rest promised to Adam, purchased by Christ, and currently celebrated by Christians in symbolic form by means of a weekly day of rest and *worship*; since the resurrection of Christ, the Sabbath is celebrated on the first day of the week.

sanctification. "A work of God's grace, whereby those whom God has, before the foundation of the world, chosen to be holy, are in time, through the powerful operation of his Spirit applying the death and resurrection of Christ to them, renewed in their whole person after the *image of God*; having the seeds of *repentance* unto life, and all other saving graces, put into their hearts, and those graces so stirred up, increased, and strengthened, that they more and more die to sin, and rise to newness of life" (WLC 75). See *benefits*; *perseverance*.

sanctorum communionem. See *communion of saints*.

seal. A confirming token or authenticating symbol. As applied to the sacraments, a seal is understood to protect a promise, emphasizing an obligation, or to solidify a *covenant*; most basically, a seal validates something. Cf. *sign*.

semen religionis ("seed of religion"). The rudimentary knowledge of God that arises in every human being because of the objective revelation of God in his work of creation and *providence*, and because of the subjective reality of a remnant of the *image of God* in each person. Because of the fall, however, the *semen religionis* gives rise not to true religion, but to idolatry and error in the name of God.[2] See *sensus divinitatis*.

sensus divinitatis ("sense of the divine"). A basic, intuitive perception of the divine existence, generated in all persons through their encounter with the providential ordering of the world. The *sensus divinitatis* is therefore the basis both of pagan religion and of natural theology. Because of the fall, the religion that arises out of this sense of the divine, or seed of religion (*semen religionis*), is idolatrous and incapable of saving or of producing true obedience before God. Our *sensus divinitatis* is thus capable only of leaving us without excuse in our rejection of God's truth.[3] See *providence*.

session. Christ's place and ministry at the right hand of the Father following his ascension into heaven.

sign. A visible action or material object that symbolizes something else. As applied to the sacraments, signs are understood to be emblems or badges that establish one's identity, indicating, for example, that the person marked belongs to God and is part of the church; most basically, a sign points to something. See *elements*. Cf. *seal*.

sonship. The concept that captures the biblical importance of sons as inheritors of special privileges. The Christian doctrine of

2. From Richard A. Muller, *Dictionary of Latin and Greek Theological Terms: Drawn Principally from Protestant Scholastic Theology*, 2nd ed. (Grand Rapids: Baker Academic, 2017), 278.

3. From Muller, *Dictionary of Latin and Greek Theological Terms*, 279.

sonship teaches that all Christians are sons, full heirs of Christ and all the benefits that are found in him alone. See *adoption; spirit of adoption*.

spirit of adoption. The Holy Spirit in his work of testifying to believers' sonship in Christ, witnessing through the Word that they are God's children even in the face of their sin and suffering. See *adoption*.

spiritual presence. The presence of Christ by his Holy Spirit in the sacrament of the Lord's Supper, a doctrine in the Reformed tradition most associated with the teaching of John Calvin.

supralapsarian. Pertaining to the order of God's decrees, particularly the relationship between God's decree of the fall into sin and his decree of election to salvation in Christ. Supralapsarians hold that God first decrees to save some and to condemn others and then decreed the fall and the work of Christ as a means to that end.[4] See *decrees of God*. Cf. *infralapsarian*.

telos. The final goal to which all things move.

theological anthropology. A study of human life in light of the knowledge of God, grounded in the Scriptures. See *image of God*.

theological presuppositions. Fundamental and foundational truths that shape how one thinks about God, oneself, and the world.

tithing. The giving of a percentage of one's income or wealth.

union with Christ. The vital, intimate union—through the Holy Spirit and by faith—by which Jesus Christ becomes the source of life and strength for his people and through which they receive every blessing of salvation. See *communion of saints; federal Calvinism; vivification*.

vivification. The bringing alive of spiritual gifts in those united to Christ, the resurrected Savior; the necessary complement to *mortification*, the putting to death of sin in those united to a crucified Savior. See *union with Christ*.

worship. The center of the Christian life, and the purpose of believers' existence. In Reformed theology, worship is to be ordered according to the Word of God only. See *dialogical principle of worship; regulative principle; Sabbath*.

4. From Ferguson and Wright, "Predestination," 529.

SINCLAIR B. FERGUSON BIBLIOGRAPHY[1]

Books Authored

Ferguson, Sinclair B. *Add to Your Faith: Biblical Teaching on Christian Maturity.* London: Pickering & Inglis, 1980.

———. *Know Your Christian Life: A Theological Introduction.* Downers Grove, IL: InterVarsity Press, 1981. Republished as *The Christian Life: A Doctrinal Introduction.* Edinburgh: Banner of Truth, 1989.

———. *Man Overboard! The Story of Jonah.* Edinburgh: Banner of Truth, 1981.

———. *Taking the Christian Life Seriously: Biblical Teaching on Christian Maturity.* Grand Rapids: Zondervan, 1981.

———. *Discovering God's Will.* Edinburgh: Banner of Truth, 1982.

———. *Handle with Care! A Guide to Using the Bible.* London: Hodder and Stoughton, 1982.

———. *A Heart for God.* Edinburgh: Banner of Truth, 1987, 1997.

———. *John Owen on the Christian Life.* Edinburgh: Banner of Truth, 1987.

———. *The Sermon on the Mount: Kingdom Life in a Fallen World.* Edinburgh: Banner of Truth, 1987.

———. *Undaunted Spirit: The Life and Testimony of Gordon Anderson-Smith.* Edinburgh: Rutherford House, 1988.

———. *Children of the Living God.* Edinburgh: Banner of Truth, 1989.

———. *Grow in Grace.* Edinburgh: Banner of Truth, 1989.

———. *Understanding the Gospel.* Eastbourne, UK: Kingsway, 1989.

———. *Deserted by God?* Edinburgh: Banner of Truth, 1993.

1. Works listed in each section of this bibliography are in chronological order by year published.

———. *The Pundit's Folly: Chronicles of an Empty Life.* Edinburgh: Banner of Truth, 1995.

———. *The Holy Spirit.* Contours of Christian Theology. Downers Grove, IL: InterVarsity Press, 1996, 1997.

———. *The Big Book of Questions and Answers.* Fearn, Scotland: Christian Focus, 1997.

———. *Let's Study Philippians.* Edinburgh: Banner of Truth, 1997.

———. *Let's Study Mark.* Edinburgh: Banner of Truth, 1999.

———. *The Big Book of Questions and Answers about Jesus.* Fearn, Scotland: Christian Focus, 2000.

———. *Daniel.* Preacher's Commentary 21. Nashville: Thomas Nelson, 2002.

———. *Jesus Teaches Us How to Be Good.* Fearn, Scotland: Christian Focus, 2004.

———. *Jesus Teaches Us How to Be Happy.* Fearn, Scotland: Christian Focus, 2004.

———. *Jesus Teaches Us How to Be Wise.* Fearn, Scotland: Christian Focus, 2004.

———. *Jesus Teaches Us How to Pray.* Fearn, Scotland: Christian Focus, 2004.

———. *Faithful God: An Exposition of the Book of Ruth.* Bridgend, Wales: Bryntirion Press, 2005.

———. *Let's Study Ephesians.* Edinburgh: Banner of Truth, 2005.

———. *In Christ Alone: Living the Gospel-Centered Life.* Orlando, FL: Reformation Trust, 2007.

———. *The Big Book of Bible Truths 1.* Fearn, Scotland: Christian Focus, 2008.

———. *The Big Book of Bible Truths 2.* Fearn, Scotland: Christian Focus, 2008.

———. *The Plan: How God Got the World Ready for Jesus.* Fearn, Scotland: Christian Focus, 2009.

———. *By Grace Alone: How the Grace of God Amazes Me.* Orlando, FL: Reformation Trust, 2010.

———. *Ignatius of Antioch: The Man Who Faced Lions.* Heroes of the Faith. Edinburgh: Banner of Truth, 2010.

———. *Irenaeus of Lyons: The Man Who Wrote Books.* Heroes of the Faith. Edinburgh: Banner of Truth, 2010.

————. *Polycarp of Smyrna: The Man Whose Faith Lasted.* Heroes of the Faith. Edinburgh: Banner of Truth, 2010.

————. *The Magnificent Amazing Time Machine: A Journey Back to the Cross.* Fearn, Scotland: Christian Focus, 2011.

————. *From the Mouth of God: Trusting, Reading, and Applying the Bible.* Edinburgh: Banner of Truth, 2014.

————. *The Trinitarian Devotion of John Owen.* Long Line of Godly Men Profile. Orlando, FL: Reformation Trust, 2014.

————. *Child in the Manger: The True Meaning of Christmas.* Edinburgh: Banner of Truth, 2015, 2016.

————. *Devoted to God: Blueprints for Sanctification.* Edinburgh: Banner of Truth, 2016.

————. *The Whole Christ: Legalism, Antinomianism, and Gospel Assurance—Why the Marrow Controversy Still Matters.* Wheaton, IL: Crossway, 2016.

————. *In the Year of Our Lord: Reflections on Twenty Centuries of Church History.* Orlando, FL: Reformation Trust, 2018.

————. *Let's Study James.* Edinburgh: Banner of Truth, 2018.

————. *Love Came Down at Christmas: Daily Readings for Advent.* [Epsom, UK]: Good Book Company, 2018.

————. *Some Pastors and Teachers: Reflecting a Biblical Vision of What Every Minister Is Called to Be.* Edinburgh: Banner of Truth, 2018.[2]

————. *Maturity: Growing Up and Going On in the Christian Life.* Edinburgh: Banner of Truth, 2019.

————. *Devoted to God's Church.* Edinburgh: Banner of Truth, 2020.

————. *To Seek and to Save: Daily Reflections on the Road to the Cross.* N.p.: Good Book Company, 2020.

————. *Lessons from the Upper Room: The Heart of the Savior.* Sanford, FL: Ligonier Ministries, 2021.

————. *What Jesus Did: 31 Devotions about the Life of Jesus.* Fearn, Scotland: Christian Focus, 2021.

————. *What Jesus Does: 31 Devotions about Jesus and the Church.* Fearn, Scotland: Christian Focus, 2021.

————. *The Dawn of Redeeming Grace: Daily Devotions for Advent.* Epsom, UK: Good Book Company, 2021.

2. *Some Pastors and Teachers* includes twenty-nine contributions to earlier publications not recorded in this bibliography. A list is found on pp. 799–802.

Books Coauthored

Oliphint, K. Scott, and Sinclair B. Ferguson. *If I Should Die before I Wake: What's beyond This Life?* Grand Rapids: Baker, 1995.

Begg, Alistair, and Sinclair B. Ferguson. *Name above All Names.* Wheaton, IL: Crossway, 2013.

Ferguson, Sinclair B., and Derek W. H. Thomas. *Ichthus: Jesus Christ, God's Son, the Saviour.* Edinburgh: Banner of Truth, 2015.

Beeke, Joel R., Michael A. G. Haykin, and Sinclair B. Ferguson. *Church History 101: The Highlights of Twenty Centuries.* Grand Rapids: Reformation Heritage Books, 2016.

Booklets

Ferguson, Sinclair B. *Healthy Christian Growth.* Edinburgh: Banner of Truth, 1991.

———. *Read Any Good Books?* Edinburgh: Banner of Truth, 1992.

———. *W. G. T. Shedd and the Doctrine of Eternal Punishment: The Evangelical Library Annual Lecture 1994.* Lewes, UK: F.C.M. Trust, 1994.

———. *The Grace of Repentance.* Repackaged ed. Today's Issues. Wheaton, IL: Crossway, 2011.

———. *The Heart of the Gospel: God's Son Given for You.* Philadelphia: Westminster Seminary Press, 2015.

———. *Wisdom Everywhere: Introducing the Treasures of John Owen Box Set.* Edinburgh: Banner of Truth, 2020.

———. *Welcome to the Library: Introducing the Puritan Classics Box Set.* Edinburgh: Banner of Truth, 2020.

Books Edited

Cameron, Nigel M. de S., and Sinclair B. Ferguson, eds. *Pulpit and People: Essays in Honour of William Still on His 75th Birthday.* Edinburgh: Rutherford House, 1986.

Ferguson, Sinclair B., and David F. Wright, eds. *New Dictionary of Theology.* Consulting ed. J. I. Packer. Downers Grove, IL: InterVarsity Press, 1988.

Still, William. *Collected Writings of William Still*. Vols. 1 & 2 edited by Nigel M. de S. Cameron and Sinclair B. Ferguson. Vol. 3 edited by Sinclair B. Ferguson and David Searle. Edinburgh: Rutherford House, 1990–94.

———. *Letters of William Still*. Selected by Sinclair B. Ferguson. Edinburgh: Banner of Truth, 1991.

Beeke, Joel R., and Sinclair B. Ferguson, eds. *Reformed Confessions Harmonized*. Grand Rapids: Baker, 1999.

Select Introductions, Forewords, and Afterwords

Cameron, Nigel M. de S., and Sinclair B. Ferguson, eds. *Pulpit and People: Essays in Honour of William Still on His 75th Birthday*. Edinburgh: Rutherford House, 1986.

Philip, George M. *Lord from the Depths I Cry: A Study in the Book of Job*. Glasgow: Nicholas Gray, 1986.

Pipa, Joseph A., Jr. *The Root & Branch: A Penetrating Look into the Person and Work of Jesus Christ*. Philadelphia: Great Commission Publications, 1989.

Fraser, James. *A Treatise on Sanctification*. Audubon, NJ: Old Paths, 1992.

Witsius, Herman. *Sacred Dissertations on the Apostles' Creed*. Translated by Donald Fraser. 2 vols. Escondido, CA: den Dulk Christian Foundation, 1993.

Fairbairn, Patrick. *The Revelation of Law in Scripture*. Phillipsburg, NJ: P&R Publishing, 1996.

Halyburton, Thomas. *Memoirs of Thomas Halyburton*. Edited by Joel R. Beeke. Grand Rapids: Reformation Heritage, 1996.

Perkins, William. *The Art of Prophesying; With, The Calling of the Ministry*. Edinburgh: Banner of Truth, 1996.

Gaffin, Richard B., Jr. *Resurrection and Redemption: A Study in Paul's Soteriology*. Phillipsburg, NJ: P&R Publishing, 1997.

McGowan, Andrew T. B. *The Federal Theology of Thomas Boston*. Rutherford Studies in Historical Theology. Edinburgh: Paternoster, 1997.

Colquhoun, John. *A Treatise on Spiritual Comfort*. Edited by Don Kistler. Morgan, PA: Soli Deo Gloria, 1998.

Beeke, Joel R. *The Quest for Full Assurance: The Legacy of Calvin and His Successors*. Edinburgh: Banner of Truth, 1999.

Calvin, John. *Heart Aflame: Daily Readings from Calvin on the Psalms*. Phillipsburg, NJ: P&R Publishing, 1999.

Venema, Cornelis P. *The Promise of the Future*. Edinburgh: Banner of Truth, 2000.

Kingdon, David. *Mysterious Ways: The Providence of God in the Life of Joseph*. Edinburgh: Banner of Truth, 2004.

Owen, John. *The Holy Spirit: His Gifts and Power*. Fearn, Scotland: Christian Heritage, 2004.

———. *Meditations on the Glory of Christ*. Fearn, Scotland: Christian Heritage, 2004.

Gale, Stanley D. *Warfare Witness: Contending with Spiritual Opposition in Everyday Evangelism*. Fearn, Scotland: Christian Focus, 2005.

Bridges, Jerry, and Bob Bevington. *The Great Exchange: My Sin for His Righteousness*. Wheaton, IL: Crossway, 2007.

Oliphint, K. Scott, ed. *Justified in Christ: God's Plan for Us in Justification*. Fearn, Scotland: Christian Focus, 2007.

Owen, John. *Communion with God*. Fearn, Scotland: Christian Heritage, 2007.

Rutherford, Samuel. *The Loveliness of Christ: Extracts from the Letters of Samuel Rutherford*. Selected by Ellen S. Lister. Edinburgh: Banner of Truth, 2007.

Shaw, Robert. *The Reformed Faith: An Exposition of the Westminster Confession of Faith*. Fearn, Scotland: Christian Focus, 2008.

Dever, Mark, and Sinclair B. Ferguson. *Westminster Directory of Public Worship*. Fearn, Scotland: Christian Heritage, 2009.

Downes, Martin. *Risking the Truth: Handling Error in the Church*. Fearn: Scotland: Christian Focus, 2009.

Martin, Hugh. *The Abiding Presence*. Fearn, Scotland: Christian Focus, 2009.

Wolfe, Paul D. *My God Is True! Lessons Learned along Cancer's Dark Road*. Edinburgh: Banner of Truth, 2009.

Alexander, Eric J. *Our Great God and Saviour*. Edinburgh: Banner of Truth, 2010.

Owen, John. *The Priesthood of Christ*. Fearn, Scotland: Christian Heritage, 2010.

Still, William. *Work of the Pastor*. Fearn, Scotland: Christian Focus, 2010.

Warfield, Benjamin Breckenridge. *The Person and Work of the Holy Spirit*. Birmingham, AL: Solid Ground Christian Books, 2010.

Zaspel, Fred G. *The Theology of B. B. Warfield: A Systematic Summary*. Wheaton, IL: Crossway, 2010.

Blanchard, John. *Does God Believe in Atheists?* 2nd ed. Darlington, UK: Evangelical Press, 2011.

Davey, Bob. *The Power to Save: A History of the Gospel in China*. Darlington, UK: Evangelical Press, 2011.

Thomas, Derek W. H. *How the Gospel Brings Us All the Way Home*. Orlando, FL: Reformation Trust, 2011.

———. *A Voyage of Discovery: The Ups and Downs of the Christian Life*. Darlington, UK: Evangelical Press, 2011.

Johnston, Mark G. *Our Creed*. Phillipsburg, NJ: P&R Publishing, 2012.

Brown, John. *The Christian's Great Enemy: A Practical Exposition of 1 Peter 5:8–11*. Edinburgh: Banner of Truth, 2013.

Manton, Thomas, and Thomas Watson Jr. *The Risen Christ Conquers Mars Hill: Classic Discourses on Paul's Ministry in Athens*. Edited by Michael Gaydosh. Birmingham, AL: Solid Ground Christian Books, 2013.

Martin, Hugh. *The Atonement: In Its Relations to the Covenant, the Priesthood, the Intercession of Our Lord*. Edinburgh: Banner of Truth, 2013.

Owen, John. *Assurance: Overcoming the Difficulty of Knowing Forgiveness*. Fearn, Scotland: Christian Heritage, 2013.

Ryle, J. C. *Thoughts for Young Men*. Birmingham, AL: Solid Ground Christian Books, 2013.

Blanchard, John. *Why Are You Here?* Darlington, UK: Evangelical Press, 2014.

Groves, Elizabeth W. D. *Grief Undone: A Journey with God and Cancer*. Greensboro, NC: New Growth Press, 2015.

Owen, John. *The Person of Christ*. Fearn, Scotland: Christian Heritage, 2015.

Randall, David J., ed. *A Sad Departure: Why We Could Not Stay in the Church of Scotland*. Edinburgh: Banner of Truth, 2015.

Crawford, Thomas J. *The Mysteries of Christianity: Revealed Truths Expounded and Defended.* Edinburgh: Banner of Truth, 2016.

Guthrie, Nancy. *One Year Praying through the Bible for Your Kids.* Carol Stream, IL: Tyndale Momentum, 2016.

Owen, John. *The Death of Death in the Death of Christ.* Fearn, Scotland: Christian Heritage, 2016.

Philip, James. *The Glory of the Cross: The Great Crescendo of the Gospel.* Peabody, MA: Hendrickson, 2016.

Fraser, J. Cameron. *Learning from Lord Mackay: Life and Work in Two Kingdoms.* Lethbridge, AB: SOS Books, 2017.

Murray, John. *O Death, Where Is Thy Sting?* Philadelphia: Westminster Seminary Press, 2017.

Van Dixhoorn, Chad. *God's Ambassadors: The Westminster Assembly and the Reformation of the English Pulpit, 1643–1653.* Grand Rapids: Reformation Heritage, 2017.

Venema, Cornelis P. *Christ and Covenant Theology: Essays on Election, Republication, and the Covenants.* Phillipsburg, NJ: P&R Publishing, 2017.

Allen, Lewis. *The Preacher's Catechism.* Wheaton, IL: Crossway, 2018.

Beeke, Joel R. *Reformed Preaching: Proclaiming God's Word from the Heart of the Preacher to the Heart of His People.* Wheaton, IL: Crossway, 2018.

Gibson, Jonathan, and Mark Earngey, eds. *Reformation Worship Liturgies from the Past for the Present.* Greensboro, NC: New Growth Press, 2018.

McCheyne, Robert Murray. *The Believer's Joy.* Fearn, Scotland: Christian Focus, 2018.

Meyer, Jason C. *Lloyd-Jones on the Christian Life: Doctrine and Life as Fuel and Fire.* Wheaton, IL: Crossway, 2018.

Poythress, Vern S. *Knowing and the Trinity: How Perspectives in Human Knowledge Imitate the Trinity.* Phillipsburg, NJ: P&R Publishing, 2018.

Davis, Dale Ralph. *Grace Be with You: Benedictions from Dale Ralph Davis.* Fearn, Scotland: Christian Focus, 2019.

Haste, Matthew D., and Shane W. Parker. *The Pastor's Life: Practical Wisdom from the Puritans.* Fearn, Scotland: Christian Focus, 2019.

Sproul, R. C. *Truths We Confess: A Systematic Exposition of the Westminster Confession of Faith.* Orlando, FL: Reformation Trust, 2019.

Beeke, Joel R., and Nick Thompson. *Pastors and Their Critics.* Grand Rapids: Reformation Heritage, 2020.

Bower, John R. *The Confession of Faith: A Critical Text and Introduction.* Grand Rapids: Reformation Heritage, 2020.

Chester, Tim. *Truth We Can Touch: How Baptism and Communion Shape Our Lives.* Wheaton, IL: Crossway, 2020.

Ellis, David W. *Through All the Changing Scenes: A Lifelong Experience of God's Unfailing Care.* Fearn, Scotland: Christian Focus, 2020.

Lawson, Steven J. *New Life in Christ: What Really Happens When You're Born Again and Why It Matters.* Grand Rapids: Baker, 2020.

Ferguson, Sinclair B., William S. Plumer, James W. Alexander, Archibald Alexander, Charles Hodge, Samuel Miller, Ashbel Green, and Nicholas Murray. *The Pastor: His Call, Character, and Work.* Edinburgh: Banner of Truth, 2020.

Warfield, B. B. *The Emotional Life of Our Lord.* Crossway Short Classics. Wheaton, IL: Crossway, 2022.

Gaffin, Richard B. *In the Fullness of Time: An Introduction to the Biblical Theology of Acts and Paul.* Wheaton, IL: Crossway, 2022.

Works Contributed

Ferguson, Sinclair B. "Prayers of Adoration." In *Worship Now: A Collection of Services and Prayers for Public Worship.* Edinburgh: St. Andrew Press, 1972.

———. "The Teaching of the Confession." In *The Westminster Confession in the Church Today: Papers Prepared for the Church of Scotland Panel on Doctrine.* Edited by Alasdair I. C. Heron. Edinburgh: St. Andrew Press, 1982.

———. "An Assembly of Theonomists? The Teachings of the Westminster Divines on the Law of God." In *Theonomy: A Reformed Critique.* Edited by William S. Barker and W. Robert Godfrey. Grand Rapids: Zondervan, 1990.

———. "Communion with God through Preaching" and "The Death of Sin: The Way to Life." In *Inside the Sermon: Thirteen Preachers Discuss Their Methods of Preparing Messages.* Edited by Richard Allen Bodey. Grand Rapids: Baker, 1990.

———. "Doubt in the Face of Suffering." In *Doubt and Assurance.* Edited by R. C. Sproul. Grand Rapids: Baker, 1993.

———. "Daniel." In *The New Bible Commentary.* Edited by Gordon J. Wenham, J. Alec Motyer, D. A. Carson, and R. T. France. 4th ed. Downers Grove, IL: InterVarsity Press, 1994.

———. "I Shall Not Want." In *If I Had Only One Sermon to Preach: Nineteen Preachers Reveal What Motivates Them.* Edited by Richard Allen Bodey. Grand Rapids: Baker, 1994.

———. "Evangelical Ministry: The Puritan Contribution." In *The Compromised Church.* Edited by John H. Armstrong. Wheaton, IL: Crossway, 1998.

———. "The Last Judgement in Puritan Preaching." In *God Is Faithful: Papers Read at the 1999 Westminster Conference.* N.p.: Westminster Conference, 2000.

———. "Pastoral Theology: The Preacher and Hell." In *Hell under Fire: Modern Scholarship Reinvents Eternal Punishment.* Edited by Christopher W. Morgan and Robert A. Peterson. Grand Rapids: Zondervan, 2004.

———. "The Heart of the Gospel." In *The Glory of the Gospel: Keswick Year Book 2005.* Milton Keynes, UK: Authentic Media, 2005.

———. "Infant Baptism View." In *Baptism: Three Views.* Edited by David Wright. Downers Grove, IL: InterVarsity Press, 2009.

———. "Christ, the Sin-Bearer." In *Atonement.* Edited by Gabriel N. E. Fluhrer. Phillipsburg, NJ: P&R Publishing, 2010.

———. "In Christ Alone—Philippians 3:8–12." In *Preaching like Calvin: Sermons from the 500th Anniversary Celebration.* Edited by David W. Hall. Phillipsburg, NJ: P&R Publishing, 2010.

———. "A Life Well Lived." In *Eyes to See; Ears to Hear: Essays in Memory of J. Alan Groves.* Edited by Peter Enns, Douglas J. Green, and Michael B. Kelly. Phillipsburg, NJ: P&R Publishing, 2010.

———. "The Christ of History." In *These Last Days: A Christian View of History.* Edited by Richard D. Phillips and Gabriel N. E. Fluhrer. Phillipsburg, NJ: P&R Publishing, 2011.

———. "'Blessed Assurance, Jesus Is Mine'? Definite Atonement and the Cure of Souls." In *From Heaven He Came and Sought Her: Definite Atonement in Historical, Biblical, Theological, and Pastoral Perspective.* Edited by David Gibson and Jonathan Gibson. Wheaton, IL: Crossway, 2013.

———. "Twenty Centuries of Church History." In *The Reformation Heritage KJV Study Bible.* Grand Rapids: Reformation Heritage, 2014.

———. "*The Glory of Christ* by John Owen." In *You Must Read: Books That Have Shaped Our Lives.* Edinburgh: Banner of Truth, 2015.

———. "Grace Alone: Luther and the Christian Life." In *The Legacy of Luther.* Edited by R. C. Sproul and Stephen J. Nichols. Orlando, FL: Reformation Trust, 2016.

———. "Preaching as Worship." In *Pulpit Aflame: Essays in Honor of Steven J. Lawson.* Edited by Joel R. Beeke and Dustin W. Benge. Grand Rapids: Reformation Heritage, 2016.

———. "The Holy Spirit and the Holy Scriptures: Inerrancy and Pneumatology." In *The Inerrant Word: Biblical, Historical, Theological, and Pastoral Perspectives*, edited by John MacArthur. Wheaton, IL: Crossway, 2016.

———. "John Owen and the Lord's Supper." In *Puritan Piety: Writings in Honor of Joel R. Beeke.* Edited by Michael A. G. Haykin and Paul M. Smalley. Fearn, Scotland: Christian Focus, 2018.

———. "All Things New." In *Our Ancient Foe: Satan's History, Activity, and Ultimate Demise.* Edited by Ronald L. Kohl. Phillipsburg, NJ: P&R Publishing, 2019.

———. "Life and Ministry." In *William Perkins: Architect of Puritanism.* Edited by Joel R. Beeke and Greg Salazar. Grand Rapids: Reformation Heritage, 2019.

———. "Solvent for the Stubborn Stains of Legalism and Antinomianism?" In *Christ Has Set Us Free: Preaching and Teaching Galatians.* Edited by D. A. Carson and Jeff Robinson Sr. Wheaton, IL: Crossway, 2019.

———. "2 Timothy 4:9–10." In *Faithful: Food for the Journey*, edited by Elizabeth McQuoid. Food for the Journey Keswick Devotionals. London: Inter-Varsity Press, 2021.

Other Contributions within the Following

Wright, David F., David C. Lachman, and Donald E. Meek, eds. *Dictionary of Scottish Church History & Theology.* Organizing ed. Nigel M. de S. Cameron. Edinburgh: T. & T. Clark, 1993.

Lewis, Donald M., ed. *A Blackwell Dictionary of Evangelical Biography 1730–1860.* 2 vols. Oxford: Blackwell, 1995.

Sproul, R. C., ed. *New Geneva Study Bible.* Nashville: Thomas Nelson, 1995.

Larsen, Thomas, ed. *Biographical Dictionary of Evangelicals.* Downers Grove, IL: InterVarsity Press, 2003.

Spirit of the Reformation Study Bible. Grand Rapids: Zondervan, 2003.

Bridges, Jerry. *How Great Is Our God: Timeless Daily Readings on the Nature of God.* Colorado Springs: NavPress, 2011.

Thomas, Derek W. H., and R. Carlton Wynne, eds. *Zeal for Godliness: Devotional Meditations on Calvin's 'Institutes.'* Darlington, UK: Evangelical Press, 2011.

Reformation Study Bible. Orlando, FL: Reformation Trust, 2015.

Journal/Magazine Articles

Ferguson, Sinclair B. "John Owen on Conversion." *Banner of Truth,* November 1974.

———. "Prayer a Covenant Work." *Banner of Truth,* February 1975.

———. "Lead Us Not into Temptation." *Banner of Truth,* October 1975.

———. "Spirit of Bondage." *Banner of Truth,* September 1976.

———. "Browsing in Banner Paperbacks." *Banner of Truth,* December 1976.

———. "More Thoughts on Preaching." *Banner of Truth,* March 1977.

———. "Westminster Conference 1976." *Banner of Truth,* September 1977.

———. "Westminster Conference 1977." *Banner of Truth,* March 1978.

———. "Leicester Ministers Conference 1978." *Banner of Truth,* June 1978.

———. "Assurance of Salvation." *Banner of Truth,* March 1979.

———. "The Scottish Influence at the Westminster Assembly." *Covenanter Witness* 95, nos. 4–5 (1979).

———. "God's Covenant the Believer's Strength." *Banner of Truth*, January 1980.

———. "Discovering God's Will." *Banner of Truth*, December 1981.

———. "Not in Vain." *Banner of Truth*, January 1982.

———. "The Book for All the People." *Christian Graduate*, June 1982.

———. "The Perspicuity of Scripture." *Christian Graduate*, June 1982.

———. "How Jesus Grew." *Discipleship Journal* (March 1984).

———. "For Jesus' Sake." *Discipleship Journal* (July 1984).

———. "Being like Jesus." *Discipleship Journal* (November 1984).

———. "Just Being There." *Discipleship Journal* (July 1985).

———. "Timing: God's and Ours." *Eternity*, May 1987.

———. "Say 'Aah': Take This Spiritual Tongue Test." *Eternity*, September 1987.

———. "John Owen on the Spirit in the Life of Christ (1)." *Banner of Truth*, February 1988.

———. "John Owen on the Spirit in the Life of Christ (2)." *Banner of Truth*, March 1988.

———. "The Whole Counsel of God: Fifty Years of Theological Studies." *Westminster Theological Journal* 50, no. 2 (September 1988): 257–81.

———. "The Fear of the Lord: Seeing God as He Is." *Discipleship Journal* (July–August 1989).

———. "Must We Also Love Them?" *Tabletalk*, November 1991.

———. "Who Is the Holy Spirit?" *Covenanter Witness*, November 1991.

———. "What in the World Can We Do?" *Decision*, May 1992.

———. "The Privileges of God's Children." *Ministry*, Fall 1992.

———. "Celebrating God's Wisdom." *Tabletalk*, February 1993.

———. "Letters of Henry Venn." *Banner of Truth*, November 1993.

———. "'Art of Prophesying': William Perkins' Famous Book Reprinted." *Banner of Truth*, February 1996.

———. "An Unexpected Journey with Martyn Lloyd-Jones." *Banner of Truth*, January 1997.

———. "Judge for Yourself." *Tabletalk*, April 1997.

———. "The Mystery of Mysteries." *Tabletalk*, September 1997.

———. "What Shall We Do?" *Banner of Truth*, November 1997.

———. "William Still: A Pastoral Theologian." *Evangel* 16, no. 3 (1998): 81–83.

———. "Exegetical Exemplar." *Tabletalk*, February 1999.

———. "The Trumpet's Blast." *Tabletalk*, October 1999.

———. "Calvin on John's Gospel." *Rutherford Journal of Church and Ministry* (Winter 2000).

———. "Living, We Die; Dying, He Lives." *Tabletalk*, April 2000.

———. "Paul's Ephesian Ministry: Discuss." *Tabletalk*, September 2000.

———. "Little Innocents?" *Banner of Truth*, February 2001. https:// banneroftruth.org/us/resources/articles/2001/little-innocents/.

———. "Medieval Mistakes and Repentance." *Banner of Truth*, March 2002. https://banneroftruth.org/us/resources/articles/2002 /medieval-mistakes/.

———. "Ministry of Reconciliation." *Banner of Truth*, May 2003. https://banneroftruth.org/us/resources/articles/2003/the-ministry -of-reconcilication-1/.

———. "The Lord of Lords." *Tabletalk*, December 2003.

———. "Apostasy and How It Happens." *Tabletalk*, April 2004.

———. "How Long Will It Last?" *Tabletalk*, May 2004.

———. "Perseverance of the Saints' God." *Banner of Truth*, May 2004.

———. "What's in Your Mind, Believer?" *Tabletalk*, June 2004.

———. "I Believe in the Holy Spirit." *Tabletalk*, September 2004.

———. "The Author of Faith." *Tabletalk*, October 2004.

———. "John Owen: Theologian of the Holy Spirit." *Tabletalk*, October 2004.

———. "A Testimony of Faithfulness." *Tabletalk*, December 2004.

———. "Princeton and Preaching." *Banner of Truth*, January 2005.

———. "Feeding the Flock of God." *Evangel* 24, no. 1 (2006): 18–24.

———. "Rutherford's Diamonds." *Banner of Truth*, October 2007.

———. "Surprised by Joy." *Tabletalk*, January 2008.

———. "Fourth of July—The View from (Slightly!) Outside." *Banner of Truth*, October 2008.

———. "Puritans: Can They Teach Us Anything Today?" *Banner of Truth*, December 2008.

———. "Speed with God." *Tabletalk*, January 2009.

———. "The Use of the Law in Evangelism." *Banner of Truth*, January 2009.

———. "James Philip (1922–2009): A Man Greatly Beloved." *Banner of Truth*, May 2009.

———. "Our Great God and Saviour." *Banner of Truth*, August–September 2010.

———. "A Catechism on the Heart." *Tabletalk*, January 2011.

———. "Time to (Re)Discover Hebrews." *Tabletalk*, January 2011.

———. "Heavenly-minded Usefulness." *Banner of Truth*, December 2011.

———. "Jesus: Our Navy SEAL." *Desiring God*, April 4, 2012. https://www.desiringgod.org/articles/jesus-our-navy-seal.

———. "Consider the Glory of God." *Tabletalk*, May 2012.

———. "Westminster Confession of Faith." *Banner of Truth*, November 2012.

———. "Union with God the Trinity." *Tabletalk*, February 2013.

———. "Faith and Repentance." *Tabletalk*, June 2013.

———. "Christian's Great Enemy." *Banner of Truth*, December 2013.

———. "John Knox." *Tabletalk*, March 2014.

———. "Guidelines for Separation." *Tabletalk*, June 2014.

———. "Authority, Sufficiency, Finality of Scripture." *Banner of Truth*, August–September 2014.

———. "Does Christology Really Matter?" *Tabletalk*, December 2014.

———. "Our New Affection." *Tabletalk*, December 2015.

———. "Sad Departure." *Banner of Truth*, December 2015.

———. "The Holy Spirit." *Tabletalk*, January 2016.

———. "Hidden Hiscocks." *Banner of Truth*, February 2016.

———. "Oh, How I Love Your Law!" *Tabletalk*, June 2016.

———. "Conversion of Saul of Tarsus." *Banner of Truth*, July 2016.

———. "Fourth Commandment." *Banner of Truth*, August–September 2016.

———. "The Whole Christ." *Tabletalk*, September 2016.

———. "Naming the Baby." *Banner of Truth*, December 2016.

———. "How the Reformers Rediscovered the Holy Spirit and True Conversion." *9Marks Journal: The Reformation and Your Church* (2017).

———. "To Enjoy Him Forever." *Tabletalk*, February 2017.

———. "The Reformation and Assurance." *Banner of Truth*, April 2017.

———. "God's Covenant People." *Tabletalk*, May 2017.

———. "Is There a God?" *Tabletalk*, August 2017.

———. "The Champion of the Kirk: John Knox (c. 1513–1572)." *Desiring God*, October 22, 2017. https://www.desiringgod.org /articles/the-champion-of-the-kirk.

———. "William Chalmers Burns." *Tabletalk*, November 2017.

———. "The Goal of Doing Theology." *Tabletalk*, February 2018.

———. "A Friend and Father in the Faith." *Tabletalk*, R. C. Sproul Commemorative Issue, 2018.

———. "The Lord Is My Shepherd; I Shall Not Want." *Tabletalk*, August 2018.

———. "He Sought to Kill Sin with a Pen: John Owen (1616–1683)." *Desiring God*, December 26, 2018. https://www.desiringgod.org /articles/he-sought-to-kill-sin-with-a-pen.

———. "John Murray's Principles of Conduct: Some Personal Reflections." *Unio Cum Christo* 5, no. 2 (2019): 222–26.

———. "Lose Particular Redemption, Lose Penal Substitution." *9Marks Journal: Penal Substitutionary Atonement* (2019).

———. "His Hymns Make Souls Feel Whole: Horatius Bonar (1808–1889)." *Desiring God*, April 8, 2019. https://www.desiringgod .org/articles/his-hymns-make-souls-feel-whole.

———. "The Faithfulness of Christ in the Little Things." *Tabletalk*, July 2019.

———. "Chalcedon: A Defining Moment for the Doctrine of Christ." *Desiring God*, December 2, 2019. https://www.desiringgod.org /articles/chalcedon.

———. "Preach like Hell Lasts Forever: Why We Must Warn—Through Tears." *Desiring God*, February 29, 2020. https://www .desiringgod.org/articles/preach-like-hell-lasts-forever.

———. "The State of Glory." *Tabletalk*, July 2021.

———. "What Is Our Theology?" *Tabletalk*, August 2021.

Book Reviews

Ferguson, Sinclair B. Review of *The New Testament Student*, edited by John H. Skilton. *Banner of Truth*, July–August 1977.

———. Review of *The Puritan Millennium: Literature and Theology, 1550–1682*, by Crawford Gribben. *Scottish Bulletin of Evangelical Theology* 21, no. 1 (2003): 80–81.

———. Review of *A Geerhardus Vos Anthology*, edited by Danny F. Olinger. *New Horizons*, January 2006.

———. Review of *Herman Bavinck on Preaching and Preachers*, by Herman Bavinck. Edited and translated by James P. Eglinton. *Unio cum Christo* 4, no. 2 (2018): 249–54.

BIBLIOGRAPHY

à Brakel, Wilhelmus. *The Christian's Reasonable Service*. Grand Rapids: Reformation Heritage Books, 1999.

———. *The Christian's Reasonable Service*. Edited by Joel R. Beeke. Translated by Bartel Elshout. 4 vols. Grand Rapids: Reformation Heritage Books; Ligonier, PA: Soli Deo Gloria, 1992.

Adams, Marilyn McCord. *Christ and Horrors: The Coherence of Christology*. Cambridge: Cambridge University Press, 2006.

à Kempis, Thomas. *The Imitation of Christ*. Translated by Ronald Knox and Michael Oakley. New York: Sheed and Ward, 1959.

Alexander, T. Desmond. *From Eden to the New Creation*. Grand Rapids: Kregel, 2009.

Allison, Gregg R. "Toward a Theology of Human Embodiment." *SBJT* 13, no. 2 (Summer 2009): 5–17.

Ames, William. *The Marrow of Theology*. Translated by John D. Eusden. Boston: Pilgrim Press, 1968.

———. *Medulla SS. Theologiae, ex sacris literis, earumque interpretibus, extracts & methodice disposita*. Amstelodami: Joannem Janssonium, 1627.

"Analyn's Head Covering Testimony: I Was One of the Last to Cover." The Head Covering Movement, June 3, 2017. https://www.head coveringmovement.com/christian-covering-videos/analyns -head-covering-testimony-one-last-cover.

Anderson, David R. *Free Grace Soteriology*. Edited by James S. Reitman. Rev. ed. The Woodlands, TX: Grace Theology Press, 2012.

Anderson, Troy S. "*Christians v. Crystal Evangelical Free Church (In re Young)*: Why Would 'Christians' Take Money Out of the Church Offering Plate?" *Regent University Law Review* 4 (1994): 177–211.

Atkinson, David J. "Emotions." In *New Dictionary of Christian Ethics & Pastoral Theology*, edited by David J. Atkinson et al., 341–43. Downers Grove, IL: InterVarsity Press, 1995.

Auerbach, Erich. *Mimesis: The Representation of Reality in Western Literature*. Translated by Willard R. Trask. New York: Doubleday/Anchor Books, 1957.

Augustine. *City of God*. Translated by Henry Bettenson. London: Penguin, 1984.

———. *Homilies on John's Gospel*. In *Lectures or Tractates on the Gospel according to St. John*, edited by Philip Schaff, 7–452. Translated by John Gibb and James Innes. Select Library of the Nicene and Post-Nicene Fathers of the Christian Church 7. 1st ser. Grand Rapids: Eerdmans, 1956.

———. "Lectures or Tractates on the Gospel according to St. John." In *St. Augustin: Homilies on the Gospel of John, Homilies on the First Epistle of John, Soliloquies*, edited by Philip Schaff, 1–452. Translated by John Gibb and James Innes. Select Library of the Nicene and Post-Nicene Fathers of the Christian Church 7. 1st ser. New York: Christian Literature Company, 1888.

Avis, Paul D. L. *The Church in the Theology of the Reformers*. London: Marshall, Morgan & Scott, 1981.

Ayres, Lewis. *Nicaea and Its Legacy: An Approach to Fourth-Century Trinitarian Theology*. Oxford: Oxford University Press, 2004.

Azurdia, Arturo G., III. *Spirit Empowered Mission: Aligning the Church's Mission to the Mission of Jesus*. Fearn, Scotland: Christian Focus, 2016.

Baillie, John. *Christian Devotion: Addresses by John Baillie*. London: Oxford University Press, 1962.

Baillie, Robert. *Ladensium autokatakrisis, the Canterburians Self-Conviction*. [Glasgow], 1640.

———. *"Smectymnuus," An Answer to a Booke Entituled, An Humble Remonstrance. In Which, the Original of Liturgy and Episcopacy Is Discussed*. London, 1641.

Bannerman, James. *The Church of Christ: A Treatise on the Nature, Powers, Ordinances, Discipline, and Government of the Christian Church*. 2 vols. Edinburgh: Banner of Truth, 1960.

Barker, William S., and W. Robert Godfrey, eds. *Theonomy: A Reformed Critique*. Grand Rapids: Zondervan, 1990.

Barrs, Jerram. *Learning Evangelism from Jesus*. Wheaton, IL: Crossway, 2009.

Barth, Karl. *Church Dogmatics*. 4 vols. Edinburgh: T. & T. Clark, 1956–75.

———. *Göttingen Dogmatics: Instruction in the Christian Religion*. Edited by Hannelotte Reiffen. Translated by Geoffrey W. Bromiley. 2 vols. Grand Rapids: Eerdmans, 1991.

Baugh, S. M. *Ephesians*. Edited by H. Wayne House. Evangelical Exegetical Commentary. Bellingham, WA: Lexham Press, 2016.

Bavinck, Herman. *Our Reasonable Faith*. Translated by Henry Zylstra. Grand Rapids: Baker, 1977.

———. *Reformed Dogmatics*. Edited by John Bolt. Translated by John Vriend. 4 vols. Grand Rapids: Baker Academic, 2003–8.

———. *Reformed Dogmatics: Abridged in One Volume*. Edited by John Bolt. Grand Rapids: Baker Academic, 2011.

———. *The Wonderful Works of God: Instruction in the Christian Religion according to the Reformed Confessions*. Translated by Henry Zylstra. Glenside, PA: Westminster Seminary Press, 2019.

Bavinck, J. H. *The Church between Temple and Mosque*. Grand Rapids: Eerdmans, 1966.

———. *The Impact of Christianity on the Non-Christian World*. Grand Rapids: Eerdmans, 1949.

———. *An Introduction to the Science of Missions*. Philadelphia: Presbyterian and Reformed, 1960.

———. *Religious Consciousness and Christian Faith*. In *The J. H. Bavinck Reader*, edited by John Bolt, James D. Bratt, and Paul J. Visser, 143–299. Grand Rapids: Eerdmans, 2013.

Baxter, Richard. *Gildas Salvianus: The Reformed Pastor*. London, 1656. In *The Practical Works of the Rev. Richard Baxter*, 14:1–400. London: James Duncan, 1830. Also available in abridged form as *The Reformed Pastor*. Edited by William Brown. Abr. eds. 1829, 1862. Reprint, Edinburgh: Banner of Truth, 1974.

Beale, G. K. *The Temple and the Church's Mission*. NSBT 17. Leicester, UK: Inter-Varsity Press, 2004.

———. *We Become What We Worship: A Biblical Theology of Idolatry.* Downers Grove, IL: IVP Academic, 2008.

Beattie, Francis R. *The Presbyterian Standards.* Brevard, NC: Southern Presbyterian Press, 1997.

Beeke, Joel R. *Heirs with Christ: The Puritans on Adoption.* Grand Rapids: Reformation Heritage Books, 2008.

———. Introduction to *The Gospel Mystery of Sanctification,* by Walter Marshall, v–xxv. Grand Rapids: Reformation Heritage Books, 1999.

———. *Knowing and Growing in Assurance of Faith.* Fearn, Scotland: Christian Focus, 2017.

———. *The Quest for Full Assurance of Faith: The Legacy of Calvin and His Successors.* Edinburgh/Carlisle, PA: Banner of Truth, 1999.

———. *A Tocha Dos Puritanos: Evangelização Bíblica.* São Paulo: Evangélicas Selecionadas, 1996.

Beeke, Joel R., and Sinclair B. Ferguson, eds. *Reformed Confessions Harmonized.* Grand Rapids: Baker, 1999.

Beekmann, Sharon, and Peter Bolt. *Silencing Satan: Handbook of Biblical Demonology.* Eugene, OR: Wipf & Stock, 2012.

Bell, Bernard Iddings. "Will the Christian Church Survive?" *Atlantic,* October 1942, 106–12.

Berger, Peter. *Questions of Faith: A Skeptical Affirmation of Christianity.* Malden, MA: Blackwell Publishing, 2004.

Bergjan, Silke-Petra. "Ecclesiology in Faith and Order Texts." *Ecumenical Review* 46, no. 1 (January 1994): 45–77.

Berkhof, Louis. *The Assurance of Faith.* Grand Rapids: Eerdmans, 1939.

———. *Systematic Theology.* Carlisle, PA: Banner of Truth, 1959.

———. *Systematic Theology.* 4th ed. Grand Rapids: Eerdmans, 1960.

Berkouwer, G. C. *The Church.* Translated by James E. Davison. Grand Rapids: Eerdmans, 1976.

———. *Man: The Image of God.* Grand Rapids: Eerdmans, 1962.

———. *The Providence of God.* Leicester, UK: Inter-Varsity Press, 1972.

———. *The Work of Christ.* Grand Rapids: Eerdmans, 1965.

Berman, Harold J. *Faith and Order: The Reconciliation of Law and Religion.* Grand Rapids: Eerdmans, 1993.

———. *The Law and Revolution: The Formation of the Western Legal Tradition.* Cambridge, MA: Harvard University Press, 1983.

Billings, J. Todd. *Union with Christ: Reframing Theology and Ministry for the Church*. Grand Rapids: Baker, 2011.

Blackburn, Danielle L. "Transcending Private Friendships to Public Hearts: Implications of Interracial Friendships for Public Life." PhD diss., Duquesne University, 2010.

Blass, Friedrich, Albert Debrunner, and Robert W. Funk. *A Greek Grammar of the New Testament and Other Early Christian Literature*. Rev. ed. Chicago: University of Chicago Press, 1961.

Blocher, Henri A. G. "Calvin on the Lord's Supper: Revisiting an Intriguing Diversity." *WTJ* 76, no. 1 (Spring 2014): 55–93 (pt. 1). *WTJ* 76, no. 2 (Fall 2014): 411–29 (pt. 2).

———. *Original Sin: Illuminating the Riddle*. Leicester, UK: Apollos, 1997.

Bock, Darrell L. *Luke 1:1–9:50*. BECNT 3A. Grand Rapids: Baker, 1994.

Bolt, John, James D. Bratt, and Paul J. Visser, eds. *The J. H. Bavinck Reader*. Grand Rapids: Eerdmans, 2013.

Bom, Klaas. "Heart and Reason: Using Pascal to Clarify Smith's Ambiguity." *Pneuma* 34, no. 3 (2012): 345–64.

Bonar, Andrew A. *Andrew A. Bonar: Diary and Life*. Edited by Marjory Bonar. Edinburgh: Banner of Truth, 1960.

Bonhoeffer, Dietrich. *Life Together*. Translated by Daniel W. Bloesch and James H. Burtness. Minneapolis: Fortress Press, 2005.

Boston, Thomas. *An Explication of the Assembly's Shorter Catechism*. In *The Whole Works of the Late Reverend Thomas Boston of Ettrick*, edited by Samuel M'Millan, 7:9–142. 12 vols. Aberdeen: George and Robert King, 1848–52.

———. *Human Nature in Its Fourfold State*. Edinburgh, 1720. Reprint, Edinburgh: Banner of Truth, 1964.

———. *Works*. Vol. 8, *A View of the Covenant of Grace*. Wheaton, IL: Richard Owen Roberts, 1980.

Bower, John R. *The Confession of Faith*. Grand Rapids: Reformation Heritage Books, 2020.

Braulik, Georg. *The Theology of Deuteronomy: Collected Essays of Georg Braulik*. Translated by Ulrika Lindblad. North Richland Hills, TX: BIBAL Press, 1994.

Breckinridge, Robert J. "Presbyterian Government Not a Hierarchy, but a Commonwealth." *Southern Presbyterian Review* 33, no. 2 (April 1882): 258–90.

Bridges, Charles. *The Christian Ministry*. 1830. Reprint, Edinburgh: Banner of Truth, 1991.

Brooks, Thomas. *A Cabinet of Jewels*. In *The Works of Thomas Brooks*, edited by Alexander B. Grosart, 3:233–504. 1864. Reprint, Edinburgh: Banner of Truth, 1980.

———. *The Crown and Glory of Christianity, or Holiness, the Only Way to Happiness*. In *The Works of Thomas Brooks*, edited by Alexander B. Grosart, 4:1–446. 1864. Reprint, Edinburgh: Banner of Truth, 1980.

———. *Heaven on Earth: A Treatise on Christian Assurance*. London: Banner of Truth, 1961.

Bruce, F. F. *Commentary on Galatians*. NIGTC. Grand Rapids: Eerdmans, 1982.

———. *The Epistles to the Colossians, to Philemon, and to the Ephesians*. NICNT 12. Grand Rapids: Eerdmans, 1984.

Bruce, Robert. *The Mystery of the Lord's Supper*. Edited and translated by Thomas F. Torrance. Richmond, VA: John Knox Press, 1958.

Brun, Jean. *L'Europe Philosophe: 25 siècles de pensée occidentale*. Paris: Stock, 1988.

Brunner, Emil. *The Misunderstanding of the Church*. Philadelphia: Westminster, 1953.

Bucer, Martin. *Concerning the True Care of Souls*. Translated by Peter Beale. 1538. Reprint, Edinburgh: Banner of Truth, 2009.

Buchanan, James. *The Doctrine of Justification*. Birmingham, AL: Solid Ground Christian Books, 2006.

———. *The Doctrine of Justification: An Outline of Its History in the Church and of Its Exposition from Scripture*. Edinburgh: T. & T. Clark, 1867.

Burgess, Anthony. *CXLV Expository Sermons upon the Whole 17th Chapter of the Gospel according to St. John*. London: Abraham Miller for Thomas Underhill, 1656.

———. *Faith Seeking Assurance*. Grand Rapids: Reformation Heritage Books, 2015.

———. *Spiritual Refining*. 1662. Reprint, Ames, IA: International Outreach, 1996.

———. *The True Doctrine of Justification Asserted and Vindicated, from the Errors of Papists, Arminians, Socinians, and More Especially Antinomians.* London: by Robert White, for Thomas Underhill, 1648.

Burns, Bob, Tasha Chapman, and Donald Guthrie. *Resilient Ministry: What Pastors Told Us about Surviving and Thriving.* Downers Grove, IL: InterVarsity Press, 2013.

Burroughs, Jeremiah. *Gospel-Worship.* London: Printed for Peter Cole, 1648.

Cahana, Jonathan. "Dismantling Gender: Between Ancient Gnostic Ritual and Modern Queer BDSM." *Theology & Sexuality* 18, no. 1 (2012): 60–75.

Calvin, John. *Calvin's New Testament Commentaries: The Epistles of Paul the Apostle to the Galatians, Ephesians, Philippians and Colossians.* Edited by David W. Torrance and Thomas F. Torrance. Grand Rapids: Eerdmans, 1965.

———. *Commentaries on the Second Epistle to Timothy.* In *Calvin's Commentaries,* translated by William Pringle, 21:177–272. Grand Rapids: Baker, 1998.

———. *Commentary on the Epistles of Paul the Apostle to the Corinthians.* Translated by John Pringle. Vol. 1. 1546. Reprint, Grand Rapids: Baker, 2003.

———. *Commentary on the Gospel according to John.* Translated by William Pringle. Vol. 2. Edinburgh: Calvin Translation Society, 1847.

———. *Commentary on the Gospel according to John: Volume First.* Translated by William Pringle. 1553. Reprint, Grand Rapids: Baker, 2003.

———. *Institutes of the Christian Religion.* Edited by John T. McNeill. Translated by Ford Lewis Battles. 2 vols. Library of Christian Classics 20–21. Philadelphia: Westminster, 1960.

———. *Institutes of the Christian Religion.* Edited by John T. McNeill. Translated by Ford Lewis Battles. 4 vols. Philadelphia: Westminster, 1967.

———. *Institutes of the Christian Religion.* Translated by Ford Lewis Battles. Louisville: Westminster John Knox, 2006.

———. *The Second Epistle of Paul the Apostle to the Corinthians and the Epistles to Timothy, Titus and Philemon.* Edited by David W. Torrance and Thomas F. Torrance. Translated by T. A. Smail. Calvin's Commentaries. Edinburgh: Oliver and Boyd, 1964.

———. *Selected Works.* Edited by Henry Beveridge. Vol. 1. Grand Rapids: Baker, 1983.

"The Canons of the Synod of Dort." In *The Creeds of Christendom, With a History and Critical Notes.* Vol. 3, *The Evangelical Protestant Creeds,* edited by Philip Schaff, 550–97. Revised by David S. Schaff. 6th ed. Grand Rapids: Baker, 1998.

Capill, Murray. *The Heart Is the Target: Preaching Practical Application from Every Text.* Phillipsburg, NJ: P&R Publishing, 2014.

Carroll, Jackson W. *God's Potters: Pastoral Leadership and the Shaping of Congregations.* Grand Rapids: Eerdmans, 2006.

Carson, D. A. *The Gospel according to John.* Pillar New Testament Commentary. Leicester, UK: Inter-Varsity Press/Grand Rapids: Eerdmans, 1991.

Case, Thomas. *The Morning Exercise Methodized.* London, 1660.

Cassidy, James J. *God's Time for Us: Barth's Reconciliation of Eternity and Time in Jesus Christ.* Bellingham, WA: Lexham Press, 2016.

Chambers, Frank M. "Pascal's Montaigne." *PMLA* 65, no. 5 (September 1950): 794–97.

Chantry, Walter J. *Today's Gospel: Authentic or Synthetic?* London: Banner of Truth, 1970.

Charnock, Stephen. *A Treatise of Divine Providence.* In *The Works of the Learned Divine Stephen Charnock,* 2:1–94. London, 1684.

Chrysostom, John. *Homilies of St. John Chrysostom, Archbishop of Constantinople, on the First Epistle of St. Paul the Apostle to the Corinthians.* Homily 26. Edited by Philip Schaff. Nicene and Post-Nicene Fathers of the Christian Church 12. New York: Christian Literature Company, 1889.

———. "Homilies of St. John Chrysostom, Archbishop of Constantinople, on the Gospel of St. John." In *Saint Chrysostom: Homilies on the Gospel of St. John and Epistle to the Hebrews,* edited by Philip Schaff, ix–333. Translated by G. T. Stupart. Select Library of the Nicene and Post-Nicene Fathers of the Christian Church 14. 1st ser. New York: Christian Literature Company, 1889.

———. *Homilies on the Epistles of Paul to the Corinthians.* Homily 27. 1889. Reprint, Peabody, MA: Hendrickson, 2004. NPNF 1, 12:161.

Ciampa, Roy E., and Brian S. Rosner. *The First Letter to the Corinthians.* Pillar New Testament Commentary. Grand Rapids: Eerdmans, 2010.

Clapp, Rodney. *Tortured Wonders: Christian Spirituality for People, Not Angels.* Grand Rapids: Brazos, 2004.

Clowney, Edmund P. *The Church.* Contours of Christian Theology. Downers Grove, IL: InterVarsity Press, 1995.

Colquhoun, John. *Repentance.* 1826. Reprint, London: Banner of Truth, 1965.

———. *A Treatise on the Law and the Gospel.* Morgan, PA: Soli Deo Gloria, 1999.

The Confession of Faith, the Larger and Shorter Catechisms with the Scripture Proofs at Large, Together with The Sum of Saving Knowledge. Applecross, Scotland: Publications Committee of the Free Presbyterian Church of Scotland, 1970.

Conn, Harvie M., ed. *Inerrancy and Hermeneutic.* Grand Rapids: Baker, 1988.

Cooper, John W. *Body, Soul, and Life Everlasting: Biblical Anthropology and the Monism-Dualism Debate.* Grand Rapids: Eerdmans, 1989.

Cortez, Marc. *ReSourcing Theological Anthropology: A Constructive Account of Humanity in the Light of Christ.* Grand Rapids: Zondervan, 2017.

Croteau, David A. "A Biblical and Theological Analysis of Tithing: Toward a Theology of Giving in the New Covenant Era." PhD diss., Southeastern Baptist Theological Seminary, 2005.

Cullmann, Oscar. "Scripture and Tradition." Translated by Joseph E. Cunneen. *Cross Currents* 3, no. 3 (1953): 262–77.

Cunningham, William. *Historical Theology.* Edinburgh: Banner of Truth, 1960.

Cyril of Alexandria. *Commentary on the Gospel according to S. John.* Vol. 2. London: Walter Smith, 1885.

Davis, Bill. *Departing in Peace: Biblical Decision-Making at the End of Life.* Phillipsburg, NJ: P&R Publishing, 2017.

de Kroon, Marijn. *We Believe in God and in Christ, Not in the Church: The Influence of Wessel Gansfort on Martin Bucer*. Louisville: Westminster John Knox, 2009.

de La Boétie, Estienne. *Œvres Complêtes*. Bordeaux: C. Gounouihou, 1892.

Denhollander, Rachael. *What Is a Girl Worth? My Story of Breaking the Silence and Exposing the Truth about Larry Nassar and USA Gymnastics*. Carol Stream, IL: Tyndale, 2019.

Dennison, James T., Jr. *Reformed Confessions of the 16th and 17th Centuries in English Translation*. Vol. 2, *1552–1556*. Grand Rapids: Reformation Heritage Books, 2010.

DeYoung, Kevin, and Greg Gilbert. *What Is the Mission of the Church? Making Sense of Social Justice, Shalom, and the Great Commission*. Wheaton, IL: Crossway, 2011.

Dick, John. *Works of John Dick*. Vol. 1, *Theology*. Philadelphia: F. W. Greenough, 1830.

Dixon, Thomas. *From Passions to Emotions: The Creation of a Secular Psychological Category*. Cambridge: Cambridge University Press, 2003.

Dowey, Edward A., Jr. "The Word of God as Scripture and Preaching." In *Later Calvinism: International Perspectives*, edited by W. Fred Graham, 5–18. Sixteenth Century Essays and Studies 22. Kirksville, MO: Northeast Missouri State University, 1994.

Downe, John. *A Treatise of the True Nature and Definition of Justifying Faith*. Oxford: I. Lichfield for E. Forrest, 1635.

Duncan, Ligon. "The Covenant Idea in Irenaeus of Lyons." Paper presented at the North American Patristics Society annual meeting, May 29, 1997. Greenville, SC: Reformed Academic Press, 1998.

Dyer, John J., and Gregory T. Jones. "Judicial Treatment of Charitable Donations in Bankruptcy before and after the Religious Liberty and Charitable Contribution Protection Act of 1998." *DePaul Business & Commercial Law Journal* 2, no. 2 (2004): 265–94.

Dykstra, Craig. "On Our Way: The Sustaining Pastoral Excellence Initiative." Plenary address presented at Lilly Endowment Annual Report, Indianapolis, May 11, 2011. Accessed April 22, 2014. http://pastoralexcellence.com/pdfs/DykstraPlenaryAddress.pdf.

Edin, Mary Hinkle. "Learning What Righteousness Means: Hosea 6:6

and the Ethic of Mercy in Matthew's Gospel." *Word and World* 18, no. 4 (Fall 1998): 355–63.

Edwards, Jonathan. *An Essay on the Trinity*. Cambridge: James Clarke, 1971.

———. *Memoirs*. In *The Works of Jonathan Edwards*, 1:xi–ccxxxiv. Edinburgh: Banner of Truth, 1974.

———. *The Works of Jonathan Edwards with a Memoir by Sereno E. Dwight*. Edited by Edward Hickman. 2 vols. Carlisle, PA: Banner of Truth, 1974.

Edwards, William R. "Participants in What We Proclaim: Recovering Paul's Narrative of Pastoral Ministry." *Themelios* 39, no. 3 (2014): 455–69.

Eglinton, James. *Trinity and Organism: Towards a New Reading of Herman Bavinck's Organic Motif*. London: Bloomsbury, 2012.

Elert, Werner. *Eucharist and Church Fellowship in the First Four Centuries*. Translated by N. E. Nagel. St. Louis: Concordia, 1966.

Emlet, Michael R. "What's in a Name? Understanding Psychiatric Diagnoses." *Journal of Biblical Counseling* 30, no. 1 (2016): 66–93.

Erskine, Ralph. "The Difference between Legal and Gospel Mortification." *Monergism*. Accessed October 15, 2020. https://www.monergism.com/blog/difference-between-legal-gospel-mortification.

Fairbairn, Patrick. *The Typology of Scripture*. Grand Rapids: Guardian Press, 1975.

Farrar, Thomas J., and Guy J. Williams. "Diabolical Data: A Critical Inventory of New Testament Satanology." *JSNT* 39, no. 1 (2016): 40–71.

———. "Talk of the Devil: Unpacking the Language of New Testament Satanology." *JSNT* 39, no. 1 (2016): 72–96.

Fee, Gordon D. *The First Epistle to the Corinthians*. NICNT. Grand Rapids: Eerdmans, 1987.

Ferguson, Everett. "The Covenant Idea in the Second Century." In *Texts and Testaments: Critical Essays on the Bible and the Early Church Fathers*, edited by W. Eugene March, 135–62. San Antonio: Trinity University Press, 1980.

Fesko, J. V. *The Theology of the Westminster Standards: Historical Context & Theological Insights*. Wheaton, IL: Crossway, 2014.

Fisher, Edward. *The Marrow of Modern Divinity*. Fearn, Scotland: Christian Focus, 2015.

"The Five Arminian Articles." In *The Creeds of Christendom, With a History and Critical Notes*. Vol. 3, *The Evangelical Protestant Creeds*, edited by Philip Schaff, 545–49. Revised by David S. Schaff. 6th ed. Grand Rapids: Baker, 1998.

Flavel, John. *The Works of John Flavel*. 1820. Reprint, Edinburgh: Banner of Truth, 1997.

———. *The Works of John Flavel*. Reprint, London: Banner of Truth, 1968.

Foxe, John. *Foxe's Book of Martyrs: Select Narratives*. Edited by John N. King. Oxford: Oxford University Press, 2009.

Frame, John M. *The Doctrine of the Word of God*. Phillipsburg, NJ: P&R Publishing, 2010.

Franklin, Adrian. "A Lonely Society? Loneliness and Liquid Modernity in Australia." *Australian Journal of Social Issues* 47, no. 1 (2012): 11–28.

Fukuyama, Francis. *Trust: The Social Virtues and the Creation of Prosperity*. New York: Free Press/Simon & Schuster Inc., 1995.

Gaffin, Richard B., Jr. "The New Testament as Canon." In *Inerrancy and Hermeneutic: A Tradition, A Challenge, A Debate*, edited by Harvie M. Conn, 165–83. Grand Rapids: Baker, 1988.

———. *Perspectives on Pentecost: New Testament Teaching on the Gifts of the Holy Spirit*. Phillipsburg, NJ: Presbyterian and Reformed, 1979.

Gamble, Whitney G. *Christ and the Law: Antinomianism at the Westminster Assembly*. Grand Rapids: Reformation Heritage Books, 2018.

Gardiner, Jeremy. *Head Covering: A Forgotten Christian Practice*. Edmonton, AB: Head Covering Movement, 2016.

Garner, David B. "Adoption in Christ." PhD diss., Westminster Theological Seminary, 2002.

Gentry, Kenneth L. *Lord of the Saved*. Chesnee, SC: Victorious Hope, 2010.

George, Timothy. *Galatians: An Exegetical and Theological Exposition of Holy Scripture*. New American Commentary 30. Nashville: Broadman & Holman, 1994.

Gibbs, Eddie, and Ryan K. Bolger. *Emerging Churches: Creating Christian Community in Postmodern Cultures.* Grand Rapids: Baker, 2005.

Gibson, David, and Jonathan Gibson, eds. *From Heaven He Came and Sought Her: Definite Atonement in Historical, Biblical, Theological, and Pastoral Perspective.* Wheaton, IL: Crossway, 2013.

Gibson, Jonathan, and Mark Earngey, eds. *Reformation Worship: Liturgies from the Past for the Present.* Greensboro, NC: New Growth Press, 2018.

Giles, Kevin. *The Eternal Generation of the Son: Maintaining Orthodoxy in Trinitarian Theology.* Downers Grove, IL: IVP Academic, 2012.

Gillespie, George. *A Dispute against the English-Popish Ceremonies, Obtruded upon the Church of Scotland.* [Leiden], 1637.

Girardeau, John L. "The Doctrine of Adoption." In *Discussions of Theological Questions,* 428–521. Harrisonburg, VA: Sprinkle, 1986.

Godbeer, Richard. *The Overflowing of Friendship: Love between Men and the Creation of the American Republic.* Baltimore: Johns Hopkins University Press, 2009.

Godfrey, W. Robert. *God's Pattern for Creation: A Covenantal Reading of Genesis 1.* Phillipsburg, NJ: P&R Publishing, 2003.

Goetz, Dave. "Tour of Duty." *Christianity Today.* April 1, 1996. https://www.christianitytoday.com/pastors/1996/spring/6l2022.html.

Goodwin, Thomas. *The Works of Thomas Goodwin.* 12 vols. Grand Rapids: Reformation Heritage Books, 2006.

Gouvea, F. Q. "The Communion of the Saints." In *The Evangelical Dictionary of Theology,* edited by Daniel J. Treier and Walter A. Elwell, 257–58. Grand Rapids: Baker, 2017.

Greaves, Richard L. *John Bunyan.* Grand Rapids: Eerdmans, 1969.

Grenz, Stanley. *The Social God and the Relational Self.* Louisville: Westminster John Knox, 2001.

Grenz, Stanley, and John Franke. *Beyond Foundationalism.* Louisville: Westminster John Knox, 2001.

Griffith, Howard. *Spreading the Feast: Instruction and Meditations for Ministry at the Lord's Table.* Phillipsburg, NJ: P&R Publishing, 2015.

Grillmeier, Aloys. *Christ in Christian Tradition*. Vol. 2, *From the Council of Chalcedon (451) to Gregory the Great (590–604)*. Part 2, *The Church of Constantinople in the Sixth Century*. Translated by Theresia Hainthaler and John Cawte. London: Mowbray, 1995.

Grudem, Wayne. *"Free Grace" Theology: 5 Ways It Diminishes the Gospel*. Wheaton, IL: Crossway, 2016.

Gunton, Colin E. *The Promise of Trinitarian Theology*. Edinburgh: T. & T. Clark, 1997.

———. "Trinity, Ontology and Anthropology." In *Persons: Divine and Human*, edited by Christoph Schwobel and Colin E. Gunton, 47–61. Edinburgh: T. & T. Clark, 1991.

Gurnall, William. *The Christian in Complete Armour*. Reprint, Edinburgh: Banner of Truth, 1964, 1974.

Hafemann, Scott J. *Suffering and the Spirit: An Exegetical Study of II Cor. 2:14–3:3 within the Context of the Corinthian Correspondence*. Wissenschaftliche Untersuchungen zum Neuen Testament, Reihe 2, 19. Tübingen: J. C. B. Mohr, 1986.

Hall, David W., and Joseph H. Hall, eds. *Paradigms in Polity*. Grand Rapids: Eerdmans, 1994.

Hallesby, Ole. *Prayer*. Minneapolis: Augsburg Publishing House, 1931.

Hamm, Jeffrey L. *Turning the Tables of Apologetics: Helmut Thielicke's Reformation of Christian Conversation*. Eugene, OR: Pickwick Publications, 2018.

Hammond, George C. *It Has Not Yet Appeared What We Shall Be: A Reconsideration of the Imago Dei in Light of Those with Severe Cognitive Disabilities*. Phillipsburg, NJ: P&R Publishing, 2017.

Hansen, David. *The Art of Pastoring: Ministry without All the Answers*. Downers Grove, IL: InterVarsity Press, 1994.

Hanson, R. P. C. *Allegory and Event: A Study of the Sources and Significance of Origen's Interpretation of Scripture*. Louisville: Westminster John Knox, 2002.

———. *The Search for the Christian Doctrine of God: The Arian Controversy 318–381*. Edinburgh: T. & T. Clark, 1988.

Harris, Harriet A. "Should We Say That Personhood Is Relational?" *Scottish Journal of Theology* 51, no. 2 (1998): 214–34.

Harris, John. *One Blood: 200 Years of Aboriginal Encounter with*

Christianity: A Story of Hope. 2nd ed. Sutherland, New South Wales, Australia: Albatross Books, 1994.

Hart, D. G., and John R. Muether. *With Reverence and Awe: Returning to the Basics of Reformed Worship.* Phillipsburg, NJ: P&R Publishing, 2002.

Hays, Steve. "Why I Believe: A Positive Apologetic." *Third Millennium Magazine Online* 5, no. 27 (2003). Accessed July 30, 2019. https://www.thirdmill.org/newfiles/ste_hays/PT.Hays.Why.Believe.apologetics.1.html.

Helm, Paul. *Calvin and the Calvinists.* Edinburgh: Banner of Truth, 1982.

———. *The Providence of God.* Leicester, UK: Inter-Varsity Press, 1993.

Henry, Matthew. *An Exposition of the New Testament.* Vol. 2. Edinburgh: J. Wood, 1759.

———. *Matthew Henry's Commentary.* Vol. 6, *Acts to Revelation.* 1723. Reprint, Peabody, MA: Hendrickson, 2003.

Heppe, Heinrich. *Reformed Dogmatics.* Edited by Ernst Bizer. Rev. ed. Eugene, OR: Wipf & Stock, 2008.

Hesselink, I. John. *Calvin's First Catechism: A Commentary: Featuring Ford Lewis Battles's Translation of the 1538 Catechism.* Louisville: Westminster John Knox, 1997.

Hill, C. E. "God's Speech in These Last Days: The New Testament Canon as an Eschatological Phenomenon." In *Resurrection and Eschatology: Theology in Service of the Church: Essays in Honor of Richard B. Gaffin, Jr.,* edited by Lane G. Tipton and Jeffrey C. Waddington, 203–54. Phillipsburg, NJ: P&R Publishing, 2008.

Hodge, Charles. *Systematic Theology.* 1873. Reprint, Peabody, MA: Hendrickson, 2003.

Hodge, J. Aspinwall. *What Is Presbyterian Law as Defined by the Church Courts? Containing the Decision of the General Assembly to 1894, Inclusive.* 7th rev. ed. Philadelphia: Presbyterian Board of Publication and Sabbath-School Work, 1894.

Hodges, Zane. *Harmony with God: A Fresh Look at Repentance.* Dallas: Redencion Viva, 2001.

Hoekema, Anthony A. *The Bible and the Future.* Grand Rapids: Eerdmans, 1994.

———. *Saved by Grace*. Grand Rapids: Eerdmans, 1989.

Hoeksema, Herman. *Reformed Dogmatics*. Grand Rapids: Reformed Free Publishing, 1966.

Hoffecker, W. Andrew. *Piety and the Princeton Theologians*. Phillipsburg, NJ: Presbyterian and Reformed, 1981.

Hoge, Dean R., and Jacqueline E. Wenger. *Pastors in Transition*. Grand Rapids: Eerdmans, 2005.

Holewa, Kathryn A., and John P. Higgins. "Palliative Care—The Empowering Alternative: A Roman Catholic Perspective." *Trinity Journal* 24, no. 2 (2003): 207–19.

Holland, Tom. *Contours of Pauline Theology: A Radical New Survey of the Influences on Paul's Biblical Writings*. Fearn, Scotland: Mentor/Christian Focus, 2004.

———. *Romans: The Divine Marriage: A Biblical Theological Commentary*. Eugene, OR: Wipf & Stock, 2011.

Horton, Michael. "Atonement and Ascension." In *Locating Atonement: Explorations in Constructive Dogmatics*, edited by Oliver Crisp and Fred Sanders, 226–50. Proceedings of the Los Angeles Theology Conference 3. Grand Rapids: Zondervan Academic, 2015.

———. *Calvin on the Christian Life: Glorifying and Enjoying God Forever*. Wheaton, IL: Crossway, 2014.

———. *The Christian Faith: A Systematic Theology for Pilgrims on the Way*. Grand Rapids: Zondervan, 2011.

———, ed. *Christ the Lord: The Reformation and Lordship Salvation*. Grand Rapids: Baker, 1992.

———. *Covenant and Eschatology: The Divine Drama*. Louisville: Westminster John Knox, 2002.

———. "Ephesians 4:1–16: The Ascension, the Church, and the Spoils of War." In *Theological Commentary: Evangelical Perspectives*, edited by R. Michael Allen, 129–53. London: T. & T. Clark, 2011.

———. *Lord and Servant: A Covenant Christology*. Louisville: Westminster John Knox, 2005.

———. "Obedience Is Better than Sacrifice." In *The Law Is Not of Faith: Essays on Works and Grace in the Mosaic Covenant*, edited by Bryan D. Estelle, J. V. Fesko, and David VanDrunen, 315–36. Phillipsburg, NJ: P&R Publishing, 2009.

———. "Post-Reformation Reformed Anthropology." In *Personal*

Identity in Theological Perspective, edited by Richard Lints, Michael S. Horton, and Mark R. Talbot, 45–69. Grand Rapids: Eerdmans, 2006.

Huber, Lynn R. *Like a Bride Adorned: Reading Metaphor in John's Apocalypse*. Emory Studies in Early Christianity 10. New York: T. & T. Clark/Bloomsbury, 2007.

Hughes, Philip Edgcumbe. *The Second Epistle to the Corinthians*. NICNT. Grand Rapids: Eerdmans, 1962.

Huijgen, Arnold. *Divine Accommodation in John Calvin's Theology: Analysis and Assessment*. Göttingen: Vandenhoeck & Ruprecht, 2011.

Hütter, Reinhard. *Bound to Be Free: Evangelical Catholic Engagements in Ecclesiology, Ethics, and Ecumenism*. Grand Rapids: Eerdmans, 2004.

Ivo of Chartres. "Prologue to the Ecclesiastical Canons." In *Prefaces to Canon Law Books in Latin Christianity: Selected Translations, 500–1245*, translated with commentary by Robert Sommerville and Bruce C. Brasington, 133–58. New Haven, CT/London: Yale University Press, 1998.

Johnson, Dennis E. "Fire in God's House: Imagery from Malachi 3 in Peter's Theology of Suffering (1 Peter 4:12–19)." *JETS* 29, no. 3 (September 1986): 285–94.

———. *The Message of Acts in the History of Redemption*. Phillipsburg, NJ: P&R Publishing, 1997.

———. *Philippians*. Reformed Expository Commentary. Phillipsburg, NJ: P&R Publishing, 2015.

Jones, L. Gregory, and Kevin R. Armstrong. *Resurrecting Excellence*. Grand Rapids: Eerdmans, 2006.

Jones, Mark. *Antinomianism: Reformed Theology's Unwelcome Guest?* Phillipsburg, NJ: P&R Publishing, 2013.

Justin Martyr. *First Apology*. In *The Apostolic Fathers with Justin Martyr and Irenaeus*, edited by Alexander Roberts, James Donaldson, and A. Cleveland Coxe, 159–87. Ante-Nicene Fathers. 1885. Reprint, Peabody, MA: Hendrickson, 1994.

Karkkainen, Veli-Matti. *An Introduction to Ecclesiology: Ecumenical, Historical & Global Perspectives*. Downers Grove, IL: InterVarsity Press, 2002.

Keller, Timothy. *Preaching: Communicating Faith in an Age of Scepticism.* London: Hodder & Stoughton, 2017.

Kelly, Douglas F. "Adoption: An Underdeveloped Heritage of the Westminster Standards." *Reformed Theological Review* 52, no. 3 (1993): 110–20.

Kelly, J. N. D. *Early Christian Creeds.* 3rd ed. New York: Longman, 1972.

Kelsey, David H. *Eccentric Existence: A Theological Anthropology.* Louisville: Westminster John Knox, 2009.

Kendall, R. T. *Tithing: A Call to Serious Biblical Giving.* Grand Rapids: Zondervan, 1983.

Kierkegaard, Søren. *Fear and Trembling.* Translated by Alastair Hannay. London: Penguin, 1985.

Kline, Meredith G. *God, Heaven and Har Magedon: A Covenantal Tale of Cosmos and Telos.* Eugene, OR: Wipf & Stock, 2006.

Knight, George W., III. *The Pastoral Epistles: A Commentary on the Greek Text.* NIGTC. Grand Rapids: Eerdmans, 1992.

Knox, John, et al. *The First Book of Discipline.* 1560. In *The Government of the Church of Scotland Fully Declared*, 24–75. London: Sold by John Sweeting at the Angel in Popes-head-Alley, 1647.

Koukl, Gregory. *Tactics: A Game Plan for Discussing Your Christian Convictions.* Grand Rapids: Zondervan, 2009.

Kruger, Michael J. *The Question of Canon: Challenging the Status Quo in the New Testament Debate.* Downers Grove, IL: InterVarsity Press, 2013.

Kruse, Colin G. *The Letters of John.* Leicester, UK: Apollos/Grand Rapids: Eerdmans, 2000.

Kuck, David W. *Judgment and Community Conflict: Paul's Use of Apocalyptic Judgment Language in 1 Corinthians 3:5–4:5.* NovTSup 66. Leiden: Brill, 1992.

Kuiper, R. B. *The Glorious Body of Christ.* Grand Rapids: Eerdmans, 1966. Reprint, London: Banner of Truth, 1967.

———. "The Glory of the Christian Church." *Presbyterian Guardian* 20, no. 12 (1951): 230–31.

Kuyper, Abraham. *The Work of the Holy Spirit.* Translated by Henri de Vries. 1900. Reprint, Grand Rapids: Eerdmans, 1956.

Lake, Meredith. *The Bible in Australia: A Cultural History.* Kensington, Australia: UNSW Press, 2018.

Lamandé, André. *La vie gaillarde et sage de Montaigne.* Paris: Librairie Plon, 1927.

Lane, Timothy S., and Paul David Tripp. *How People Change.* Winston-Salem, NC: Punch Press, 2006.

Lane, Tony. "The Wrath of God as an Aspect of the Love of God." In *Nothing Greater, Nothing Better: Theological Essays on the Love of God,* edited by Kevin J. Vanhoozer, 138–67. Grand Rapids: Eerdmans, 2001.

Laniak, Timothy S. *Shepherds after My Own Heart: Pastoral Traditions and Leadership in the Bible.* Downers Grove, IL: IVP Academic, 2006.

Lasater, Phillip Michael. "'The Emotions' in Biblical Anthropology? A Genealogy and Case Study with ירא." *Harvard Theological Review* 110, no. 4 (2017): 520–40.

LeFebvre, Michael. *Collections, Codes, and Torah: The Re-Characterization of Israel's Written Law.* New York: T. & T. Clark/Bloomsbury, 2006.

Leith, John H., ed. *Creeds of the Churches.* 3rd ed. Atlanta: John Knox Press, 1982.

Letham, Robert. *The Holy Trinity: In Scripture, History, Theology, and Worship.* Rev. and expanded ed. Phillipsburg, NJ: P&R Publishing, 2019.

———. "The Relationship between Saving Faith and Assurance of Salvation." ThM thesis, Westminster Theological Seminary, 1976.

———. *Systematic Theology.* Wheaton, IL: Crossway, 2019.

———. *Union with Christ: In Scripture, History, and Theology.* Phillipsburg, NJ: P&R Publishing, 2011.

———. *The Westminster Assembly: Reading Its Theology in Historical Context.* Phillipsburg, NJ: P&R Publishing, 2009.

———. *The Work of Christ.* Contours of Christian Theology. Leicester, UK: Inter-Varsity Press, 1993.

Lewis, A. J. *Zinzendorf, the Ecumenical Pioneer: A Study in the Moravian Contribution to Christian Mission and Unity.* London: SCM Press, 1962.

Lewis, C. S. *The Four Loves.* New York: Harcourt, 1960.

Lightfoot, J. B. *Saint Paul's Epistle to the Philippians: A Revised Text with Introduction, Notes and Dissertations*. 1913. Reprint, Grand Rapids: Zondervan, 1953.

Lillback, Peter A., ed. *The Practical Calvinist: An Introduction to the Presbyterian and Reformed Heritage*. Fearn, Scotland: Mentor/Christian Focus, 2002.

Lim, Michelle. *Australian Loneliness Report*. Melbourne: Australian Psychological Society, 2018. Accessed August 25, 2019. https://apo.org.au/node/202286.

Lloyd-Jones, D. Martyn. *The Assurance of Our Salvation*. Wheaton, IL: Crossway, 2013.

———. *Revival*. London: Marshall Pickering, 1986.

———. *Spiritual Depression: Its Causes and Cures*. London: Pickering & Inglis, 1965.

Lull, Timothy F., and William R. Russell, eds. *Martin Luther's Basic Theological Writings*. 3rd ed. Minneapolis: Fortress Press, 2012.

Lunn, Nicholas P. "'Let My People Go!' The Exodus as Israel's Metaphorical Divorce from Egypt." *Evangelical Quarterly* 86, no. 3 (2014): 239–51.

Luther, Martin. *Luther's Works*. Edited by Jaroslav Pelikan. St. Louis: Concordia, 1955–58.

———. *On Christian Liberty*. Minneapolis: Fortress Press, 2003.

———. *The Works of Martin Luther*. Translated by Henry Eyster Jacobs. Philadelphia: Muhlenberg Press, 1943.

Machen, J. Gresham. *Christianity and Liberalism*. Rev. ed. Grand Rapids: Eerdmans, 2009.

———. "The Minister and His Greek New Testament." In *Machen: Selected Shorter Writings*, edited by D. G. Hart, 210–13. Phillipsburg, NJ: P&R Publishing, 2004. Originally published in *The Presbyterian* 88 (February 7, 1918): 8–9.

Macleod, Donald. *A Faith to Live By: Understanding Christian Doctrine*. Fearn, Scotland: Christian Focus, 1998.

———. *Therefore the Truth I Speak: Scottish Theology 1500–1700*. Fearn, Scotland: Mentor, 2020.

Marcel, Pierre C. *The Relevance of Preaching*. Edited by William Childs Robinson. Translated by Rob Roy McGregor. New York: Westminster, 2000.

Marshall, Walter. *The Gospel Mystery of Sanctification*. Grand Rapids: Reformation Heritage Books, 1999, 2013.

Marthaler, Berard L. *The Creed*. Mystic, CT: Twenty-Third Publications, 1987.

Martin, Hugh. *The Atonement*. Edinburgh: Banner of Truth, 2013.

———. *The Atonement*. Edinburgh: Knox Press, 1976.

———. *The Atonement: In Its Relations to the Covenant, the Priesthood, the Intercession of Our Lord*. Edinburgh: Lyon and Gemmell, 1877.

———. *Christ for Us: Sermons of Hugh Martin*. Edinburgh: Banner of Truth, 1998.

———. *Christ Victorious: Selected Writings of Hugh Martin*. Edited by Matthew J. Hyde and Catherine E. Hyde. Edinburgh: Banner of Truth, 2019.

———. "Co-Ordination of Grace and Duty." *British and Foreign Evangelical Review* 32 (1883): 305–35.

———. "Justification." *British and Foreign Evangelical Review* 29 (1880): 393–408.

McCheyne, Robert Murray. "Sermon XI: Ordination Sermon." In *The Works of the Late Rev. Robert Murray McCheyne*, 2:76–88. New York: Robert Carter, 1847.

McClean, John. "'Do Not Conform': Thinking about Complementarianism as Contextualisation." In *The Gender Conversation: Evangelical Perspectives on Gender, Scripture, and the Christian Life*, edited by Edwina Murphy and David Starling, 173–85. Macquarie Park, Australia: Morling Press/Eugene, OR: Wipf & Stock, 2016.

———. Review of *Known by God: A Biblical Theology of Personal Identity*, by Brian Rosner. *Themelios* 43, no. 3 (December 2018): 516–20.

McLelland, Joseph C., ed. and trans. *The Peter Martyr Library*. Vol. 4, *Philosophical Works*. Sixteenth Century Essays and Studies. Kirksville, MO: Sixteenth Century Journal Publishers, 1996.

McNeill, John T. "Natural Law in the Teaching of the Reformers." *Journal of Religion* 26, no. 3 (1946): 168–82.

McWilliams, David B. *Galatians: A Mentor Commentary*. Fearn, Scotland: Christian Focus, 2009.

Meador, Jake. *In Search of the Common Good: Christian Fidelity in a Fractured World*. Downers Grove, IL: InterVarsity Press, 2019.

Meyendorff, John. *Christ in Eastern Christian Thought*. Crestwood, NY: St. Vladimir's Seminary Press, 1975.

Migne, J.-P., et al., eds. *Patrologia Graeca*. Paris, 1857–66.

Miller, Holly G. "Sustaining Pastoral Excellence: A Progress Report on a Lilly Endowment Initiative." Durham, NC: Leadership Education at Duke Divinity, 2011. Accessed April 22, 2014. http://pastoralexcellence.com/pdfs/Final_SPE_Report2011.pdf.

Milligan, William. *The Resurrection of Our Lord*. New York: Macmillan, 1917.

Moltmann, Jürgen. *The Trinity and the Kingdom*. Minneapolis: Fortress Press, 1993.

Montaigne, Michel de. *Apologie de Raymond Sebond*. 1573. Republished in English as *In Defense of Raymond Sebond*. Translated by Arthur H. Beattie. Milestones of Thought in the History of Ideas. New York: Frederick Ungar, 1959.

———. "On Affectionate Relationships." In *Les Essais, livre Ier, chapitre XXVIII*, trans. M. A. Screech, 205–19. New York: Penguin, 1993.

Morris, Leon. *The Gospel according to John: The English Text with Introduction, Exposition and Notes*. NICNT. Grand Rapids: Eerdmans, 1995.

Moulton, James Hope. *A Grammar of New Testament Greek*. Edinburgh: T. & T. Clark, 1949.

Muller, Richard A. *Dictionary of Latin and Greek Theological Terms: Drawn Principally from Protestant Scholastic Theology*. 2nd ed. Grand Rapids: Baker Academic, 2017.

———. *Post-Reformation Reformed Dogmatics*. Vol. 2, *Holy Scripture*. Grand Rapids: Baker Academic, 2003.

Muller, Richard A., and Rowland S. Ward. *Scripture and Worship: Biblical Interpretation and the Directory for Worship*. Phillipsburg, NJ: P&R Publishing, 2007.

Murray, David P. "A Theology of Sleep." *PRJ* 6, no. 2 (2014): 318–27.

Murray, John. "The Agency in Definitive Sanctification." In *Collected Writings of John Murray*, vol. 2, *Systematic Theology*, 285–93. Edinburgh: Banner of Truth, 1977.

———. "The Attestation of Scripture." In *The Infallible Word: A Symposium by the Members of the Faculty of Westminster Theological Seminary*, edited by Ned B. Stonehouse and Paul Woolley, 1–54. 2nd ed. Phillipsburg, NJ: P&R Publishing, 2002. First published 1946.

———. "Calvin on the Sovereignty of God." In *Collected Writings of John Murray*, vol. 4, *Studies in Theology*, 191–204. Edinburgh: Banner of Truth, 1982.

———. *Collected Writings*. Edinburgh: Banner of Truth, 1980.

———. *Collected Writings of John Murray*. Vol. 2. Edinburgh: Banner of Truth, 1977.

———. "Common Grace." *WTJ* 5, no. 1 (1942): 1–28.

———. *The Covenant of Grace*. London: Tyndale Press, 1977.

———. "Definitive Sanctification." In *Collected Works of John Murray*, vol. 2, *Systematic Theology*, 277–84. Edinburgh: Banner of Truth, 1977.

———. "The Dynamic of the Biblical Ethic." In *Principles of Conduct*, 202–28. Grand Rapids: Eerdmans, 1997.

———. *The Epistle to the Romans*. 2 vols. NICNT. Grand Rapids: Eerdmans, 1959, 1968, 1997.

———. *Redemption Accomplished and Applied*. Grand Rapids: Eerdmans, 1955, 2015.

Myers, A. C. "Heart." In *The Eerdmans Bible Dictionary*, 471. Grand Rapids: Eerdmans, 1987.

Neusner, Jacob. *Making God's Word Work: A Guide to the Mishnah*. New York: Continuum, 2004.

———, trans. *The Mishnah: A New Translation*. New Haven, CT: Yale University Press, 1988.

Newman, Randy. *Bringing the Gospel Home*. Downers Grove, IL: InterVarsity Press, 2011.

Newton, John. *The Works of John Newton*. New ed. 4 vols. Edinburgh: Banner of Truth, 2015.

Nichols, Terence. *Death and Afterlife: A Theological Introduction*. Grand Rapids: Brazos, 2010.

Nickles, Lynn. "The Only Thing That Matters." *Reach Out Columbia*, November 2009, 6–8.

Novak, David. *Covenantal Rights: A Study in Jewish Political Theory.* Princeton, NJ: Princeton University Press, 2000.

———. *Jewish-Christian Dialogue: A Jewish Justification.* New York: Oxford University Press, 1989.

Old, Hughes Oliphant. *The Reading and Preaching of the Scriptures in the Worship of the Christian Church.* 7 vols. Grand Rapids: Eerdmans, 1998–2010.

———. *Worship: Reformed according to Scripture.* Rev. ed. Louisville: Westminster John Knox, 2002.

Olson, Roger E. "Free Church Ecclesiology and Evangelical Spirituality." In *Evangelical Ecclesiology: Reality or Illusion?*, edited by John G. Stackhouse Jr., 161–78. Grand Rapids: Baker, 2003.

Ortlund, Gavin. "Resurrected as Messiah: The Risen Christ as Prophet, Priest, and King." *JETS* 54, no. 4 (December 2011): 749–66.

Owen, John. "Christologia: Or, A Declaration of the Glorious Mystery of the Person of Christ—God and Man." In *The Works of John Owen*, vol. 1, *The Person of Christ*, 1–272. Edinburgh: Banner of Truth, 1972.

———. *Communion with God.* Edinburgh: Banner of Truth, 1991.

———. *A Discourse concerning the Holy Spirit.* In *The Works of John Owen*, edited by William H. Goold, 3:1–651. Edinburgh: Banner of Truth, 1994.

———. *The Doctrine of Justification by Faith.* In *The Works of John Owen*, edited by William H. Goold, 5:1–400. Edinburgh: Banner of Truth, 1965.

———. *An Exposition upon Psalm CXXX.* In *The Works of John Owen*, edited by William H. Goold, 6:323–648. Edinburgh: Banner of Truth, 1995.

———. *The Glory of Christ: His Office and Grace.* 1684. Reprint, Fearn, Scotland: Christian Focus, 2004.

———. *The Mortification of Sin.* Edinburgh: Banner of Truth, 2004.

———. *The Mortification of Sin.* In *The Works of John Owen*, edited by William H. Goold, 6:1–86. Edinburgh: Banner of Truth, 1995.

———. *On the Dominion of Sin and Grace.* In *The Works of John Owen*, edited by William H. Goold, 7:499–560. Edinburgh: Banner of Truth, 1994.

———. *Pneumatologia, or, A Discourse concerning the Holy Spirit.*

Vol. 3 of *The Works of John Owen*. Edited by William H. Goold. Edinburgh: Banner of Truth, 1994.

———. *Pneumatologia, or, A Discourse concerning the Holy Spirit*. Vol. 3 of *The Works of John Owen*. Edited by William H. Goold. 1850–53. Reprint, London: Banner of Truth, 1965.

———. *The Works of John Owen*. 23 vols. Edinburgh: Banner of Truth, 1992.

Packer, J. I. *Concise Theology: A Guide to Historic Christian Beliefs*. Wheaton, IL: Tyndale, 1993.

———. *Knowing God*. London: Hodder & Stoughton, 2013.

Padgett, Alan G. "Faith Seeking Understanding: Collegiality and Difference in Theology and Philosophy." In *Faith and Reason: Three Views*, edited by Steve Wilkens, 89–91. Downers Grove, IL: InterVarsity Press, 2014.

Pardigon, Flavien. *Paul against the Idols: A Contextual Reading of the Areopagus Speech*. Eugene, OR: Pickwick Publications, 2019.

Pascal, Blaise. *Pensées*. Translated by A. J. Krailsheimer. London: Penguin, 1966.

Payne, Philip B. *Man and Woman, One in Christ: An Exegetical and Theological Study of Paul's Letters*. Grand Rapids: Zondervan, 2009.

Pearcey, Nancy R. *Love Thy Body: Answering Hard Questions about Life and Sexuality*. Grand Rapids: Baker, 2018.

Pearson, John. *An Exposition of the Creed*. 6th ed. Oxford: Clarendon, 1877.

Pelikan, Jaroslav. *Jesus through the Centuries: His Place in the History of Culture*. New Haven, CT: Yale University Press, 1985.

Peppiatt, Lucy. *Women and Worship at Corinth: Paul's Rhetorical Arguments in 1 Corinthians*. Cambridge: James Clarke & Co., 2017.

Percival, Henry R. *The Seven Ecumenical Councils of the Undivided Church: Their Canons and Dogmatic Decrees*. Select Library of Nicene and Post-Nicene Fathers of the Christian Church 14. 2nd ser. Reprint, Edinburgh: T. & T. Clark, 1997.

Peterson, Eugene H. *The Pastor: A Memoir*. New York: HarperCollins, 2012.

Pipa, Joseph A., and David W. Hall, eds. *Did God Create in 6 Days?* Dallas, GA: Tolle Lege, 2006.

Piper, John. *Bloodlines: Race, Cross, and the Christian.* Wheaton, IL: Crossway, 2011.

———. *Brothers, We Are Not Professionals: A Plea to Pastors for Radical Ministry.* Nashville: B&H Publishing, 2013.

Ployd, Adam. *Augustine, the Trinity, and the Church: A Reading of the Anti-Donatist Sermons.* Oxford: Oxford University Press, 2015.

Powlison, David. "Crucial Issues in Contemporary Biblical Counseling." In *Counsel the Word,* 107–22. 2nd ed. Glenside, PA: Christian Counseling & Educational Foundation, 2002.

Poythress, Vern S. *God-Centered Biblical Interpretation.* Phillipsburg, NJ: P&R Publishing, 1999.

———. *In the Beginning Was the Word: Language—A God-Centered Approach.* Wheaton, IL: Crossway, 2009.

Reisinger, Ernst C. *Lord and Christ: The Implications of Lordship for Faith and Life.* Phillipsburg, NJ: P&R Publishing, 1994.

———. *What Should We Think of the Carnal Christian?* Edinburgh: Banner of Truth, 1978.

Reynolds, Adrian. *And So to Bed . . . A Biblical View of Sleep.* Fearn, Scotland: Christian Focus, 2014.

Reynolds, Edward. *Three Treatises: Of the Vanity of the Creature. The Sinfulness of Sinne. The Life of Christ.* London: B. B. for Rob Bastocke and George Badger, 1642.

Ridderbos, Herman N. "The Canon of the New Testament." In *Revelation and the Bible: Contemporary Evangelical Thought,* edited by Carl F. H. Henry, 189–201. Grand Rapids: Baker, 1958.

———. *The Epistle of Paul to the Churches of Galatia.* NICNT. Grand Rapids: Eerdmans, 1953.

———. *Paul: An Outline of His Theology.* Translated by John Richard de Witt. Grand Rapids: Eerdmans, 1975.

———. *Redemptive History and the New Testament Scriptures.* 2nd rev. ed. Phillipsburg, NJ: P&R Publishing, 1988. First published 1963.

Ridgeley, Thomas. *A Body of Divinity.* 2 vols. New York: Robert Carter, 1855.

Roberts, Christopher Chenault. *Creation and Covenant: The Significance of Sexual Difference in the Moral Theology of Marriage.* New York: T. & T. Clark, 2007.

Robertson, O. Palmer. *Christ and the Covenants.* Phillipsburg, NJ: Presbyterian and Reformed, 1987.

———. *The Christ of the Covenants.* Phillipsburg, NJ: Presbyterian and Reformed, 1980.

Robinson, Stuart. *The Church of God as an Essential Element of the Gospel, and the Idea, Structure, and Functions Thereof. A Discourse in Four Parts.* Philadelphia: Joseph M. Wilson, 1858. Reprint (and edited with a foreword by A. Craig Troxel), Willow Grove, PA: Committee on Christian Education of the Orthodox Presbyterian Church, 2009.

Rogers, John. *The Doctrine of Faith: Wherein Are Particularly Handled Twelve Principall Points, Which Explaine the Nature and Use of It.* London: N. Newbery and H. Overton, 1629.

Rosner, Brian S. *Known by God.* Grand Rapids: Zondervan, 2017.

———. *Paul and the Law: Keeping the Commandments of God.* Nottingham, UK: Apollos, 2013.

Ross, Philip S. *From the Finger of God: The Biblical and Theological Basis for the Threefold Division of the Law.* Fearn, Scotland: Mentor, 2010.

Rutherford, Samuel. *A Survey of the Spirituall Antichrist.* London: by J. D. & R. I. for Andrew Crooke, 1648.

———. *The Trial and Triumph of Faith.* Edinburgh: Collins, 1845.

Ryken, Leland, James C. Wilhoit, and Tremper Longman III, eds. *Dictionary of Biblical Imagery.* Downers Grove, IL: InterVarsity Press, 1998.

Ryle, J. C. *Expository Thoughts on Matthew.* Edinburgh: Banner of Truth, 2012.

———. *Holiness.* Darlington, UK: Evangelical Press, 2001, 2014.

Sanders, Fred, and Scott R. Swain. *Retrieving Eternal Generation.* Grand Rapids: Zondervan, 2017.

Schaeffer, Francis A. *Genesis in Space and Time.* Downers Grove, IL: InterVarsity Press, 1972.

Schaff, Philip. *The Creeds of Christendom.* 3 vols. Grand Rapids: Baker, 1993.

———. *The Creeds of Christendom.* 3 vols. New York: Harper & Row, 1931. Reprint, Grand Rapids: Baker, 2007.

———, ed. *A Select Library of the Nicene and Post-Nicene Fathers of the Christian Church.* Translated by John Gibb and James Innes. 1st ser. New York: Christian Literature Company, 1888. Reprint, Peabody, MA: Hendrickson, 1994.

Schweitzer, Ivy. *Perfecting Friendship: Politics and Affiliation in Early American Literature.* Chapel Hill, NC: University of North Carolina Press, 2006.

Scudder, Henry. *The Christian's Daily Walk.* Reprint, Harrisonburg, VA: Sprinkle, 1984.

Seneca. "On Providence." In *Seneca: Dialogues and Essays,* translated by John Davie, 3–17. Oxford: Oxford University Press, 2007.

Shaw, Robert. *The Reformed Faith: An Exposition of the Westminster Confession of Faith.* 8th ed. Edinburgh: Blackie and Son, 1857.

Shedd, W. G. *Dogmatic Theology.* Edited by Alan W. Gomes. 3rd ed. Phillipsburg, NJ: P&R Publishing, 2003.

Sibbes, Richard. *Works of Richard Sibbes.* Edited by Alexander Grant. 7 vols. 1862–64. Reprint, Edinburgh: Banner of Truth, 1973.

Silva, Moisés. "Freedom." In *The Evangelical Dictionary of Biblical Theology,* edited by Walter A. Elwell, 270–72. Grand Rapids: Baker, 1996.

Simeon, Charles. *Galatians–Ephesians.* Vol. 17 of *Horae Homileticae.* London: Holdsworth and Ball, 1833.

Smeaton, George. *The Doctrine of the Holy Spirit.* 2nd ed. 1889. Reprint, Edinburgh: Banner of Truth, 1974.

Smith, Claire. *God's Good Design: What the Bible Really Says about Men and Women.* Kingsford, Australia: Matthias, 2012.

Smith, James K. A. *You Are What You Love: The Spiritual Power of Habit.* Grand Rapids: Brazos, 2016.

Snyder, Rachel Louise. *No Visible Bruises: What We Don't Know about Domestic Violence Can Kill Us.* New York: Bloomsbury, 2019.

Sonderegger, Katherine. *Systematic Theology.* Vol. 1, *The Doctrine of God.* Minneapolis: Fortress, 2015.

Spicq, Ceslas. *Saint Paul: Les Épîtres Pastorales.* Paris: Librairie Lecoffre, 1947.

Spurgeon, Charles Haddon. "Foretastes of the Heavenly Life." In *Spurgeon's Sermons,* 3:138–48. Grand Rapids: Baker, 2004.

———. "The Marvelous Magnet." *Spurgeon's Sermons (1717).* Vol. 29

(1883). Accessed July 30, 2019. https://www.ccel.org/ccel/spurgeon/sermons29.xx.html.

———. "The Minister's Self-Watch." In *Lectures to My Students*, 1–18. Edinburgh: Banner of Truth, 2008.

———. "The Way to Honor." Christian Classics Ethereal Library. Accessed March 7, 2018. https://www.ccel.org/ccel/spurgeon/sermons19.xxx.html.

———. "The Word a Sword." In *The Metropolitan Tabernacle Pulpit Sermons*, 34:109–20. London: Passmore & Alabaster, 1888.

Spurstowe, William. *The Wells of Salvation Opened: or, A Treatise Discerning the Nature, Preciousness, and Usefulness of the Gospel Promises and Rules for the Right Application of Them.* London: T. R. & E. M. for Ralph Smith, 1655.

Stibbs, Alan M. *The First Epistle General of Peter.* Tyndale New Testament Commentaries. Grand Rapids: Eerdmans, 1959.

Still, William. *Dying to Live.* Fearn, Scotland: Christian Focus, 1991.

———. *The Work of the Pastor.* Rev. ed. Fearn, Scotland: Christian Focus, 2010.

Stone, Jordan. *A Communion of Love: The Christian-Centered Spirituality of Robert Murray M'Cheyne.* Eugene, OR: Wipf & Stock, 2019.

———. *Love to Christ: Robert Murray M'Cheyne and the Pursuit of Holiness.* Grand Rapids: Reformation Heritage Books, 2020.

Stonehouse, Ned B. "The Authority of the New Testament." In *The Infallible Word: A Symposium by the Members of the Faculty of Westminster Theological Seminary*, edited by Ned B. Stonehouse and Paul Woolley, 92–140. 2nd ed. Phillipsburg, NJ: P&R Publishing, 2002. Originally published 1946.

Stott, John R. W. *Between Two Worlds: The Art of Preaching in the Twentieth Century.* Grand Rapids: Eerdmans, 1982.

Strange, Daniel. "Never Say 'the Phones Are Quiet.'" *Themelios* 44, no. 2 (2019): 216–25.

———. *Plugged In: Connecting Your Faith with What You Watch, Read, and Play.* Epsom, UK: Good Book Company, 2019.

———. *Their Rock Is Not like Our Rock: A Theology of Religions.* Grand Rapids: Zondervan, 2014.

Strong, William. *Communion with God in Ordinances, The Saints Priviledge and Duty.* London: by R. W. for Fra. Tryton, 1656.

———. *The Saints Communion with God, and God's Communion with Them in Ordinances.* London: for George Sawbridge, 1656.

Swain, Scott R. "Divine Trinity." In *Christian Dogmatics: Reformed Theology for the Church Catholic,* edited by Michael Allen and Scott R. Swain, 78–106. Grand Rapids: Baker Academic, 2016.

Swete, Henry B. *The Holy Catholic Church: The Communion of Saints.* London: Macmillan, 1916.

Taylor, Charles. *A Secular Age.* Cambridge, MA: Belknap/Harvard University Press, 2007.

Taylor, Howard. *Hudson Taylor in the Early Years: The Growth of a Soul.* 6th ed. London: China Inland Mission, 1923.

Taylor, Jeremy. *Holy Living and Holy Dying.* Vol. 2, *Holy Dying.* Edited by P. G. Stanwood. 1651. Reprint, Oxford: Oxford University Press, 1981.

Thielicke, Helmut. *Man in God's World.* Translated by John W. Doberstein. New York: Harper & Row, 1963.

Thiselton, Anthony C. *The First Epistle to the Corinthians.* NIGTC. Grand Rapids: Eerdmans, 2000.

Thompson, Bard. *Liturgies of the Western Church.* Minneapolis: Fortress Press, 1980.

Thompson, John Lee. *John Calvin and the Daughters of Sarah: Women in Regular and Exceptional Roles in the Exegesis of Calvin, His Predecessors, and His Contemporaries.* Genève: Librairie Droz S.A., 1992.

Thornwell, James Henley. *Collected Writings.* 4 vols. Edinburgh: Banner of Truth, 1974.

Tipton, Lane G. "Christocentrism and Christotelism: The Spirit, Redemptive History, and the Gospel." In *Redeeming the Life of the Mind: Essays in Honor of Vern Poythress,* edited by John M. Frame, Wayne Grudem, and John J. Hughes, 129–45. Wheaton, IL: Crossway, 2017.

———. "Christology in Colossians 1:15–20 and Hebrews 1:1–4: An Exercise in Biblico-Systematic Theology." In *Resurrection and Eschatology: Theology in Service of the Church: Essays in Honor* of *Richard B. Gaffin, Jr.*, edited by Lane G. Tipton and Jeffrey Waddington, 177–202. Phillipsburg, NJ: P&R Publishing, 2008.

Tolkien, J. R. R. *The Fellowship of the Ring*. New York: Houghton Mifflin, 2014.

Tönnies, Ferdinand. *Community and Society*. Edited and translated by Charles P. Loomis. 1887. Reprint, Lansing, MI: Michigan State University Press, 1957.

Towner, Philip H. *The Letters to Timothy and Titus*. NICNT. Grand Rapids: Eerdmans, 2006.

Trumper, Tim. "Adoption: The Forgotten Doctrine of Westminster Soteriology." In *Reformed Theology in Contemporary Perspective*, edited by Lynn Quigley, 87–123. Edinburgh: Rutherford House, 2006.

———. "An Historical Study of Adoption in the Calvinistic Tradition." PhD diss., University of Edinburgh, 2001.

Turretin, Francis. *Institutes of Elenctic Theology*. Edited by James T. Dennison Jr. Translated by George Musgrave Giger. 3 vols. Phillipsburg, NJ: P&R Publishing, 1992–97.

Urbach, Ephraim E. *The Sages: Their Concepts and Beliefs*. Translated by Israel Abrahams. Jerusalem: Magnes Press, Hebrew University of Jerusalem, 1990.

Vainio, Olli-Pekka. "*Imago Dei* and Human Rationality." *Zygon* 49, no. 1 (March 2014): 121–34.

Vanbrugge, David. "Sinclair Ferguson: A Plain Preacher." *PRJ* 10, no. 1 (January 2018): 227–43.

van der Kooi, Cornelis, and Gijsbert van den Brink. *Christian Dogmatics: An Introduction*. Grand Rapids: Eerdmans, 2017.

Van Dixhoorn, Chad. *Confessing the Faith: A Reader's Guide to the Westminster Confession of Faith*. Edinburgh: Banner of Truth, 2014.

VanDoodewaard, William. *The Quest for the Historical Adam*. Grand Rapids: Reformation Heritage Books, 2015.

VanDrunen, David. *Natural Law and the Two Kingdoms: A Study in the Development of Reformed Social Thought*. Emory University Studies in Law and Religion. Grand Rapids: Eerdmans, 2009.

van Mastricht, Petrus. *Theoretical-Practical Theology*. Vol. 1, *Prolegomena*. Edited by Joel R. Beeke. Translated by Todd M. Rester. Grand Rapids: Reformation Heritage Books, 2018.

Van Nieuwenhove, Rik. *An Introduction to Medieval Theology*. Cambridge: Cambridge University Press, 2012.

Van Til, Cornelius. *Christian Apologetics*. Edited by William Edgar. 2nd ed. Phillipsburg, NJ: P&R Publishing, 2003.

———. *The Defense of the Faith*. Philadelphia: Presbyterian and Reformed, 1955.

———. *An Introduction to Systematic Theology*. Nutley, NJ: Presbyterian and Reformed, 1974.

———. *Why I Believe in God*. Philadelphia: Committee on Christian Education, Orthodox Presbyterian Church, 1948.

Van Til, Cornelius, and Eric H. Sigward. "A Letter to Francis Schaeffer." In *Unpublished Manuscripts of Cornelius Van Til*. Electronic ed. New York: Labels Army Co., 1997.

Venema, Cornelis P. *The Promise of the Future*. Edinburgh: Banner of Truth, 2000.

Visser, Paul J. *Heart for the Gospel, Heart for the World: The Life and Thought of a Reformed Pioneer Missiologist, Johan Herman Bavinck (1895-1964)*. Eugene, OR: Wipf & Stock, 2003.

Vitello, Paul. "Taking a Break from the Lord's Work." *New York Times*, August 1, 2010. Accessed December 14, 2013. http://www.ny times.com/2010/08/02/nyregion/02burnout.html?pagewanted= all&_r=0.

Volf, Miroslav. *After Our Likeness: The Church as the Image of the Trinity*. Grand Rapids: Eerdmans, 1998.

———. *Exclusion and Embrace: A Theological Exploration of Identity, Otherness, and Reconciliation*. Nashville: Abingdon, 1996.

Vos, Geerhardus. *Biblical Theology*. Grand Rapids: Eerdmans, 1948. Reprint, Carlisle, PA: Banner of Truth, 2007.

———. *Biblical Theology: Old and New Testaments*. Grand Rapids: Eerdmans, 1991.

———. "Doctrine of the Covenant in Reformed Theology." In *Redemptive History and Biblical Interpretation*, 234-67. Phillipsburg, NJ: P&R Publishing, 1980.

———. "Eschatology in the New Testament." In *Redemptive History and Biblical Interpretation*, 25-58. Phillipsburg, NJ: Presbyterian and Reformed, 1980.

———. *The Eschatology of the Old Testament*. Edited by James T. Dennison Jr. Phillipsburg, NJ: P&R Publishing, 2001.

———. "Eschatology of the Psalter." In *Pauline Eschatology*, 321–65. Phillipsburg, NJ: Presbyterian and Reformed, 1991.

———. *Grace and Glory: Sermons Preached in the Chapel of Princeton Theological Seminary*. Grand Rapids: Reformed Press, 1922.

———. "The Idea of Biblical Theology as a Science and as a Theological Discipline." In *Redemptive History and Biblical Interpretation: The Shorter Writings of Geerhardus Vos*, edited by Richard B. Gaffin Jr., 3–24. Phillipsburg, NJ: P&R Publishing, 2001.

———. "The More Excellent Ministry." In *Grace and Glory*, 82–102. Edinburgh: Banner of Truth, 1994.

———. *The Pauline Eschatology*. Phillipsburg, NJ: Presbyterian and Reformed, 1979.

———. *Reformed Dogmatics*. Edited and translated by Richard B. Gaffin Jr. 5 vols. Bellingham, WA: Lexham Press, 2012–14.

———. "The Structure of the Pauline Eschatology." In *The Pauline Eschatology*, 1–41. Phillipsburg, NJ: Presbyterian and Reformed, 1991.

Wakefield, Gordon S. *Puritan Devotion: Its Place in the Development of Christian Piety*. London: Epworth Press, 1957.

Walker, Andrew T. *God and the Transgender Debate: What Does the Bible Actually Say about Gender Identity?* Centralia, WA: Good Book Company, 2017.

Ware, Timothy. *The Orthodox Church*. New York: Penguin, 1997.

Warfield, Benjamin B. "The Biblical Doctrine of Faith." In *The Works of Benjamin B. Warfield*. Vol. 2, *Biblical Doctrines*, 467–508. 1929. Reprint, Grand Rapids: Baker, 1981.

———. "The Essence of Christianity and the Cross of Christ." In *The Person and Work of Christ*, 479–530. Philadelphia: Presbyterian and Reformed, 1970.

———. *The Inspiration and Authority of the Bible*. Edited by Samuel Craig. 1894. Reprint, Philadelphia: Presbyterian and Reformed, 1948.

———. *The Plan of Salvation*. Philadelphia: Presbyterian Board of Publication, 1915. Reprint, Avinger, TX: Simpson Publishing, 1989.

———. "The Significance of the Confessional Doctrine of the Decree."

In *Benjamin B. Warfield: Selected Shorter Writings*, 2:93–102. Phillipsburg, NJ: P&R Publishing, 2001.

———. "The Spirit of God in the Old Testament." In *Biblical and Theological Studies*, 127–56. Philadelphia: Presbyterian and Reformed, 1952.

Waters, Brent. "Man Reconstructed: Humanity beyond Biology." *Concordia Theological Quarterly* 77, no. 3 (2013): 271–85.

Watson, Thomas. *All Things for Good*. Edinburgh: Banner of Truth, 1986. Reprint of *A Divine Cordial*. London, 1663.

———. *Heaven Taken by Storm*. Morgan, PA: Soli Deo Gloria, 1994.

———. "Sermon VIII: How We May Read the Scriptures with Most Spiritual Profit." In *Puritan Sermons 1659–1689*, edited by James Nichols, 2:57–71. Wheaton, IL: Richard Owen Roberts, 1981.

Webb, R. A. *Christian Salvation: Its Doctrine and Experience*. Richmond, VA: Presbyterian Committee of Publication, 1921.

Webster, John. *God without Measure: Working Papers in Christian Theology*. Vol. 1, *God and the Works of God*. London: Bloomsbury T. & T. Clark, 2016.

———. "Providence." In *Mapping Modern Theology: A Thematic and Historical Introduction*, edited by Kelly M. Kapic and Bruce L. McCormack, 203–26. Grand Rapids: Baker Academic, 2012.

———. "The Self-Organizing Power of the Gospel: Episcopacy and Community Formation." In *Word and Church: Essays in Christian Dogmatics*, 191–210. Edinburgh: T. & T. Clark, 2001.

Wells, Bob. "Which Way to Clergy Health?" Accessed October 15, 2020. https://faithandleadership.com/programs/spe/resources /dukediv-clergyhealth.html.

Wheeler, Henry. *The Apostles' Creed: An Examination of Its History and an Exposition of Its Contents*. New York: Eaton & Mains, 1912.

Whitefield, George. *Works*. London, 1771.

Whitehead, Alfred North. *Religion in the Making*. New York: Meridian, 1960.

Wilbourne, Rankin C. *Union with Christ: The Way to Know and Enjoy God*. Colorado Springs: David C. Cook, 2016.

Wilson, Jared C. *The Pastor's Justification: Applying the Work of Christ in Your Life and Ministry*. Wheaton, IL: Crossway, 2013.

Witsius, Herman. *The Apostles' Creed.* 2 vols. 1823. Reprint, Escondido, CA: den Dulk Christian Foundation, 1993.

Young, Edward J. *The Book of Isaiah, Chapters 1–18.* Vol. 1. Grand Rapids: Eerdmans, 1965.

———. *Thy Word Is Truth: Some Thoughts on the Biblical Doctrine of Inspiration.* 1957. Reprint, Carlisle, PA: Banner of Truth, 2008.

INDEX OF SCRIPTURE

INDEX OF SUBJECTS
AND NAMES

116–17, 133, 153–54, 157–58,
197, 408, 490, 493
kingdom of, 490
as last Adam, 46, 68, 116, 118–
19, 139–41, 157, 262, 308–9,
413, 420, 496
Logos, 134
mediator, 117, 120
obedience of, 118–19, 366
offices, 117
passive obedience of, 164
perseverance of, 310
preaching of, 480, 482–85
resurrection of, xxii–xxiv, 8, 10,
21, 32, 59–60, 66, 133, 139,
140–42, 150, 158, 160–61, 172,
174–77, 181, 185–91, 194, 199,
201, 222, 224, 226, 263–66,
268, 272, 274–75, 307, 371,
381, 433–34, 481, 483–84,
490–91, 493–94, 527, 540
return of, 465
sufficiency of, 484
suretyship of, 119
threefold office, 158, 160–61
two natures, 116, 471
union with, xxii, xxv, 32, 45–46,
48–49, 62, 127, 141, 144, 165–
66, 171–74, 176–78, 180–82,
184–85, 188, 190, 193–94,
196, 233, 244, 285, 291, 308,
310–11, 318–19, 371–72, 377,
430, 435, 449, 455, 462, 466,
483, 534, 540–41
victory of, 66, 105
work of, 119
Christendom, 217, 232, 305, 429,
432–33, 486
Christian liberty, 245, 366–68, 372,
374–75, 378–83, 421
Christocentric, 52

Chrysostom, John, 21, 352–53, 463
church, the, 403, 427, 437, 555
as bride, 407
as mediocosm, 408, 422
Cicero, 422, 546, 558
coiffure, 353
common grace, 105–6, 498
lex interior, 500
verbum externum, 499
verbum internum, 498
communion of saints, 426, 428–29,
432–38, 440–41, 444–46
communitarianism, 426, 434, 446
historic Reformed view, 432
sacramental view, 430
sancta, 429–30
sancti, 429–30
sanctorum communio, 428–29,
431, 434
sanctorum communionem, 428–
29, 434
supernatural foundation, 436–37
community
ecumenical, 27, 129, 428, 435
congregational government, 428
conscience, 152, 167, 303, 367, 375,
378–80, 421
consummation, xxiv, 18, 124, 140,
163, 251, 489–91, 494, 496,
501, 508, 527
covenant fellowship, 16, 125, 505
covenant of grace, xxv, 110–28,
163, 234, 245, 259, 285, 287,
303, 450, 452, 498, 500–501
covenant of works, 111, 118, 122,
135, 140, 245, 360, 499, 501,
503
covenant theology
federal headship, 499
suzerain treaty, 495
Cranmer, Thomas, 86

443, 456, 522–23, 530, 532–
34, 540
preaching, xxiv, 1, 4, 6–8, 11, 14,
19, 23, 25, 32–35, 52–53, 71,
83, 86, 97, 125, 127, 149, 158,
165, 172, 177, 179, 185, 187–
90, 192, 201, 205–7, 218, 228,
231–32, 237, 240, 242–43,
248, 251–52, 258, 279, 282,
286, 288, 295–98, 311–13,
319, 324, 331, 333, 343, 345–
46, 354, 358–62, 364, 378,
380, 392, 442–43, 449, 454,
464–65, 472–73, 480–481,
487, 489, 513, 516, 519, 521,
524, 526, 531–35, 537, 540
presbyterianism, 409, 411–12, 416,
418, 421
priesthood, Levitical, 151
problem of evil, 81
prophets, xxiii, 5, 158, 178–79, 188,
197, 199–200, 206, 211, 219,
301, 325, 369, 396, 414, 420,
452, 543
Protestant conception, 130–34, 139,
146, 373
providence, xxv, 11, 71–78, 80–87,
198, 250–51, 276, 408
public worship, 80, 208, 351, 353,
379, 386, 397, 399–400, 437,
440, 447
Puritans, 13, 171, 174, 192, 204,
239, 243, 322, 324, 326–27,
329–330, 333–37, 339–40,
342–44, 521, 532–33

rebellion, 57, 62–63, 111, 388
redemption
new creation, 16, 81, 113, 124,
139, 161, 173, 229, 490, 507
redemption, covenant of, 44

Reformation, xxv, 1, 4, 14, 69,
75–76, 91, 98, 126, 162, 171,
180, 217, 232, 239–40, 252,
258, 277, 290, 296, 299, 322,
327, 330, 346–47, 367, 382,
385, 398, 401, 432, 449, 460,
475, 514, 518, 522–23
Reformation Bible College, 522
Reformed Theological Seminary,
238, 317, 513, 522
regeneration, 44, 196, 198, 213,
238, 286, 307, 322, 527
relation of origin, 132–33
Remonstrants, 304, 499
repentance, xxv, 18–19, 44, 121, 210,
265–66, 277–85, 292–99, 333,
342, 481, 483, 514, 520, 543
repristination, 66
Ridderbos, Herman, xxiv, 4, 18, 22,
132–35, 147, 209, 511
Ridley, Nicholas, 86
righteousness, 2, 7–8, 16, 41, 44, 51,
55–56, 60, 111, 119, 145, 149,
156, 160, 164, 171, 197, 203,
212, 218–21, 224–27, 229–31,
238, 244, 246, 257, 259–60,
266, 270–71, 273–74, 282–83,
288, 338, 359, 362, 414–16,
450, 464, 499, 501, 509
imputed, 227
Robinson, Stuart, 411
Roman Catholic Church, 430, 454,
549, 551
Dogmatic Constitution on the
Church, 430
The Fourth Lateran Council, 431
Vatican Council, 430
Vatican Council II, 430
Roseveare, Helen, 181–82
Rosner, Brian, 99, 106, 352
Ryle, J. C., 220, 263, 278

CONTRIBUTORS

Joel R. Beeke is president and professor of systematic theology and homiletics at Puritan Reformed Theological Seminary, and is a pastor of the Heritage Reformed Congregation in Grand Rapids. He has written extensively in the areas of Reformed theology and ministry; his recent works include *Reformed Preaching, Knowing and Growing in Assurance of Faith*, and *Reformed Systematic Theology* (4 vols.).

Ligon Duncan is chancellor and CEO of Reformed Theological Seminary, where he also serves as the John E. Richards Professor of Systematic and Historical Theology. For seventeen years (1996–2013), he was senior pastor of the historic First Presbyterian Church, Jackson, Mississippi (1837). He served as moderator of the PCA General Assembly in 2004–5, and president of the Alliance of Confessing Evangelicals (2004–12).

William Edgar is professor of apologetics at Westminster Theological Seminary, Philadelphia, where he has taught since 1989. He is ordained in the Presbyterian Church in America. Recent publications include *Created and Creating: A Biblical Theology of Culture, Does Christianity Really Work?, Truth in All Its Glory*, and *Schaeffer on the Christian Life: Countercultural Spirituality*. He also directs the gospel-jazz band *Renewal*.

William R. Edwards is assistant professor of pastoral theology at Westminster Theological Seminary. Rob previously served in pastoral and university ministry for twenty years. He is the author of *Study Guide for John Owen's "The Mortification of Sin"* and has contributed articles to the *Westminster Theological Journal*, the *Journal of Biblical Counseling*, and *Themelios*.

John C. A. Ferguson is minister of the Inverness Associated Presbyterian Church, which meets at Kingsview Christian Centre in Inverness, Scotland. He is editor of the *Scottish Bulletin of Evangelical Theology* published by the Scottish Evangelical Theology Society in association with Highland Theological College UHI (University of the Highlands and Islands).

Mark A. Garcia is associate professor of systematic theology at Westminster Theological Seminary and founding president and fellow in Scripture and theology at Greystone Theological Institute. He is author of *Life in Christ: Union with Christ and Twofold Grace in Calvin's Theology* and many journal articles and essays.

David Gibson is minister of Trinity Church in Aberdeen, Scotland. He has authored *Living Life Backward: How Ecclesiastes Teaches Us to Live in Light of the End* and *Reading the Decree: Exegesis, Election and Christology in Calvin and Barth*. He is also coeditor of *From Heaven He Came and Sought Her: Definite Atonement in Historical, Biblical, Theological, and Pastoral Perspective*.

W. Robert Godfrey is president emeritus and professor emeritus of church history at Westminster Seminary California. He is a minister in the United Reformed Churches in North America. He is currently serving as chairman of the board of Ligonier Ministries, and is a teaching fellow there. His publications include *Saving the Reformation, Learning to Love the Psalms*, and *Pleasing God in Our Worship*.

Ian Hamilton is professor of historical theology at Westminster Presbyterian Theological Seminary (England) and adjunct professor of applied theology at Greenville Presbyterian Theological Seminary (South Carolina). Ian also serves on the boards of GPTS and Banner of Truth Trust. His most recent book is a commentary on Ephesians in the *Lectio Continua* series.

Michael Horton is J. Gresham Machen Professor of Systematic Theology and Apologetics at Westminster Seminary California and a minister in the United Reformed Churches in North America. He is editor in chief of *Modern Reformation* magazine and has authored many books, including *The Christian Faith: A Systematic Theology for Pilgrims on the Way.*

Dennis E. Johnson is professor emeritus of practical theology at Westminster Seminary California and assistant pastor of Westminster Presbyterian Church in Dayton, Tennessee. His written works include *Him We Proclaim: Preaching Christ from All the Scriptures, Triumph of the Lamb: A Commentary on Revelation,* and books on Acts, Hebrews, and Philippians.

Douglas Kelly was professor of systematic theology at Reformed Theological Seminary (1983–2016). He also served as minister of First Presbyterian Church, Dillon, South Carolina, for eight years. His publications include the first two volumes of his *Systematic Theology* and *Preachers with Power: Four Stalwarts of the South,* and *Creation and Change.*

Robert Letham is professor of systematic and historical theology at Union School of Theology. He has twenty-five years of pastoral experience, including as senior minister of Emmanuel Orthodox Presbyterian Church, Wilmington, Delaware (1989–2006). He has written a number of books, including *The Work of Christ, The Holy Trinity,* and *Union with Christ.*

John McClean is vice principal of Christ College, Sydney, where he teaches systematics and ethics, and is ordained in the Presbyterian Church of Australia. He has authored a short introduction to Christian doctrine (*The Real God for the Real World*) and is currently completing a book on the doctrine of revelation. He has also written a number of theological works as book chapters and journal articles.

Michael McClenahan is professor of systematic theology at Union Theological College in Belfast, and an Irish Presbyterian minister. He is also the executive director of BibleMesh and contributing editor for www.kairosjournal.org. He is the author of *Jonathan Edwards and Justification by Faith.*

David B. McWilliams is senior minister at Covenant Presbyterian Church in Lakeland, Florida. Formerly, he served Westminster Theological Seminary in the Department of Systematic Theology. He has published in the *Westminster Theological Journal* and elsewhere. He is author of *Galatians: A Mentor Commentary* and of a *Lectio Continua* commentary on Hebrews.

Philip S. Ross is minister of the Associated Presbyterian Church in Dundee, Scotland. He is the author of *From the Finger of God: The Biblical and Theological Basis for the Threefold Division of the Law* and *Anthems for a Dying Lamb*. He also worked extensively on the Christian Heritage editions of *The Marrow of Modern Divinity* and several John Owen titles.

Philip Graham Ryken is the eighth president of Wheaton College, where he also teaches theology. He is the former senior minister of Tenth Presbyterian Church, Philadelphia. Ryken has also authored many Bible commentaries and other books, including *When Trouble Comes*, *Art for God's Sake*, and *City on a Hill: Reclaiming the Biblical Pattern for the Church.*

David Strain is senior minister of First Presbyterian Church in Jackson, Mississippi. He serves on the council of the Gospel Reformation Network and is the convener of the Twin Lakes Fellowship. He has authored expository commentaries on Ruth, Esther, and Philippians, and is a frequent contributor to *Tabletalk* magazine.

Daniel Strange is director of Crosslands Forum, a center for cultural engagement and missional innovation. Previously he was director of Oak Hill College, London, and an elder of East Finchley Baptist Church. He is a contributing editor of *Themelios*, and author of *Their Rock Is Not like Our Rock: A Theology of Religions*, *Plugged In*, and *Making Faith Magnetic*.

Lane G. Tipton is pastor of Trinity Orthodox Presbyterian Church (Easton, Pennsylvania) and a fellow of systematic and biblical theology for Reformed Forum. He has authored many articles, and coedited

Revelation and Reason: New Essays in Reformed Apologetics and *Resurrection and Eschatology: Theology in Service of the Church: Essays in Honor of Richard B. Gaffin, Jr.*

A. Craig Troxel is professor of practical theology at Westminster Seminary California. Previously, he pastored Bethel Presbyterian Church in Wheaton, Illinois, and Calvary Presbyterian Church in Glenside, Pennsylvania. His publications include *With All Your Heart: Orienting Your Mind, Desires and Will toward Christ*, and the titles *What Is Man?* and *What Is the Priesthood of Believers?* in the Basics of the Faith series by P&R.

Chad Van Dixhoorn is professor of Church History at Westminster Theological Seminary. Previously, he served as associate pastor at Cambridge Presbyterian Church (UK) and then at Grace Presbyterian Church (Vienna, Virginia). He is the editor of *The Minutes and Papers of the Westminster Assembly, 1643–1652*, and is the author of *God's Ambassadors: The Westminster Assembly and the Reformation of the English Pulpit, 1643–1653*.

Cornelis P. Venema is president and professor of doctrinal studies at Mid-America Reformed Seminary, and is an ordained minister in the United Reformed Churches in North America. He has authored several books, including *Heinrich Bullinger and the Doctrine of Predestination, The Promise of the Future, Christ and Covenant Theology*, and *Chosen in Christ: Revisiting the Contours of Predestination*.

Paul D. Wolfe serves as senior pastor of New Hope Presbyterian Church in Fairfax, Virginia. He is the author of *My God Is True: Lessons Learned along Cancer's Dark Road* and *Setting Our Sights on Heaven: Why It's Hard and Why It's Worth It*.

R. Carlton Wynne serves as assistant pastor at Westminster Presbyterian Church in Atlanta and is adjunct professor of systematic theology at Reformed Theological Seminary in Atlanta. He has coedited *Zeal for Godliness: Devotional Meditations on Calvin's Institutes*.

P&R ACADEMIC

Reliable. Relevant. Reformed.

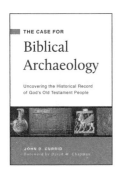

"I strongly recommend this."
—**H. Wayne House**

"Fills an important gap."
—**Michael Horton**

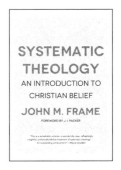

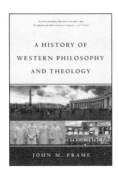

"[An] outstanding achievement."
—**J. I. Packer**

"Refreshingly insightful, profoundly biblical."
—**Wayne Grudem**

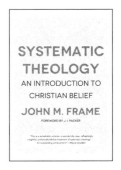

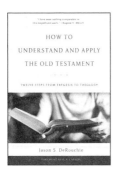

"[A] magnificent work."
—**Eugene H. Merrill**

"Accessible and user-friendly."
—**Timothy Keller**

Discover our wide-ranging academic resources at www.prpbooks.com.

We offer desk, examination, and personal copies of textbooks to qualifying professors. See www.prpbooks.com/academic-copies.